CENTURY PSYCHOLOGY SERIES

Kenneth MacCorquodale
Gardner Lindzey
Kenneth E. Clark

editors

Deborah Skinner

FESTSCHRIFT for B. F. SKINNER

edited by

P. B. DEWS

Harvard Medical School

APPLETON-CENTURY-CROFTS

educational division

NEW YORK MEREDITH CORPORATION

770-1

Library of Congress Card Number: 76-133193

ACKNOWLEDGEMENTS

Pages 1 to 21 reprinted from A HISTORY OF
PSYCHOLOGY IN AUTOBIOGRAPHY,
VOLUME V by Edwin G. Boring and
Gardner Lindzey. Copyright © 1967 by
Meredith Corporation.

Pages 49 to 405 reproduced with the kind per-
mission of the Society for the Experimental Analysis of Behavior.

PRINTED IN THE UNITED STATES OF AMERICA
390- 26645-0

TABLE OF CONTENTS

PREFACE

The papers in this volume are dedicated to one of the great men of our times on his sixty-fifth birthday. The papers included are a highly selected more or less random collection of contributions to fields started by B. F. Skinner's work.

Most men who have profoundly assisted the development of science have required four types of skills. First, the ability to recognize and to define important problems susceptible to scientific elucidation, and to define them clearly; that is, to see distant goals clearly and to formulate strategy. Second, the tactical ability to conceive and conduct experiments sufficiently limited in scope to be rigorous, but advancing science according to the general strategy. Third, the innovative ingenuity and technical skill needed for the actual conduct of elegant experiments. Fourth, the ability to see how the results of experiments contribute to understanding, and to use the results to guide the tactics of future experiments. Most scientists have one or two of these skills, but few have all four; most have one or more glaring deficiencies. There are hundreds of reports in the *Journal of Comparative and Physiological Psychology* which give evidence of clear distant goals and technical skill but which show inadequate tactics. There are dozens of reports in the *Journal of the Experimental Analysis of Behavior* (a younger journal) which show experimental skill and the ability to recognize results, but which fail to advance science appreciably because they cannot be seen to advance or modify understanding in the broader picture. The different types of skills can be added to a common pool in collaborative work between people. But when all the skills are present in an individual, they are mutually enhanced, so that the scientific potency of the individual is far greater than that of four people, each contributing one of the skills. Skinner has all four skills and in unusual measure. In the contemporary academic vernacular, he is very bright, good in the lab, good with his hands, and sharp: witness the theoretical papers of the thirties, the elegant experiments of *The Behavior of Organisms,* the cumulative recorder, and the recognition of the extraordinary properties of schedules of reinforcement. His contributions to science, moreover, reflect the multiplicative enhancement of these skills; the instrumental ingenuity which made the cumulative recorder enabled the explosive exploration of the properties of schedules, while the theoretical skills guided the thrust into a trajectory of great efficiency.

Massive advances in science can affect society either by changing man's views of himself or by leading to substantive changes in his environment. The contributions of Copernicus and Darwin profoundly affected society through their philosophical implications, though they have made little difference to the contents of one's house or how one does things. Dalton's Atomic Theory and Faraday's Electromagnetism had little influence on the nineteenth century Establishment, although they led, through chemistry and electricity, to profound changes in man's surroundings. The work of a few people has affected society both ways; Pasteur's germs affected both people's view of life and also their beer, wine, and medical treatment. Skinner's discoveries in the field of the transactions of a higher organism with its environment will have a greater and more enduring effect on man's view of himself than the views of Freud. Meanwhile, slowly but increasingly, education is being influenced by Skinner's findings, and perhaps someday they may influence broadly how men dispense justice and punishment, raise children, handle neuroses, organize an economic system and conduct international relations.

The breadth and depth of Skinner's contributions presented problems to the Festschrift Committee. So many people of so many different kinds have been influenced by Skinner's work and writings; who should be invited to contribute to a Festschrift volume? Under what conditions should the invitations be issued? Who would control quality, and how? The Committee avoided the first two questions by deciding not to issue invitations and the third by relying on the policies and editors of the *Journal of the Experimental Analysis of Behavior*. Many people were informed of the plans for a Festschrift and told that the management of *JEAB* had agreed to permit a dedicatory footnote on papers published in Volume 12 of the Journal. These decisions made the work of the Committee intellectually tolerable; without them, there would have been no Festschrift. They were not free, of course, from inevitable undesirable consequences. Workers in fields other than those that *JEAB* is organized to serve were automatically excluded from contributing, as was anyone temporarily lacking publishable experimental results during the short period when manuscripts could be submitted for inclusion. To such would-be well wishers we can only apologize and plead our incompetence to compile a volume by any other mechanism. Since no paper carrying a dedicatory note in Volume 12 was excluded from the Festschrift volume, the result is, as stated previously, a highly selected more or less random collection of papers. Fortunately for the breadth of coverage in the Festschrift volume, the editorial policy of *JEAB* has shifted in recent years to permit the inclusion of other than strictly experimental papers, so we are able to include contributions by MacCorquodale, Schoenfeld, Huntley, Day, and Herrnstein. The editors of the *Journal of Applied Behavior Analysis* permitted a dedicatory footnote so we were able to welcome a contribution by Bijou. As its only acts of arbitrary authority, the Committee invited F. S. Keller to write about the early Harvard years and C. B. Ferster to write about the Pigeon Lab. We hope readers will agree that the end justified the means.

Mention must be made of the inclusion of the brief autobiography in the Festschrift volume. When he heard of our intentions, Fred demurred: it is not seemly, he averred, that a man's own writings should appear in a volume intended to do him honor. The Committee and publisher felt that the autobiography added flesh and blood to the bones of the bibliography, and that the Festschrift Volume would reach many different hands from those that have held the Boring and Lindzey volumes. Since the autobiography is already in print, it cannot be construed as a narcissistic intrusion into the Festschrift. Under the impact of these arguments, Fred withdrew his veto.

The volume would not have been possible without the expert help of Charles Catania and the organizational energies and bright ideas of Vic Laties, these two being the other members of the Festschrift Committee, nor without the mysterious but vital work of Kay Dinsmoor and Garth Hopkins who trafficked in blues and four-ups and so brought print to page. Thank you all.

P. B. Dews
FOR THE FESTSCHRIFT COMMITTEE

FESTSCHRIFT for B. F. SKINNER

B. F. SKINNER . . . AN AUTOBIOGRAPHY

EARLY ENVIRONMENT

My Grandmother Skinner was an uneducated farmer's daughter who put on airs. She was naturally attracted to a young Englishman who came to America in the early 1870's looking for work, and she married him. (He had not found just the work he wanted when he died at the age of ninety.) My grandmother's aspirations were passed on to her son, William, who "read law" while apprenticed as a draftsman in the Erie Railroad shops in Susquehanna, a small town in north-eastern Pennsylvania. He went on to a law school in New York City and passed his bar examination in Susquehanna County before getting a degree. He suffered from his mother's ambitions all his life. He was desperately hungry for praise, and many people thought him conceited; but he secretly—and bitterly—considered himself a failure, even though he eventually wrote a standard text on Workmen's Compensation Law which was in its fourth edition when he died.

My mother, Grace Burrhus, was bright and beautiful. She had rigid standards of what was "right," and they never changed. Her loyalties were legendary. At eleven she began to correspond with a friend who had moved away, and they wrote to each other in alternate weeks, without missing a week, for seventy years. Her father was born in New York State. He lied about his age to enlist as a drummer boy in the last year of the Civil War. After the war he came to Susquehanna looking for work as a carpenter, and eventually he became foreman of the Erie Carpenter Shops there. My Grandmother Burrhus had the only claim to quality in the family: an ancestor, a Captain Potter, had fought under Washington.

My home environment was warm and stable. I lived in the house I was born in until I went to college. My father, mother, and I all graduated from the same high school. I saw a great deal of my grandparents. I had a brother two and a half years younger than I. As a child I was fond of him. I remember being ridiculed for calling him "honey," a term my mother used for both of us at home. As he grew older he proved to be much better at sports and more popular than I, and he teased me for my literary and artistic interests. When he died suddenly of a cerebral aneurism at the age of sixteen, I was not much moved. I probably felt guilty because I was not. I had once made an arrowhead from the top of a tin can, and when I made a test shot straight up into the air, the arrow fell back and struck my brother in the shoulder, drawing blood. I recalled the event with a shock many years later when I heard Lawrence Olivier speaking Hamlet's lines:

> . . . . Let my disclaiming from a purpos'd evil
> Free me so far in your most generous thought,
> That I have shot mine arrow o'er the house,
> And hurt my brother.

Susquehanna is now half deserted, and it was even then a rather dirty railroad town, but it is situated in a beautiful river valley. I roamed the hills for miles

[1] Preparation of this manuscript has been supported by grant K6-MH-21,775–01 of the National Institute of Mental Health of the U. S. Public Health Service and by the Human Ecology Fund.

around. I picked arbutus and dogwood in early Spring, chewed sassafras root and wintergreen berries and the underbark of slippery elm, killed rattlesnakes, and found flint arrowheads. With another boy I built a shack in the hills alongside a creek, and I learned to swim in the pool we made by blocking the creek with a sod-and-stone dam, sharing the pool with a poisonous watersnake. Four other boys and I once went three hundred miles down the Susquehanna River in a fleet of three canoes. I was fifteen at the time and the oldest in the party.

I was always building things. I built roller-skate scooters, steerable wagons, sleds, and rafts to be poled about on shallow ponds. I made seesaws, merry-go-rounds, and slides. I made slingshots, bows and arrows, blow guns and water pistols from lengths of bamboo, and from a discarded water boiler a steam cannon with which I could shoot plugs of potato and carrot over the houses of our neighbors. I made tops, diabolos, model airplanes driven by twisted rubber bands, box kites, and tin propellers which could be sent high into the air with a spool-and-string spinner. I tried again and again to make a glider in which I myself might fly.

I invented things, some of them in the spirit of the outrageous contraptions in the cartoons which Rube Goldberg was publishing in the *Philadelphia Inquirer* (to which, as a good Republican, my father subscribed). For example, a friend and I used to gather elderberries and sell them from door to door, and I built a flotation system which separated ripe from green berries. I worked for years on the design of a perpetual motion machine. (It did not work.)

I went through all twelve grades of school in a single building, and there were only eight students in my class when I graduated. I *liked* school. It was the custom for students to congregate outside the building until a bell rang and the doors were opened. I was a constant problem for the janitor, because I would arrive early and ask to be let in. He had been told to keep me out, but he would shrug, open the door just enough to let me through, and lock it after me. As I see it now, the school was good. I had four strong years of high school mathematics using no-nonsense texts by Wentworth. In my senior year I could read a bit of Virgil well enough to feel that I was getting the meaning in Latin. Science was weak, but I was always doing physical and chemical experiments at home.

My father was a sucker for book salesmen ("We are contacting a few of the town's more substantial citizens"), and as a result we had a fairly large library consisting mostly of sets—*The World's Great Literature, Masterpieces of World History, Gems of Humor,* and so on. Half a dozen small volumes on applied psychology, published by an "institute," were beautifully bound, with white spines and embossed seals on blue covers. I remember only one sample: it was said that an advertisement for chocolates showing a man shovelling cocoa beans into a large roasting oven was bad psychology.

An old-maid school teacher named Mary Graves was an important figure in my life. Her father was the village atheist and an amateur botanist who believed in evolution. Miss Graves once showed me a letter he had received from the Prince of Monaco offering to exchange specimens of pressed plants. Miss Graves was a dedicated person with cultural interests far beyond the level of the town. She organized the Monday Club, a literary society to which my mother belonged. The club would spend a winter reading Ibsen's *Doll's House.* Miss Graves did her best to bring the little town library up to date. When I was in high school, she once whispered to me in a conspiratorial tone, "I have just been reading the strangest book. It is called *Lord Jim.*"

Miss Graves was my teacher in many fields for many years. She taught a Presbyterian Sunday school class, taking six or eight of us boys through most of the Old Testament. She taught me drawing in the lower grades, and she was later promoted to teaching English, both reading and composition. I think it was in the eighth grade that we were reading *As You Like It*. One evening my father happened to say that some people believed that the plays were not written by Shakespeare but by a man named Bacon. The next day I announced to the class that Shakespeare had not actually written the play we were reading. "You don't know what you are talking about," said Miss Graves. That afternoon I went down to the public library and drew out Edwin Durning-Lawrence's *Bacon is Shakespeare* (1910). The next day I *did* know what I was talking about, and I must have made life miserable for Miss Graves for the next month or two. Durning-Lawrence had analyzed act five, scene one of *Love's Labours Lost*, proving that the word *honorificabilitudinitatibus* was a cipher which, when properly interpreted, read, "These works, the offspring of Francis Bacon, are preserved for the world." To my amazement I discovered that the same act and scene in *As You Like It* was also cryptic. The philosopher Touchstone (who else but Bacon?) is disputing with the simple William (who else but Shakespeare?) for the possession of the fair Audrey (what else but the authorship of the plays?). The clincher was that William says that he was born in the Forest of Arden, and Shakespeare's mother's name was Arden. (O, the lovely adolescent obscenity of that "forest"!) I have long since lost interest in the Bacon-Shakespeare controversy, but in my defensive zeal I read biographies of Bacon, summaries of his philosophical position, and a good deal of *The Advancement of Learning* and *Novum Organum*. How much it meant to me at the age of fourteen or fifteen I cannot say, but Francis Bacon will turn up again in this story.

Miss Graves was probably responsible for the fact that in college I majored in English literature and afterwards embarked upon a career as a writer, and probably also for the fact that I have dabbled in art. I have never painted or sculpted really well, but I have enjoyed trying to do so.

My father had played the trumpet (then called the cornet) in a small orchestra, but he gave it up when he married. I never heard him play more than a few notes; he had "lost his lip." My mother played the piano well and had an excellent contralto voice. She sang at weddings and funerals—and the same songs at both. I still have her copy of J. C. Bartlett's "A Dream." It begins, "Last night I was dreaming of thee, love, was dreaming . . ." A sacred text for use at funerals is added in her own hand: "Come, Jesus, Redeemer, abide thou with me-e . . ." At the age of eight or nine I studied the piano for a year with an old man who sucked Sens-sens and jabbed me in the ribs with a sharp pencil whenever I made a mistake. For a while I gave up the piano in favor of the saxophone. My father was then local attorney for the Erie Railroad, and he arranged for me to play with an employee's band. We never got beyond "Poet and Peasant," "Morning Noon and Night in Vienna," and other overtures by von Suppe, but I learned to love ensemble playing. I played in a jazz band during my high school years. When I returned to the piano again, a friend of the family who taught piano noticed that I was limited to my mother's sentimental music and a few volumes of *Piano Pieces the Whole World Loves,* and she sent me a copy of Mozart's Fourth Sonata. Shortly afterward I bought all the Mozart sonatas, playing at first only short passages here and there. Later I came to play them all through once a year in a kind of ritual.

I was never physically punished by my father and only once by my mother. She washed my mouth out with soap and water because I had used a bad word. My father never missed an opportunity, however, to inform me of the punishments which were waiting if I turned out to have a criminal mind. He once took me through the county jail, and on a summer vacation I was taken to a lecture with colored slides describing life in Sing Sing. As a result I am afraid of the police and buy too many tickets to their annual dances.

My mother was quick to take alarm if I showed any deviation from what was "right." Her technique of control was to say "tut-tut" and to ask, "What will people think?" I can easily recall the consternation in my family when in second grade I brought home a report card on which, under "Deportment," the phrase "Annoys others" had been checked. Many things which were not "right" still haunt me. I was allowed to play in the cemetery next door, but it was not "right" to step on a grave. Recently in a cathedral I found myself executing a series of smart right-angle detours to avoid the engraved stones on the floor. I was taught to " respect books," and it is only with a twinge that I can today crack the spine of a book to make it stay open on the piano.

My Grandmother Skinner made sure that I understood the concept of hell by showing me the glowing bed of coals in the parlor stove. In a travelling magician's show I saw a devil complete with horns and barbed tail, and I lay awake all that night in an agony of fear. Miss Graves, though a devout Christian, was liberal. She explained, for example, that one might interpret the miracles in the Bible as figures of speech. Shortly after I reached puberty, I had a mystical experience. I lost a watch which I had just been given by my family, and I was afraid to go home ("You would lose your head if it were not screwed on"). I took my bicycle and rode up along the river and followed the creek up to our shack. I was miserably unhappy. Suddenly it occurred to me that happiness and unhappiness must cancel out and that if I were unhappy now I would necessarily be happy later. I was tremendously relieved. The principle came with the force of a revelation. In a mood of intense exaltation I started down along the creek. Halfway to the road, in a nest of dried grass beside the path, lay my watch. I have no explanation; I had certainly "lost" it in town. I took this as a Sign. I hurried home and wrote an account in biblical language and purple ink. (The ink I had made by dissolving the lead from an indelible pencil, and it had an appropriate golden sheen.) No other signs followed, however, and my new testament remained only one chapter in length. Within a year I had gone to Miss Graves to tell her that I no longer believed in God. "I know," she said, "I have been through that myself." But her strategy misfired: I never went *through* it.

COLLEGE

A friend of the family recommended Hamilton College, and I did not think of going anywhere else. It was then at the nadir of its long career. I took an absurd program of courses, but in some curious way I have made good use of every one of them. I majored in English and had good courses in Anglo-Saxon, Chaucer (for which I wrote a modern translation of "The Pardoner's Tale"), Shakespeare, Restoration drama, and Romantic poetry. I minored in Romance languages. Hamilton was proud of its reputation for public speaking, and I had four thin compulsory years of that. I elected biology as my freshman science and went on to advanced courses in embryology and cat anatomy.

The most important thing that happened to me at Hamilton was getting to know the Saunders family. They were abroad during my freshman year, recovering from the tragic death of their elder son, a brilliant student who had been killed in a hazing accident the year before. All the Saunders children were prepared for college at home; and when the family returned, they asked my mathematics professor to suggest a tutor for their younger son. I agreed to serve.

Percy Saunders was then dean. Hamilton College students called him "Stink" because he taught chemistry, but his great love was hybrid peonies. He and his family lived in a large frame house alongside the campus. It was full of books, pictures, sculpture, musical instruments, and huge bouquets of peonies in season. Dean Saunders played the violin, and there were string quartets at least one night a week. Louise Saunders took in a few students each year to prepare them for college, among them usually a pretty girl with whom I would fall in love. We would walk through the Root Woods, returning for tea before a fire in the music room in the late afternoon. Once in a while on a clear night a telescope would be set up among the peonies, and we would look for the moons of Mars or Saturn's rings. Interesting people came to stay—writers, musicians, and artists. Beside my chair as I listened to Schubert or Beethoven I might find a copy of the avant-garde *Broom* or a letter from Ezra Pound. I remember a page from the score of George Antheil's *Ballet Mécanique* with the words COMPLETELY PERCUSSIVE printed diagonally across it. Percy and Louise Saunders made an art of living, something I had not known was possible.

I never fitted into student life at Hamilton. I joined a fraternity without knowing what it was all about. I was not good at sports and suffered acutely as my shins were cracked in ice hockey or better players bounced basketballs off my cranium—all in the name of what was ironically called "physical education." In a paper I wrote at the end of my freshman year, I complained that the college was pushing me around with unnecessary requirements (one of them daily chapel) and that almost no intellectual interest was shown by most of the students. By my senior year I was in open revolt.

John K. Hutchens and I began that year with a hoax. Our professor of English composition, Paul Fancher, was a great name-dropper in the field of the theater. Hutchens and I had posters printed reading, in part: "Charles Chaplin, the famous cinema comedian, will deliver his lecture 'Moving Pictures as a Career' in the Hamilton College Chapel on Friday, October 9." The lecture was said to be under Fancher's auspices. In the early hours of October 9 we went down to the village, plastered the posters on store windows and telephone poles, threw a few into lobbies of apartment houses, and went back to bed. That morning Hutchens called the afternoon paper in Utica, the nearest city, and told them that the president had announced the lecture at morning chapel. By noon the thing was completely out of hand. The paper ran Chaplin's picture on the front page and even guessed at the time he would arrive at Union Station, which, I am ashamed to say, was swarming with children at the appointed hour. In spite of police road-blocks it was estimated that 400 cars got through to the campus. A football pep meeting was mistaken for a Chaplin rally, and a great throng began to mill around the gymnasium. The editorial which appeared next day in the college paper ("No man with the slightest regard for his alma mater would have done it") was one of the best things Hutchens ever wrote.

As a nihilistic gesture, the hoax was only the beginning. Through the student publications we began to attack the faculty and various local sacred cows. I published a parody of the bumbling manner in which the professor of public speaking would review student performances at the end of a class. I wrote an editorial attacking Phi Beta Kappa. At commencement time I was in charge of Class Day exercises, which were held in the gymnasium, and with the help of another student (Alf Evers, later a well known illustrator) I covered the walls with bitter caricatures of the faculty.

One of the most sacred of Hamilton institutions was the Clark Prize Oration. Students submitted written orations, six of which were selected to be spoken in an evening contest, from which a winner was chosen by a committee of judges. Four of us decided to wreck the institution. We submitted orations which we thought would be selected but which were potentially so bombastic that we could convert the evening into an uproarious farce. We misjudged the judges, however. Only mine was selected. I found myself on the program with five serious speakers. I decided there was nothing for it but to go through with the joke alone, hoping that my friends would understand. Very few did. We also made a shambles of

the commencement ceremonies, and at intermission the President warned us
sternly that we would not get our degrees if we did not settle down.

LITERARY INTERLUDE

My Hamilton College activities seemed to be pointing toward a career as a
writer. As a child I had had an old typewriter and a small printing press, and
during my grade school years I wrote poems and stories and typed or printed
them "artistically." I started a novel or two—sentimental stuff on the model of
James Oliver Curwood: Pierre, an old trapper, lived in the woods of colonial
Pennsylvania with his lovely daughter, Marie (how they got down from Quebec
I never thought it necessary to explain). In high school I worked for the local
Transcript. In the morning before school I would crib national and international
news from the Binghamton papers which had come in on the morning train.
Occasionally I did a feature story or published a poem in the manner of Edgar
Guest. When I got to college I contributed serious poems to the *Hamilton
Literary Magazine*. Free verse was coming in, and I tried my hand at it. Here
is a sample:

CONCUPISCENCE

An old man, sowing in a field,
Walks with a slow, uneasy rhythm.
He tears handfuls of seed from his vitals,
Caressing the wind with the sweep of this hand.
At night he stops, breathless,
Murmuring to his earthly consort,
"Love exhausts me!"

And I had not yet heard of Freud. Once, when in love, I wrote five or six
rather derivative Shakespearean sonnets and enjoyed the strange excitement of
emitting whole lines ready-made, properly scanned and rhymed.

The summer before my senior year I attended the Middlebury School of
English at Breadloaf, Vermont. I took a course with Sidney Cox, who one day
invited me to have lunch with Robert Frost. Frost asked me to send him some
of my work, and I sent him three short stories. His comments came the following
April. The letter is printed in the *Selected Letters of Robert Frost*, edited by
Lawrance Thompson (1964). It was encouraging, and on the strength of it I
definitely decided that I would be a writer. My father had always hoped that I
would study law and come into his office. My birth had been announced in the
local paper in that vein: "The town has a new law firm: Wm. A. Skinner & Son."
I had taken a course in political science my senior year just in case I might indeed
go into law. My father was naturally unhappy that I had decided against it. He
thought I should prepare myself to earn a living—say, as a lawyer—and *then*
try my hand at writing. He eventually agreed, however, that I should live at home
(in Scranton, Pennsylvania, to which my family had moved) and write for a year
or two. I built a small study in the attic and set to work. The results were dis-
astrous. I frittered away my time. I read aimlessly, built model ships, played the
piano, listened to the newly-invented radio, contributed to the humorous column
of a local paper but wrote almost nothing else, and thought about seeing a
psychiatrist.

Before the year was out, I rescued myself and my self-respect by taking on a
hack job. The FBI has occasionally expressed interest in that two-year gap in my

educational history, but I was not writing for the *Daily Worker*. On the contrary, I was way out on the right wing. In 1904, after a bitter coal strike, President Theodore Roosevelt had set up a Board of Conciliation to settle grievances brought by unions and companies. The decisions which had since been handed down were increasingly cited as precedents, and the coal companies wanted them digested so that their lawyers could prepare cases more effectively. I read and abstracted thousands of decisions and classified them for ready reference. My book was privately printed under the title *A Digest of Decisions of the Anthracite Board of Conciliation*. (My father was listed as coauthor, but for prestige only.) The book was intended to give the coal companies an advantage, but the lawyer who prepared all the union cases had a copy within the year.

After I had finished the book, I went to New York for six months of bohemian living in Greenwich Village, then to Europe for the summer, and on to Harvard in the fall to begin the study of psychology. In New York I worked in a book shop, dined at Chumleys', and drank hot rum Punchino's at Jimmy's, a speakeasy on Barrow Street. My friends were liberal and even intellectual. On Saturday nights eight or ten of us would somehow manage to have an all-night party on one quart of prohibition gin. That summer Paris was full of literary ex-patriots and I met some of them, but a violent reaction against all things literary was setting in.

I had failed as a writer because I had had nothing important to say, but I could not accept that explanation. It was literature which must be at fault. A girl I had played tennis with in high school—a devout Catholic who later became a nun—had once quoted Chesterton's remark about a character of Thackeray's: "Thackeray didn't know it but she drank." I generalized the principle to all literature. A writer might portray human behavior accurately, but he did not therefore understand it. I was to remain interested in human behavior, but the literary method had failed me; I would turn to the scientific. Alf Evers, the artist, had eased the transition. "Science," he once told me, "is the art of the twentieth century." The relevant science appeared to be psychology, though I had only the vaguest idea of what that meant.

TOWARD PSYCHOLOGY

Many odds and ends contributed to my decision. I had long been interested in animal behavior. We had no household pets, but I caught and kept turtles, snakes, toads, lizards, and chipmunks. I read Thornton Burgess and Ernest Thompson Seton and was interested in folk wisdom about animals. The man who kept the livery stable once explained that the cowboys in the rodeo let themselves be thrown just before "breaking the spirit" of the bucking broncos to avoid spoiling them for future performances. At a county fair I saw a troupe of performing pigeons. The scene was the facade of a building. Smoke appeared from the roof, and a presumably female pigeon poked her head out of an upper window. A team of pigeons came on stage pulling a fire engine, smoke pouring from its boiler. Other pigeons with red fire hats rode on the engine, one of them pulling a string which rang a bell. Somehow a ladder was put up against the building, and one of the firepigeons climbed it and came back down followed by the pigeon from the upper window.

Human behavior also interested me. A man in Binghamton who gave me advanced lessons on the saxophone had entertained soldiers during the war with a vaudeville act. He wrote the alphabet forward with his right hand and backward with his left while adding a column of figures and answering questions—all at the same time. It gave him a headache. I remember being puzzled by an episode at some kind of church fair where there was a booth in which you could throw baseballs at dolls mounted on a rack. The dolls were restored to their place by pulling a rope from the front of the booth. When the woman who ran the concession was gathering balls near the dolls, some wag pulled the rope. Everyone laughed as the woman dropped to the ground in alarm. Why had she confused the sound of the rack with the sound of a ball?

Some of the things I built had a bearing on human behavior. I was not allowed to smoke, so I made a gadget incorporating an atomizer bulb with which I could "smoke" cigarettes and blow smoke rings hygienically. (There might be a demand for it today.) At one time my mother started a campaign to teach me to hang up my pajamas. Every morning while I was eating breakfast, she would go up to my room, discover that my pajamas were not hung up, and call to me to come up immediately. She continued this for weeks. When the aversive stimulation grew unbearable, I constructed a mechanical device that solved my problem. A special hook in the closet of my room was connected by a string-and-pulley system to a sign hanging above the door to the room. When my pajamas were in place on the hook, the sign was held high above the door out of the way. When the pajamas were off the hook, the sign hung squarely in the middle of the door frame. It read: "Hang up your pajamas!"

My earliest interest in psychology was philosophical. In high school I began a treatise entitled "Nova Principia Orbis Terrarum." (That sounds pretentious, but at least I got it out of my system early. Clark Hull published his Principia at the age of fifty-nine.) Two pages of this great work survive. It begins: "Our soul consists of our mind, our power of reasoning, thinking, imagining, weighing, our power to receive impressions, and stimulate action of our body; and our conscience, our inner knowledge of write (sic)." I engaged in a good deal of self-observation, and I kept notes. Once in a rather noisy street I was trying to talk to a friend in a store window. Though I strained to hear him, I could not make out what he was saying. Then I discovered that there was no glass in the window and that his voice was reaching me loud and clear. I had dismissed it as part of the ambient noise and was listening for a fainter signal.

College did little to further my interest in psychology. The only formal instruction I received lasted ten minutes. Our professor of philosophy (who had actually studied under Wundt) once drew a pair of dividers from his desk drawer (the first Brass Instrument I had ever seen) and demonstrated the two-point limen. My term paper for a course in Shakespeare was a study of Hamlet's madness. I read rather extensively on schizophrenia, but I should not care to have the paper published today. At Breadloaf I wrote a one-act play about a quack who changed people's personalities with endocrines, a subject which was then beginning to attract attention in the newspapers.

After college my literary interests carried me steadily toward psychology. Proust's *A La Recherche du temps perdu* was just being translated. I read all that was available in English and then carried on in French. (I bought Part VIII, *Le Temps retrouvé,* in Algiers in 1928. The uncut pages indicate that I abandoned literature on page ninety-six.) Proust intensified my habit of self-observation and of noting and recording many tricks of perception and memory. Before going to Harvard I bought Parson's book on perception, and I suppose it was only my extraordinary luck which kept me from becoming a Gestalt or (so help me) a cognitive psychologist.

The competing theme which saved me was suggested by "Bugsy" Morrell, my biology teacher at Hamilton. He had called my attention to Jacques Loeb's *Physiology of the Brain and Comparative Psychology* (1900), and later he showed me Pavlov's *Conditioned Reflexes* (1927). I bought Pavlov's book and read it while living in Greenwich Village. The literary magazine called *The Dial,* to which I subscribed, was publishing articles by Bertrand Russell, and they led me to Russell's book, *Philosophy,* published in 1925, in which he devoted a good deal of time to John B. Watson's *Behaviorism,* emphasizing its epistemological implications. I got hold of Watson's *Behaviorism* (1924–25) (but not his *Psychology from the Standpoint of a Behaviorist,* 1919), and in the bookstore in New York I read the store's copy of his *Psychological Care of Infant and Child* (1928) between customers.

The Department of Psychology at Harvard did not strengthen any particular part of this hodgepodge of interests, but two graduate students did. Fred S. Keller, who was teaching part time at Tufts, was a sophisticated behaviorist in every sense of the word. I had seen the regal name of Charles K. Trueblood spread across the pages of *The Dial,* for which he wrote many reviews. Now I found Trueblood himself, in white coat and gumshoes, moving silently through the corridors of Emerson Hall carrying cages of rats, the performances of which he was studying in a rotated maze. I welcomed the support of another renegade from literature.

At Harvard I entered upon the first strict regimen of my life. I had done what was expected of me in high school and college but had seldom worked hard. Aware that I was far behind in a new field, I now set up a rigorous schedule and maintained it for almost two years. I would rise at six, study until breakfast, go to classes, laboratories, and libraries with no more than fifteen minutes unscheduled during the day, study until exactly nine o'clock at night and go to bed. I saw no movies or plays, seldom went to concerts, had scarcely any dates, and read nothing but psychology and physiology.

My program in the department was not heavy. Boring was on leave, writing his history. Troland gave a course, but I found it unbearably dull and withdrew after the first day. Carroll Pratt taught psychophysical methods and was always available for discussions. I took Harry Murray's course in Abnormal Psychology the first year he gave it. I could reach French but needed German as well, so I took an intensive course which met five days a week. To pass statistics I simply read G. Udney Yule's *An Introduction to the Theory of Statistics* (1911). His use of Greek letters to refer to the absence of attributes explains my symbols S^D and S^Δ, the awkwardness of which has plagued many psychologists since.

The intellectual life around the department was of a high order. A weekly colloquium, loosely structured, was always exciting and challenging. We argued with Pratt, Beebe-Center, and Murray on even terms. The informality is shown by a letter which I wrote to Harry Murray, of which he recently reminded me. He had given a colloquium on his theory of "regnancy." I wrote to tell him that there were some things about himself I felt he ought to know. When he was a child, he had obviously been led to believe that it was urine which entered the female in sexual intercourse. This had wreaked havoc in his scientific thinking, and he was still trying to separate *p* from *pregnancy.*

A joint reception for new students in philosophy and psychology was held each year at Professor Hocking's. My first year I turned up at the appointed hour, which was, of course, too early. A little old man with a shiny bald head and deep-set eyes soon arrived and came straight toward me in the friendliest way. He wore a wing collar and ascot tie. He stammered slightly and spoke with an English accent. I sized him up as a clergyman—perhaps an imported preacher in one of the better Boston churches. He asked me where I had gone to college and what philosophy I had studied. He had never heard the name of my professor and was only puzzled when I tried to help by explaining that he was an Edwardian (meaning a disciple of Jonathan Edwards). He told me that a young psychologist should keep an eye on philosophy, and I told *him,* fresh from my contact with Bertrand Russell, that it was quite the other way around: we needed a psychological epistemology. This went on for fifteen or twenty minutes, as the room filled up. Others began to speak to my new friend. Finally a student edged in beside me, explaining that he wanted to get as close to the professor as possible. "Professor who?" I asked. "Professor Whitehead," he said.

My thesis had only the vaguest of Harvard connections. Through a friend who had come to Harvard to study under Percy Bridgman I got to know the *Logic of Modern Physics* (1927). I read Poincaré and Mach. I began to spend a good deal of time in the Boston Medical Library and in the summer of 1930 wrote a paper on the concept of the reflex, adopting the semihistorical method from Mach's *Science of Mechanics*. Early that fall I was discussing my future with Beebe-Center. I outlined the work I intended to cover in my thesis. His comment was typical: "Who do you think you are? Helmholtz?" He encouraged me to get a thesis in at once. I was already well along in my work on changes in rate of eating and had written two short papers on drive and reflex strength. I combined these with my paper on the reflex and submitted them as a thesis to Professor Boring, who was now back in residence. I still have his long reply. He was bothered by my selective use of history. A thesis on the history of the reflex should be quite different. He suggested an alternative outline. I felt that he had missed my point, and I resubmitted the thesis without change. Suspecting that he was bothered by my behavioristic learnings, I attached a quotation from Thomas Hood:

> Owning her weakness,
>   Her evil behavior,
> And leaving, with meekness,
>   Her sins to her Savior.

Boring accepted the role of Savior. He appointed a thesis committee of which he himself was not a member; the thesis was approved, and I passed my orals at the end of the fall term of 1930–31. I stayed in my laboratory, supported by the balance of a Harvard Fellowship, until June.

Meanwhile I had come into close contact with W. J. Crozier and Hudson Hoagland. Hoagland had taken his Ph.D. in psychology but was teaching in Crozier's department of General Physiology. It was felt, I think, that Crozier was stealing students from psychology. He certainly offered enthusiastic encouragement, and after I got my degree he put me up for National Research Council Fellowships for two years, but I was never under any pressure to adopt his principles or move into his field. During my first postdoctoral year I spent every other day working on the central nervous system at the medical school under Alexander Forbes and Hallowell Davis. For the rest of my time Crozier offered me a subterranean laboratory in the new biology building. I moved my animal equipment into it and worked there for five years, the last three as a Junior Fellow in the Harvard Society of Fellows.

I have traced the development of my research in detail elsewhere. Russell and Watson had given me no glimpse of experimental method, but Pavlov had: control the environment and you will see order in behavior. In a course with Hoagland I discovered Sherrington and Magnus. I read *Körperstellung* and proposed to do a translation (fortunately I failed to find a publisher). I felt that my thesis had exorcised the physiological ghosts from Sherrington's synapse, and I could therefore maintain contact with these earlier workers. In writing *The Behavior of Organisms* (1938) I held doggedly to the term "reflex." Certain characteristics of operant behavior were, however, becoming clear. My first papers were challenged by two Polish physiologists, Konorski and Miller. It was in my answer to them that I first used the word "operant." Its function, then as now, was to identify behavior traceable to reinforcing contingencies rather than to eliciting stimuli.

MINNESOTA

In the spring of 1936, the low point of the depression, the end of my Junior Fellowship was approaching and I had no job. The best offer the Department of Psychology could pass along to me was from a YMCA college; but Walter Hunter was teaching that summer at Minnesota, and he mentioned me to R. M. Elliott, who was looking for someone to teach small sections of a big introductory course. The beginning salary was $1900.

At Minnesota I not only taught for the first time, I began to learn college psychology, keeping a jump or two ahead of my students in Woodworth's text. I chose two sections of twenty students each from about eight hundred in the beginning course. Many of them were already committed to particular careers, such as medicine, law, journalism, and engineering, but five percent of the students I had during five years went on to get Ph.D.'s in psychology and many more to get M.A.'s. I stole W. K. Estes from engineering and Norman Guttman from philosophy. I have never again been so richly reinforced as a teacher.

VERBAL BEHAVIOR

I did not quite give up literature. At Harvard I met I. A. Richards, who managed somehow to blend psychology and literary criticism, and I discussed books and techniques with other literary friends. I wrote an article for the *Atlantic Monthly* under the editor's title of "Has Gertrude Stein a Secret?" In it I showed that a paper which Gertrude Stein had published when at Radcliffe contained samples of her own automatic writing which resembled material she later published as literature. Gertrude Stein wrote to the editor in reply: "No, it is not so automatic as he thinks. If there is anything secret it is the other way too. I think I achieve by xtra consciousness, xcess, but then what is the use of telling him that, he being a psychologist and I having been one."

I began to look at literature, not as a medium for portraying human behavior, but as a field of behavior to be analyzed. A discussion with Whitehead after dinner at the Society of Fellows set me to work on my book *Verbal Behavior* (1957). The chairman of the Society, L. J. Henderson, cautioned me that such a book might take five years. The following summer he sent a postcard from France: "A motto for your book—'Car le mot, ç'est le verbe, et le verbe, ç'est Dieu'—Victor Hugo."

As a boy I knew two interesting cases of verbal behavior. My Grandmother Skinner was an almost pathological talker. My grandfather had stopped listening to her while still a young man, and when any visitor came to her house she would begin talking and would repeat, without pausing, a string of anecdotes and stereotyped comments which we all knew by heart. More predictable verbal behavior I have never seen. The other case was Professor Bowles, the principal of my high school, who taught mathematics. He had a long list of favorite topics, and almost any stimulus would set him off on a digression. He would eventually return to mathematics with a perfunctory bow to the comment which had first set him off. One day I made running notes of the topics he was touching upon. There were two long harangues that day, and to my surprise he concluded the second by returning to the topic with which he had begun and concluded the first!

When I was in the Society of Fellows, another verbal phenomenon came to my attention. On a beautiful Sunday morning I was in my subterranean, sound-proofed laboratory writing notes against a background of rhythmic noise from my apparatus. Suddenly I found myself joining in the rhythm, saying silently, "You'll never get out, you'll never get out, you'll never get out." The relevance of the remark seemed worth investigating. I built a phonographic system in which patterns of vowels (separated by glottal stops) could be repeated as often as desired. Playing each sample softly to a subject, I could maintain the illusion that it was actual speech and could collect a large sample of "projective" verbal responses. Harry Murray supplied me with subjects from his research on thematic apperception.

My renewed interest in literature was encouraged by my marriage in 1936 to Yvonne Blue. She had majored in English at the University of Chicago, where she had taken a course in English composition with Thornton Wilder. She is an active reader (and a rapid one—she reads exactly twice as fast as I), and there were always new books around the house. When I had a chance to give a summer school course in the psychology of literature, she attended my lectures and reinforced me appropriately. I gave the course again and broadcast it over an educational radio station. To fill out the term I roamed rather widely, from *The Meaning of Meaning* (1945) through psychoanalysis, and thus explored the field of verbal behavior rather more widely than I should otherwise have done. As a rule the material in which I had least confidence proved to be most popular, but I did not wholly abandon my scientific principles. After several persuasive demonstrations of alliteration as a verbal process, for example, I became suspicious and made a statistical analysis of a hundred of Shakespeare's sonnets. I found that, although an occasional line might have as many as four stressed initial *s's,* such lines occurred almost exactly as often as one would predict from chance. (A similar study of Swinburne, I was glad to find, not only demonstrated alliteration, but showed an alliterative tendency extending over several syllables.)

In the fall of 1941 on a Guggenheim Fellowship I began to write a final draft of *Verbal Behavior.* The war intervened, but I picked up the Fellowship again in 1944–45 and finished the greater part of the manuscript. I gave a course from it in the summer of 1947 at Columbia, and my William James Lectures at Harvard that fall were based on it. I put off a final version in order to write *Science and Human Behavior* (1953). *Verbal Behavior* was published, not five, as Henderson had predicted, but twenty-three years after it was begun, in 1957. It was completed under heavy competition from research and from another book, *Schedules of Reinforcement* (1957), which Charles Ferster and I published at about the same time.

PROJECT PIGEON

By the end of the 1930's the Nazis had demonstrated the power of the airplane as an offensive weapon. On a train from Minneapolis to Chicago in the spring of 1939, I was speculating rather idly about surface-to-air missiles as a possible means of defense. How could they be controlled? I knew nothing about radar, of course, but infrared radiation from the exhaust of the engines seemed a possibility. Was visible radiation out of the question? I noticed a flock of birds flying alongside the train, and it suddenly occurred to me that I might have the answer in my own research. Why not teach animals to guide missiles? I went back to Minneapolis and bought some pigeons. The rest of the story of Project Pigeon has already been told (1960).

THE "BABY BOX"

Toward the end of the Second World War, we decided to have another child. My wife remarked that she did not mind bearing children but that the first two years were hard to take. I suggested that we mechanize the care of a baby. There is nothing natural about a crib. Wrapping a baby in several layers of cloth— undershirt, nightie, sheets, and blankets, with a mattress underneath—is an inefficient way of maintaining a proper temperature, and it greatly restricts the child's movements. I built, instead, an enclosed space in which the baby, wearing only a diaper, could lie on a tightly stretched woven plastic sheet, the surface of which feels rather like linen and through which warm air rises, moved by convection or a fan, depending on the outside temperature.

When our second daughter, Deborah, came home from the hospital, she went directly into the device and used it as sleeping space for two and a half years. I reported our happy experience in an article in the *Ladies' Home Journal,* and many hundreds of babies have been raised in what is now called an Aircrib. Child care is conservative, and the method has been adopted fairly slowly, but medical and behavioral advantages should be studied. Predictions and tales of dire consequences have not been supported. Deborah broke her leg in a skiing accident but presumably not because of "the box." Otherwise she has had remarkably good health. She is now in college, interested in art and music, from Bach to Beatle, and she usually beats me at chess. To complete the story of the shoemaker's children, our older daughter, Julie, is married to a sociologist, Ernest Vargas, and is finishing her work for a Ph.D. in educational research. Their first child, Lisa, is, of course, being raised in an Aircrib.

WALDEN TWO

In the spring of 1945 at a dinner party in Minneapolis, I sat next to a friend who had a son and a son-in-law in the South Pacific. I expressed regret that when the war was over they would come back and take up their old way of life, abandoning their present crusading spirit. She asked me what I would have them do instead, and I began to discuss an experimental attitude toward life. I said that some of the communities of the nineteenth century represented a healthy attitude. She pressed me for details and later insisted that I publish them. I was unaware that I was taking her seriously. A paper on "The Operational Analysis of Psychological Terms" (1945) was due on June 1, and I met that deadline. Then, to my surprise, I began to write *Walden Two* (1948). It began simply as a description of a feasible design for community living. I chose the unoriginal utopian strategy of having a few people visit a community. The characters soon took over.

In general I write very slowly and in longhand. It took me two minutes to write each word of my thesis and that is still about my rate. From three or four hours of writing each day I eventually salvage about one hundred publishable words. *Walden Two* was an entirely different experience. I wrote it on the typewriter in seven weeks. It is pretty obviously a venture in self-therapy, in which I was struggling to reconcile two aspects of my own behavior represented by Burris and Frazier. Some of it was written with great emotion. The scene in Frazier's room, in which Frazier defends *Walden Two* while admitting that he himself is not a likeable person or fit for communal life, I worked out while walking the streets near our house in St. Paul. I came back and typed it out in white heat.

I receive a steady trickle of letters from people who have read *Walden Two,* want to know whether such a community has ever been established, and, if so, how they can join. At one time I seriously considered an actual experiment. It could be one of the most dramatic adventures in the twentieth century. It needs a younger man, however, and I am unwilling to give up the opportunity to do other things which in the long run may well advance the principles of *Walden Two* more rapidly. A conference organized to consider an actual experiment was recently attended by nearly one hundred people.

INDIANA

In the fall of 1945 I became chairman of the Department of Psychology at Indiana. I took with me from Minnesota the unfinished manuscript of *Verbal Behavior,* the manuscript of *Walden Two,* the Aircrib with its lovely occupant, and a miscellaneous lot of apparatus. I was inexperienced as an administrator, but the department survived my brief chairmanship. I did no undergraduate teaching, but the chapter in *Science and Human Behavior* on self-control is to a large extent the joint product of a seminar in which, for almost the only time in my life, I successfully managed group thinking. In spite of my administrative responsibilities I ran a number of experiments—all with pigeons—on reaction time, differential reinforcement of slow responding, two operanda, and matching-to-sample. These studies are mostly reported in "Are Theories of Learning Necessary?" (1950)

THE EXPERIMENTAL ANALYSIS OF BEHAVIOR

Other people were now beginning to do research along the same lines. W. K. Estes, who went on to get a Ph.D. at Minnesota, wrote a thesis on the effects of punishment which became a classic. At Columbia Fred Keller was teaching graduate students from *The Behavior of Organisms* and, with W. N. Schoenfeld, was planning a revolutionary introductory course in the college. A problem in communication arose, and Keller and I started what became a series of annual conferences on the Experimental Analysis of Behavior. Those who attended the first of these at Indiana in the spring of 1946 are pictured in volume five (1962) of the *Journal of the Experimental Analysis of Behavior.* Eventually we began to meet at the same time as the American Psychological Association and later as part of its program. When Division 3 could no longer provide space or arrange time for our expanding activities, we took the probably inevitable step of forming a separate division—Division 25.

Meanwhile, the need for a special journal had become clear. I proposed an inexpensive newsletter, but more constructive opinions prevailed. A small holding society was formed and the *Journal of the Experimental Analysis of Behavior* founded. The history of the discipline can also be traced in the increasing availability of excellent apparatus, reflecting the growing complexity and subtlety of the contingencies of reinforcement under analysis.

HARVARD AGAIN

While giving the William James Lectures at Harvard in 1947, I was asked to become a permanent member of the department, and we moved to Cambridge in 1948. Remembering my introductory teaching at Minnesota I proposed to add a course in human behavior to the Harvard list. The first year was nearly a disaster. More than four hundred students, anticipating a "gut" course, signed up.

I had no appropriate text and could only supply hastily prepared mimeographed sheets. My section men were loyal but puzzled. Later the course was incorporated into the General Education program and gradually improved. By 1953 *Science and Human Behavior* was available as a text.

Meanwhile I had set up a pigeon laboratory in which Charles Ferster and I worked very happily together for more than five years. It was the high point in my research history. Scarcely a week went by without some exciting discovery. Perhaps the behavior we dealt with most effectively was our own. Near the end of our collaboration we found ourselves with a vast quantity of unanalyzed and unpublished data, and we proceeded to design an environment in which we could scarcely help writing a book. In it we both worked as we had never worked before. In one spring term and one long hot summer we wrote a text and a glossary and prepared over a thousand figures, more than 900 of which were published.

The success of my laboratory in the 1950's and early 1960's was due in large part to many excellent graduate students, not all of them under my direction, of whom I may mention Douglas G. Anger, James A. Anliker, Donald S. Blough, Richard J. Herrnstein (now my colleague on the Harvard faculty), Alfredo V. Lagmay, William H. Morse, Nathan H. Azrin, Ogden R. Lindsley, Lewis R. Gollub, Matthew L. Israel, Harlan L. Lane, George S. Reynolds, A. Charles Catania, Herbert S. Terrace, and Neil J. Peterson. With very little direct help from me they all made and are continuing to make important contributions.

TECHNOLOGICAL APPLICATIONS

At Minnesota W. T. Heron and I had studied the effects of certain drugs on operant behavior. In the 1950's a strong interest in psychopharmacology suddenly developed. Almost all the large drug companies set up operant laboratories, some only for the screening of new compounds but many providing an opportunity for basic research. Much of this interest was generated by Joseph V. Brady of the Walter Reed Army Medical Center. Peter Dews of the Department of Pharmacology in the Harvard Medical School began to work in close cooperation with my laboratory and soon organized an active program in his own department.

In the early 1950's Dr. Harry Solomon, then chairman of the Department of Psychiatry at the Harvard Medical School, helped me set up a laboratory for the study of the operant behavior of psychotics at the Metropolitan State Hospital in Waltham, Massachusetts. Ogden R. Lindsley took over, and the work he initiated there has now been carried forward in many other laboratories. Azrin and others have extended operant principles to the management of psychotic patients in hospital wards, and there is increasing interest in applications to personal therapy.

Sporadic research on operant behavior in children goes back to the 1930's. Sidney Bijou, among others, has been particularly active in applying the principles of an experimental analysis to the behavior of children in nursery schools, clinics, and the home. Ferster turned from our work on schedules to the study of autistic children, and there are now many operant laboratories for the study of retardates. Almost all these practical applications have contributed to our understanding of behavior. Fortunately, they have not overshadowed the basic science; many laboratories continue to study operant behavior apart from technological significances.

In the late 1930's, looking ahead to the education of our first child, I began to write a book called *Something to Think About*. It was never completed, though I got as far as having an artist work on the illustrations. It contained examples of what later came to be called programmed instruction. When our daughters went to school, I showed the usual interest as a parent but carefully refrained from speaking as a specialist in the field of learning. In 1953 our younger daughter was in fourth grade in a private school in Cambridge. On November 11, as a Visiting Father, I was sitting in the back of the room in an arithmetic class. Suddenly the situation seemed perfectly absurd. Here were twenty extremely valuable organisms. Through no fault of her own the teacher was violating almost everything we knew about the learning process.

I began to analyze the contingencies of reinforcement which might be useful in teaching school subjects and designed a series of teaching machines which would permit the teacher to provide such contingencies for individual students. At a conference on Current Trends in Psychology at the University of Pittsburgh in the spring of 1954 I demonstrated a machine to teach spelling and arithmetic. Within a year I found myself caught up in the teaching machine movement. A series of projects at Harvard led eventually to a Committee on Programmed Instruction, in which I had the invaluable collaboration of James G. Holland.

Economics, government, and religion are farther from psychology than linguistics, psychotherapy, or education, and few people have the kind of joint interest needed for an examination of common principles. I have seen myself moving slowly in this direction, however, and I am now working under a Career Award from the National Institutes of Health which will permit me to explore the social sciences from the point of view of an experimental analysis of behavior.

MY BEHAVIOR AS A SCIENTIST

It is often said that behaviorists do not view themselves as they view their subjects—for example, that they regard what they say as true in some sense which does not apply to the statements of the people they study. On the contrary, I believe that my behavior in writing *Verbal Behavior,* for example, was precisely the sort of behavior the book discusses. Whether from narcissism or scientific curiosity, I have been as much interested in myself as in rats and pigeons. I have applied the same formulations, I have looked for the same kinds of causal relations, and I have manipulated behavior in the same way and sometimes with comparable success. I would not publish personal facts of this sort if I did not believe that they throw some light on my life as a scientist.

I was taught to fear God, the police, and what people will think. As a result I usually do what I have to do with no great struggle. I try not to let any day "slip useless away." I have studied when I did not feel like studying, taught when I did not want to teach. I have taken care of animals and run experiments as the animals dictated. (Some of my first cumulative records are stamped December twenty-fifth and January first.) I have met deadlines for papers and reports. In both my writing and my research I have fought hard against deceiving myself. I avoid metaphors which are effective at the cost of obscuring issues. I avoid rhetorical devices which give unwarranted plausibility to an argument (and I sometimes reassure myself by making lists of the devices so used by others). I avoid the unwarranted prestige conferred by mathematics, even, I am afraid, when mathematics would be helpful. I do not spin impressive physiological theories from my data, as I could easily do. I never convert an exploratory experiment into an *experimentum crucis* by inventing a hypothesis after the fact. I write and rewrite a paper until, so far as possible, it says exactly what I have to say. (A constant search for causes seems to be another product of that early environment. When my wife or one of my daughters tells me that she has a headache, I am likely to say, "Perhaps you have not been eating wisely" or "You may have been out in the sun too much." It is an almost intolerable trait in a husband, father, or friend, but it is an invaluable scientific practice.)

I must admit that all these characteristics have been helpful. Max Weber could be right about the Protestant Ethic. But its effect is only cautionary or restrictive. Much more important in explaining my scientific behavior are certain positive reinforcements which support Feuer's answer to Weber in which he shows that almost all noted scientists follow a "hedonistic ethic." I have been powerfully reinforced by many things: food, sex, music, art, and literature—and my scientific results. I have built apparatuses as I have painted pictures or modelled figures in clay. I have conducted experiments as I have played the piano. I have written scientific papers and books as I have written stories and poems. I have *never* designed and conducted an experiment because I felt I ought to do so, or to meet a deadline, or to pass a course, or to "publish rather than perish." I dislike experimental designs which call for the compulsive collection of data and, particularly, data which will not be reinforcing until they have been exhaustively analyzed. I freely change my plans when richer reinforcements beckon. My thesis was written before I knew it was a thesis. *Walden Two* was not planned at all. I may practice self-management for Protestant reasons, but I do so in such a way as to maximize non-Protestant reinforcements. I emphasize positive contingencies. For example, I induce myself to write by making production as conspicuous as possible (actually, in a cumulative record). In short, I arrange an environment in which what would otherwise be hard work is actually effortless.

I could not have predicted that among the reinforcers which explain my scientific behavior the opinions of others would not rank high, but that seems to be the case. Exceptions are easily traced to my history. I take a silly pride in the fact that "Freedom and the Control of Men" (1955–1956) appears as an example of good contemporary prose in textbooks written for college freshmen; Miss Graves would have been pleased. But in general my effects on other people have been far less important than my effects on rats and pigeons—or on people as experimental subjects. That is why I was able to work for almost twenty years with practically no professional recognition. People supported me, but not my line of work; only my rats and pigeons supported *that*. I was never in any doubt as to its importance, however, and when it began to attract attention, I was wary of the effect rather than pleased. Many notes in my files comment on the fact that I have been depressed or frightened by so-called honors. I forego honors which would take time away from my work or unduly reinforce specific aspects of it.

That I have never been interested in critical reactions, either positive or negative, is probably part of the same pattern. I have never actually read more than a dozen pages of Chomsky's famous review of *Verbal Behavior*. (A quotation from it which I have used I got from I. A. Richards.) When Rochelle Johnson sent me a reprint of her reply to Scrivin's criticism of my position, it only reminded me that I had never read Scrivin. Clark Hull used to say that I did not make hypotheses because I was afraid of being wrong. Verbal statements are, indeed, right or wrong, and in some sense I want my statements to be right. But I am much more interested in measures for the control of a subject matter. Some relevant measures are verbal, but even so they are not so much right or wrong as effective or ineffective, and arguments are of no avail. For the same reason I am not interested in psychological theories, in rational equations, in factor analyses, in mathematical models, in hypothetico-deductive systems, or in other verbal systems which must be *proved* right.

Much of this attitude is Baconian. Whether my early and quite accidental contact with Bacon is responsible or not, I have followed his principles closely. I reject verbal authority. I have "studied nature not books," asking questions of the organism rather than of those who have studied the organism. I think it can be said, as it was said of Bacon, that I get my books out of life, not out of other books. I have followed Bacon in organizing my data. I do not collect facts in random "botanizing," for there are principles which dictate what Poincaré called *le choix des faits,* and they are not, as Poincaré argued, hypotheses. I classify not for the sake of classification but to reveal properties.

I also follow Bacon in distinguishing between observation and experimentation. Bacon no doubt underestimated the importance of extending the range of human sense organs with instruments, but he did so in emphasizing that knowledge is more than sensory contact. I would put it this way: *Observation* overemphasizes stimuli; *experimentation* includes the rest of the contingencies which generate effective repertoires. I have also satisfied myself that Bacon's four Idols can be translated into an acceptable behavioral analysis of faulty thinking.

My position as a behaviorist came from other sources. Perhaps, like Jeremy Bentham and his theory of fictions, I have tried to resolve my early fear of theological ghosts. Perhaps I have answered my mother's question, "What will people think?" by proving that they do not think at all (but the question might as well have been "What will people *say?*"). I used to toy with the notion that a behavioristic epistemology was a form of intellectual suicide, but there is no suicide because there is no corpse. What perishes is the homunculus—the spontaneous, creative inner man to whom, ironically, we once attributed the very scientific activities which led to his demise.

To me behaviorism is a special case of philosophy of science which first took shape in the writings of Ernst Mach, Henri Poincaré, and Percy Bridgman. Bridgman himself could never make the extension to behavior. He is one man I *did* argue with. When he published *The Way Things Are* (Bridgman, 1959), he sent me a copy with a note: "Here it is. Now do your damnedest!" I was busy with other things and did nothing. But I could never have convinced him, for it is not a matter of conviction. Behaviorism is a formulation which makes possible an effective experimental approach to human behavior. It is a working hypothesis about the nature of a subject matter. It may need to be clarified, but it does not need to be argued. I have no doubt of the eventual triumph of the position— not that it will eventually be proved right, but that it will provide the most direct route to a successful science of man.

I have acknowledged my indebtedness to Bertrand Russell, Watson, and Pavlov. I never met or even saw Watson, but his influence was, of course, important. Thorndike (not a behaviorist but still an important figure in a science of behavior) I met briefly. He knew of my interest in verbal behavior and sent me his *Studies in the Psychology of Language* (Thorndike, 1938). When I wrote to thank him, I told him about my analysis of alliteration and added, "Hilgard's review of my book [*The Behavior of Organisms*] in the *Bulletin* has reminded me of how much of your work in the same vein I failed to acknowledge . . . I seem to have identified your point of view with the modern psychological view taken as a whole. It has always been obvious that I was merely carrying on your puzzle box experiments but it never occurred to me to remind my readers of the fact." Thorndike replied, "I am better satisfied to have been of service to workers like yourself than if I had founded a 'school.'"

Walter Hunter I knew well. He gave me professional advice. I recall his wry smile as he told me, "It only takes one little idea to be a success in American psychology." (He measured the idea with thumb and forefinger.) Clark Hull visited my laboratory in Cambridge and made suggestions, which I never followed. I talked to his seminar at Yale and was invited to the unveiling of his portrait shortly before he died. I have a bound volume of my papers which was once on his shelves under the title *Experimental Studies in Learning.*

Tolman taught summer school at Harvard in 1931, and we had many long discussions. I had been analyzing the concept of hunger as a drive. In my thesis I had called it a "third" variable—that is, a variable in addition to stimulus and response occupying the intervening position of Sherrington's synaptic states. I have always felt that Tolman's later formulation was very similar. When *The Behavior of Organisms* appeared, he wrote:

I think the two words *operant* and *respondent* are swell . . . I do think, as I have said so many times before, that what you ought to do next is to put in two levers and see what relationships the functions obtained from such a discrimination set up will bear to your purified functions where you have only one lever. No doubt you were right that the "behavior-ratio" is a clumsy thing for getting the fundamental laws, but it is a thing that has finally to be predicted and someone must show the relation between it and your fundamental analysis. I congratulate you on coming through Harvard so beautifully unscathed! . . .

P.S. And, of course, I was pleased as Hell to be mentioned in the Preface.

Another behaviorist whose friendship I have valued is J. R. Kantor. In many discussions with him at Indiana I profited from his extraordinary scholarship. He convinced me that I had not wholly exorcised all the "spooks" in my thinking.

THE CONTROL OF BEHAVIOR

I learned another Baconian principle very slowly: "Nature to be commanded must be obeyed." Frazier in *Walden Two* speaks for me here:

I remember the rage I used to feel when a prediction went awry. I could have shouted at the subjects of my experiments, "Behave, damn you! Behave as you ought!" Eventually I realized that the subjects were always right. They always behaved as they should have behaved. It was I who was wrong. I had made a bad prediction.

But that coin has another face: once obeyed, nature can be commanded. The point of Solomon's House in the *New Atlantis,* as of The Royal Society founded on Bacon's model, was that knowledge should be useful. A hundred years later— in an epoch in which I feel especially at home—Diderot developed the theme in his *Encyclopédie*. A hundred years after that, the notion of progress took on new significance in the theory of evolution. *Walden Two* is my *New Atlantis;* I suppose it could also be said that in applying an experimental analysis to education I returned to a motto which Bacon as a child saw in his father's house: *Moniti Meliora* (instruction brings progress). I believe in progress, and I have always been alert to practical significances in my research.

I began to talk explicitly about the control of human behavior after I had written *Walden Two*. Control was definitely in the air during my brief stay at Indiana. In *Science and Human Behavior* and the course for which it was written, I elaborated on the theme. In the summer of 1955, on the island of Monhegan, Maine, where we had a cottage, I wrote "Freedom and the Control of Men" for a special issue of the *American Scholar* (1955–1956). In it I took a much stronger stand on freedom and determinism. My position has been rather bitterly attacked, especially by people in the humanities, who feel that it is in conflict with Western democratic ideas and that it plays down the role of the individual. I have been called Machiavellian, a Communist, a Fascist, and many other names. The fact is, I accept the ends of a democratic philosophy, but I disagree with the means which are at the moment most commonly employed. I see no virtue in accident or in the chaos from which somehow we have reached our present position. I believe that man must now plan his own future and that he must take every advantage of a science of behavior in solving the problems which will necessarily arise. The great danger is not that science will be misused by despots for selfish purposes but that so-called democratic principles will prevent men of goodwill from using it in their advance toward humane goals. I continue to be an optimist, but there are moments of sadness. I find the following in my notebook, dated August 5, 1963.

End of an Era

Last night Deborah and I went to the Gardner Cox's for some music in their garden. A group of young people, mostly current or former Harvard and Radcliffe students, sang a Mass by William Byrd. It was *a cappella* and, for most of the singers, sight reading. Very well done. The night was pleasant. Ragged clouds moved across the sky, one of them dropping briefly a fine mist. The garden has a circular lawn surrounded by shrubs and a few old trees. Half a dozen lights burned among green branches. Several kittens played on the grass. We sat in small groups, in folding chairs. Except for a few jet planes the night was quiet and the music delightful. *Kyrie eleison* . . . I thought of *Walden Two* and the B-minor Mass scene. And of the fact that this kind of harmless, beautiful, sensitive pleasure was probably nearing the end of its run. This was Watermusic, floating down the Thames and out to sea. And why?

Phyllis Cox may have answered the question. As I said good night, she motioned toward the young man who had conducted the music and said, "You know, he thinks you are a terrible person. Teaching machines . . . a fascist . . ."

Possibly our only hope of maintaining any given way of life now lies with science, particularly a science of human behavior and the technology to be derived from it. We need not worry about the scientific way of life; it will take care of itself. It would be tragic, however, if other ways of life, not concerned with the practice of science as such, were to forego the same kind of support through a misunderstanding of the role of science in human affairs.

The garden we sat in that evening once belonged to Asa Gray. In high school I studied Botany from a text by Gray, called, as I remember it, *How Plants Grow.* One passage impressed me so much that I made a copy which I have kept among my notes for nearly fifty years. It is the story of a radish. I would reject its purposivism today but not its poetry, for it suggests to me a reasonable place for the individual in a natural scheme of things.

So the biennial root becomes large and heavy, being a storehouse of nourishing matter, which man and animals are glad to use for food. In it, in the form of starch, sugar, mucilage, and in other nourishing and savory products, the plant (expending nothing in flowers or in show) has laid up the avails of its whole summer's work. For what purpose? This plainly appears when the next season's growth begins. Then, fed by this great stock of nourishment, a stem shoots forth rapidly and strongly, divides into branches, bears flowers abundantly, and ripens seeds, almost wholly at the expense of the nourishment accumulated in the root, which is now light, empty, and dead; and so is the whole plant by the time the seeds are ripe.

PUBLICATIONS CITED

Bridgman, P. *Logic of modern physics.* New York: Macmillan, 1927.

———. *The way things are.* Cambridge: Harvard, 1959.

Durning-Lawrence, E. *Bacon is Shakespeare.* London: Gay and Hancock, 1910.

Feuer, L. *The scientific intellectual.* New York: Basic Books. 1963.

Loeb, J. *Physiology of the brain and comparative psychology.* New York: Putnam, 1900.

Mach, E. *The science of mechanics, a critical and historical account of its development.* LaSalle: Ind. Open Court Publ. Co., 1942.

Magnus, R. *Körperstellung.* Berlin: Springer, 1924.

Pavlov, I. *Conditioned reflexes.* London: Oxford, 1927.

Richards, I. A. & Ogden, C. K. *The meaning of meaning.* New York: Harcourt, Brace & World, 1923.

Russell, B. *Philosophy.* New York: Norton, 1925.

Sherrington, C. S. *The integrative action of the nervous system.* New Haven: Yale, 1906.

Thompson, L. (Ed.) *Selected letters of Robert Frost.* New York: Holt, Rinehart and Winston, 1964.

Thorndike, E. L. Studies in the psychology of language. *Arch. Psychol.*, 1938, No. 231.

Watson, J. B. *Behaviorism.* New York: People's Institute Publ. Co., 1924–25.

———. *Psychological care of infant and child.* New York: Norton, 1928.

———. *Psychology from the standpoint of a behaviorist.* Philadelphia: Lippincott, 1919.

Yule, G. *An introduction to the theory of statistics.* London: Griffin, 1911.

PUBLICATIONS OF B. F. SKINNER

On the conditions of elicitation of certain eating reflexes. *Proceedings of the National Academy of Sciences,* 1930, *16,* 433–438.

The progressive increase in the geotropic response of the ant *Aphaenogaster* (with T. C. Barnes). *Journal of General Psychology,* 1930, *4,* 102–112.

On the inheritance of maze behavior. *Journal of General Psychology,* 1930, *4,* 342–346.

The concept of the reflex in the description of behavior. *Journal of General Psychology,* 1931, *5,* 427–458.

Drive and reflex strength I. *Journal of General Psychology,* 1932, *6,* 22-37.

Drive and reflex strength II. *Journal of General Psychology,* 1932, *6,* 38–48.

On the rate of formation of a conditioned reflex. *Journal of General Psychology,* 1932, *7,* 274–286.

A paradoxical color effect. *Journal of General Psychology,* 1932, *7,* 481–482.

On the rate of extinction of a conditioned reflex. *Journal of General Psychology,* 1933, *8,* 114–129.

The abolishment of a discrimination. *Proceedings of the National Academy of Sciences,* 1933, *19,* 825–828.

The measurement of " spontaneous activity." *Journal of General Psychology,* 1933, *9,* 3–24.

The rate of establishment of a discrimination. *Journal of General Psychology,* 1933, *9,* 302–350.

Resistance to extinction in the process of conditioning. *Journal of General Psychology,* 1933, *9,* 420–429.

Some conditions affecting intensity and duration thresholds in motor nerve, with reference to chronaxie of subordination (with E. F. Lambert and A. Forbes). *American Journal of Physiology,* 1933, *106,* 721–737.

Has Gertrude Stein a secret? *Atlantic Monthly,* January 1934, *153,* 50–57.

The extinction of chained reflexes. *Proceedings of the National Academy of Sciences,* 1934, *20,* 234–237.

A discrimination without previous conditioning. *Proceedings of the National Academy of Sciences*, 1934, *20*, 532–536.

The generic nature of the concepts of stimulus and response. *Journal of General Psychology*, 1935, *12*, 40–65.

Two types of conditioned reflex and a pseudo type. *Journal of General Psychology*, 1935, *12*, 66–77.

A discrimination based upon a change in the properties of a stimulus. *Journal of General Psychology*, 1935, *12*, 313–336.

A failure to obtain "disinhibition." *Journal of General Psychology*, 1936, *14*, 127–135.

The reinforcing effect of a differentiating stimulus. *Journal of General Psychology*, 1936, *14*, 263–278.

The effect on the amount of conditioning of an interval of time before reinforcement. *Journal of General Psychology*, 1936, *14*, 279–295.

Conditioning and extinction and their relation to drive. *Journal of General Psychology*, 1936, *14*, 296–317.

Thirst as an arbitrary drive. *Journal of General Psychology*, 1936, *15*, 205–210.

The verbal summator and a method for the study of latent speech. *Journal of Psychology*, 1936, *2*, 71–107.

Two types of conditioned reflex: A reply to Konorski and Miller. *Journal of General Psychology*, 1937, *16*, 272–279.

Changes in hunger during starvation. *Psychological Record*, 1937, *1*, 51–60.

Distribution of associated words. *Psychological Record*, 1937, *1*, 71–76.

Effects of caffeine and benzedrine upon conditioning and extinction (with W. T. Heron). *Psychological Record*, 1937, *1*, 340–346.

The behavior of organisms. New York: Appleton-Century-Crofts, 1938.

An apparatus for study of animal behavior. *Psychological Record*, 1939, *3*, 166–176.

Some factors influencing the distribution of associated words. *Psychological Record*, 1939, *3*, 178–184.

The alliteration in Shakespeare's sonnets: A study in literary behavior. *Psychological Record*, 1939, *3*, 186–192.

The rate of extinction in maze-bright and maze-dull rats. *Psychological Record*, 1940, *4*, 11–18.

A method of maintaining an arbitrary degree of hunger. *Journal of Comparative Psychology*, 1940, *30*, 139–145.

A quantitative estimate of certain types of sound-patterning in poetry. *American Journal of Psychology*, 1941, *54*, 64–79.

Some quantitative properties of anxiety (with W. K. Estes). *Journal of Experimental Psychology,* 1941, *29,* 390–400.

Processes involved in the repeated guessing of alternatives. *Journal of Experimental Psychology,* 1942, *30,* 495–503.

Reply to Dr. Yacorzynski. *Journal of Experimental Psychology,* 1943, *32,* 93–94.

Operational analysis of psychological terms. *Psychological Review,* 1945, *52,* 270–281.

Baby in a box. *Ladies' Home Journal,* October, 1945, 30.

An automatic shocking-grid apparatus for continuous use (with S. Campbell). *Journal of Comparative and Physiological Psychology,* 1947, *40,* 305–307.

"Superstition" in the pigeon. *Journal of Experimental Psychology,* 1948, *38,* 168–172.

Walden Two. New York: The Macmillan Company, 1948.

Card-guessing experiments. *American Scientist,* 1948, *36,* 456–458.

Are theories of learning necessary? *Psychological Review,* 1950, *57,* 193–216.

Human use of human beings. *Psychological Bulletin,* 1951, *48,* 241.

How to teach animals. *Scientific American,* 1951, *185,* 26–29.

The experimental analysis of behavior. *Proceedings and Papers of the Thirteenth International Congress of Psychology,* 1951, 62–91.

Some contributions of an experimental analysis of behavior to psychology as a whole. *American Psychologist,* 1953, *8,* 69–78.

Science and human behavior. New York: The Macmillan Company, 1953.

The science of learning and the art of teaching. *Harvard Educational Review,* 1954, *24,* 86–97.

Critique of psychoanalytic concepts and theories. *Scientific Monthly,* 1954, *79,* 300–305.

The control of human behavior. *Transactions of the New York Academy of Science,* 1955, *17,* 547–551.

Some issues concerning the control of human behavior (with C. R. Rogers). *Science,* 1956, *124,* 1057–1066.

Freedom and the control of men. *American Scholar,* 1956, *25,* 47–65.

A case history in scientific method. *American Psychologist,* 1956, *11,* 221–233.

What is psychotic behavior? In *Theory and treatment of the psychoses: Some newer aspects* (dedication of Renard Hospital, St. Louis), Washington University Studies, 1955, 77–99.

The experimental analysis of behavior. *American Scientist,* 1957, *45,* 343–371.

A second type of superstition in the pigeon (with W. H. Morse). *American Journal of Psychology*, 1957, *70*, 308–311.

Concurrent activity under fixed-interval reinforcement (with W. H. Morse). *Journal of Comparative and Physiological Psychology*, 1957, *50*, 279–281.

Schedules of reinforcement (with C. B. Ferster). New York: Appleton-Century-Crofts, 1957.

Verbal behavior. New York: Appleton-Century-Crofts, 1957.

Diagramming schedules of reinforcement. *Journal of the Experimental Analysis of Behavior*, 1958, *1*, 67–68.

Some factors involved in the stimulus control of operant behavior (with W. H. Morse). *Journal of the Experimental Analysis of Behavior*, 1958, *1*, 103–107.

Reinforcement today. *American Psychologist*, 1958, *13*, 94–99.

Teaching machines. *Science*, 1958, *128*, 969–977.

Sustained performance during very long experimental sessions (with W. H. Morse). *Journal of the Experimental Analysis of Behavior*, 1958, *1*, 235–244.

Fixed–interval reinforcement of running in a wheel (with W. H. Morse). *Journal of the Experimental Analysis of Behavior*, 1958, *1*, 371–379.

John Broadus Watson, behaviorist. *Science*, 1959, *129*, 197–198.

Pigeons in a pelican. *American Psychologist*, 1960, *15*, 28–37.

The analysis of behavior (a programmed text with J. G. Holland). New York: McGraw-Hill, 1961.

Cumulative record, Revised edition. New York: Appleton-Century-Crofts, 1961.

The design of cultures. *Daedalus*, 1961, *90*, 534–546.

Why we need teaching machines. *Harvard Educational Review*, 1961, *31*, 377–398.

Technique for reinforcing either of two organisms with a single food magazine (with G. S. Reynolds). *Journal of the Experimental Analysis of Behavior*, 1962, *5*, 58.

Operandum. *Journal of the Experimental Analysis of Behavior*, 1962, *5*, 224.

Squirrel in the yard: certain sciurine experiences of B. F. Skinner. *Harvard Alumni Bulletin*, May 26, 1962, *64*, 642–645.

Two "synthetic social relations." *Journal of the Experimental Analysis of Behavior*, 1962, *5*, 531–533.

Conditioned and unconditioned aggression in pigeons (with G. S. Reynolds and A. C. Catania). *Journal of the Experimental Analysis of Behavior*, 1963, *6*, 73–74.

Behaviorism at fifty. *Science*, 1963, *140*, 951–958.

Operant behavior. *American Psychologist*, 1963, *18*, 503–515.

Reflections on a decade of teaching machines. *Teachers College Record*, 1963, *65*, 168–177.

Reply to Thouless. *Australian Journal of Psychology*, 1963, *15*, 92–93.

New methods and new aims in teaching. *New Scientist*, 1964, *122*, 483–484.

Man. *Proceedings of the American Philosophical Society*, 1964, *108*, 482–485.

The technology of teaching. *Proceedings of the Royal Society*, Series B, 1965, *162*, 427–443.

Why teachers fail. *Saturday Review*, October 16, 1965, *48*, 80–81.

Contingencies of reinforcement in the design of a culture. *Behavioral Science*, 1966, *11*, 159–166.

What is the experimental analysis of behavior? *Journal of the Experimental Analysis of Behavior*, 1966, *9*, 213–218.

The phylogeny and ontogeny of behavior. *Science*, 1966, *153*, 1205–1213.

An operant analysis of problem solving. In *Problem solving: Research, method, and theory*, edited by B. Kleinmuntz. New York: John Wiley & Sons, Inc., 1966, 225–257.

Operant behavior. In *Operant behavior: Areas of research and application*, edited by W. K. Honig. New York: Appleton-Century-Crofts, 1966, 12–32.

Visions of Utopia. *The Listener*, January 5, 1967.

Utopia through the control of human behavior. *The Listener*, January 12, 1967.

The technology of teaching. New York: Appleton-Century-Crofts, 1968.

Teaching science in high school. *Science*, 1968, *159*, 704–710.

The design of experimental communities. *International Encyclopedia of the Social Sciences, 16*, 271–275. New York: The Macmillan Company, 1968.

Contingencies of reinforcement: A theoretical analysis. New York: Appleton-Century-Crofts, 1969.

PSYCHOLOGY AT HARVARD (1926–1931)
A REMINISCENCE

FRED S. KELLER

WESTERN MICHIGAN UNIVERSITY

Harvard University, in the late twenties of this century, was not the only center of American psychology. Yale, Pennsylvania, Cornell, Clark, Chicago, Princeton, Columbia, California (Berkeley), Stanford, and Minnesota boasted good departments, as did a few other universities. But Harvard was important—important in the eyes of the scholarly world, of its carefully chosen staff, and of each little band of students admitted yearly to its graduate classes. It may not have been the most American of psychology departments, but it was probably the most prestigious.

Admission to graduate study within its halls was not a complicated matter or fraught with undue worry. Applicants were few and decisions were made without the pretence of measuring a candidate's potentiality for success. A letter of recommendation, a personal introduction to the Chairman (with a few words of supporting comment), and an interview of perhaps five minutes' duration, were enough to launch a career. One had to have his A.B., or B.S., but not necessarily with distinction or in a special field of study. "We'll try to make an experimentalist out of you," said the Chairman, and one's acceptance was assured.

To a young man with a bad secondary-school education and a baccalaureate of dubious quality from a small New England college, Harvard was nevertheless a frightening place, once classes had begun. Not just because of its Yard, its ivied brick and classic columns, or academic fame; not just because of the forbidding silence and pervasive gloom of Emerson Hall, where one climbed daily to the third-floor home of the Department; but also because of an indefinable atmosphere, a certain ectoplasm of erudition, remoteness, and austerity that exuded from the Staff itself—from the directors of one's destiny.

As I call them up now in free association, they were an impressive group. Professor Boring, our Head, our principal lecturer, our mentor, and our conscience, was able to excite our respect, affection, fear, and amusement, in roughly that rank order of frequency. His were the unofficial *core* courses, rich in content and presented with the same compelling animation, semester after semester, at the same morning hour. Under him we studied *history, sensation, perception,* and *association and determination.* For none of these was there a textbook, so we sometimes came early to class to copy the suggested readings from the blackboard. Since many of these references were in German, we relied heavily upon our lecture notes in satisfying course requirements.

Professor Pratt, a Quaker, like Boring, who had come with the latter from Clark, seemed as much at home in art as in science, in German as in English. He lectured, sometimes explosively, in beautifully resonant tones that always commanded attention; and he had, as I recall it, some skill in vocal mimicry. (I seem to remember an impressive imitation of suction-cup tires on a wet pavement.) Through him I was introduced (barely) to *psychophysics* and, in a term of *aesthetics,* came to enjoy Santayana.

Professor Troland, once called "the young Helmholtz," excited our awe and admiration not by his lectures, which were sleep-inducing, but by his many text-

29

books, "written from dictation," someone said, "like Edgar Wallace mysteries," and by his recognition in the practical world of Technicolor. His knowledge seemed encyclopaedic, his laboratory a marvel of mirrors, tubes, and lenses, and his manner shy to the extreme. (I'll never forget our mutual embarrassment when, following a Christmas recess, I met him in the hallway, loaded down with mail, and impulsively extended my hand in greeting.) I attended his lectures on *physiological psychology* and *motivation,* and his evening seminar on *vision.*

Professor Beebe-Center was impressive, too, and not just because of the hyphen. Tall and slightly stooped, always running-away in his manner, he spoke French "like a native," was said to have a chateau in Tours, to teach at Harvard simply *pour le sport,* and to turn back his salary regularly to the University. He was also warm and responsive, but this I did not know for several years. With him I spent a term on *affectivity* (thus catalogued in deference to Radcliffe's Dean, for whom *affection* had improper overtones), while he was writing his *Pleasantness and Unpleasantness.* Beebe-Center was crystal clear in classroom exposition and unusually stimulative of research, even by undergraduates. He graded our French and German, too.

Professor Murray, at the Clinic, was the most approachable of all, seeming to welcome lecture interruptions and the exchange of ideas with students. He was, of course, not a *real* psychologist, like those of Emerson Hall, being interested in such concepts as *thematic apperception,* such measuring devices as the *psycho-galvanic reflex,* and such an area of study as that of unconscious motivation. He had an M.D. from Columbia, a Ph.D. from Cambridge, and rumor gave him "a wealthy Back Bay private practice." He was a provocative person, with a twinkling eye and an endearing speech defect, and I liked him very much, but he was clearly of a foreign population.

These were the central figures in our citadel of learning. Upon their teachings we depended most in passing two of our three main examinations on the way to our doctorates—the written "prelims" and the oral "general." Their courses would later serve as models, or at least as starting points, for courses of our own. From them we would draw not only facts and theories, but anecdotes and gossip, as well as our classroom styles.

They did, indeed, leave their marks upon us. Even now, more than forty years later, I can see Professor Boring, eyes rolled upwards, shoulders hunched, palms together before him, marching to and fro, with occasional darting smiles in our direction, as he explained Korte's Laws, praised Heymans' approach to the Müller-Lyer problem, summarized John Locke on the qualities of objects, distinguished between *Kundgabe* and *Beschreibung,* and discussed Rubin on figure-ground, Helmholtz on unconscious inference, Johannes Müller on specific nerve energies, or G. E. Müller on the method of *right associates.*

I can see Professor Troland, a study in preoccupation, discoursing in monotone on *retroflex* action (and smiling faintly as he disclaimed a personal reference in the *tro* of retroflex); on the relation of *P* and *U* to synaptic resistance; and on the merits of the three hedonisms—of the past, the present, and the future. I can also see Professor Beebe-Center, concernedly evaluating the tridimensional theory of feeling or the existence of an indifference point on the *P-U* continuum; Professor Pratt, showing us, with the aid of a recording, the lack of resolution in *Tristan and Isolde,* or illustrating the accrual of *context* to *core* by vocalizing

> When fur stews can the sill Lear I'm
> Toot rye tomb ache the mean ink leer
> Yule thin kits own lea way sting thyme . . . . etc.;

and Professor Murray, relating self-assertive to self-corrective compulsions, or introducing to his class a middle-aged nurse with "automatic speech." These and many other scenes are readily reinstated and they bring, I must confess, a certain nostalgia with them.

These men were not the only ones to whom I was, or could have been, exposed in the late twenties. Nearby, in physiology, was Professor Crozier, reputedly addicted to who-dun-its, working in the Loeb tradition and exciting the behaviorally inclined among us who were not mathematically illiterate. At the Medical School, there were Professors Davis and Forbes, for those who wanted the latest in nervous-system function and were hardy enough for the cross-town trip. Professor Dearborn was accessible, but seldom used, in education and statistics; Professor Sarton could be enjoyed (in the History of Science) without leaving Emerson Hall, as could Professors Whitehead, Perry, and a few other philosophers and logicians. We had a bountiful fare which, unfortunately, my own early training did not fully prepare me to appreciate.

Then there were our Visiting Professors, who spent a Summer Session with us, or even a regular term or two. I remember with especial pleasure the classes of Professors Hunter (Clark), Tolman (Berkeley), Perrin (Texas), and Bühler (Vienna). Koffka was also there from Smith, Robinson from Chicago, and Stone from Stanford, but I had no room for them within my workday schedule. None of the men under whom I did sit was very skilled at the podium; they excited me, I think, because they told about their unsolved problems, exposed their half-formed theories, and encouraged us to struggle with each. Our regular mentors were impressive in their scholarship, but commonly left us gasping with all that we had to learn; there was little time for thinking.

Professor Bühler, an expressive and *gemütvoll* person, brought us his theory of language, with a strong European flavor and some special English-language problems of his own. Professors Tolman, Hunter, and Perrin brought us animal researches, principally maze-learning studies, and provided us with our first respectable, academic taste of behaviorism. What's more, they gave us a glimpse of a fresh, free-swinging, non-Wundtian, "Western" world, in which teachers sometimes hobnobbed with students, in which issues were debated at kitchen-table seminars over mugs of prohibition beer, and where scholarship was probably defective (from our cloistered point of view), but where something new and possibly significant was stirring. For a few of us, their influence was actually greater than that of our regular staff.

Also a part of our educational scene was a long line of short-time visitors who came to give an address (e.g., a Lowell Lecture), to speak at our Colloquium, to attend the 1927 meeting of the Society of Experimental Psychologists, or simply to visit the laboratories. I recall, in particular, talks by W. B. Cannon, on emotion and bodily changes (dull); Selig Hecht, on visual theory (brilliantly impressive, he made you want to be a scientist); A. V. Hill, on fatigue (impressively British); L. Lapicque, on chronaxie (very French, but quite clear); Wolfgang Köhler, on "insight" (charming, but elusive); K. S. Lashley, on brain extirpation and maze learning (ghoulish); John Paul Nafe, on feeling (sepulchral); Johnson O'Connor, on aptitude testing (wrong audience); and J. B. Rhine, McDougall's assistant, agonizedly defending his chief's position on the Lamarckian inheritance of maze-swimming skill in the rat.

I can remember Professor McDougall himself, marching down the corridor, a short and chesty Roman senator, with a former pupil in tow; Professors Dallenbach and Langfeld, conversing in an empty classroom, Van Dykes wagging; and Professor Titchener ("T"), a stern little Santa, unconsciously presiding over his Society's meeting as Harold Schlosberg, a young graduate student from Princeton, reported his work on knee-jerk conditioning (to be tagged immediately as a "biological" study by the unofficial Chairman).

We saw our regular professors mainly in the classroom, or at Colloquium over tea and coffee. The atmosphere was never unfriendly, but there was little social interaction between the students and the staff. In five years of half-time study at Harvard, I was twice at Professor Boring's home, and once, I believe, at Professor Pratt's. On the two or three occasions when I conferred with Professor Boring in his office, it was under pressure from the timer on his desk, which could abruptly end our meeting. No one of the teachers I have mentioned ever called me by my given name, and I, of course, was never less formal than "Professor" or "Doctor"—a habit that was not really shaken in my later contacts with them.

With some of the younger men, at the instructor level, we enjoyed an easier relationship, especially as we neared the end of our studies. Frank Pattie, tall, languid, and suspected of genius, permitted "Frank;" Morgan Upton was "Kelly" to everyone who worked in the new animal laboratory at the top of Boylston Hall; and M. H. Elliott, a Tolman Ph.D., whom I assisted in Undergraduate Experimental, was "Hugh" to me and several others. Such intimacy was rare, however, and seldom led further than coffee together at the Georgian. The roles of teacher and pupil, master and apprentice, senior and junior, or worker and player, were clearly discriminated in the twenties.

When I asked myself what *students* I knew at Harvard during the time that I was there, I find that I'm in trouble. There were many more of them than teachers, and both the quality and quantity of my relations with them varied through a wider range. In a couple of hours, I was able to list the names of about thirty comrades-in-study [1] with whom I had some contact in the years between 1926 and 1931. Within this group, there were fifteen or twenty whom I knew quite well from having sat in class with them regularly, worked with them on laboratory exercises, or studied with them for examinations; and, finally, there were eight or ten of these whom I learned to know intimately through extra-curricular connections of one sort or another—at mealtimes, in the evenings, or on social safaris. Especially memorable are the hours I spent with Wes Bousfield, Jim Coronios, Paul Huston, Mac McCarthy, Obie Oberlin, Burrhus Skinner,[2] Bill Turner, and Jack Volkmann. (Briefer association was enjoyed with Hyung Lin Kim, Ed Newbury, Muzafer Sherif, and Bill Stavsky.)[3]

These men differed greatly in their origins and in their destinies. Of the former I can say little, but I know they ended up in widely different *ambientes*. Bousfield, Coronios, Newbury, Sherif, Skinner, and Volkmann remained in academic psychology; Huston went on to psychiatry and administration, with a medical degree; Oberlin soon turned from teaching to counselling and psychotherapy; Stavsky became a clinician; Turner's interests shifted to social work

---

[1] Here they are: Herbert Barry, Jr.; Weston A. Bousfield; Edw. N. Brush; A. Hadley Cantril, Jr.; Merton E. Carver; Dwight W. Chapman; James D. Coronios; Harry R. DeSilva; Crawford Goldthwait; Albert J. Harris; Wm. A. Hunt; Paul E. Huston; Theodore F. Karowski; Hyung Lin Kim; Donald W. McKinnon; Eugene F. McCarthy; Ross A. McFarland; Edw. Newbury; Kermit W. Oberlin; R. Nevitt Sanford; David Shakow; Muzafer Sherif; B. F. Skinner; Carl E. Smith; Wm. H. Stavsky; Chas. K. Trueblood; Wm. D. Turner; John Volkmann; and Robert W. White. (There were others whom I never saw, one whose name I cannot remember, and perhaps a couple I may have overlooked.)

[2] B. F. Skinner was, and is, known to most of his friends as *Fred*, but I gradually adopted *Burrhus*, hoping, I suppose, to avoid confusion in small group conversation. The hope was not realized, but my habit persists.

[3] I must also mention H. C. Gilhousen, already a Ph.D., from Tolman's laboratory, who was a research assistant and a tutor, but with us in spirit. A dedicated student of behavior and a talented commentator on the social scene, "Gil" was one of the bright spots in my last two graduate years, and our friendship still endures.

and administration; Kim went into business; and McCarthy, I believe, went into ophthalmology. Oddly enough, from a Department dedicated to the furtherance of normal, adult, human, experimental psychology in the classical tradition, Bousfield and Volkmann alone have borne the standard of such a science throughout their long and productive careers. A similar ratio holds when the larger group is considered.

When I am asked to talk about my days at Harvard, the focal point of interest is sometimes not exclusively in Harvard or my days, but in Burrhus Frederic Skinner and what I knew about him when we were there together. This is understandable. Among all of us who walked the Yard to Emerson and Boylston Halls in the twenties, he is the one whose name is known around the world today. Moreover, he has mentioned me in print on several occasions and honored me with a textbook dedication, while I have paid homage to his genius at various times and places. It is no wonder that strangers ask me about the relationship between us; that loyal pupils sometimes imagine influences upon him that I never exercised; that unfriendly critics cry "disciple," or worse; and that curious colleagues look to me for "inside" stories. (Sometimes I am even asked to defend the mode of life in *Walden Two,* discuss the "baby box" in pediatric detail, or give the *coup de grâce* to Dr. Chomsky.)

I don't know where or when I first met Burrhus Skinner. Let us just say in a Harvard classroom, in 1927; I doubt that anyone will check. And it could not have been long thereafter when he rented basement quarters in the Arlington Street apartment house in which I lived. From then on, we began to see each other fairly often, and discovered a number of things we had in common.

Our tastes in food, for example. Each of us had been sensitized by travel abroad, especially in Paris. I remember a good onion soup that we concocted in our kitchen, aiming, I suppose, to recover Left Bank savors; and the time when my friend bought a keg of wine-to-be, which was delivered with full instructions for aging, but which never really grew to vintage stature. Best of all, I remember excursions to Boston, by subway, to favorite eating places. We went to Jake Wirth's for *bratwurst and shell beans, sauerbraten, apfel strudel,* and other delicacies, topped off with seidels of point-three beer, in a high-ceilinged room with sawdust on the floor, *Suum Quique* over the bar, and the good-natured service of harried waiters who sometimes recognized our faces. We went to the Athens-Olympia, also on Stuart Street, for chicken *pilaf,* strong dark wine (presumably "needled") in coffee cups, and *baklava;* or to Locke-Ober's, dressed for the occasion, at a window table on the street floor (for gentlemen only), where we had dishes with sherry in them and chatted like true cosmopolites. Less lavishly, but more frequently, we enjoyed a simple Chinese meal, with chopsticks, in a little upstairs place near Harvard Square.

We each liked bicycling and we bought two Columbia wheels, which our boyhood expertise had recommended as the best. We often rode them to work and sometimes took trips together. We went to Walden Pond, where we stood beside the pile of stones that were thought to mark the site of Thoreau's hut, and talked about *Life in the Woods.* Our longest journey was to Providence, for an overnight stay at Brown, where Charley Trueblood and Jim Coronios were doing their doctoral research. My bike was finally stolen, from in front of Boylston Hall; I don't know what happened to his.

On a less positive note, there were other sources of affinity. Each of us had resisted parental wishes in choosing a vocation; each had openly renounced his early religious teachings; each had attacked such college prescriptions as "physical education" and compulsory chapel attendance; each had felt himself out of step with his fellow undergraduates; and each was as "un-American" as he could be without endangering any of his basic rights or privileges. (We didn't

wear attention-getting costumes; we didn't march in the streets for Sacco and
Vanzetti; we didn't join our expatriate contemporaries in Paris; we didn't burn
our college diplomas; and we didn't even buy the *American Mercury* openly on
Boston Common, in defiance of the Watch and Ward Society. I would say that
we were *tamely* un-American, not at all like our present-day "activists.")

We were also budding *behaviorists,* in a department that was basically
structuralistic. Skinner had read Pavlov, Loeb, and Watson (*Behaviorism*) before
coming to Harvard, and I had been led back into college in 1925 by reading
Psychology from the Standpoint of a Behaviorist. We defended the position in
many lively debates with our peers and occasionally spoke out in the classroom.
I was greatly flattered once when Professor Murray referred to us as "lions in
debate." I should probably have been embarrassed, but psychology in the twenties
was not yet the experimental science that it is today. The relative merits of the
various *schools* were still of major concern to anyone who planned, as we did,
to spend his life in teaching.

So much for the things we shared. I haven't included them all, and I don't
mean to suggest that we shared them exclusively. Each of us had his own socio-
gram, which included friends that never met each other. And it should go without saying that there were many other things which we did not have in common.
Besides the obvious difference in genetic constitution, we were brought up on
different sides of the track, we had different occupational histories, military
experience, and quality of education. We enjoyed different kinds of prose and
poetry, had liked different kinds of music, had felt differently about competitive
sports, and had fallen in love with different types of girls. Had we been reared
in the same town, we might never have met.

We had very different patterns of work and play. At nine in the morning,
when I was still rubbing sleep from my eyes, his working day was well advanced;
but he was no good at all socially after nine in the evening, when I was wide
awake. It used to irritate me mildly to see him playing pingpong with Bill Stavsky
or some other denizen of Boylston Hall in the middle of the "working day," and I
was faintly annoyed that he found time to play the piano or make marionettes
for Hallowell Davis's children. I don't know how we had as many hours together
as we did.

In view of the fact that most of my academic life has since been spent in the
advancement of reinforcement theory and its application, it may seem strange
that my real interest in "Skinnerian" research did not begin at Harvard in the
twenties, when my friend was developing his experimental techniques, collecting
early data, and starting to build a system. The fact is, however, that it didn't,
and, at the risk of too much self-reference, I'll try to explain why.

First, in addition to my teaching and laboratory duties, I had my doctoral
research to look after (a follow-up of Hunter's work with the temporal maze),
a dissertation to write (without an active sponsor), and examinations to pass. This
left me with little time for thinking about the work of other graduate students.
(Actually, Skinner took more account of my research than I of his. Observing my
tedious daily task of running rats, he once constructed an automatic temporal
maze that would permit an animal to carry out a left-left-right-right sequence of
choices twenty-four hours a day, receiving all his food and drink within the
apparatus. Had the procedure been successful, I would probably have had to
alter my theory of the learning process involved. More helpful than this was
the editorial aid he gave me when I was writing under pressure of a thesis
deadline.)

Secondly, Burrhus was a solitary worker (*Schedules of Reinforcement* is the
principal exception) and a very cautious one. He didn't describe his experiments

in advance of their execution; he never responded hastily to a challenging question (sometimes the answer was delayed for years); and he didn't announce a finding until he felt it was secure. He was not the kind to discuss his hopes or plans or half-analyzed data around the laboratory coffee-pot, at the dinner table, or with a drink in hand at some convention. Such prudence may win respect, but is unlikely to initiate joint enterprise.

There is still another reason for our lack of important interaction in the twenties. In spite of his genius in experimental research, Burrhus Skinner was primarily a systematist, even then, and I was essentially a teacher. While he was doing the spade-work for his paper on the reflex, I was translating mentalistic terms into stimulus-response and peddling the result to college undergraduates as a kind of ready-to-wear behaviorism. Nothing I ever got from him helped me much in composing lectures, and he got even less from me with which to further his ends. He was a producer of system; I was a promoter, and he had nothing yet ready for promotion.

I was, however, fully aware of his talent and I never expected less than a brilliant future for him. I was impressed by his study, reported at Colloquium, of eating behavior in the rat, although I did not recognize that *responses* could have replaced *pellets* on the y-axes of his plots. Later on, in the years between 1931 and 1938, I read his other papers as they came along, and even bought a *Skinner Box* (for $45.00), but I saw his contributions as mainly methodological. It was not until the summer of '38, when I began to read my copy of *The Behavior of Organisms,* that I finally saw what had been happening. Then, at last, I had something systematically exciting to give my classes, and a new phase of my own career began. But that is another story.

The changes in experimental-theoretical psychology during the past forty years have been far greater than commonly recognized by younger workers in our field. Within this period, for example, "schools" of psychology have passed quietly into history; "theories of learning" have come and gone (or should have); the laboratory experiment has replaced the polemic; and a self-supporting science of individual human behavior has emerged, along with an increasingly effective *praxis.* These changes are closely related to the fact that, within this same time span, a field of research called "learning" was crudely circumscribed, integrated, and extended.

In 1926, we could study, each in its own special chapter, textbook, or course: (a) memory and forgetting, (b) transfer of training, (c) maze learning, problem-box solution, and delayed-reaction capacity, (d) ball-tossing, dart-throwing, and Morse-code mastery, (e) concept formation, (f) language development, and (g) the newly-reported conditioned reflex. (Kohler's *Mentality of Apes* had barely reached us, hence "insight" and the *Umweg* method were not part of our usual offerings.) Each of these topics was uncontaminated by contact with the others, and any meaningful relation found between them was largely accidental and sometimes a source of worry.

In 1926, the most popular instruments for the laboratory study of behavior change were the maze and the memory drum; the principal measures of such change were those of *time and errors per trial;* the subjects were mainly white rats and college students. Great interest was shown in "learning curves," based on group data, and in the validity of certain "laws" of memory and habit formation (e.g., *frequency, recency, primacy, vividness, effect, completeness of response,* and *contiguity*). *Forgetting* was of some interest, especially in the case of nonsense syllables and other verbal material, and a few procedures had been suggested for the breaking of "bad habits;" but the concept of *extinction* was still around the corner, and that of behavior *maintenance* was ten years' distant or more. Pavlov's system was unknown, and so were Guthrie's views on the Russian's basic paradigm. Hull and his pupils were still several years away from taking the concept into the laboratory.

In 1926, learning research was hypothesis-oriented, crude in design, and instrumentally primitive. The picture of a psychologist was that of a man in a laboratory coat, pencil in one hand and stopwatch in the other, seated behind a screen through a hole in which he could observe a white rat on an elevated maze. Replications of research were rarely attempted and even more rarely achieved. Results were not trusted, sometimes not even by the investigator himself. Orderliness of change in an individual organism's behavior, except in the case of sensory studies, was unheard-of.

This was the situation in 1926, as well as I can remember. It is not the situation that exists today in the great centers of advanced psychological study. Memory, maze-learning, conditioning, and concept formation are now to be found within the same universe of scientific discourse and are now part of a theoretical formulation that also has within it a place for such traditionally unrelated elements as those of motivation, instinct, emotion, sensation, perception, and imagery. The field of "learning," as distinct from the field of psychology itself, is increasingly difficult to identify, and the word *learning* itself is passing from our technical vocabulary. Problems of long-term behavior maintenance have taken the play from those of simple acquisition and elimination.

The maze and the memory drum are ticketed for the *omnium gatherum* of psychological relics; the old "laws" of memory and learning have lost their allure; and the search for "the learning curve" no longer attracts volunteers. But smooth curves of behavioral change are now common, for the individual as well as the group; successful replication of experimental findings is the rule; and the day approaches, perhaps, when the application of mathematics to the description of human and animal behavior will be systematically meaningful.

Where and when did the movement begin which made the difference between 1926 and now? Historians will give better answers to this question than I could possibly provide. But I shall trade upon my own before-and-after status to suggest that it all started at Harvard University, during the late twenties and early thirties, in the experimental and theoretical labors of Burrhus Frederic Skinner.

As for my part in all this, I would now like to quote the inscription in my dog-eared copy of *The Behavior of Organisms: To Fred Keller—for friendship and faith when they were most needed—Burrhus.*

SCHEDULES OF REINFORCEMENT WITH SKINNER

C. B. FERSTER

THE AMERICAN UNIVERSITY

To tell about the pigeon laboratory at Harvard during the period I was there, I must first describe the state of the science at Columbia while I was a graduate student there. The comparison provides a "before and after" which will help me to communicate what happened at Harvard during the years when B. F. Skinner and I worked on *Schedules of Reinforcement*.

The pigeon lab was already operating at Harvard in the fall of 1950 when word reached Columbia that Skinner was looking for someone to assist him. Columbia was the obvious place to look because there was so much activity and excitement there about operant conditioning and a functional analysis of behavior. Keller and Schoenfeld had just completed *Principles of Psychology*, and the introductory course at Columbia was in full swing. We learned of the impact of a laboratory science of behavior on biological science, pressing community problems such as mental illness, education, and rearing children for a better life and a basic understanding of human nature. Everyone had conditioned a rat, read *Walden Two,* and most were impatient for a chance to try out a science of behavior. Some students fantasied a new Institute for Operant Behavior with buildings, equipment and full-time research. Others dreamed of an actual planned community modeled after *Walden Two* where the products of laboratory research could be lived and applied. I'm sure many of today's laboratories exceed what were then our wildest expectations. For in those days the typical operant experimenter either manually operated switches in a darkened room, or programmed a half dozen relays cannibalized from vending machines. A pressing instrumentation problem was a reliable pellet dispenser, but recording problems were not serious because only a small amount of behavior was recorded. Experiments, seldom more than an hour long, took place just before the rats were fed.

I was a third-year graduate student when, hearing of the chance to work with Skinner, I made an appointment to go to Cambridge for an interview. I took the midnight train to Boston and wandered around Harvard Square nervously from six in the morning until what I thought would be a respectable hour to appear at Skinner's office. The interview was easy once I got there. We had a coke, he showed me some of the equipment in the lab, and I was scarcely aware of at what point I knew that I was to come to work in February. Within two hours I was on my way back to New York and Skinner was back in his office writing.

I had finished almost all of my course work at Columbia and was doing exploratory experiments on chaining. A retractable lever came into the cage when the rat pulled a chain suspended from the ceiling. These were called exploratory experiments because they preceded the real experiment; because only one or two animals were used; because the procedures as well as the apparatus were constantly adjusted during the experiments; and because it was impossible to know in advance what was going to happen. Experiments in which an animal served as its own control were not quite acceptable at Columbia as yet.

Because Skinner wanted me to be in Cambridge by the first of February, completing a Ph.D. dissertation before I left posed a large problem. At Columbia, getting a thesis topic approved was quite an involved process. First there were informal tests with faculty and student. These consisted of discussions in the corridor with other graduate students and visits to several professors' offices. The proposed experiment was received very differently in different places. First, there were the kind ear and probing questions of Professor Keller who listened gently until there was no more time. Later in the day of my "test" with Keller, I found myself redoing the plan as I tried to explain answers to his questions. Others were not so gentle. A thesis plan also had to pass muster of a formal departmental meeting. Since I had not even gotten by the informal test when I returned from my interview with Skinner, it was clear that the usual process was much too long and labored to meet Skinner's deadline, so chaining was put aside, for the time being. Instead I formulated a hypothesis, built equipment, ordered fifty genetically controlled Wistar rats, and tested the hypothesis that a stimulus present during conditioning would influence the number of performances the rat would emit when reinforcement was discontinued.

The laboratory was in operation when I arrived in Cambridge. Several graduate students were preparing pigeon demonstrations for Skinner's introductory course and there were several pigeon boxes with relay control apparatus. The newest behavioral discovery was aperiodic or random-reinforcement (variable-interval) schedules which were programmed by a metal phonograph recording disc covered with plastic. A slow motor turned the disc. A wiper, operating on the outside groove of the disc, like the recording arm of a phonograph, picked up an electric pulse whenever the covering was scraped away. The distribution of scratches around the periphery of the disc made the variable schedule, and the number of scratches determined the average interval of reinforcement.

When I reported to Skinner on my first day, he showed me parts and plans for a variable-ratio programmer for Elinor Maccoby, then completing her Ph.D. in the Social Relations Department. She needed the equipment for an experimental thesis with pigeons, which extended the experiments on random-interval to random-ratio schedules as they were then called. The programmer, already designed by Skinner, was to be built from a stepping switch much along the principle of the motor-driven disc used to arrange a variable-interval schedule.

My first months in the pigeon lab were a strange contrast of days adjusting equipment and experimental procedures for one or two pigeons, and nights at

Fig. 1 The relay programming and recording equipment for the chained VI FI equipment. There were three parallel pairs of bars on the tables into which the relay and other control panels were fastened. The pigeon box rested on the shelf below the table and the recorder sat on a bridge across it.

the calculating machine trying log and trigonometric transformations of the thesis data to make an analysis of covariance possible. Fortunately, the increase of the frequency of rewards of the former activity could be paced with the early completion of the latter.

While I was building the variable-ratio programmer, I spent the rest of the time during my first week in the lab exploring all of the parts in the drawers and cabinets, reorganizing them according to my own habits, and labeling them to my custom. I found a large store of small electrical and mechanical parts: springs, phosphor bronze, string, glue, bakelite, plexiglas, surplus relays, assortments of capacitors and resistors, cable clamps, lacing cord, soldering supplies, bits and pieces of rubber and plastic, a large box of accumulated nuts and bolts, small odd pieces of metal, wire and cable, surplus electronic relays and electrical devices that could be disassembled for parts, cardboard and paper, motors and a host of the miscellany that seems to come in handy at odd times for unexpected uses. Gerbrands' machine shop down the hall had seemingly endless drawers of bolts and nuts, cotter pins, hex nuts, brass nuts, steel nuts, lock washers, Allen nuts, Phillips head, round-head, flat-head, oval-head, and spline-head screws, wood, machine and metal screws, brass and steel washers and lock washers. All were stocked in every length, diameter and thread. Further down the hall were the psycho-acoustic laboratory shops, directed by Rufus Grason, where resistors, capacitors and all of the rest were found in the same rows of cabinets and in the same profusion of varying wattages, resistances and capacitance values, accuracy levels and shapes. The pigeon laboratory already had a room dedicated as a shop with a drill press, two long work benches and the usual assortment of hand tools.

Instrumentation was easy and natural, and all components for innovative apparatus construction were immediately at hand. Herbach and Rademan sold surplus electrical equipment by mail order catalogue, even then, and it was the tradition then as it is now to scan the catalogue each month to buy parts and devices that "might be useful sometime." One of the first steps for solution of an instrumentation problem was always to look through the drawers and cabinets to see what suggested itself.

The physical arrangements of the laboratory, the supplies, the equipment and the shop were important factors in determining the kind of research that went on. There were sufficient parts immediately on hand for construction to begin the moment an experiment required new instrumentation. Skinner usually built the first model from what was on hand, seldom waiting because parts needed to be ordered. The prototype was usually makeshift and not quite reliable enough, but it served long enough to prove itself. By then there had been time enough to order proper parts and to build a well-constructed model.

Probably the most serious and pressing instrumentation problem we faced was the design of a reliable cumulative recorder, and the construction of enough of them to service the large number of experiments that ran concurrently. Even more recorders were needed because we developed the habit of using several at once on a single experiment, as in a multiple schedule, to treat the data during recording rather than by numerical manipulations later. The first model used a Ledex rotary switch to drive the pen on the performance scale. By this time the paper drive worked well, using a typewriter platen, with its associated mechanism for holding the paper, and the Leeds-Northrup glass reservoir pen solved the problem of providing a reliable ink line. Twelve recorders were hardly completed, however, when the experimental sessions lengthened because we learned how to sustain high rates of performance with our pigeons for ten-hour sessions or more. Experiments which recorded two or three thousand pecks at the start of our research soon required 100,000 or more pecks to be recorded during a single experimental session. For a long while, I spent much of my time replacing and repairing rotary solenoids which lasted only a few hundred thousand operations. The discovery of the Automatic Electric stepping switch mechanism, which stood up to the billions of pecks which were recorded on each instrument, freed much time and energy for other purposes.

It was an enormous source of support to move into a laboratory which Skinner had already arranged and stocked. A beginner faces so many anxieties and new problems that without this support I doubt that there would have been enough energy both for producing the physical arrangement of shops, supplies and equipment that is so critical in order to be able to do innovative research, and for actually carrying out an experiment. The pigeon lab set the pattern for all of my later laboratories. For example, I always saved and carried with me a large box of nuts, screws, hardware, assorted junk and parts and devices that accrued when the bench top was swept and that "might be useful someday." For almost ten years, I carried around a 244 pole stepping switch (purchased from surplus for a dollar or two) before I finally threw it out.

During my first months with Skinner and the pigeon lab, I learned a great deal about how to run a laboratory, design and interact with experiments, and think through instrumentation and research problems. The teaching process was so natural but subtle, that I had no awareness that I was learning anything new or that the research we were carrying out was a departure from the existing body of knowledge. It was not until months later, around the time we gave our first paper on schedules (Skinner on mixed and I on multiple schedules), that I began to consciously sense that our work was extending and departing from the current literature.

I think that part of the reason for the delicacy and smoothness of the learning process was Skinner's natural style of creating the conditions which allowed learning to take place rather than teaching or telling me things. In retrospect, my personal experience in the spring of 1950 contained many examples of how the laboratory environment contained supplementary and collateral variables which supported my behavior so long as they were needed, and which faded out as I developed my own ways of providing the same support. The first task assigned to me in the laboratory, constructing the random-ratio (variable-ratio) programmer for Elinor Maccoby's experiment, served to move me into action at my own pace and with support. The device had already been designed and the components were at hand. Although it was a simple device which I could now complete in an hour or two, I spent two or three days poking away at it, redoing it several times and at the same time getting used to the color of the walls and the other features of my new working space. No one checked on the progress of the device during these several days and the most important consequence of finishing it was its installation in the control circuits of Elinor Maccoby's pigeon experiment.

I began two experiments as soon as I had straightened out the cabinets, swept the floor, and built the random-ratio programmer. One was variable-interval baseline with a time out between reinforcement and the performance that preceded. I don't remember now why I did this experiment except perhaps it was the only one I could think of. Fortunately, no one asked me. I was surprised that the delay between the performance and the operation of the food magazine did not decrease the frequency of pecking, so I continued to extend the delay period. No one noticed this experiment for some time. Skinner suggested the second experiment. He thought we should do something with "ratios" and we talked about how number of pecks could control the bird's behavior in a ratio schedule and I suggested that we reinforce for a long time on FR 50 and see whether we could see the evidence of the reinforcement after fifty performances, when reinforcement was discontinued. Skinner suggested a random alternation between a small and a large fixed-ratio schedule (two-valued ratio) so that the control by the smaller ratio would show up in the effect on the large ratio on a continuing basis. The idea of a stable state experiment ended the discussion and began the experiment.

Thereafter our discussion about experiments occurred at "rounds," usually the first thing each morning when we toured the laboratory to look at the harvest from the day and night before. This was when we discovered the apparatus failures, particularly in cumulative recorders, which were so frequent and discouraging during the early days of the pigeon lab. Failures of programming and recording sometimes set an experiment back the days or even weeks that were necessary to recover the baseline. On these occasions Skinner always commented on what caused the failure and we discussed changes that would reduce the likelihood of failure in the future. Although both of us felt keen disappointment in the delay in the experiment, our remarks always concerned possible remedial action rather than the current failure of the experiment (or perhaps the experimenter). Rounds took thirty minutes to an hour, depending on the press of other activities, and it was a lively activity with much rolling and unrolling of cumulative records, comment on what had happened, ooo's and aaah's about a new degree of orderliness and planning of the next procedure. Conversations did not include references to who had pulled the switch, first mentioned the idea for the experiment, built the apparatus, or predicted the outcome of the experiment. It took almost a year before I stopped predicting. The pigeon really did know best what it was he was likely to do and the conditions under which he would do it. Free of Skinner's praise, I was also free of his censure, real or imagined. Yet I still had the advantage of an inspiring model I could observe, whose behavior prompted me to greater accomplishments. I remember how easy it was for me to talk with Skinner about experiments and psychology in general. I sometimes wondered how it was that this young man could face the feeling that almost anything he could do Skinner could do better. I think the reason I could contribute my portion without uneasiness was that I was never evaluated, rewarded or punished; nor was my behavior ever measured against his. I found Skinner's repertoire an ever-present source of prompts and supports which I could use whenever I was able to. It was a very fortunate young man from Columbia who had an opportunity to carry out his work with so much intellectual and practical support and with such exciting chances to "brainstorm." Nor was it a small measure of support to be able to watch B. F. Skinner in the laboratory designing new instruments, or to be able to turn over a problem to him.

But I give the reader the wrong impression if I suggest that there was no reinforcement for the results of experimentation other than the actual behavior generated in the birds. There were many personal, natural consequences of completing a successful experiment. A successful experiment led to conversations about the data, the new devices we could build, the new experiments that had to be started and the new ways we could organize our past experience from the laboratory.

When we discovered a new degree of orderliness or an unexpected but rewarding result on morning rounds, there was always much excitement and talk about where the experiment might go next and how to manage the equipment for the next experiment that was burning to be done because of the new result. When new discoveries accumulated too fast to be digested during morning rounds, there were planning sessions which were always great fun and very exciting. It was during these sessions that I learned the value of large sheets of paper which we used to aid our thought and to chart our progress. Every experimental result appeared as an entry someplace on paper about ten square feet in size. The theoretical structures and programmatic aspects of our work appeared

Fig. 2 The room where the graphs were pasted up and where schedules of reinforcement were written.

as the spatial arrangement of the headings. Later, these headings were to appear as chapter and subchapter titles in *Schedules of Reinforcement*. Each entry prompted rearrangements of the theoretical pattern and suggested new experiments and programs which in turn prompted further rearrangements of the data. The interactions between these theoretical exercises and changes in on-going experiments in the laboratory were continuous and constituted an important reinforcer. Although almost all of the entries on the large sheet of paper were in Skinner's hand, I took part significantly by providing facts and prompts, and by reacting to the patterns which emerged. Mostly we arranged and rear-ranged the findings and procedures we had discovered and worked with, and reacted to the new experimental procedures that were suggested by the arrange-ments. Skinner did most of the talking, just as he did most of the writing, but even when I was silent, I was always intensely involved because he generally spoke for both of us. It was sometimes like playing a well-tuned organ that could play itself if the right key were pressed and a properly reactive listener were present. We came to share such an extensive repertoire that not everything had to be said by each person. When one person spoke, the other frequently could have said the same thing a few minutes later, or he might have been so close to saying it that a small amount of supplementary stimulation was enough to pro-duce the same performance.

Our interaction as speakers and listeners was an apt illustration of the verbal process described in *Verbal Behavior* where Skinner wrote, in the chapter on supplementary stimulation, about strengthening the behavior of the listener. To a degree we were in the same position as speakers and listeners as the pro-verbial prisoners who told jokes by code numbers, indicating stories that they already knew. "When no one laughed when the taps on the pipe indicated Joke

Number Ten, it was explained to a visitor that this prisoner didn't tell jokes very well."

One of the unspoken rules of these thinking, planning and theory sessions was to avoid criticism or contradiction. The performances which occurred were delicate and of such high frequency that criticism or contradiction produced a large and sudden change. I learned that there were natural consequences of unproductive or incorrect suggestions or formulations which shaped them and altered their frequency. Any thought was fair game and the worst that could result from an error, an inept or an inappropriate suggestion was that it would be ignored or have no consequences in prompting or aiding other activities. If one or the other of us had strong behavior which was not shared, a record was made on the work sheets, apparatus was built, or an experiment was started, but there was no requirement for both to participate or speak about it. In some cases an unshared line of work disappeared because the performances it led to were not useful. In other cases it persisted successfully.

I don't remember any experiment being called "great" or "bad" or anyone being given credit for doing something especially useful or valuable. Some experiments led to further planning, new apparatus, exciting conversations, new theoretical arrangements of data and procedures or a rush to tell everyone about them, while others enabled less behavior of this kind. I don't know whether Skinner was conscious of the lack of personal praise in interpersonal relations in the laboratory. I certainly was not. My behavior was generated by the natural reinforcement of the laboratory activity. But some of the graduate students found the absence of personal support difficult.

Recently a distinguished psychologist, who had come to Harvard when he was a student to study under Skinner in the pigeon lab, reminded me of an incident which illustrated the personal styles around the laboratory then. After completing the professional seminar, the main classroom experience in the Harvard curriculum, he appeared before Skinner saying that he was ready to do research in the pigeon laboratory. He asked what he should start on. The conversation was awkward; the student did not receive the kind of support and encouragement that he expected, especially since he had come to Harvard for the single purpose of working under Skinner. Finally, in the heat of frustration, he complained, "Aren't I even going to get a pigeon box?" This remark galvanized Skinner who dashed out of his office into the pigeon laboratory around the corner shouting, "Charlie, he needs a pigeon box," and left. I dutifully took one of the unused Sears and Roebuck ice chests we used as the shells for pigeon experimental spaces, handed it to him, and left. The student was then left with the problem of assembling all of the components and constructing the equipment he needed. Although neither Skinner nor I remembered the incident, the anger and disappointment could be detected after all these years. Yet he went on to complete an experiment which was an original departure from the main experimental program of the pigeon laboratory and which still remains in the literature as a base for much research and thinking. I don't know whether this particular student would have gone on to do the same valuable work had Skinner supported his ideas personally, or had I given him equipment and supervised his day to day work in an experiment related to ours. But I think many others would have become pale imitations of Skinner and Ferster rather than the original, imaginative, aggressive scientists they did become.

The pigeon staff meeting where we reviewed current experiments with graduate students and others was one of the traditions of the laboratory. We met, usually weekly, in the seminar room, reviewing and talking about one or two birds. Ogden Lindsley introduced the symbol of the pigeon feather at this time when he made up a sign with a pigeon feather that was hung on the bulletin board on

Fig. 3 The members of the pigeon staff meeting posed for a picture toward the end of one of the meetings. Left to right are: B. F. Skinner, Clair Marshall, W. H. Morse, R. J. Herrnstein, Tom Lohr, Nate Azrin, and James Anliker. Murray Sidman was visiting. Others attending frequently were Peter Dews, Ogden Lindsley, and Michael Harrison.

days that there were meetings. Later, he sent a white feather to the charter subscribers of *JEAB*. The seminar presentation consisted of either Skinner or me going through the cumulative records, a day at a time and a bird at a time, reacting to the small details of the results. The substance of the meetings was a very detailed examination of the results, even if some participants had to learn to read cumulative records upside down. There were frequent interruptions with questions, suggestions, or comments, and usually a prolonged discussion at the end. When the prolonged discussion occurred before all of the data in the experiment had been covered, we continued with the same bird the next time. Later, when students and others had experiments under way, they brought in their data in a similar way. The presentations of the pigeon staff meetings were seldom a summarized formal report of what had happened in the experiment, but rather an informal scanning of the raw data. I think the feeling of participating in the formulation and identification of the results contributed to strong interest in the meetings.

Most of the research for schedules of reinforcement was completed by 1953, when we began to plan a written report. As more of my time shifted to organizing the data and writing, the laboratory was turned over to Morse, Herrnstein, and others at Harvard. By the end of 1954, Skinner and I were writing full time. The first problem we faced was how to present the large amount of data we had collected, not only from long experimental sessions and protracted experiments, but also from a large number of separate experiments. By the end of our research there were about a dozen separate experiments in progress. The problem was to compromise between the need to report enough detail of our descriptive experiments and the need to reduce the bulk of the thousands of feet of cumulative curves. Three inventions—the collapsed record, a razor blade, and a standard cardboard stock thirty inches long—got the final report under way. Collapsing the record by cutting out blank paper along the time axis allowed us to present as much as fifty to seventy-five thousand pecks in a single figure; the razor blade made it possible to cut the records swiftly and effortlessly; and the card stock permitted a storage system that was easily handled. Skinner usually pasted records on the cards while I cut excerpts from the folders. Decisions about what to excerpt were made quickly, usually without much discussion because we were both so familiar with the records. Skinner took justifiable pride in his skill and speed with a razor blade. The ultimate test was to cut on several layers of paper, piercing an exact number of layers. The figures were pasted up, experiment by experiment, and the categories under which the figures were filed turned out to be the chapter and section headings of the book. On our best days we could do thirty figures, but this was a grueling pace which could not be kept up. Once the figures were completed, the writing turned out to be a relatively routine job of describing the main features of a record and indicating procedures. It became clear very early in our writing that we could not discuss the experiments theoretically or spell out the implications for the casual reader.

We worked slowly at first, but the need to finish before my scheduled departure in June 1955 led us to organize our environment and to develop several ways of self-management. All our work was done in a room dedicated to writing and not used at other times. Interruptions were the first problem, which we handled by a decision not to take phone calls. When visitors appeared at the door, we routinely stepped in the corridor to speak with them briefly. The frequency of interruptions became very low and the writing room came to control our behavior. Usually we began before nine and stopped by lunch time. There was frequently a temptation to continue in the afternoon when we were working especially well or when the data was especially interesting, but our recently acquired data on fixed-ratio performances convinced us to seek a work schedule that kept our performance at maximum frequency for the period we were actually writing. The procedure worked very well. There were no warm-up or inactive periods in the writing room. Naturally we did not write elsewhere nor did we converse about outside matters nor do anything but work on schedules of reinforcement so long as we were in the writing room. At times the pace of the writing was so intense, and rewarding, that we began to control our outside activities in the fear that they might compete with or decrease the frequency of writing and graph-making. Bridge, chess and late social evenings were out.

The professional record speaks for the "before and after" of the pigeon laboratory. There were personal results too, however. B. F. Skinner has already written his feelings about our collaborative activities. For my part, besides the satisfaction of a very rewarding association, I remember most of all how I came away from the pigeon lab with a firmly developed attitude toward discovery and unknown things.

There is a fear of the unknown in research just as there is a fear of dealing with new people. We approach a new problem or a new person with a repertoire that comes from our past experience. When we are successful, the new person or problem differentially reinforces our existing repertoire, and we acquire a new means of dealing with a new environment. Unfortunately, the old repertoire often continues without significant influence of the new contingencies. Such a repertoire is called compulsive or neurotic by clinicians. The analogue, in research, is the experimenter who is controlled primarily by the social and professional consequences—his colleagues' verbal behavior—and to a lesser degree by the behavior he produces and measures in his experiment. I don't think we were ever worried in the pigeon lab that we would have nothing to show for our time or that an experiment would waste time and money. The pigeon lab was a place where an unknown problem became an occasion which led to discovery and accomplishment rather than a cause for worry. The more a new situation could be seen as very different from our current experience, the more it signalled an experiment that would bring results which we valued. Perhaps my experience in the pigeon lab with B. F. Skinner prompted me to write in 1958: "A potential reinforcing environment exists for every individual, however, if he will only emit the required performances on the proper occasions. One has merely to paint the picture, write the symphony, produce the machine, tell the funny story, give affection artfully, (manipulate the environment and observe the behavior of the animal) and the world will respond in kind with prestige, money, social response, love (and recognition for scientific achievement)." [1]

[1] C. B. Ferster, "Reinforcement and punishment in the control of human behavior by social agencies," *Psychiatric Research Reports*, Dec. 1958, 101–118.

GENERALIZATION GRADIENT SHAPE AND SUMMATION IN STEADY-STATE TESTS[1]

DONALD S. BLOUGH

BROWN UNIVERSITY

Pigeons' pecks at one or two wavelengths were reinforced intermittently. Random series of adjacent wavelengths appeared without reinforcement. Gradients of responding around the reinforced wavelengths were allowed to stabilize over a number of sessions. The single (one reinforced stimulus) and summation (two reinforced stimuli) gradients were consistent with a statistical decision account of the generalization process.

Generally speaking, if an operant response is reinforced in the presence of a stimulus, the response will later occur with relatively high probability when that stimulus is present. What happens if the response is reinforced in the presence of two or more stimuli? Two cases, limited to two stimuli for simplicity, may be distinguished: (a) Responses are measured to the two stimuli presented singly, and to the two presented together. If joint stimulation produces a greater response than either stimulus alone, "summation" is said to have occurred. (b) Responses are measured to a set of unreinforced stimuli related in some way to the two reinforced stimuli. The response to each of the unreinforced stimuli yields one point on a "generalization gradient". Gradients following single-stimulus reinforcement are compared with those following reinforcement of two stimuli. If the two-stimulus gradient is higher at some point than either single-stimulus gradient, "generalization gradient summation" is said to have occurred at that point.

This paper is about generalization gradient summation, but no implications are intended about the nature of the discriminative processes that may be involved. Unfortunately, terms concerned with stimulus control have not been precisely used, and they often have unintended theoretical connotations. "Gener-alization" and "discrimination" are notorious examples, since they do not even imply distinct procedures. The confusing consequences are typified in the present studies, which some readers might prefer to call "generalization" experiments, others "discrimination" experiments.

A distinction of value, however, is that between transient and steady-state situations (Sidman, 1960). Conditioning and extinction typify behavioral transients. The generalization method pioneered by Guttman and Kalish (1956) shows stimulus control during the extinction transient. Though the transient data from the Guttman and Kalish method have provided important qualitative information, attempts to state the shape of functions and to account for combination effects such as gradient summation (Kalish and Guttman, 1957, 1959) and generalization peak shift (Hanson, 1959) have been inconclusive. Perhaps this results partly from the fact that the measurements involve complex changes and response components that are difficult to sort out (Blough, 1963).

The complexities introduced by transient testing may be reduced by treating generalization as a psychophysical problem (Boneau and Cole, 1967; Blough, 1967). For this purpose, gradients are obtained repeatedly under the same conditions for many sessions (Pierrel, 1958). The present experiments generated steady-state gradients centered around several reinforced stimuli on a wavelength dimension. A recently developed reinforcement schedule (Blough, 1966) kept responding stable yet relatively unstereotyped throughout the experiment. Both single and summated gradients

[1]Dedicated to B. F. Skinner in his sixty-fifth year. This research was supported in part by USPHS grants MH-02456 and MH-08355. Mrs. Patricia Blough contributed to the research by running the subjects and computer programming. Reprints may be obtained from the author, Walter S. Hunter Laboratory of Psychology, Brown University, Providence, Rhode Island 02912.

were collected for each of three subjects; these were regularized somewhat by rescaling the stimuli, and their form was related to possible controlling mechanisms.

METHOD

Subjects

Three White Carneaux pigeons were maintained at approximately 75% of free-feeding weight by supplementary feeding, if necessary, after each experimental session. The birds had all served previously in an experiment on reinforcement schedules (Blough, 1966), and Birds 556 and 812 had a variety of discrimination training prior to that.

Apparatus

The birds worked simultaneously in three standard Grason Stadler pigeon chambers. These chambers were dark except for a stimulus spot projected upon the response key. The key switches closed on application of about 10-g force. Each chamber was equipped with a ventilating fan and a loudspeaker that supplied white masking noise.

Stimuli were provided by a Bausch & Lomb 250-mm grating monochromator equipped with a ribbon filament lamp operated at 17 amp ac. Entrance and exit slits were set to provide a half-width dispersion of 6.6 nm. Light of this limited wavelength passed through a set of shutters to focus on the ends of three fiber-optics light guides of $\frac{1}{8}$ in. diameter by 3 ft. length. The terminal ends of the light guides were mounted approximately $\frac{1}{4}$ in. behind the translucent plastic response keys in the pigeon chambers. The stimulus patch supplied by the wires consisted of a fuzzy spot of approximately $\frac{3}{8}$ in. diameter, centered on the circular response key. The luminance of the spot was approximately six foot lamberts at 580 nm. The spot appeared on the key at all times except during reinforcement, during intertrial intervals, and for 0.6 sec after each peck. The key went dark after each peck to provide feedback to the subject for effective responses, and because responses at shorter interresponse times (IRTs) are not generally under stimulus control (Blough, 1963, 1966).

A small general-purpose computer, the LINC, (Clark and Molnar, 1964) sensed closures of the key switches. The LINC stored response latencies and interresponse times in its magnetic core memory; the data were periodically written onto magnetic tape. During the session, the LINC programmed stimulus presentations, drove a stepping motor to adjust stimulus wavelength, and operated shutters to control presentation intervals. The machine also delivered reinforcements via its output relays, according to programmed instructions outlined below. Following each session, the LINC printed key data tables and graphs on a teletype; subsequently, other data analyses were performed and the results either printed or graphically displayed on the machine's oscilloscope.

Procedure

The experiment ran daily for seven months, each daily session lasting 134 min. The session consisted of a sequence of 30-sec trials, during which the stimulus spot illuminated the response key. Three-second blackout periods separated the trials. On some of the trials reinforcement was available on an intermittent schedule; these will be called "S+" trials. These S+ trials were mixed with unreinforced trials ("test trials") according to a semi-random sequence as follows. Each session began with four S+ trials. Following this warmup, the session was divided into 15 stimulus sequences, presented serially. Each sequence consisted of 12 test trials, each a different wavelength, and four S+ trials, all 16 mixed in random order. It is important to note that if any wavelength appeared in the sequence as an S+, it also appeared once, unreinforced, as a test stimulus. The data presented in this paper are from test trials only.

Reinforcement consisted of 3-sec access to mixed grain. The reinforcement schedule in effect during S+ presentations was a somewhat simplified version of a schedule, described in detail elsewhere (Blough, 1966), called the "reinforcement of least-frequent interresponse times" or "LF" schedule. This schedule reinforced only those responses that terminated IRTs that the bird emitted least often, relative to the distribution of IRTs that would be expected were responses to occur on the average of 1 per sec, but randomly in time. On S+ trials, each peck that met the IRT criterion momentarily in force produced reinforcement. For reinforcement purposes, the latency of a peck from the beginning of a trial counted as an IRT. After each reinforcement and each trial, the LINC recomputed the IRT next required for reinforcement. Only response data from previous S+ trials entered the computation, and of these, only the most-recent 72 IRTs. For a full explanation of the details of this computation, see Blough (1966). In respects here unspecified, the schedule was as reported in that paper. The birds obtained approximately 60 to 70 reinforcements per session.

The LF schedule produces a pattern of reinforcement and of behavior much like that of a variable-interval schedule. It has the advantage for the present study of maintaining relatively constant response rates across subjects and through long experimental procedures. In previous work (unpublished) similar to that reported here, VI schedules have produced rates that climbed dramatically from session to session, in some birds approaching the high rate characteristically generated by a ratio schedule.

Single and double S+ sessions. As outlined above, each session started with four S+ trials and continued with 15 series of 16 trials each, a series comprising 12 test trials and four S+ trials. For single S+ runs, just one of the test wavelengths appeared on the four S+ trials in each sequence. During these S+ trials, reinforcement was available on the schedule just described.

During most of the experiment, two wavelengths rather than a single one, were selected for reinforcement. During these sessions, each of these two stimuli appeared on two of the four warmup S+ trials, and each appeared on two of the four S+ trials interspersed with the 12 test trials of each sequence. The LF reinforcement schedule was maintained independently for each of the two S+ wavelengths.

Stimulus ranges and S+ placements. Stimulus wavelengths over a 44-nm range from 558 nm to 602 nm were presented during the experiment. This range was selected because of the relatively high energies available from the monochromator, and the high and relatively constant luminance of the stimuli for the pigeon (Blough, 1958) over this part of the spectrum. Sometimes the entire range was used, with the 12 test stimuli spaced 4 nm apart across the spectrum; on other occasions, a narrower part of the spectrum was used, with correspondingly closer spacing of the stimuli. In general, the wide range was employed with two widely spaced S+s, and the range narrowed for a single S+ or two closely spaced S+s. Each range and combination of S+s appeared repeatedly until the data collected from day to day appeared to be stable. Table 1 lists the stimulus conditions and the number of days spent on each.

Table 1

Stimulus Conditions Employed in the Experiment

S+ in nm	Test stimuli, nm	Number of sessions
570 (pretraining)	570 only	17
570	560-582, 2-nm steps	43*
570	558-602, 4-nm steps	13
570, 590	same	27*
570, 586	same	20*
574, 586	same	15*
578, 586	562-598 in 4-nm steps, plus 580, 584	15*
580, 584	same	4
same	566-594 in 4-nm steps, plus 576, 580, 584, 588	12*
582	same	2
same	570-592 in 2-nm steps	8*
578, 586	same	2
574, 586	558-602 in 4-nm steps	1
570, 590	same	26*
590	578-600 in 2-nm steps	24*
582	576-587 in 1-nm steps	31*

*Last six sessions analyzed and shown in Figures.

As Table 1 shows, single S+ gradients were obtained around three wavelengths, 570, 582, and 590 nm. Double S+ gradients were obtained around combinations of these and intermediate wavelengths. In a number of cases (see Table 1), a few transition sessions intervened between prolonged runs on a given condition. These helped to prevent the subjects' behavior from being disrupted, particularly when marked shifts in S+ wavelength were in progress.

RESULTS

Single Gradients

Each bird produced single S+ gradients around three wavelengths, 570 nm, 582 nm, and 590 nm, with test stimuli spaced at 2-nm intervals. The gradient around 582 nm was replicated with 1-nm spacing in two birds. Figure 1 shows the results of all these single S+ conditions. The data are means over the

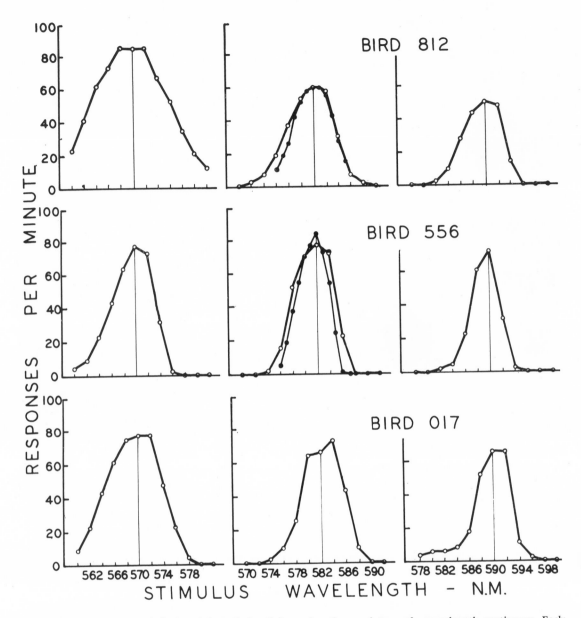

Fig. 1. Gradients around single reinforced stimuli located at three points on the wavelength continuum. Each function represents the mean of six sessions. Test stimuli were spaced at 2-nm intervals except for replications (filled circles) with stimuli 1-nm apart.

last six days of the given procedure. These and subsequent data include only responses from unreinforced test presentations, and also omit responses to the first of the 15 daily stimulus series. In all graphs, "response rate" means responses per minute when the stimulus was on; this quantity includes a correction for the 0.6-sec off period after each peck, since such off periods were sometimes extended by rapid multiple pecks.

Figure 1 shows that the birds gave rather regular gradients of similar form. Individual differences across birds are largely consistent differences in the width of the functions, those of Bird 812 being relatively wide and those of Bird 556 relatively narrow. Across wavelengths, a consistent effect is seen with all the birds: the curves tend to be steeper to the right of the reinforced wavelength than to the left, and they are narrower at the right of the figure (around 590 nm) than the left (around 570 nm). Both of these observations are consistent with the idea that equal wavelength steps are not the most appropriate way to space the stimuli. Hence, rescaling of the abscissa was attempted, as described below.

Gradients with two S+s. Considered now are gradients generated by the reinforcement of responses at two stimulus wavelengths, rather than just one. Once again, the data consist of mean response frequencies for each bird over the final six days of a given reinforcement condition. On the basis of these sets of data, together with the single gradient data presented in Fig. 1, a rough rescaling of the stimulus continuum was attempted along the lines suggested by Shepard (1965). Since the single gradients did not overlap extensively, and the bimodal gradients posed a complex analytical problem, an analytical solution that would yield the desired uniform gradient shape was not attempted. Instead, a graphical approximation was performed which resulted essentially in stretching the continuum at the longer wavelength end and compressing it at the shorter, to yield roughly symmetrical curves. The single-stimulus gradients were plotted on cumulative probability paper, and the two limbs around each S+ were fitted with straight lines. The abscissa scale was adjusted to make the slope of these lines as equal as possible. Since there were some apparently systematic differences between birds, the resulting scale is not optimum for any individual bird.

The dual S+ gradients are shown on this new abscissa in Fig. 2. The curves in this figure include one single S+ gradient around 582 nm (leftmost curve), and also include the replication of the widest separation of S+s (570 nm and 590 nm), shown by the dashed curve in the rightmost rank. The implications of these curves will be touched on below. Note the individual differences, with Bird 812 yielding unimodal curves for all conditions (except a suggestion of bimodality in the replication curve) and the other birds showing a regular progression from a bimodal to a unimodal curve.

Components of gradients. The shape of some of the gradients in Fig. 1 and 2, especially the flat ones of Bird 017, prompts inquiry about possible components that may combine to produce these curves. Such inquiry

is appropriate, too, because this study attempts to approach as simple a steady-state situation as possible, eliminating sequential components inherent in the standard generalization testing procedure.

The data were examined for the effects of several possible variables that might be expected to introduce variability in the curves. No trend could be detected in the data across the six days that entered into the means shown in Fig. 1, 2, 3, and 4, nor were consistent within-session effects evident in data over that portion of each session (the last 14 stimulus series) presented here. However, a consistent effect appeared when the results were broken down by time within 30-sec stimulus presentations. Responding when the stimuli first appeared was less well-controlled (flatter gradients) than was responding after the stimulus had been present for some seconds. This effect can be seen in Fig. 3, where responses occurring in successive thirds of each 30-sec trial are segregated, and functions constructed for each time period. This sample, consisting of gradients around 590 nm, shows the first 10-sec gradients higher in two cases, but in all cases proportionally wider, than the gradients from the latter two time periods. This effect appeared in all sets of data from all birds, with both single and dual S+ curves.

Working with discrete trials, Boneau, Holland, and Baker (1965) found that when responses to trials following reinforced trials were collected according to stimulus, broader gradients resulted than on other trials. Comparable gradients were constructed by locating all stimulus presentations after the appearance of a reinforced S+ and adding up (for each stimulus) the responses emitted during such trials. Since random stimulus sequences were used, the resulting sums were corrected by dividing each by the number of times the given stimulus actually appeared after a reinforced trial. The same procedure was followed for stimuli separated from reinforced presentations by two intervening trials. The resulting gradients did not differ in any systematic way from each other or from the overall gradients, though small differences may have been obscured by the relatively high variability of the curves. It is possible that this result differs from that of Boneau *et al.* (1965) because the extended trials allowed reinforcement effects to dissipate within the reinforced

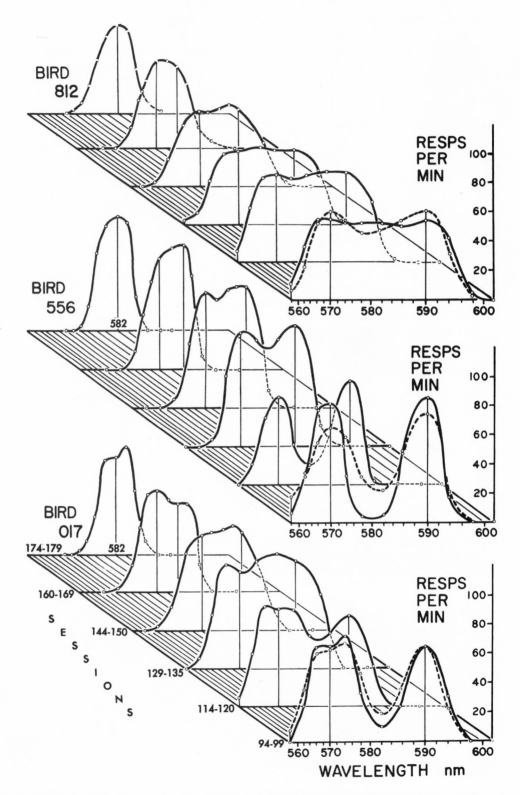

Fig. 2. Summation gradients for various S+ separations. Thin vertical lines indicate reinforced stimuli; dashed curves are replications. Note that the abscissa is distorted; see text for explanation.

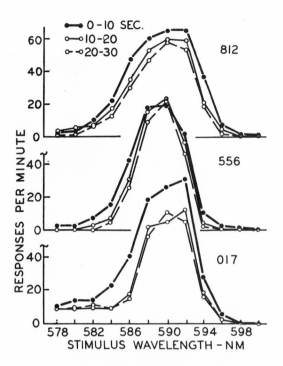

Fig. 3. Sample data showing effect upon gradient shape of time within each 30-sec stimulus presentation. Note that gradients from the first part of the presentation are broader than those from later parts. These curves are representative; all data sets showed the effect.

trial itself, rather than extending across trials. Boneau *et al.* used 2-sec trials and the effect had disappeared by the second trial after reinforcement.

Finally, the probability of response as a joint function of stimulus wavelength and of time since preceding response was estimated. On the basis of previous results (Blough, 1963 and unpublished data) it is to be expected that responses terminating IRTs of less than 1 sec will be less affected by stimulus value than by longer IRT responses. The procedure of inserting a 0.6-sec blackout after each peck eliminated many of these short IRTs. The remaining short IRTs were compared with longer IRTs in the following way. The IRTs/ Op statistic, which estimates the probability of response conditional upon IRT (Anger, 1956), was computed for responses to each stimulus. For this purpose, IRTs were divided into four bins: 0.6 to 1 sec, 1 to 2 sec, 2 to 4 sec, and greater than 4 sec. The results for all sets of data were similar, but the largest number of meaningful points came from the sessions involving 1-nm stimulus spacing. These were

single-stimulus gradients around 582 nm, and they appear in Fig. 4. Where few or no responses occur to a stimulus, IRTs/Op becomes quite variable, and such points are omitted. Also omitted are points for the last IRT bin (IRTs greater than 4 sec), since this transformation always yields "1" in the last bin. It is evident here that the stimulus controlled response probability effectively only in the 2- to 4-sec range, and even there the curves are quite flat compared with overall response rate curves. (The overall response rate curves appear in Fig. 1, center column, black points.)

Why are the overall rate curves steeper than the conditional probability functions in Fig. 4? The effect is largely a result of the fact that at stimuli relatively distant from S+, a rather high proportion of trials yield very few or no responses. Since at least two responses are required to define an interresponse time, trials yielding 0 or 1 response contribute nothing to the curves in Fig. 4, while trials with few responses contribute relatively little. On the other side of the coin, trials to these stimuli that do happen to yield more responses, and hence contribute to Fig. 4, are a portion of the population of trials selected on the basis of high momentary response probability. Blough (1967) found this variability in rate to different trials with the same stimulus useful in analyzing stimulus control in these situations; no more will be said of the matter here.

The data of Bird 017 deserve special mention, since they differ in several respects from those of the other birds. Particularly in evidence are irregular and flat-topped gradients (Fig. 1 and 2). The difficulty in this case can probably be traced to the nature of the bird's behavior and its interaction with the LF schedule of reinforcement. This bird tended to start each trial with a burst of responses (Fig. 3). Therefore, to meet the LF schedule criterion of balanced IRT distribution, the bird was required to "wait" to an excessive degree in the remainder of the trial. This constituted, in effect, a differential-reinforcement-of-low-rate (DRL) component in the reinforcement schedule. Such a contingency is known to flatten generalization gradients (Hearst, Koresko, and Poppen, 1964) and also steady-state gradients (Gray, 1966). It is possible that this flattening is due to stimulus control of "waiting" as a response separable from peck-

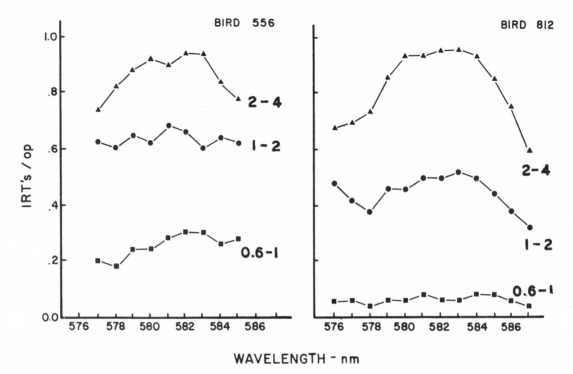

Fig. 4. Gradients showing probability of response as a joint function of wavelength and of interresponse time. The numbers next to each curve indicate the IRT bins in seconds. The overall level of the curves varies with the size of the time bin contributing to the curve; the shape of the curves is their significant aspect. See text.

ing, though further evidence is needed on this point. In any case, it is evident that the LF schedule needs modification to take into account response sequences and stimulus periodicity, as well as overall IRT distribution.

If different response patterns were found to be correlated with each of two reinforced stimuli, "summation" would be hard to interpret. Figure 2 indicates that where reinforcement was delivered in the presence of two stimuli, the rates to these two stimuli tended to remain about the same. Response patterning to the two stimuli as indicated by distributions of IRTs likewise showed no indication that different patterns of response were differentiated.

DISCUSSION

It is hard to compare these data with previously collected generalization functions, because the present data come from a situation that involved maintained reinforcement instead of extinction. As suggested above, it appears easier to cope with data of the present sort, for several reasons. First, the major variables controlling the gradient seem reasonably

well in hand, while a number of studies have suggested important effects of prior (often uncontrolled) experience upon the typical generalization gradient (*e.g.*, Friedman and Guttman, 1965; Peterson, 1962). Secondly, the maintained procedure substitutes the steady state for the complexities attendant on a transient process. In the usual generalization test, the changes due to extinction interact with those attributable to stimulus change. It is also likely that effects upon responding of stimulus novelty as such are separable from generalization effects as usually conceived. Finally, the steady state enables us to define gradients rather precisely within subjects, and to minimize the variability common to most generalization data.

Gradient shape and summation. These maintained gradients differ from typical operant generalization functions in being considerably narrower, as one would expect from the repeated presentation of reinforced stimuli against a background of unreinforced stimuli. Some readers may be struck by the rounded modes characteristic of these gradients, having been accustomed to think in terms of the "tent-shaped" gradient popularized in textbooks. It is interesting to note that a large proportion of published generalization gradients are also best characterized by rounded modes. Where this is not the case, the apparent sharp point often arises from a lack of data points near the mode; by convention, the single high mode is then connected by straight lines to the lower points, yielding a sharp peak. The shape of the gradient at the mode is of interest with regard to summation and discrimination hypotheses. For example, if tent-shaped gradients describe both the "excitation" and "inhibition" functions, Hanson's "peak shift" (1955) cannot be derived from simple summation of the curves. Rounded modes, however, do permit prediction of the shift.

As for summation, Fig. 5 shows the relation between dual and single gradients for two birds. In this figure, the single S+ gradients (thin lines) are literally empirical curves only in the bottom row. For the other rows, which involve S+s never used singly, the curve used is the mean of the bird's three single gradients (Fig. 1) after rescaling the abscissa (as in Fig. 2). Where necessary, these single gradients were multiplied by a constant to match their peaks to the peaks of the dual S+ gradients from Fig. 2. It is, of course, impossible to collect gradients in a single S+ experiment in a manner entirely comparable to that used in a double S+ situation. In the present case, the single S+ appeared as a reinforced stimulus twice as frequently as did either of the S+s in the summation sessions. The fact that the outer limbs of the summation gradients are generally similar to the corresponding limbs of the single gradient (Fig. 5) suggests that this difference was not crucial.

All birds in all dual S+ conditions showed "summation" in the sense that the height of the dual S+ gradient exceeded that of the "component" gradients between the S+ wavelengths. There was no evidence of "summation" on the outer limbs of the gradients, a point that has been noted before (Mednick and Freedman, 1960, p. 192). There was no suggestion of any mode between the S+ wavelengths, as might be implied by theoretical accounts of a summation process (see below). In certain cases, though, the inter-S+ curve is much higher than one might expect from an additive process. For example, the individual

gradients for Bird 812 around 570 and 590 nm both fall near zero at 580 nm, yet when these wavelengths are reinforced in the same session the responding at 580 nm almost equals that at the reinforced stimuli (lower right, Fig. 5).

Theory. It is now time to examine possible combination rules that will enable prediction of dual-stimulus gradients from single-stimulus gradients. Four such rules have been stated. Three of them are mentioned by Guttman and Kalish (1956). The first states that the dual S+ gradient can be found simply by superimposing the two single S+ gradients and tracing their outline; that is, it assumes that there is no interaction or summation of the effects of dual stimulus reinforcement. Figure 5 makes it evident that this rule does not fit the present data; the portions of the dual S+ gradients between the S+s are almost all much too high.

The second rule states that the dual S+ gradient can be computed by adding the values of single gradients at corresponding points on the abscissa. This rule is equally untenable from the present data; the dual gradients are too high for widely spaced S+s and too low for closely spaced S+s.

The third rule is the "exponential addition" proposed by Hull, and derives from his Postulate 5, Corollary I: "All effective habit tendencies to a given reaction, whether positive or negative, which are active at a given time summate according to the positive growth principle exactly as would the reinforcements which would be required to produce each." (1943, p. 199) Because habit strength exponentially approaches a "physiological maximum" as asymptote, increments of strength from different sources combine to yield something less than their algebraic sum. How much less the combined strength will be depends upon the free parameter that specifies the asymptote of habit strength. Guttman and Kalish (1956) assume that response rate varies linearly with response strength, and they set the limit at 180 responses per minute. However, no matter what value is assigned to the limit, Hull's rule generates predictions at odds with the present data. A high limit is clearly untenable, since closely spaced S+ values would then generate a peak in the dual curve lying between the modes of the single gradients. A low limit could account for the

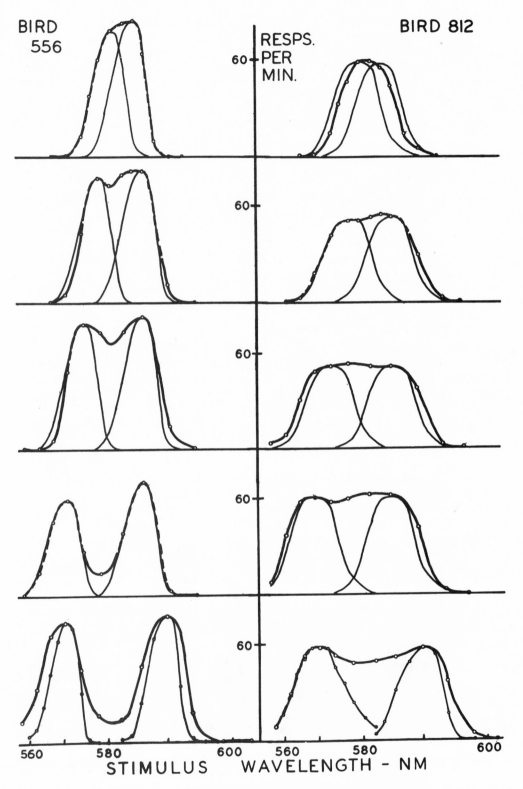

Fig. 5. Data reproduced from Fig. 2 showing the relationship of empirical "summation" gradients to single gradients derived from the same bird's data (thin lines).

lack of such peaks, but would still not account for the height of dual gradients between widely spaced S+ values (the prediction is too low) or the height of the lateral tails on dual gradients with closely spaced S+ values (the prediction is too high).

The fourth proposal for summation comes from stimulus sampling theory (Carterette, 1961; LaBerge and Martin, 1964). Here it is assumed that gradients will be linear on a properly scaled "substitutive" continuum, and summation reduces to an algebraic addition of the single S+ gradients up to a maximum given by the gradient peaks. The stimulus continua employed, the response measures used, the methods, and the subjects all differ in important ways from these items in the present research. However, insofar as the analysis can be applied to the present data, it seems inappropriate. Individual highly reliable gradients are not linear, nor will any scale transformation applicable to several gradients make them so. Also, as already mentioned, algebraic addition does not predict the present data, even when an upper limit is imposed.

It appears, then, that no formulation previously proposed adequately accounts for the present results. One could argue that no theory of "true generalization" could be expected to apply to the present data, since the steady-state procedure used does not constitute a generalization test in the usual sense of the word. This argument has a hollow ring, for there is in fact no current formulation that deals adequately with phenomena of stimulus control, call them what you will, either of the present sort, or from the more common generalization tests in extinction—such phenomena as the peak shift (Hanson, 1959) or gradient sharpening in extinction (Friedman and Guttman, 1965).

Statistical decision theory offers a possible approach to the present data and also to other findings. Though its broad implications will not be explored in detail here, it appears to offer a framework within which a variety of generalization data can be fitted with reasonable comfort. Boneau and Cole (1967) recently applied decision theory to a steady-state situation like that used in the present experiments. Let us briefly review their argument and see how it applies to generalization data.

Decision theory supposes that variations in response arise from decisions as to whether the reinforced stimulus is present or absent. That is, when the subject sees stimulus values close to the S+, it sometimes acts as if the stimulus were the S+ and sometimes as if it were not. (In contrast, the Hullian view attributes variations in response to differences in response strength associated with each of the several test stimuli.) A physical stimulus is said to arouse within the organism a corresponding "discriminal process". Given a constant stimulus, this process varies somewhat. For differing wavelengths we might imagine, as a heuristic device, that the discriminal process corresponds to differing "hues". The probability that for a given stimulus the process takes on various values ("hues") is given by the "discriminal distribution". Figure 6 (top) suggests the discriminal distributions corresponding to two stimulating wavelengths. Criteria divide the continuum on which the discriminal process varies into regions. If, at a given moment, the state generated by a stimulus falls within the "response" region, the bird will perform that behavior which is reinforced in the presence of the discriminative stimulus. If the state falls outside the response regions, this behavior will not be emitted. In Fig. 6, 590 nm is the reinforced stimulus, and this wavelength generates states that almost

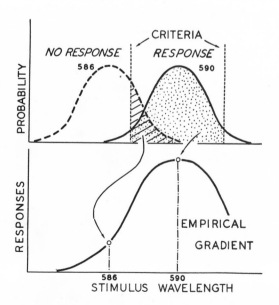

Fig. 6. Diagram suggesting how response criteria partition discriminal distributions of the several stimuli to generate the empirical gradient. Response rate to a given stimuli depends on the proportion of its distribution falling within the "response" region.

always fall within the criterion limits associated with responses. The proportion of the area under the curve that falls within these limits corresponds to the proportion of the time that this wavelength will be called "S+" and responded to accordingly. Figure 6 suggests that as the physical stimulus retreats from S+ = 590 nm, this proportion falls, and hence the number of responses emitted to the more distant wavelengths falls accordingly. One such case is shown, that of 586 nm. Its discriminal process falls within the criterion limits only about one-fourth of the time, and hence responding will be proportionately lower than at 590 nm.

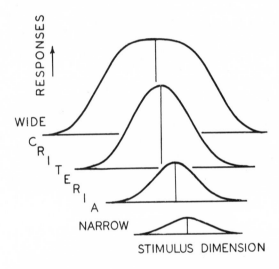

Fig. 7. Diagram suggesting how empirical gradient would be expected to vary as a result of shifts in response criteria. A Gaussian discriminal distribution is assumed here; other assumptions yield somewhat differing shapes, but all are broad and flat for wide criteria.

This way of viewing generalization gradients can handle variations in gradient width and shape as outcomes of criterion change. Figure 7 shows the gradients that result from varying the inter-criterion distance, on the assumption of Gaussian discriminal distributions. The gradients are flat for widely separated criteria, and they contract to a Gaussian form that gradually falls in height as the criteria encroach upon the discriminal distribution associated with the S+. Boneau and Cole show how conditions of reinforcement may be expected to determine an animal subject's criteria by affecting the relative payoff to be expected from various decisions. Variables such

as amount and schedule of reinforcement, deprivation, punishment, and extinction might reasonably be expected to operate in this way. Shifted peaks and asymmetries may arise if, under some conditions, the criteria on the two sides of S+ shift independently.

Detectability analysis handles summation as a simple extension of the single gradient situation. We assume two "response" regions, one associated with each of the reinforced stimuli. A stimulus between these two S+s may generate a discriminal process that sometimes falls between the two regions, and hence generates no response, and sometimes falls within one of the regions, and hence generates responses. As the S+s come closer together, intermediate stimuli will more often fall within the response region of one or the other S+. At some point, the zone between the response regions vanishes. At this point, the empirical gradient loses its twin peaks and flattens on top.

The present data seem reasonably consistent with this formulation, if one assumes rather widely spaced criteria. The summated gradients are no higher than single gradients, and when their bimodality vanishes they become flat instead of having a mode between the S+s (Fig. 2). If payoff conditions were such that response regions were very narrow, and the discriminal distribution of the S+ itself extended much beyond the criteria on either side, the theory predicts a peak between the S+s in the summation case. It would be interesting to test this prediction by manipulating payoff in the summation situation. We have already noted that summation between widely separated modes is greater than a simple algebraic sum of the single participating gradients (Fig. 2 and 5). This is also consistent with the theory, because, as the S+s approach one another, their associated response regions not only approach but also widen to meet each other. This happens because payoff determines the placement of response criteria, and the probability of reinforcement of "hues" between the S+s goes up somewhat as the S+s approach. Details of the relevant calculations can be found in Boneau and Cole (1967). Unfortunately, the expected enhancement of summation is not large enough to account entirely for the data.

Conclusion. The major contribution of decision theory to psychophysics is often said to lie in its ability to separate effects of motivational or payoff variables from effects of stimulus or sensitivity variables. The present data do not permit a "test" of the decision model, in that a separation of these variables is not possible. With no independent estimates of distribution shape or criterion locus, it is possible to say only that the data seem more compatible with the model than with the alternatives now available. But this application of decision theory represents current changes in thinking about stimulus control that are considerably more far-reaching than such a specific test. The classic view of stimulus control, exemplified in the thinking of Pavlov, held implicitly that each event distinguished by an experimenter is a "stimulus". If such a stimulus evokes a response, yet is not itself an eliciting stimulus, and has never been associated with reinforcement, its evocative power must have "spread" or generalized somehow from stimuli that were reinforced. The current view holds, of course, that environmental events are classified by organisms; if they evoke responses, it is because they fall into the class of "reinforced stimuli". The focus thus shifts from association and the spread of associative connections to the selection and classification of stimuli.

Given this reorientation, it seems worthwhile to apply the ideas of decision, criterion, and payoff to behavioral transients such as the common generalization testing procedure. For example, the narrowing of gradients during the test (Friedman and Guttman, 1965) would be expected, since a decrease in payoff should narrow the inter-criterion range. If the theory seems to make sense, we can expect experiments directed to finding what variables affect criteria in stimulus control situations. We may also expect modifications in the theory. For example, we will probably want to attribute a large measure of variance not to discriminal distributions but rather to moment-to-moment changes in criteria. It can be shown (Swets, 1964, p. 396) that models assuming criterion variance are analytically equivalent to models assuming discriminal distribution variance. Allowing criterion variance would, however, suggest that we seek variables controlling criterion variance as well as criterion locus. With this additional degree of freedom, such things as variations in summation, very broad gradients, and asymmetrical gradients could be accommodated.

Even if such speculations prove fruitful, it is clear that decision theory will not provide a complete picture of stimulus control. Discriminations are still learned somehow; the response tendencies involved may compete, be subject to inhibition, and so on. Many situations involve multiple responses that are chained or interact in complex ways; responses signifying detection may vary in rate or topography; observing behavior may be highly significant. Just as "learning theory" has dealt inadequately with stimulus problems, psychophysics has little to say of response and associative processes.

REFERENCES

Anger, D. The dependence of interresponse times upon the relative reinforcement of different interresponse times. *Journal of Experimental Psychology*, 1956, **52**, 145-161.

Blough, D. S. Spectral sensitivity in the pigeon. *Journal of the Optical Society of America*, 1957, **47**, 827-833.

Blough, D. S. Interresponse time as a function of continuous variables: a new method and some data. *Journal of the Experimental Analysis of Behavior*, 1963, **6**, 237-246.

Blough, D. S. The reinforcement of least-frequent interresponse times. *Journal of the Experimental Analysis of Behavior*, 1966, **9**, 581-591.

Blough, D. S. Stimulus generalization as signal detection in pigeons. *Science*, 1967, **158**, 940-941.

Boneau, C. A. and Cole, J. L. Decision theory, the pigeon, and the psychophysical function. *Psychological Review*, 1967, **74**, 123-135.

Boneau, C. A., Holland, M. K., and Baker, W. M. Color discrimination performance of pigeons: effects of reward. *Science*, 1965, **149**, 1113-1114.

Carterette, T. S. An application of stimulus sampling theory to summated generalization. *Journal of Experimental Psychology*, 1961, **62**, 448-455.

Clark, W. A. and Molnar, C. E. The LINC: a description of the Laboratory Instrument Computer. *Annals of the New York Academy of Sciences*, 1964, **115**, 653-668.

Friedman, H. and Guttman, N. A. A further analysis of the effects of discrimination upon stimulus generalization. In D. I. Mostofsky (Ed.), *Stimulus generalization*. Stanford: Stanford Univer. Press, 1965. Pp. 255-267.

Gray, V. A. *The stimulus control of temporally spaced responses.* Master's thesis, Brown University, 1966.

Guttman, N. and Kalish, H. I. Discriminability and stimulus generalization. *Journal of Experimental Psychology*, 1956, **51**, 79-88.

Hanson, H. M. Effects of discrimination training on stimulus generalization. *Journal of Experimental Psychology*, 1959, **58**, 321-334.

Hearst, E., Koresko, M. B., and Poppen, R. Stimulus generalization and the response-reinforcement contingency. *Journal of the Experimental Analysis of Behavior*, 1964, **7**, 369-380.

Hull, C. L. *Principles of behavior*. New York. Appleton-Century, 1943.

Kalish, H. I. and Guttman, N. Stimulus generalization after equal training on two stimuli. *Journal of Experimental Psychology*, 1957, **53**, 139-144.

Kalish, H. I. and Guttman, N. Stimulus generalization after training on three stimuli: a test of the summation hypothesis. *Journal of Experimental Psychology*, 1959, **57**, 268-272.

LaBerge, D. and Martin, D. R. An analysis of summated generalization. *Journal of Experimental Psychology*, 1964, **68**, 71-79.

Mednick, S. A. and Freedman, J. L. Stimulus generalization. *Psychological Bulletin*, 1960, **57**, 170-200.

Morse, W. H. and Skinner, B. F. A second type of superstition in the pigeon. *American Journal of Psychology*, 1957, **70**, 308-311.

Peterson, N. Effect of monochromatic rearing on the control of responding by wavelength. *Science*, 1962, **136**, 774-775.

Pierrel, R. A generalization gradient for auditory intensity in the rat. *Journal of the Experimental Analysis of Behavior*, 1958, **1**, 303-313.

Shepard, R. N. Approximation to uniform gradients of generalization by monotone transformations of scale. In D. I. Mostofsky (Ed.), *Stimulus generalization*. Stanford: Stanford Univer. Press, 1965. Pp. 94-110.

Sidman, M. *Tactics of scientific research*. New York: Basic Books, 1960.

Swets, J. A. (Ed.) *Signal detection and recognition by human observers*. New York: Wiley, 1964.

Switalski, R. W., Lyons, J., and Thomas, D. R. Effects of interdimensional training on stimulus generalization. *Journal of Experimental Psychology*, 1966, **72**, 661-666.

Received 19 January 1968.

EXTINCTION OF A DISCRIMINATIVE OPERANT FOLLOWING DISCRIMINATION LEARNING WITH AND WITHOUT ERRORS[1]

H. S. TERRACE

COLUMBIA UNIVERSITY

Different groups of pigeons were trained to respond to red and not to green with and without errors (responses to green) under a free operant procedure, in which responding to red was intermittently reinforced, and under a trial procedure in which all responses to red were reinforced. The response to red was then extinguished under a procedure in which the discriminative stimuli were successively alternated as during discrimination training. The performances of those birds that learned the discrimination without errors under the trial procedure were seriously disrupted during extinction; the birds persistently responded to green for the first time. The performances of those subjects that learned the discrimination without errors under the free operant procedure were not disrupted during extinction. In a second experiment, the same discrimination was trained without errors under a trial procedure in which the response to red was intermittently reinforced. Extinction did not disrupt discrimination performance. Thus, errorless discrimination performance was shown to remain intact during extinction so long as the response to red was intermittently reinforced during discrimination training.

A series of earlier studies showed that performances following discrimination learning with and without errors (responses to S−) differ in several respects. Gross "emotional" responses (Terrace, 1966a), drug-induced disruption of discrimination performance (Terrace, 1963a), behavioral contrast (Terrace, 1963b, 1963c, 1966a), post-discrimination generalization peak shifts (Terrace, 1964), and gradients of inhibition with minima at S− (Terrace, 1966b) were observed to occur only after discrimination learning with errors. These phenomena were in each case assumed to result from the aversiveness of S− that was established by the occurrence of non-reinforced responding to S−.

It is conceivable, however, that there exist other differences following discrimination learning with and without errors that are not immediately related to the aversiveness of S−. The present experiments stemmed from the hypothesis that performances during extinction following discrimination learning with and without errors may differ and that these differences are the result of variables other than the aversiveness of S−.

Experiment I is the final (but unpublished) phase of an earlier study on errorless discrimination learning (Terrace, 1963b). Briefly stated, Exp. I was concerned with the extinction of the response to S+ following discrimination learning with and without errors. All subjects in Exp. I were trained on a successive discrimination between a red (S+) and a green (S−) circular patch of light. Half of the subjects were trained by a trial procedure that reinforced each response to S+ and terminated each trial after a single response. The remaining subjects were trained by a free operant procedure in which responding to S+ was intermittently reinforced and which allowed many responses to occur during each presentation of S+ or S−.

In the case of both the trial and the free operant groups, one sub-group was trained to discriminate between S+ and S− without errors.[2] In each case this was accomplished by

[1]Dedicated to B. F. Skinner in his sixty-fifth year. Experiment I of this paper is based on a portion of a dissertation submitted to the Dept. of Psychology, Harvard University, in partial fulfillment of the requirements of the Ph.D. degree. Experiment I was supported by NSF grant G-8621 and was conducted while the author was a PHS pre-doctoral fellow. Experiment II was carried out under the auspices of NSF grant GB-4686 and NIH grant HD-00930. Reprints may be obtained from the author, Dept. of Psychology, Schermerhorn Hall, Columbia University, New York, N.Y. 10027.

[2]While none of the subjects of Exp. I acquired a discrimination with zero errors, none of the subjects in

starting discrimination training immediately after the key-peck response had been conditioned with a large S+—S— difference that was progressively reduced to the final S+—S— value. Because discrimination training began early in the conditioning history of these subjects, with a pair of discriminative stimuli, the difference between which was progressively reduced, this procedure was called the "early-progressive" procedure. The remaining subjects of the trial and free operant groups were trained on one of three variations of the "early-progressive" procedure: "early-constant", "late-progressive", and "late-constant". The relevant details of these procedures are described below.

Experiment II employed a modification of the early-progressive procedure that was followed under the trial paradigm. As in Exp. I, the value of the probability of reinforcement for responding to S+ was 1.0 at the start of discrimination training. However, during the course of discrimination training, the probability of reinforcement for responding to S+ was gradually reduced from 1.0 to 0.10. This was done to provide the subjects that made no errors during the acquisition of the discrimination with a history of intermittent reinforcement for responding to S+.

EXPERIMENT I

Method

Subjects

Twenty four male White Carneaux pigeons had all served in an earlier study of discrimination learning (Terrace, 1963*b*). The specific history of each subject is discussed below. Each

bird was maintained at 80% of its free-feeding body weight throughout its experimental history.

Apparatus

An experimental chamber containing a response key and food and stimulus-presenting devices, was identical to the apparatus used in an earlier study (Terrace, 1963*b*). The stimulus-presenting device, adapted from an Industrial Electrical Engineering Corporation display unit, was mounted directly behind the key and could transilluminate the key with either a red (S+) or a green (S—) light.

Procedure

The conditioning history of each subject is described in detail in Terrace (1963*b*). This study was primarily concerned with: (1) variables that affect the number of errors that occurred during the acquisition of a discrimination, and (2) interactions within multiple schedules (*e.g.*, behavioral contrast, *cf.* Reynolds, 1961). As a result, these subjects had a relatively complex history of alternation between differential and non-differential reinforcement training before extinction. The essential details of each group's conditioning history are summarized below. To avoid possible confusion, the reader is again reminded that the only portion of the subjects' training history not reported previously is the extinction procedure. The sketchy summaries of the non-differential and differential reinforcement history of each subject described below are intended solely to provide a basis for interpreting the results of the extinction procedure.

Trial Procedure

Each session consisted of a series of discrete, automatically scheduled trials. A trial was defined as the period of time during which the response key was transilluminated by either a red (S+) or a green (S—) light. All trials were terminated by a response or by a failure to respond within 5 sec of the onset of the trial. Thus, only one response could occur during each trial. Responses during an S+ trial were immediately reinforced. Between trials, the houselight remained on, but the key was dark. The duration of the intertrial interval was

---

Exp. II, which were trained on a more refined version of the training procedure that progressively introduced S—, made *any* errors in acquiring the same discrimination. The same discrimination procedure was successful in 12 out of 12 instances in a study carried out subsequent to Exp. I (Terrace, 1963*c*) and also in experiments using the free-operant procedure (Terrace, 1964, 1966*a*). It should be noted also that the performances of those subjects that learn a discrimination with zero or near-zero number of errors differ in many respects from those that make many errors. For these reasons, discriminations acquired with zero or near-zero number of errors will both be referred to as discriminations acquired without any errors.

determined by an irregular series of intervals with a range of 9 to 30 sec and a mean of 15 sec. Responding during the intertrial interval delayed the onset of the next trial for 10 sec.

Each subject was given both non-differential and differential reinforcement training. A non-differential reinforcement session consisted of 60 S+ trials. A differential reinforcement session consisted of 60 S+ and 60 S— trials. The S+ and S— trials alternated in an irregular series except when a correction procedure was invoked. The correction procedure required S+ trials, during which no response occurred, and S— trials, during which responses did occur, to repeat as the next trial. Both the S+ and the S+—S— sessions were terminated after 60 reinforcements. The upper portion of Table I summarizes the numbers of sessions using each procedure and their order of occurrence for each experimental group. The order of occurrence of the S+ (non-differential reinforcement) and the S+—S— (differential reinforcement) sessions depended on whether or not S— was introduced immediately after the key peck was conditioned ("early"), or after extended S+ training ("late"). If S— was introduced early, discrimination training began during the first experimental session. The sequence of training conditions under the early condition was: S+—S—, S+, S+—S—. If S— was introduced

late, discrimination training began after 14 S+ sessions. Under the late condition, the sequence of training conditions was: S+, S+—S—, S+, S+—S—.

Discrimination Training

The procedures described in the following section were used to train the red-green discrimination during the first series of S+—S— sessions. The second series of S+—S— sessions began abruptly with no special training procedure.

Early-progressive discrimination training (Subjects 118, 119, 120). Discrimination training began immediately after the key-peck response had been conditioned. During the first session, S— was progressively changed from a dark key of 0.5-sec duration to a fully intense green key of 5-sec duration.

Early-constant discrimination training (Subjects 139, 144, 145). Discrimination training began immediately after the key-peck response had been conditioned. From the outset of discrimination training, S— was at full intensity and of 5-sec duration.

Late-progressive discrimination training (Subjects 140, 142, 146). Discrimination training began after 14 S+ sessions. The changes in the intensity and the duration of S— were the same as those made for the early-progressive group.

Table 1

Sequence and Number of S+, S+—S—, and Ext. Sessions for Trial and Free-Operant Groups

Type of Session (in order of occurrence)	Extinction Early-Progressive Group (118, 119, 120)	Early-Constant Group (139, 144, 145)	Late-Progressive Group (142, 146, 140)	Late-Constant Group (141, 128, 127)
TRIAL PROCEDURE				
S+			14	14
S+—S—	14	14	14	14
S+	14	14	7	7
S+—S—	14	14	14	14
Extinction	20	20	20	20
FREE OPERANT PROCEDURE				
	(114, 116, 155)	(150, 151, 152)	(147, 148, 149)	(131, 132, 154)
S+			21	21
S+—S—	21	21	14	14
S+	14	14	7	7
S+—S—	7	7	14	14
Extinction	7	7	7	7

Late-constant discrimination training (Subjects 127, 128, 141). Discrimination training began after 14 S+ sessions. S— was initially at full intensity and of 5-sec duration.

Extinction

Following the second series of discrimination sessions, each group received 20 extinction sessions. During each extinction session, S+ and S— alternated as previously, but no responses were reinforced. A response made during an S— trial resulted in the repetition of that trial. Responding or not responding during an S+ trial, however, had no effect on the nature of the next trial. Each extinction session was terminated after 60 S+ trials had occurred.

FREE OPERANT PROCEDURE

The free operant and the trial procedures differed with respect to (1) the probability of reinforcement for a response to S+ and (2) the number of responses that could occur during each presentation of a discriminative stimulus. Under the trial procedure, the probability that a response to S+ would be reinforced was always 1.0 and a single response terminated the presentation of each S+ and S—. In the free operant procedure, however, responses to S+ were intermittently reinforced, and many responses could occur during each presentation of S+ and S—.

Four groups of pigeons were used. As in the trial procedure, each group differed with respect to when and how discrimination training began. During discrimination training, a two-component, multiple variable-interval extinction (*mult* VI *ext*) schedule was used. During the first component, the key was red (S+), and responses were reinforced on a VI 1-min schedule of reinforcement. The S+ component lasted 3 min and was immediately followed by the onset of S—. During S—, the key was green and responding was never reinforced. The duration of the S— component was, in part, controlled by whether or not responding to S— occurred. If no responding to S— occurred, the second component lasted 3 min. If responding to S— did occur, the onset of the next S+ component was delayed until 3 min without a response to S— had occurred. This correction procedure was used to minimize the possibility of accidental reinforcement of

responding to S— by the subsequent presentation of the S+ component.

The order of occurrence of the S+ and the S+—S— sessions depended on whether or not S— was introduced early or late. The number of each type of session and their order of occurrence for the four experimental groups appear in the lower half of Table 1. Both the non-differential (S+) and the differential (S+—S—) reinforcement sessions were terminated after 60 reinforcements had occurred.

Discriminating Training

The procedures described in the following section were used to train the red-green discrimination during the first S+—S— series. As was the case for the trial procedure, the second S+—S— series began abruptly with no special training procedure.

Early-progressive discrimination training (Subjects 114, 116, 155). Discrimination training began approximately 30 sec after the key peck had been conditioned. During the first three sessions, the schedules of reinforcement associated with S+ were changed from continuous reinforcement (CRF) to VI 30-sec to VI 60-sec and S— was changed from a dark key of 5-sec duration to a fully intense green key of 3-min duration.

Early-constant discrimination training (Subjects 150, 151, 152). Discrimination training started for this group also during the first experimental session. The duration and the brightness of S—, however, were initially at their maximum values: 3 min and full intensity, respectively. Approximately 30 sec after the key peck had been conditioned, the schedule of reinforcement was changed from CRF to VI 30-sec. Three minutes later the first S— component began, and the S+—S— procedure went into effect. After the first session, responding in the S+ component was reinforced on a VI 60-sec schedule.

Late-progressive discrimination training (Subjects 147, 148, 149). Discrimination training was started after 21 S+ sessions. The changes in the intensity and the duration of S— were the same as those made for the early-progressive group. Throughout discrimination training, the duration of the S+ component was 3 min, and the schedule of reinforcement during the S+ component was VI 60-sec.

Late-constant discrimination training (Subjects 131, 132, 154). Discrimination training was started after 21 S+ sessions. S− was initially at full intensity and of 3-min duration.

Extinction

Following the second series of S+—S− sessions, each group was given seven extinction sessions. The only differences between the S+—S− and the extinction sessions were that (1) no responses to S+ were reinforced, and (2) each extinction session was terminated after 20 S+—S− cycles.

RESULTS

Before considering the extinction performances of the trial and the free operant groups, it is important to consider first the number of errors that each subject made during discrimination training. This information is summarized in Table 2 along with the number of responses to S+ and to S− emitted by each subject during extinction, the median latency of the response to S+ during the last five S+—S− sessions of each subject trained under the trial procedure, and the mean rate of responding to S+ during the last five sessions of each subject trained under the free operant procedure. The analysis of performance during extinction that follows below considers (1)

the number and distribution of responses to S+ and to S− during extinction, (2) the relationship between the number of errors during discrimination training and the number of responses to S+ and to S− during extinction, and (3) the relationship between the number of responses to S+ during extinction and either the latency of the response to S+ at the end of discrimination training (trial group) or the rate of responding to S+ at the end of discrimination training (free operant group).

Trial procedure: responding to S−. The cumulated number of responses to S+ and to S− emitted by each subject over each extinction session is shown in Fig. 1. The most striking aspect of these results is the performance of the early-progressive group, which had acquired the discrimination between S+ and S− with virtually no errors. Each of these subjects made at least five times as many responses to S− during extinction as they had during discrimination training. It should also be noted that during extinction the number of responses to S− of the early-progressive group approached the number of responses to S− made during acquisition by the subjects of the late-constant group, the group that made the largest number of responses to S− during discrimination training. The Spearman rank-

Table 2

| Discrimination Training Procedure | Trial Procedure | | | | | Free Operant Procedure | | | | |
| | Bird No. | Discrimination Training | | Extinction | | Bird No. | Discrimination Training | | Extinction | |
		No. of Responses to S−	Median Latency of Responding to S+ (sec)	No. of Responses to S−	to S+		No. of Responses to S−	Mean Rate of Responding to S+ (resp/ min)	No. of Responses to S−	to S+
Early-Progressive	118	8	0.74	40	400	114	26	45	24	1648
	119	4	0.96	299	411	116	39	52	41	8105
	120	3	0.38	286	558	155	42	63	34	4455
Early-Constant	139	44	1.32	16	279	150	812	128	182	9660
	144	40	0.91	19	197	151	376	94	214	5826
	145	187	0.65	0	80	152	405	91	164	7889
Late-Progressive	142	20	1.12	133	309	147	1418	78	86	6483
	146	38	1.26	0	79	148	855	85	74	6113
	140	25	0.97	4	97	149	1091	130	103	4260
Late-Constant	141	176	0.63	24	475	131	5056	83	925	18231
	128	295	0.82	45	208	132	2018	118	471	9920
	127	314	0.92	21	202	154	4425	125	486	4061

ABRUPT EXTINCTION — TRIAL PROCEDURE

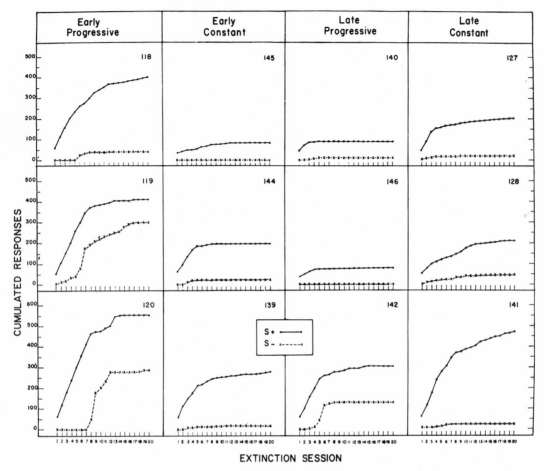

Fig. 1. The cumulated number of responses of each subject trained under the trial procedure during 20 extinction sessions.

order correlation coefficient between responding to S— during discrimination training and during extinction was −0.37.

By the eighth extinction session, each of the subjects of the early-progressive group began to respond to S—. In two out of three cases, the onset of responding to S— occurred one or two sessions before the session in which the probability of responding to S+ fell below 1.0 for the first time. Subject 120, for example, responded to each of the 60 S+ presentations during each of the first eight extinction sessions. During the ninth session, Subject 120 made only 48 responses to S+. Subject 120 began responding to S— during the eighth extinction session during which it responded to S— 51 times. Subject 118 began responding to S— during the sixth extinction session, the

second session during which fewer than 60 responses to S+ had occurred.

Subject 119, an apparent exception to this rule, began responding to S— during the second extinction session. It was not, however, until the sixth and seventh extinction sessions that the probability of Subject 119's responding to S— reached its maximum value. The sixth extinction session was the first in which Subject 119 did not respond on all of the S+ trials.

A similar pattern of responding to S— can be seen in the performance of Subject 142 of the late-progressive group. This subject responded to S— on only 20 trials during discrimination training, the smallest number of responses outside of the early-progressive group. Subject 142 began responding to S—

during the third extinction session. The maximum frequency of responding to S— occurred during the fifth and sixth extinction sessions. The probabilities of an S+ response during the second, third, fourth, fifth, and sixth sessions were, respectively, 0.72, 0.92, 0.70, 0.73, and 0.30. It thus appears that the highest frequency of responding to S—, during extinction, of those subjects that learned the discrimination with a few responses to S— occurred at the time that responding to S+ began to weaken.

None of the remaining subjects (the early-constant group, Subjects 140 and 146 of the late-progressive group and the late-constant group) emitted more than 45 responses to S— during extinction. Responding to S— in each of these instances was sporadic (*cf.* Fig. 1). Thus, unlike the sharply rising response functions of the subjects that learned the discrimination with few errors, the S— response functions of the subjects that learned the discrimination with many errors showed a gradual rise during the course of extinction.

Responding to S+. The early-progressive group made the largest number of responses to S+ during extinction. Subjects 120, 119, and 118 of the early-progressive group made, respectively, the first, third, and fourth highest number of responses to S+. With the exception of Subject 141 of the late-constant group, the number of responses to S+ of the remaining groups were uniformly distributed among the early-constant, the late-progressive, and the late-constant groups.

Correlation between latency of responding to S+ during discrimination training and responding to S+ and to S— during extinction. The latency of the response to S+ at the end of discrimination training (*cf.* Table 2) was a poor predictor of the number of responses to S+ and to S— during extinction. The Spearman rank-order correlation coefficients between latency of responding to S+ at the end of discrimination training and the number of responses to S+ and to S— during extinction were, respectively, +0.37 and +0.33.

Free operant procedure: responding to S—. The cumulated number of responses emitted by each subject to S+ and to S— during each extinction session is shown in Fig. 2. It should be noted that in Fig. 2 the left-hand ordinate is larger than the right-hand ordinate by a factor of 20.

The accuracy of discrimination performance of the early-progressive group, the group that learned the discrimination with a near-zero number of errors, was not disrupted by extinction. Table 2 and Fig. 2 show that responding to S— of the subjects of the early-progressive group remained at a near-zero level throughout extinction. Thus, the effects of extinction on errorless discrimination performance following discrimination training under a free operant procedure differed from the effects of extinction following discrimination training under a trial procedure. Errorless performance was disrupted only during extinction following training under a trial procedure.

The cumulated response to S— functions shown in Fig. 2 indicate that there was no overlap of the number of responses emitted to S— among the subjects of each group. The smallest number of responses to S— was made by the subjects of the early-progressive group (range: 24 to 41). Between these extremes were the subjects of the late-progressive group (range: 74 to 103) and the early-constant group (range: 164 to 214).

The number of responses emitted to S— during extinction was correlated with the number of responses to S— during discrimination training. (Spearman rank-order correlation coefficient = +0.78). The only reversal between the number of responses to S— during discrimination training and extinction involved the early-constant and late-progressive groups. Curiously, the subjects of the early-constant group made fewer responses to S— during discrimination training than did any of the subjects of the late-progressive group. During extinction, however, all subjects of the early-constant group made more responses to S— than did any of the subjects of the late-progressive group.

Responding to S+. The number of responses to S+ during extinction did not differ across the four experimental groups. While the smallest number of responses to S+ was made by Subject 114 of the early-progressive group (1648 responses) and the largest number to S+ by Subject 131 of the late-progressive group (18,231 responses), there was much overlap among the four experimental groups trained under the free operant procedure.

Correlation between rate of responding to S+ during discrimination training and re-

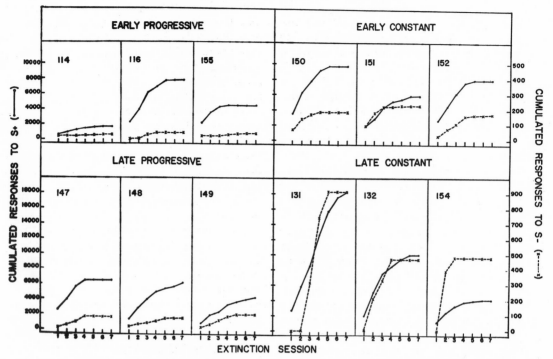

Fig. 2. The cumulated number of responses to S+ and to S— of each subject trained under the free operant procedure during seven extinction sessions. Note that the scale of the ordinate on the left showing the cumulative number of responses to S+ differs from the scale of the ordinate on the right showing the cumulated number of responses to S— by a factor of 20.

sponding to S+ and to S— during extinction. The number of responses that occurred in extinction to S— showed little relation to the rate of responding to S+ at the end of discrimination training. The value of the Spearman rank-order correlation coefficient between the rate of responding to S+ at the end of discrimination training and the number of responses to S— during extinction was +0.38. A higher correlation was obtained, however, between the rate of responding to S+ at the end of discrimination training and the number of responses to S+ during extinction ($\Gamma = 0.58$).

DISCUSSION

The major finding of this experiment was that errorless discrimination performance was seriously disrupted during extinction following discrimination training in which the probability of reinforcement for responding to S+ was 1.0. Extinction following discrimination training in which responses to S+ were inter-

mittently reinforced had no adverse effect on errorless discrimination performance.

These results suggest that the abrupt transition from a probability of reinforcement for responding to S+ of 1.0 to 0.0, in going from discrimination training to extinction, was responsible for the disruption of errorless discrimination performance. The most obvious benefit of intermittent reinforcement of the response to S+ during discrimination training appears to be the establishment of what is popularly called "frustration tolerance".

Unfortunately, "frustration tolerance" carries with it only the weight of popular usage (*cf.* Rosenzweig, 1938, 1944; Freeman, 1948, p. 115; Keller and Schoenfeld, 1950, p. 91; Cofer and Appley, 1965, p. 331) and has not been the subject of an empirical or conceptual analysis. It seems clear, however, that intermittent reinforcement is one of the basic variables involved in establishing what various psychologists have referred to as frustration tolerance. Skinner (1938, p. 138) cited the relationship between "equanimity" (an apt synonym for frustration tolerance) and intermittent reinforcement in describing the extinction process:

"The stability of reflex strength under periodic reconditioning and the prolongation of the extinction curve following it are important properties of normal behavior. They are responsible for a measure of equanimity in a world in which the contingency of reinforcing stimuli is necessarily uncertain. Behavior would be clumsy and inefficient if the strength of an operant were to oscillate from one extreme to another with the presence or absence of its reinforcement."

It should be noted that this analysis is also consistent with the generalization-decrement explanation of why resistance to extinction is greater after partial reinforcement than after regular reinforcement (*cf.* Kimble, 1961, pp. 299 ff). Just as the uncertainty of when reinforcement can occur increases the difficulty of discriminating between conditioning and extinction, this factor may also increase frustration tolerance by reducing anticipatory responses of when reinforcement might occur.

Given that frustration occurs when a reinforcement that has regularly followed a response is withheld, one would expect that frustration tolerance would be greater after irregular intermittent reinforcement than after continuous reinforcement. Experiment II attempted to establish frustration tolerance during discrimination training, in which a trial procedure is used, by gradually reducing the probability of reinforcement for responding to S+ during the course of discrimination training.

The results of Exp. I are also relevant to Jenkins' observation (1961) that non-reinforced responding to S— during the acquisition of a discrimination functions like intermittent reinforcement in a non-differential reinforcement situation by increasing resistance to extinction. Jenkins used three groups of subjects: (1) intermittent reinforcement, (2) discrimination training, and (3) continuous reinforcement. Each subject from the intermittent group was matched with a subject from the discrimination group. For each intermittent subject, both the number and the temporal location of non-reinforced trials were determined by the performance of the discrimination subject with which it was matched. On those trials in which a discrimination subject responded to S—, reinforcement availability was cancelled for the subject of the intermittent group with which it was matched. The third group was given continuous reinforcement in the presence of one stimulus. No differences were observed between the intermittent and the discrimination groups with respect to the number of responses to S+ that occurred during extinction. Since all three groups had an equal number of reinforcements before extinction, these results demonstrated that the effect of unreinforced responses to S— (errors) during the acquisition of a discrimination was equivalent to the effect of intermittent reinforcement in that they both increased resistance to extinction by similar amounts. Jenkins concluded (1961, p. 115):

"discrimination training increased resistance to extinction over regular reinforcement. . . . [The results] further show that the pattern of intermittent reinforcement . . . which occurs in discrimination training is capable, when applied to a single stimulus, of producing an increase in resistance to extinction over regular reinforcement as large or larger than the increase resulting from discrimination training itself. . . . [This] implied that the increase in resistance to extinction is not directly related to the fact that S_1+ is eventually discriminated from S_2-. Rather, it is related to the occurrence of non-reinforced responses in the process of learning the discrimination. If the stimuli were very dissimilar, so that after training on S_1+, only a few responses were made to S_2-, then a smaller increase in resistance to extinction would be expected to result from discrimination training."

Jenkins' analysis of non-reinforced responding during discrimination training suggests that the resistance to extinction in the group that learned the discrimination without errors would be equivalent to the resistance to extinction of a group which had the same number of continuous reinforcements under non-differential reinforcement training. Unfortunately, the design of the present experiment did not provide a non-differential group that received continuous reinforcement. The design of this experiment did, however, allow a check of another implication of Jenkins' analysis. Since the number of responses to S− during discrimination training varied as a function of the discrimination training procedure, one would expect that the resistance to extinction of the response to S+ would vary directly with the number of responses to S− during discrimination training. The results obtained from the free operant group supported this prediction; the results obtained from the trial group did not.

For the free operant group, the number of responses to S− during discrimination training varied directly with the resistance to extinction of the response to S+ (Spearman rank-order correlation coefficient = +0.78). Thus, the greater the level of non-reinforced responding to S− during discrimination training, the larger the frequency of responding to S+ during extinction. It should, however, also be noted that an alternative account of the correlation between the number of responses to S+ and to S− during extinction is equally compatible with the results obtained in Exp. I. The resistance to extinction of the response to S+ was correlated, to a slightly lesser degree, with the rate of responding to S+ at the end of discrimination training. Since behavioral contrast (*cf.* Reynolds, 1961) occurred only in the case of those subjects that learned the discrimination with errors, and since the amount of contrast was generally related to the number of errors during discrimination training, it is not possible to distinguish between the rate of responding to S+ at the end of discrimination training and the number of errors during the formation of the discrimination in accounting for the resistance to extinction of the response to S+.

A different state of affairs emerged with respect to the relationship between the number of errors during discrimination training and the resistance to extinction of the response to S+ in the case of the trial group. It should be noted that the present trial procedure closely approximated Jenkins' procedure. It was, therefore, all the more surprising not to have obtained a relationship between the number of errors during discrimination training and the resistance to extinction of the response to S+.

Following discrimination training under the trial procedure, the resistance to extinc-

tion of the response to S+ was greatest for the early-progressive group, the group that acquired the discrimination with virtually no errors. The high resistance to extinction of the response to S+ following errorless discrimination learning may have been due to the emotional reaction generated by non-reinforcement. It should be remembered that until extinction training began, the subjects of the early-progressive group had virtually no history of non-reinforcement in the experimental situation. For those subjects that acquired the discrimination with errors, the emotional responses generated by non-reinforcement had presumably diminished in strength before the onset of extinction. In another experiment (Terrace, 1966c) it was shown that behavioral contrast and the peak shift, two characteristics of discrimination performance following discrimination learning with errors that were also presumed to result from extinction-induced emotional responses, diminished during extended discrimination training.

Emotional reactions have been invoked by various researchers to account for a temporary strengthening of the response at the start of extinction. Skinner (1938, p. 76), for example, noted that the rate of responding may temporarily increase after the onset of extinction. Likewise, Notterman and Mintz (1965) and Halasz (1963) reported an increase in the force of responding at the start of extinction, and Azrin, Hutchinson, and Hake (1966) reported the occurrence of aggressive responses at the onset of extinction. It is interesting to note that in all of these instances, the temporary increase in the strength of the response at the onset of extinction was most apparent after a history of continuous reinforcement.

In the present study, emotional responses generated by extinction appeared to be a more important factor than the absence of non-reinforced responding to S− in determining resistance to extinction. It might, however, be the case that if these emotional responses were eliminated, as for example, following the administration of certain tranquilizers (*cf.* Terrace, 1963a), the resistance to extinction of the response to S+ might be lowest following errorless discrimination training. Under these kinds of conditions, it might also be the case that errorless discrimination performance would remain intact throughout extinction.

EXPERIMENT II

In Exp. I, only the early-progressive group, trained under the trial procedure did not have a history of non-reinforced responding before extinction. All of the remaining groups, however, emitted non-reinforced responses to either S+ or to S− during discrimination training. It was hypothesized that discrimination performance during extinction was disrupted following early-progressive discrimination training under the trial procedure, in three out of three instances, because these subjects had not had a history of intermittent reinforcement for responding to S+ during discrimination training. Experiment II tested this hypothesis by gradually lowering the probability of reinforcement for responding to S+ from 1.0 to 0.10. Thus, unlike Exp. I, in which the probability of reinforcement on an S+ trial was abruptly reduced in going from discrimination training to extinction, in Exp. II the value of this probability was gradually reduced during discrimination training.

METHOD

Subjects

Three male White Carneaux pigeons (B-120, B-124, and B-125) with no experimental history were maintained at 80% of their free-feeding weights throughout the experiment.

Apparatus

The apparatus was identical to that used in Exp. I.

Procedure

Each subject was trained under the early-progressive discrimination procedure used in Exp. I. After the first five S+−S− sessions, during which the probability of reinforcement was 1.0, the probability of reinforcement was reduced as follows: two sessions of 0.75 probability of reinforcement; two sessions of 0.50; three sessions of 0.25; and three sessions in which the probability of reinforcement was 0.10. Each subject was then given 30 extinction sessions using the extinction procedure of Exp. I. It should be noted that in Exp. II, there was no alternation between S+ and S+−S− sessions as there was in Exp. I. In Exp. II, only the S+−S− and the extinction procedures were used.

RESULTS

None of the subjects responded to S− during the S+−S− sessions. The reduction of the probability of reinforcement for responding to S+, from 1.0 to 0.10, affected neither the probability of responding to S+ nor the latency of responding to S+.

After the key peck was conditioned during the first experimental session, the probability of responding to S+ was 1.0 for each subject during each of the 14 discrimination sessions. Thus, discrimination performance was perfect before extinction. The median latencies of the response to S+ during the last five S+−S− sessions of Subjects B-120, B-124, and B-125 were, respectively, 0.45, 0.73, and 0.68 sec. These medians are virtually indistinguishable from the median latency of responding to S+ of the subjects of the early-progressive group of Exp. I (cf. Terrace, 1963b, Fig. 6).

The cumulative number of responses of each subject to S+ and to S− is shown in Fig. 3. In each case, extinction had no effect on S− responding; none of the subjects responded to S− during any of the 30 extinction sessions.

Another difference in the extinction performance of the early-progressive groups in Exp. I and II can be seen in the resistance to extinction of the response to S+. In Exp. I,

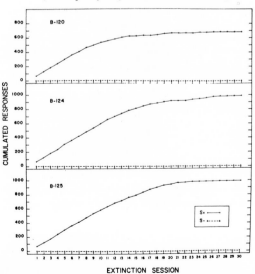

TRIAL PROCEDURE - PROGRESSIVE EXTINCTION
(Following Early Progressive Discrimination Training)

Fig. 3. The cumulated number of responses to S+ and to S− of each of the subjects of Exp. II during 30 extinction sessions.

the average number of responses to S+ during extinction was 456. In Exp. II, the average number of responses emitted to S+ was 888. This difference was undoubtedly the result of the intermittent reinforcement of the response to S+, rather than the 10 additional extinction sessions that the early-progressive group of Exp. II received. Inspection of Fig. 3 shows that responding to S+ had essentially ceased by the end of the twentieth extinction session, the point at which extinction was terminated in Exp. I.

DISCUSSION

Experiment II demonstrated that errorless discrimination performance under a trial procedure could be maintained throughout extinction if the response to S+ had a history of intermittent reinforcement during discrimination training. In the Discussion of Exp. I, it was noted that a reasonable explanation of the maintenance of errorless performance during extinction in the case of the free operant group was the development of frustration tolerance by the intermittent reinforcement of responding to S+ during discrimination training. Presumably, the high level of frustration tolerance in Exp. II was also the result of the intermittent reinforcement of responding to S+ during discrimination training.

Another important implication of the results of both Exp. I and II is that errorless discrimination learning is not an unmixed blessing if the response to S+ is continuously reinforced. To ensure that errorless performance continues during extinction, it is necessary to reinforce intermittently responding to S+ during discrimination training.

REFERENCES

Azrin, N. H., Hutchinson, R. R., and Hake, D. F. Extinction-induced aggression. *Journal of the Experimental Analysis of Behavior*, 1966, **9**, 191-204.

Cofer, C. N. and Appley, M. H. *Motivation: theory and research*. New York: J. Wiley & Sons, Inc., 1965.

Freeman, G. L. *The energetics of human behavior*. Ithaca: Cornell University Press, 1948.

Halasz, M. F. Emotional response to nonreinforcement. (ltr.) *Science*, 1963, **139**, 1128-1129.

Jenkins, H. M. The effect of discrimination training on extinction. *Journal of Experimental Psychology*, 1961, **61**, 111-121.

Keller, F. S. and Schoenfeld, W. N. *Principles of psychology*. New York: Appleton-Century-Crofts, 1950.

Kimble, G. A. *Hilgard & Marquis' conditioning and learning*. 2d ed.; New York: Appleton-Century-Crofts, 1961.

Notterman, J. M. and Mintz, D. E. *Dynamics of response*. New York: J. Wiley & Sons, Inc., 1965.

Reynolds, G. S. An analysis of interactions in a multiple schedule. *Journal of the Experimental Analysis of Behavior*, 1961, **4**, 107-117.

Rosenzweig, S. A general outline of frustration. *Character and Personality*, 1938, 7, 151-160.

Rosenzweig, S. An outline of frustration theory. In J. McV. Hunt (Ed.), *Personality and the behavior disorders*. New York: Ronald, 1944.

Skinner, B. F. *The behavior of organisms*. New York: Appleton-Century-Crofts, 1938.

Terrace, H. S. Errorless discrimination learning in the pigeon: Effects of chlorpromazine and imipramine. *Science*, 1963, **140**, 318-319. (*a*)

Terrace, H. S. Discrimination learning with and without errors. *Journal of the Experimental Analysis of Behavior*, 1963, **6**, 1-27. (*b*)

Terrace, H. S. Errorless transfer of a discrimination across two continua. *Journal of the Experimental Analysis of Behavior*, 1963, **6**, 223-232. (*c*)

Terrace, H. S. Wavelength generalization after discrimination learning with and without errors. *Science*, 1964, **144**, 78-80.

Terrace, H. S. Stimulus control. In Honig, W. K. (Ed.), *Operant behavior: areas of research and application*. New York: Appleton-Century-Crofts, 1966. (*a*) Pp. 271-344.

Terrace, H. S. Discrimination learning and inhibition. *Science*, 1966, **154**, 1677-1680. (*b*)

Terrace, H. S. Behavioral contrast and the peak shift: effects of extended discrimination training. *Journal of the Experimental Analysis of Behavior*, 1966, **9**, 613-617. (*c*)

Received 23 February 1968.

GENERALIZATION GRADIENTS AND STIMULUS CONTROL IN DELAYED MATCHING-TO-SAMPLE[1]

Murray Sidman

Massachusetts General Hospital

Neurological patients were subjects in delayed visual matching-to-sample. The sample and choice stimuli were ellipses of varying size. By measuring the difference in size between the sample on a given trial and the ellipse the subject chose on that trial, gradients of differences between samples and choice stimuli could be plotted. These difference gradients broadened with increasing delays. Sharp gradients were controlled by the samples. Flat gradients were controlled by features of the choice display, independently of the samples. Intermediate gradients reflected combined control by the samples and by the choice displays.

A flat stimulus-generalization gradient may tell us simply that the stimuli specified within the continuum have failed to control the measured behavior differentially. A sharply peaked gradient may tell us that the positive or some other specified stimulus exerts precise differential control relative to the stimuli tested. These descriptive statements, involving little more than the reading of graphs, are consistent with the point of view, reviewed and amplified by Prokasy and Hall (1963), and Terrace (1966), that the stimulus generalization gradient is neither more nor less than a technique for measuring stimulus control.

This descriptive treatment, however, ignores a major implication of the position taken by Prokasy and Hall, who pointed out that the central issue is the definition of the effective stimuli:

"What represents an important dimension of the physical event for the experimenter may not even exist as part of the

effective stimulus for the subject. Similarly, the subject may perceive aspects of an experimenter event which have been ignored by, or are unknown to, the experimenter." (Prokasy and Hall, 1963, p. 312).

In these terms, one may consider a sharp gradient to mean that experimenter-specified stimuli are the effective ones, a flat gradient to mean that other stimuli are the effective ones, and an intermediate gradient to indicate that both experimenter-specified and one or more other identifiable stimuli are effective in controlling the subject's behavior. (An intermediate gradient may indicate that the experimenter-specified stimuli are effective, but that they control more than one response (Ray and Sidman, in press). The present discussion will be confined to the stimulus side of the controlling stimulus-response relation.) The assumption here is that changes of gradient shape reflect shifts in the stimuli which exert control, shifts not merely in differential control among the same stimuli, but shifts to stimuli not identified by the coordinates of the generalization curves.

The descriptive stimulus-control interpretation of the gradient assumes that only the amount of differential control within the stimuli of the test dimension changes. The flat gradient becomes peaked because (or when) the amount of differential control increases. The sharp gradient becomes less sharp because (or when) differential control decreases. An unstated assumption is that the same stimuli have

[1]Dedicated to B. F. Skinner in his sixty-fifth year. This research was supported by Research Grants NB 03535 from the Institute of Neurological Diseases and Blindness, and MH 05408 from the National Institute of Mental Health. The author is indebted to Martha Willson and F. Garth Fletcher for their help with the experimental procedures, to Cynthia Basillio for manuscript preparation, and to Barbara A. Ray, Lawrence T. Stoddard, and Jonathan Leicester for their constructive suggestions concerning the data analysis. Reprints may be obtained from Murray Sidman, Neurology Research, Massachusetts General Hospital, Boston, Mass. 02114.

controlled the subject's behavior both before and after the gradient changed.

Lashley and Wade (1946) interpreted the flat gradient as a failure of the subject to discriminate the relevant stimulus, and were challenged by Brown, Bilodeau, and Baron (1951) to define failure of discrimination "independently of the particular generalization reaction it is supposed to explain." The assumption that "failure to discriminate" reflects control by other stimuli makes independent definition possible. What is required is to demonstrate that the flat gradient reflects complete control by stimuli other than the ones specified by the experimenter, that the sharp gradient reflects little or no control from other sources, and that the gradient of intermediate slope is, indeed, the resultant of control shared by two or more identifiable stimuli. Such demonstrations are a major aim of the present paper.

Ray and Sidman (in press) have reported data from two monkeys, one of which gave a relatively sharp and the other, a relatively flat gradient along the dimension of line tilt. An eight-key simultaneous-discrimination procedure was used, with a different line tilt on each key. Key position, although a constant feature of the test situation and not systematically related to line tilt, was a likely alternative source of stimulus control. Indeed, both animals preferred certain key positions. It was possible to plot tilt generalization gradients separately for responses to the most-preferred key position, and for the combined responses to all other key positions. When they pressed nonpreferred keys, both animals had sharp tilt-generalization gradients. One animal's tilt gradient, however, was sharp for the preferred key position also; the other animal's tilt gradient for the preferred key was flat. The latter animal had the relatively flat overall tilt gradient. In this instance tilts, the training stimuli, and key position, a stimulus outside the training dimension, controlled each animal's responses. When key position interacted compatibly with line tilt, the overall tilt gradient was sharp; when key position exerted control that was relatively independent of line tilt, the overall tilt gradient was nearly flat.

This finding demonstrated that the slope of a generalization gradient along one stimulus dimension may be an inverse function of the amount of independent control exerted by other identifiable stimuli, even when the other stimuli are not systematically correlated with reinforcement. The term, independent, is critical. Different aspects of complex stimuli may exert either compatible (nonindependent) or incompatible (independent) control; only incompatible control will yield shallow gradients.

It is not to be expected that one will be able to identify the alternative sources of independent control which account for every observed instance of a flat or intermediate gradient. Therefore, many such demonstrations will be needed. This report will help serve that function, although it will not concern itself with factors that might influence the relative compatibility of different stimuli.

All reference in this paper is to differential control by stimuli, not to control by stimulus dimensions. Discussion of this point would lead us far afield; let it suffice to note here that the language is deliberate, stemming from the conviction that control by a whole dimension is unverifiable. Differential behavioral control may be exerted by stimuli classifiable along the same or different dimensions, but subjects respond differentially to the stimuli, not to the dimensions.

METHOD

Subjects

Although many subjects, brain-damaged and normal, have provided data on the delayed-matching procedure (*e.g.*, Rosenberger, Mohr, Stoddard, and Sidman, 1968; Sidman, Stoddard, and Mohr, 1968), only certain of the patients were affected adversely by the delays. These patients constituted a useful "preparation" for studying changes of stimulus control in individual subjects, and the data from seven of them are presented here. Although the concern here is not with brain damage *per se*, a brief description of each patient will accompany the presentation of his data.

Apparatus and Procedure

The subject sat in a small, sound-resistant room and faced a square matrix of nine translucent windows. The windows were each 2-in. square and were separated by 0.75-in. barriers. Light finger pressure on a window activated a switch mounted behind that window. Stimuli were rear-projected from slides onto the windows. The slides were punch-coded so that each could be identified by photocells that initiated appropriate electronic programming and recording signals to be correlated with the subject's responses.

Each trial began with a sample stimulus projected on the center window of the matrix; shutters, operated by rotary solenoids, kept the outer windows dark. The subject then pressed the sample window. In simultaneous matching, the sample press immediately exposed the choice stimuli on the outer windows. Then, the subject was to press the choice stimulus that matched the sample.

In delayed matching, the sample disappeared when the subject pressed it. After a delay, during which no stimuli were present, the choices appeared without the sample. Again, the subject was to press the choice stimulus which matched the (absent) sample.

When the subject matched correctly, a chimes sounded, a nickel (penny, for Subject H.M.) was delivered from an automatic dispenser, and all stimuli disappeared. After an intertrial interval of 1.5 sec, the next sample appeared on the center window. If the subject pressed an incorrect choice, the intertrial interval began without either chimes or nickel. The procedure was noncorrection.

Delay intervals were 0, (simultaneous disappearance of the sample and appearance of the choice stimuli), 8, 16, 24, 32, and 40 sec. Not all subjects were exposed to every delay. Most had 24 trials per delay, but some had 48. Some experienced the delays successively, starting with the shortest, and others were given the delays in a mixed sequence, in blocks of six trials at each delay. These variations, although not germane to the theses of this paper, will be noted. All subjects had experience with delayed-matching tasks that involved other stimuli than the ones used here, and no additional instructions were necessary. However, all were given preliminary practice at simultaneous and zero-delay matching in order to acquaint them with the stimuli of this experiment.

The stimuli were ellipses, with 1.00-in. major (horizontal) axes and minor axes of 0.17, 0.31, 0.39, 0.46, 0.61, 0.77, 0.89, and 1.00 inch. They are shown, actual size, in Fig. 1. The ellipses were not evenly spaced along any physical or subjective continuum; adjacent sizes were selected, by rough estimate, to be as easily discriminable from each other as possible. All ellipses appeared as choice stimuli on every trial, but the two extreme sizes (0.17 and 1.00) were never used as samples. Each of the remaining six ellipses appeared as a sample four (or eight) times at every delay. Consecutive trials presented different samples and different arrangements of ellipses on the outer windows.

Stimulus and Response Measurement

The ellipses can be classified along any of several dimensions, the most prominent of which are shape (ratio of minor to major axis), height (length of minor axis), and area. The specific dimension to which the subjects attended is not at issue here, and all are referred to indiscriminately as "size". It may be noted,

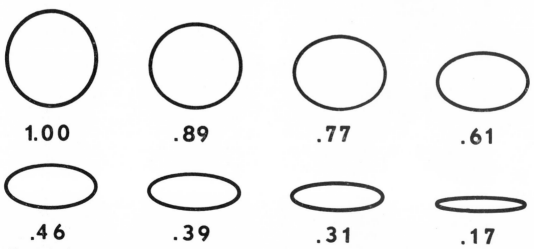

Fig. 1. The stimuli, actual size. Each is identified by its minor axis length (or the ratio of minor to major axis) in inches. The 1.00 ellipse is actually a circle.

however, that the constant 1-in. major axis makes the axis ratio and height numerically equal, and that the formula for area reduces to $\frac{\pi h}{4}$, where h is the minor axis. Therefore, area is directly proportional to height. For these reasons the ellipses have been classified in the results along the height dimension, inches.

The ellipses the subject selected from the choice display served to classify his responses. The datum of primary interest, the *gradient of sample control*, will summarize the differences between the sample ellipses and the ellipses actually chosen by the subject. To obtain the gradient of sample control each ellipse chosen was classified as a deviation from the sample, and the number of times the subject selected each deviation was recorded. If the subject matched correctly, the deviation between sample and choice was zero; if he chose, say, the 0.89 ellipse when the sample was the 0.77 ellipse, his choice was classified as a deviation of +0.12 inches; if he chose the 0.61 ellipse in response to the 0.77 sample, the deviation was −0.16 inches. Positive deviations may be regarded as overestimations of the sample size, and negative deviations as underestimations.

All deviations were not equally probable because adjacent ellipse sizes were not equally spaced, and because the size of the sample automatically restricted the range of possible deviations on a given trial. To illustrate the latter point, consider the extreme cases, with reference to Fig. 1. Suppose the sample on a given trial was the 0.89 ellipse. The only positive deviation available as a choice would be +0.11 (the 1.00 ellipse), but there would be six negative deviations from which to choose. If the sample was the 0.31 ellipse, one negative and six positive deviations would be available as choices. A middle-sized sample, *e.g.*, the 0.46 or the 0.61 ellipse, would eliminate the possibility of extremely large positive or negative deviations. Therefore, the subject had many more opportunities to select smaller than larger deviations. Because of these inequalities, the number of times the subject selected each deviation was divided by the number of opportunities available to the subject for each selection. Gradients of sample control were then plotted as choices of each deviation per opportunity.

Other classifications of stimulus control will be described in conjunction with the results.

RESULTS

Subject H.M.

H.M., male, age 41, had undergone radical bilateral excision of temporal-lobe structures 12 years earlier. Since then, he has been severely amnesic (Scoville and Milner, 1957; Milner, 1966; Milner, Corkin, and Teuber, 1968). The presentation of H.M.'s ellipse matching data will set the pattern to be followed with the other subjects.

Sample control. Solid curves in the left column of Fig. 2 show gradients of control by the sample stimuli at each delay. The point above zero on each abscissa represents correct choices (zero deviation in size from the sample). Points at the left of zero represent choices of ellipses increasingly smaller than the samples (negative deviations). Points at the right of zero represent choices of ellipses increasingly larger than the samples (positive deviations).

The simultaneous-matching gradient shows relatively sharp sample control. Seventy-seven per cent of the choices were correct, and most of the few incorrect choices were ellipses slightly smaller than the samples.

Control by the samples diminished with increasing delays. Although negative deviations (underestimations) predominated at 0- and 8-sec delays, H.M. shifted to overestimation at 16-sec delays. At 32-sec delays his choices per opportunity were spread relatively evenly from zero to the largest positive deviations.

Choice control. Was the change from a sharply peaked to a broad gradient accompanied by a shift in stimulus control from sample size to other stimuli? H.M.'s sample-control gradient at 32 sec suggested that he might have been selecting large ellipses indiscriminately, regardless of the sample size. Therefore, his choices were classified as absolute ellipse sizes, without reference to the samples, and were expressed as relative frequencies (number of choices/number of trials). The choice gradients in the center column of Fig. 2 show how frequently he selected each ellipse at each delay.

In simultaneous matching, H.M.'s choices were relatively evenly distributed among the six ellipses that were also used as samples, as was to be expected from his accurate performance. But with increasing delays, choice preferences developed. At 8- and 16-sec delays, H.M. preferred the middle-sized ellipses, but

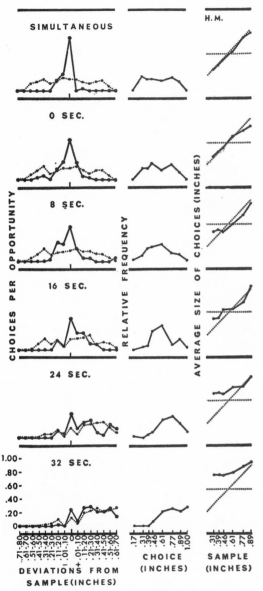

Fig. 2. H.M.'s actual sample-control gradients (solid curves in left column), choice gradients (center column), theoretical sample-control gradients (dotted curves in left column), and interaction analysis (right column), as described in the text. Delay intervals are consistent across rows. All ordinates have the same numerical scales, indicated at the lower left, but the numbers represent different variables in each column, as indicated by the ordinate labels. On the left-column abscissa, deviations from the samples have been grouped into classes 0.1-in. wide. This subject experienced the delays in ascending order and had 48 trials at each delay.

he shifted to larger choices at 24 and 32 sec. The choice display came to exert some control over his behavior.

"Control by the choice display" was, of course, involved even in accurate sample matching. The term, choice control, used here in a more restricted sense, may refer to any property of the choice display *except* the relation of the choice ellipses to the sample on a given trial.

Did control by the choice display influence the shape of the sample-control gradient? This possibility was evaluated by assuming that the subject's choices were actually independent of the samples. Such an assumption, if true, would require that the subject distribute his choices among the samples strictly in proportion to the relative frequency of each choice. For example, suppose H.M. had selected the circle (1.00 ellipse) on 50% of the trials at a given delay. If his choices were, in fact, independent of the sample sizes, he would have selected the circle on 50% of the presentations of each sample. Similarly, the relative frequency of each choice ellipse (center column) would determine its frequency of occurrence in response to each of the samples.

Theoretical sample-control gradients, based on the assumption that the choice display exerted control independently of the samples, were plotted. These are the dotted curves in the left column of Fig. 2. Because they depend on the actual distribution of the subject's choices among the various ellipses, the theoretical gradients differ from delay to delay and from subject to subject.

If the assumption of independent choice control were valid, the theoretical (dotted) and actual (solid) sample-control gradients would coincide. As was to be expected, the two curves for simultaneous matching were quite different. H.M. selected zero deviations much more often, and large positive and negative deviations much less often, than the assumption of independent choice-control predicted. But with increasing delays, the actual sample-control gradient conformed more closely to the prediction. Relatively complete sample control in simultaneous matching shifted to relatively complete control by the choice stimuli at 32-sec delays.

It should be pointed out that the experimental procedures and methods of data analysis do not, by themselves, artificially determine the predictability of one gradient from the other. There are only two extreme constraints: Only if the subject always chooses the same ellipse will the sample-control gradient necessarily be predictable from the choice preferences; only if the subject always chooses the correct matching ellipse will the choice gradient be completely determined. At the other extremes, even a flat choice gradient may be accompanied by either a sharp or a flat sample-control gradient; or a flat sample-control gradient may be accompanied by either a sharp or a flat choice gradient. If the actual and predicted sample-control gradients were flat and identical, but the choice gradients were flat also, then, of course, it could not be said that the choice display determined the shape of the sample-control gradient. In that instance, neither samples nor choices could be said to control the subject's behavior. Thus, before asking if the choice gradient determined the shape of the sample-control gradient, it was necessary to show that choice preferences did exist.

Although H.M.'s choice preferences became more pronounced, at least up to 16-sec delays, and the area between theoretical and actual sample-control gradients decreased steadily, the correspondence between theoretical and actual gradients was never complete. Even at 32 sec, accurate choices (zero deviations) occurred slightly more often than was predicted from the choice preferences. The inference to be drawn is that both sources of control contributed to the shape of the sample-control gradients, but that the relative contribution of each varied as a function of the delay interval.

Combined control. Having established that the actual controlling stimuli shifted as the sample-control gradients broadened, and that both sources of control contributed to the shape of the intermediate gradients, it becomes relevant to inquire more precisely into the nature of the combined control over the subject's behavior.

To evaluate the combined control by sample sizes and choice displays, the average size of the ellipses chosen by the subject was determined for each sample separately. The solid curves in the right column of Fig. 2 show the average choice size as a function of the sample size at each delay.

If the average size of the subject's choices was completely determined by the samples, without bias toward over- or underestimation, the solid curve would coincide with the diagonal dotted line, as it did fairly closely in simultaneous matching. Here, H.M. slightly underestimated 0.89 and 0.61 sample ellipses. At zero delay, he underestimated the 0.89 and 0.77 samples.

If the average choice was controlled by the samples but was inaccurate, the solid curve would be parallel to, but displaced from the diagonal dotted line. For example, at 8-sec delays H.M. slightly underestimated the four largest sample ellipses, but the slope of the curve indicated that his average choices were related to these samples.

If the subject's selections were unrelated to the samples, and were, instead, completely determined by stimuli in the choice display, the solid curve would be horizontal. Its location relative to the horizontal dotted line would depend on the size of the preferred choices. (The horizontal dotted line is located at the median of the choice-ellipse sizes.) Control by the choice display began to develop at 8-sec delays; when the samples were 0.31, 0.39, and 0.46 ellipses, the average size of H.M.'s choices remained constant and just below the median.

Slopes between the diagonal line and the horizontal reflect combined sample and choice control, the steepness of the curve indicating which source of control predominated. H.M.'s curves changed in slope from 45 degrees to near-horizontal with increasing delays, indicating a shift from exclusive sample control at simultaneous matching, to combined sample and choice control at intermediate delays, and to nearly exclusive choice control at 32 sec.

Combined control by samples and choices is demonstrated not only by intermediate linear slopes, but by nonlinear curves also. It is tempting to interpret the right-column, 8-sec curve, as showing that features of the choice display completely determined the subject's responses to the smallest samples; that the sample sizes completely determined his responses to the largest samples; and that only when the data were averaged over all samples, as in the left column, did the two sources of control seem to combine. The averaging process in the left column did, indeed, hide the varying degrees of control by different samples, but it would not be correct to say that either choice or sample control was complete at any *one* sample size. The evaluation of stimulus control always requires measurement of responses to at least two stimuli. If lines were drawn from the average choice at each of the smallest samples to the average choice at each of the largest samples, the steep slopes would show considerable differential control within each small-large pair. The 0.31 sample, for example, exerted no differential control with respect to the 0.46 sample, but considerable differential control when measured against the 0.89 sample. An accurate interpretation of the 8-sec curve in the right column is that there was no differential sample control among the three smallest samples, relative to each other; nearly maximum differential sample control among the four largest samples, relative to each other; and combined sample and choice-display control within all small-large sample pairs. Thus, choice or sample control which varies with sample size demonstrates an interaction between the two sources of control, and produces a nonlinear curve in the righthand column.

At 16-sec delays the slope became shallow between the 0.46 and the 0.77 ellipses, indicating that sample sizes within this range were beginning to lose differential control, relative to each other. The trend continued until, at 32-sec delays, there was no longer any sign of exclusive differential sample control. All samples were overestimated, and the shallow overall slope revealed all pairs of samples to exert either no differential control at all or to share control with the choice display. The small residue of combined control is consistent with the nonindependence of the choice control which was revealed by the comparison of actual and predicted gradients in the left column.

Summary of H.M.'s data. Sample-control gradients became broader with increasing delays (solid curves in left column). Choice preferences developed (center column) as sample control deteriorated. Choice control became increasingly independent of the samples at longer delays, and the sample-control gradients became more predictable from the choice preferences alone (comparison of dotted and solid curves in the left column). Exclusive sample control shifted to combined sample and choice control (right column) when the initially sharp sample-control gradient assumed intermediate slopes. Combined control faded into nearly independent choice control as the gradient approached the horizontal.

Data from other patients will demonstrate

that the findings are not confined to any particular neurological condition. Furthermore, not all patients preferred the same ellipses, nor were their forms of combined sample and choice control identical. These variations will demonstrate that the phenomena are not artifacts of the ellipse series or other constant aspects of the experimental procedure.

Subject J.B.

J.B., male, age 51, had been left unconscious after a physical assault, and was found to have a large mass lesion deep in the left posterofrontal-temporal region. An intracerebral clot was surgically removed. His oral speech was severely impaired, but he had no obvious memory disturbance. The present data were obtained 3 yr after he suffered the lesion.

Sample control. The solid curves in the left column of Fig. 3 show a sharp deterioration of sample control upon the change from simultaneous to zero-delay matching. J.B.'s choices

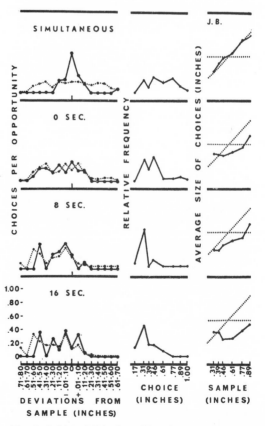

Fig. 3. Subject J.B.'s data, like Fig. 2 except that he had 48 trials each at simultaneous and zero delay, and 24 trials at 8 and 16 sec.

were predominantly ellipses smaller than the samples (negative deviations) at delays of 0, 8, and 16 sec. Even at 16-sec delays, however, he avoided the extreme negative deviations.

Choice control. When sample control deteriorated, J.B. developed a preference for small ellipses (center column of Fig. 3).

At delays of 0 to 16 sec, the theoretical sample-control gradients (dotted curves in the left column), computed from the choice frequencies alone, predicted the actual gradients fairly closely. Differences between the two gradients were inconsistent, except for the theoretical overestimation of the number of large negative deviations at 8 and 16 sec, and of large positive deviations at 0 and 8 sec.

Combined control. Nearly exclusive sample control was apparent in simultaneous matching (right column of Fig. 3).

In zero-delay matching, the horizontal slope from 0.31 to 0.46 samples shows choice control within this range. The 0.77 and 0.89 samples showed exclusive but inaccurate differential sample control. All other pairs of samples revealed combined sample and choice control.

Even though the choice preference sharpened at 8-sec delays, control by the choices became less independent of the samples, as indicated by the somewhat steeper slope of the 8-sec curve in the right column. Although sample control increased, it was still inaccurate (underestimation). This is consistent with the peak at small negative deviations in the 8-sec sample-control gradient, and with the excess of actual over predicted deviations at and near the peak.

At 16-sec delays control by the small choices predominated, with a remnant of exclusive but inaccurate differential sample control within the largest samples.

Although J.B. preferred small ellipses and H.M. (Fig. 2) preferred large ellipses, choice control was strongest in both subjects within the range of small samples. Therefore, no consistent correlation need exist between the range of ellipse sizes preferred by the subject and the sample range within which choice control predominates.

Subject S.J.K.

S.J.K., male, age 20, suffered a concussion in an automobile accident, followed by a period of amnesia which eventually became restricted to the events immediately before the accident.

The present data were obtained when the general amnesia had almost completely disappeared.

Sample control. The gradients of sample control were relatively sharp at all delays (left column of Fig. 4), but from 0 to 40 sec the peak shifted to the right, indicating slight overestimation of the sample sizes.

Choice control. Evidence of choice control was present from 0 to 40 sec (middle column) but, as might have been expected from the relatively sharp sample-control gradients, choice control proved only a poor predictor of the sample-control gradients. Differences between predicted and actual gradients, shown only at 40-sec delays, were similar at all delays.

Combined control. Choice control was evident within the range of the smallest sample

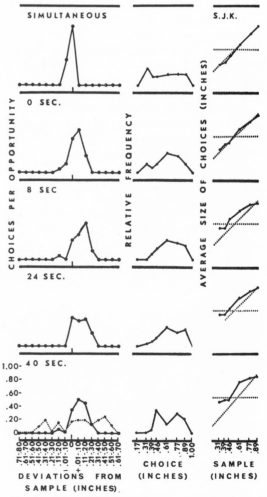

Fig. 4. Subject S.J.K., like Fig. 2, except that he had 24 trials at each delay.

ellipses (right column; 8, 24, and 40-sec delays), but the steepness of the curves indicated that S.J.K.'s behavior was almost completely controlled by the samples, with some tendency toward overestimation. Even though S.J.K.'s choice preferences at 8, 24, and 40 sec (middle column) were at least as sharp as H.M.'s at 40 sec (Fig. 2), S.J.K.'s choice control was clearly less independent of the samples; hence, his choice gradients had less influence on the shape of his sample-control gradients.

Subject V.C.C.

V.C.C., female, age 60, suffered a cerebral infarction, affecting the distribution of the left middle cerebral artery. She was aphasic, with no obvious memory disorder. The present data were obtained one month after the stroke.

Sample control. The solid curves in the left column of Fig. 5 show the peak of V.C.C.'s sample-control gradient shifting gradually toward larger positive deviations with increasing delays. As the peak shifted, the gradient broadened. A suggestion of sample control remained at 24 sec, where the subject never selected extremely large positive or negative deviations.

Choice control. The center column of Fig. 5 shows the development of a relatively sharp choice gradient, peaked at the 0.61 ellipse. With increasing delays, theoretical sample-control gradients, computed from choice frequencies alone (dotted curves in the left column), accounted more completely for the actual gradients. Theoretical gradients, however, consistently underestimated actual choices per opportunity at the shifting peaks.

Combined control. At zero delays, differential sample control predominated between sample pairs that included the largest and smallest ellipses (right column of Fig. 5), but the slope of the curve in the middle range of sample sizes revealed combined sample and choice control within that range.

The interaction between sample and choice control was similar at 8-sec delays except for the subject's tendency to choose larger ellipses in response to smaller samples at the low end of the sample-size range.

At 16-sec delays, the trend which began at 0 sec became more pronounced. Nearly exclusive differential sample control remained between ellipses at the extreme ends of the curve, although it was inaccurate (overestimation) at small sample sizes. But the combined control

that occurred within the middle range of sample sizes at shorter delays shifted to choice control at 16 sec; the curve became flat in the middle range of samples.

Exclusive but inaccurate differential sample control remained at 24-sec delays only between the smallest sample ellipses. Otherwise, the choice display exerted nearly complete control. Thus, control by the small samples, which took the form of consistent overestimation, was largely responsible for the discrepancy between the actual and theoretical gradients at 24 sec in the left column.

There was more sample control at 16-sec than at 24-sec delays, even though V.C.C.'s choice gradient was sharper at 16 sec. This again illustrates the principle that the sample-control gradient is a function not simply of

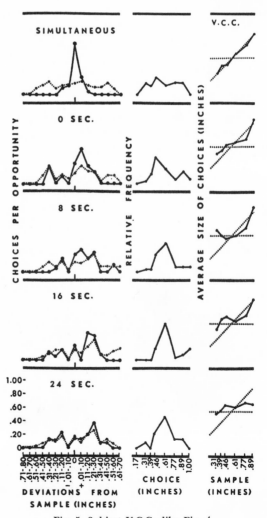

Fig. 5. Subject V.C.C., like Fig. 4.

concurrent choice control, but also of the degree to which choice control is independent of the samples.

V.C.C.'s data revealed the strongest choice control when preferred ellipses were also the samples. This type of interaction between sample and choice control was similar to that of J.B. (Fig. 3), except that J.B. preferred small ellipses and V.C.C. preferred middle-sized ellipses. In contrast, H.M. (Fig. 2) showed strongest control by the choices when nonpreferred ellipses were the samples.

Subjects E.J.R., M.D., and E.T.T.

These patients were nearly-classic examples of Korsakoff's disease, and showed the severe memory disturbance characteristic of this disorder. E.J.R. and M.D. were female, age 48 and 57, respectively. E.T.T., male, was 59 yr of age. Their data, shown in Fig. 6, 7, and 8, are intended to serve the following functions: A. Replication of the findings already described; B. Controls for the order in which the delays were presented. Unlike the previous subjects, who experienced the delays in ascending order, these subjects were given the mixed sequence (see Method); C. Controls for disease category; D. To illustrate certain additional features of the data analysis and interpretation.

These subjects, particularly M.D. (Fig. 7), were somewhat more variable than the others, possibly because of the mixed scheduling of the delays. All sample-control gradients, however, deteriorated with increasing delays (solid curves in the left columns). All subjects displayed choice preferences (middle columns) when the sample-control gradients broadened. Sample-control gradients were more strongly determined by the choice gradients as a function of increasing delays (comparison of solid and dotted curves in the left columns). For all subjects, combined control emerged from exclusive sample control as the delays lengthened, and became exclusive or nearly exclusive choice control at those delays that were the longest.

E.J.R.'s choice gradient at zero delay (Fig. 6, center column) was sharply bimodal. Yet, the corresponding sample-control gradient was markedly peaked. Similarly, M.D.'s bimodal choice gradient at 24-sec delays (Fig. 7) was correlated with a pronounced, though displaced, peak in the corresponding sample-control gradient. However, at delays of 32 and 40

sec, M.D.'s bimodal choice gradients were correlated with relatively weak sample control. These observations demonstrate once again that in the absence of specific and complete choice control, or of perfect sample control, it is not possible to reconstruct one gradient by knowing the other. The type of interaction between the two sources of control becomes the determining factor, and the interaction is a feature of the individual subject's behavior, not of the analytic methods.

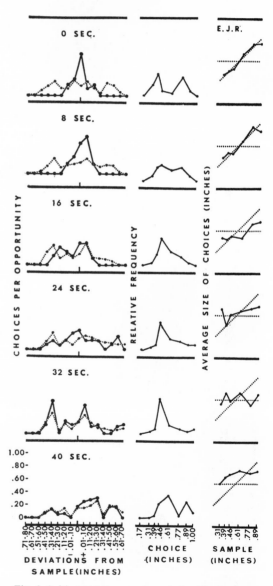

Fig. 6. Subject E.J.R. experienced the mixed sequence of delays and had 24 trials at each. Her simultaneous matching, not shown here, was only slightly better than the zero-delay performance.

DISCUSSION

Two sources of stimulus control were identified in delayed matching-to-sample. One source was the sample stimuli. The other was the choice display. With increasing delays, behavioral control shifted from the samples to the choice displays, independently of the samples. Sharply peaked gradients of sample control were shown to reflect nearly exclusive control of the subjects' behavior by the sample stimuli. Broad gradients of sample control reflected nearly exclusive control by the choice displays. Intermediate sample-control gradients resulted when samples and choice displays combined to control the subjects' behavior.

These data are not consistent with the view that the same stimuli control a subject's behavior both before and after a change in gradient shape, and that the new gradient only reflects shifting differential control among stimuli of the test dimension. Rather, the data demonstrate that gradient changes are accompanied by shifts to new sources of stimulus control. Furthermore, the greater the independence of the new sources of control, the more they de-

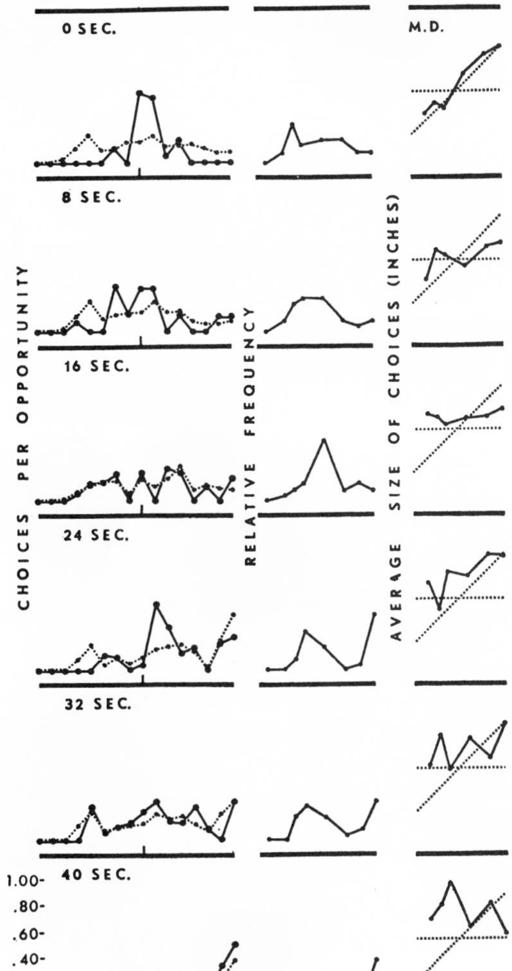

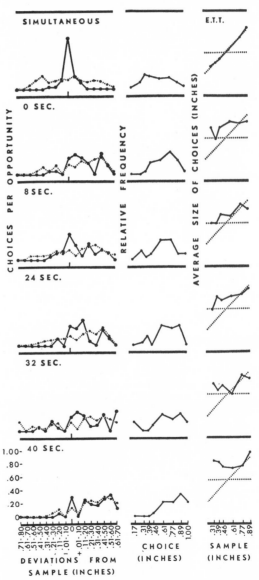

Fig. 8. Subject E.T.T., like Fig. 6 and 7. His 16-sec delay performance, omitted here, was like the one at 24 sec.

Fig. 7. Subject M.D., like Fig. 6.

termine the shape of the gradient along the original dimension.

Although a major purpose of this paper was to demonstrate that the shape of the sample-control gradient was a function of combined control from two sources, that purpose, once accomplished, diminished in importance. Intermediate and flat gradients became exposed as devices for masking multiple sources of control. The masking was accomplished by inaccurate experimenter-specification of the relevant stimuli and by averaging across them. It then became of greater importance to separate out the several sources. When this was done, various patterns of control were revealed. In some instances, samples or choice displays exerted nearly exclusive control over the subject's responses. In other instances, samples and choices exerted joint control; the subject selected the preferred choices when they were within a certain range of size deviations from the sample. Intermediate between exclusive and joint control were instances in which the average choice was invariant within one range of sample sizes, but within another range was determined either by the samples alone or by samples and choices combined.

The present data do not answer the question: does combined, or even joint, control refer to simultaneous action of both stimuli? The alternative possibility is that one stimulus or the other, sample or choice display, actually exerted exclusive control on any given trial but that the pooling of data over several trials masked fluctuations from trial to trial. By presenting all choice stimuli to the subject simultaneously, the amount of information gained from each response was increased, and the number of trials necessary for the averaging process was greatly reduced (Ray and Sidman, in press). But until methods are devised that permit identification of the controlling stimulus after the subject has responded only once, the problem of simultaneous *vs.* exclusive but fluctuating control will be answerable only by theoretical inference (*e.g.*, Cross, 1965*a*).

Although control by the samples was consistent with the reinforcement contingencies, the development of control by the choice display was not predictable on behavioral or logical grounds. It might easily have proven impossible to discover any source of control to account for the intermediate and flat gradients. Competing control might have shifted so frequently among several sources other than samples or choice displays as to be unidentifiable; or the experimenter simply might not have been aware of all the possibilities. In this experiment there were undoubtedly sources of control besides those selected for analysis. A relatively obvious candidate was key position. Some patients (none in this report at the time these experiments were done) have, in fact, preferred keys on the left or right side of the matrix. Three-way control by samples, choices, and key positions, however, could not be evaluated because of the small number of trials.

These considerations emphasize that the identification of alternative sources of stimulus control remains a problem of empirical discovery. Failures do not disprove the existence of such control. The very absence of a theoretical basis for evaluating negative evidence, however, requires that there be many confirmatory demonstrations. Competing control of the individual subject's behavior by several aspects of complex stimuli has been identified in simple discriminations, matching, and oddity (*e.g.*, Blough, 1963; Cumming and Berryman, 1965; Ferster and Hammer, 1966; Harlow, 1950; Jenkins, 1965; Johnson and Cumming, 1968; Revesz, 1925; Shepard, 1964; Sidman and Stoddard, 1967; Skinner, 1965). The rules by which reinforced unidimensional stimuli may combine to produce multidimensional control have been investigated (*e.g.*, Atkinson, Calfee, Sommer, Jeffrey, and Shoemaker, 1964; Butter, 1963; Cross, 1965*a*, *b*; Johnson, 1966; Shepard, 1964; White, 1958). However, apart from the present data, there has been only one demonstration (Ray and Sidman, in press) that an experimentally irrelevant gradient of stimulus control can influence the shape of a gradient along another stimulus dimension, and that the extent of its influence is related to the type of interaction between the two gradients. The number of such demonstrations required for the stimulus-control interpretation of the generalization gradient to be accepted will be a matter of individual preference.

It should not be inferred that the development of control by the choice display was responsible for the breakdown of sample control. The suggestion has been presented elsewhere, on independent grounds, that stimulus control other than that intended by the experimenter develops as a result of factors which render the subject unable to respond in concordance with the scheduled contingencies (Sidman and Stoddard, 1966, 1967; Stoddard and Sidman, 1967). Here, the increasing delays, interposed between sample disappearance and presentation of the choice stimuli, were directly responsible for the loss of sample control over the subject's choice responses. The development of control by the choice display must be considered a consequence, not a cause, of the deterioration of sample control.

Although choice control did not initiate the breakdown of sample control, it did contribute to the shape of the sample-control gradients once the latter began to broaden. Furthermore, because choice control was not systematically reinforced, its gradient shape and its interaction with sample control varied, even among subjects who showed markedly similar changes in their sample-control gradients, and among subjects with the same neurological diagnosis.

REFERENCES

Atkinson, R. C., Calfee, R. C., Sommer, G. R., Jeffrey, W. E., and Shoemaker, R. A test of three models for stimulus compounding with children. *Journal of Experimental Psychology*, 1964, **67**, 52-58.

Blough, D. S. Interresponse time as a function of continuous variables: a new method and some data. *Journal of the Experimental Analysis of Behavior*, 1963, **6**, 237-246.

Brown, J. S., Bilodeau, E. A., and Baron, M. R. Bidirectional gradients in the strength of a generalized voluntary response to stimuli on a visual-spatial dimension. *Journal of Experimental Psychology*, 1951, **41**, 52-61.

Butter, C. M. Stimulus generalization along one and two dimensions in pigeons. *Journal of Experimental Psychology*, 1963, **65**, 339-346.

Cross, D. V. Metric properties of multidimensional stimulus control. Doctoral dissertation, University of Michigan, 1965. (*a*)

Cross, D. V. *Metric properties of multidimensional stimulus control*. Doctoral dissertation, University of *Stimulus generalization*. Stanford: Stanford University Press, 1965. Pp. 72-93. (*b*)

Cumming, W. W. and Berryman, R. The complex discriminated operant: studies of matching-to-sample and related problems. In D. I. Mostofsky (Ed.), *Stimulus generalization*. Stanford: Stanford University Press, 1965. Pp. 284-330.

Ferster, C. B. and Hammer, C. E., Jr. Synthesizing the components of arithmetic behavior. In W. K. Honig (Ed.), *Operant behavior: areas of research and application*. New York: Appleton-Century-Crofts, 1966. Pp. 634-676.

Harlow, H. F. Analysis of discrimination learning by monkeys. *Journal of Experimental Psychology*, 1950, **40**, 26-39.

Jenkins, H. M. Measurement of stimulus control during discriminative operant conditioning. *Psychological Bulletin*, 1965, **64**, 365-376.

Johnson, D. F. *Determiners of selective discriminative stimulus control*. Doctoral dissertation, Columbia University, 1966.

Johnson, D. F. and Cumming, W. W. Some determiners of attention. *Journal of the Experimental Analysis of Behavior*, 1968, **11**, 157-166.

Lashley, K. S. and Wade, M. The Pavlovian theory of generalization. *Psychological Review*, 1946, **53**, 72-87.

Milner, B. Amnesia following operation on the temporal lobes. In O. L. Zangwill and C. W. M. Whitty (Eds.), *Amnesia*. London: Butterworths, 1968. Pp. 109-133.

Milner, B., Corkin, S., and Teuber, H. -L. Further analysis of the hippocampal amnesic syndrome: 14-year follow-up study of H.M. *Neuropsychologia*, 1968, **6**, 215-234.

Prokasy, W. F. and Hall, J. F. Primary stimulus generalization. *Psychological Review*, 1963, **70**, 310-322.

Ray, B. A. and Sidman, M. Reinforcement schedules and stimulus control. In W. N. Schoenfeld and J. Farmer (Eds.), *Theory of reinforcement schedules*. New York: Appleton-Century-Crofts (in press).

Revesz, G. Experimental study in abstraction in monkeys. *Journal of Comparative Psychology*, 1925, **5**, 293-343.

Rosenberger, P. B., Mohr, J. P., Stoddard, L. T., and Sidman, M. Inter- and intramodality matching deficits in a dysphasic youth. *Archives of Neurology*, 1968, **18**, 549-562.

Scoville, W. B. and Milner, B. Loss of recent memory after bilateral hippocampal lesions. *Journal of Neurology, Neurosurgery and Psychiatry*, 1957, **20**, 11-21.

Shepard, R. N. Attention and the metric structure of the stimulus space. *Journal of Mathematical Psychology*, 1964, **1**, 54-87.

Sidman, M. and Stoddard, L. T. Programming perception and learning for retarded children. In N. R. Ellis (Ed.), *International review of research in mental retardation*, Vol. II. New York: Academic Press, 1966. Pp. 151-208.

Sidman, M. and Stoddard, L. T. The effectiveness of fading in programming a simultaneous form discrimination for retarded children. *Journal of the Experimental Analysis of Behavior*, 1967, **10**, 3-15.

Sidman, M., Stoddard, L. T., and Mohr, J. P. Some additional quantitative observations of immediate memory in a patient with bilateral hippocampal lesions. *Neuropsychologia*, 1968, **6**, 245-254.

Skinner, B. F. Stimulus generalization in an operant: a historical note. In D. I. Mostofsky (Ed.), *Stimulus generalization*. Stanford: Stanford University Press, 1965. Pp. 193-209.

Stoddard, L. T. and Sidman, M. The effects of errors on children's performance on a circle-ellipse discrimination. *Journal of the Experimental Analysis of Behavior*, 1967, **10**, 261-270.

Terrace, H. S. Stimulus control. In W. K. Honig (Ed.), *Operant behavior: areas of research and application*. New York: Appleton-Century-Crofts, 1966. Pp. 271-344.

White, S. W. Generalization of an instrumental response with variations in two attributes of the CS. *Journal of Experimental Psychology*, 1958, **56**, 339-343.

Received 3 January 1969.

FURTHER OBSERVATIONS ON OVERT "MEDIATING" BEHAVIOR AND THE DISCRIMINATION OF TIME[1]

Victor G. Laties, Bernard Weiss, and Ann B. Weiss

UNIVERSITY OF ROCHESTER

When the lever-pressing behavior of five rats was maintained by a DRL schedule (reinforcement was scheduled only when a specified waiting time between successive responses was exceeded), collateral behavior developed that apparently served a mediating function. In two cases this behavior did not arise until the experimental environment included pieces of wood that the rats started to nibble. When collateral behavior first appeared, it was always accompanied by an increase in responses spaced far enough apart to earn reinforcement. If collateral behavior was prevented, the number of reinforced responses always decreased. Extinction of lever pressing extinguished the collateral behavior. Adding a limited-hold contingency to the schedule did not extinguish collateral behavior. It appears that the rat can better space its responses appropriately when concurrently performing some overt collateral activity. The amount of this activity apparently comes to serve as a discriminative stimulus. To assume the existence of internal events that serve as discriminative stimuli in temporal discriminations is, at least under some circumstances, unnecessary.

Questions concerning the discrimination of time are often phrased in terms of the discrimination of on-going physiological events. Dimond (1964) reflected this viewpoint when, in reviewing the "structural basis of timing", he wrote:

"The stream of sensory impulses gathered from the environment is distributed in time. It is supposed that the duration of stimuli and the intervals between them are compared with an internal standard. Such a standard could be represented by the steady functioning of some mechanism of the body."

The notion of some sort of internal standard or "clock" appears in much of the literature in the traditional field of time perception (Fraisse, 1963; Treisman, 1963). The discrimination of stimuli associated with mechanisms of this type may, indeed, play some part in the discrimination of duration, especially when an effort is made to exclude other discriminative stimuli, such as those associated with human counting (*e.g.*, Laties and Weiss, 1962). But recent work has shown that the externally observable behavior emitted by an organism between responses on a lever (collateral behavior) may adventitiously come to be important in determining response distributions on temporally defined schedules (*e.g.*, Davis and Wheeler, 1967; Hodos, Ross, and Brady, 1962; Laties, Weiss, Clark, and Reynolds, 1965; Nevin and Berryman, 1963; Segal-Rechtschaffen, 1963). A previous report from this laboratory described a rat with a stereotyped pattern of behavior between lever presses maintained by a schedule—DRL (for Differential Reinforcement of Low rate)—that arranged reinforcement only for responses separated from the immediately preceding response by a minimum interval of time (Laties *et al.*, 1965). The rat gnawed its tail between responses (without breaking the skin), and we concluded that this unscheduled collateral behavior was "mediating" behavior; *i.e.*, it appeared to be ". . . behavior . . . used by the organism as a controlling stimulus in subsequent behavior . . ." (Ferster and Skinner, 1957, p. 729). The present series of ob-

[1]Dedicated to B. F. Skinner in his sixty-fifth year. From the Department of Radiation Biology and Biophysics, University of Rochester. A portion of this study was conducted at the Johns Hopkins University, supported in part by grants MH-03229, MH-08353, and MH-07498, from the National Institute of Mental Health; a portion was conducted at the University of Rochester, supported in part by grant MH-11752 from the National Institute of Mental Health, and performed under contract with the U. S. Atomic Energy Commission at the University of Rochester Atomic Energy Project and has been assigned Report No. UR-49-845. Reprints may be obtained from Victor G. Laties, Department of Radiation Biology and Biophysics, University of Rochester School of Medicine and Dentistry, Rochester, New York 14620.

servations further explored the nature of the collateral behavior often seen in rats maintained on this schedule.

METHOD

The subjects were five male albino rats (Carworth Farms, CFN), maintained with dry Purina lab chow at about 75% of their predicted free-feeding weight. When 14 weeks old, they were trained to eat from the dipper that delivered the reinforcer (sweetened condensed milk, diluted 1:1 with tap water). Next, the first 50 lever presses were each reinforced. The reinforcement schedule then became DRL 18-sec; that is, reinforcement occurred only when a response on the lever followed the preceding response by at least 18 sec. If a response was reinforced, the 18-sec period was timed from the end of the reinforcement cycle. With rare exceptions, the rats were tested at approximately the same time, five days a week. Except when otherwise indicated, sessions were 1-hr long.

A force of 35 g was necessary to depress the lever 4 mm and close a microswitch. A telegraph sounder gave a feedback click for each such response. The lever, a 0.5-in. diameter, 2-in. long steel rod, was mounted 3.5 in. above the grid floor on the front wall. A tone sounded during the upswing of the 0.1-cc dipper that delivered the milk reinforcer. The reinforcement cycle lasted 6 sec. A broadband masking noise was on continuously.

The experimental chamber (Foringer and Company, Rockville, Md.) was 10.5-in. long by 10-in. wide. The glass top was 6 in. from the floor at the front of the box and 7 in. from it at the rear. The 0.25-in. diameter stainless steel bars that comprised the floor were 0.8-in. apart. The chamber had been modified in the following way. Doors had been cut in the two side walls; when open, they led to a 7-in. wide by 7-in. high alley that surrounded the chamber on three sides. The outside lengths of the three legs of the alley were 26, 24, and 26 in. The floor of the alley was of pressed fiberboard (Masonite) and the outer side and top were of wire mesh, supported by small wooden posts. The apparatus was set into a larger box of wall board; one side and the top of this box were Plexiglas. The scheduling and recording equipment were located in an adjoining room. A one-way mirror in the door

of this room, plus a mirror mounted at a 45-degree angle over the chamber, allowed the experimenter to watch the subject.

The general plan was to await the development of collateral behavior that appeared to serve a mediating function, then thwart its expression and record the effects on the DRL performance (*cf.*, Davis and Wheeler, 1967; Deadwyler and Segal, 1965; Hodos, Ross, and Brady, 1963; Laties *et al.*, 1965). With three of the rats (randomly chosen), the doors to the alley remained closed. These were to constitute the control group of an experiment that, as will be seen, did not work out as planned. The other two rats always had access to the alley so that it would be possible for their movement through the alley to be reinforced adventitiously, thereby making instances of collateral behavior especially easy to observe and measure. Various one- and two-rat subgroups were used for the several supplementary studies listed in Table 1 and outlined in detail below.

Table 1
Summary of Procedures

	Subjects				
	2-1	3-1	3-2	2-0	3-0
Development and thwarting of collateral behavior	X	X	X	X	X
Extinction and reconditioning				X	X
Addition of limited-hold requirement	X	X			
Addition of collateral behavior to limited-hold performance				X	
Comparison of two types of collateral behavior			X		X
Increase in lower limit of DRL requirement		X			

RESULTS

Initial Development of Collateral Behavior and Effects of Interference

All five subjects developed patterns of overt collateral behavior. In each case, it could be shown that interfering with the collateral behavior changed the DRL performance. However, provision of the alley through which two of the subjects could run did not generate any stable collateral behavior. We can only guess why this procedure failed. Perhaps it was because a circuit of the alley took only a few seconds. Both subjects were seen to run through it early in training but the frequency with which such a circuit was followed by a reinforced lever press may not have been great enough to support the behavior.

Rat 2-1, which worked with the alley doors open, rarely left the inner chamber after the first few sessions. Beginning with the eighth session, it spent most of the time between lever presses nibbling and licking the front bar of the grid floor. Before the eighth session, it had earned between 30 and 50 reinforcements. From the eighth to the twentieth session, the number of reinforcements varied between 68 and 98, increasing gradually over time. In order to determine the relationship between this oral behavior and the increased number of reinforcements, a Plexiglas floor was installed before the twenty-first session, thereby preventing the rat from reaching the grid bar. The floor effectively prevented nibbling of the grid bar, although midway in the session the rat started to lick the front wall. The results were dramatic (Fig. 1). The response rate increased markedly, the number of reinforced responses decreased, and as a result the "efficiency ratio" of reinforcements to responses fell (Brady and Conrad, 1960). These measures returned to about their pretreatment levels when the false floor was removed and the rat could (and immediately did) return to gnawing the front grid bar.

Rat 3-1 also had access to the alley and spent more time there than Rat 2-1. Occasionally, it would run halfway through the alley, spend some time exploring, then run back to the inner chamber and press the lever. Such be-havior occurred during the early sessions on many occasions and frequently would occur before each of a sequence of responses, but it was unstable and did not persist. Beginning with Session 21, the rat started to display a stereotyped pattern of behavior that proved quite stable: after a response it would leave the inner chamber, go to one of three wooden posts that comprised part of the framework of the alley, gnaw on it for some time, then move rapidly back to the lever. As can be seen in Fig. 2, the number of reinforcements doubled in the first session during which it gnawed wood in the alley. When the doors to the alley were closed, the number of reinforcements dropped almost to the original level. This was the only rat that showed an increase in interresponse-time variability when showing overt collateral behavior, a finding perhaps related to the fact that it did not appear to favor any one post over the others.

The other three rats at no time had access to the outside alley.

Rat 3-2 developed collateral behavior that took advantage of a design peculiarity of the apparatus. The pressed wood (Masonite) floor of the alley projected under the doors to the chamber by about 0.5 in. Sometime before the tenth session, this rat began to gnaw between lever responses at the pressed wood under one door. The number of reinforcements per session rose quickly. Figure 3 shows the effects of a Plexiglas barrier that prevented the rat from gnawing the pressed wood; of the rat transferring its gnawing activity to the

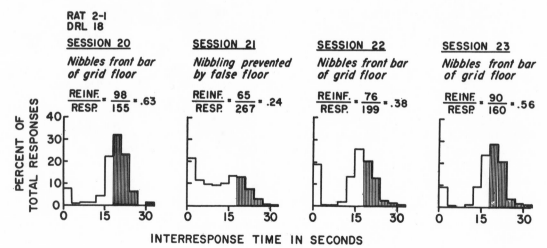

Fig. 1. Effects of barring Rat 2-1 from access to the grid floor it had been nibbling and licking between lever presses. A false floor was added only for Session 21. Shading indicates interresponse times that led to reinforcement.

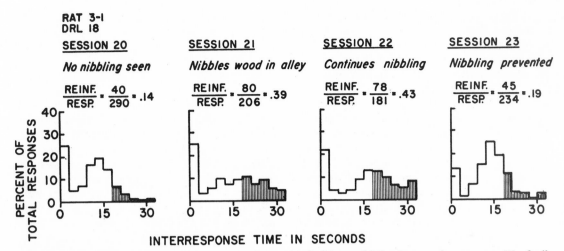

Fig. 2. Effects of barring Rat 3-1 from access to the wood it had been nibbling between lever presses. Wood nibbling was first seen during Session 21. The entrances to the alley containing the wood were closed just before Session 23. Shading indicates interresponse times that led to reinforcement.

wood under the other door; and of a second barrier to prevent gnawing there, too. It seems clear that the gnawing played an important role in maintaining appropriately spaced responding.

Rat 2-0 did not display any consistent collateral behavior during its first 31 sessions. At the end of that time it was earning fewer reinforcements than the three rats that had developed stereotyped chains. In hopes of stimulating the formation of such behavior, a piece of wood (pine), 1 in. by 2 in. by 10 in., was wedged into the rear half of the chamber before the thirty-second session. The rat sniffed the wood occasionally but did not gnaw it. After the first 10 min of the next session, with the same piece of wood again in place, it started to gnaw between most lever presses. The wood chips were later collected from the waste pan; they weighed 5.5 g. The number of reinforcements doubled. The same piece of wood was reinserted for the next

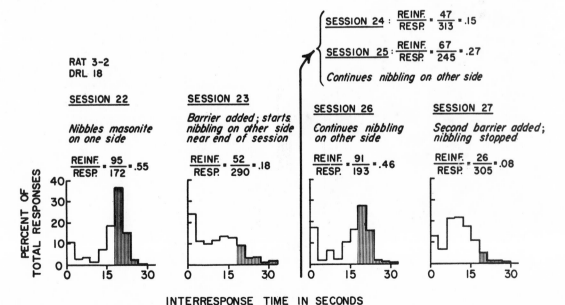

Fig. 3. Effects of barring Rat 3-2 from access to the pressed wood it had been nibbling between lever presses. Shading indicates interresponse times that led to reinforcement.

several sessions and reinforcements continued to increase, as one would expect if the amount of gnawing was serving as a discriminative stimulus. Two aspects of the behavior of the rat are summarized in the left half of Fig. 4, top. (The data on extinction shown in the right half are discussed in the next section.) This chart shows the number of reinforcements earned during each session; those sessions during which wood was available to the rat are indicated by the use of an "X" instead of a dot. In addition, the amount of wood that had dropped through to the waste pan is charted for sessions where that measure is relevant. After the fourth session with wood in the chamber, the wood was removed for one session. The number of reinforcements halved. Replacing the wood for the next session raised the number of reinforcements to its previous level.

Rat 3-0, the fifth subject, did not develop a reliable sequence of overt behavior between lever responses during its first 22 sessions. An attempt to induce licking of the front bar of the grid floor was then made, in the twenty-third through the thirtieth sessions, by smearing sweetened condensed milk on the bar before the rat was placed in the chamber. Each time, it licked off the milk immediately and then proceeded to respond as it had during the preceding sessions, earning about 30 reinforcements each time (Fig. 4, bottom). A piece of wood (similar to that used with Rat 2-0) was wedged in the chamber from the thirty-first through the thirty-fifth sessions, removed for the thirty-sixth, and returned for the thirty-seventh, with results that replicated the findings with Rat 2-0. The drop in reinforcements earned for the session without wood was smaller than for the comparable session for Rat 2-0. Midway through this hour, Rat 3-0 started nibbling on its tail, and from that point in the session reinforcement rate increased markedly. This tail nibbling disappeared when wood was reintroduced for the next session.

Collateral Behavior During Extinction

The responses of both Rat 2-0 and Rat 3-0 were put on extinction in order to explore further the relation of wood nibbling and lever pressing. (The milk was removed but the

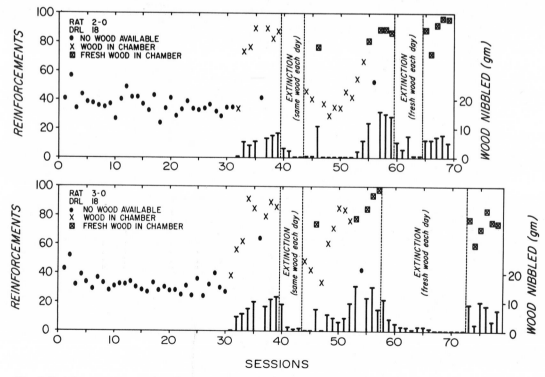

Fig. 4. Reinforcements earned and amount of wood nibbled (vertical bars) during 1-hr sessions by Rat 2-0 (top) and Rat 3-0 (bottom) as a function of various experimental manipulations.

dipper continued to operate.) Each rat had its own piece of wood wedged into the chamber at the beginning of each session, as before. Over four extinction sessions the amount of wood nibbled decreased, in both cases, to less than 1 g per session (Fig. 4). During the fourth session, Rat 2-0 made 70 responses (*vs.* 148 during the last pre-extinction session), while Rat 3-0 made 30 (*vs.* 129). In each case the subject made very few responses during the last half of the fourth session, lying on the floor most of the time. Thus, gnawing ceased before lever pressing, confirming the extinction results of the single tail-nibbling rat of Laties *et al.* (1965) and demonstrating again the status of the collateral behavior as a member of a heterogeneous chain. This disappearance of wood nibbling also argues against any interpretation of it as merely competing behavior which would keep the rat away from the lever in the way that running did in the Skinner and Morse (1957) study of fixed-interval performance.

We expected the rats to resume gnawing wood during the first reconditioning session. Instead, both rats ignored the wood during this and the succeeding session. The number of reinforcements earned was appropriate to the previous no-wood sessions. It seemed possible that extinction of wood nibbling may have been specific to the particular piece of wood present during the extinction sessions. When a fresh piece of wood was used for each rat during Session 46, both subjects gnawed vigorously and earned many more reinforcements than during the two prior sessions. The pieces of wood present during extinction were returned before the next session and neither animal gnawed. Reinforcement frequency halved. Further sessions were then conducted with the original wood present to see if and when the rats would resume gnawing. Rat 2-0 ignored the wood until its ninth session with the original wood. Rat 3-0 started to gnaw during the fourth session.

After the rats were gnawing the original wood regularly, they both were switched to a regimen of a fresh piece of wood each day. When the wood piece was again withdrawn, reinforcement frequency declined substantially (Session 56 for Rat 2-0, Session 54 for Rat 3-0). Extinction was now tried once more, this time with a fresh piece of wood available each day, to test whether or not gnawing had, indeed, previously come under the discriminative control of the particular piece of wood present during extinction. (Each rat was first given three sessions, each with new wood, before the milk was withdrawn for the extinction sessions.) Rat 2-0 had five extinction sessions; at the end of these it was once more responding at a very low rate and nibbling very little wood. When the milk was replaced for Session 65, the rat immediately began to gnaw the wood, although only half as much as before extinction. Rat 3-0 was given 15 extinction sessions, each with fresh wood available. During its last session it made only a few responses and gnawed only 0.05 g of wood. After milk was returned for the next session, it nibbled 9.3 g of a fresh piece of wood. It seems clear that regular changing of the wood present during extinction prevented the build-up of discriminative properties.

Effect on Collateral Behavior of Adding a Limited Hold

If an upper bound is added to the interresponse times required by the DRL schedule, a DRL with limited hold (DRL LH) results. Kelleher, Fry, and Cook (1959) suggested that "the development of chains of behavior should be less probable [on such a schedule], since the animal must discriminate a discrete point on the temporal continuum. The time occupied by overt behavior other than lever pressing could occupy enough time to enable the animal to meet the minimum requirement; but this chain of responses would be unreinforced whenever it extended beyond the maximum requirement." In fact, they found no overt chaining in animals they trained on DRL with limited holds.

In order to see what the addition of a limited hold would do to the collateral behavior that had already developed, two animals with stable collateral behavior were shifted from DRL 18 to DRL 18 LH 3; *i.e.,* only responses at least 18 sec but no more than 21 sec since the previous response were reinforced.

Rat 2-1's last 1-hr session on DRL 18 is shown in the upper portion of Fig. 5. This subject, which usually nibbled on the front bar of the grid floor, was then shifted to the 3-sec limited-hold contingency and maintained on that regimen for 26 one-hour sessions. The first effect of the shift was to abolish nibbling of the front bar and increase markedly the amount of time the animal spent out in the alley. (The doors were open throughout for this rat.) Some licking of the front wall was seen during the second and third sessions. By the fourth session, however, the rat was back to bar nibbling, and it remained at that task between lever presses throughout the rest of the limited-hold sessions. The numbers of reinforced responses were 11, 23, 27, 38, 27, and 31, respectively, for the last six. The cumulative record from Session 50 is shown in Fig. 5 (bottom). Notice especially the increased density of the marks made by the pen that monitored contacts with the first bar, reflecting an increase in bar nibbling.

The responding of Rat 3-1, the subject that usually gnawed the wooden stanchions in the alley, was placed on a limited hold immediately after the last session shown in Fig. 2 and kept on it for ten 1-hr sessions. It did not gnaw the stanchions during the first session and earned 20 reinforcements. It then returned to gnawing the wooden posts. The amount chewed was not measured but it appeared to remain fairly constant during the course of the 10 sessions on limited hold. Reinforcements varied between 18 and 30.

We conclude that the imposition of a limited hold with rats that had already developed stable collateral behavior does not lead to the extinction of the collateral behavior. Instead, it appears that reinforcements received on a limited-hold schedule are sufficient to keep the collateral behavior in full strength.

Effect of Adding Collateral Behavior to Stable Behavior on DRL 18-sec LH 3-sec

We also examined whether or not the opportunity to gnaw wood for a rat with a history of wood nibbling would modify its behavior on the limited-hold version of the DRL schedule. Rat 2-0 was given five 2-hr sessions on DRL 18 LH 3 with no wood available. During these sessions, with no systematic collateral behavior visible, it produced 56, 76, 64, 51, and 41 reinforcements, respectively.

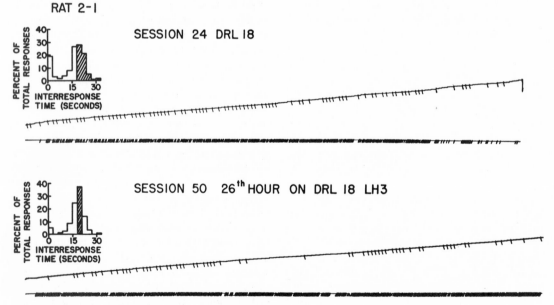

Fig. 5. Effects on nibbling front bar of grid floor by Rat 2-1 of adding a 3-sec limited hold to DRL 18-sec. Downward deflections of the operations pen (bottom line of each pair of records) denote contacts with front bar. A Lehigh Valley Electronics drinkometer was used to monitor contacts with the front bar, with the sensitivity set so that only juxtaposition of wet mouth and the bar produced these deflections. The oblique pips on the cumulative records represent reinforcements which, for the top record, occurred whenever the subject responded at least 18 sec after the last response and, for the bottom record, whenever the subject had paused between 18 and 21 sec before making a response. The shaded portions of the interresponse-time graphs also indicate reinforced responses. The recorder did not run during the reinforcement cycle. The rat made 183 responses during Session 24, 100 during Session 50.

Before the beginning of the next session a fresh piece of wood was introduced, and this procedure was followed for four more sessions. During these sessions it produced 82, 75, 100, 104, and 102 reinforcements, respectively, and the amount of wood gnawed varied between 2.8 and 6.0 g, with no correlation apparent between amount nibbled and number of reinforcements (see below for more data on such correlations). Figure 6 (bottom) displays the interresponse-time distributions derived from the last two sessions under each condition. The shift of the distribution is similar to that seen on a regular DRL. That more than a simple shift of the distribution is involved is shown by the conditional probability function (Fig. 6, top). Clearly, the rat showed a more precise discrimination when it spent its time between responses gnawing wood. An attempt to recapture the "no-wood" performance proved only partially successful: the rat started nibbling on one of the bars of the grid floor part way through the first session without wood and continued to do so through two more sessions. The conditional probabil-

ity curve from the first session fell neatly between the two curves plotted in Fig. 6, top.

Comparison of Two Varieties of Collateral Behavior in the Same Rat

Several rats were seen to change from one type of collateral behavior to another. For example, Rat 2-1 (see above) was seen to lick the front wall when prevented from nibbling on the bars of the grid floor. Two rats developed collateral behaviors that allowed comparison of the DRL performances associated with each.

Rat 3-2. Directly after the experiment summarized in Fig. 3, this rat was used in a drug experiment. The effects of amphetamine were assessed as a function of the opportunity to gnaw the pressed wood projecting into the chamber (Weiss and Laties, 1966). Data from control sessions (two of every four) are summarized in Fig. 7. Gnawing occurred with great regularity during sessions in which the rat was permitted access to the wood and the interresponse-time distributions consistently peaked in the 18- to 21-sec bin. At first, preventing access to the pressed wood with Plexiglas barriers led to a marked shift toward lower interresponse-time values. This regularity broke down at approximately the fiftieth session. From then on, behavior with and without barriers in place became progressively more similar, the rat producing almost as many reinforcements with barriers in place as not. The reason for this seems clear: whenever it was denied access to the pressed wood, it gnawed its tail. This nibbling was not as systematic as the wood nibbling and obviously was a poor substitute for the latter, for whenever the barriers were removed, the rat went back to nibbling wood.

Rat 3-0. This rat was exposed to DRL 18 LH 3 (no wood available) to replicate the experiment with Rat 2-0 (see above). However, during one of its first few 2-hr sessions, it began systematically to nibble its tail (the exact time was not noted). After seven sessions, wood was placed in the chamber to determine if wood nibbling would now displace tail nibbling (Fig. 8). It did so, briefly. During the first of these sessions, the animal gnawed 4.4 g of wood and also nibbled its tail frequently. During the next four sessions, it gnawed less and less wood, dropping finally

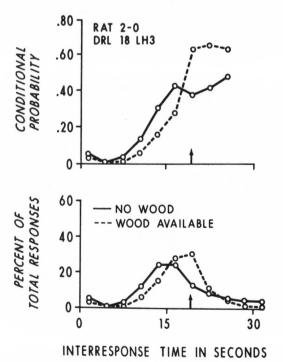

Fig. 6. Effects of collateral behavior on the interresponse distribution (bottom) and conditional probability function (top) of Rat 2-0 when it worked with a 3-sec limited-hold requirement added to the DRL 18-sec schedule.

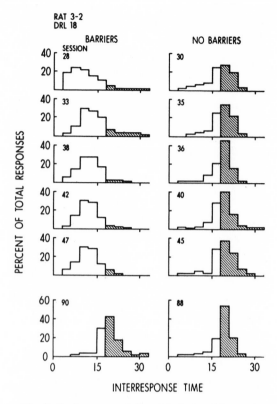

RAT 3-2
DRL 18

Fig. 7. Performance of Rat 3-2 during 1-hr sessions with (right) and without (left) access to the pressed wood that it nibbled between lever presses. Interresponse times shorter than 3 sec have been ignored in casting up these distributions (see Hodos, 1963).

pected mediating behavior during DRL (Wilson and Keller, 1953) and of the "active employment" near the dipper described by Azzi, Fix, Keller, and Rocha e Silva (1964) for a delayed reinforcement procedure. Reinforcements had reached 101 when the experiments had to be discontinued.

This rat obviously favored tail nibbling to the previously quite strong wood nibbling, and interfering with the former markedly reduced reinforcements. This animal had shown tail nibbling once before when wood was withdrawn earlier in its experimental history (see above). But at that time the tail nibbling disappeared as soon as wood was again made available.

Collateral Behavior at Higher DRL Values

A single subject, Rat 3-1, was used to see whether or not wood nibbling would continue to serve a mediating function at values of the minimum reinforced interresponse time higher than 18 sec. This rat, which previously had worked on DRL 18 LH 3 with the alley doors open, was placed on DRL 18 with the

to 0.1 g, and spent more and more of the time between lever presses with tail in mouth. Reinforcements rose with tail nibbling. Next, the tail was painted with a substance used to dissuade rats from gnawing wires, a 1.0% solution of cycloheximide (Weeks, 1962; Laties et al., 1965), in order to see if the rat would go back to wood nibbling when tail nibbling was made less likely. This procedure did abolish tail nibbling and reinforcements decreased to 23 during the first such session. The rat did not immediately resume chewing wood, nibbling only 0.4 g, and it spent a great deal of time grabbing its tail and dropping it after touching it to its mouth. For five more 2-hr sessions, the tail was painted before the session and wood was made available to the animal. During these sessions the rat ignored its tail, nibbled amounts of wood varying from 0.9 to 3.2 g, and spent much time with its nose near the dipper hole in a manner reminiscent of the original descriptions of sus-

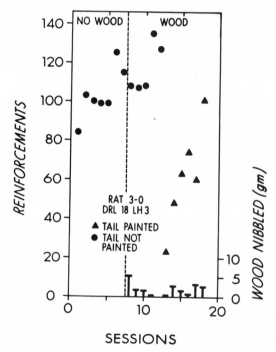

Fig. 8. Performance of Rat 3-0 on DRL 18-sec LH 3 without and with wood available to it. Vertical bars indicate amount of wood nibbled. Tail nibbling developed sometime before the fourth session. Tail nibbling was disrupted when wood was first returned and was suppressed completely by the cycloheximide.

limited-hold contingency removed, and with the doors to the alley closed. A piece of wood similar to that used successfully with Rat 2-0 and Rat 3-0 was then wedged in the chamber. Within three 1-hr sessions the rat was gnawing consistently between bar presses. After about 10 hr more of training, the minimum required pause for reinforcement was raised to 24 sec for three sessions, to 30 sec for three sessions, and then to 36 sec for 17 sessions. Figure 9 shows the development of the latter performance to the point where the rat was earning about 40 reinforcements and was making approximately 90 responses per hour. It nibbled 4.1 g of wood during the seventeenth session with wood available to it. When the wood was removed, responses rose sharply to 129. Reinforcements obtained correspondingly decreased to 15. Seven more sessions without wood did not materially change the IRT distribution, and no other regular pattern of overt behavior was seen. Responses totaled 136 and reinforcements 12 during the twenty-fifth session on DRL 36. The minimum required pause length was then increased to 48 sec and the wood replaced. During the last of eight such sessions the rat made 82 responses, 34 of which were reinforced. It nibbled 5.4 g of wood. The wood was then removed, again with dramatic effect: responses increased to 145 and reinforcements earned decreased to five. During the eighth session without wood the rat made 171 responses and received only three reinforcements. It had developed no substitute overt

collateral behavior during that time. Replacement of the wood quickly reversed matters; during the first session the rat made 127 responses, 20 of which were reinforced, and gnawed 5.1 g of wood. During the third such session, the rat made only 73 responses and earned 37 reinforcements, while gnawing 7.9 g of wood. The opportunity to gnaw wood clearly has effects that are not limited to a minimum pause of 18 sec.

Correlation Between Amount of Wood Nibbled and Number of Reinforcements

It is possible to examine some of the data already discussed to see how closely amount of collateral behavior covaried with the number of reinforcements earned. This has been done for three instances where extensive wood nibbling data are available. Figure 10 summarizes these data for Rat 2-0 and Rat 3-0. In both cases the scatter diagrams contain data collected on all the occasions shown in Fig. 4 when wood was available to the subject. Shown as well in each case are results from the session immediately before wood was introduced and the two test sessions for which wood had been removed from the box. When no wood was available, number of reinforcements was low; when wood was available but not nibbled, reinforcements remained low; and, as amount of wood nibbled increased, so did number of reinforcements. The Spearman rank-difference correlation coefficients for sessions with wood present are 0.73 for Rat 2-0 and 0.68 for Rat 3-0.

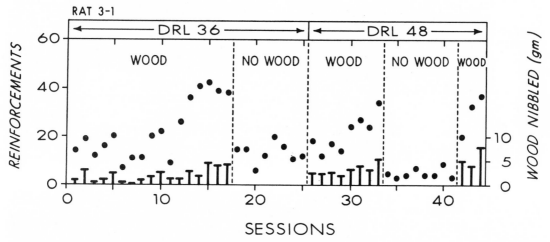

Fig. 9. Performance of Rat 3-1 with and without wood available at higher values of the minimum reinforced interresponse time. Vertical bars indicate amount of wood nibbled.

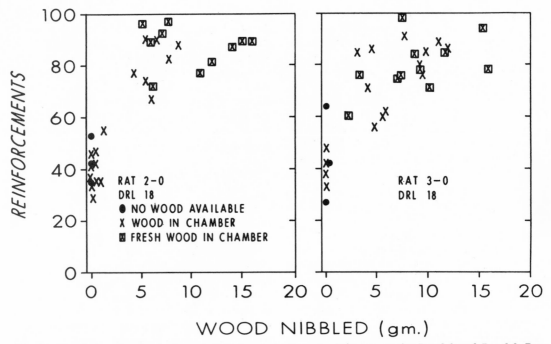

Fig. 10. Covariation of amount of wood nibbled and number of reinforcements for Rat 2-0 and Rat 3-0. Data from all sessions with wood available have been plotted (see Fig. 4). These started with Session 32 for Rat 2-0, with Session 31 for Rat 3-0. In addition, three occasions on which no wood was available have been included for each rat—the one just before the first wood-available session, and the two sessions that were interpolated among the wood-available sessions. Extinction sessions, during which reinforcements were, of course, not present, have been excluded.

A similar analysis of the data from Fig. 9 of Rat 3-1 is displayed in Fig. 11. Here, the correlations are higher, with rho = 0.82 for the DRL 36 data and 0.89 for the DRL 48 data. Given the crude nature of the measure of collateral behavior—the weight of wood chips gnawed from a bar of pine—these correlation coefficients, which (assuming causality) can be interpreted as indicating that between 45 and 80% of the variance has been accounted for, are heartening. But the coefficients are not unity, a fact that suggests that the collateral behavior studied here, when present, is not the only factor controlling lever-pressing behavior. Also, any lines fitted to the plotted points would intersect the ordinate far above zero: the rats did space a substantial number of their responses far enough apart for reinforcement even in the absence of wood nibbling.

DISCUSSION

The wood nibbling and other collateral behaviors that developed between lever presses on the DRL schedule appear to have been related to the frequency with which rats refrained from lever pressing long enough to insure reinforcement. It proved possible to vary this frequency by varying the opportunity to engage in nibbling behavior, either by preventing the rats from using the object nibbled or by extinguishing nibbling. In general, when collateral behavior was present, large amounts of such behavior were correlated with large numbers of reinforcements, while small amounts were correlated with small numbers of reinforcements. And fewest reinforcements were earned when the animals did not show any collateral behavior at all. This relationship held even when a limited hold was in effect, evidence that the collateral behavior was more than merely competing with lever pressing, keeping the rat away from the lever long enough for the minimum interval to have elapsed. Further evidence that the collateral behavior had a mediating function comes from the sharpening of the discrimination in the single case when the opportunity to nibble wood was given a rat on a limited-hold schedule (Fig. 6).

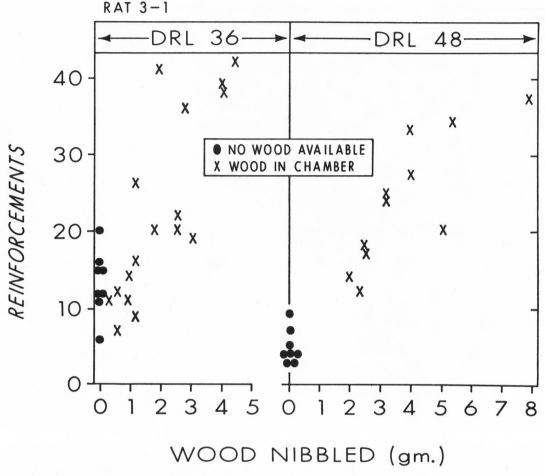

Fig. 11. Covariation of amount of wood nibbled and number of reinforcements for Rat 3-1 on DRL 36 and on DRL 48. Data from all sessions with wood available have been plotted (see Fig. 9). In addition, the number of reinforcements for those occasions on which no wood was available has been indicated.

Anger (1963, p. 479) took as the cornerstone of his analysis of temporal discrimination the proposition "that animals have available some events, either internal *or in their behavior*, that change in a consistent way with time after the last response, reinforcement, *etc.* These events function like external stimuli, at least to the extent that differences in responding can be conditioned to these organism differences." (Italics ours.) The data from both this and our preceding paper on overt "mediating" behavior (Laties *et al.*, 1965) are consistent with this analysis. But what are the "events"? At least some seem to be overt activities, the manipulation of which can change profoundly the distribution of responses in time. Under the conditions of the present experiments, both stimuli from internal physiological events and stimuli from unobservable behavior appear to be of little importance. In particular, discriminative stimuli arising from non-behavioral activity, such as heart rate, are unlikely to play much of a role in controlling the spacing in time of the rat's responses on the lever. Although such internal events may "change in a consistent way with time", they would presumably be undisturbed by such procedures as introducing a piece of wood into the experimental chamber. If anything, they would become less, rather than more, regular. The assumption that they are important, therefore, seems gratuitous. But in what way does behavior such as wood nibbling "change" with time? We have not seen long chains of topographically distinct responses, each response setting the occasion for the next; *i.e.*, heterogeneous response chains.[2] If these were present, the discrimination of time would reduce to the simple discrimination of the last member of the chain, since the probability of reinforcement would be greatest at the time of its emission. Instead, behavior develops that possesses great apparent homogeneity, resembling response sequences rather than response chains (Kelleher, 1966, p. 163). Some physical property of this activity taken as a whole must therefore come to exert discriminative control over responding.

The fact that the behavior of the rat can readily be brought under the discriminative control of a particular amount of its own behavior is documented by much prior work; *e.g.*, Ferster and Skinner, 1957, p. 590; Hurwitz, 1963; Keehn, 1965; Mechner and Guevrekian, 1962; Notterman and Mintz, 1965; Schlosberg and Katz, 1943; Solomon, 1949; Weissman, 1960).[3] Although many of the preceding references confound number (or amount) and duration, the Mechner and Guevrekian (1962) experiment strongly suggests that the discrimination may well be primarily of amount rather than duration. Rats trained to emit four or more responses on one lever before switching to a second lever that then, and only then, produced reinforcement continued to emit the same mean number of responses even when the response rate was markedly slowed by a low condition of deprivation.

Another possible discriminative property of a homogeneous chain, one about which even less is known, may lie in sequential dependencies among members of the chain. It is known that a long series of lever presses exhibits such properties (*cf.*, Weiss, Laties, Siegel, and Goldstein, 1966; Weiss, in press). We should not be surprised to find similar properties in long chains of nibbles, licks, sniffs, *etc.*, after appropriate techniques have been developed to measure the intensive and temporal characteristics of these behaviors.

The precise topography of the collateral behavior that may appear in a subject maintained on a DRL schedule depends, of course, on the behavioral predilections of the subject and the experimental environment. Gnawing probably arose here because oral activity predominated in our rats, as it does in all rats. The mouth area is known to have extensive representation in the rat's somatosensory cortex (Woolsey, 1958), a fact reflecting, in part, this organ's acuity in tactile discrimination and the role it plays in the rat's behavior (Rose and Mountcastle, 1959, p. 402). One would thus expect the rat to be able to discriminate amount of gnawing with fair precision. If the environment of rats on DRL schedules includes objects that lend themselves to oral activity, such activity will have a high operant level and a substantial probability of being reinforced adventitiously.

Although the activity studied here seems to serve as "mediating" behavior, it is unlikely that all overt behavior emitted between lever responses on the DRL schedule does so. For instance, the drinking of great quantities of water between lever presses by rats working for dry food apparently sometimes does and sometimes does not serve as mediating behavior (Clark, 1962; Deadwyler and Segal, 1965; Falk, 1961; Segal, 1965; Segal and Deadwyler, 1964, 1965*a*, 1965*b*; Segal and Holloway, 1963; Segal and Oden, 1965; Stein, 1964). It is also necessary to recall that, as Morse (1966, p. 91) has pointed out: ". . . the temporal correlation of a response with a reinforcer has inherent effects that will necessarily be operating in any situation in which temporal discriminations may be operating. Since these inherent dynamic factors control patterns of responding in time, the continued appeal to temporal discriminations and timing as 'pure' stimulus events obverts progress in the analysis of temporally patterned responding." It thus is particularly important that the precise stimulus function of each example of collateral behavior be established independently.

---

[2] We are here attending only to the collateral behavior itself. If the lever press is also considered, the entire chain is, of course, heterogeneous. And we also are defining homogeneity in terms of our own, rather than the rat's discriminative capacities; while a sequence of nibbles may look alike to us, they may constitute a very heterogeneous chain to the rat.

[3] That other animals can discriminate amount of emitted behavior is suggested by, *e.g.*, Pliskoff and Goldiamond (1966) and Rilling and McDiarmid (1968) for the pigeon, and Laties and Weiss (1963) for man. See Kelleher (1966) for a recent analysis of much of this work.

REFERENCES

Anger, D. The role of temporal discriminations in the reinforcement of Sidman avoidance behavior.

Journal of the Experimental Analysis of Behavior, 1963, **6**, 477-506.

Azzi, R., Fix, D. S. R., Keller, F. S., and Rocha e Silva, M. I. Exteroceptive control of response under delayed reinforcement. *Journal of the Experimental Analysis of Behavior,* 1964, **7**, 159-162.

Brady, J. V. and Conrad, D. G. Some effects of brain stimulation on timing behavior. *Journal of the Experimental Analysis of Behavior,* 1960, **3**, 93-106.

Clark, F. C. Some observations on the adventitious reinforcement of drinking under food reinforcement. *Journal of the Experimental Analysis of Behavior,* 1962, **5**, 61-63.

Davis, H. and Wheeler, L. The collateral pretraining of spaced responding. *Psychonomic Science,* 1967, **8**, 281-282.

Deadwyler, S. A. and Segal, E. F. Determinants of polydipsia VII. Removing the drinking solution midway through DRL sessions. *Psychonomic Science,* 1965, **3**, 185-186.

Dimond, S. J. The structural basis of timing. *Psychological Bulletin,* 1964, **62**, 348-350.

Falk, J. Production of polydipsia in normal rats by an intermittent food schedule. *Science,* 1961, **133**, 195-196.

Ferster, C. B. and Skinner, B. F. *Schedules of reinforcement.* New York: Appleton-Century-Crofts, 1957.

Fraisse, P. *The psychology of time.* New York: Harper & Row, 1963.

Hodos, W. A simple method for the description of inter-response time distribution. *Journal of the Experimental Analysis of Behavior,* 1963, **6**, 90.

Hodos, W., Ross, G. S., and Brady, J. V. Complex response patterns during temporally spaced responding. *Journal of the Experimental Analysis of Behavior,* 1962, **5**, 473-479.

Hurwitz, H. M. B. Facilitation of counting-like behaviour. *Animal Behavior,* 1963, **11**, 449-454.

Keehn, J. D. Temporal alternation in the white rat? *Journal of the Experimental Analysis of Behavior,* 1965, **8**, 161-168.

Kelleher, R. T. Chaining and conditioned reinforcement. In W. K. Honig (Ed.), *Operant behavior: areas of research and application.* New York: Appleton-Century-Crofts, 1966. Pp. 160-212.

Kelleher, R. T., Fry, W., and Cook, L. Inter-response time distribution as a function of differential reinforcement of temporally spaced responses. *Journal of the Experimental Analysis of Behavior,* 1959, **2**, 91-106.

Laties, V. G. and Weiss, B. Effects of alcohol on timing behavior. *Journal of Comparative and Physiological Psychology,* 1962, **55**, 85-91.

Laties, V. G. and Weiss, B. Effects of a concurrent task on fixed-interval responding in humans. *Journal of the Experimental Analysis of Behavior,* 1963, **6**, 431-436.

Laties, V. G., Weiss, B., Clark, R. L., and Reynolds, M. D. Overt "mediating" behavior during temporally spaced responding. *Journal of the Experimental Analysis of Behavior,* 1965, **8**, 107-116.

Mechner, F. and Guevrekian, L. Effects of deprivation upon counting and timing. *Journal of the Experimental Analysis of Behavior,* 1962, **5**, 463-466.

Morse, W. H. Intermittent reinforcement. In W. K. Honig (Ed.), *Operant behavior: areas of research and application.* New York: Appleton-Century-Crofts, 1966. Pp. 52-108.

Nevin, J. A. and Berryman, R. A note on chaining and temporal discrimination. *Journal of the Experimental Analysis of Behavior,* 1963, **6**, 109-113.

Notterman, J. M. and Mintz, D. E. *Dynamics of response.* New York: J. Wiley, 1965.

Pliskoff, S. S. and Goldiamond, I. Some discriminative properties of fixed-ratio performance in the pigeon. *Journal of the Experimental Analysis of Behavior,* 1966, **9**, 1-9.

Rilling, M. E. and McDiarmid, C. G. Signal detection in fixed-ratio schedules. *Science,* 1965, **148**, 526-527.

Rose, J. E. and Mountcastle, V. B. Touch and kinesthesis. In J. Field (Ed.), *Handbook of physiology I. Neurophysiology,* Vol. I. Washington, D. C.: American Physiological Society, 1959. Pp. 387-429.

Schlosberg, H. and Katz, A. Double alternation lever pressing in the white rat. *American Journal of Psychology,* 1943, **56**, 274-282.

Segal-Rechtschaffen, E. Reinforcement of mediating behavior on a spaced-responding schedule. *Journal of the Experimental Analysis of Behavior,* 1963, **6**, 39-46.

Segal, E. F. The development of water drinking on a dry food free-reinforcement schedule. *Psychonomic Science,* 1965, **2**, 29-30.

Segal, E. F. and Deadwyler, S. A. Amphetamine differentially affects temporally spaced bar pressing and collateral water drinking. *Psychonomic Science,* 1964, **1**, 349-350.

Segal, E. F. and Deadwyler, S. A. Determinants of polydipsia in rats II. DRL extinction. *Psychonomic Science,* 1965, **2**, 203-204. (a)

Segal, E. F. and Deadwyler, S. A. Determinants of polydipsia VI. Taste of the drinking solution on DRL. *Psychonomic Science,* 1965, **3**, 101-102. (b)

Segal, E. F. and Holloway, S. M. Timing behavior in rats with water drinking as a mediator. *Science,* 1963, **140**, 888-889.

Segal, E. F. and Oden, D. L. Determinants of polydipsia in rats: a reply to Stein. I. Emptying the water bottle. *Psychonomic Science,* 1965, **2**, 201-202.

Skinner, B. F. and Morse, W. H. Concurrent activity under fixed interval reinforcement. *Journal of Comparative and Physiological Psychology,* 1957, **50**, 279-281.

Solomon, R. L. The role of effort in the performance of a distance discrimination. *Journal of Experimental Psychology,* 1949, **39**, 73-83.

Stein, L. Excessive drinking in the rat: superstition or thirst? *Journal of Comparative and Physiological Psychology,* 1964, **58**, 237-242.

Treisman, M. Temporal discrimination and the indifference interval: implications for a model of the "internal clock." *Psychological Monographs,* 1963, **77** (13, Whole No. 576).

Weeks, J. Methods and materials for chronic intravenous injections in relatively unrestrained rats. Document No. 7304, ADI, Auxiliary Publications Project, Library of Congress, Washington, D. C., 1962.

Weiss, B. The fine structure of operant behavior during transition states. In W. N. Schoenfeld and J. Farmer (Eds.), *Theory of reinforcement schedules.* New York: Appleton-Century-Crofts, in press.

Weiss, B. and Laties, V. G. Time as a dimension of

behavior in interaction with drugs. *Proceedings of the 18th International Congress of Psychology,* 1966, **8,** 22-40.

Weiss, B., Laties, V. G., Siegel, L., and Goldstein, D. A computer analysis of serial interactions in spaced responding. *Journal of the Experimental Analysis of Behavior,* 1966, **9,** 619-626.

Weissman, A. The behavioral effects of repeated exposure to three mixed extinction schedules. *Journal of the Experimental Analysis of Behavior,* 1960, **3,** 115-122.

Wilson, M. P. and Keller, F. S. On the selective reinforcement of spaced responses. *Journal of Comparative and Physiological Psychology,* 1953, **46,** 190-193.

Woolsey, C. N. Organization of somatic sensory and motor areas of the cerebral cortex. In H. F. Harlow and C. N. Woolsey (Eds.), *Biological and biochemical bases of behavior.* Madison: University of Wisconsin, 1958. Pp. 63-81.

Received 16 October 1967.

REINFORCEMENT CONTINGENCIES MAINTAINING COLLATERAL RESPONDING UNDER A DRL SCHEDULE[1]

D. E. McMILLAN[2]

DOWNSTATE MEDICAL CENTER
STATE UNIVERSITY OF NEW YORK

Two-key conjunctive schedules were studied with one key (food key) under a differential-reinforcement-of-low-rate 20-sec schedule, while the consequences of responding on another key (collateral key) were varied. When food depended not only upon a food-key interresponse time in excess of 20 sec, but also upon the occurrence of one or more collateral-key responses during the food-key interresponse time, the rate of collateral-key responding was low and food-key interresponse times rarely exceeded 20 sec. When collateral-key responses could produce a discriminative stimulus correlated with the availability of food under the DRL schedule, the discriminative stimulus functioned as a conditioned reinforcer to maintain higher rates of collateral-key responding, and the spacing of food-key responses increased. If the occurrence of the discriminative stimulus was independent of collateral-key responses, the rate of collateral-key responding was again low, but the spacing of food-key responses was still controlled by the discriminative stimulus. Both the conditioned reinforcer and the explicit reinforcement contingency could maintain collateral-key responding, but the adventitious correlation between collateral-key responses and the delivery of food could not maintain very much collateral-key responding. The pattern of responding on the food-key was determined to a much greater extent by the correlation between the discriminative stimulus and the delivery of food than by the pattern of responding on the collateral key.

CONTENTS

[1]Dedicated to B. F. Skinner in his sixty-fifth year. Supported by U.S. Public Health Service General Research Support Grant 12-8517. Reprints may be obtained from the author, Department of Pharmacology, Downstate Medical Center, State University of New York, 450 Clarkson Avenue, Brooklyn, N.Y. 11203.

[2]I wish to thank P. B. Dews, W. H. Morse, J. W. McKearney, and J. M. Frankenheim for suggestions concerning the manuscript. I also wish to thank Mrs. Rosemarie Sortino for typing several drafts of the manuscript.

Collateral behavior, first observed by Wilson and Keller (1953), often has been considered to mediate (Segal-Rechtschaffen, 1963; Laties, Weiss, Clark, and Reynolds, 1965) the spacing of responses under schedules that selectively reinforce long interresponse times (DRL schedules). Originally, the purpose of the present experiments was to establish collateral behavior on an operandum, as Segal-Rechtschaffen (1963) did, in order to study the relationship between collateral behavior and the spacing of responses on a second key reinforced according to a DRL schedule. However, this objective became of secondary importance when it was discovered that the procedures separated the roles of explicit, adventitious, and conditioned reinforcement in maintaining collateral behavior.

Under all of the two-key conjunctive schedules studied, DRL 20-sec was scheduled on one key (food key), while the response requirements on the other key (collateral key) during the food-key interresponse time were varied. Under some schedules, a collateral-key response was required during the food-key interresponse time before food-key responses could produce food. These schedules measured the combined effects of explicit and adventitious reinforcement contingencies in maintaining collateral-key responding. When the explicit contingency was eliminated the role of the adventitious contingency could be studied in isolation. Under other schedules, collateral-key responses produced a discriminative stimulus correlated with availability of food under the DRL schedule. Under these schedules, the discriminative stimulus came to function as a conditioned reinforcer. By comparing patterns of collateral-key responding under schedules where collateral-key responses produced a discriminative stimulus with schedules where the discriminative stimulus was independent of collateral-key responding, or where no discriminative stimulus could be produced, the function of the discriminative stimulus as a conditioned reinforcer could be studied.

METHODS

Subjects

Two male White Carneaux pigeons, weighing 475 to 625 g with free access to food and water, were food-deprived to 80% of their free-feeding body weights, and maintained at these weights for the duration of the experiments. Both birds had been trained to peck a key under various schedules of food presentation and had some experience with a two-key DRL schedule; they had not been used in any experiments for about nine months before the present one.

Apparatus

The experimental chamber, after Ferster and Skinner (1957), was sound attenuating. Two translucent, plastic pigeon keys, 20 mm in diameter, were mounted on a false wall inside the experimental chamber about 9 cm

apart and 18 cm above the chamber floor. One key could be transilluminated by either white or green lamps (collateral key) and the other by red lamps (food key). A feedback relay behind the wall operated whenever 15 g of force was applied to either key. Centered between the two keys at a point about 4 cm above the floor of the chamber was a rectangular opening through which a pigeon could gain 3-sec access to grain. The chamber was illuminated by a 25-w bulb and white noise was present at all times. Scheduling and recording apparatus were housed in a different room from the one containing the experimental chamber.

Procedure

Sessions were 30 min in duration. The two birds were retrained to peck the food key, which was always red, and then were exposed to one session during which every response on the food key produced food. In the second and third sessions, delivery of food was made contingent upon one or more responses on the collateral key, which was white, followed by a response on the food key. Responses on the collateral key never produced food directly. The collateral-key contingency remained in effect, while the minimum reinforced interresponse time (IRT) on the food key was gradually increased to 20 sec. In subsequent experiments, the DRL 20-sec schedule on the food key was held constant, while the contingencies on the collateral key were varied. The schedules to which the birds were exposed and the order of exposures are outlined in Table 1.

RESULTS

Responding under a DRL 20-Sec Schedule with a Collateral Response Required on a Second Key (No-Stimulus Schedule or NS Schedule)

The purpose of this experiment was to assure that at least some of the behavior occurring during the IRT on a food key under a DRL schedule could be measured objectively. This was accomplished by requiring that one of the collateral responses during the food-key IRT be pecks on a collateral key. Therefore, the food key was under a DRL 20-sec schedule, but before a food-key response could produce food, at least one response had to be made on the collateral key during the food-key IRT. This schedule is referred to as the

Table 1

Summary of Schedules Investigated

Schedule	Food Key Contingency	Collateral Key Contingency (To "Set Up" Food)	Conditions Producing Stimulus Change on Collateral Key	Sessions on Schedule	
				Bird 284	Bird 337
No-stimulus schedule (NS)	DRL 20 Red Key	One or more responses during food-key IRT	Key always white, no programmed change	35-62	63-90
Optional response-produced-stimulus schedule (ORPS)	DRL 20 Red Key	Same as NS schedule	First response after 20-sec IRT on food key changes color from white to green	7-34	35-62
Clock-stimulus schedule (CS)	DRL 20 Red Key	Same as NS schedule	Key changes color from white to green automatically after 20-sec IRT on food key	63-90	7-34
Response-produced-stimulus schedule (RPS)	DRL 20 Red Key	One or more responses after 20-sec IRT on food key	First response after 20-sec IRT on food key changes color from white to green	104-131	103-130
CS, no collateral response required	DRL 20 Red Key	None	Same as CS	91-97	Not tested
ORPS, no collateral response required	DRL 20 Red Key	None	Same as ORPS	98-103	Not tested
NS, no collateral response required	DRL 20 Red Key	None	Same as NS	Not tested	91-97
NS, no collateral response required, no collateral-key light	DRL 20 Red Key	None	White key light turned off, no stimulus change	Not tested	98-102

no-stimulus schedule (NS schedule) since no stimulus change was scheduled as a result of collateral-key reponses.

Both birds were exposed to the NS schedule for 28 sessions in the order shown in Table 1. Performance was stable over approximately the final 10 sessions. Figure 1 shows IRT frequency distributions in 4-sec class intervals for the food key and the total number of collateral-key responses during each food-key class interval, averaged over the final five sessions under the NS schedule.

For both birds, IRT distributions peaked in the fourth class interval (12 to 16 sec) with a smaller peak in the first class interval (0 to 4 sec). Neither bird terminated many IRTs longer than 20 sec, so food rarely was delivered. Similar short spacing of responses has been reported for pigeons under conventional DRL schedules (Reynolds and Catania, 1961; Reynolds, 1964; Staddon, 1965). The few IRTs longer than 20 sec usually produced food (22 of 25 times for Bird 284, and 38 of 42 times for Bird 337, over the last five ses-

sions), since the birds usually pecked the collateral key at least once during the food-key IRT.

Figure 1 also shows that collateral-key responses occurred with greatest frequency in the class interval just before the peak of the IRT distribution (8 to 12 sec) and in the same class interval as the peak of the IRT distribution (12 to 16 sec). These data suggest that collateral-key responses immediately preceded food-key responses.

Bird 284 had about a one-to-one ratio of collateral-key responses to food-key responses. Since a one-to-one ratio matched the minimum requirement of the NS schedule, it is not likely that adventitious correlation of food delivery with collateral-key responses maintained this bird's collateral-key responding. Bird 337 made more collateral-key responses than required by the schedule. These "extra" collateral-key responses might represent unextinguished responses from a previous schedule (see Table 1). However, the rate of collateral-key responding was quite stable

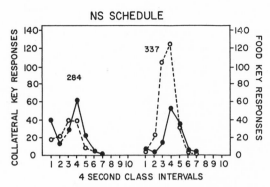

Fig. 1. Interresponse-time and collateral-key frequency distributions for both birds under the NS schedule. Each point represents the number of responses (food key is the solid line with closed circles, and collateral key is the broken line with open circles) occurring at each class interval, averaged over the last five sessions under the NS schedule. Each class interval is 4-sec wide, and food becomes available at the beginning of the sixth class interval.

quency of food delivery. In the sense that temporal discrimination is reflected by a peak in the IRT distribution during the fourth and fifth class intervals (8 to 16 sec), performance deteriorated when the collateral-key requirement was eliminated; however, in the sense that more reinforcements occurred, performance improved.

After seven days under the NS schedule without a collateral-key contingency, the collateral-key light was turned off for five sessions. Turning off the collateral-key light further decreased collateral-key responding, which was again accompanied by a flattening of the food-key IRT distribution (not shown). Thus, both methods of eliminating collateral-key responses were accompanied by a flattening of the food-key IRT distribution and an increased frequency of food delivery.

for Bird 337 over the final 10 of 28 sessions under the NS schedule, and since there was a temporal relationship of collateral-key to food-key responses, the "extra" collateral-key responses probably were maintained by their adventitious correlation with food delivery. However, the IRT distributions were similar for both birds despite differences in the rate of collateral-key responding.

Elimination of the Collateral-Response Requirement from the NS Schedule (Bird 337). Turning off the Collateral-Key Light (Bird 337)

The purpose of these experiments was to determine if collateral-key responding could be decreased by removing the collateral-key contingency from the NS schedule and later decreased further by turning off the collateral-key light, and finally to determine what effects these manipulations had on the patterns of food-key responding. Table 2 shows that when the collateral-key requirement was eliminated from the NS schedule, the rate of collateral-key responding decreased during the first session. Over the remaining six sessions collateral-key responding continued to decrease (not shown).

Table 2 shows also that the decreased rate of collateral-key responding under the NS schedule without a collateral-response requirement was accompanied by a flattening of the food-key IRT distribution, and a higher fre-

Responding under a DRL 20-Sec Schedule, Where Required Responses on a Collateral Key Can Produce a Discriminative Stimulus Correlated with the Availability of Food under the DRL Schedule (Optional-Response-Produced-Stimulus Schedule or ORPS Schedule)

The purposes of this experiment were to see if a discriminative stimulus, correlated with the availability of food under the DRL schedule and produced by collateral-key responses, could reinforce collateral-key responding, and to determine if the response-produced discriminative stimulus could control the pattern of food-key responding. The food-key schedule was DRL 20-sec, and reinforcement again was contingent upon one or more collateral-key responses during the food-key IRT (as under the NS schedule). In addition, the first collateral-key response occurring after a 20-sec IRT on the food key changed the color of the collateral key from white to green. Under this schedule, food-key responses could produce food (assuming an IRT in excess of 20 sec) in the presence of either a white or a green collateral-key light. If all collateral-key responses occurred before the 20-sec food-key IRT, the food-key response would produce food in the presence of a white collateral-key light (exactly as under the NS schedule; see Table 1). However, a collateral-key response after 20 sec without a food-key response produced the discriminative stimulus. In so far

Table 2

Changes in the pattern of responding when the collateral-key requirement was removed from the NS schedule. Data represent the last session before the collateral-key requirement was eliminated from the NS schedule for Bird 337 and the first session after the collateral-key requirement was eliminated.

4-Sec Class Interval	IRT Frequency Distribution		Frequency Collateral-Key	
	NS Schedule	NS-No Collateral	NS Schedule	NS-No-Collateral
1	5	5	3	8
2	3	14	23	36
3	14	27	103	50
4	54	30	134	50
5	32	25	35	29
6	7	15	3	6
7	1	3	1	2
8	0	3	0	1
9	0	0	0	0
10	1	0	2	0

as obtaining food was concerned, production of the discriminative stimulus on the collateral key was optional; hence, this schedule will be referred to as the optional-response-produced-stimulus schedule (ORPS schedule).

Both birds were exposed to 28 sessions under the ORPS schedule. Figure 2 shows frequency distributions of IRTs on the food key in 4-sec class intervals and the number of collateral-key responses during each class interval, averaged over the last five sessions under the ORPS schedule.

The IRT frequency distributions of both birds peaked in the fifth class interval (16 to

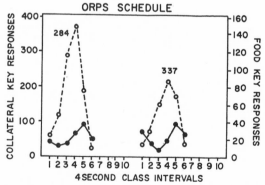

Fig. 2. Interresponse-time and collateral-key frequency distributions for both birds under the ORPS schedule. Each point represents the number of responses (food key is the solid line with closed circles, and collateral key is the broken line with open circles) occurring at each class interval, averaged over the last five sessions under the ORPS schedule. Each class interval is 4-sec wide, and food becomes available at the beginning of the sixth class interval.

20 sec), with a secondary peak in the first class interval (0 to 4 sec). The shape of the IRT distribution under the ORPS schedule was bimodal, as under the NS schedule, but under the ORPS schedule the distribution was shifted one class interval to the right (closer to reinforcement), and many more food-key responses were reinforced. Thus, adding the discrimination stimulus after collateral-key responses clearly increased the spacing of food-key responses. Nevertheless, the major proportion of food-key responses terminated IRTs of less than 20 sec, and did not produce food. The failure of the discriminative stimulus to exert better control over food-key responding was probably because food-key responses could produce food in the absence of the discriminative stimulus, which would strengthen the tendency to make food-key responses at short IRTs when the collateral key was white.

Only rarely did IRTs greater than 20 sec terminate without the delivery of food because no collateral-key responses were made. For Bird 337, 131 of 132 IRTs longer than 20 sec terminated with food, while 113 of 116 IRTs longer than 20 sec terminated with food for Bird 284 (summed over the last five sessions). Unfortunately, the recording methods did not permit a determination of the proportion of times food delivery occurred in the presence of the white collateral-key light, relative to the green collateral-key light.

Figure 2 shows that the rate of responding on the collateral key was many times higher under the ORPS schedule than under the NS schedule (Fig. 1), indicating that the stimulus change on the collateral key also functioned as a conditioned reinforcer to maintain collateral-key responding.

Collateral-key responses occurred with greatest frequency in the class interval (12 to 16 sec) just before the class interval (16 to 20 sec) where food-key responses occurred with greatest frequency. Such data suggest that the rate of collateral-key responding was highest just before a food-key response, a suggestion supported by the cumulative-response records of Fig. 3.

Elimination of the Collateral-Response Requirement from the ORPS Schedule (Bird 284)

This experiment sought to determine whether or not the conditioned reinforcer could maintain collateral-key responding when food delivery was no longer dependent upon collateral-key responses. Immediately before this experiment, Bird 284 had been under a schedule that eliminated collateral-key responding completely (see Table 1). Under the ORPS schedule without a collateral response requirement, the number of collateral-key responses increased from 0 to 62 responses during the first session, to 154 during the second session, and to 192 during the third session. These data were a further indication that the green collateral-key light was a conditioned reinforcer, capable of establishing responding in the absence of a scheduled food contingency.

Responding under a DRL 20-Sec Schedule Where Collateral-Key Responses Must Produce a Discriminative Stimulus Correlated with the Availability of Food before a Food-Key Response Can Be Reinforced (Response-Produced-Stimulus Schedule or RPS Schedule)

Under the ORPS schedule, the spacing of food-key responses was not as efficient as expected, and it was suggested that this was because food-key responses could produce food both with and without collateral responses producing the discriminative stimulus. Therefore, the ORPS schedule was modified so that at least one collateral-key response was required after 20 sec without a food-key response before a food-key response could produce food. Since the first collateral-key response after a

20-sec IRT on the food-key also produced a discriminative stimulus for the availability of food under the DRL schedule, food could be delivered only after collateral-key responses had produced the discriminative stimulus. Since the discriminative stimulus was no longer an optional event in the sequence leading to food, this schedule was called the

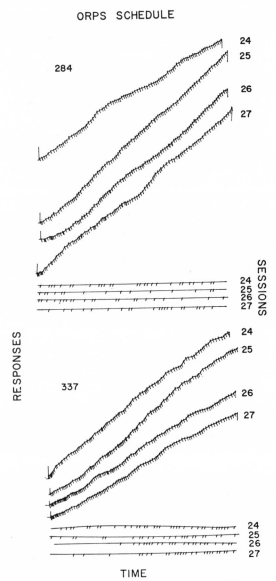

ORPS SCHEDULE

Fig. 3. Cumulative-response records of performances of both birds during four of the last five sessions under the ORPS schedule. Ordinate: cumulative number of collateral-key responses (left axis) and session number (right axis). Abscissa: time. Diagonal offsets of the pen on the horizontal lines indicate delivery of food. Diagonal offsets of the pen on the cumulative response lines indicate food-key responses.

response-produced-stimulus schedule (RPS schedule).

Both birds were exposed to the RPS schedule for 28 days, although behavior had stabilized after 18 days. Distributions of IRT frequency for the food key and the number of collateral-key responses in each class interval have been averaged over the final five sessions under the RPS schedule in Fig. 4.

Figure 4 shows that almost all IRTs on the food key were terminated during the sixth class interval (20 to 24 sec) and produced food. The near optimal spacing of food-key responses under the RPS schedule strongly suggests that the closer spacing of responses under the ORPS schedule resulted from the reinforcement of some food-key responses in the presence of the white collateral-key light. The tendency to respond on the food key in the presence of the white collateral-key light might have generalized to shorter IRTs which could not terminate in food delivery.

The rate of responding on the collateral key was much higher under the RPS schedule than under any other except the ORPS schedule, the rate under the RPS schedule being only slightly higher than under the ORPS schedule. This slight increase in rate was correlated with a more frequent production of the conditioned reinforcer under the RPS schedule.

If premature food-key responses did not occur under the RPS schedule, the green collateral-key light was scheduled according to a 20-sec fixed interval. Figure 5 shows that a fixed-interval pattern (a pause followed by an increased rate of responding) of collateral-key responding developed. By shaping a fixed-interval pattern of collateral-key responding, the conditioned reinforcer controlled responding in the same manner as other reinforcers.

Responding under a DRL 20-Sec Schedule Where a Discriminative Stimulus Is Presented Automatically (Clock-Stimulus Schedule or CS Schedule)

The purpose of this experiment was to determine if the discriminative stimulus for the

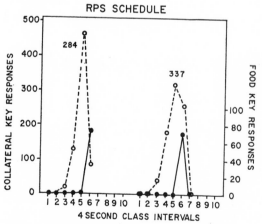

Fig. 4. Interresponse-time and collateral-key frequency distributions for both birds under the RPS schedule. Each point represents the number of responses (food key is solid line with closed circles, and collateral-key is broken line with open circles) occurring at each class interval, averaged over the last five sessions under the RPS schedule. Each class interval is 4-sec wide and food becomes available at the beginning of the sixth class interval.

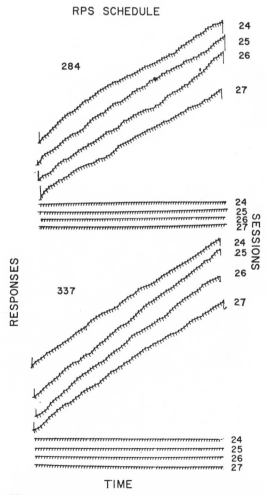

Fig. 5. Cumulative-response records of performances of both birds during four of the last five sessions under the RPS schedule. Recording as in Fig. 2.

availability of food under the DRL schedule could maintain collateral-key responding when it was independent of collateral-key responses, and to determine to what extent the discriminative stimulus controlled the pattern of food-key responding under these conditions. The schedule requirements were identical with those of the NS schedule (one collateral response was required during a food-key IRT greater than 20 sec, see Table 1), except that after 20 sec without a food-key response, the color on the collateral key changed automatically from white to green. By analogy with the terminology used to describe fixed-interval schedules with time-correlated stimuli (Ferster and Skinner, 1957), the present schedule was designated as the clock-stimulus schedule (CS schedule). Food-key IRT frequency distributions in 4-sec class intervals and the number of collateral-key responses in each class interval have been plotted in Fig. 6.

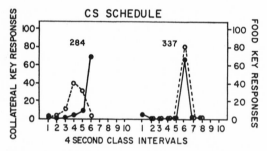

Fig. 6. Interresponse-time and collateral-key frequency distributions for both birds under the CS schedule. Each point represents the number of responses (food key is the solid line with closed circles, and collateral key is the broken line with open circles) occurring at each class interval, averaged over the last five sessions under the CS schedule. Each class interval is 4-sec wide and food becomes available at the beginning of the sixth class interval.

Under the CS schedule the food-key IRT frequency distribution peaked in the sixth class interval (20 to 24 sec) and the frequency of IRTs in all other class intervals was very low. Thus, automatic presentation of the discriminative stimulus correlated with the availability of food exerted about the same degree of control over food-key responding as occurred under the RPS schedule. Despite the efficient spacing of food-key responses under the CS schedule by both pigeons, Bird 284 produced only 225 reinforcements following termination of 359 IRTs on the food key that

were longer than 20 sec. Therefore, during many IRTs longer than 20 sec, Bird 284 did not make collateral-key responses. For Bird 337, reinforcement almost always occurred after termination of IRTs longer than 20 sec (315 out of 321 times).

The rate of collateral-key responding under the CS schedule was quite low, lower even than under the NS schedule (Fig. 1). Although the ratio of collateral-key responses to food-key responses was about one-to-one for both birds, the temporal relationship of collateral-key to food-key responses was different for each bird under the CS schedule. Bird 284, which failed to make collateral-key responses during some IRTs, made collateral-key responses most often during the fourth and fifth class intervals (12 to 20 sec). During some IRTs, Bird 284 must have made several collateral-key responses and during other IRTs, no collateral-key responses at all. Figure 6 shows that Bird 337 did not respond until the discriminative stimulus appeared and then pecked the collateral key and the food key in sequence. The green collateral-key light appears to have served as a discriminative stimulus for both food-key and collateral-key responding for Bird 337, rather than as a conditioned reinforcer. Thus, the evidence indicates that the green collateral-key light controlled the pattern of food-key responding, but it had little effect as a conditioned reinforcer for collateral-key responding when it was not response-contingent.

Elimination of the Collateral-Response Requirement from the CS Schedule (Bird 284)

After 28 days under the CS schedule, the collateral-key requirement was eliminated for Bird 284. By the seventh day under the CS schedule without a collateral-key contingency, collateral-key responses no longer occurred. These results suggest that under the CS schedule, collateral-key responding was maintained almost entirely by the requirement that at least one collateral response was necessary during the food-key IRT before food could be produced.

DISCUSSION

At least three reinforcement contingencies might have contributed to the maintenance of collateral-key responding during these experiments. First, under some of these schedules collateral-key responses were required before food could be delivered under the DRL schedule. Second, collateral-key responses in excess of the one required by most schedules might be strengthened by adventitious correlation with the reinforcer if they occurred in close temporal proximity to it. Third, under some schedules collateral-key responding produced a discriminative stimulus for the availability of food under the DRL schedule, and such stimuli are potential conditioned reinforcers (Kelleher and Gollub, 1962). By varying the consequences of responding on the collateral key, the role of each of these contingencies in maintaining collateral-key responding could be determined.

Under the NS schedule, where only one collateral-key response was required, the extent to which the rate on the collateral key exceeded the rate on the food key probably reflected the degree to which collateral-key responding was maintained by adventitious correlation with food delivery. This contingency maintained responding under the NS schedule in only one of the two birds (Bird 337). When the collateral-key contingency was eliminated under the NS schedule for this same bird, a low rate of collateral-key responding was maintained after seven sessions, providing some evidence that adventitious correlation between collateral-key responding and food delivery might be maintaining a limited amount of responding. However, the failure of collateral-key responding to occur at a higher rate than food-key responding under the NS schedule for Bird 284, the failure of collateral-key responding to be maintained in excess of the schedule requirements under the CS schedule in both birds, and the rapid extinction of collateral-key responding when the collateral-key requirement was eliminated from the CS schedule (Bird 284), all indicate that adventitious correlations played a relatively small role in maintaining responding on the collateral-key. Collateral-key responding observed under these schedules must have been maintained largely by the requirement that collateral-key responses had to occur before food could be obtained under the DRL schedule.

Under the ORPS and RPS schedules, collateral-key responses could produce a stimulus correlated with the availability of food (after a food-key response). That this stimulus also came to function as a conditioned reinforcer of collateral-key responding when it was response-produced is suggested by the high rate of responding under the RPS and ORPS schedules. Further, the fixed-interval patterns of responding, seen especially under the RPS schedule, indicated that the conditioned reinforcer maintained responding in a manner similar to that of unconditioned reinforcers.

A second question upon which these experiments bear is the degree to which the pattern of food-key responding was controlled by the discriminative stimulus and by the pattern of responding on the collateral key. Under the RPS and CS schedules, practically all food-key responses terminated IRTs between 20 and 24 sec. Under both of these schedules, food-key responses were reinforced only in the presence of a green collateral-key light. However, under the CS schedule the green collateral-key light occurred automatically, while under the RPS schedule it was response-produced. That the rate of collateral-key responding was much higher under the RPS schedule, while the food-key patterns were much the same under both schedules, suggests that the pattern of food-key responding was controlled much more by the discriminative stimulus than by the responses which occurred during the food-key IRT.

Under variations of the ORPS schedule, the discriminative stimulus did not exert as much control over the pattern of food-key responding as under the other schedules where a discriminative stimulus was available. This was probably because food could be obtained under ORPS schedules in the absence of the discriminative stimulus. Nevertheless, spacing of responses on the food key was considerably better under the ORPS schedule than it was under the NS schedule, where no discriminative stimulus was scheduled.

Removing the collateral-key requirement from the NS schedule provided inconclusive evidence as to whether or not collateral-key responding could mediate food-key responding in the absence of a scheduled discriminative stimulus. When collateral-key responding was decreased by extinguishing it, or by turning off the collateral-key light, the IRT distribution on the food key was flattened, indicating a disruption of the temporal pattern of responding. However, this disruption resulted in a higher frequency of reinforcement, which might be interpreted as an improved performance.

REFERENCES

Ferster, C. B. and Skinner, B. F. *Schedules of reinforcement.* New York: Appleton-Century-Crofts, 1957.

Kelleher, R. T. and Gollub, L. R. A review of positive conditioned reinforcement. *Journal of the Experimental Analysis of Behavior,* 1962, **5,** 543-597.

Laties, V. G., Weiss, B., Clark, R. L., and Reynolds, M. D. Overt "mediating" behavior during temporally spaced responding. *Journal of the Experimental Analysis of Behavior,* 1965, **8,** 107-116.

Reynolds, G. S. Temporally spaced responding by pigeons: development and effects of deprivation and extinction. *Journal of the Experimental Analysis of Behavior,* 1964, **7,** 415-421.

Reynolds, G. S. and Catania, A. C. Behavioral contrast with fixed-interval and low-rate reinforcement. *Journal of the Experimental Analysis of Behavior,* 1961, **4,** 387-391.

Segal-Rechtschaffen, E. F. Reinforcement of mediating behavior on a spaced responding schedule. *Journal of the Experimental Analysis of Behavior,* 1963, **6,** 39-46.

Staddon, J. E. R. Some properties of spaced responding in pigeons. *Journal of the Experimental Analysis of Behavior,* 1965, **8,** 19-30.

Wilson, M. P. and Keller, F. S. On the selective reinforcement of spaced responses. *Journal of Comparative and Physiological Psychology,* 1953, **46,** 190-193.

Received 21 May 1968.

COLLATERAL RESPONDING DURING DIFFERENTIAL REINFORCEMENT OF LOW RATES[1]

G. E. ZURIFF

WHEATON COLLEGE

Two pigeons were trained to peck either of two response keys for food, under two different variable-interval schedules. When responding stabilized, the schedule on the left key (reinforcement-key) was changed to a differential-reinforcement-of-low-rates schedule, and responses on the right key (extinction-key) were no longer reinforced. The mean interresponse time of responses on the reinforcement-key approximated the temporal requirement of the reinforcement schedule on that key. Collateral responding on the extinction-key was maintained by one of the birds. A "run" of these collateral responses was defined as a sequence of responses on the extinction-key occurring between two responses on the reinforcement-key. For this one bird, collateral behavior, measured by mean time per run and mean number of responses per run, was an increasing function of the temporal requirements of the reinforcement schedule on the reinforcement key, and it was strongly positively correlated with the mean interresponse time of responses on the reinforcement-key. However, from an analysis of the results, the collateral behavior did not appear to have mediated the temporal spacing of responses on the reinforcement-key.

An organism can be said to be "timing" when its responses are temporally spaced so as to correspond to the temporal requirements of a reinforcement contingency. This timing is conspicuous in behavior under the differential-reinforcement-of-low-rates (DRL) schedule of reinforcement. Under this schedule, a response is reinforced if and only if it occurs a specified time after a certain prior event, usually the previous response or reinforcement. Timing can be measured by the degree of correspondence between the interresponse time (IRT) and the interval required by the DRL schedule.

It is often reported (*e.g.*, Wilson and Keller, 1953; Holz, Azrin, and Ulrich, 1963) that under a DRL schedule, a collateral chain of behavior that fortuitously precedes the reinforced response is maintained due to an adventitious temporal correlation with the reinforcer. Some authors have theorized that this collateral chain of behavior mediates timing behavior and is instrumental in its maintenance. It is suggested either that the collateral chain fills up the necessary temporal delay between responses (Bruner and Revusky, 1961), or that the collateral behavior is used by the organism as a stimulus controlling subsequent behavior (Ferster and Skinner, 1957, p. 729). On the other hand, in many experiments in which subjects timed accurately, no overt chains of collateral behavior were observed (Anger, 1956; Kelleher, Fry, and Cook, 1959).

In order to assess the role played by this collateral behavior many studies have attempted to measure and control collateral responses under a DRL schedule. Using human subjects under a DRL schedule, Kapostins (1963) established a collateral chain of verbal responses which he was able to record and measure. Other experiments with DRL schedules have shown that the collateral responding can be brought under the same stimulus control as the timing response and that experimental manipulations affect both collateral behavior and DRL responding in related ways (Hodos, Ross, and Brady, 1962; Laties, Weiss, Clark, and Reynolds, 1965; Laties, Weiss, and Weiss, 1969).

The fact that collateral behavior often occurs under DRL schedules and may possibly mediate timing behavior has been used as an

[1]Dedicated to B. F. Skinner in his sixty-fifth year. This research was performed while the author was a National Science Foundation Graduate Fellow at Harvard University. The experiment was conducted with the technical assistance of Mrs. Antoinette C. Papp and Mr. Wallace R. Brown. Dr. R. J. Herrnstein provided helpful and well-appreciated comments. Reprints may be obtained from the author, Wheaton College, Norton, Massachusetts, 02766.

explanatory concept in dealing with other phenomena related to DRL schedules. Hearst, Koresko, and Poppen (1964) suggested that features of the post-DRL-reinforcement generalization gradient may be attributed to collateral behavior during the DRL schedule. Similarly, Weiss, Laties, Siegel, and Goldstein (1966) tentatively appealed to a mediating chain of collateral behavior to explain certain features of interresponse time sequences under a DRL schedule. Schedule-induced polydipsia has been explained in terms of collateral chains (Clark, 1962; but see Falk, 1966). In addition, local interactions in concurrent schedules (*conc*), in which two or more responses are reinforced according to independent schedules, have been attributed in some cases to collateral chains (Catania and Cutts, 1963; Catania, 1966, p. 229).

The concurrent schedule has also been used in several experiments to study collateral behavior under a DRL schedule. Because the concurrent schedule provides additional manipulanda on which collateral responses may occur, these collateral responses, often merely casually observed and reported, can be objectively measured and recorded. Bruner and Revusky (1961) reinforced responses on only one of four response keys under a DRL schedule. Collateral responses occurring on the other keys were never reinforced, yet these collateral responses were maintained by the subject and could, therefore, be measured and studied. In another series of experiments (Segal-Rechtschaffen, 1963), it was found possible to examine how DRL behavior and collateral, possibly mediating, behavior interact by concurrently reinforcing responses collateral to responses under a DRL schedule.

The purpose of the present experiment was to establish, control, and study collateral behavior on a DRL schedule in which reinforcement is not contingent on the collateral response. To examine the relationship between timing and collateral behavior, the contingency controlling the timing response was manipulated, and the resulting change in the collateral behavior was measured.

METHOD

Subjects

Two adult male White Carneaux pigeons, 274 and 342, with previous experience in a variety of experiments, were maintained at about 80% of their free-feeding body weights throughout the experiment.

Apparatus

A standard experimental chamber for the pigeon contained two translucent response keys. The left one was transilluminated by a white light, and the right one by a red light. During reinforcement (4-sec access to mixed grain) both key lights were extinguished, and the feeder illuminated. For both keys, a peck of at least 10-g force was recorded and produced a feedback click. The chamber was illuminated by a white overhead light, and white masking noise was continuously present.

Procedure

Preliminary training. Pecks on the right key were reinforced according to a variable-interval schedule with a mean interval of 15 sec (VI 15-sec), and pecks on the left key were concurrently reinforced according to a VI 45-sec schedule. This preliminary training, *conc* VI 15-sec VI 45-sec, was maintained for 15 sessions at the end of which responding on both keys had reached a fairly high and steady rate.

Conc DRL EXT. The reinforcement schedule for pecks on the left key was changed to DRL 3-sec: a response on the left key (DRL-key) was reinforced if and only if it followed by 3 sec or more: (a) the previous response on the DRL-key, (b) the end of the previous reinforcement, or (c) the start of the session, whichever was most recent. Responses on the right key were now never reinforced (EXT). The DRL 3-sec was maintained for 30 sessions, at which point behavior showed no systematic changes. Thereafter, every six sessions the DRL requirement on the DRL-key was increased. One day with no session separated each six-session group. The DRL requirements used in the order presented were (in sec): 3.0, 3.5, 4.0, 4.5, 5.5, 6.0, 6.5, 7.0, 8.0, 8.5, 9.0, 9.5, and 10.0. Sessions terminated when 40 reinforcements had occurred.

RESULTS

Behavior on the DRL-key is presented in Fig. 1 for Subject 274 and in Fig. 2 by the filled circles for Subject 342. These functions show the mean interresponse time (IRT) on the DRL-key as a function of the DRL requirement. The data represent the medians of the means for each of the last three sessions at each DRL value. The solid lines fitted to the obtained points are the regression lines. The equation for the line fitted to the points in Fig. 1 is $Y' = 0.686 X + 1.61$ with a standard error of estimate $S_{Y·X} = 0.620$. The equation for the line fitted to the filled circles in Fig. 2 is $Y' = 0.784 X + 1.08$ and $S_{Y·X} = 0.238$.

other hand, continued to respond on the EXT-key although reinforcement was not contingent on responses on that key. Moreover, this collateral behavior continued, even though on occasion no responses on the EXT-key intervened between reinforcements. All the data on collateral behavior represent the medians of the means for each of the last three sessions at each DRL value for Subject 342.

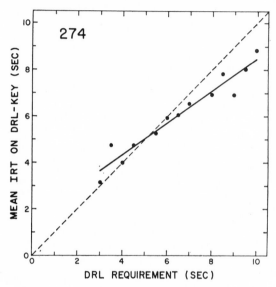

Fig. 1. Mean interresponse time of responses on the DRL-key as a function of the DRL requirement of a *conc* DRL EXT schedule for Subject 274. The equation for the regression line fitted to the obtained points is given in the text. The broken line represents the function that would be obtained if timing were perfect so that the mean interresponse time of responses on the DRL-key equaled the DRL requirement.

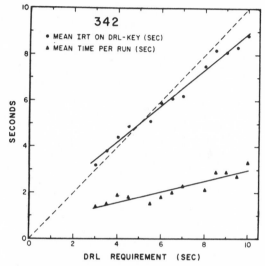

Fig. 2. The filled circles represent the mean interresponse time of responses on the DRL-key as a function of the DRL requirement of a *conc* DRL EXT schedule for Subject 342. The triangles represent the mean time per run on the EXT-key as a function of the DRL requirement. The equations for the regression lines fitted to the obtained points are given in the text. The broken line represents the function that would be obtained if timing were perfect so that the mean interresponse time of responses on the DRL-key equaled the DRL requirement.

The broken line represents the function that would be obtained if the mean IRT were equal to the DRL requirement in either figure. As is often found with DRL schedules (*e.g.*, Staddon, 1965), the obtained function approximates the 45° line although it falls increasingly short of the 45° line as the DRL requirement increases. "Timing" on the part of the organism will be defined as this correspondence between the mean IRT and the DRL requirement.

Both subjects at first continued to respond on the right key (EXT-key) when responses on that key were no longer reinforced. However, over the next few sessions under DRL 3-sec, the response rate on the EXT-key declined to near zero for Subject 274. Subject 342, on the

Following Nevin and Berryman (1963), collateral behavior will be analyzed in terms of "runs" where a "run" will be defined as a sequence of responses starting with the first response on the EXT-key following either a reinforcement or a response on the DRL-key, and terminating with the next response on the DRL-key. The mean interval of time per run for Subject 342 as a function of the DRL requirement is described by the lower function in Fig. 2 (triangles). The equation of the regression line fitted to the obtained points is $Y' = 0.237 X + 0.62$, and $S_{Y·X} = 0.254$. Thus, as Fig. 2 shows, both the mean time per run and the mean IRT on the DRL-key are increasing functions of the DRL requirement, and the correlation coefficient between mean time per run on the EXT-key and mean IRT on the DRL-key is 0.913.

For those IRTs on the DRL-key during which a run occurred, the IRT between response A and response B on the DRL-key equals the time per run plus the pause between response A and the next response to the EXT-key (pre-run pause). Since runs occurred during almost all IRTs on the DRL-key, the mean time per pre-run pause is closely approximated by the difference between the two functions in Fig. 2. The fact that the difference between the functions increases as the DRL requirement increases indicates that the pre-run pause increased with increases in the DRL requirement and thus was also controlled by the DRL contingency.

Figure 3 shows the mean number of responses per run (not including the response on the DRL-key which terminates the run) for Subject 342 as a function of the DRL requirement. The regression line fitted to the obtained points has the equation $Y' = 0.432\,X + 1.78$, and $S_{Y \cdot X} = 0.487$. The mean number of responses per run is also an increasing function of the DRL requirement, and the correlation coefficient between mean number of responses per run and the mean IRT on the DRL-key is 0.901.

Although both measures of collateral behavior, responses per run and time per run,

are increasing functions of the DRL requirement, they are not monotonically increasing functions. For both functions there is an inversion in each case in which the DRL requirement was increased by a full second rather than the more usual 0.5 sec. On the other hand, the increases of 1 sec did not have the same disruptive effect on the DRL response rate.

Response rate during a run did not vary systematically with the DRL requirement. With DRL requirements between 4.5 and 6.5 sec, the response rate was stable between 140 and 160 responses per minute. At longer and shorter DRL requirements, response rate during a run was between 110 and 120 responses per minute.

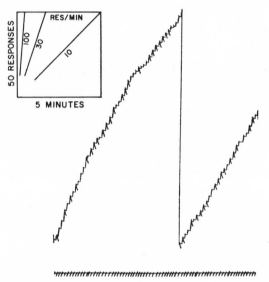

Fig. 4. A cumulative record of responses on the EXT-key under a *conc* DRL EXT schedule for Subject 342. The record represents the entire final session (about 12.3 min) when the DRL requirement was 10 sec. The diagonal pips represent reinforcement after a response on the DRL-key, and the event markers at the bottom of the record responses on the DRL-key. The recorder stopped only during reinforcement.

The pattern of responding on the EXT-key is shown in Fig. 4, which is a cumulative record of all responses on the EXT-key during an entire session when the DRL requirement was 10 sec. Typically, after a response on the DRL-key or a reinforcement, there is a short pause in all responding. After the pause (the pre-run pause), there is a rapid burst of responding on the EXT-key, followed immedi-

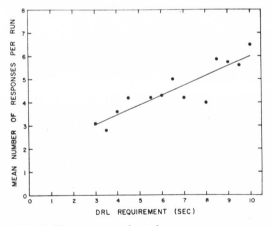

Fig. 3. The mean number of responses per run on the EXT-key under a *conc* DRL EXT schedule as a function of the DRL requirement for Subject 342. The response on the DRL-key which terminated the run was not included in calculating the number of responses per run. The equation of the regression line fitted to the obtained points is given in the text.

ately by a response on the DRL-key. Then the pattern repeats. This "pause-run" pattern was also found by Segal-Rechtschaffen (1963) for collateral behavior on a DRL schedule.

DISCUSSION

There are at least three possible reasons why responses on the EXT-key were maintained under the *conc* DRL EXT schedule even though they were no longer reinforced: (1) response induction from responses on the DRL-key; (2) previous strengthening during the *conc* VI VI schedule; and (3) strengthening due to adventitious temporal correlations with reinforcements following responses on the DRL-key. The fact that responding on the EXT-key was maintained throughout the experiment by only one of the subjects suggests, however, that accidental circumstances controlled the collateral responding, thus supporting the third of the putative explanations.

Both response measures of collateral behavior on the EXT-key—time per run and responses per run—were functionally related to the DRL contingency, indicating that the collateral behavior came under the control of the same contingency which controlled responding on the DRL-key. Moreover, the response measure of the DRL-key, *i.e.*, mean IRT, was strongly positively correlated with the two measures of collateral behavior. Beyond the mere correlation of the DRL behavior and the collateral behavior, can it be said that the collateral chain *mediated* timing under the DRL schedule?

Clearly, collateral responding to the EXT-key was not necessary for timing on the DRL-key, since Subject 274 timed but did not respond on the EXT-key at any appreciable rate. Furthermore, the fact that at all values of the DRL requirement, the mean time per run was less than the mean IRT on the DRL-key (see Fig. 2) indicates that the responses on the EXT-key alone were not even sufficient to mediate the entire interval between temporally spaced responses on the DRL-key. As noted in the Results section, the pre-run pause also increased with increases in the DRL requirement and thus was under the control of the DRL contingency. If timing was mediated, the mediating behavior consisted not only of responses on the EXT-key, but in addition,

included unrecorded behavior during the pre-run pause.

If then, responding on the EXT-key were mediating the timing behavior at least in part, it would be expected that the collateral behavior would be no more variable and at least as accurate as the timing behavior, just as would a clock in comparison with the behavior of the person using it. However, in Fig. 2, the standard error of estimate of the equation fitted to the collateral behavior is slightly greater than the standard error of estimate of the equation fitted to the timing behavior. Furthermore, the coefficient of determination, *i.e.*, the proportional reduction in the variance of the dependent values in Fig. 2, given the DRL requirement and the linear equations fitted to the points, is greater for the timing behavior (0.982) than for the collateral behavior (0.892). Therefore, the timing behavior shows a stronger linear functional relationship with the DRL contingency than does the collateral behavior, which is supposed to mediate the control exerted by the DRL contingency. Thus, the collateral behavior on the EXT-key appears to be more variable and less strongly related to the DRL requirement than the timing behavior, and therefore, hardly seems qualified to serve as a clock.

Considerations that cast doubt on the hypothesis that the collateral behavior mediated the timing also tend to raise the question as to why it is necessary to assume that timing behavior is mediated. Under the proper set of reinforcement contingencies, subtle properties of a response, such as its force, location, and duration can be selected and shaped. The IRT of a response can also be considered a differentiable property of a response (Morse, 1966, p. 67), and timing can be construed as the successful shaping of selected IRTs.

Alternately, timing behavior can be interpreted as temporal discrimination. Under the proper set of contingencies, the behavior of an organism can be brought under the control of subtle features of a stimulus such as the orientation of a line, the intensity of a light or the frequency of a tone. Duration, too, is a discriminable feature of a stimulus (Stubbs, 1968), and timing can be viewed as the successful discrimination of stimulus duration. Since the complex stimulus from which duration is abstracted by a timing organism under a DRL schedule is ordinarily unidentified, there is no good reason to assume, *a priori*, that the stimulus whose duration is the discriminative stimulus for timing behavior must be either an internal stimulus, as Anger (1956) suggests that it might be, or is a chain of responses, as proponents of the mediation hypothesis maintain. Any stimulus, external, internal, or generated by behavior might possibly serve as the stimulus from which duration could be abstracted.

When viewed as response differentiation or stimulus discrimination, timing loses much of the uniqueness that makes the mediation hypothesis an appealing theory.

REFERENCES

Anger, D. The dependence of interresponse times upon the relative reinforcement of different interresponse times. *Journal of Experimental Psychology*, 1956, **52**, 145-161.

Bruner, A. and Revusky, S. H. Collateral behavior in humans. *Journal of the Experimental Analysis of Behavior*, 1961, **4**, 349-350.

Catania, A. C. Concurrent operants. In W. K. Honig (Ed.), *Operant behavior: areas of research and application*. New York: Appleton-Century-Crofts, 1966. Pp. 213-270.

Catania, A. C. and Cutts, D. Experimental control of superstitious responding in humans. *Journal of the Experimental Analysis of Behavior*, 1963, **6**, 203-208.

Clark, F. C. Some observations on the adventitious reinforcement of drinking under food reinforcement. *Journal of the Experimental Analysis of Behavior*, 1962, **5**, 61-63.

Falk, J. Schedule-induced polydipsia as a function of fixed interval length. *Journal of the Experimental Analysis of Behavior*, 1966, **9**, 37-39.

Ferster, C. B. and Skinner, B. F. *Schedules of reinforcement*. New York: Appleton-Century-Crofts, 1957.

Hearst, E., Koresko, M. B., and Poppen, R. Stimulus generalization and the response-reinforcement contingency. *Journal of the Experimental Analysis of Behavior*, 1964, **7**, 369-380.

Hodos, W., Ross, G. S., and Brady, J. V. Complex response patterns during temporally spaced responding. *Journal of the Experimental Analysis of Behavior*, 1962, **5**, 473-486.

Holz, W. C., Azrin, N. H., and Ulrich, R. E. Punishment of temporally spaced responding. *Journal of the Experimental Analysis of Behavior*, 1963, **6**, 115-122.

Kapostins, E. E. The effects of DRL schedules on some characteristics of word utterance. *Journal of the Experimental Analysis of Behavior*, 1963, **6**, 281-290.

Kelleher, R. T., Fry, W., and Cook, L. Inter-response time distribution as a function of differential reinforcement of temporally spaced responses. *Journal of the Experimental Analysis of Behavior*, 1959, **2**, 91-106.

Laties, V. G., Weiss, B., Clark, R. L., and Reynolds, M. D. Overt "mediating" behavior during temporally spaced responding. *Journal of the Experimental Analysis of Behavior*, 1965, **8**, 107-116.

Laties, V. G., Weiss, B., and Weiss, A. B. Further observations on overt "mediating" behavior and the discrimination of time. *Journal of the Experimental Analysis of Behavior*, 1969, **12**, 43-57.

Morse, W. H. Intermittent reinforcement. In W. K. Honig (Ed.), *Operant behavior: areas of research and application*. New York: Appleton-Century-Crofts, 1966. Pp. 52-108.

Nevin, J. A. and Berryman, R. A note on chaining and temporal discrimination. *Journal of the Experimental Analysis of Behavior*, 1963, **6**, 109-113.

Segal-Rechtschaffen, E. Reinforcement of mediating behavior on a spaced-responding schedule. *Journal of the Experimental Analysis of Behavior*, 1963, **6**, 39-46.

Staddon, J. E. R. Some properties of spaced responding in pigeons. *Journal of the Experimental Analysis of Behavior*, 1965, **8**, 19-27.

Stubbs, A. The discrimination of stimulus duration by pigeons. *Journal of the Experimental Analysis of Behavior*, 1968, **11**, 223-238.

Weiss, B., Laties, V. G., Siegel, L., and Goldstein, D. A computer analysis of serial interactions in spaced responding. *Journal of the Experimental Analysis of Behavior*, 1966, **9**, 619-626.

Wilson, M. P. and Keller, F. S. On the selective reinforcement of spaced responses. *Journal of Comparative and Physiological Psychology*, 1953, **46**, 190-193.

Received 17 March 1969.

SOME VARIABLES AFFECTING THE SUPERSTITIOUS CHAINING OF RESPONSES[1,2]

JOHN J. BOREN

WALTER REED ARMY INSTITUTE OF RESEARCH

This study was based upon a repeated acquisition technique that systematically generated superstitious chains of responses. Several procedures were investigated in an effort to modify the amount of superstitious chaining. The effects of a large work requirement, a stimulus correlated with non-reinforcement after inappropriate responses, an equivalent time delay after inappropriate responses, and extensive training were examined. The presentation of a stimulus correlated with non-reinforcement was found to be the most effective technique for reducing superstitious chaining; the time delay was the least effective.

Reinforcement strengthens any behavior it happens to follow. When an organism makes a response that is not actually part of the reinforcement contingency but that is nevertheless followed by reinforcement, the behavior so strengthened can be described as superstitious and the reinforcement contingency as adventitious. A notable step toward understanding and analyzing experimentally such superstitious behavior was taken by Skinner in 1948. He arranged for a food magazine simply to operate automatically every 15 sec in the same chamber with a hungry pigeon. When he returned some time later, he found that the pigeons were performing such behaviors as turning, bowing, and hopping. The birds had apparently been conditioned by accidental coincidences between the behavior and reinforcement. Skinner noted the similarity between these behaviors in his pigeons and certain human superstitions, such as a card-player's rituals for changing his luck and a bowler's "body-English" for guiding the ball into the pins. These behaviors, too, were probably strengthened by an accidental coincidence between the ritual and a reinforcing state of

affairs, although a causal relationship was lacking.

Since Skinner's original work, a number of studies with a variety of experimental situations have implicated superstitious behavior. One example is the collateral behavior observed by Wilson and Keller (1953) to intervene between the lever-pressing responses on a differential reinforcement of low rate (DRL) schedule. They noticed that their rats developed stereotyped behaviors, such as grooming or nose poking, which occupied enough time so that the next lever press was often reinforced. Although it may have increased the probability of reinforcement of the next lever press, the collateral behavior can still be regarded as superstitious, since the behavior was not part of the reinforcement contingency. Analogous superstitious behaviors during DRL schedules have been found in various settings and with several species. Hodos, Ross, and Brady (1962) observed excessive licking and head jerking in monkeys restrained in primate chairs. Laties, Weiss, Clark, and Reynolds (1965) studied a rat that nibbled its tail in a stereotyped way between spaced responses. Bruner and Revusky (1961) and Randolph (1965) found that humans would operate extra pushbuttons before the response reinforced by the DRL schedule; Catania and Cutts (1963) made a similar finding with a variable-interval schedule. Kapostins (1963) discovered systematic patterns of intervening verbal behavior in an human experiment on word utterance. While they may have filled time, the various collateral behaviors in all of

---

[1]Dedicated to B. F. Skinner in his sixty-fifth year. His pioneering work on superstition in 1948 formed the background for the present research.

[2]A version of this paper was delivered at the meetings of the Eastern Psychological Association in Atlantic City in 1965. Reprints may be obtained from John J. Boren, Department of Experimental Psychology, Walter Reed Army Institute of Research, Washington, D. C. 20012. The author is indebted to Dennis D. Devine for his able technical assistance.

these studies formed no part of the actual reinforcement contingency.

Other examples of superstitious behavior have been observed with quite different procedures. Migler (1963) and Keehn and Chaudrey (1964) presented a shock that was automatically turned off after a fixed duration. Nevertheless, the rats in these experiments continued to press a lever during the shock as if the lever press terminated the shock. Migler also observed one rat to press a spare second lever during the shock, even though that lever had never had any effect. The superstitious escape behavior in these experiments was maintained by the accidental correlation of the response and shock termination. Accidental relationships may also arise in the sensory control of behavior. Morse and Skinner (1957) trained pigeons with food reinforcement delivered after variable intervals to peck a key in an orange light. Occasionally a blue light was presented independently of the reinforcement schedule. Pigeons that accidentally received a few reinforcements in the blue light began to peck at high rates in blue. Other pigeons that received no reinforcements in blue responded infrequently during the stimulus. Such superstitious discriminations can be explained in terms of adventitious reinforcement (or accidental failure to receive reinforcement) during the incidental stimulus.

An experiment particularly relevant to the present study was performed by Herrnstein and Morse (reported in Herrnstein, 1966). A pigeon was trained to peck a disk on a short fixed-interval schedule (FI 11-sec). Then the reinforcement contingency was removed, but the reinforcer was delivered every 11 sec regardless of the bird's behavior. The results over 21 daily sessions showed that a substantial rate of pecking (about one peck every 2 sec) was maintained, even though the reinforcement was purely accidental. This study departed from those discussed above in that the behavior was conditioned with a deliberate reinforcement contingency and then was maintained superstitiously.

In a study of the repeated acquisition of new behavioral chains (Boren and Devine, 1968), a large amount of superstitious behavior was observed. In that study, monkeys were trained with food reinforcement in a chamber containing four groups of three levers. During each session, the monkey's task was to learn a new four-response chain by pressing in sequence the correct lever from each group. At the beginning of the session, the monkey pressed a random assortment of incorrect levers, as one might expect in the acquisition situation. However, by about the twentieth repetition of the reinforced chain, a semi-stable mixture of correct and incorrect responses usually developed. At this point, the same incorrect responses would often appear in the same sequence within the reinforced chain. For example, if the reinforced ("correct") sequence of levers was 1-4-8-12, the monkey might repeatedly press in the sequence 2-1-4-8-12. This elongated sequence was reinforced even though the press on lever 2 was irrelevant. The unnecessary lever press had apparently become chained adventitiously with the correct levers upon which the reinforcement was in fact contingent. Under appropriate conditions, new patterns of superstitious chaining were reestablished from session to session, so it appeared that the superstitious behavior was being systematically generated.

Using this superstitious behavior as a baseline, the purpose of the present study was to examine several variables that might change the frequency of such behavior. One variable was the amount of behavior required for each member of the chain. If the monkey could maintain a lengthy superstitious chain only by putting out a great deal of work, the amount of superstitious behavior might decrease. Other variables explored were: (1) the effects of a timeout stimulus (or S^Δ—a stimulus in the presence of which responses were not reinforced); (2) the effect of a time delay without a stimulus to determine if the delay alone could decrease superstitious chaining; and (3) the effect of extended training on one sequence to determine if (as suggested by Herrnstein, 1966) superstitious behavior would drift toward minimal forms.

METHOD

Subjects

Three rhesus monkeys (*macaca mulatta*) served. Their past history included more than 300 sessions in the apparatus described below, so their familiarity with the experimental environment and their pattern of relearning had reached a stable state. The monkeys were deprived of food for 24 hr before each session. Their major source of food was the 80 pellets (0.7-g D & G monkey lab chow pellets) delivered as reinforcers during the session. The only other food was an orange given to the monkeys several hours after the session.

The principles of laboratory animal care as promulgated by the National Society for Medical Research were observed.

Apparatus

The experimental environment was a metal chamber, 2 ft (0.6 m) in each dimension. Twelve levers, in four groups of three, were mounted on one wall, and above each lever was a pilot light. Behind each lever was a relay that produced an audible click when the lever was pressed. A pellet tray was mounted in the center of the wall below the levers.

The experimental procedure was scheduled automatically by relays, timers, pre-determining counters, *etc.* The clicks of the equipment were masked by white noise in the experimental room. Magnetic counters and a 20-pen event recorder automatically recorded the subjects' lever-pressing behavior.

General Procedure

The basic procedure was to train the monkey to learn or re-learn a four-response chain during an experimental session. As the monkey faced the 12-lever panel, the pilot lights were on over the first three levers on the left. When the monkey pressed the correct lever, the first three lights went out and the next three to the right came on. Next, the monkey had to press the correct one of levers 4-5-6 in order to advance the lights. Finally, when the correct one of levers 10-11-12 was pressed, the food-pellet dispenser operated. Then, the first three lights came on again to set the occasion for another response chain.

Several specific details of the basic procedure require comment. The food-pellet reinforcer was delivered after the completion of every second sequence, although the pellet dispenser operated (clicked) after each sequence. As another procedural detail, the monkeys were required to learn a new chain on alternate sessions. In other words, the second session of each pair was devoted to relearning the same response sequence as in the first session of the pair. Counterbalanced sets of six lever sequences were devised for the segments of the

study to be compared. An example of one such set is as follows: 3-4-9-11, 2-6-7-12, 1-5-8-10, 3-6-7-11, 1-4-8-12, and 2-5-9-10. The rules for constructing a set were: the same levers were not selected for the next sequence; repeated pairings of two lever sequences were not permitted; and each lever appeared equally often (twice) in each set. It has been found in this laboratory that the number of errors made in learning different sets constructed in this way do not differ substantially. Furthermore, in going through the same set several times, the monkeys make about the same number of errors each time. However, to avoid any small differences in the sets, a given set was always used in studying comparable conditions. Thus, for example, in studying one ascending-descending order of work requirements, the same set of lever sequences was used. Another set was used for the second ascending-descending order, *etc.* Each monkey served under all control and experimental conditions of the study.

Experiment I

The first variable examined was the work requirement on each lever. Fixed ratios (FRs) of 1, 5, 10, and 20 presses on each correct lever were required to change the pilot lights and to advance the chain toward the terminal food reinforcement. Thus, with FR 10 and the sequence 1-4-8-12, the monkey must press lever 1 at least 10 times, then lever 4 ten times, and so on, until the tenth press on lever 12 operated the pellet dispenser (no pellet). When this entire sequence was completed the second time, the dispenser delivered a pellet. The fixed-ratio sizes were studied in an ascending and a descending order on two occasions. The exact order is also indicated in the figures to follow. The assumption behind this experiment was that the increased work imposed by the larger fixed ratios would reduce the superstitious chaining of incorrect levers because the maintenance of superstitious behavior would also involve increased work.

Experiment II

The second phase of the study was concerned with a manipulation of the consequences of the non-essential behavior. One such consequence was a stimulus (S^Δ) correlated with non-reinforcement. When the monkey pressed a lever that was not part of the required chain, an S^Δ was produced. More specifically, after an incorrect response, the pilot lights over the levers and the houselights went out, and the levers did not produce food. After the S△ terminated, the pilot lights came on over the same levers where the error was made, and the monkey began again in the same part of the chain where it had previously made the inappropriate response. The work requirement on each correct lever was FR 1. Based upon a prior study of a range of S△ durations (Boren and Devine, 1968), S△s of 1 sec and 15 sec were used. Any lever press during the S△ prolonged it, so that 1 sec or 15 sec of no responding was required to terminate the S△ period. In the prior study, an effect of error-produced S△ was to stop responding and to insert a delay between an incorrect response and a correct one. Thus, an S△ might well prevent adventitious reinforcement by the mechanism of inserting a temporal space between the incorrect response and the reinforcement produced by a correct one. To determine if the delay itself (rather than the delay plus the exteroceptive stimulus) could prevent the superstitious chaining, the stimuli making up the S△ were removed. In other words, when the monkey pressed an incorrect lever, a delay was scheduled but the pilot lights and the houselight remained on. All other conditions remained exactly the same, including the requirement of 1 sec or of 15 sec of no responding before the delay was terminated. The object was to compare the control over superstitious behavior exercised by the time delay alone with that exercised by the time delay plus the stimulus.

In all of the experiments described above, a given experimental condition was maintained for at least 12 sessions. This number of sessions was found to be sufficiently long for the monkey's performance to reach a stable state. Indeed, the performance usually changed within the first session of a new experimental condition.

Experiment III

The final phase of the study was directed at the question: "Can the superstitious chaining eventually be reduced by extended training?" The monkeys were permitted to relearn the same sequence of correct levers for five consecutive sessions. Four different sequences were scheduled for five sessions each. The work re-

quirement on each correct lever was held to the simplest schedule, FR 1.

RESULTS

Experiment I

The behavior treated quantitatively in this study was the number of times the monkeys pressed a lever that was not part of the reinforced response chain. Such lever presses will be referred to as nonreinforced, incorrect, and inappropriate responses, or more simply, as errors. The vast majority of the errors observed were of two types and were observed in two parts of a session. (1) The irregular, scattered "learning" error where the monkey hit various unreinforced levers in a non-systematic order. This type of error occurred at the beginning of a session while the monkey was learning a new response chain. (2) The systematic "performance" error which the monkey regularly included within the response chain. This type of error was typically observed later in the session while the monkey was rapidly performing the chain.

The two types of errors are illustrated in Fig. 1 with event records from the beginning and the middle of a typical session. The upper

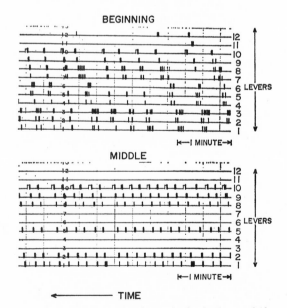

Fig. 1. Event recordings from the beginning and the middle of a session. The reinforced sequence of lever presses was 2-5-9-10. The upper record illustrates the scattering of responses typical of the acquisition of a new response chain and the lower record illustrates a well-formed superstitious chain (levers 1-2-5-8-9-10).

record from the beginning of the session shows that the monkey scattered its responses over a variety of unreinforced levers. The variable performance might be expected because the monkey was relearning a new sequence of levers which it had not experienced for many sessions. A different picture is seen in the record from the middle of the same session. By this time the monkey was rapidly pressing the levers (2-5-9-10) upon which reinforcement depended. In addition, two non-reinforced levers (1 and 8) were included in the response chain so that the total chain was 1-2-5-8-9-10. Levers 1 and 8 were included far too frequently and repetitively to be considered non-systematic. Note that the extended sequence was reinforced even though the presses on levers 1 and 8 were irrelevant. The unnecessary lever presses had apparently become chained superstitiously with the correct levers upon which reinforcement was actually contingent. Such lever presses form the basic subject matter of the results.

By recording the errors made after the twentieth chain, one finds that the vast majority of the errors are of the systematic repetitive type. Considering the lack of any but accidental reinforcement contingencies, these errors will be referred to as superstitious.

Figures 2 and 3 show how the superstitious errors varied with changes in the fixed-ratio size. The measures plotted in these figures were derived by several steps. First, the number of presses on non-reinforced levers (errors) was recorded from the twenty-first to the one hundred-sixtieth chain, for the reason indicated in the previous paragraph. Next, the median number of errors per session was computed for an individual monkey based upon the last eight sessions (four pairs) under a given FR. The details of the computation were as follows: using the errors in the four initial learning sessions (where a given lever sequence was first scheduled), a median was computed. In the same way, a separate median was computed for the four relearning sessions where the same lever sequence was scheduled a second time. Finally, the value representing the median errors per session was divided by the size of the fixed ratio. This division was done because more errors should be expected from the larger fixed ratios. For example, on FR 20 the monkey must press an incorrect lever 20 times before any stimuli are available that

this lever is not part of the reinforced chain. On FR 1, the monkey need press only once. Thus, to correct for this factor, the number of errors was divided by the FR size. This computation yielded an error measure in terms of FR units.

Figure 2 shows how the error measure described above varied as a function of the fixed-ratio size. The data in the upper graph came from the initial sessions on a given lever se-

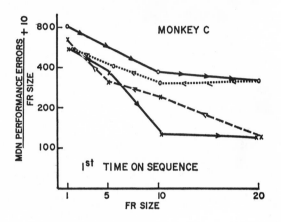

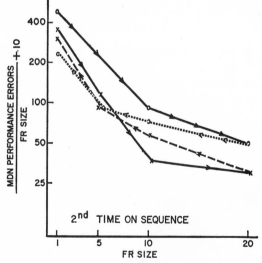

Fig. 2. Performance errors in FR units as a function of the fixed-ratio size (Monkey C). For convenience in plotting the error measure, the ordinate is on a logarithmic scale; to avoid zero, 10 has been added to each error measure. The first study of an ascending-descending order of FR sizes is plotted by round points; the replication is plotted by x's. The arrows on the lines indicate whether the FR was being increased or decreased. The data for the first time on a given lever sequence are shown in the upper graph, and the data for the second time on a sequence are in the lower graph.

quence and the data in the lower graph came from the second sessions on the sequence. Both functions show a systematic decrease in the error measure as FR increased. As might be expected, the two functions differ largely in that more errors were made during the initial sessions than during the second sessions.

Similar data for a second monkey are shown in Fig. 3. As in Fig. 2, the general trend of the functions was for the error measure to decrease

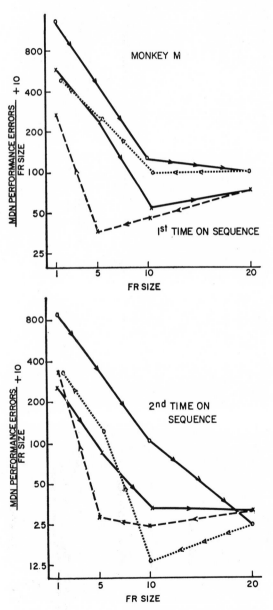

Fig. 3. Performance errors in FR units as a function of the fixed-ratio size (Monkey M). The construction of this figure is the same as for Fig. 2.

as the fixed ratio increased. However, examination of the order in which the points were determined reveals a certain lack of reversibility from one FR condition to another. For example, the errors for FR 10 tended to be lower when the previous condition was FR 20 than when it was FR 5. In spite of this tendency, however, the FR 1 condition always produced an elevation in the error measure. The data for the third monkey (Monkey S) demonstrated the same functional relation as in Fig. 2 and 3.

The inverse relation between FR size and superstitious errors does not reliably hold if the absolute number of errors is plotted, rather than errors in FR units as in Fig. 2 and 3. The reader can confirm this statement by multiplying the points above FR by 5, the points over FR 10 by 10, etc. Furthermore, although the evidence on resistance to extinction as a function of FR size (Mowrer and Jones, 1945; Boren, 1961) indicates that the consideration of errors in FR units is an approximation in the right direction, it may be argued that division by the FR size is somewhat arbitrary and probably inexact. In order to develop a less arbitrary measure of errors, the recordings were analyzed for the number of occasions an incorrect lever was pressed, regardless of how many times. An occasion was defined as one or more presses on an incorrect lever without interruption by a press on another lever. The usefulness of the "number of occasions" analysis was that the measure avoids the problem of FR size and of the number of lever presses made during an occasion. The behavior during the last 20 reinforcements was used for this analysis not only for simplicity but also because the superstitious chaining could be seen most clearly late in the session. The results of this analysis for Monkey C appear in Fig. 4. The function is a declining one. As the FR size increased, the number of occasions the monkey pressed an incorrect lever decreased.

The same was true of Monkey M, as shown in Fig. 5, with somewhat less non-systematic variability. The carry-over from one fixed ratio to another, already noted in Fig. 3 for Monkey M, is apparent here. This partial irreversibility is especially clear because it occurred both times the fixed ratio size was increased and decreased. The main effect, however, shows that if a monkey must emit a number of responses to maintain a superstitious chain, it will do so

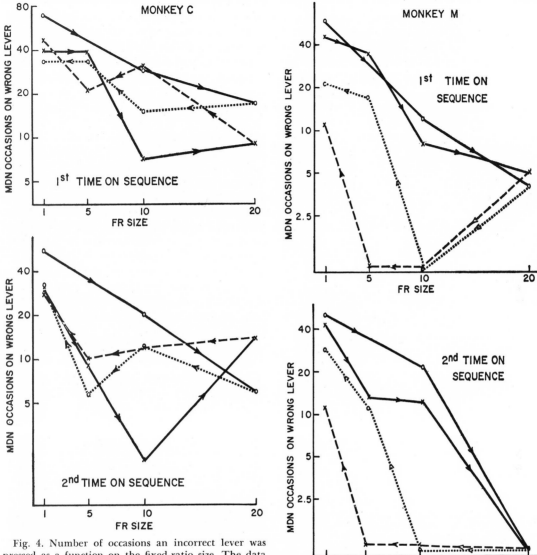

Fig. 4. Number of occasions an incorrect lever was pressed as a function on the fixed-ratio size. The data are for Monkey C.

Fig. 5. The number of occasions Monkey M pressed incorrect levers at the various fixed-ratio sizes. This figure was constructed in the same way as Fig. 4, except that the data are for Monkey M. Note that the number of errors (especially for FR 10) depended partly on whether the previous FR was larger or smaller.

on fewer occasions than if it must emit only one response. Thus, by this measure, as by the measure in terms of FR units shown in Fig. 2 and 3, the results are in agreement. When the monkeys were coerced by a large FR to put out large amounts of work to perform the superstitious behavior, then the superstitious behavior was less well maintained.

In a final analysis, the data of Exp. 1 were examined to determine the location of errors within the four-response chain. Because of the large volume of data and because of the variability, only representative data are shown in Table 1. The data are for the initial sessions

on lever sequences for FR 1 and FR 20 (two replications each). The median and the range of errors for four sessions are presented. Inspection of Table 1 reveals a great deal of variability. Nevertheless, Monkeys C and M tended to make fewer errors on the part of the chain (levers 10-11-12) closest to primary reinforcement. The variability makes other com-

Table 1

The frequency of errors in different parts of the response chain.

Levers	FR 1		FR 20	
	Mdn	Range	Mdn	Range
Monkey C				
1-2-3	266	167-863	3026	588-9247
4-5-6	196	142-297	2389	1950-3038
7-8-9	140	70-214	2516	882-5098
10-11-12	45	29-73	959	235-1425
1-2-3	440	244-588	1900	1468-5250
4-5-6	174	94-192	1638	503-2819
7-8-9	226	135-268	1491	11-2588
10-11-12	44	21-77	741	417-1273
Monkey M				
1-2-3	151	23-265	2540	108-2849
4-5-6	308	14-601	734	646-2168
7-8-9	150	44-258	1450	1142-1615
10-11-12	20	5-101	546	314-803
1-2-3	152	2-317	1695	1163-2603
4-5-6	20	10-360	1405	122-2295
7-8-9	78	51-188	712	326-1336
10-11-12	16	14-17	810	427-1119
Monkey S				
1-2-3	12	0-60	1170	454-2240
4-5-6	68	21-73	925	500-1292
7-8-9	23	6-36	935	186-1150
10-11-12	31	13-44	459	216-788
1-2-3	30	0-103	304	83-762
4-5-6	35	6-57	225	104-443
7-8-9	39	11-57	336	141-582
10-11-12	38	33-40	147	64-234

parisons difficult, a difficulty probably arising from the superstitious nature of the errors.

Experiment II

In this experiment certain consequences were made contingent upon the superstitious behavior. In a previous study (Boren and Devine, 1968), a response on an incorrect lever was followed immediately by a stimulus correlated with non-reinforcement (an S^Δ). This procedure effectively reduced the superstitious behavior, although it was not clear whether the stimulus *per se* was critical in producing the effect or whether the time delay was the major factor. The object of Exp. II was to extend the previous observation and to compare the effect of the S^Δ with the effect of an equivalent delay minus the stimulus.

Figure 6 shows the median errors of Monkey M under the various conditions of the experiment. Since a given sequence of reinforced lever presses was scheduled in two consecutive sessions, the data for the first and second times on a sequence are shown in Fig. 6. As in Fig. 2 to 5, the two times on a sequence can be considered partial replications which permit estimates of the reliability of the effect within a subject.

In Fig. 6, a comparison of the errors under S^Δ conditions with the errors under delay conditions shows that the S^Δ were much more effective in reducing errors. It was of little consequence whether the S^Δs were 1 sec or 15 sec; they were about equally effective, thus confirming the previous study (Boren and Devine, 1968). Although the delays produced considerable variability (compare the two times a 1-sec delay was studied), the delays *per se* were relatively ineffective in reducing errors. For example, if the equivalent delays and S^Δs are compared, the S^Δ errors are 2% or less of the delay errors.

In Fig. 7, the data for another subject, Monkey C, show similar main effects. In every

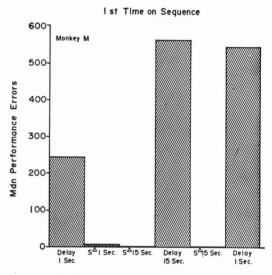

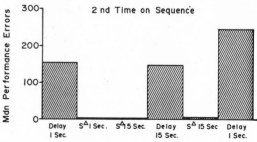

Fig. 6. Median performance errors of Monkey M under the various S^Δ and delay conditions of Exp. II. The order of studying the conditions follows the order on the abscissa.

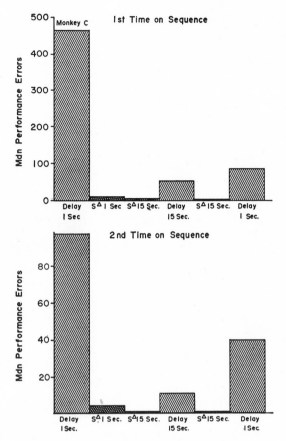

Fig. 7. Median performance errors of Monkey C under the various S^Δ and delay conditions of Exp. II.

case, the S^Δs reduced the frequency of inappropriate responding much more than did the delays. The average errors under S^Δ conditions were about 6% of the errors under the equivalent delay conditions. It is clear from both Fig. 6 and 7 that merely inserting a temporal space between an incorrect response and reinforcement is a relatively ineffective way to attenuate superstitious chaining of responses.

Why was the delay relatively ineffective in comparison with an S^Δ? One reason is that the delay made poor contact with the inappropriate behavior. After the monkey pressed the wrong lever, no discriminable change occurred. When the error produced an S^Δ, on the other hand, the lights went out immediately. The clear and immediate stimulus change, indicating that the monkey no longer had access to reinforcement, exercised effective control.

A second factor was also present. Once a delay period without stimuli was started, the monkey often pressed other levers, thus pro-

longing the delay. During this time, both correct and incorrect levers could be pressed, but in either case nothing in the monkey's environment changed. Thus, many incorrect responses were without consequence, and many correct responses went unreinforced. In contrast, the S^Δ procedure was much more exacting. Incorrect responses were immediately followed by an S^Δ. Furthermore, since the monkeys did not respond during the S^Δ, correct responses were always reinforced, either by the pilot lights or by the food pellet. This set of exact contingencies arising from the S^Δ procedure and its associated delay seems to account for much of its relatively greater effect.

The changeover delay used by Catania and Cutts (1963) to separate the superstitious response from reinforcement was considerably more effective than the post-error delay of the present study. One reason may be that the two delays were scheduled differently. The changeover-delay interval was reset only by another superstitious response, whereas the delay of the present study was reset also by correct responses. Nevertheless, in partial agreement with the present study, Catania and Cutts found that the changeover delay varied considerably in its effect and that some subjects continued to respond superstitiously in spite of it.

Experiment III

The problem of the final experiment was to determine whether extended training on a given sequence would reduce the superstitious chaining to negligible amounts. The problem was approached by training the monkeys on the same sequence of correct levers for five consecutive sessions. This was done with four different sequences. The work requirement on each correct lever was FR 1, which in Exp. I had proved most likely to generate superstitious behavior.

The number of errors was recorded for each of the five sessions on a given lever sequence. Then, using the error values for the first session (Day 1) on each of the four lever sequences, a median was calculated. In the same way, a median was calculated separately for the second, third, fourth, and fifth sessions on a sequence.

A session-by-session plot of these median errors per session is shown in Fig. 8. With all three monkeys, the number of errors declined systematically with repeated training. The curves were negatively accelerated with the bulk of the errors (an average over the three monkeys of 77%) occurring in the first two sessions. By the fifth session, all monkeys were making relatively few errors, and an extrapolation of the curves suggests that the errors would probably have decreased further with additional training.

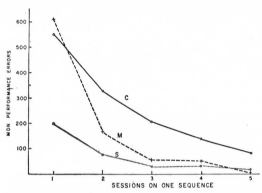

Fig. 8. The reduction in errors caused by retraining the monkeys on one sequence of lever presses. Each curve shows the performance of one monkey.

In summary, extended training on the same sequence of levers reduced the amount of superstitious chaining. This result is consistent with Herrnstein's (1966) proposal that superstitious behavior should drift toward minimal forms. The findings in Fig. 8 may have been due to one or both of the following processes: (1) consistent and repeated reinforcement may have strengthened the correct lever presses, while (2) the delays and extra responding inherent in superstitions may have weakened the superstitious behaviors.

DISCUSSION

There is every reason to believe that superstitious behavior obeys the same laws as other behavior. Herrnstein (1966), in an excellent review of this question, found no exception. In the present study, the superstitious behavior included within the reinforced response chain seemed to be determined by an accidental reinforcement contingency, in the same way as the non-superstitious behavior was determined by an actual reinforcement contingency. While neither a new theoretical analysis nor a new set of principles is required, there remains the technical problem of how to

control such behavior. The problem is especially difficult because the adventitious reinforcement that maintains the superstition may still be present and may counteract efforts at control.

This study has investigated three ways of decreasing superstitious behavior. One way is to increase the response cost of the superstition. When the number of responses required to maintain the superstition was increased, the superstitious behavior was attenuated, at least if the appropriate correction for FR size or the number of occasions was considered. A second way to decrease superstitious behavior is to follow such behavior with an S^Δ. The use of an S^Δ is a simple and highly effective means of control. In comparison, interposing a delay between the superstitious response and the reinforcement was both behaviorally complex and relatively ineffective. The third way explored in this study was repeated training. When a number of sessions was devoted to training the desired responses, the superstitious responses were gradually reduced. Of the variables studied, however, the use of an S^Δ was the most immediate, reliable, and effective means to control superstitious chaining.

REFERENCES

Boren, J. J. and Devine, D. D. The repeated acquisition of behavioral chains. *Journal of the Experimental Analysis of Behavior*, 1968, **11**, 651-660.

Boren, J. J. Rate and resistance to extinction as a function of the fixed ratio. *Journal of Experimental Psychology*, 1961, **61**, 304-308.

Bruner, A. and Revusky, S. H. Collateral behavior in humans. *Journal of the Experimental Analysis of Behavior*, 1961, **4**, 349-350.

Catania, A. C. and Cutts, D. Experimental control of superstitious behavior in humans. *Journal of the Experimental Analysis of Behavior*, 1963, **6**, 203-208.

Herrnstein, R. J. Superstition: A corollary of the principles of operant conditioning. In W. K. Honig (Ed.), *Operant behavior: areas of research and application*. New York: Appleton-Century-Crofts, 1966. Pp. 33-55.

Hodos, W., Ross, G. S., and Brady, J. V. Complex response patterns during temporally spaced responding. *Journal of the Experimental Analysis of Behavior*, 1962, **5**, 473-479.

Kapostins, E. E. The effects of DRL schedules on some characteristics of word utterance. *Journal of the Experimental Analysis of Behavior*, 1963, **6**, 281-290.

Keehn, J. D. and Chaudrey, S. Superstitious escape behavior during Sidman avoidance training. *Journal of the Experimental Analysis of Behavior*, 1964, **7**, 26.

Laties, V. G., Weiss, B., Clark, R. L., and Reynolds, M. D. Overt "mediating" behavior during temporally spaced responding. *Journal of the Experimental Analysis of Behavior*, 1965, **8**, 107-116.

Migler, B. Experimental self-punishment and superstitious escape behavior. *Journal of the Experimental Analysis of Behavior*, 1963, **6**, 371-385.

Morse, W. H. and Skinner, B. F. A second type of superstition in the pigeon. *American Journal of Psychology*, 1957, **70**, 308-311.

Mowrer, O. H. and Jones, H. M. Habit strength as a function of the pattern of reinforcement. *Journal of Experimental Psychology*, 1945, **35**, 293-311.

Randolph, J. J. A further study of collateral behavior in humans. *Psychonomic Science*, 1965, **3**, 227-228.

Skinner, B. F. Superstition in the pigeon. *Journal of Experimental Psychology*, 1948, **38**, 168-172.

Wilson, M. P. and Keller, F. S. On the selective reinforcement of spaced responses. *Journal of Comparative and Physiological Psychology*, 1953, **46**, 190-193.

Received 28 April 1969.

STUDIES ON RESPONDING UNDER FIXED-INTERVAL SCHEDULES OF REINFORCEMENT: THE EFFECTS ON THE PATTERN OF RESPONDING OF CHANGES IN REQUIREMENTS AT REINFORCEMENT[1]

P. B. Dews

HARVARD MEDICAL SCHOOL

In pigeons responding under a 180-sec fixed-interval schedule of reinforcement, the frequency distribution of the duration of the final interresponse time before the reinforcer was compared with the distribution of the preceding two interresponse times. The results confirmed qualitatively and quantitatively the expected preferential reinforcement of longer interreinforcement times under fixed-interval reinforcement. Requirements at reinforcement were then changed to eliminate the preferential reinforcement of longer interresponse times. Local patterns and mean rate of responding could change, without the characteristic fixed-interval pattern of increasing responding through the interval (scalloping) being much affected. It is concluded that this characteristic pattern of fixed-interval responding does not depend crucially on effects of the reinforcer at the moment of reinforcement, but rather on effects extending over much longer periods of time than just the last interresponse time.

Under a fixed-interval schedule of reinforcement (FI) a response is followed by reinforcing stimuli only when some fixed interval of time has elapsed since the onset of a particular environmental stimulus that is present at reinforcement. With a variety of species, responses, reinforcers, and parameters, FI generates an increasing rate of responding through the interval, asymptoting to a relatively constant average rate in the terminal segment (Ferster and Skinner, 1957; Dews, 1958; Kelleher and Morse, 1968). The present experiments are part of a continuing program to measure the contribution of the various attributes of an FI schedule to the determination of the characteristic pattern (notably the scallop) and the rates of responding under the schedule. Since Skinner pointed out that "the effects of a schedule are due to the contingencies which prevail at the moment of reinforcement under it" (Skinner, 1953, p. 105), students of schedules have sought to explain *all* the effects of schedules in terms of characteristics of responding at the moment of reinforcement, despite the broader implications of the term "contingencies". An alternative view, that the effects on future responding of the occurrence of the reinforcer depends directly on the pattern of responding during considerable intervals of time preceding the moment of reinforcement, has been stated, and evidence to support it in the case of FI responding has been presented (Dews, 1962). The intervals of time are measured from the moment of reinforcement and so are temporally contingent on the moment of reinforcement. The present paper examines the effects on responding under FI of the precise temporal pattern of responding at reinforcement.

The average rate of responding in the terminal segment (say the terminal tenth) of an interval is fairly constant, though there is a considerable variation in the duration of individual interresponse times (IRTs), the times from the beginning of one response to the beginning of the next. Since the timing of the fixed interval continues independently of responding, the fixed interval is relatively more likely to end during a long IRT than during a short one (Skinner, 1938, p. 275; Anger, 1956). A general account of the necessary, mathematical consequences of interval-type schedules of reinforcement on the distribution of reinforced IRTs[2] in relation to the distribution of

[1]Dedicated to B. F. Skinner in his sixty-fifth year. This research was supported by Grants MH 02094 and MH 07658 from the U. S. Public Health Service. I am indebted to Miss Leona M. Delaney for help with the experiments, and to Miss Frances Reagan for measurement of the polygraph records. Reprints may be obtained from the author, Dept. of Psychiatry, Harvard Medical School, 25 Shattuck St., Boston, Mass. 02115.

[2]Following customary practice, the response whose occurrence triggers the reinforcing stimuli by means of the controlling apparatus will be called the reinforced response. I have argued elsewhere that other responses may be equally entitled to the designation reinforced, in the behavioral sense, even though they do not similarly affect the hardware (Dews, 1962).

adjacent but non-reinforced IRTs has been presented by Revusky (1962). His arguments apply to FI when an IRT of t sec occurs, the fixed-interval is twice as likely to conclude during it as when an IRT of $t/2$ sec occurs. Generally, provided the durations of IRTs are small compared to the length of the interval, the conditional probability of an interval concluding in an IRT of duration t sec is directly proportional to t. IRTs of different durations, however, occur with different frequencies. The actual probability that the fixed interval will conclude during an IRT of a particular duration is equal to the proportion of the total time occupied by IRTs of that duration during the terminal segment of the interval. Consider the terminal segment of the interval (duration T sec) during which the mean rate and the relative frequencies of the various IRTs are constant. If the frequency of IRTs of duration t_i is f_i, then the probability of the reinforced response concluding an IRT of duration t_i is $f_i t_i/T$. Since the entire time is occupied by IRTs, $\Sigma f_i t_i$ over all values of i must equal T. If there is a large preponderance of short IRTs, most of the reinforced responses might conclude short IRTs, even though the conditional probability that an IRT of a given duration will conclude with a reinforced response is higher the longer the IRT (in direct proportion to the duration).

The quantitative consequences of these theoretical considerations have been examined. Derived and directly measured IRT distributions of three pigeons responding under an FI schedule of parameter value 180 sec (3 min) have been compared. The distributions were similar, so the hardware faithfully implemented the schedule in this regard. The magnitude of the differences between reinforced and non-reinforced IRT distributions differed considerably among the subjects. The importance of preferential reinforcement of longer IRTs in determining the characteristic pattern and rates of FI responding was then assessed by changing the distribution of the reinforced IRTs. Circumstances at the time of reinforcement affected the average rate of responding and the local patterns of responding, that is, the pattern over series of a few consecutive responses. The preferential reinforcement of longer IRTs was not, however, of importance in maintaining the characteristic general FI pattern of increasing rate through the interval.

The results complement previous evidence indicating the importance of reinforcement of whole patterns of responding rather than of single responses (Dews, 1962; Dews, 1966).

MATERIALS AND METHODS

Subjects were three male White Carneaux pigeons, numbered 44, 152, and 260, with extensive and varied previous experience under a variety of schedules. The free-feeding weights were about 500, 525, and 490 g, respectively. During the experiment they were maintained at 400, 450, and 400 g respectively. The apparatus, response mechanism, reinforcer (food), and other stimuli were as in previous experiments on FI responding (Dews, 1962), and were in all matters of significance according to Ferster and Skinner (1957). The response key was transilluminated by white bulbs (GE Nova C 7 1/2). No houselight was present.

SCHEDULES

The schedules of reinforcement were FI 180-sec and variations thereof. The details are more easily presented with the following nomenclature (Dews, 1960). An elapsed time requirement of the schedule of reinforcement is designated by T followed by the requirement in seconds, *e.g.*, T 180-sec. Response requirements are designated by N followed by the number requirement. T 180-sec N 1 means that 180 sec must elapse and then one response occur whereupon the reinforcer supervenes; and so represents FI 180-sec. The schedules studied were T 180-sec N 1, T 180-sec N 2, T 180-sec N 10, and T 180-sec N 1 T 1-sec. The schedules T 180-sec N 2 and T 180-sec N 10 could be called tandem FI 180-sec FR 1 and tandem FI 180-sec FR 9 respectively; the last schedule has no familiar designation. All are diagrammed in Fig. 1. The key light was present continuously except during a 30-sec timeout of complete darkness which followed each presentation of reinforcing stimuli.

Procedure

Subjects were exposed to a schedule for a minimum of 20 sessions, consisting of 30 schedule cycles each concluded by reinforcing stimuli before definitive information for tabulation was collected. The final 20 cycles from a further 10 sessions were used in tabulation, giving a sample of 200 cycles for each subject

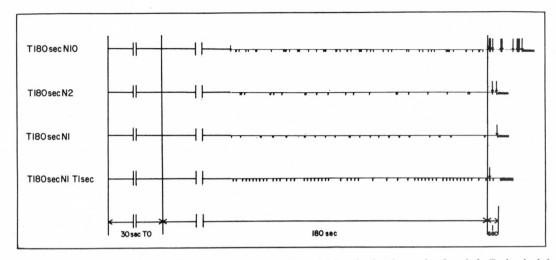

Fig. 1. Diagram of schedules. The abscissas represent time, with breaks showing omitted periods. Each schedule cycle started with a 30-sec timeout (TO) period of complete darkness followed by a 180-sec period with the key light present but with responses having no scheduled consequence. Responses are shown as brief downward deflections of the pen making the horizontal record. The key light continued until the reinforcer. The responses required by the different schedules are identified by arrows pointing to the individual responses. Finally, the first part of the period of food presentation is shown as a thickening of the line. The lines showing responses and reinforcer are polygraph records of performances on the various schedules and illustrate what was measured to obtain the distributions shown in Fig. 3, 4, and 5. The records were chosen to illustrate the schedule contingencies, *e.g.*, the possibility of continued responding in the terminal 1 sec under T 180-sec N 1 T 1-sec rather than the patterns of responding, which are shown in Fig. 3, 4, and 5. The record of T 180-sec N 1 T 1-sec, however, does illustrate the absence of short IRTs even though this particular record shows an unusually large number of responses in the 20-sec sample for this schedule. *Schedules.* T 180-sec N 10: when the key light had been present 180 sec, the reinforcer followed the tenth subsequent response. T 180-sec N 2: when the key light had been present 180 sec, the reinforcer followed the second subsequent response. T 180-sec N 1: when the key light had been present 180 sec, the reinforcer followed the first subsequent response. T 180-sec N 1 T 1-sec: when the key light had been present 180 sec, the reinforcer occurred 1 sec after the first subsequent response. Notice that the response requirements of the various schedules lead to only trivial changes in the time elapsing between onset of the key light and occurrence of the reinforcer; the difference between T 180-sec N 1 and T 180-sec N 10 in the cycles shown is about 1% of the total key-light duration.

under each procedure. Times were measured from an ink polygraph (Gerbrands Ink Writing Event Recorder) record drawn with a paper speed of 10 mm/sec (see Fig. 1). Scheduling was performed using Grason-Stadler Series 1300 Solid State Modules.

RESULTS

The characteristic pattern of FI responding, increasing rate up to the terminal rate, developed under T 180-sec N 1 (Fig. 2).

The relative frequency distributions of the durations of the three IRTs up to the reinforcing stimuli are shown in Fig. 3. For all three birds there is a deficit of short IRTs in the distribution of the last IRT before the reinforcing stimuli (L in Fig. 3) as compared to the distributions of the previous two IRTs (L-1 and L-2 respectively in Fig. 3). Short IRTs were un-

common for Birds 152 and 260, even for L-1 and L-2: they disappear altogether from the distribution of reinforced IRTs. For Bird 44, short IRTs (less than 0.1 sec) were frequent for L-1 and L-2, but short IRTs were only very infrequently concluded by reinforcing stimuli even for this bird.

Quantitative relations were examined. Panel M in Fig. 3 shows the mean of L-1 and L-2 for Bird 44. The relative frequency of responses in the different class intervals in the distribution (f_i) were multiplied by the corresponding IRT durations (t_i) to give the time occupied by IRTs of those durations $(f_i t_i)$. The relative distribution of times in IRTs of various durations $(f_i t_i / \Sigma f_i t_i)$ was then drawn (44 calc. of Fig. 3). Since the conclusion of the 180-sec requirement should occur in IRTs of different durations in proportion to the total time occupied by the different IRTs, the 44 calc. distribution should be the same as the distribution of reinforced IRTs.[3] The resemblance between 44 calc. and the observed distribution of reinforced IRTs for Bird 44 can be seen from Fig. 3 to be very close. Similar calculations and comparisons were made for Birds 152 and 266 with similar results, though since the difference in distribution between the last IRT and preceding ones was slight the demonstration was less dramatic. It is concluded that the preferential reinforcement of long IRTs under FI is qualitatively and quantitatively as would be expected from a program faithfully implementing the schedule.

The preferential reinforcement of a longer IRT should not occur if two responses, instead of one response, are required after the elapse of 180 sec (*i.e.*, under the schedule T 180-sec N 2), since the reinforcer occurs at the second response after the 180 sec quite independently of the time between the first and second responses (the L IRT). Detailed analyses are presented of the data of Pigeon 44; the data of Pigeons 152 and 260 showed the same effects although quantitatively the effects were much less. Under T 180-sec N 2, in fact, no preferential reinforcement of long IRTs was found; the distribution of the L IRT and the L-2 IRT were quite similar (Fig. 4). The distribution of the L-1 IRT, however, shows a strong shift towards longer IRTs; since this is the IRT during which the 180-sec interval must conclude, such a shift is according to expectations. When the number requirement was increased to 10 (T 180-sec N 10) the IRT distributions for the L, the L-1, and the L-2 became indistinguishable (Fig. 4). There was no differential reinforcement of classes of IRTs.

Another means of modifying the FI schedule to change the relations between IRTs and the occurrence of the reinforcer is to present the reinforcer at a fixed time after a response without regard to intervening responses. Under T 180-sec N 1 T 1-sec, the reinforcer was presented 1 sec after the first response occurring after elapse of the 180-sec interval (Fig. 1).

---

[3]An additional assumption is involved here: that the distribution of L-1 and L-2 IRTs from a number of intervals in a number of sessions is the same as the distribution of IRTs during the period of the constant terminal rate in a given interval. The good quantitative agreements between observed values and calculated values justify the assumption (see below and Discussion section).

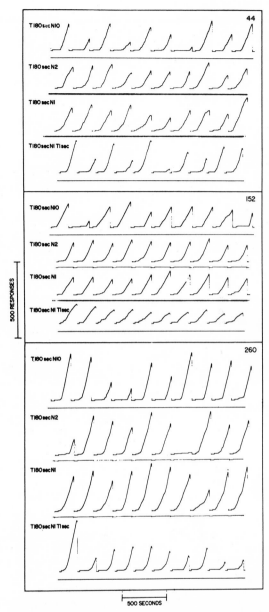

Fig. 2. Cumulative records of terminal performances under each of the schedules. Abscissa represents time, continuously through the session, including the timeout periods, which are identified by a downsetting of the response pen. The lower horizontal line on each record provides no additional information and was used merely as a help in making the chart. The details of the various schedules are given in Fig. 1 and in the text.

There are under this schedule, strictly speaking, no terminal IRTs; the last "IRTs" are truncated by the presentations of the reinforcer, and are therefore response-reinforcer times (RRfTs). The distribution of the RRfTs

T 180sec NI

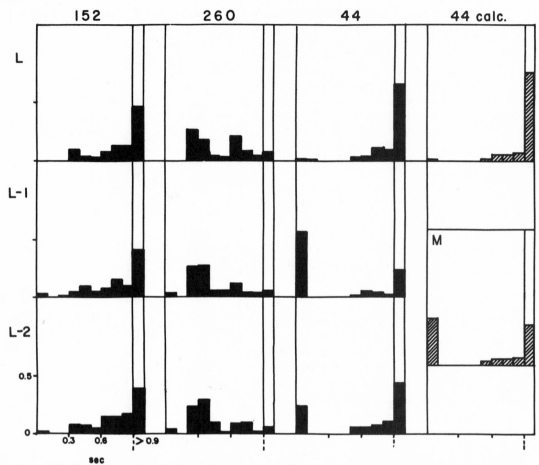

Fig. 3. Relative frequency distributions of IRTs of different durations. Abscissa: duration of IRTs in 100-msec compartments. IRTs of greater than 900 msec were pooled in the tenth compartment. Ordinate: relative frequency of IRTs. L: last IRT, *i.e.* IRT concluded by response which occasioned the reinforcer. L-1: IRT preceding L. L-2: IRT preceding L-1. M (for Bird 44): mean of distributions of L-1 and L-2. 44 calc.: proportion of total time spent in IRTs of different durations as estimated from M distribution. Notice how closely the L distribution for 44 follows the theoretically predicted distribution (44 calc.) as calculated from the independent measurements of L-1 and L-2.

is quite different from the distribution of last IRTs under the schedules previously described (Fig. 5). Again, the data of Pigeon 44 are presented.

The expected distribution of RRfTs can be calculated from the distribution of preceding IRTs. From the mean of the distributions of L-1 and L-2 (Fig. 5) the proportion of the total time spent in IRTs of different lengths was calculated, as for Fig. 2. This gives the probability that the 1-sec time period will be completed during what starts out to be an IRT of that length. But timing of the 1 sec is independent of responding so that if a reinforcer

truncates an IRT that started out to be 0.4 sec long, it is equally likely to do so in the 0.0 to 0.1, 0.1 to 0.2, 0.2 to 0.3, and 0.3 to 0.4-sec class intervals. The probability of a particular IRT being truncated is therefore partitioned equally among the class intervals shorter than the IRT. The various partial probabilities for each class interval are summed to give the calculated distribution of Fig. 5. The procedure is, in a way, the converse of Anger's (1956) IRT/Ops calculation. All IRTs that would have been longer than 1 sec were, of course, truncated by the reinforcer, and were so treated in the calculation; IRTs of this length

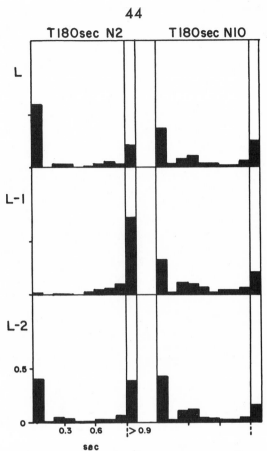

Fig. 4. Relative frequency distributions of IRTs of different lengths. Conventions as in Fig. 3. Note the deficit of short IRTs in the L-1 distribution under T 180-sec N 2, which are the IRTs during which the 180 sec must conclude. In contrast, note the similarities of the L, L-1, and L-2 distributions under T 180-sec N 10.

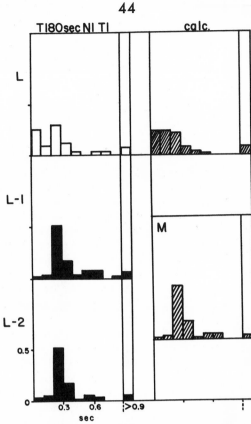

Fig. 5. Relative frequency distributions of IRTs of different lengths. Conventions as in Fig. 3 except the open bars for the L distribution draw attention to this being a response-reinforcer time distribution (RRfT) rather than an interresponse time distribution (IRT). Note the relatively flat, generally declining RRfT distribution, which is as predicted under the assumption of a random truncation of IRTs (the "calc" distribution).

occurred too infrequently to affect the distributions appreciably. The agreement with the observed distribution is fair (Fig. 5); there is a deficit in the second class interval of the observed distribution compared to the calculated. However, the total of the first three class intervals for the observed and calculated distributions is closely similar.

The effects of the changes in the occurrence of the reinforcer in relation to the final response on the general pattern of responding are shown in Fig. 2. The most striking feature is the similarity of the performances both in the patterns of the cumulative records (Fig. 2) and in the averaged data (Fig. 6). Under all schedules, a progressive increase of rate through the interval, characteristic of FI re-

sponding, occurs. Even the rate of increase is much the same under all the schedules except T 180-sec N 1 T 1-sec (Fig. 6). Under T 180-sec N 1 T 1-sec the rates of responding are uniformly less than under the other schedule, but since the rate in each segment is reduced in approximately the same proportion, the *pattern* of the changing responding is similar under all the schedules. The general pattern of FI responding is therefore not importantly dependent on the preferential reinforcement of longer IRTs nor, apparently, on any particular conditions just at the time the reinforcer is presented. The only uniform features of the schedules were the T 180-sec segment and a response requirement; the characteristic fixed-interval pattern of responding seems to de-

Table 1

Mean Rates of Responding (Responses per Second) under the Various Schedules Studied

	Schedule			
Bird	T 180-sec N 10	T 180-sec N 2	T 180-sec N 1	T 180-sec N 1 T 1-sec
44	0.72	0.74	0.93	0.55
152	0.61	0.70	0.67	0.40
260	1.21	1.10	1.10	0.45
Mean	0.85	0.85	0.90	0.47

pend directly on the fixed-interval characteristic of the schedule.

The modifications of the schedule caused substantial changes in aspects of the responding other than the general pattern. While T 180-sec N 1, T 180-sec N 2, and T 180-sec N 10 engendered similar mean rates, the mean rate under T 180-sec N 1 T 1-sec was only about half of that under T 180-sec N 1 (Fig. 2 and Table). Short IRTs were reduced under T 180-sec N 1 T 1-sec (Fig. 3 and 5) even though the mean RRfT was less than 250 msec for each of the birds. Inspection of Fig. 2 suggests that change from T 180-sec N 1 to T 180-sec N 2 or T 180-sec N 10 lead to a prolongation of the initial pause in the intervals and a more abrupt acceleration to terminal rates of responding. But this suggestion does not emerge in the averaged figures (Fig. 6). Further analysis of such small but possibly significant changes in the pattern of FI responding must await better mathematical description of the pattern.

DISCUSSION

The argument of Skinner (1938, p. 275), that under a fixed-interval schedule of reinforcement ("periodic reconditioning"), if there are local variations in rate, then "a reinforced response will more frequently follow a relatively long interval" without a response, has been confirmed experimentally. Local variations in rate are clearly apparent in Fig. 1. The trend to longer IRTs for the reinforced IRTs is best discerned as a virtual elimination of very short (<0.1-sec) IRTs from the distribution of reinforced IRTs (Fig. 3). Such an effect followed necessarily from the actual distributions of the preceding IRTs, but the computation could not have been made without the numerical information.

In making the calculations, it was assumed that at the end of the interval the rate of re-

sponding had asymptoted, so that the distribution of L, L-1, and L-2 IRTs would have been the same if the reinforcer had not intervened. Several pieces of evidence support the assumption: the great similarities of the L-1 and L-2 distributions under T 180-sec N 1 (Fig. 3); the L and L-2 distributions under T 180-sec N 2 (Fig. 4); the L-1 and L-2 distributions under T 180-sec N 1 T 1-sec (Fig. 5) and of the L, L-1,

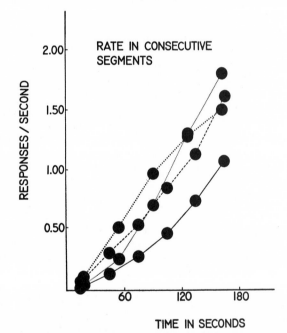

Fig. 6. Mean rates of responding in consecutive segments of intervals. Abscissa: time from start of interval. Ordinate: rate in responses per second. Heavy dotted line: T 180-sec N 10. Dashed line: T 180-sec N 1. Light dotted line: T 180-sec N 2. Solid line: T 180-sec N 1 T 1-sec. Responding in 30-sec segments of T 180-sec N 1 and T 180-sec N 1 T 1-sec and in 36-sec segments of T 180-sec N 2 and T 180-sec N 10 was accumulated over the cycles of a session and over the 10 definitive sessions on a schedule and, finally, over the three birds to obtain the graphed figures. There is no obvious difference in the progression of rates under the different modifications, nor in the rates themselves except for T 180-sec N 1 T 1-sec.

and L-2 distributions under T 180-sec N 3 (Fig. 4) all point to a constant terminal mean rate.

The distributions of the L, L-1, and L-2 IRTs under T 180-sec N 10 (tandem FI 3-min FR 9) give no support to the notion that a fixed-ratio schedule of reinforcement (FR) "favors the reinforcement of responses following relatively short intervals" (Skinner, 1938, p. 284). Under FR, the probability that an IRT will be reinforced is exactly equal to the probability of occurrence of the IRT in the terminal mean rate of responding (*i.e.*, the L distribution is the same as the L-1 and L-2 distributions in Fig. 4). Some other mechanism for the tendency of FR to lead to high rates of responding must be sought, such as a positive feedback loop (Dews, 1962).

The persistence of the FI pattern of responding under tandem FI FR schedules confirms the findings of Ferster and Skinner (1957, p. 416 *et seq*). These authors also noted an increase in overall mean rate of responding in going from FI to tandem FI FR, an effect not seen in the present series of experiments. The difference may be due to the parameter values; Ferster and Skinner worked with a long interval of 2700 sec in contrast to the 180 sec of the present experiments. Ferster and Skinner superimposed the tandem FR on very low mean rates of responding, whereas in the present experiments the tandem FR was superimposed on already quite high rates of responding (0.5 to 1.0 responses/sec). The same considerations may explain the much lower tendency for a burst and pause pattern of local responding to occur in the present experiments than in the experiments of Ferster and Skinner (1957). The grouping of responses in bursts, seen by Ferster and Skinner (1957) is an important phenomenon seen also under tandem schedules such as N 18 $\overline{\text{T 2-sec}}$ N 4[4] (an initial ratio of 18, a minimum pause of 2 sec, and a terminal ratio of 4) (Morse and Herrnstein, 1956) and under second-order schedules of reinforcement (Kelleher, 1966). All this evidence supports the present conclusion that the effect of a reinforcer in a schedule of reinforcement exerts its effects directly over much longer periods of time than the last IRT or the last few IRTs. At the same time, the change from essentially simultaneous presentation of the reinforcer at the reinforced response (under T 180-sec N 1) to an average delay between last response and reinforcer of less than 250 msec (under T 180-sec N 1 T 1-sec) lead to an approximate halving of number of responses made per interval. So, circumstance very close in time to the occurrence of the reinforcer can be very important, because of that proximity, in determining certain attributes of responding under a schedule of reinforcement.

Anger has studied the distribution of reinforced IRTs in rats responding under VI 300-sec (Anger, 1956). He chose VI to minimize systematic changes in IRT distributions with time since reinforcement (such systematic changes giving the FI scallop have been the major focus of attention in the present work). Anger used a 4-sec (or 8-sec) class interval for his IRT distributions and found that the IRT/Op distribution seemed to follow the Rf/Hr distribution for the different IRT lengths, resulting in favoring of "short" (<8-sec) IRTs. In the present work, class intervals of 0.10 sec have been used; all the IRTs would have been "short" by Anger's scale, being almost exclusively less than 1 sec. In the present work, Rf/Hr of IRTs of less than 0.10 sec were essentially zero under T 180-sec N 1, yet such short IRTs persisted. The gross differences in time scales prevent the present results from either confirming or conflicting with Anger's. Parenthetically, the importance of taking into account absolute times is obvious from these considerations. Had Anger presented his results in terms of per cent success or any other derived measure eliminating absolute time, we would have been faced with an uninterpretable and irreconcilable contradiction. As things are, it can be seen at what parameter values more experimental results are needed.

---

[4]The bar over the T 2-sec $\overline{\text{(T 2-sec)}}$ in this nomenclature means that the 2 sec must elapse *without* a response to fulfill the schedule requirements.

REFERENCES

Anger, D. The dependence of interresponse times upon the relative reinforcement of different interresponse times. *Journal of Experimental Psychology,* 1956, **52**, 145-161.

Dews, P. B. Analysis of effects of psychopharmacological agents in behavioral terms. *Federation Proceedings,* 1958, **17**, 1024-1030.

Dews, P. B. Free operant behavior under conditions of delayed reinforcement, I. CRF-type schedules. *Journal of the Experimental Analysis of Behavior,* 1960, **3**, 221-234.

Dews, P. B. The effect of multiple S^Δ periods on responding on a fixed-interval schedule. *Journal of the Experimental Analysis of Behavior*, 1962, **5**, 369-374.

Dews, P. B. The effect of multiple S^Δ periods on responding on a fixed-interval schedule: IV. Effect of continuous S^Δ with only short S^D probes. *Journal of the Experimental Analysis of Behavior*, 1966, **9**, 147-151.

Dews, P. B. The theory of fixed-interval responding. In W. N. Schoenfeld and J. Farmer (Eds.), *Theories of reinforcement schedules*. New York: Appleton-Century-Crofts. (in press)

Ferster, C. B. and Skinner, B. F. *Schedules of reinforcement*. New York: Appleton-Century-Crofts, 1957.

Kelleher, R. T. Chaining and conditioned reinforcement. In W. K. Honig (Ed.), *Operant behavior: areas of research and application*. New York: Appleton-Century-Crofts, 1966. Pp. 160-212.

Kelleher, R. T. and Morse, W. H. Determinants of the specificity of behavioral effects of drugs. *Ergebnisse der Physiologie*, 1968, **60**, 1-56.

Morse, W. H. and Herrnstein, R. J. Effects of drugs on characteristics of behavior maintained by complex schedules of intermittent positive reinforcement. *Annals of New York Academy of Science*, 1956, **65**, 303-317.

Revusky, S. H. Mathematical analysis of the durations of reinforced interresponse times during variable interval reinforcement. *Psychometrika*, 1962, **27**, 307-314.

Skinner, B. F. *The behavior of organisms*. New York: Appleton-Century-Crofts, 1938.

Skinner, B. F. *Science and human behavior*. New York: Macmillan, 1953.

Received 1 November 1967.

COMBINED ACTION OF DIAZEPAM AND d-AMPHETAMINE ON FIXED-INTERVAL PERFORMANCE IN CATS[1]

Marc Richelle

UNIVERSITY OF LIÈGE—BELGIUM

Cats trained under a fixed-interval 5-min schedule of milk presentation were injected with diazepam, amphetamine, and combinations of amphetamine and diazepam. Diazepam increased overall response rate as a function of the dose and disrupted the temporal pattern of responding. Low doses of amphetamine (0.5 mg/kg) usually increased the response rate; higher doses (1 to 2 mg/kg) either decreased the response rate or had little effect. Amphetamine always disrupted the temporal pattern of responding, even though it did not affect the overall rate. When doses of amphetamine that increased the response rate or left it unchanged were combined with diazepam, a potentiated increase in response rate occurred. When doses of amphetamine that decreased the response rate were combined with diazepam, the amphetamine-induced rate decreases were reversed at least partially. Less clear potentiation of disruption of the temporal pattern of responding was observed when amphetamine and diazepam were combined.

The present research sought to describe the effects of diazepam (DZP) and d-amphetamine (AMPH) on positively reinforced behavior in cats, and to analyze the behavioral effects obtained when these two compounds, belonging to different pharmacological classes, were combined.

Frequently, pharmacologists have attempted to determine the mode of action of one drug by combining it with a second drug of known action. A similar approach at the behavioral level might provide important evidence about the mechanisms by which drugs affect behavior. Drug-combination studies in behavioral pharmacology are especially useful in testing the relevance of behavioral hypotheses in interpreting the effects of psychotropic compounds.

METHOD

Subjects

Six adult cats were used, Nr 20 (male) and 21 (male) in Exp. 1, Nr 22 (female), 23 (female), 24 (male), and 25 (male) in Exp. 2. All had an experimental history, ranging from 1 to 2 yr, on fixed-interval (FI) schedules, but had never been given drugs. They lived in groups of two to three animals in large home cages, were fed a standard ration (50 g) of wet food for cats, and received milk as the reinforcer in the experimental cage. When no experi-

ment took place, on weekends, an equivalent amount of milk was given in the home cage.

Apparatus

The cats were studied in a cubic experimental cage (edge: 45 cm) equipped with a response lever 7.5 cm above the floor and protruding 5 cm from the wall. An electrically operated tap was used to dispense milk automatically. Each reinforcement consisted of 0.2 ml of milk, delivered in a tray to the left of the response lever. A 15-w bulb provided light during the experiment. The experimental cage was enclosed in an isolating compartment, providing partial sound isolation. The controlling units, composed of standard relay circuits, counters, and cumulative recorder, were located in another room.

Procedure

Subjects were put in the experimental cage for 90 min daily, at approximately the same hour each day, Monday to Friday. Stable behavior under FI 5-min was obtained after four

[1]Dedicated to B. F. Skinner in his sixty-fifth year. Compounds used in this study were kindly supplied by Hofmann-Laroche (Valium) and Laboratoire Delagrange (Maxiton). I thank both for their help. Reprints may be obtained from the author, Dept. of Experimental Psychology, University of Liège, 32, Boulevard de la Constitution, Liège, Belgium. The technical assistance of N. Fayen, C. Guffens, and C. Rigo is gratefully acknowledged.

to eight weeks. The results averaged from the last 10 sessions were used as control values.

The drug study was then started, according to a schedule slightly different in the successive Exp. 1 and 2.

Experiment 1 sought to obtain the dose-effect relationship for five doses of DZP and three doses of AMPH, and for the 15 possible combinations of the two drugs. Doses in mg per kg of body weight were as follows:

DZP   :   0.03, 0.0625, 0.125, 0.25, 0.50
AMPH :   0.5, 1, 2

Experiment 2 attempted to verify in four other cats the potentiated rate increase observed in Exp. 1 when DZP and AMPH were combined. Two doses of each drug were selected and administered alone and in the four possible dose combinations. The doses were in both cases the smallest and the largest doses used in Exp. 1, *i.e.*, 0.03 and 0.5 DZP and 0.5 and 2 AMPH. In addition, the effects of drug combination were determined during one session under an extinction schedule.

The drugs were administered i.p. 15 to 20 min before the session. AMPH was dissolved in natrium chloride solution. DZP was administered in the injectable solvent supplied for clinical use.[2] When the effects of two compounds were studied, two injections were made. Drug sessions took place every other day, provided that the subject's behavior had returned to the control baseline the day before. Drugs were never administered on a day following a weekend without experimental session.

Data Recording and Analysis

Responses and reinforcements were recorded on a cumulative recorder and digital counters. In addition, responses were counted on a set of eight counters. Each of these counters recorded the responses emitted during one of the successive fractions of 37.5 sec that divided the 5-min interval.

The analysis of results is based on the overall response rate and on the pattern of responding during the fixed interval. The rate under drug was compared to the control value

---

[2]The formula of the solvent for 5-mg DZP is: benzylic alcohol, 15.7 mg, aethylic alcohol, 80.6 mg, N,N-dimethylacetamid, 94 mg, tetrahydrofurfuryl alcohol polyaethylen glycol, 434 mg, aqua q.s. ad. 1 ml (Hoffmann-Laroche, Valium[R]).

by computing the output ratio, obtained by dividing the number of responses under drug by the number of responses averaged from 10 control sessions preceding the pharmacological tests (Smith, 1964). As a measure of the pattern of responding during the fixed interval, the index of curvature proposed by Fry, Kelleher, and Cook (1960) was computed.

The numbers of responses recorded in the eight 37.5-sec subdivisions of the 5-min interval were divided by the number of intervals in the session. These averaged values were used as a basis to compute the curvature index. As for overall rate, pre-drug controls were derived from 10 sessions.

The index of curvature is given by the formula

$$I = \frac{(n-1) \; R_n - 2 \sum_{i=1}^{n-1} R_i}{nR_n}$$

where n is the number of subdivisions in the time interval; Rn the cumulated number of responses obtained by summing up the responses emitted in the last subdivision plus all the responses emitted in the $(n-1)$ preceding subdivisions. The maximal value of the index depends on the number of subdivisions used. With eight subdivisions the maximum is 0.875. As the positively accelerated rate typical of FI schedule was preserved throughout the pharmacological tests, the index retained its positive value.

RESULTS

Experiment 1

Pre-drug control. The stabilized pattern of responding under FI 5-min shows the "scalloping" seen in many different species. A typical cumulative record is shown in Fig. 1A. The mean number of responses emitted per minute was 4.3 for Cat 20 and 2.9 for Cat 21. The index of curvature was 0.64 and 0.67 respectively.

Effects of DZP. In both Cats 20 and 21, DZP produced an increase in the rate of responding, striking at doses of 0.125, 0.25, and 0.50 mg/kg for Cat 20, and at doses of 0.25 and 0.50 mg/kg for Cat 21. The number of responses was multiplied by a factor of 2 to 4, as can be seen from Fig. 2.

Cumulative curves for Cat 20 are shown in Fig. 1, B to F.

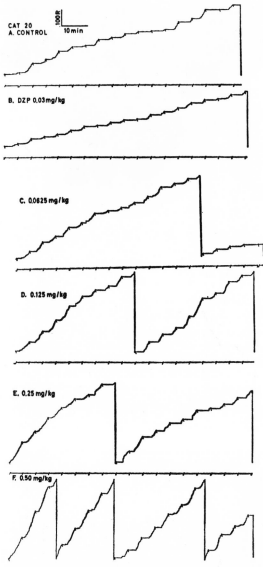

Fig. 1. Cumulative response records of Cat 20 on FI 5-min, showing the dose-effect relationship for DZP. A: Control; B to F: increasing doses of DZP. The pen tracing the horizontal line at the bottom of each graph was deflected when the 5 min elapsed; it came back to the initial position when the reinforced response was emitted.

The temporal pattern of responding obtained after stabilization of FI 5-min was altered by the drug. This is apparent from cumulative curves in Fig. 1, B to F. Figure 3 shows the decrease of the index of curvature as a function of the dose.

Effect of AMPH. The effects of AMPH administered alone are indicated in Fig. 2 and 3 by horizontal lines across the graphs.

In Cat 20, AMPH produced no increase in response rate at the doses selected. No significant effect was obtained at the dose of 0.5 and 1 mg/kg. Responding was almost completely suppressed after 2 mg/kg.

In Cat 21, AMPH at the dose of 0.5 mg/kg doubled the number of responses. A less significant increase was observed for the two higher doses (see Fig. 2).

A disruption of the temporal pattern of responding, as expressed by the index of curvature, was observed; this disruption was not correlated with increases in overall response rate. In Cat 20, the index dropped sharply with 1 mg/kg, though the number of responses did not deviate significantly from the control value. In Cat 21, the temporal pattern was disrupted increasingly with dosage, though the output ratio was at a maximum with the smallest dose (see Fig. 3).

Table 1 shows the effect of the three doses of AMPH on the rate in each of the successive subdivisions of the interval for Cat 21. Results are expressed in responses per minute. Larger doses tended to increase the low rate in the first parts of the interval and to decrease the high rate typical in the last subdivisions.

Table 1

Number of responses/min in each of the eight subdivisions of FI 5-min under AMPH for Cat 21.

	Successive Subdivisions of FI							
	1	2	3	4	5	6	7	8
control	0	0	0.2	0.3	1.3	3.0	6.6	12.2
0.5 mg/kg AMPH	0	0	0	3.2	5.6	8.5	13.4	17.6
1 mg/kg AMPH	0	0.5	0.8	2.7	4.9	8.6	7.0	10.4
2 mg/kg AMPH	0	0.8	2.6	6.2	5.8	6.7	7.7	8.8

Effect of DZP + AMPH combinations. The most frequent effect, when the two drugs were combined, was a potentiation of the rate-increasing effect of DZP (see Fig. 2).

In Cat 21, where AMPH alone increased response rate slightly, and where the rate increase due to DZP was negligible below the dose of 0.25 mg/kg, a sharp increase was observed when the two drugs were combined, even at the smallest doses. The control rate was multiplied by a factor of 6 to 9 when the highest dose of DZP or of AMPH was included in the combination. The potentiation was

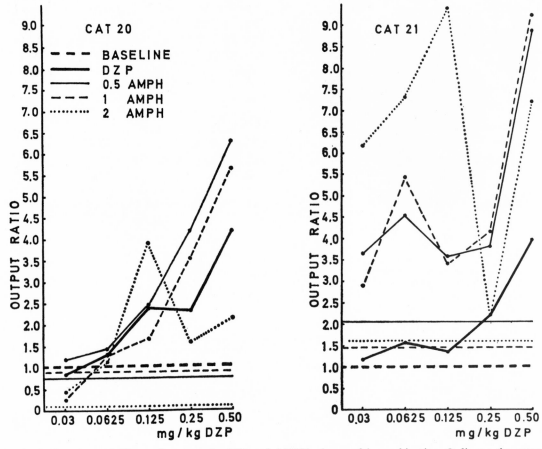

Fig. 2. Experiment I. Change in rate under DZP and AMPH, alone and in combination. Ordinate: the output ratio, computed by dividing the total output under drug by the control output. Abscissa: doses of DZP. The heavy solid curve is for DZP alone. The other curves are for doses of AMPH + DZP, as indicated in the upper-left corner. Results obtained with AMPH alone are given by the horizontal lines.

observed with 14 of the 15 possible combinations (one atypical result was obtained with 0.25 mg/kg DZP + 2 mg/kg AMPH). The phenomenon is illustrated by sample cumulative curves in Fig. 4.

In Cat 20, where AMPH either decreased response rate or had little effect, DZP usually partially reversed the AMPH rate decrease, or DZP rate increases were potentiated by those AMPH doses that had little effect when given alone. These relationships were particularly true when the dose of DZP was high.

The effect of the drug combination on the temporal pattern of responding cannot be summarized in a single relationship. The changes in the index of curvature shown in Fig. 3 do not strictly correlate with the variations in rate as seen in Fig. 2. At the higher end of the DZP dose-response curve, AMPH

combined with DZP did nothing that DZP alone did not do: the index was close to the value obtained with DZP alone. At lower doses of DZP combined with 0.5 mg/kg AMPH, AMPH potentiated the changes seen after DZP alone. The effects on rate of the same dose combinations were negligible in Cat 20. In Cat 21, the potentiated increase in rate was far less pronounced than with higher doses, while the index of curvature reached the lowest value obtained in this experiment. Finally, the deteriorating effect of high doses of AMPH was at least partially antagonized by low and medium doses of DZP.

This complex picture clearly indicates that the effects of the combined drugs on the temporal pattern of responding are not merely a reflection of the effects on overall rate. It must be noted that the potentiated increase in over-

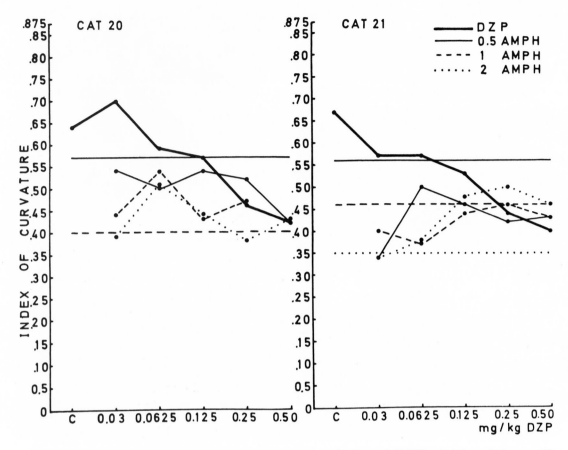

Fig. 3. Experiment I. Change in curvature index as a function of DZP and AMPH, administered alone and in combination. Ordinate: index of curvature computed from Fry, Kelleher, and Cook's formula. Abscissa: C = pre-drug control value, followed by the doses of DZP. The heavy solid curve is for DZP alone. The other curves are for doses of AMPH + DZP, as indicated in the upper right corner. Results obtained with AMPH alone are given by the horizontal lines; the index of curvature was not computed for Cat 20 under 2 mg/kg AMPH because responding was almost completely suppressed at that dose.

all rate never concealed a sharp increase of output during the first part of the interval (the classical "pausing period" of the FI) that would counterbalance an unchanged or reduced rate during the final part. An analysis of the proportions of responses emitted in each of the eight successive subdivisions of the 5-min interval, the details of which are not reported here, did not show any differential effect on "low" and "high" control rates that were typical of the first and the last part of the interval respectively.

Expressed in absolute figures, the increase was far more marked during the last 37.5-sec subdivision, despite the higher initial value, than during any of the first four periods, in which the initial value was close to zero.

Table 2 shows a typical example, drawn

from the results of Cat 21, for the combination 0.5 mg/kg DZP + 0.5 mg/kg AMPH, corresponding to cumulative curve F in Fig. 4.

Table 2

Number of R/min in each of the eight subdivisions of the FI under one DZP + AMPH combination in Cat 21.

	Successive Subdivisions of FI							
	1	2	3	4	5	6	7	8
[1]control	0	0	0.2	0.3	1.3	3.0	6.6	12.2
0.5 mg/kg [2]DZP + 0.5 mg/kg AMPH	0	1.9	8	20.8	35.5	41.8	46.9	54.6
increase (2 minus 1)	0	1.9	7.8	20.5	34.2	38.8	40.3	42.4

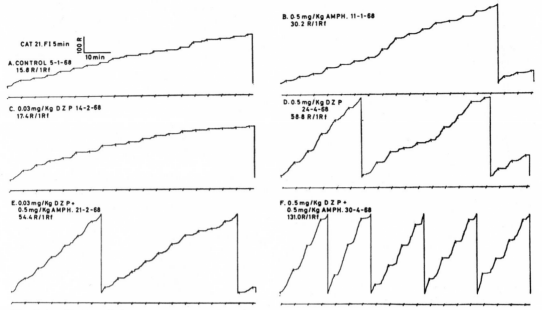

Fig. 4. Cat 21. Cumulative response records illustrating the potentiation between DZP and AMPH. The average number of responses per interval is given with each curve (n R/1Rf).

Experiment 2

Pre-drug control. The mean numbers of responses per minute, giving the reference value for computing the output ratio, are as follows:

Cat Nr	responses/min
22	5.4
23	5.9
24	5.7
25	8.6

The general pattern of responding was the same as in Exp. 1, but the total output was higher than in Cat 20 and 21. Except for Cat 24, the temporal pattern of responding was somewhat different from that of the subjects in Exp. 1. Control values of the index of curvature are shown on the first point of solid curves in Fig. 6.

Effect of DZP. The effects of DZP on the rate of responding are shown in Fig. 5. An increase in the number of responses was observed in all subjects after administration of 0.5 mg/kg. It was most pronounced in Cat 22 and 24, the output under drug corresponding to 250 and 256% of the control, respectively. The dose of 0.03 mg/kg produced either an increase (Cat 22 and 24) or a slight decrease (in Cat 23 and 25, practically negligible in the former animal). These results are in line with the results of Exp. 1.

The temporal pattern of responding was altered after administration of the higher dose in all subjects except Cat 25. The smaller dose either: failed to affect the index of curvature (Cat 22), reduced it less markedly than the higher dose (Cat 24), or increased it (Cats 23 and 25) (see Fig. 6).

Effect of AMPH. The response rate was clearly increased after 0.5 mg/kg for all animals except Cat 25. Under 2 mg/kg, the number of responses was close to the control value except for Cat 24, which showed a decrease. The index of curvature was altered to approximately the same extent for the two doses.

Effect of DZP + AMPH combinations. As can be seen from Fig. 5, a potentiation of the rate increase was observed in Cat 22 for all four combinations; in Cat 23 when DZP was combined with 0.5 mg/kg AMPH, and in Cat 24 and 25 for the combination 0.5 mg/kg DZP + 0.5 mg/kg AMPH. An antagonizing effect of the amphetamine-induced depression in rate was observed in Cat 24 with the combination of 0.5 mg/kg DZP + 2 mg/kg AMPH.

Two atypical results were obtained. In Cats 23 and 24 with the combination of 0.03 mg/kg DZP + 2 mg/kg AMPH, the response rate was markedly reduced. In Cat 24, it resembled the effect of AMPH alone, and the results obtained with the larger dose of DZP indicate that the

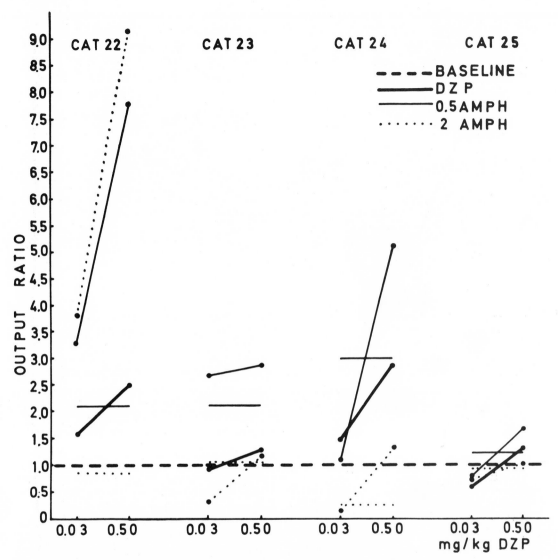

Fig. 5. Experiment II. Change in rate under DZP and AMPH, alone and in combination. Ordinate: output ratio; abscissa: doses of DZP. See Fig. 2 for key to reading.

smaller dose was insufficient to antagonize the effect of AMPH. In Cat 23, both drugs injected alone left the number of responses unaltered. A similar result was noted once in Exp. 1, in Cat 20 (DZP 0.03 mg/kg + AMPH 1 mg).

The index of curvature reflected in some cases a potentiation of the decreasing effect of both drugs and in some cases an antagonizing action, the decreasing effect of AMPH being partially attenuated by DZP (see Fig. 6).

Experimental extinction. When no milk was placed in the automatic dispenser and no drug was injected, experimental extinction showed the usual pattern: the rate of respond-

ing was high right after the first operation of the empty dispenser. Subjects were always placed in the experimental cage when a fixed-interval cycle was completed, so that their first response was reinforced. The high rates, typical of a beginning extinction session, occurred during the first and second interval. By the third interval, responding was almost completely eliminated. Cumulative curves for the four subjects are shown in Fig. 7A.

Contrasting with this pattern, the curves obtained under drug (0.5 mg/kg DZP + 0.5 mg/kg AMPH), indicate a surprising resistance to extinction. The rate of responding

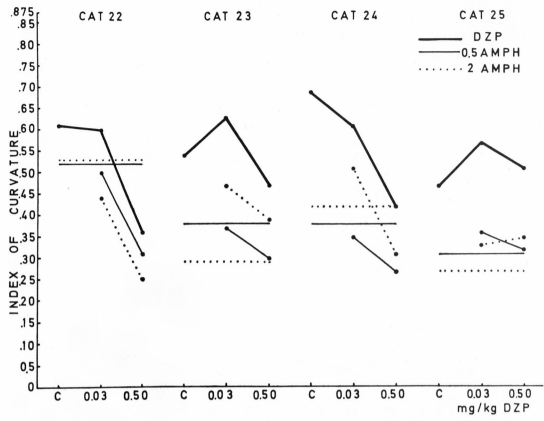

Fig. 6. Experiment II. Change in index of curvature under DZP and AMPH, alone and in combination. Ordinate: index of curvature. Abscissa: C = pre-drug control value, followed by doses of DZP. See Fig. 3 for key to reading.

was sustained throughout the session, reaching a level close to the one observed under identical pharmacological conditions in a normal fixed-interval session (see Fig. 7B).

Increased food deprivation test. It is highly improbable that an increase in hunger would explain the increased rate of responding under DZP, AMPH, or their combination. A similar hypothesis was discarded in a study on chlordiazepoxide (Richelle, 1962) in which food deprivation was extended over a 72-hr period, in addition to the permanent deprivation maintained throughout the experiment. Moreover, AMPH is known as an anorexic drug and, supposing that a change in hunger might explain the effect of DZP, it would not explain the potentiation of AMPH, nor the cases of antagonism.

For four subjects deprived of food in their home cage for 48 hr, the rate of responding was not changed.

DISCUSSION

The rate-increasing effect of benzodiazepines has been confirmed repeatedly for chlordiazepoxide (Richelle, 1962; Richelle and Djahanguiri, 1964; Richelle, Xhenseval, Fontaine, and Thone, 1962; Cook and Kelleher, 1963). DZP has been reported to increase the response rate in rats in intracranial self-stimulation experiments (Olds, 1966). Our results show that this action on operant behavior is not restricted to one species and is not specific to hypothalamic electric reinforcement. Olds' interpretation of her results, resorting to "specific facilitatory effects on hypothalamic reward systems" seems too simple to account for the rather widespread rate increasing action of diazepines on operant behavior. We cannot *a priori* rule out the possibility that this action is related to an effect on hypothalamic reward systems, or, in other words, to some basic motivational mech-

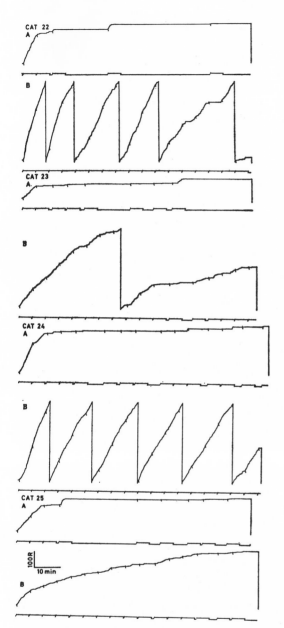

Fig. 7. Experiment II. Experimental extinction without drug (curves marked A) and under 0.5 mg/kg DZP + 0.5 mg/kg AMPH (curves B) in four individual subjects.

diazepoxide in the same schedule when a locomotor response was used, and Cook and Catania (1964) under chlordiazepoxide in a fixed-interval shock escape schedule.

The present results with AMPH confirm, on the whole, the numerous reports on the behavioral action of this drug. The quantitative analysis of the change in rate in the different subdivisions of the fixed interval indicates the well-known tendency of AMPH to increase low rates and to decrease high rates at appropriate doses (Kelleher and Morse, 1968). However, at the dose of 0.5 mg/kg, an increase in rate was observed in the final part of the interval and is negligible in the first part. The resistance of the pause might be due to the long training of the present subjects, especially in the two cats used in Exp. 1.

The rate-increasing effects of diazepam were frequently potentiated by amphetamine; DZP also antagonized the rate-decreasing effect found with high doses of the latter drug. Potentiation by amphetamine of the rate-increasing effects of another diazepine, chlordiazepoxide, has been described by Rushton and Steinberg (1966). Similar phenomena were observed after combined administration of amphetamine and barbiturates (Rushton and Steinberg, 1963; Rutledge and Kelleher, 1965). The mechanism of this potentiation and antagonism are unknown.

Behavioral analysis shows that the potentiation of DZP effects by amphetamine is not a general effect: it is not observed for each dose combination in all individuals. The effects of amphetamine alone show great interindividual variability, but do not help to predict unequivocally the potentiation of diazepam effects. Another complication comes from the fact that the type of behavior being studied might be an important variable, the potentiation appearing in some cases and not in other cases, as was shown for amphetamine-barbiturate combinations. Further research should seek to verify the potentiation effect on behavior maintained by other schedules.

anism supposedly common to all positively reinforced behavior. However, a number of studies have shown that increases in response rate due to diazepines are not limited to positively reinforced behavior: Heise and Boff (1962) observed it in a Sidman avoidance schedule under nitrazepam and diazepam, Fontaine and Richelle (1969) under chlor-

REFERENCES

Cook, L. and Catania, A. C. Effects of drugs on avoidance and escape behavior. *Federal Proceedings*, 1964, **23**, 818-835.

Cook, L. and Kelleher, R. T. Effects of drugs on behavior. *Annual Review of Pharmacology*, 1963, **3**, 205-222.

Fontaine, O. and Richelle, M. Etude comparative de la chlorpromazine et du chlordiazepoxide sur une série de comportements avec renforcement positif et négatif chez le rat. *Psychologica Belgica*, 1969, **9,** 17-29.

Fry, W., Kelleher, R. T., and Cook, L. A mathematical index of performance on fixed-interval schedules of reinforcement. *Journal of the Experimental Analysis of Behavior*, 1960, **3,** 193-199.

Heise, G. A. and Boff, E. Continuous avoidance as a baseline for measuring behavioral effects of drugs. *Psychopharmacologia*, 1962, **3,** 264-282.

Kelleher, R. T. and Morse, W. H. Determinants of the specificity of behavioral effects of drugs. *Ergebnisse der Physiologie*, Band 60, Springer-Verlag, Berlin 1968, 1-56.

Olds, M. E. Facilitatory action of diazepam and chlordiazepoxide on hypothalamic reward behavior. *Journal of Comparative and Physiological Psychology*, 1966, **62,** 136-140.

Richelle, M. Action du chlordiazepoxide sur les régulations temporelles dans un comportement conditionné chez le chat. *Archives internationales de Pharmacodynamie*, 1962, **140,** 434-449.

Richelle, M., and Djanhanguiri, B. Effet d'un traite-ment prolongé au chlordiazepoxide sur un conditionnement temporel chez le rat. *Psychopharmacologia*, 1964, **5,** 106-114.

Richelle, M., Xhenseval, B., Fontaine, O., and Thone, L. Action of chlordiazepoxide on two types of temporal conditioning in rats. *International Journal of Neuropharmacology.*, 1962, **1,** 381-391.

Rushton, R. and Steinberg, H. Combined effects of chlordiazepoxide and dexamphetamine on activity of rats in an unfamiliar environment. *Nature*, 1966, **211,** 1312-1313.

Rushton, R. and Steinberg, H. Dose-response relations of amphetamine-barbiturate mixtures. *Nature*, 1963, **197,** 1017-1018.

Rutledge, Ch. O. and Kelleher, R. T. Interactions between the effects of methamphetamine and pentobarbital on operant behavior in the pigeon. *Psychopharmacologia*, 1965, **7,** 400-408.

Smith, C. B. Effects of *d*-amphetamine upon operant behavior of pigeon: enhancement by reserpine. *Journal of Pharmacology and Experimental Therapeutics*, 1964, **146,** 167-174.

Received 1 February 1969.

EFFECTS OF INSTRUCTIONS AND REINFORCEMENT-FEEDBACK ON HUMAN OPERANT BEHAVIOR MAINTAINED BY FIXED-INTERVAL REINFORCEMENT[1]

ALAN BARON, ARNOLD KAUFMAN, AND KATHLEEN A. STAUBER

UNIVERSITY OF WISCONSIN—MILWAUKEE

In three experiments, human subjects were trained on a five-component multiple schedule with different fixed intervals of monetary reinforcement scheduled in the different components. Subjects uninstructed about the fixed-interval schedules manifested high and generally equivalent rates regardless of the particular component. By comparison, subjects given instructions about the schedules showed orderly progressions of rates and temporal patterning as a function of the interreinforcement intervals, particularly when feedback about reinforcement was delivered but also when reinforcement-feedback was withheld. Administration of the instructions-reinforcement combination to subjects who had already developed poorly differentiated behavior, however, did not make their behavior substantially better differentiated. When cost was imposed for responding, both instructed and uninstructed subjects showed low and differentiated rates regardless of their prior histories. It was concluded that instructions can have major influences on the establishment and maintenance of human operant behavior.

Several experiments have demonstrated the influence of instructions on the acquisition and maintenance of human operant performance. One finding has been that when instructions about the desired response are omitted, substantial numbers of subjects may fail to acquire the response despite scheduling of reinforcing contingencies deemed favorable for acquisition (*e.g.*, Ader and Tatum, 1961; Ayllon and Azrin, 1964; Turner and Solomon, 1962). By comparison, addition of instructions about the desired response results in rapid adoption of the response (*e.g.*, Ayllon and Azrin, 1964; Baron and Kaufman, 1966) but also may induce inappropriately high rates, particularly on temporally based schedules (Kaufman, Baron, and Kopp, 1966; Weiner, 1962). More detailed instructions about reinforcing contingencies, as well as the response itself, typically produce response rates approximating the requirements of the reinforcement schedule (*e.g.*, Dews and Morse, 1958; Kauf-

man *et al.*, 1966; Weiner, 1962). Finally, several studies have shown that instructions about the reinforcement schedule may have effects overriding those of the schedule itself. Thus, instructions can induce behavior in the absence of reinforcement (Ayllon and Azrin, 1964; Kaufman *et al.*, 1966), and can produce behaviors more in accord with instructions than with actually scheduled reinforcement (Kaufman *et al.*, 1966; Lippman and Meyer, 1967).

The present experiment dealt with performances by human subjects on fixed-interval schedules of reinforcement, and, in particular, the influences of instructions on such performance. Holland (1958) reported that uninstructed subjects exhibited the temporal patterning characteristic of subhuman subjects on fixed-interval schedules, with overall response rates decreasing with increases in the duration of the fixed interval. Other researchers (*e.g.*, Blair, 1958; Weiner, 1962), however, observed high, undifferentiated rates under analogous conditions. In addition, Weiner (1962) showed that one way of producing lower rates and temporal patterning on fixed-interval schedules is by making "response cost" contingent upon responding, as when in his study each response resulted in loss of the points used to maintain the fixed-interval behavior.

[1]Dedicated to B. F. Skinner in his sixty-fifth year. This research was supported by NSF grants GB 4004 and GB 8234. During some phases of the research, Kathleen Stauber was an undergraduate research participant supported by NSF Undergraduate Research Grant GY 2639 (Harry L. Madison, Director). Judy Kosovich and Susan Slavick assisted in the collection of the data. Reprints may be obtained from Alan Baron, Department of Psychology, University of Wisconsin–Milwaukee, Milwaukee, Wisconsin 53201.

The three experiments of the present series trained subjects on a five-component multiple schedule with different fixed-interval schedules of monetary reinforcement in the different components. Experiment I compared the controlling influences of instructions with those exerted by the reinforcement schedule itself. Subjects were trained under either standard conditions, *i.e.*, when uninstructed about the schedule of reinforcement, or with one of several combinations of the instructions and reinforcement conditions, *i.e.*, when instructed about the schedule but without feedback about reinforcement in the experimental environment, with both instructions and reinforcement, and with neither instructions nor reinforcement. Experiment II was concerned with the reversibility of the effects observed in Exp. I. Finally, Exp. III examined the effects of response-cost when introduced in conjunction with some of the above procedures.

METHOD

Subjects

Eighteen female college students served as paid subjects for an extended series of experimental sessions: Subjects 1 to 14 in Exp. I, Subjects 1, 2, 5, 6, 9, and 10 in Exp. II, and Subjects 15 to 18 in Exp. III. Subjects were paid $0.75 for each 50-min experimental session and could earn up to $0.88 more depending upon performance.

Apparatus

The subject sat at a table in a 6-ft (1.82-m) sq sound-attenuated room. Mounted on the table was an 11 by 18 in. (279 by 457 mm) sloping panel with a plastic pushbutton in the center (Grason-Stadler, E8670A) that required a force of 50 to 90 g to operate. A five-digit electrical-reset counter was situated 2.5 in. (64 mm) to the left of the pushbutton. For some subjects in Exp. I and II and for all subjects in Exp. III, a second counter was located symmetrically to the right of the response key. This second counter was not part of the procedure when present in Exp. I and II; it always read zero and subjects were told to disregard it.

Spaced at 2.5-in. (64-mm) intervals at the top of the panel were five small lights covered with different colored plastic caps, 0.5 in. (13 mm)

in diameter. The colors, in the order left to right, were: blue, red, green, yellow, and orange. Control and recording equipment were located in an adjacent room.

Preliminary Orientation

Before the preliminary training session, which lasted for only 10 min, each subject read a printed description of the job for which she had applied. She was informed that: (a) no information could be provided about the purpose of the research but that it was neither physically nor psychologically harmful; (b) that she would be able to earn, on the average, from $1.00 to $1.50 per session; (c) she must await payment until the end of the experiment; (d) she would be fined $1.00 for each absence without prior notice and excuse; (e) she would forfeit all earnings if she dropped out before the end of the experiment.

Experimental Procedure

Before entry into the experimental room, personal belongings were taken from the subject including her purse, books, watch, and any writing materials. The session began shortly afterwards and, except for the preliminary session, always lasted 50 min.

After each session, subjects were given a written voucher indicating their earnings for that session. Actual payment usually was given only at the end of the experiment, although in a few cases fractional payments were made earlier because of the subject's financial need.

The same five-component multiple schedule operated during all sessions. Each session was divided into five 10-min periods during each of which a different colored light was presented. Four of the lights, blue, red, green, and yellow, were associated with fixed-interval schedules of reinforcement with temporal intervals of 10, 30, 90, and 270 sec respectively. The fifth, orange light was associated with extinction.

The first interval of a given schedule was timed from the onset of the component and subsequent intervals from preceding reinforcements. The order of components was varied in a semi-random order from session to session in such a way that each component preceded every other component an equal number of times. Changes from one component to another were separated by 3-sec timeout periods when all stimulus lights were off and responding had no scheduled consequences. During the preliminary 10-min session, only the FI 90-sec schedule was used.

During the training under the *feedback* condition, the left-hand counter in the experimental room advanced as the reinforcer was delivered. During training under the *no-feedback* condition, the left-hand counter never advanced, but a record was kept in the control room of the number of reinforcements. For the *cost* condition (Exp. III only), the right-hand counter advanced each time the response key was operated.

Instructions

Five sets of printed instructions, corresponding to the different conditions studied in the three experiments, were used. These instructions, which the subject was asked to read before the first session, remained in the room for the duration of the condition.

Schedule Instructions-Feedback (I-F). The most comprehensive instructions were given to subjects exposed to this condition, and are given in their entirety below. Instructions used for other conditions, described later, primarily involved deletion and/or substitution of certain sections. Numeration of paragraphs has been added below for ease of reference to these sections.

(1) This is how you will earn money. First, you always will be paid at least 75¢ for each session you work regardless of what you do. You can earn money in addition to the 75¢ by pressing the button located in the center of the panel. To work properly, the button must be pressed all the way down and then released.

(2) Now look at the counter to the left. Right now it registers zero. Each time that the counter advances, it means that you have earned 1¢. If, for example, at the end of the session the counter registers 70, it means that you have earned 70¢ by pressing the button. When added to the 75¢ mentioned above, you would have earned $1.45 for that session.

(3) Here is how the counter works. When the button is pressed, the counter sometimes will advance. The counter can work only after a fixed

period of time has elapsed since the last time it worked. This means that if you press the button before the period of time is up, nothing will happen. Once the time is up, the counter will be ready to work when you press the button. Upon pressing the button, the counter will register and the fixed period of time will begin over again. If you delay pressing the button when the counter is ready to work, you will be losing time when you could be making money.

(4) Now, look at the five lights at the top of the panel. During different portions of the session, one of these lights will be on. These lights will serve as signals to you.

(5) The color of the light indicates the duration of the time interval associated with the working of the counter, that is, how soon it can work after its last operation: BLUE = 10 seconds; RED = 30 seconds; GREEN = 90 seconds; YELLOW = 270 seconds; ORANGE = the counter does not work at all. One other thing about the signal lights and the time intervals: when there is a change from one color to another, the particular time interval starts when the light goes on.

Subsequent parts of the instructions indicated that: (a) the onset of one of the signal lights on the darkened panel would indicate the beginning of the session and offset of all lights the end of the session; (b) responding would be ineffective during the brief interval when the colors changed; (c) earnings based on the counter reading would be entered on a payment sheet at the end of the session; and (d) no questions could be answered.

Schedule Instructions-No Feedback (I-NF). For subjects exposed to this condition, the following paragraph, indicating that the left-hand (reinforcement) counter would not operate, was substituted for paragraph (2) in the I-F instructions:

(2a) Now look at the counter to the left. This counter does not work and will always register zero. However, each time that a counter just like it in the adjacent room advances, you have earned 1¢. If, for example, at the end of the session, the counter in the adjacent room registers 70, it means that you have earned 70¢ by pressing the button. When added to the 75¢ mentioned above, you would have earned $1.45 for that session.

No Schedule Instructions-Feedback (NI-F). For subjects trained with this condition, paragraphs (3) and (5) of the I-F instructions, those parts pertaining to the fixed-interval schedules, were deleted.

No Schedule Instructions-No Feedback (NI-NF). For subjects trained with this condition, paragraphs (3) and (5) of the I-F instructions were deleted, and in place of paragraph (2) the alternative no-feedback paragraph (2a), described for the I-NF condition, was used.

Cost (C). This condition was employed only in Exp. III and always in combination with one of the above sets of instructions. Following paragraph (5) in the NI-F instructions, or in the analogous place in the other instructions, the following paragraph about the right-hand, cost-counter was inserted:

Finally, notice the counter to your right. It now registers zero. This counter will advance each time you press the center button. It has nothing to do with how much money you earn; it just advances each time the button is pressed.

Subsequently in Exp. III, when the cost condition was introduced, the following additional instructions were given:

From now on, each time the right-hand counter advances it means that you have lost one-tenth of a cent from your earnings on the left-hand counter. Every 10 counts on the right-hand counter, then, means the loss of 1¢. When the session is over, I will subtract the money you have lost, as indicated on the right-hand counter, from the money you have earned, as indicated on the left-hand counter, up to the limits of those earnings. As before, you always will earn 75¢ for each session regardless of the counter readings at the end of the session.

EXPERIMENT I: INSTRUCTIONS AND FEEDBACK, ALONE AND IN COMBINATION

Subjects 1 to 14 served in Exp. I. As summarized in Table 1, four subjects (S1, S2, S3,

and S4) were assigned to the I-F condition, *i.e.*, they were given instructions about the reinforcement schedule, and reinforcement-feedback was provided on the left-hand counter in the experimental room. The four subjects (S5, S6, S7, and S8) assigned to the I-NF condition also were given schedule instructions, but the reinforcement counter remained inoperative.

Table 1
Assignment of subjects and sequence of conditions in Experiments I and II.

Subjects	*Exp. I* Sessions 1-20	*Exp. II* Sessions 21-40
1, 2	I-F	I-NF
3, 4	I-F	—
5, 6	I-NF	I-F
7, 8	I-NF	—
9, 10	NI-F	I-F
11, 12	NI-F	—
13, 14	NI-NF	—

The four subjects (S9, S10, S11, and S12) assigned to the NI-F condition were uninstructed about the schedule, but reinforcement-feedback was provided. Finally, two subjects (S13, S14) were assigned to the NI-NF condition, *i.e.*, they were neither instructed about the schedule nor given reinforcement-feedback.

As indicated by the instructions, at the end of each session subjects in the feedback condition were told their additional earnings based on $0.01 for each count registering on the left-hand counter at the end of the session. Subjects in the no-feedback condition were told their earnings based on the number of times the counter would have registered had it been operative.

All subjects were trained for twenty 50-min sessions.

EXPERIMENT II: SEQUENTIAL EFFECTS OF CHANGES IN INSTRUCTIONS AND FEEDBACK

Subjects 1, 2, 5, 6, 9, and 10, all of whom had served in Exp. I, were used. Beginning with Session 21, and continuing for a total of twenty 50-min sessions, the following procedural changes shown in Table 1 were made: (a) S1 and S2, trained originally in Exp. I with the I-F procedure, were shifted to the I-NF procedure, *i.e.*, the reinforcement counter now was inoperative; (b) S5 and S6, trained originally in Exp. I with the I-NF procedure, were shifted to the I-F procedure, *i.e.*, reinforcement-feedback now was added to the schedule instructions; (c) S9 and S10, trained originally in Exp. I with the NI-F procedure, also were shifted to the I-F procedure, *i.e.*, schedule instructions now were added to reinforcement-feedback. In all cases, subjects were asked to read, before Session 21, the instructions appropriate to the new condition, and these new instructions remained in the room thereafter.

EXPERIMENT III: ADDITION OF RESPONSE COST TO INSTRUCTIONS AND FEEDBACK

Four subjects (S15, S16, S17, and S18), who had not previously served, were used. As indicated in Table 2, three (S15, S16, and S17) were trained for twenty 50-min sessions using the NI-F procedure, while the fourth subject (S18) was trained using the I-NF procedure. During these 20 sessions, the right-hand counter advanced each time a response was made, but, as stated in the instructions, these counts were unrelated to earnings.

During Sessions 21 to 40, the cost instructions were introduced for all four subjects, and one cent was deducted from left-hand counter earnings for each 10 counts that registered on the right-hand counter at the end of the session.

Finally, during Sessions 41 to 60, S15 and S16 were observed under the I-NF condition with cost while S18 was observed under the I-F procedure with cost.

Table 2

Assignment of subjects and sequence of conditions in Experiment III.

Subjects	Sessions		
	1 to 20	*21 to 40*	*41 to 60*
15, 16	NI-F	NI-F (C)	I-NF (C)
17	NI-F	NI-F (C)	—
18	I-NF	I-NF (C)	I-F (C)

RESULTS

The main concern was with the functions relating response rates to rates in the different components of the schedule. Direct graphic presentation of these data was complicated by wide variations between rates of different subjects and within rates of individual subjects. To deal with this problem, and to reduce the effects of occasional discrepant rates, the number of responses in each 10-min component of each session of the experiments were converted to common logarithms (with the value of one added to each daily total to eliminate scores of zero). These logarithms of response rates then were averaged in five-day blocks and graphed as a function of the reinforcement rate within each of the components. In referring to the response rate-reinforcement rate functions given below, it may be helpful to note the response-rate equivalents (antilogarithms) of the integers on the logarithmic ordinate: $0 = 0$ responses/10 min; $1 = 9$ responses/10 min; $2 = 99$ responses/10 min; and $3 = 999$ responses/10 min.

EXPERIMENT I: INSTRUCTIONS AND FEEDBACK, ALONE AND IN COMBINATION

The results summarized in Fig. 1 show performances of the members of each of the four groups during Days 1 to 5 (top panels) and Days 16 to 20 (bottom panels) of training. The data in the top four panels indicate systematic differences involving the instructions variable during the first five training days. Five of the eight subjects given instructions, three trained with the I-F procedure (S1, S2, S3), and two with the I-NF procedure (S7, S8), responded at rates appropriate to the schedule, *i.e.*, their response rates generally were low (within the range 0 to 100 responses/min) and were close to the minimum required to produce all scheduled reinforcements. Rates of the remaining three instructed subjects, S4 trained with the I-F procedure and S5 and S6 trained with the I-NF procedure, also varied as a function of component, but rates were somewhat higher and the progression of rates was less orderly. By comparison with modal performances of instructed subjects, rates of the six uninstructed subjects (NI-F and NI-NF) during Days 1 to 5 were considerably higher and, with the possible exception of S10 in the NI-F condition, no tendencies can be seen for response rates to vary as a function of reinforcement rates.

The top panels of Fig. 1 also show that the feedback condition had little or no initial effect. Thus, average performances of subjects trained with the I-F procedure were not markedly dissimilar from performances of subjects trained with the I-NF procedure. Similarly, no differences of any great magnitude can be discerned between the NI-F and NI-NF subjects.

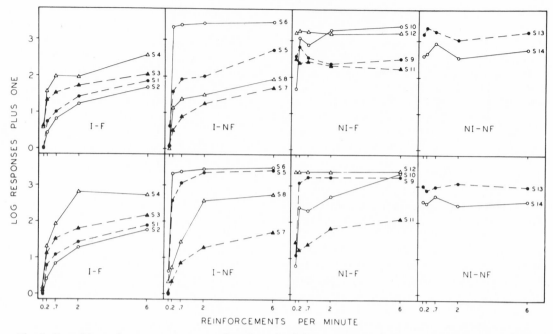

Fig. 1. Logarithms of response rates as a function of reinforcement rates in Exp. I. The response rate equivalents (antilogarithms) of the logarithmic values represented on the ordinate are: 0 = 0 responses/10 min; 1 = 9 responses/10 min; 2 = 99 responses/10 min; 3 = 999 responses/10 min. The top four panels show average response rates for each subject early in training (Sessions 1 to 5) and the bottom panel shows response at the end of training (Sessions 16 to 20). Reading from left to right, the conditions were: Instructions and Feedback (I-F), Instructions and No Feedback (I-NF), No Instructions and Feedback (NI-F), and No Instructions and No Feedback (NI-NF). The five points for each subject correspond to the five components of the multiple schedule expressed as reinforcement rates: Extinction or 0 reinforcements/min; FI 270-sec or 0.2 reinforcements/min; FI 90-sec or 0.7 reinforcements/min; FI 30-sec or 2 reinforcements/min; and FI 10-sec or 6 reinforcements/min.

The bottom four panels of Fig. 1 summarize performances during Sessions 16 to 20, the last five sessions of the experiment. Comparison of performances during these sessions with initial performances indicates that previously described differences were maintained but in somewhat reduced form. Attenuation of differences associated with the instructions variable may be seen to have stemmed from the following changes: (a) the discrepant I-F subject (S4) showed further increases in overall rates, although an orderly progression of rates still was maintained; (b) response rates increased in three of the four I-NF subjects (S5, S6, S8), although rates continued to vary systematically; and (c) response rates of three of the four NI-F subjects (S9, S10, S11) declined somewhat and tendencies appeared for differential responding as a function of schedule component.

Despite these modifications, performances during Sessions 16 to 20 support the conclusion that instructions both with and without

feedback enhanced sensitivity to the different components of the multiple schedule. One way of assessing relative degrees of sensitivity is to count the number of irregularities in the performance curves of individual subjects, *i.e.*, the number of times response rates did not increase with increases in reinforcement rates. From this standpoint, Fig. 1 indicates that seven of the eight instructed subjects showed a monotonic relationship between response and reinforcement rates (although differences for S6 in the range 0.7/min–6/min appear small on the logarithmic ordinate of the graph). The remaining instructed subject (S4) showed one inversion involving 2/min and 6/min. By comparison, of the four subjects given feedback but no instructions, one (S12) did not show any degree of differentiation, as was the case with both of the NI-NF subjects. A number of irregularities are apparent in the curves of the remaining three NI-F subjects: for S10, 0.7/min is less than 0.2/min; for S9, 6/min is less than 2/min and 0.7/min, and for S11,

EXT is greater than 0.2/min and 0.7/min.

Aside from the overall differences in rate described above, the instructions and feedback variables also influenced temporal patterning within schedule components. Figure 2 presents cumulative records obtained during a given session at the end of training for a subject in each condition. Pen deflections on the records indicate reinforcement (advancement of the subject's counter) for the feedback conditions, and the points at which reinforcement would have occurred for the no-feedback conditions. The records have been assembled in 10-min segments in order of reinforcement rates within the five components, from FI 10-sec to extinction.

Figure 2 shows that the subject trained with the I-F procedure (upper left) developed precise temporal patterning of responses within the fixed-interval components, with most responses occurring near the end of the intervals, and that no responses occurred in the extinction component. By comparison, the subject trained with the NI-F procedure (lower left) responded at steady rates with the shorter fixed intervals (10 and 30 sec). Tendencies for temporal patterning appeared with FI 90-sec and FI 270-sec, but marked irregularities also were present. Some responding occurred during the extinction component for this subject. The subject trained with the I-NF procedure (upper right) performed at levels intermediate between the performances of the I-F and NI-F subjects. Temporal patterning occurred with fixed intervals of 30, 90, and 270 sec, but, as might be expected, without feedback these patterns were not coordinated with the actual times when reinforcement would have been delivered. Also to be noted is the absence of responding during the extinction component. Finally, the subject trained with the NI-NF procedure (lower right) showed no evidence of temporal patterning. Rate differences among the different components for this subject stemmed from progressive decreases in rates during the course of the session.

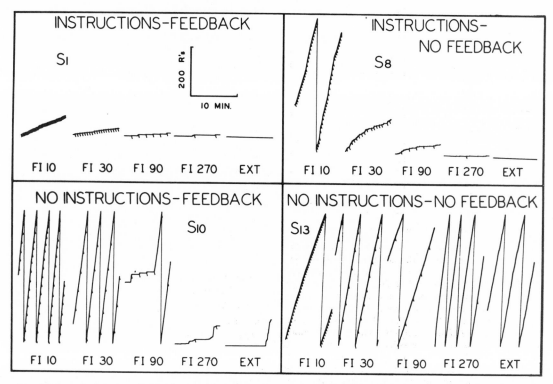

Fig. 2. Cumulative records for four subjects, one from each of the four conditions of Exp. I. Pen deflections on the records indicate occurrences of reinforcement (advancement of the subject's counter) for the feedback conditions, and points at which reinforcement would have occurred for the no-feedback conditions. The records have been assembled in 10-min segments in order of reinforcement rates within the five components of the multiple schedule, *i.e.*, from FI 10-sec to EXT (extinction).

Experiment II: Sequential Effects of Changes in Instructions and Feedback

Figure 3 compares rates during the last five sessions of Exp. I (solid lines) with rates during the last five sessions of Exp. II (dashed lines).

The top two panels show the consequences of changing from the I-F procedure to the I-NF procedure. For the two subjects studied (S1 and S2), the differentiated behavior previ-

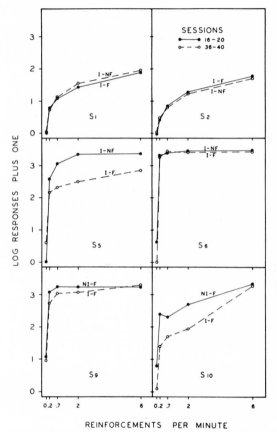

Fig. 3. Logarithms of response rates as a function of reinforcement rates during the last five sessions of Exp. II (Sessions 36 to 40). Also presented are the last five sessions of Exp. I (Sessions 16 to 20). The response rate equivalents (antilogarithms) of the logarithmic values represented on the ordinate are: $0 = 0$ responses/10 min; $1 = 9$ responses/10 min; $2 = 99$ responses/10 min; $3 = 999$ responses/10 min. Subjects 1 and 2 were trained with Instructions and No Feedback (I-NF) in Exp. II, while Subjects 5, 6, 9, and 10 were trained with Instructions and Feedback (I-F). The five points for each subject correspond to the five components of the multiple schedule expressed as reinforcement rates: Extinction or 0 reinforcements/min; FI 270-sec or 0.2 reinforcements/min, FI 90-sec or 0.7 reinforcements/min, FI 30-sec or 2 reinforcements/min., and FI 10-sec or 6 reinforcements/min.

ously controlled by the instructions-feedback combination was well maintained when feedback no longer was provided. The cumulative records for these subjects indicated that temporal patterning, previously established with the I-F procedure, also continued when feedback was omitted. But, as was the case in Exp. I, in the absence of feedback, patterning was not always closely coordinated with the points at which reinforcement would have been delivered.

The remaining panels of Fig. 3 show the effects of changing to the I-F procedure after training with either the NI-F procedure or the I-NF procedure. It may be seen in the middle two panels that addition of feedback to instructions (S5 and S6) had relatively small influence and did not produce the low rates and differentiated behaviors associated with the I-F procedure in Exp. I. To be noted is that these two subjects were the least efficient of the four originally trained with the I-NF procedure in Exp. I. The bottom two panels show that addition of instructions to feedback (S9 and S10) also did not produce the high degree of differentiation observed with the I-F procedure in Exp. I, although rates declined somewhat for both subjects.

Experiment III: Addition of Response Cost to Instructions and Feedback

The results summarized in Fig. 4 indicate that during Sessions 16 to 20, when cost was not contingent upon responding (solid line), two of the three NI-F subjects (S15 and S17) showed the high rates and relatively poor differentiation previously observed under this condition. The remaining NI-F subject (S16) was atypical in comparison with other subjects trained with this procedure, insofar as rates were quite low and approached the minimal rates required by the schedule. Finally, the subject trained with the I-NF procedure evidenced intermediate rates of responding, but as was observed previously, rates exceeded the minimal requirements of the schedule.

Introduction of the cost procedure during Sessions 21 to 40 (closed circles, dashed lines) had similar effects on all four subjects despite previous variations in their performances. In all cases, there were marked reductions in response rates with terminal performances approximating the minimal required rates. Additional details of the effects of cost on tem-

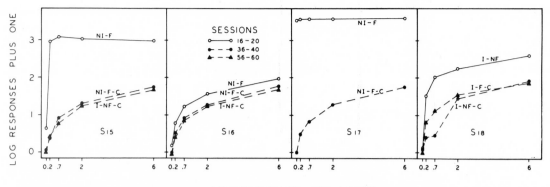

Fig. 4. Logarithms of response rates as a function of reinforcement rates in Exp. III. The response rate equivalents (antilogarithms) of the logarithmic values represented on the ordinate are: $0 = 0$ responses/10 min; $1 = 9$ responses/10 min; $2 = 99$ responses/10 min; $3 = 999$ responses/10 min. Shown are the last five training sessions without cost (Sessions 16 to 20), and the last five sessions in the first and second cost series (Sessions 36 to 40 and Sessions 56 to 60). The five points for each subject correspond to the five components of the multiple schedule expressed as reinforcement rates: Extinction or 0 reinforcements/min; FI 270-sec or 0.2 reinforcements/min; FI 90-sec or 0.7 reinforcements/min; FI 30-sec or 2 reinforcements/min, and FI 10-sec or 6 reinforcements/min.

poral patterning may be seen in Fig. 5, which gives the cumulative record of a subject trained with the NI-F procedure. At the end of training without cost (top panel), this subject showed no evidence of temporal patterning and poor differentiation of rates among the various components. By comparison, the record obtained at the end of training with NI-F plus cost for each response (bottom panel) shows highly precise temporal patterning with most responses occurring close to the end of the fixed intervals, and with no response occurring during the EXT component.

Finally, Fig. 4 also shows the outcome with respect to overall rates during Sessions 41 to 60 (triangles, dashed lines) when feedback was removed and instructions added (S15 and S16) and when feedback was added to instructions (S18). It may be seen that in all cases, differentiated patterns of responding were maintained.

DISCUSSION

Performances of subjects given feedback without instructions about the schedule provide parametric data about reactions of humans to fixed-interval schedules of reinforcement. Although the work of Holland (1958), using sequential presentations of fixed-interval schedules and a signal-detection procedure, suggested that uninstructed subjects would develop good differentiation of different fixed-intervals incorporated into a multiple sched-

ule, this expectation was not borne out by the present results. In Exp. I and III, over a total of twenty 50-min sessions, only one of seven uninstructed subjects showed an orderly progression of response rates as a function of reinforcement intervals, and response rates generally were much higher than the minimum required by the schedules. Another indication of the insensitivity of the subjects was that even at the end of training, six of the seven

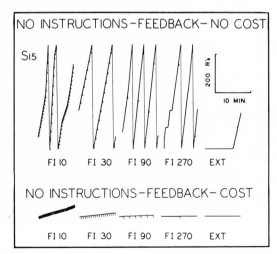

Fig. 5. Cumulative records for a subject trained with the No Instructions-Feedback procedure without cost (top) and with cost (bottom). The records have been assembled in 10-min segments in order of reinforcement rates within the five components of the multiple schedule, from FI 10-sec to EXT (extinction).

subjects continued to respond during the extinction component, although reinforcement never occurred in this component. The basis for the atypical performance of the one uninstructed subject who did adjust to the schedule cannot be specified; it may be noteworthy that each response by this subject advanced the counter subsequently used to indicate response cost.

A number of factors may be relevant to the lack of sensitivity to reinforcing contingencies observed in the present experiment. An obvious possibility is that exposure to the schedule was not sufficiently prolonged. However, consideration of sequential changes over the 20 sessions indicated that whatever systematic decreases in rate did occur were completed by the fifteenth session and no changes of great magnitude occurred thereafter. A different account of these results stresses the conditioning histories that human subjects may bring into the experimental situation (*cf.* Kaufman *et al.*, 1966; Long, 1962; Weiner, 1964). If it is correct to assume that such natural histories characteristically involve ratio schedules, thus generating tendencies for high rates, then human subjects might be expected to respond at unnecessarily high rates when reinforcement is provided on the basis of time, rather than on the basis of work output. In this regard, Weiner (1964) demonstrated that a prior experimental history of ratio reinforcement produces inappropriately high rates on interval schedules. A further possibility is related to the relative effortlessness of the response used in the present study. High rates on interval schedules have been attributed to the lack of substantial "cost" per response (Weiner, 1962); an inherent feature of interval schedules is that while reinforcement may be lost if rates are too low, there is no penalty for unnecessarily high rates, save for the effort required to respond.

Evidence for the importance of response cost in the development of differentiated fixed-interval behavior was obtained in Exp. III. The results indicated that introduction of monetary cost for responding generated highly differentiated behavior for both uninstructed and instructed subjects. This outcome, which is similar to that reported by Weiner (1962) using an FI 1-min schedule, occurred in the present study regardless of prior rates. Thus, both S16 and S18, who had shown relatively good adjustment to the schedule, and S15 and S17, who showed little or no differentiation, were brought to the same level of maximum differentiation when cost was introduced. These findings add to those of Weiner by showing the generality of response-cost effects in a multiple schedule that included fixed intervals ranging from FI 10-sec to FI 270-sec, as well as an EXT component.

The other major finding of the present investigation concerns the effects of instructions on fixed-interval performance. When schedule instructions were given initially in Exp. I, with or without reinforcement-feedback, differentiated behavior developed rapidly and was maintained to the end of the experiment. While there was some indication that instructions were more effective when combined with reinforcement-feedback, differences in this regard were small in comparison to the effects of instructions in general. These results concerning the controlling influences of instructions differ from those reported by Ayllon and Azrin (1964), who found with psychiatric-patient subjects that instructions without immediate reinforcement did not maintain behavior in many cases. The greater degree of sensitivity to instructional control observed in the present study may be related to the use of young-adult college students; as Ayllon and Azrin indicate, a defining characteristic of psychiatric patients is their inability to follow instructions. A further indication of control by instructions was seen in the performances of those subjects in Exp. I instructed to respond but given neither schedule-instructions nor reinforcement-feedback. Although, as might be expected, differentiated behavior as a function of schedule component did not appear, these subjects continued to respond at high and persistent levels for the 20 sessions of the experiment.

While Exp. I indicated that a combination of instructions and reinforcement-feedback characteristically resulted in differential responding to different schedule components, the results of Exp. II suggested that this outcome is related in complex ways to the subject's experimental history. Experiment II showed that when control initially was established with both instructions and reinforcement, low and differentiated rates were maintained even when reinforcement-feedback was no longer provided. When, however, the instructions-reinforcement combination was introduced after previous establishment of high and undifferentiated rates, the instructions-reinforcement combination was relatively ineffective in producing discrimination of schedule contingencies. It would appear, then, that extended training unaccompanied by differential responding to the contingencies of a schedule may reduce the effectiveness of a set of conditions that otherwise would produce sensitivity if introduced at the start of training. This general finding has occurred in other studies of human operant behavior in our laboratory (Kaufman and Baron, 1969).

It is of interest to consider the present results from the standpoint of the place of instructions in the experimental analysis of human operant behavior. Under the heading, "The circumvention of an operant analysis", Skinner (1966) raised the question of whether instructions about contingencies have the same behavioral effects as actual exposure to the same contingencies. Skinner suggested that since subjects usually cannot verbalize accurately the contingencies to which they actually have been exposed, they cannot be expected to react appropriately to descriptions of contingencies provided by experimenters. On these grounds, he contended that verbal instructions should not be used as a substitute for the actual arrangement and manipulation of contingencies, although he did concede that instructions may be of value as an alternative to shaping when concern is with eventual performance of a response rather than with its acquisition.

The present study provides needed experimental evidence about establishment and maintenance of human operant behavior as a function of instructions about contingencies and as a function of direct exposure to the same contingencies. The results appear to bear out Skinner's contention that these two procedures lead to different consequences, but in a surprising way. In the absence of instructions about contingencies, reactions to actual contingencies were imprecise, and differed markedly from what might be expected on the basis of the contingencies themselves, or from studies with subhuman subjects employing similar contingenices. By comparison, instructions about contingencies had the consequence of producing the kinds of differentiated behaviors that might be expected from the animal literature and from the contingencies themselves, particularly when instructions

about contingencies were combined with actual exposure to contingencies and when the combination was present from the start of training.

The present findings, as well as those of other recent studies of instruction effects, suggest two broad conclusions. First, insofar as the goal of an experimental analysis of behavior is to identify variables with major controlling influences, these studies indicate that investigation of instruction effects with humans is a necessary step toward this goal. Worth stressing is that instructions represent an external, observable determinant of behavior whose influences, although complex, can be investigated in a straightforward, objective manner. Second, as Ayllon and Azrin (1964) pointed out, instructions given to humans provide a means of evoking and controlling operant behaviors whose establishment in other ways would be impractical, if not impossible. Once behavior has been established, various experimental contingencies become accessible to study, as were effects of fixed-interval reinforcement in the present study. Thus, use of instructional manipulations in the study of human behavior may be viewed as playing a role parallel to such manipulations as deprivation and drug administration in work with subhuman subjects; by increasing the probability of desired behaviors in this way a means is provided whereby the controlling influences of reinforcement contingencies may be studied effectively.

REFERENCES

Ader, R. and Tatum, R. Free-operant avoidance conditioning in human subjects. *Journal of the Experimental Analysis of Behavior*, 1961, **4**, 275-276.

Ayllon, T. and Azrin, N. H. Reinforcement and instructions with mental patients. *Journal of the Experimental Analysis of Behavior*, 1964, **7**, 327-331.

Baron, A. and Kaufman, A. Human, free-operant avoidance of "time out" from monetary reinforcement. *Journal of the Experimental Analysis of Behavior*, 1966, **9**, 557-565.

Blair, W. C. Measurement of observing responses in human monitoring. *Science*, 1958, **128**, 255-256.

Dews, P. B. and Morse, W. H. Some observations on an operant in human subjects and its modifications by dextro amphetamine. *Journal of the Experimental Analysis of Behavior*, 1958, **1**, 359-364.

Holland, J. G. Human vigilance. *Science*, 1958, **128**, 61-63.

Kaufman, A. and Baron, A. Discrimination of periods of avoidance-extinction by human subjects. *Psychonomic Monograph Supplements*, 1969, No. 5 (Whole No. 37), 53-60.

Kaufman, A., Baron, A., and Kopp, R. M. Some effects of instructions on human operant behavior. *Psychonomic Monograph Supplements*, 1966, **1**, No. 11, 243-250.

Lippman, L. G. and Meyer, M. E. Fixed interval performance as related to instructions and to subjects' verbalizations of the contingency. *Psychonomic Science*, 1967, **8**, 135-136.

Long, E. R. Additional techniques for producing multiple-schedule control in children. *Journal of the Experimental Analysis of Behavior*, 1962, **5**, 443-455.

Skinner, B. F. Operant behavior. In W. K. Honig (Ed.), *Operant behavior*. New York: Appleton-Century-Crofts, 1966. Pp. 12-32.

Turner, L. H. and Solomon, R. L. Human traumatic avoidance learning. *Psychological Monographs*, 1962, **76**, No. 40 (Whole No. 559).

Weiner, H. Some effects of response cost upon human operant behavior. *Journal of the Experimental Analysis of Behavior*, 1962, **5**, 201-208.

Weiner, H. Conditioning history and human fixed-interval performance. *Journal of the Experimental Analysis of Behavior*, 1964, **7**, 383-385.

Received 11 February 1969.

DELAYED REINFORCEMENT VERSUS REINFORCEMENT AFTER A FIXED INTERVAL[1]

ALLEN J. NEURINGER

FOUNDATION FOR RESEARCH ON THE NERVOUS SYSTEM

When interreinforcement intervals were equated, pigeons demonstrated little or no preference between reinforcement after a delay interval and reinforcement presented on a fixed-interval schedule. The small preferences sometimes found for the fixed interval (a) were considerably smaller than when the delay and fixed intervals differed in duration, and (b) were caused by the absence of light during the delay. These results suggest that the effects of delayed reinforcement on prior responding can be reproduced by imposing a temporally equal fixed-interval schedule in place of the delay; and, therefore, that the time between a response and reinforcement controls the probability of that response, whether other responses intervene or not.

Reinforcement is delayed by interposing an interval between a response and the reinforcement for that response. The delay is found to weaken responding: rates of responding are lower than when reinforcement immediately follows a response, pauses are longer, new responses and discriminations take more time to learn, and a delayed reinforcement is less likely to be chosen than an immediate one (Skinner, 1938, p. 139 ff; Perin, 1943; Perkins, 1947; Grice, 1948; Chung, 1965; Smith, 1967). Such results cause most experimenters to treat the effects produced by schedules of delayed reinforcement as different from those produced by schedules of immediate reinforcement. However, the work of Ferster and his associates suggests that when the temporal parameters of these schedules are equated, the effects produced with delayed reinforcements are replicated with immediate ones. For example, Ferster (1953) showed that pigeons' rates of responding prior to a 1-min delay period were comparable to their rates prior to reinforcement presented on a 1-min fixed-interval schedule; furthermore, superstitious responses—perhaps analogous to responses during the fixed-interval schedule—were observed during the interval of delay. Similarly, Ferster and Hammer (1965) demonstrated that the behavior of monkeys prior to a 24-hr delay of reinforcement interval was approximately the same as that prior to a 24-hr fixed-interval schedule. Technically, these experiments employed chain schedules, with responses in the initial link of the chain leading to a fixed-interval terminal link in one case and a delay-of-reinforcement link in the other. The two terminal links differed in the following ways: responses were emitted throughout the fixed interval and the final response was immediately followed by reinforcement; during the delay interval, effective responses could not be emitted and a response-independent reinforcement (*i.e.*, one presented without regard to the animal's behavior) occurred at the end of the delay. The two schedules were identical with respect to other parameters, most important of which was reinforcement frequency.

The present work extended Ferster's experiments by permitting pigeons to choose between delayed reinforcement and reinforcement on a temporally equal fixed-interval schedule. If, when other parameters are equated, delayed and immediate reinforcers have the same effects on responding, subjects should choose equally between these two alternatives. On the other hand, if delaying a reinforcer has special effects on behavior, a lesser preference for the delay would be predicted.

[1]Dedicated to B. F. Skinner in his sixty-fifth year. This research was supported by grant M. H. 12108 from the National Institutes of Health to the Foundation for Research on the Nervous System, Dr. Shin-Ho Chung, principal investigator. I gratefully acknowledge the cheerful assistance of Vivian Goldman, Mary Miskella, Maria Oliva, and Andrea Schein. Reprints may be obtained from the author, Foundation for Research on the Nervous System, 36 The Fenway, Boston, Massachusetts 02215.

METHOD

Subjects

Ten male White Carneaux pigeons, all with previous experience in a variety of experiments, were fed enough after each experimental session to maintain them at approximately 85% of their free-feeding body weights. Only five of these (Subjects 280, 281, 282, 31, and 34) were used in Exp. I.

Apparatus

A standard operant conditioning chamber consisted of two Plexiglas Gerbrands response keys and a Gerbrands food hopper below the keys. The keys could be transilluminated by 7-w white or 7-w red bulbs, and the hopper was illuminated by a 7-w white bulb whenever grain was presented. Except in Exp. III, to be discussed below, these lights provided the only illumination in the chamber (*i.e.*, there was no houselight). Reinforcement consisted of 3-sec access to mixed grain from the hopper. Pecks of at least 15 g force on a lighted key were recorded and produced feedback clicks from a dc relay mounted behind the front panel. The experiment was automatically controlled by relays, stepping switches, counters, and timers.

EXPERIMENT I
EQUAL DELAY AND
FIXED INTERVALS

Procedure

In the preliminary condition, pecks on the two response keys were reinforced according to two independent variable-interval (VI) 90-sec schedules, one VI scheduling reinforcement on the left key and the other on the right. The interreinforcement intervals, identical on the two schedules, were 120, 14, 23, 148, 44, 70, 11, 162, 80, 96, and 222 sec. The VIs were presented concurrently so that subjects could freely respond on either key and thereby choose between the two schedules. The only restriction was that a switch from one key to the other prevented reinforcement for 1.5-sec. (This restriction is called a change-over delay, or COD, and was scheduled in the same way as in Herrnstein, 1961.) When the numbers of responses became stable and approximately equal on the two keys, the procedure was changed to a concurrent chain

(Herrnstein, 1964). Figure 1 is a schematic diagram of this procedure. The same 90-sec VIs and 1.5-sec COD as used above were presented in the concurrent initial links of two chain schedules. Responses during the initial link on one key now resulted in the occasional presentation (as determined by the respective VI) of a terminal link composed of a fixed-interval (FI) schedule of reinforcement. Responses during the initial link on the other key resulted in the occasional presentation of a delay-of-reinforcement terminal link. Whereas the initial links were presented concurrently, the terminal links were presented exclusive of one another, *i.e.*, the subject was confronted with either a fixed-interval schedule or a delay of reinforcement. During the initial links, both keys were lighted by white bulbs. During the fixed-interval terminal link, the light transilluminating the "fixed-interval key" was changed from white to red, and the other key, the "delay key," became dark and inoperative. The first peck on the fixed-interval key after the fixed interval terminated produced immediate access to grain. During the delay-of-reinforcement terminal link, the chamber was totally dark (blackout) and both keys were inactivated. The delay was terminated by the response-independent presentation of grain. After either a delayed reinforce-

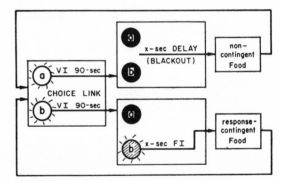

Fig. 1. Diagram of one cycle of the experimental procedure. Each box represents a possible condition in the chamber. A white circle indicates that the key is operative and lighted by a white bulb, a striped circle indicates that the key is operative and lighted by a red bulb, and a black circle indicates that the key is dark and inoperative. Responding in the choice link (left) leads either to a delay (upper-middle) which is followed by response-independent reinforcement (upper-right) or to a fixed interval (lower-middle) which is followed by response-produced reinforcement (lower-right). After reinforcement in either condition, the choice link is again presented.

ment or reinforcement on the fixed-interval schedule, the initial links were again presented. Thus, subjects could freely respond on two keys during the initial links and thereby choose to enter either a delay-of-reinforcement or a fixed-interval terminal link. The basic differences between the delay and fixed-interval periods were: (1) the chamber was totally dark during the delay, whereas the fixed-interval key was red during the fixed interval; therefore, (2) as was expected, few or no pecks were emitted in the darkened chamber during the delay, whereas many responses were emitted on the lighted fixed-interval key during the fixed-interval; and (3) reinforcement was presented without regard to the subject's behavior at the end of the delay period, whereas a response produced reinforcement at the end of the fixed interval.

The duration of the delay always equalled the duration of the fixed interval in this experiment; both will be referred to as the "time to reinforcement". This time was varied in the following order: 8, 2, 30, 60, 18, and 45 sec. Subjects could first choose between an 8-sec delay-of-reinforcement and an 8-sec fixed-interval schedule, then between a 2-sec delay and 2-sec fixed interval, *etc.* A total of 35 to 50 sessions was given at each time-to-reinforcement value, with the functions of the keys being interchanged after a minimum of 15 sessions; thus, a minimum of 15 sessions was given with the delay on the left and a minimum of 15 with the delay on the right. Each session was terminated after the fortieth reinforcement.

Preference was determined from the number of responses emitted on each key during the concurrently presented initial links. The number of initial-link responses emitted on the fixed-interval key was divided by the total number of initial-link responses on both keys. This datum, FI choices divided by total choices, will be referred to as the "per cent choice of the fixed-interval schedule". According to this per cent choice measure, 50% indicates that an equal number of responses were emitted on the two keys during the initial links, 67% indicates that the FI key was chosen twice for each choice response on the delay key, 75% indicates three to one, *etc.* Also to be discussed are (a) the overall rate of responding during the initial links, defined as the total number of initial-link responses on both keys

divided by the total time spent in these links; and (b) the rate of responding during the fixed-interval terminal link, defined as the number of responses emitted during the fixed-interval divided by the time spent in the interval. Arithmetic average performances over 14 sessions—the last seven sessions when the delay was on the left plus the last seven when the delay was on the right—were used for all data to be discussed in all of the following experiments.

RESULTS

Figure 2 shows the per cent choices of the fixed-interval key as a function of time to reinforcement. Most points lie close to, but above, the 50% line, indicating a small preference for the FI condition. This preference was approximately constant as time to reinforcement varied. The average of all points is 55%, shown by the dashed line, or an average preference for FI over delay of about 1.2 to 1. Note that these preferences did not greatly influence the relative number of reinforcements obtained from the two conditions. At the 30-sec time-to-reinforcement value, where the difference was greatest, 52.6% of the reinforcements were from the FI condition and 47.4% were from the delay.

The approximate invariance of the choices might indicate that time to reinforcement had no effect in the present experiment. That this was not the case is seen in Fig. 3, where overall rates of responding in the initial links are shown to decrease as time to reinforcement in the terminal links increased. Similarly, Fig. 4 shows that the rates of responding within the terminal fixed-interval component decreased as the duration of the fixed interval increased. Thus, although preferences did not vary, the rates at which choices were emitted and the response rates within the fixed interval decreased as time to reinforcement increased.

EXPERIMENT II
UNEQUAL DELAY AND
FIXED INTERVALS

This experiment compared the magnitude of the 55% choice value in Exp. I with preferences for the shorter of two times to reinforcement. Subjects were therefore permitted to choose between unequal delay and fixed intervals.

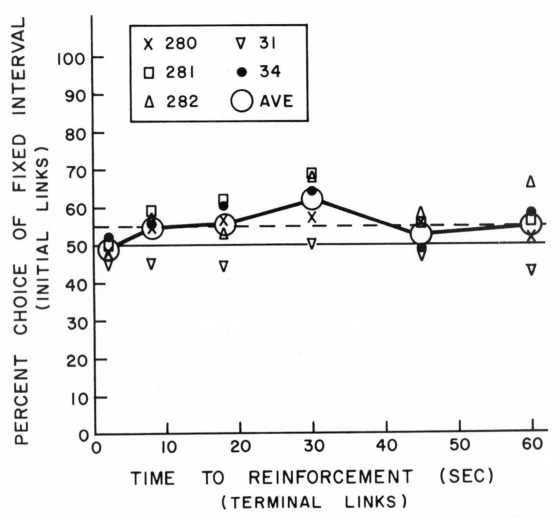

Fig. 2. Per cent choice of the fixed-interval key (initial-link responses on the fixed-interval key divided by the total number of initial link responses on both fixed-interval and delay keys) as a function of the times to reinforcement during the fixed-interval and delay-of-reinforcement terminal links. The fixed and delay intervals were equal.

Procedure

A concurrent-chain schedule was again used. As in Exp. I, the initial concurrent links were identical VI 90-sec schedules with COD 1.5-sec, and the terminal links consisted of a fixed-interval schedule on one key and a delay-of-reinforcement schedule on the other. The only difference between this experiment and Exp. I is that now the durations of the delay and fixed intervals differed. The same subjects used in Exp. I, now referred to as Group I, first chose between a 10-sec fixed-interval and a 2-sec delay, and then between a 10-sec fixed-interval and 20-sec delay. Each of these com-

parisons was presented for a minimum of 35 sessions, with the fixed interval on the left for at least 15 sessions and then on the right for another 15 sessions. A second group of pigeons, Subjects 1, 5, 11, 26, and 45, received the same experience as Group I, except that the 10-sec condition was a delay of reinforcement while the fixed interval was 2 sec in one case and 20 sec in the other. Thus, while the time-to-reinforcement values were identical for the two groups, the schedule conditions were reversed, *i.e.*, the fixed interval was 10 sec for Group I whereas the delay was 10 sec for Group II. Two groups were used in order to factor out the effects of the type of sched-

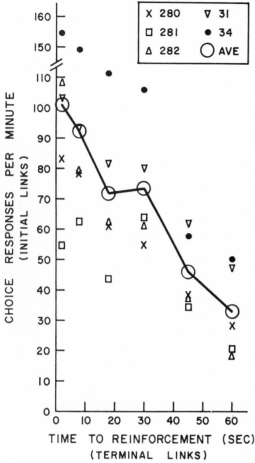

Fig. 3. Choice responses per minute (total initial-link responses on both keys divided by the total time in the initial link) as a function of the times to reinforcement during the terminal links. The durations of the fixed- and delay-interval terminal links were equal.

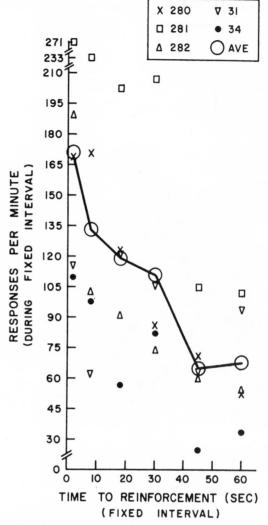

Fig. 4. Rate of responding during the fixed-interval terminal link as a function of the duration of the fixed interval.

ule (delay *versus* FI) from the effects of the times to reinforcement. The schedule effects can be seen by comparing Group I and Group II performances; the effects of time to reinforcement can be seen by comparing choices during the 10-sec *versus* 2-sec condition with choices during the 10-sec *versus* 20-sec condition.

RESULTS

Figure 5 shows the percentage of initial-link choice responses on the "10-sec key", *i.e.*, the key on which the terminal link was either a 10-sec fixed interval (Group I) or 10-sec delay (Group II). The average Group I performances are shown by the open bars and

the average Group II performances by the striped bars. Consider first the effects of changing the comparison time to reinforcement from 2 sec to 20 sec. This change caused the average Group I choices of the 10-sec key to increase from 31% to 72%; Group II choices similarly increased from 25% to 67%. Consider next the effects of the type of schedule. Note again that any difference between the two groups' choices must be attributed to the difference in schedule conditions. The Group I choices of the 10-sec condition were, on average, six and five percentage points higher than the Group II choices. Thus, whereas an

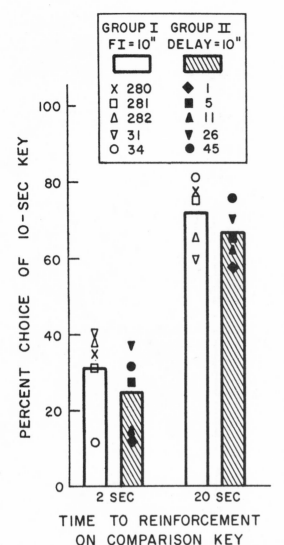

Fig. 5. Per cent choices of the 10-sec fixed-interval condition when the delay condition was 2 sec and 20 sec, respectively (Group I, open bars), and of the 10-sec delay of reinforcement condition when the fixed-interval was 2 sec and 20 sec (Group II, striped bars). The between-group differences show the effects of the different schedule conditions (FI *versus* delay), whereas the within-group changes show the effects of the increase in time to reinforcement.

increase in time to reinforcement caused per cent choices to increase by approximately 42 points, the difference between FI and delay schedules caused per cent choices to differ by only six points. These results are consistent with the small preferences for FI over delay found in Exp. I and, furthermore, suggest that those preferences were indeed relatively small.

EXPERIMENT III
CONTROLLING FOR THE BLACKOUT

Attempts were next made to determine whether the blackouts *per se* were responsible for the small preferences for FI over delay obtained in Exp. I and II. The blackout was removed from the delay condition in Exp. IIIA and added to the fixed interval in Exp. IIIB.

Procedure

Experiment IIIA: a 7-w yellow houselight was added to the experimental chamber, and was lighted throughout the session; thus, there were no blackouts. Subjects 280, 281, 282, 31, and 34 chose between a 20-sec fixed-interval terminal link and a 20-sec delay of reinforcement. During the delay, while both keys were dark and inoperative, the chamber remained lighted by the houselight. Except for the absence of blackout, this procedure was identical to that in Exp. I. If the blackout caused the slightly lower preference for delay in Exp. I and II, the subjects would now be expected to respond equally in the initial links of the chains; on the other hand, if the preferences were due to some other characteristic of the delay operation (*e.g.*, the response-independent presentation of grain), the same 55% choice value would be predicted. Subjects received at least 30 sessions' experience under this condition, with the position of the delay and fixed-interval conditions being interchanged after approximately 15 sessions.

Experiment IIIB: Subjects 1, 5, 11, 26, and 45 chose between a 20-sec delay of reinforcement and a 20-sec "delay-plus-FR 1" (delay plus one response) terminal link. The delays in both conditions were identical to those in Exp. I, *i.e.*, the chamber was completely dark (blackout). The delay consisted of a 20-sec period of blackout at the end of which response-independent reinforcement occurred. The delay-plus-FR 1 condition also contained a 20-sec period of blackout; however, at the end of this blackout the "delay-plus-FR 1 key" was transilluminated by a yellow 7-w bulb and a single peck on this lighted key produced immediate reinforcement. Except for the delay-plus-FR 1 contingency, the present procedure was identical to that used in Exp. I. If the blackout stimulus alone caused the obtained preferences, subjects would now be expected to respond equally in the initial links. On the other hand, if another attribute of delayed reinforcement caused the previous results, the subjects should now prefer the immediate reinforcement in the delay-plus-FR 1 condition. Subjects received approximately 30 sessions under this condition, with the positions of the keys being interchanged after approximately 15 sessions.

RESULTS

The basic data were the percentages of initial-link responses emitted on the fixed-interval key in Exp. IIIA (or per cent choices of the fixed interval) and the percentages of initial-link responses to the delay-plus-FR 1 key in Exp. IIIB. The per cent choices of the FI key in Exp. IIIA were 56, 42, 48, 49, and 56 for the subjects in the order given in the procedure above. The average of these is 50%, indicating indifference between the two alternatives. Some subjects responded on the darkened and inoperative key during the delay (since the houselight was on) whereas other subjects responded little or not at all. There was no correlation between this responding and per cent choice. The per cent choices of the delay-plus-FR 1 key for subjects in Exp. IIIB, in the order given above, were 57, 47, 50, 55, and 47, respectively, for an average of 51%. Once again, this average indicates an approximate indifference between the two alternatives. In neither Exp. IIIA, where blackouts were absent in both delay-of-reinforcement and fixed-interval conditions, nor in Exp. IIIB, where blackouts were present in both conditions, were the Exp. I preferences (55%) obtained. These results therefore suggest that the lower preferences for delayed reinforcement in Exp. I and II were caused by the blackout stimulus *per se.*

DISCUSSION

Hull (1952, p. 126 ff) distinguished between two basic types of delay-of-reinforcement experiments: in the first, response chains are required during the "delay" interval and the last response in the chain is immediately followed by reinforcement, *e.g.*, as in a multiple unit maze; in the second, no specific response is required during the delay and response-independent reinforcement occurs at the end

of the delay, *e.g.*, as in an operant chamber where the operandum is removed during the delay interval. Most studies on delayed reinforcement use the second type of situation: the operandum is inactivated or removed, the chamber is darkened, or responding during the delay is punished (Perin, 1943; Ferster, 1953; Dews, 1960; Chung, 1965). Studies of Hull's first type of "delay" are now found under the rubric of "schedules of reinforcement" and, more specifically, under "chain schedules". The basic question raised in the present work is whether these two situations, now to be referred to as delay of reinforcement and chain schedules of reinforcement, can be integrated within a single framework. To put the question another way, are the behavioral effects of a delayed reinforcement due to attributes unique to delay (*e.g.*, an interval of "no responding" between response and response-independent reinforcement) or to attributes common to all chain schedules (*e.g.*, the interval between initiation of the chain's terminal link and reinforcement)?

To answer this question, pigeons were permitted to choose between a schedule of delayed reinforcement and a temporally equal fixed-interval schedule. It was found that an average of 55% of the choice responses were emitted on the "fixed-interval key", indicating a 1.2 to 1 preference for fixed interval rather than delay. While this preference might suggest that attributes unique to delayed reinforcement affect responding, the preference was both approximately constant over a range of intervals (Exp. I) and relatively small (Exp. II), suggesting that some factor other than the delay might have been responsible. That factor was shown to be the blackouts present during the delay interval: removing (Exp. IIIA) or controlling for (Exp. IIIB) the blackouts caused the subjects to choose equally between the delay and fixed-interval alternatives. (Note that whereas some studies similarly suggest that blackouts are aversive, *e.g.*, Ferster, 1958, other studies demonstrate the opposite effect, *e.g.*, Neuringer and Chung, 1967). Thus, it is concluded that pigeons demonstrate relatively little or no preference in their choices between a delayed reinforcement and a temporally equal fixed-interval schedule of reinforcement.

This conclusion does not imply that the interval between a response and reinforcement is an unimportant variable. To the contrary, Fig. 3 and 4 show that as this interval increases, response rates decrease, and Fig. 5 shows that subjects prefer the shorter of two times to reinforcement. The present results, together with those of Ferster (1953) and Ferster and Hammer (1965), do imply, however, that the main effects of a delay interval on behavior are due to the interval rather than to attributes unique to the delay operation; in other words, whether or not further responding occurs during the interval, and whether or not a response is immediately followed by reinforcement at the end of the interval, make little or no difference in subjects' preferences.

Other studies similarly suggest that interreinforcement responses exert relatively little influence over behavior, whereas interreinforcement intervals exert a relatively great control. For example, Anger (1956) and Herrnstein (1964) showed that responding by rats in a single operandum situation and pigeons in a choice situation, respectively, was better correlated with reinforcements per unit time than with reinforcements per response. Dews (1962, 1965, 1966a, 1966b) argued that pigeons' rates of responding under fixed-interval schedules were controlled by the time between reinforcements and did not depend upon the responses emitted during this time. Autor (1960) and Killeen (1968) demonstrated that the choices of pigeons varied with reinforcement rates whether or not responses were required for reinforcement (see, however, Fantino, 1968 for different results). And Neuringer and Schneider (1968) found that the response latencies of pigeons increased linearly with interreinforcement time but were completely unrelated to the number of interreinforcement responses. These studies, together with the present findings, suggest the following hypothesis: the probability (or rate, or latency) of a response is controlled by the interval between that response and reinforcement (a) independently of the number of other responses intervening in the interval, and (b) independently of whether such intervening responses are required or prohibited. (Note that a single response, the one that produces reinforcement, is required under the fixed-interval schedule, whereas effective responses are prohibited under the delay schedule.) More research is of course necessary to substantiate this hypothesis. For example, it must be determined whether the effects of delay of reinforcement intervals on the learning of new responses and discriminations might also be explained by the intervals rather than by attributes unique to the delay.

The series of experiments by Dews (1962, 1965, 1966a, 1966b) has suggested that the scalloped patterns of responding found under fixed-interval schedules are caused not by hypothetical response chains but by the passage of time. The present work suggests a similar alternative to the notion that "superstitious chains of responses" must be invoked to explain the control exerted by delayed reinforcers. As indicated in the Introduction, Ferster (1953), as well as other experimenters (Blough, 1959; Hearst, 1962) have reported superstitious responses during the delay period. However, the animal often is not observed during the delay (e.g., Chung and Herrnstein, 1967), and, when observed, superstitious chains are sometimes not found (Mabry, 1965; Smith, 1967). Thus, the more general, as well as more parsimonious, hypothesis is the present one, i.e., that the time between a response and reinforcement controls the probability of that response, whether other responses intervene or not.

REFERENCES

Anger, D. The dependence of interresponse times upon the relative reinforcement of different interresponse times. *Journal of Experimental Psychology,* 1956, **52**, 145-161.

Autor, S. M. *The strength of conditioned reinforcers as a function of the frequency and probability of reinforcement.* Unpublished doctoral dissertation, Harvard University, 1960.

Blough, D. S. Delayed matching in the pigeon. *Journal of the Experimental Analysis of Behavior,* 1959, **2**, 151-160.

Chung, S-H. Effects of delayed reinforcement in a concurrent situation. *Journal of the Experimental Analysis of Behavior,* 1965, **8**, 439-444.

Chung, S-H. and Herrnstein, R. J. Choice and delay of reinforcement. *Journal of the Experimental Analysis of Behavior,* 1967, **10**, 67-74.

Dews, P. B. Free-operant behavior under conditions of delayed reinforcement. I. CRF-type schedules. *Journal of the Experimental Analysis of Behavior,* 1960, **3**, 221-234.

Dews, P. B. The effect of multiple S^Δ periods on responding on a fixed-interval schedule. *Journal of the Experimental Analysis of Behavior,* 1962, **5**, 369-374.

Dews, P. B. The effect of multiple S^Δ periods on responding on a fixed-interval schedule: III. Effect of changes in pattern of interruptions, parameters and stimuli. *Journal of the Experimental Analysis of Behavior*, 1965, **8**, 427-435.

Dews, P. B. The effect of multiple S$^\Delta$ periods on responding on a fixed-interval schedule:IV. Effect of continuous S$^\Delta$ with only short S^D probes. *Journal of the Experimental Analysis of Behavior*, 1966, **9**, 147-151. (*a*)

Dews, P. B. The effect of multiple S$^\Delta$ periods on responding on a fixed-interval schedule: V. Effect of periods of complete darkness and of occasional omissions of food presentations. *Journal of the Experimental Analysis of Behavior*, **9**, 1966, 573-578. (*b*)

Fantino, E. Effects of required rates of responding upon choice. *Journal of the Experimental Analysis of Behavior*, 1968, **11**, 15-22.

Ferster, C. B. Sustained behavior under delayed reinforcement. *Journal of Experimental Psychology*, 1953, **45**, 218-224.

Ferster, C. B. Control of behavior in chimpanzees and pigeons by time out from positive reinforcement. *Psychological Monographs*, 1958, **72**, No. 14 (Whole No. 461).

Ferster, C. B. and Hammer, C. Variables determining the effects of delay in reinforcement. *Journal of the Experimental Analysis of Behavior*, 1965, **8**, 243-254.

Grice, G. R. The relation of secondary reinforcement to delayed reward in visual discrimination learning. *Journal of Experimental Psychology*, 1948, **38**, 1-16.

Hearst, E. Delayed alternation in the pigeon. *Journal of the Experimental Analysis of Behavior*, 1962, **5**, 145-161.

Herrnstein, R. J. Relative and absolute strength of response as a function of frequency of reinforcement. *Journal of the Experimental Analysis of Behavior*, 1961, **4**, 267-272.

Herrnstein, R. J. Secondary reinforcement and rate of primary reinforcement. *Journal of the Experimental Analysis of Behavior*, 1964, **7**, 27-36.

Hull, C. L. *A behavior system.* New Haven: Yale University Press, 1952.

Killeen, P. Response rate as a factor in choice. *Psychonomic Science*, 1968, **12**, 34.

Mabry, J. H. Discriminative functions based on a delay in the reinforcement relation. *Journal of the Experimental Analysis of Behavior*, 1965, **8**, 97-103.

Neuringer, A. J. and Chung, S-H. Quasi-reinforcement: control of responding by a percentage-reinforcement schedule. *Journal of the Experimental Analysis of Behavior*, 1967, **10**, 45-54.

Neuringer, A. J. and Schneider, B. A. Separating the effects of interreinforcement time and number of interreinforcement responses. *Journal of the Experimental Analysis of Behavior*, 1968, **11**, 661-667.

Perin, C. T. The effect of delayed reinforcement upon the differentiation of bar responses in white rats. *Journal of Experimental Psychology*, 1943, **32**, 95-109.

Perkins, C. C. Jr. The relation of secondary reward to gradients of reinforcement. *Journal of Experimental Psychology*, 1947, **37**, 377-392.

Skinner, B. F. *The behavior of organisms.* New York: Appleton-Century-Crofts, 1938.

Smith, L. Delayed discrimination and delayed matching in pigeons. *Journal of the Experimental Analysis of Behavior*, 1967, **10**, 529-533.

Received 16 October 1968.

CONCURRENT PERFORMANCES: INHIBITION OF ONE RESPONSE BY REINFORCEMENT OF ANOTHER[1]

A. Charles Catania

NEW YORK UNIVERSITY

In an analysis of interactions between concurrent performances, variable-interval reinforcement was scheduled, in various sequences, for both keys, for only one key, or for neither key of a two-key pigeon chamber. With changeover delays of 0.5 or 1.0 sec, and with each key's reinforcements discriminated on the basis of key-correlated feeder stimuli, reinforcement of pecks on one key reduced the pecking maintained by reinforcement on the other key. The decrease in pecking early after reinforcement was discontinued on one key was not substantially affected by whether pecks on the other key were reinforced, but after reinforcement was discontinued on both keys, reinstatement of reinforcement for one key sometimes produced transient increases in pecking on the other key. Correlating the availability of right-key reinforcements with a stimulus, which maintained right-key reinforcement while reducing right-key pecking to negligible levels, demonstrated that these interactions depended on concurrent reinforcement, not concurrent responding. Thus, reinforcement of a response, but not necessarily the occurrence of the response, inhibits other reinforced responses. Compared with accounts in terms of excitatory effects of extinction, often invoked in treatments of behavioral contrast, this inhibitory account has the advantage of dealing only with observed dimensions of behavior.

In concurrent schedules, two or more component schedules operate simultaneously but independently, each for a different response. In multiple schedules, two or more component schedules operate successively for a single response, each in the presence of a different stimulus. The two types of schedules are both formally and behaviorally related in that the analysis of either must be concerned with the relative frequencies of the component responses.

Concurrent performances ordinarily consist of the successive emission of the concurrent responses as the organism switches from one to the other. Simultaneous concurrent responses are possible in principle, but attempts are usually made to eliminate such responses in practice because independence of the concurrent performances cannot be maintained if each response is not separated in time from subsequent consequences of the other response (Catania, 1962). Thus, in typical concurrent performances the organism successively confronts different stimuli as it moves from one response to another.

In multiple schedules, the component responses and stimuli also occur in succession, with the major difference that changes from one to the other are determined by the experimenter rather than by the organism. This formal equivalence of the two types of schedules is clearest within a concurrent procedure that arranges a separate changeover response (Findley, 1958). For example, when such a procedure is scheduled for a pigeon the concurrent responses consist of pecks in the presence of different stimuli on one key, and the pigeon changes over from one stimulus to another by pecking a second key. This changeover-response procedure has been shown to be functionally as well as formally equivalent to a two-response concurrent procedure (e.g., Catania, 1963).

Because concurrent performances involve changeover responses, which cannot occur in

[1]Dedicated to B. F. Skinner in his sixty-fifth year, with the hope that its concern with the experimenter's verbal behavior makes it fitting. This research was supported by NSF Grant GB 3614 and by NIH Grant MH 13613 to New York University. Some data were presented at the Eastern Pyschological Association (Catania and Tallen, 1968). Thanks are due to Barry Schwartz, Philip Silverman, and Barrington Graham for help in various phases of the experiment, and to Mrs. Geraldine Hansen for unfailing secretarial assistance during the preparation of the manuscript. Reprints may be obtained from the author at the Department of Psychology, University College of Arts and Science, New York University, New York, New York 10453.

multiple schedules, the two types of schedules differ in details of data treatment. The interactions that occur within each type of schedule are, however, qualitatively similar. For example, an increase in the reinforcement of one response produces a decrease in the rate of the other response both in concurrent schedules (*e.g.*, Catania, 1963) and in multiple schedules (*e.g.*, Reynolds, 1961*a*). The interactions in concurrent schedules tend to be larger in magnitude than the analogous interactions in multiple schedules, but it has been shown that both types can be dealt with in terms of a single quantitative account (Lander and Irwin, 1968). The two types of schedules are also similar with respect to interactions involving both reinforcement and punishment. For example, when both component responses are punished in either concurrent or multiple schedules, the absolute rates of each response are reduced but their relative rates are not affected (*e.g.*, in concurrent schedules, Holz, 1968; in multiple schedules, Tullis and Walters, 1968), and when the two component responses are each maintained by reinforcement and only one is punished, the decrease in the rate of the punished response is accompanied by an increase in the rate of the unpunished response (*e.g.*, in concurrent schedules, Reynolds, 1963; Catania, 1966, pp. 245-246; in multiple schedules, Brethower and Reynolds, 1962).

Interactions between component responses have been examined in detail in multiple schedules (*e.g.*, Reynolds, 1961*b*, 1964, 1968). Concurrent performances are characterized by interactions analogous to those observed in multiple schedules, and their quantitative properties have been described on the basis of data from two-response concurrent procedures (*e.g.*, Herrnstein, 1961), from changeover-response concurrent procedures (*e.g.*, Catania, 1963), and from concurrent chained schedules (in which the concurrent responses are each reinforced by a stimulus in the presence of which a schedule of primary reinforcement operates; *e.g.*, Herrnstein, 1964). The present study of two-response concurrent performances extends the analysis of schedule interactions by examining exhaustively the possible sequences of concurrent schedules when either reinforcement or extinction is scheduled for pigeons' pecks on each of two keys. In this two-response concurrent proce-

dure, as in changeover-response and concurrent-chain procedures, reinforcement can be scheduled for both responses, for only one response, or for neither response. Thus, sequences of concurrent schedules can be arranged in which reinforcement of both responses is followed by extinction either of one or of both responses, in which extinction of both responses is followed by reinforcement either of one or of both responses, and in which reinforcement of only one response is followed either by reinforcement of both responses, by extinction of both responses, or by extinction of that response and reinforcement of the other response. Within such sequences, continued reinforcement, continued extinction, and the change from reinforcement to extinction or from extinction to reinforcement of one response can be observed both when accompanied by reinforcement of the other response and when unaccompanied by reinforcement of the other response.

METHOD

Subjects

Six adult male White Carneaux pigeons, with varied histories in earlier concurrent procedures, were maintained at about 80% of free-feeding body weight. Of the four experimental series described below, Series 1 and 2 included Pigeons 150, 43, 44, and 45, Series 3 included Pigeons 150, 43, 50, and 45, and Series 4 included Pigeons 150, 43, 50, and 72. During Series 1 and 2, Pigeons 44 and 45 showed both physical and behavioral symptoms of illness (loss of feathers, vomiting, difficulty in standing erect, and occasional instances of extreme variability in performance from day to day). Pigeon 44 died and Pigeon 50 was substituted near the end of Series 2 and Pigeon 45 was dropped from the experiment and Pigeon 72 was substituted during Series 3; the data from these pigeons in these series were not incorporated into the data presentation.

Apparatus

The two-key experimental chamber included the following standard devices: a houselight that provided general illumination; a speaker that produced white masking noise; a relay, mounted behind the panel, that could produce feedback clicks when either key was pecked; a Gerbrands feeder; and a ventilating fan. The two Gerbrands pigeon keys, adjusted for approximately equal 15-g (0.14 N) forces of operation, were mounted above the feeder at a height of 9 in. (230 mm) from the floor and were spaced 2.5 in. (64 mm) apart, center-to-center. The left key was ordinarily illuminated green and the right amber. Pecks on a given key produced feedback clicks only when the key was illuminated. During Series 1, 2, and 3, two white 6-w lamps in the feeder were lit during reinforcement, when all other lights in the chamber were turned off and key pecks were ineffective. During Series 4, the feeder was modified (Fig. 1), and a green and an amber lamp were substituted for the two white lamps.

Procedure

Throughout the experiment, reinforcement duration was 3 sec, daily sessions were 100 min (excluding the duration of reinforcement), and variable-interval reinforcement, arranged according to the specifications of Catania and Reynolds (1968, Appendix II), was scheduled with an average interval of 180 sec. Each key's intervals were timed from the end of reinforcement, the order of the intervals in the schedule for one key was the reverse of that for the other key, and each key's schedule stopped operating during reinforcement produced by pecks on the other key.

Each session consisted of one of four possible combinations of variable-interval (VI) and extinction (EXT) schedules for the two keys (VI VI, VI EXT, EXT VI, and EXT EXT, where the terms of each pair represent the left-key and the right-key schedules, respectively). Various sequences of changes from one to another of the schedule combinations were arranged in the four experimental series outlined in Table 1: Series 1 and 2 examined the effects of schedule changes with two different changeover delays; Series 3 separated effects of concurrent reinforcement from effects of concurrent responding; and Series 4 examined the effects of schedule changes when discriminated reinforcers were arranged for the two responses.

In sessions of Series 1 and 2, the left key was lit green and the right key amber at all times except during reinforcement. The two series differed in the changeover delay (COD: Herrnstein, 1961) that was scheduled: COD 0.5-sec in Series 1 and COD 1.0-sec in Series 2. The changeover delay arranged that no peck could be reinforced until at least the delay interval had elapsed after changeovers from one key to the other; the delay was timed from the first peck on one key after a peck on the

Table 1

Sequence of concurrent schedules for the left key (green) and the right key (amber), in that order, within the successive series. Numbers indicate sessions. Changeover delays (CODs) were timed from the first peck on one key after a peck on the other. The mean interval of each variable-interval (VI) schedule was 180 sec. In Series 3, the right key lit only when reinforcement became available for pecks on that key (SCVI: stimulus-correlated VI schedule); the key was dark when extinction (EXT) was scheduled.

Series 1			Series 2			Series 3			Series 4					
COD 0.5-sec			COD 1.0-sec			COD 1.0-sec Right key: SCVI			COD 0.5-sec Key-correlated feeder stimuli					
VI	VI	14	VI	EXT	5	VI	SCVI	12	VI	VI	28	EXT	VI	12
VI	EXT	12	EXT	EXT	7	VI	EXT	7	EXT	VI	7	VI	VI	14
EXT	VI	10	VI	VI	10	VI	SCVI	14	EXT	EXT	8	VI	EXT	7
VI	VI	11	VI	EXT	6	VI	EXT	11	EXT	VI	5	EXT	VI	14
EXT	EXT	6	EXT	VI	6	EXT	EXT	10	EXT	EXT	5	VI	VI	10
VI	EXT	8	EXT	EXT	6	EXT	SCVI	7	VI	EXT	7	VI	EXT	7
VI	VI	9	VI	EXT	6	VI	SCVI	9	VI	VI	10	EXT	VI	10
EXT	VI	20	VI	VI	5	EXT	SCVI	16	EXT	EXT	5	VI	VI	14
EXT	EXT	6	EXT	EXT	4	EXT	EXT	7	VI	VI	6			
VI	EXT	16	EXT	VI	8	VI	EXT	6	EXT	VI	9			
EXT	EXT	6	VI	VI	9	EXT	SCVI	9	VI	EXT	7			
VI	VI	8				VI	EXT	9	EXT	EXT	5			
VI	EXT	8							VI	EXT	9			

other. By interposing a minimum interval of time between a peck on one key and a subsequent reinforced peck on the other, the COD contributes to the independence of the concurrent responses (Catania, 1962).

In Series 3, the left key was lit green as in the preceding series, but the right key was lit amber only when the schedule for that key had arranged reinforcement for a subsequent peck. A 1-sec COD remained in effect for changeovers in either direction, and each key was operative only when lit. The correlation of a stimulus with the right-key VI schedule (Catania, 1963) reduced responding on the right key to a few pecks (satisfying the COD) on the average of once every 3 min, when reinforcement was scheduled; the key was rarely pecked when dark. Reinforcement of right-key pecks, however, occurred at essentially the same rate as in the equivalent VI schedules for the right key in Series 1 and 2. To reduce the likelihood that the pigeon's looking toward the right key would affect the rate of left-key pecking (*cf.* Rachlin and Baum, 1969), the left key was darkened whenever the right key lit. The right key remained dark at all times when EXT was scheduled for that key.

In sessions of Series 4, a COD of 0.5 sec was in effect and both keys were again lit at all times except during reinforcement, but the feeder was modified so that discriminated reinforcers could be scheduled for each key. According to the VI schedule for the left key (green), the reinforced peck turned off the lights in the chamber, made the keys inactive, and lit a green lamp in the feeder; a peck on a switch within the left side of the feeder then raised the food hopper for 3 sec. According to the VI schedule for the right key (amber), the reinforced peck turned off the lights in the chamber, made the keys inactive, and lit an amber lamp in the feeder; a peck on a switch within the right side of the feeder then raised the food hopper for 3 sec. (The procedure is equivalent to concurrent chained schedules, as in Herrnstein, 1964, with the modification that the terminal responses of each chain occur inside the feeder instead of on the keys.)

The arrangement of the switches inside the feeder is illustrated schematically in Fig. 1. Establishment of feeder-switch pecking was facilitated by placing several small black spots above the bottom edge of each switch

plate at the start of training. Two of the pigeons began to operate the switches within a single session during which the concurrent schedules of Series 4 were fully in operation. The responses of the other two pigeons were shaped within a single subsequent session by selectively reinforcing head movements inside the feeder when the feeder was lit. Once the feeder was lit, the time preceding a peck on the appropriate switch was not restricted (no limited hold), nor did pecks on the inappropriate switch have any effect. Before the first schedule change of Series 4, each pigeon was responding accurately and with short latencies with respect to the key-correlated feeder stimuli and their respective switches.

RESULTS

The data obtained in each experimental series are summarized in Fig. 2. The rows show the four series, with the order of Series 3 and 4 reversed because the data of Series 3 differ in labelling and treatment from those of

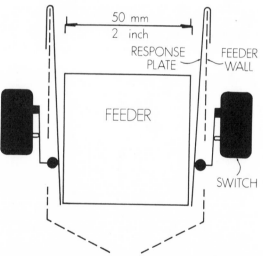

Fig. 1. Arrangement of feeder switches in sessions of Series 4. Centered in the side walls of a standard Gerbrands feeder, two square 0.75-in. (19 mm) holes each accommodated the roller of a light-force extended-roller miniature switch (Cherry E23-70K). Two 4-in. by 1.125-in. (100-mm by 28-mm) plates of 1/64 in. (0.4-mm) aluminum were bent to fit over the top edges of the side walls. The lower surface of each plate rested against the corresponding miniature switch roller, so that pecks on the plates operated the respective switches. A peck on the left plate when the feeder was lit green (left-key color) or a peck on the right plate when the feeder was lit amber (right-key color) raised the food hopper for 3 sec.

the other series. The columns show the various sequences of concurrent schedules. For convenience of presentation, the data for Series 1, 2, and 4 have been treated so that a given schedule within a concurrent pair is represented by a single set of data points rather than by two sets that distinguish whether the schedule operated for the left key or for the right key. For example, in the change from EXT EXT to VI VI (column 1), the data from the two keys were averaged together because the schedules were the same for each key; in the changes from VI EXT to VI VI and from EXT VI to VI VI (column 2), the data from the left key in the first sequence were averaged together with the data from the right key in the second sequence because in their respective sequences the schedules for these two keys were the same. Symmetrical concurrent sequences (identical except for the reversal of keys, as in the preceding example) could not occur in Series 3 because different types of schedules were arranged for the two keys; the stimulus-correlated schedules for the right key reduced responding on that key to negligible levels, and therefore all the data shown for Series 3 are from the left key only.

The concurrent VI and EXT sequences are treated exhaustively in Fig. 2: reinforcement of pecks on both keys (VI VI) could follow either extinction on both keys (column 1) or reinforcement of pecks on only one key (column 2); reinforcement of pecks on only one key (VI EXT or EXT VI) could follow either reinforcement of pecks on both keys (column 3), reinforcement of pecks on only the other key (column 4), or extinction on both keys (column 5); extinction on both keys (EXT EXT) could follow either reinforcement of pecks on only one key (column 6) or reinforcement of pecks on both keys (column 7).

The subsequent presentation emphasizes the data obtained in Series 4 and in Series 3. The data for Series 1 and 2 were obtained from only two pigeons and were based on fewer repetitions of a given schedule change than the data for Series 4 (*cf.* Table 1). In addition, data from the early exposures to schedule changes in Series 1 probably were affected by the order in which the changes were examined as well as by the properties of the concurrent schedules, especially in those cases in which either schedule changed from VI to EXT.

These considerations may account for the somewhat greater session-to-session variability for a given schedule in Series 1 and 2 than in Series 4.

Nevertheless, the data from the four series are qualitatively similar even if they differ in quantitative detail. The rates of EXT responding were typically higher in Series 1 with COD 0.5-sec than in Series 2 with COD 1-sec, but no other substantial effects were evident. The difference in rates of EXT responding may be attributed both to the order in which the series were scheduled and to the different CODs, which have been shown to affect some properties of concurrent performances (*e.g.*, Catania, 1966, pp. 241-243; Shull and Pliskoff, 1967). The addition of key-correlated feeder stimuli in Series 4, which guaranteed that the reinforcers correlated with each key were discriminated, also did not substantially alter the general characteristics of the interactions. The arrangement of different reinforcers for concurrent responses (*e.g.*, food and shock avoidance: Catania, Deegan, and Cook, 1966) sometimes can reduce concurrent interactions, but the arrangement of reinforcers discriminated only on the basis of the responses that produced them apparently does not have this effect.

The interactions in Series 3 were similar to those in the other series even though there were no symmetrical concurrent sequences in that series. In each graph for Series 3 that shows two sets of data, the two sets were obtained successively in different schedule changes, whereas corresponding data for the other series were obtained simultaneously. For example, the change from VI EXT to VI VI or from EXT VI to VI VI in the other series always provided the data both from the key for which VI reinforcement was maintained and from the key for which the schedule was changed from EXT to VI. These two sets of data were obtained successively in Series 3: one set from the left key in the change from VI EXT to VI SCVI (stimulus-correlated VI), and the other set also from the left key in the change from EXT SCVI to VI SCVI. Because the interactions in Series 3 occurred even though right-key responding was reduced to negligible levels, concurrent reinforcement rather than concurrent responding is implicated as the variable that determined the properties of the concurrent interactions.

These interactions may now be examined by comparing the concurrent performances shown in different columns of Fig. 2. The presentation considers how the following aspects of performance were affected by concurrent reinforcement: the rate of responding maintained by VI reinforcement; the rapidity with which the rate of responding increased after the change from EXT to VI reinforcement; the rate of responding maintained during EXT; and the rapidity with which the rate of responding decreased after the change from VI reinforcement to EXT.

Responding Maintained by VI Reinforcement

The rate of responding maintained by VI reinforcement was consistently lower when concurrent responding was reinforced (columns 1 and 2) than when concurrent respond-

ing was not reinforced (column 3, unfilled circles, and columns 4 and 5, filled circles). For example, with key-correlated feeder stimuli in Series 4, a VI schedule maintained about 40 resp/min during VI VI and about 60 resp/min during VI EXT or EXT VI. The unfilled circles in columns 2 and 3 show the changes in rate that are usually spoken of in terms of behavioral contrast in analogous multiple schedules (*e.g.*, Reynolds, 1961*b*): when reinforcement was introduced for a concurrent response (column 2), the rate of responding maintained by VI reinforcement decreased; when the concurrent response was extinguished (column 3), the rate of responding maintained by VI reinforcement increased. These two changes in rate occurred without exception in each of about 40 observations of each of these schedule changes throughout the

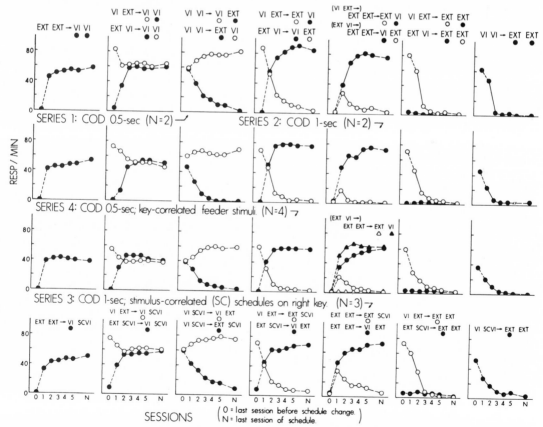

Fig. 2. Summary of data obtained within each experimental series. Each graph shows arithmetic means taken across the schedule changes for each pigeon in a given series and, as labelled above each graph, across corresponding keys of symmetrical schedule changes (*e.g.*, the left key in the change from VI EXT to VI VI and the right key in the change from EXT VI to VI VI). The number of pigeons contributing data to each series is indicated. The order of Series 3 and Series 4 has been reversed for convenience of exposition. VI—variable-interval schedule (180 sec); EXT—extinction; COD—changeover delay. Additional details in text.

four series (including data from Pigeons 44 and 45, which were not incorporated into Fig. 2; see Method).

The data from Series 3, obtained with stimulus-correlated VI schedules for the right key, demonstrate that these changes in rate depended directly on concurrent reinforcement rather than on competition between concurrent responses; an increase in the rate of right-key responding in the other series did not reduce the rate of left-key responding by limiting the time available for its emission, because the same reduction in rate occurred when right-key responding was reduced to negligible levels in Series 3.

The Change from EXT to VI Reinforcement

The schedule for a given key could change from EXT to VI reinforcement either accompanied by VI reinforcement of a concurrent response (columns 1 and 2) or unaccompanied by VI reinforcement of a concurrent response (columns 4 and 5). When concurrent responding was reinforced, the change to the rate of responding maintained by VI reinforcement was reached more rapidly after EXT EXT (column 1) than after VI EXT or EXT VI (column 2, filled circles). In Series 4, for example, a rate of about 40 resp/min was reached within the first session after the change from EXT EXT to VI VI, whereas a rate of only about 30 resp/min was reached after the change from VI EXT or EXT VI to VI VI.

When concurrent responding was not reinforced, however, the change to the rate of responding maintained by VI reinforcement was reached more slowly after EXT EXT (column 5, filled circles) than after VI EXT or EXT VI (column 4, filled circles). In Series 4, for example, the rate of responding continued to increase for several sessions after the change from EXT EXT, whereas a relatively stable rate of about 60 resp/min was reached by the second session after VI EXT or EXT VI. This difference may have depended on the sequence of preceding schedules and on effects on the extinguished concurrent response; these factors are considered below.

The Rate of EXT Responding

When EXT was scheduled for a given key, responding was usually maintained at higher rates during VI reinforcement of concurrent responding (column 3, filled circles, and columns 4 and 5, unfilled circles) than during extinction of concurrent responding (columns 6 and 7), although this difference was small in absolute terms. In Series 4, for example, the rate of EXT responding was 2 or 3 resp/min after at least seven sessions of VI EXT or EXT VI (column 3, filled circles; *cf.* Table 1), whereas the rate of EXT responding was already essentially 0 resp/min after only five sessions of EXT EXT (column 7). This difference indicates that a low rate of EXT responding may be maintained when it can occasionally be followed by reinforcement scheduled for a concurrent response (*cf.* Catania and Cutts, 1963). In Series 1, 2, and 4, the COD imposed a minimum delay between EXT responses and subsequent reinforcements of concurrent responses, but did not eliminate the incidental delayed reinforcement of the EXT responses. In Series 3, the effects of concurrent reinforcement on EXT responding were somewhat greater than in the other series, even though right-key reinforcements were delayed by a COD, presumably because left-key EXT responding could sometimes be followed without any scheduled delay by the stimulus correlated with right-key reinforcements. The available data do not allow speculation on how reinforcement of one response would affect the rate of a concurrent extinguished response if incidental delayed effects on one response of reinforcement of the other could be completely eliminated.

The effect of concurrent reinforcement on responding for which EXT was maintained is shown in columns 5 (unfilled circles) and 6 (filled circles). The introduction of VI reinforcement for one of two extinguished responses, in the change from EXT EXT to either EXT VI or VI EXT, typically produced a transient increase in the rate of the other response. The analogous case in multiple schedules (Reynolds, 1964) has been discussed in terms of an inductive effect on one response of reinforcement of another response. The effect cannot be attributed to a discriminative effect of reinforcement on the responding that follows reinforcement (Reid, 1957), because it occurred in Series 4 with discriminated reinforcers as well as in Series 1 and 2; nor can it be attributed directly to the increase in the rate of the reinforced response, because it occurred when right-key responding was reduced to negligible levels by stimulus-correlated schedules in Series 3.

Series 4 assessed the contribution of the schedules in preceding sessions to this inductive effect. In the other series, the effect had been observed in sequences such that the extinguished response had been reinforced in the pair of concurrent schedules that preceded EXT EXT (see bracketed schedules in the labels for column 5). During Series 4, two sequences were arranged so that the extinguished response was not reinforced in the pair of concurrent schedules that preceded EXT EXT (unfilled and filled triangles in column 5 of Series 4; *cf.* Table 1). These sequences of schedule changes did not produce an inductive effect on EXT responding (unfilled triangles), and the rate of responding maintained by VI reinforcement of the other response was reached more rapidly than when the VI reinforcement was accompanied by an inductive effect (filled triangles *versus* filled circles). These differences do not in any sense account for the observed phenomenon of induction, but they do illustrate its dependence either on the preceding sequence of schedules or on the number of sessions for which EXT was maintained for the response in the preceding sequences.

When EXT was maintained for one response while VI reinforcement was discontinued for the other response, the rate of the maintained EXT responding ordinarily decreased (column 6, filled circles). This effect was small in absolute magnitude, and exceptions were sometimes observed during the early sessions after the change in schedules (*e.g.*, in Series 2, a slight increment in responding in Sessions 1 and 2 was followed by a decrease to a final EXT rate lower than that in the session before the schedule change). In Series 4, the rate decreased from 2 or 3 resp/min during VI EXT or EXT VI to essentially 0 resp/min in the last of the sessions of EXT EXT; in Series 3, the rate decreased from 4 or 5 resp/min during EXT SCVI to less than 1 resp/min in the last EXT EXT sessions. These effects of concurrent reinforcement on maintained EXT responding are consistent with the other effects on EXT responding considered above.

The Change from VI Reinforcement to EXT

The change from VI reinforcement to EXT for a given response could occur either accompanied by concurrent VI reinforcement (columns 3 and 4) or unaccompanied by concurrent VI reinforcement (columns 6 and 7). When the change followed VI VI (columns 3 and 7), the decrement in responding during EXT began from a lower rate of responding than when the change followed VI EXT or EXT VI (columns 4 and 6).

Responding in EXT after VI VI decreased more slowly when VI reinforcement continued for the concurrent response (column 3, filled circles) than when VI reinforcement did not continue for the concurrent response (column 7). In Series 4, for example, the rate of responding during the first session of EXT dropped only to about 30 resp/min when reinforcement continued for the other response but to about 20 resp/min when reinforcement was discontinued for both responses. This difference was fairly consistent across pigeons and series; the reversal in Series 1 probably depended on the order in which the schedule changes were examined during the initial exposures of each pigeon to EXT in this series (*cf.* Method).

Concurrent reinforcement did not have consistent effects on the decrements in EXT responding after VI EXT or EXT VI (columns 4 and 6). The rate of EXT responding in the first session of EXT VI after VI EXT or in the first session of VI EXT after EXT VI (column 4, open circles) was higher in Series 2 and 4 and lower in Series 1 and 3 than the rate in the first session of EXT EXT after VI EXT or EXT VI (column 6, open circles). Two effects may have operated together in these cases: a direct reduction of EXT responding by concurrent VI reinforcement may have been balanced by an inductive effect of VI reinforcement like that shown in column 5. In the absence of data separating two such effects, however, it is more appropriate to conclude that concurrent reinforcement does not affect the decrease in responding during EXT. This conclusion is consistent with the observation that reinforcement of one response has different effects on concurrent responding also maintained by reinforcement than on concurrent responding that is only maintained at operant level (Catania, 1966, p. 259).

The change from VI reinforcement to EXT in column 4 (unfilled circles) has a unique characteristic: because VI reinforcement was initiated for concurrent responding when

EXT began, it is the only case in which the dependency between responses and reinforcers was terminated while the rate of delivery of reinforcers continued unchanged. Thus, this example of extinction may be uncontaminated by effects of the termination of reinforcers (*e.g.*, emotional behavior) that typically accompany the termination of a dependency between responses and reinforcers. This schedule change may have special relevance for the

analysis of extinction, but its advantages may be offset by the need to evaluate the inductive effects of concurrent reinforcement on the extinguishing response.

Data obtained in successive schedule changes for Pigeon 150 in Series 4 and Series 3 are shown in Fig. 3, to illustrate the extent to which the summary data in Fig. 2 are representative of individual performances. Data from Series 3 show left-key responding only,

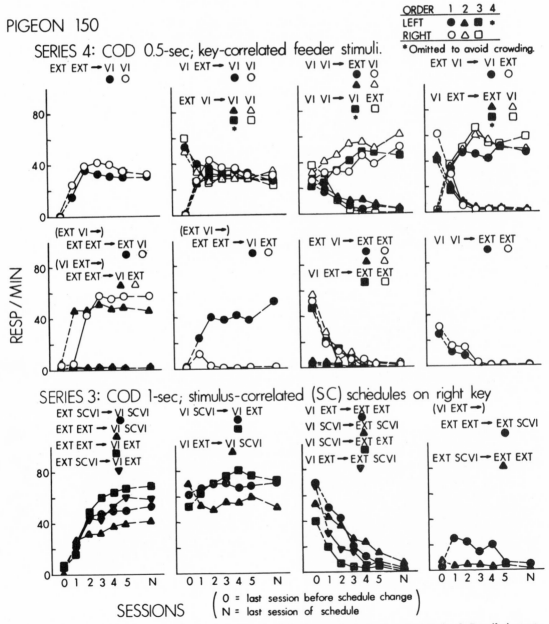

Fig. 3. Data from Pigeon 150, showing successive schedule changes in Series 4 and in Series 3. Details in text.

because right-key responding occurred at near-zero rates throughout that series. For this pigeon, the rate of responding maintained by VI reinforcement in Series 4 tended to be slightly higher on the right key (unfilled symbols) than on the left key (filled symbols), a difference that might be referred to as a response bias in favor of the right key. Nevertheless, the interactions were qualitatively similar to those illustrated in Fig. 2.

DISCUSSION

In summary, the present findings show that the rate of one reinforced response is reduced by the reinforcement of a concurrent response, that this interaction depends on concurrent reinforcement rather than on competition between the concurrent responses, and that reinforcement of one response sometimes has transient inductive effects on concurrent extinguished responses but does not accelerate the reduction in rate when extinction begins for the concurrent response. These findings are consistent with a quantitative account of concurrent performances (Catania, 1963) in which the rate of one of two concurrent responses is described by the following equation:

$$R_1 = \frac{Kr_1}{(r_1 + r_2)^n}.$$

In this equation, R_1 is the rate of Response 1, r_1 and r_2 are the respective rates of reinforcement of the two responses, and K is a constant that depends on the units of measurement. The exponent, n, is slightly less than 1.0 (in a related account by Herrnstein, 1964, n = 1.0). According to this equation, the rate of Response 1 decreases as the rate of reinforcement of Response 2 increases; the rate of Response 1 is determined solely by the rates of reinforcement of the two responses, because the rate of Response 2 does not enter into the equation; and the rate of Response 1 is zero when its rate of reinforcement is zero, but the rapidity with which rates may change when reinforcement is discontinued or reinstated for either response is not specified.

The relationship described by the above equation can be expressed in the following way: reinforcement of one response inhibits the rate of other reinforced responses. This application of the vocabulary of inhibition is

descriptive, and has the advantage that both the inhibited and the inhibiting processes are precisely and quantifiably specified in terms of concrete experimental operations. Thus, the vocabulary of inhibition can provide a convenient way of speaking about certain properties of behavior. But this vocabulary is inconsistent with the vocabulary applied to interactions in multiple schedules, which often have been attributed to excitatory properties of extinction. The discussion that follows therefore will be concerned with some characteristics of the vocabulary of inhibition and its implications for the analysis of interactions in both concurrent and multiple schedules. What follows, in other words, is not so much about the empirical findings as it is about the ways in which these findings may be spoken of.

The trouble with the concept of inhibition, as it is often applied to behavior, is that it is difficult to say unambiguously what is inhibited by what. If the inhibited and the inhibiting events are not clearly specified, the conditions that actively reduce responding may not be distinguishable from those that simply fail to maintain responding (*cf.* Skinner, 1938, p. 96). In the classical account (Pavlov, 1927), extinguished responding was said to be inhibited, but the process that did the inhibiting was not so concretely identified. The process was inferred not only from the response decrement produced by extinction, but also from accompanying increments in other responses (positive induction).

This inhibitory account is paralleled in current treatments of behavioral contrast in multiple schedules (*e.g.*, Reynolds, 1961c; Terrace, 1968). When reinforcement in the presence of two successive stimuli is followed by extinction in the presence of one of them, the rate of responding in the presence of the other typically increases (Reynolds, 1961a). This increase, an example of behavioral contrast, is usually treated as an excitatory side-effect of extinction. Such accounts have not always been formulated in the vocabulary of inhibition, but like the inhibitory account they speak of two processes: a direct effect on the extinguished response, and an indirect effect on other responses.

There is an alternative way of talking about what is inhibited by what in behavior: the maintenance of one response may be said to inhibit other responses (*cf.* Hovland, 1936).

Although this account may be expressed solely in terms of observed interactions between responses and therefore need not appeal to an unobserved inhibitory process, the common vocabulary of inhibition has tended to obscure the distinction between the two formulations (*cf.* Wendt, 1936). Figure 4 illustrates the way in which they differ.

An interaction characterized in terms of an excitatory effect of extinction is shown in *A*. Response 1 is maintained by reinforcement. When extinction reduces the rate of Response 2, the rate of Response 1 increases from *x* to *y*. When reinforcement is reinstated for Response 2, Response 1 returns to *x*, its original level. The arrows show the locus of the effect: extinction of Response 2 produces an increment in Response 1.

In *B*, the same interaction is shown in terms of inhibition of one response by reinforcement of another. When Response 2 is extinguished,

Response 1 is maintained by itself, at rate *y*. When reinforcement is reinstated for Response 2, the rate of Response 1 is reduced from *y* to *x*. Again, the arrows show the locus of the effect: reinforcement of Response 2 produces a decrement in Response 1.

The hypothetical data in *A* and *B* are the same. Yet the first characterizes extinction as the effective process and takes the reinforcement of both responses as the baseline level from which effects are measured (solid line at *x*). The second characterizes reinforcement as the effective process and takes the reinforcement of one response alone as the baseline level from which effects are measured (solid line at *y*). What is an effect in one formulation is the baseline level in the other. Because both formulations are consistent with the data, there is no simple empirical basis for choosing between them. But the second has a logical advantage, in that it treats reinforcement, an experimental operation, rather than extinction, the discontinuation of that operation, as a causal variable in the control of behavior. This treatment is consistent with the view that the extinction process is fundamentally nothing more than a manifestation of reinforcement (*cf.* Morse, 1966, pp. 53-54): the effects of reinforcement persist in time even after reinforcement is discontinued, and the time course of this persistence is called extinction. In any particular case, the analysis of this time course may be complicated because other effects are superimposed, but such effects need not force us to regard reinforcement and extinction as dichotomized processes. For example, the generalized changes in behavior called emotional probably depend directly on the termination of reinforcers. This termination is not a necessary accompaniment of extinction and its effects can be separated experimentally from the effects of its defining property, the termination of a dependency between responses and reinforcers (*cf.* Fig. 2, column 4).

The essential property of inhibition is not merely the reduction of an activity or process, but rather the dependence of this reduction on an increment in some other activity or process. Such a relationship precisely describes concurrent performances: the rate of a reinforced response is inhibited by the reinforcement of other responses. The inverse relationship, that extinction of a response produces increments

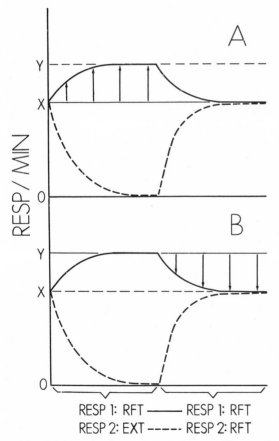

Fig. 4. Interaction between two responses illustrated as an excitatory effect of extinction (A) or as an inhibitory effect of reinforcement (B). Details in text.

in the rate of other responses, has never seemed a plausible description of concurrent performances because, in a given experimental situation, there are always any number of unreinforced concurrent responses that could be taken into account. For multiple schedules, too, the description of performances in terms of inhibitory effects of reinforcement has been suggested (Catania and Gill, 1964; Staddon, 1967), but the description in terms of excitatory effects of extinction has been predominant (*e.g.*, Reynolds, 1961*c*; Nevin and Shettleworth, 1966; Terrace, 1968).

The alternative ways of speaking are also evident in the description of punishment interactions in concurrent and multiple schedules. For example, when two responses are each maintained by reinforcement and only one is punished, the decrease in the rate of the punished response may be accompanied by an increase in the rate of the unpunished response (*e.g.*, Brethower and Reynolds, 1962). In a description that parallels the description of behavioral contrast as an excitatory effect of extinction, the increment in the unpunished response has been spoken of as a facilitative effect of the punishment of another response. But it is also possible to say that punishment counteracts the effect of reinforcement, and in so doing releases the unpunished response from inhibition by reinforcement. In this vocabulary, the effect of punishment on unpunished responding is disinhibiting rather than facilitating (in order of magnitude, the increments that punishment produces in unpunished responding are consistent with this interpretation).

The formal and functional similarities between concurrent and multiple schedules suggest that if the vocabulary of inhibitory effects of reinforcement is preferable to the vocabulary of excitatory effects of extinction in the concurrent case, it should also be preferable in the multiple case. The alternative is to retain two incompatible accounts of behavioral phenomena that may be fundamentally related but that differ perhaps in only superficial properties of the baseline schedule within which they have been observed.

What stands in the way of extending the present inhibitory vocabulary to multiple as well as to concurrent schedules? One substantial factor is that the phenomenon of behavioral contrast has been studied predominantly by manipulating conditions during the extinction component of the multiple schedules within which contrast is observed. (This experimental strategy itself arises from the assumption that behavioral contrast is a consequence of excitatory effects of extinction.) Various schedules of reinforcement (*e.g.*, differential–reinforcement-of-long–interresponse–time or DRL schedules: Terrace, 1968; Reynolds and Limpo, 1968) have been substituted in the extinction component to reduce the rate of responding in that component while maintaining presentations of the reinforcer (the rationale is related to that for the stimulus-correlated schedules of Series 3 in the present experiment). Such procedures must deal with the possible induction of the differentially reinforced response properties (*e.g.*, interresponse times) from one component to another (*cf.* Segal, 1961). Other procedures have involved changes in the parameters of reinforcement schedules, without the scheduling of extinction (*e.g.*, transitions among various multiple VI VI schedules, in Terrace, 1968). Such schedules tend to reduce the emphasis on absolute rates of responding, favoring the direction of change of the component rates, and can deal with excitatory effects of extinction only with difficulty in terms of the effects of reductions in reinforcement. The graded effects on one response produced by graded changes in the reinforcement of other responses (*e.g.*, as in Nevin, 1968) are handled more comfortably by the vocabulary of inhibition by reinforcement than by the vocabulary of excitation by extinction. Finally, procedures for establishing stimulus control without extinction responding ("errorless" discrimination: Terrace, 1963*a*, 1963*b*) eliminate behavioral contrast while maintaining alternating periods of VI reinforcement and extinction. This finding supports the argument that the absence of extinction responding during the acquisition of stimulus control prevents extinction from having its usual excitatory effect. But emotional effects or the incidental reinforcement of unspecified classes of responses may also be involved in the outcome, and from the conclusion that an extinction component in a multiple schedule may have aversive properties it does not necessarily follow that extinction is inhibitory.

Each of these cases may involve different empirical problems and different problems of interpretation, and this is not the place to evaluate all the possibilities. But it is possible to reformulate some of the questions. If it is plausible to state that reinforcement of one response inhibits other reinforced responses in concurrent schedules and that this vocabulary can appropriately be extended to multiple schedules, then it follows that the appropriate baseline condition for studying reinforcement interactions is one response reinforced alone. The present account in terms of inhibitory effects of reinforcement suggests, therefore, that rather than asking why most multiple VI EXT schedules produce the increase in VI responding that is spoken of in terms of behavioral contrast while those in errorless-discrimination procedures do not (Terrace, 1963a, 1963b), it may be profitable to ask instead why errorless-discrimination procedures produce a decrease in VI responding compared to the rates typically maintained in other multiple VI EXT schedules.

REFERENCES

Brethower, D. M. and Reynolds, G. S. A facilitative effect of punishment on unpunished behavior. *Journal of the Experimental Analysis of Behavior*, 1962, 5, 191-199.

Catania, A. C. Independence of concurrent responding maintained by interval schedules of reinforcement. *Journal of the Experimental Analysis of Behavior*, 1962, 5, 175-184.

Catania, A. C. Concurrent performances: reinforcement interaction and response independence. *Journal of the Experimental Analysis of Behavior*, 1963, 6, 253-263.

Catania, A. C. Concurrent operants. In W. K. Honig (Ed.), *Operant behavior: areas of research and application.* New York: Appleton-Century-Crofts, 1966. Pp. 213-270.

Catania, A. C. and Cutts, D. Experimental control of superstitious responding in humans. *Journal of the Experimental Analysis of Behavior*, 1963, 6, 203-208.

Catania, A. C., Deegan, J. F., and Cook, L. Concurrent fixed-ratio and avoidance responding in the squirrel monkey. *Journal of the Experimental Analysis of Behavior*, 1966, 9, 227-231.

Catania, A. C. and Gill, C. A. Inhibition and behavioral contrast. *Psychonomic Science*, 1964, 1, 257-258.

Catania, A. C. and Reynolds, G. S. A quantitative analysis of the responding maintained by interval schedules of reinforcement. *Journal of the Experimental Analysis of Behavior*, 1968, 11, 327-383.

Catania, A. C. and Tallen, R. R. *Concurrent performances: Inhibition and induction in sequences of variable-interval and extinction schedules for pigeons' pecks on two keys.* Paper presented at Eastern Psychological Association, Washington, D.C., 1968.

Findley, J. D. Preference and switching under concurrent scheduling. *Journal of the Experimental Analysis of Behavior*, 1958, 1, 123-144.

Herrnstein, R. J. Relative and absolute strength of response as a function of frequency of reinforcement. *Journal of the Experimental Analysis of Behavior*, 1961, 4, 267-272.

Herrnstein, R. J. Secondary reinforcement and rate of primary reinforcement. *Journal of the Experimental Analysis of Behavior*, 1964, 7, 27-36.

Holz, W. C. Punishment and rate of positive reinforcement. *Journal of the Experimental Analysis of Behavior*, 1968, 11, 285-292.

Hovland, C. I. "Inhibition of reinforcement" and the phenomena of experimental extinction. *Proceedings of the National Academy of Science*, 1936, 22, 430-433.

Lander, D. G. and Irwin, R. J. Multiple schedules: effects of the distribution of reinforcements between components on the distribution of responses between components. *Journal of the Experimental Analysis of Behavior*, 1968, 11, 517-524.

Morse, W. H. Intermittent reinforcement. In W. K. Honig (Ed.), *Operant behavior: areas of research and application.* New York: Appleton-Century-Crofts, 1966. Pp. 52-108.

Nevin, J. A. Differential reinforcement and stimulus control of not responding. *Journal of the Experimental Analysis of Behavior*, 1968, 11, 715-726.

Nevin, J. A. and Shettleworth, S. J. An analysis of contrast effects in multiple schedules. *Journal of the Experimental Analysis of Behavior*, 1966, 9, 305-315.

Pavlov, I. P. *Conditioned reflexes.* Tr. G. V. Anrep. London: Oxford Univ. Press, 1927.

Rachlin, H. and Baum, W. M. Response rate as a function of amount of reinforcement for a signalled concurrent response. *Journal of the Experimental Analysis of Behavior*, 1969, 12, 11-16.

Reid, R. L. The role of the reinforcer as a stimulus. *British Journal of Psychology*, 1958, 49, 202-209.

Reynolds, G. S. Behavioral contrast. *Journal of the Experimental Analysis of Behavior*, 1961, 4, 57-71. (a)

Reynolds, G. S. An analysis of interactions in a multiple schedule. *Journal of the Experimental Analysis of Behavior*, 1961, 4, 107-117. (b)

Reynolds, G. S. Contrast, generalization, and the process of discrimination. *Journal of the Experimental Analysis of Behavior*, 1961, 4, 289-294. (c)

Reynolds, G. S. Potency of conditioned reinforcers based on food and on food and punishment. *Science*, 1963, 139, 838-839.

Reynolds, G. S. Operant extinction near zero. *Journal of the Experimental Analysis of Behavior*, 1964, 7, 173-176.

Reynolds, G. S. Induction, contrast, and resistance to extinction. *Journal of the Experimental Analysis of Behavior*, 1968, 11, 453-457.

Reynolds, G. S. and Limpo, A. J. On some causes of behavioral contrast. *Journal of the Experimental Analysis of Behavior*, 1968, 11, 543-547.

Segal, E. F. Behavioral interactions under concurrent spaced-responding, variable-interval schedules of reinforcement. *Journal of the Experimental Analysis of Behavior*, 1961, 4, 263-266.

Shull, R. L. and Pliskoff, S. S. Changeover delay and concurrent schedules: some effects on relative performance measures. *Journal of the Experimental Analysis of Behavior*, 1967, **10,** 517-527.

Skinner, B. F. *The behavior of organisms.* New York: Appleton-Century-Crofts, 1938.

Staddon, J. E. R. Attention and temporal discrimination: factors controlling responding under a cyclic-interval schedule. *Journal of the Experimental Analysis of Behavior*, 1967, **10,** 349-359.

Terrace, H. S. Discrimination learning with and without "errors". *Journal of the Experimental Analysis of Behavior*, 1963, **6,** 1-27. (a)

Terrace, H. S. Errorless transfer of a discrimination across two continua. *Journal of the Experimental Analysis of Behavior*, 1963, **6,** 223-232. (b)

Terrace, H. S. Discrimination learning, the peak shift, and behavioral contrast. *Journal of the Experimental Analysis of Behavior*, 1968, **11,** 727-741.

Tullis, C. and Walters, G. Punished and unpunished responding in multiple variable-interval schedules. *Journal of the Experimental Analysis of Behavior*, 1968, **11,** 147-152.

Wendt, G. R. An interpretation of inhibition of conditioned reflexes as competition between reaction systems. *Psychological Review*, 1936, **43,** 258-281.

Received 27 March 1969.

CONCURRENT RESPONDING WITH FIXED RELATIVE RATE OF REINFORCEMENT[1]

D. ALAN STUBBS AND STANLEY S. PLISKOFF

NEW YORK UNIVERSITY AND UNIVERSITY OF MAINE

Responding by pigeons on one key of a two-key chamber alternated the color of the second key, on which responding produced food according to a variable-interval schedule of reinforcement. From time to time, reinforcement would be available for a response, but in the presence of a particular stimulus, either red or green light on the key. Red or green was chosen irregularly from reinforcement to reinforcement, so that a proportion of the total number of reinforcements could be specified for each color. Experimental manipulations involved variations of (1) the proportions for each color, (2) changeover delay, or, alternatively, (3) a fixed-ratio changeover requirement. The main findings were: (1) relative overall rates of responding and relative times in the presence of a key color approximated the proportions of reinforcements obtained in the presence of that color, while relative local rates of responding changed little; (2) changeover rate decreased as the proportions diverged from 0.50; (3) relative overall rate of responding and relative time remained constant as the changeover delay was increased from 2 to 32 sec, with reinforcement proportions for red and green of 0.75 and 0.25, but they increased above 0.90 when a fixed-ratio changeover of 20 responses replaced the changeover delay; (4) changeover rate decreased as the delay or fixed-ratio was increased.

Concurrent schedules specify that two (or more) reinforcement schedules function simultaneously. There are two (or more) operants, and reinforcement for each is scheduled independently. By one method, each operant and its schedule are assigned to an individual response key. By a second, all of the schedules are assigned to the same key (main key) and different exteroceptive stimuli are associated with each operant-schedule pair. Responses on a second key (changeover key) alternate the exteroceptive stimulus and the schedule in effect on the main key. Each schedule functions continuously, whether or not it is assigned to the main key at a given moment. The two procedures appear to be equivalent (Catania, 1966), but the second provides an advantage: since a changeover is explicit, contingencies and recording functions may be defined more directly.

A feature of concurrent variable-interval (VI) schedules that has been found under certain conditions is the "matching relationship" between relative response rates and reinforcement rates. The relative rate of responding and the proportion of time spent on each schedule approximate the relative rate of reinforcement for a schedule. With concurrent VI 1-min VI 3-min schedules, for example, about 0.75 of the feeder operations are assigned by the VI 1-min schedule. Of the total number of responses emitted, approximately 0.75 are on the VI 1-min key; of the total time, approximately 0.75 is spent responding on that key (Brownstein and Pliskoff, 1968; Catania, 1963, 1966; Herrnstein, 1961).

Because each of the VI schedules functions independently, the subject can confine its responding to one alternative and produce all reinforcements arranged by that schedule without changing over and responding on the other. If one of the schedules is extinction, changeovers are infrequent and the relative rates of reinforcement are always exactly 1.00 and 0.00. If neither of the schedules is extinction, the changeover rate is ordinarily high enough to prevent extreme variability in obtained relative rates of reinforcement from session to session. However, it remains true

[1]Dedicated to B. F. Skinner in his sixty-fifth year. The research was performed at the Institute for Behavioral Research and was supported by grants to that Institute: Grant NsG 450 from the National Aeronautics and Space Administration and by an NIH General Research Support Grant #5 501 FR 05636. Reprints may be obtained from D. Alan Stubbs, Department of Psychology, New York University, New York, New York 10453.

that the relative frequency of reinforcement is to some extent controlled by the subject. The present procedure was designed to guarantee a specified relative rate of reinforcement regardless of changeover rate—session-to-session variability was virtually eliminated by requiring that a scheduled feeder operation occur before another was arranged by either schedule. This procedure is similar to concurrent VI schedules in that responses are reinforced intermittently at variable intervals, and also in that a relative frequency of reinforcement can be specified for each main-key color. It is unlike the procedure of concurrent schedules in that reinforcement is not scheduled independently for each response class.

The desired relation between VI schedules may be arranged by halting both VI tape drives when either assigns a reinforcement, instead of the usual procedure of halting only the drive making the assignment. Alternatively, a single VI schedule may be employed to assign all reinforcements in conjunction with a second circuit that specifies a key color. Only a response in the presence of the specified key color is reinforced, and a specified proportion of all of the reinforcements is thereby assigned to the key color.[2] The latter method was employed here.

The present experiment studied two problems. First, does the matching relationship (Herrnstein, 1961) obtain, given the nonindependence between the two VIs required by the procedure? To answer that question, the proportion of the total number of reinforcements produced by responding in the presence of a given key color was varied. Each proportion yielded a relative rate of reinforcement that was compared with a relative rate of responding. A second question concerned the effects of changeover delays (COD) in choice. The COD specifies a minimum duration that must elapse between a changeover and the possibility of reinforcement. Herrnstein (1961) found that a COD was necessary to yield matching. Shull and Pliskoff (1967) also found that the distribution of responses was a function of COD duration. With concurrent VI 1-min VI 3-min schedules, COD duration was

varied between 0 and 20 sec. As the COD duration increased, the proportion of responses emitted and the time spent with respect to the VI 1-min schedule increased to approximately 0.90. However, as the relative rate of responding and time increased, the relative rate of reinforcement increased for the VI 1-min schedule. In the present experiment, the probability of reinforcement for a given main-key color was fixed by the procedure, while relative response rate and time could vary.

METHOD

Subjects

Three experimentally naive Silver King pigeons were maintained at 80% of their free-feeding weights throughout the experiment.

Apparatus

The two keys (Ralph Gerbrands Company) of the pigeon chamber were mounted 9.25 in. (23.5 mm) above the floor, 2.50 in. (6.35 mm) between centers. A force of 15 g (0.147 N) was required to operate each key; each operation produced a click from a relay located behind the work panel. The keys could be transilluminated by different colored lights. Mixed grain was presented by a Lehigh Valley Electronics pigeon feeder.

Procedure

Before the experimental procedure began, the birds were pretrained for 7 to 11 days. Pretraining consisted in establishing the key peck followed by training on a variable-interval schedule of reinforcement.

The experimental procedure was as follows. Left-key (main key) responses were reinforced according to a variable-interval 1.5-min schedule of reinforcement; the intervals were arranged according to a method described by Catania and Reynolds (1968, p. 381). The left key was transilluminated by either red or green light. Each response on the right key (changeover key) changed the color of the left key; the right key was transilluminated by yellow light.

A main-key response could be reinforced once the VI programmer had assigned a reinforcement, but only for a key peck emitted in the presence of a particular stimulus. The specific stimulus (red or green) was changed

---

[2]This procedure is closely related to that of Shimp (1966, 1969) and that of Graf, Bullock, and Bitterman (1964). It is sufficiently different in detail, however, and the intents of the several experiments are sufficiently diverse to obviate a lengthy comparison.

irregularly from reinforcement to reinforcement. The overall sequence of reinforcements was scheduled by a 33-position stepping switch. The sequence was changed at irregular intervals during the various experimental conditions.

Right-key responses (changeovers) produced a minimum delay before the possibility of reinforcement. The minimum time was the changeover delay. The VI tape programmer operated during the COD. Once a changeover was emitted, a second could be emitted without a main-key response intervening. Changeovers occurring during the COD initiated a new delay interval. Each session lasted until a bird received 60 food presentations of 3.5-sec access to mixed grain. During food presentation, the keylights and houselights were turned off and the grain tray was illuminated. Sessions were run daily.

The following manipulations were studied.

Changes in relative reinforcement rate. The procedure allows for a specification of the relative rate of reinforcement indirectly by adjusting the proportion of reinforcements that had to be produced in the presence of a specified key color. The relative rates, arranged with respect to the red key color, were: 0.50, 0.75, 0.00, 0.25, 0.90. The duration of the COD was 2 sec for all conditions. The number of sessions for each condition is shown in the last column of Table 1.

Changes in COD. The relative reinforcement rate was maintained at 0.75, and the duration of the COD was varied. The COD durations were: 8, 16, 32, and 0 sec. The numbers of sessions are shown in Table 1.

Fixed-ratio changeover requirement. With no COD, the number of responses required to changeover was varied: fixed-ratio (FR) changeover requirements of one (equivalent to COD = 0 sec) and 20 responses were used (see Table 1). Two changes in procedure were introduced for the FR 20 condition. Once a response was emitted on the changeover key, the main key was darkened and inactivated. After the FR was completed, the alternate main-key color came on; during the ratio requirement, the VI programmer was stopped. For the FR 1 condition, the procedure led simply to an immediate change from red to green or from green to red. After the changeover requirement of the one or the 20 responses was completed, at least one response on the main key was necessary before another changeover could be effected.

RESULTS

The following calculations with respect to the red key color were made: relative overall response rate, relative time, relative local response rate, relative reinforcement rate, main-key response rate, and the changeover-key response rate.

1. Relative overall response rate reduces to (Shull and Pliskoff, 1967):

$$\frac{R_R}{R_R + R_G}$$

Responses on the red key (R_R) were divided by total responses, responses on the red key plus responses on the green key (R_G).

2. Relative time:

$$\frac{T_R}{T_R + T_G}$$

Time spent in the presence of the red key was divided by total session time, exclusive of reinforcement cycles (and changeover time during the FR 20 changeover condition).

3. Relative local response rate:

$$\frac{R_R/T_R}{R_R/T_R + R_G/T_G}$$

Responses on the red key were divided by the time spent in the presence of the red key; the result was divided by the sum of those quantities for the red and the green keys.

4. Relative reinforcement rate reduces to:

$$\frac{r_R}{r_R + r_G}$$

The number of reinforcements produced by responding on the red key (r_R) was divided by the total number of reinforcements.

5. Main-key response rate: The total number of responses on the main key (color ignored) was divided by the total time, exclusive of reinforcement time (and changeover time during the FR 20 changeover condition).

Table 1

The Original Data from Which Calculations Were Made. Data Were Totaled Across the Last Five Sessions

Rein. Prop. (Red key)	CO Requirement	Responses		Time (sec)		Changeovers		Reinforcements		Sessions
		Red	Green	Red	Green	Red	Green	Red	Green	
PIGEON 103										
0.50	COD 2-sec	11855	9822	17824	14530	1212	1211	150	150	41
0.75	COD 2-sec	21883	4699	26562	4655	675	675	227	73	31
0.0	COD 2-sec	20	27223	133	28729	100	100	0	300	21
0.25	COD 2-sec	10057	26496	7622	22404	1322	1322	72	228	44
0.90	COD 2-sec	18670	2001	29527	1886	571	572	280	20	30
0.75	COD 8-sec	28536	6307	28913	4808	284	284	224	76	32
0.75	COD 16-sec	29043	6235	30996	4446	151	150	223	77	33
0.75	COD 32-sec	37132	7387	42477	5025	130	133	222	78	32
0.75	COD 0-sec	26064	3952	23336	5900	2801	2802	225	75	33
0.75	FR 1	18006	5533	21274	8112	4089	4093	228	72	8
0.75	FR 20	30157	1163	31902	2607	213	213	227	73	19
0.75	FR 1	17341	5691	20983	8412	4243	4242	225	75	9
PIGEON 104										
0.50	COD 2-sec	16278	15689	15670	16228	662	662	151	149	39
0.75	COD 2-sec	31514	3847	28196	3287	403	404	225	75	32
0.0	COD 2-sec	25	29705	75	28832	50	50	0	300	21
0.25	COD 2-sec	5954	33565	5110	26627	547	548	76	224	43
0.90	COD 2-sec	30644	1876	28696	1695	258	258	280	20	30
0.75	COD 8-sec	33643	6442	27687	5536	304	304	227	73	32
0.75	COD 16-sec	35189	4731	30359	6699	255	255	225	75	33
0.75	COD 32-sec	53217	2608	38107	4977	115	116	226	74	32
0.75	COD 0-sec	27990	6365	21805	7523	2066	2066	225	75	33
0.75	FR 1	26611	7670	20934	8466	2160	2160	224	76	8
0.75	FR 20	44786	541	31834	2733	197	198	225	75	18
0.75	FR 1	31659	5397	23081	6276	2061	2061	226	74	10
PIGEON 108										
0.50	COD 2-sec	14524	13927	16376	14687	1129	1132	149	151	37
0.75	COD 2-sec	17755	4681	25638	5811	660	660	226	74	32
0.0	COD 2-sec	4	13690	11	29093	1	1	0	300	21
0.25	COD 2-sec	6128	17994	6849	24883	677	676	74	226	44
0.90	COD 2-sec	19950	1851	28828	1925	399	399	280	20	30
0.75	COD 8-sec	19783	5824	26195	6402	379	380	223	77	32
0.75	COD 16-sec	17124	5076	30597	6040	186	186	226	74	33
0.75	COD 32-sec	16422	5431	36180	6102	119	120	224	76	32
0.75	COD 0-sec	9190	2846	22206	7829	2050	2050	223	77	32
0.75	FR 1	10558	3241	22960	6751	2178	2178	225	75	9
0.75	FR 20	17135	1766	27932	4434	316	313	223	77	16*
0.75	FR 1	10790	3096	23965	6245	2337	2338	226	74	11

*Pigeon 108 was run two additional sessions during which the pigeon did not respond due to an injury to its beak.

187

6. Changeover-key response rate: The total number of responses on the changeover key was divided by the total time as defined above.

Table 1 shows the original data summed for the final five sessions under each experimental condition. All calculations were made from those five-day sums.

Figure 1 was plotted from data obtained with the COD equal to 2 sec and shows the relative overall response rate, relative time, and relative local response rate as a function of the relative overall rate of reinforcement. The relative response rates and time measures approximated the relative rates of reinforcement. There was, however, a tendency for relative overall response rate and for relative time to exceed relative reinforcement rate for values of the latter greater than 0.50. Relative local response rate reasonably approximated 0.50 over all conditions for the three subjects. This outcome indicates that the birds responded on the main key at a constant rate under each condition and partitioned time so that relative time (and hence relative response rate) approximated relative reinforcement rate. (Note that if relative overall response rate and relative time are equal, then relative local response rate necessarily must be 0.50.) No point was plotted for relative local response rate at the relative reinforcement rate of 0.0, since only a negligible number of responses was emitted on the red key.

Figure 2 shows response rates on both the main key and the changeover key as functions of relative reinforcement rate. Main-key response rate varied across conditions; however, there was no consistent trend in relation to reinforcement rate. Changeover rate, on the other hand, decreased as the relative reinforcement rate diverged from 0.50. An exception was Bird 103, which demonstrated the highest changeover rate at the relative reinforcement rate 0.25 rather than 0.50.

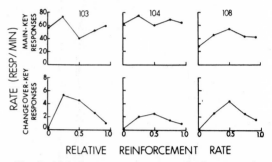

Fig. 2. Main-key response rate and changeover-key response rate as functions of the relative rate of reinforcement.

Figure 3 shows relative overall response rate, relative time, and relative local response rate as functions of the changeover delay with the relative reinforcement rate fixed at 0.75. The points at the COD of 2 sec are the same as those plotted in Fig. 1 at the relative reinforcement rate of 0.75. Relative response rate and relative time remained approximately constant across CODs; however, relative time was generally closer to 0.75 at the COD equal to 0 sec than at other values of the COD. Only Bird 104 showed the same effect for relative response rate. The range of variation across conditions was less than 0.10 for Birds 103 and 108 and less than 0.15 for Bird 104. Excluding the 0-sec COD, the range was less than 0.10 in every case. Both relative response rate and relative time measures were generally above 0.75, the relative reinforcement rate; the only exceptions were that relative time was lower than 0.75 for Birds 104 and 108 at the 0-sec COD and that relative response rate was lower for Bird 108 at the 32-sec COD. As the COD increased, relative local response rate decreased below 0.50 for Bird 103 and 108 and increased above 0.50 for Bird 104. Relative

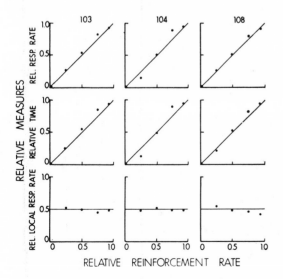

Fig. 1. Relative rate of responding, relative time spent and relative local response rate as functions of the relative rate of reinforcement. Calculations were made with respect to the red key color.

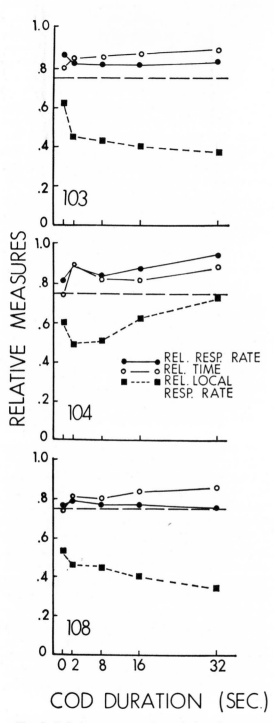

Fig. 3. Relative response rate, relative time spent, and relative local response rate as functions of variations in the duration of the COD. The relative rate of reinforcement was 0.75. Calculations were made with respect to the red key color.

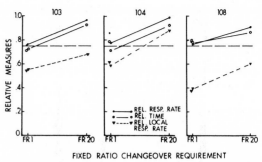

Fig. 4. Relative response rate, relative time spent, and relative local response rate as functions of variation of the fixed-ratio changeover requirement. The relative rate of reinforcement was 0.75. Calculations were made with respect to the red key color.

local response rate was greater than 0.50 for all birds at the 0-sec COD.

Figure 4 shows relative measures obtained with the two fixed-ratio changeover requirements. The unconnected points at FR 1 are from the redetermination shown in the final row of Table 1. Relative overall response rate and relative time increased when the changeover requirement was changed from FR 1 to FR 20. Relative overall response rate and relative time were higher with the FR 20 condition than they had been under any value of the COD. Relative local response rate also increased under the FR 20 requirement. With reinstatement of the FR 1 condition, the pigeons' performances were quite similar to those established under the original determination. Only for Bird 104 did two comparison measures (relative overall response rate) differ by more than 0.05.

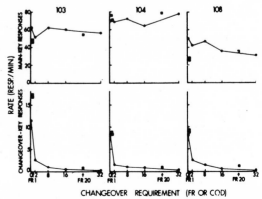

Fig. 5. Main-key response rate and changeover-key response rate as functions of differences in the changeover requirement. Variations in COD and FR requirements are both shown, and their placement on the same horizontal is for convenience of comparison only.

Figure 5 shows main-key and changeover-key response rates as functions of the change-over requirement. The several COD durations and the two FR requirements are plotted on the horizontal axis. For the FR 20 condition, the vertical axis of the lower row shows changeovers per minute, rather than change-over-key responses per minute. Also, the changeover delays and fixed-ratio requirements are presented together only to emphasize the similar effects on performance obtained by increasing either; correspondence in any other sense is not intended. Main-key response rates were somewhat variable across conditions. For Bird 108, main-key response rate decreased with increases in the COD. There was a decrease in changeover rate for all birds as a function of increases in the COD. Finally, changeover rate decreased also for the FR 20 requirements as compared with the FR 1 requirement.

DISCUSSION

The procedure provided that responses produce food intermittently in the presence of different stimuli, and the proportion of the feeder operations that had to occur in the presence of a given stimulus was specified. Certain behavioral effects observed in the present experiment are similar to those observed with the more usual procedure for concurrent VI VI schedules. It was seen that: (1) the relative overall rate of responding broadly approximated the relative rate of reinforcement; (2) the relative amount of time spent in the presence of each stimulus also approximated the relative rate of reinforcement; (3) given brief COD values, relative local rate tended to be equal in the presence of the different stimuli; (4) with a fixed COD (2 sec), changeover rate decreased the greater the divergence of the relative reinforcement rate from 0.50; (5) with a fixed rate of reinforcement (0.75), change-over rate decreased as a function of increases in the COD.

A matching relation between relative rate of responding and relative rate of reinforcement has been observed for pigeons with concurrent VI VI schedules (Catania, 1963, 1966; Herrnstein, 1961). In those experiments, relative reinforcement rate was manipulated by varying the average interreinforcement interval for each of the VI schedules.

Pigeons have been observed to match relative time and relative rate of reinforcement (Brownstein and Pliskoff, 1968; Catania, 1966). Catania observed the relation between relative time and relative reinforcement rate with concurrent VI VI schedules. Brownstein and Pliskoff observed such a relation with response-independent concurrent VI VI schedules. Food was delivered independently of behavior; responses on the only available key changed from one response-independent VI to the other. Whereas in Catania's experiment, the relative rate of responding also was related to relative reinforcement rate, responding was absent in the experiment by Brownstein and Pliskoff.

It has been suggested that the relation between relative rates of responding and reinforcement may be a byproduct of the way in which animals partition time between concurrent VI VI schedules (Catania, 1966; Brownstein and Pliskoff, 1968; Shull and Pliskoff, 1967). If pigeons partition only time, then responding should occur at the same local rate in the presence of either stimulus. Changes in relative response rate result simply from changes in the number of responses emitted in the presence of the different stimuli. The local response rates should therefore be equal. Catania (1966) found in fact that both relative overall response rate and relative time matched reinforcement rate with concurrent VI VI schedules (given a 2-sec COD). Thus, the relative local rate of responding would necessarily approximate 0.50, as was the case in the present experiment.

With concurrent VI VI schedules, change-over rate has been found to decrease as a function of the divergence of relative reinforcement rate from 0.50 (Brownstein and Pliskoff, 1968; Herrnstein, 1961). Herrnstein demonstrated this relation with concurrent VI VI schedules and Brownstein and Pliskoff found that the relation obtained also with the response-independent procedure previously described.

Changeover rate decreases as a function of increases in the COD (Brownstein and Pliskoff, 1968; Herrnstein, 1961; Shull and Pliskoff, 1967). Herrnstein demonstrated that change-over rate was lower with a 1.5-sec COD than with no COD. Brownstein and Pliskoff (1968), with the response-independent procedure, found that changeover rate was a decreasing function of the COD. Using rats as subjects and brain stimulation as the reinforcer, Shull and Pliskoff (1967) also found that changeover rate was a decreasing function of the COD; changeover rate decreased both with concurrent VI 1.5-min VI 1.5-min schedules and with concurrent VI 1-min VI 3-min schedules of reinforcement.

There are also differences between the present procedure and results and the usual procedure and results with concurrent VI VI schedules. In the present experiment, relative overall response rate and relative time remained approximately constant as the COD increased. Shull and Pliskoff (1967) found, with concurrent VI 1-min VI 3-min schedules, that both relative response rate and relative time, computed with respect to the VI 1-min schedule, increased as the COD increased in duration. The difference in results between the present study and the study by Shull and Pliskoff could have resulted from differences in the effect of responding on relative rate of reinforcement. With concurrent schedules, changes in the relative rate of responding can affect the relative reinforcement rate. Shull and Pliskoff found that as relative response rate and relative time increased on the VI 1-min schedule, the relative rate of reinforcement also increased. In the present study, changes in relative overall response rate and relative time could not result in changes in the relative reinforcement rate. Relative reinforcement rate was constant at 0.75 while the COD varied. However, there were other differences between the two studies. In the experiment by Shull and Pliskoff, rats rather than pigeons were subjects, brain stimulation rather than food was used as a reinforcer, and Shull and Pliskoff had fewer sessions per condition (5 to 10 sessions).

It is not clear how the changeover delay serves to modulate responding on concurrent VI VI schedules of reinforcement so as to produce matching. Shull and Pliskoff (1967, p. 526) suggested that the COD in conjunction with relative reinforcement rate determines the distribution of responses between the two variable-interval schedules during the session. Their analysis assumed that the organism responds at a uniform local rate throughout the session, or, in other words, that the local response rates for the two schedules of a concurrent pair are the same. How-

ever, the COD affects local response rate when the latter is examined in detail, rather than calculated from data collected over an entire experimental session. As yet unpublished data by Silberberg and Fantino and by Pliskoff and Green show that the local response rate is higher during the interval following a changeover when the COD is timing than after that interval has expired. Local response rate is, therefore, bivalued when examined in detail, and the "uniform" local rate is an average of the two values. Presumably, the higher response rate immediately following a changeover results from the complex contingencies existing at that moment, i.e., a COD superimposed upon a VI schedule with a probability of reinforcement at the expiration of the COD dependent upon (a) the length of the VI interval currently timing, (b) the duration of the COD, and (c) the time since that schedule was last sampled.

The FR changeover requirement that we examined was designed to simplify the post-changeover contingencies to some extent. The experiment is essentially halted as soon as the first response of the FR is emitted on the changeover key—the VI tapes stop, the main key is darkened and inactivated, and the cumulating-time recorders are stopped. When the final response of the FR is emitted, the changeover is completed and the experiment is reinstated. The schedule at that moment on the main key is a variable interval without the added complexity of a superimposed COD. Whether the FR changeover requirement is a procedural factor more useful than the COD remains to be determined.

REFERENCES

Brownstein, A. J. and Pliskoff, S. S. Some effects of relative reinforcement rate and changeover delay in response-independent concurrent schedules of reinforcement. *Journal of the Experimental Analysis of Behavior*, 1968, **11**, 683-688.

Catania, A. C. Concurrent performances: reinforcement interaction and response independence. *Journal of the Experimental Analysis of Behavior*, 1963, **6**, 253-263.

Catania, A. C. Concurrent operants. In W. K. Honig (Ed.), *Operant behavior: areas of research and application*. New York: Appleton-Century-Crofts, 1966. Pp. 213-270.

Catania, A. C. and Reynolds, G. S. A quantitative analysis of the responding maintained by interval schedules of reinforcement. *Journal of the Experimental Analysis of Behavior*, 1968, **11**, 327-383.

Graf, V., Bullock, D. H., and Bitterman, M. E. Further experiments on probability-matching in the pigeon. *Journal of the Experimental Analysis of Behavior*, 1964, **7**, 151-157.

Herrnstein, R. J. Relative and absolute strength of response as a function of frequency of reinforcement. *Journal of the Experimental Analysis of Behavior*, 1961, **4**, 267-272.

Shimp, C. P. Probabilistically reinforced choice behavior in pigeons. *Journal of the Experimental Analysis of Behavior*, 1966, **9**, 443-455.

Shimp, C. P. The concurrent reinforcement of two interresponse times: the relative frequency of an interresponse time equals its relative harmonic length. *Journal of the Experimental Analysis of Behavior*, 1969, **12**, 403-411.

Shull, R. L. and Pliskoff, S. S. Changeover delay and concurrent schedules: Some effects on relative performance measures. *Journal of the Experimental Analysis of Behavior*, 1967, **10**, 517-527.

Received 11 July 1969.

CHOICE AND RATE OF REINFORCEMENT[1,2]

EDMUND FANTINO

UNIVERSITY OF CALIFORNIA, SAN DIEGO

Pigeons' responses in the presence of two concurrently available (initial-link) stimuli produced one of two different (terminal-link) stimuli. The rate of reinforcement in the presence of one terminal-link stimulus was three times that of the other. Three different pairs of identical but independent variable-interval schedules controlled entry into the terminal links. When the intermediate pair was in effect, the pigeons distributed their (choice) responses in the presence of the concurrently available stimuli of the initial links in the same proportion as reinforcements were distributed in the mutually exclusive terminal links. This finding was consistent with those of earlier studies. When either the pair of larger or smaller variable-interval schedules was in effect, however, proportions of choice responses did not match proportions of reinforcements. In addition, matching was not obtained when entry into the terminal links was controlled by unequal variable-interval schedules. A formulation consistent with extant data states that choice behavior is dependent upon the amount of reduction in the expected time to primary reinforcement, as signified by entry into one terminal link, relative to the amount of reduction in expected time to reinforcement signified by entry into the other terminal link.

Many of the variables controlling an organism's choice behavior have been studied with concurrent chain schedules of reinforcement (*e.g.*, Autor, 1960; Herrnstein, 1964*a, b;* Fantino, 1967, 1968; Fantino and Herrnstein, 1968; Pliskoff and Hawkins, 1967; Rachlin, 1967; Reynolds, 1963). In this procedure, the organism responds on two concurrently available keys, each of which is illuminated by the stimulus associated with the initial link of one of the chains. Responses on each key occasionally produce the stimulus for the terminal link of the chain on that key. Responses in the presence of either of the mutually exclusive terminal-link stimuli are reinforced with food. The independent variable has generally involved some difference in the conditions arranged during the terminal links. The dependent variable is the measurement of choice: the distribution of responses in the initial, concurrently presented links of the chain.

One of the more interesting findings in the literature on choice is that of Autor (1960) and Herrnstein (1964*a*), who showed that the organism distributes its responses during the initial links in the same proportion as reinforcements are distributed in the terminal links; *i.e.*, the organism matches proportions of responses to proportions of reinforcements. For example, the rate (in reinforcements per minute) at which reinforcement is obtained in the terminal link of the chain associated with the left key may be three times greater than the rate of reinforcement in the terminal link of the chain associated with the right key. In this case, the organism emits three times as many responses on the left key as on the right key during the concurrently presented initial links of the two chains.

This formulation may be represented by a simple mathematical equation. Let R_L and R_R represent the number of responses emitted during the initial links of the left and right keys respectively; let t_L and t_R represent the expected time, in minutes, required to obtain reinforcement, as calculated from the onset of the terminal links of the left and right keys respectively. This model states that

$$\frac{R_L}{R_L + R_R} = \frac{\frac{1}{t_L}}{\frac{1}{t_L} + \frac{1}{t_R}} \tag{1}$$

[1]This paper is dedicated to B. F. Skinner in his sixty-fifth year.

[2]This research was supported by NSF Grant GB-6659 to the University of California, San Diego. Reprints may be obtained from the author, Department of Psychology, University of California, San Diego, P.O. Box 109, La Jolla, California 92037.

An implication of equation (1) is that choice, *i.e.*, the distribution of responses in the initial links represented by the left side of the equation, is independent of the expected time required to reach the terminal links. Intuitively, this does not seem plausible: a constant difference between t_L and t_R should be less influential in affecting choice, the greater the time required to reach the terminal links. For example, if the first response on either key produces the stimulus of the associated terminal link, a stimulus associated with a t_L of 10 sec should be strongly preferred to one associated with a t_R of 20 sec; preference should be negligible, however, if an hour's responding is required before these stimuli may be obtained.

Despite this possible shortcoming, equation (1) has been successful in providing reasonably close approximations to all of the relevant published data. This may be due to the widespread use of variable-interval (VI) 1-min schedules in the initial links. With much larger or smaller VIs, however, equation (1) may not hold. In other words, the generality of equation (1) has not been examined. There is, however, an alternative model that has different properties, is consistent with the earlier work, and is empirically distinguishable from equation (1). This formulation stipulates that the critical variable determining choice is the amount of reduction in expected time to primary reinforcement signified by entry into one terminal link relative to the reduction in expected time to reinforcement signified by entry into the other terminal link. For example, if the reduction of expected time to reinforcement is twice as great for the left terminal link as for the right, then the organism should distribute two-thirds of its choice responses to the left key. To express this more generally, one additional term is needed: T, the average time to reinforcement calculated from the onset of the initial links. This new formulation and the calculation of T can be made clearer with an example based on an experiment reported below. Responses during each of the concurrently presented initial links produce entry into the terminal links after a mean interval of 600 sec for each key. Thus, the expected time required to reach a terminal link is 300 sec. The expected times to reinforcement for the left and right terminal links (t_L and t_R) are 30 sec and 90 sec, respectively. Since the left and right terminal links are equiprobable, in this ex-

ample, T, the expected time to reinforcement, is: $300 \text{ sec} + [(\frac{1}{2}) \cdot (30 \text{ sec}) + (\frac{1}{2}) \cdot (90 \text{ sec})] = 360 \text{ sec}$. Thus, when the left terminal link is obtained, the organism is $360\text{-}30 = 330$ sec *closer* to reinforcement than it had been at the outset; when the right terminal link is obtained, the organism is only $360\text{-}90 = 270$ sec closer. This new formulation predicts that the organism will distribute the following proportion of its choice responses to the left: $330/(330 + 270) = 0.55$. Thus, formulation (2) states (by definition):

$$\frac{R_L}{R_L + R_R} \begin{cases} = \dfrac{T - t_L}{(T - t_L) + (T - t_R)} & \text{when } t_L < T, t_R < T \\ = 1 & \text{when } t_L < T, t_R > T \\ = 0 & \text{when } t_L > T, t_R < T \end{cases} \quad (2)$$

Of course, the case in which *both* t_L and t_R are greater than T is impossible.

In the example discussed above, formulation (1) predicts that the organism will distribute the following proportion of its choice responses to the left: $\frac{1}{30}/(\frac{1}{30} + \frac{1}{90}) = 0.75$. Indeed, equation (1) predicts 0.75 regardless of the time required to enter the terminal links. These times help determine T, which affects equation (2) only. Thus, one test that would allow a choice between these formulations is one that varied T while holding t_L and t_R constant. If the organism's choice were unaffected by this manipulation, formulation (1) would be supported. Formulation (2) would be supported if choice varied in the predicted direction. In a second test of the two models, the mean times required to enter the terminal links of the two keys are unequal. In previous studies, these times have been equal; when they are unequal, formulations (1) and (2) generally make different predictions.

The predictions made by these formulations are shown in Fig. 1 for the terminal-link values used in the present study (VI 30-sec and VI 90-sec). Formulation (1) always predicts a choice proportion of 0.75; it should be added, however, that neither Autor (1960) nor Herrnstein (1964a) stated whether or not formulation (1) applies when the initial link schedules are different. Figure 1 suggests values of the initial-link VIs that would permit straightforward experimental tests to determine whether formulation (1) or (2) provides a better description of choice. The present study examined this question.

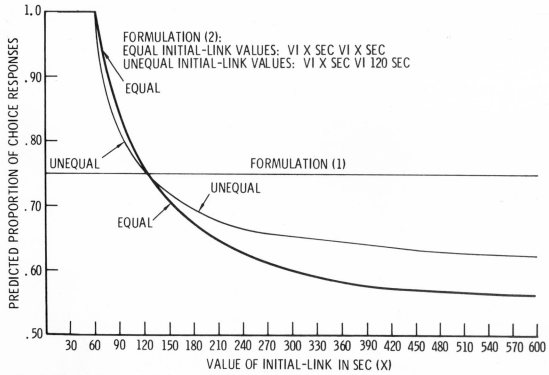

Fig. 1. The predictions made by formulations (1) and (2) for the terminal-link values used in the present study (VI 30-sec and VI 90-sec). The required proportions of choice responses to the key with VI 30-sec in the terminal link are plotted against different initial-link values. In the case of unequal initial-link values, the VI of the initial link leading to the VI 30-sec is varied (VI X-sec) along the abcissa while the VI of the initial link leading to the VI 90-sec is always VI 120-sec. In the case of equal initial links, of course, the VI values covary.

METHOD

Subjects

Six adult male White Carneaux pigeons were maintained at approximately 80% of their body weights measured while they had free access to grain. They were experimentally naive at the start of the experiment.

Apparatus

The experimental chamber was a modified picnic icebox (Ferster and Skinner, 1957) containing a solenoid-operated grain hopper, two 6-w lamps for general illumination and two translucent response keys 3 in. (7.6 cm) apart, mounted 9 in. (22.9 cm) above the floor. The right key was transilluminated by either a white or red light, the left key by either a white or green light. Transillumination was accomplished by stimulus lights mounted behind the response keys (Westinghouse D18, C-7-1/2 Christmas bulbs). A minimum force of 10 g (0.01 N) was required to operate each response

key. Each response produced auditory feedback by operating a 110-v ac relay. Standard scheduling and recording equipment was located in an adjacent room.

Procedure

The concurrent chains procedure is schematized in Fig. 2. As indicated, VI schedules[3] controlled access to the stimuli of the terminal links. When such access was scheduled by

---

[3]The nominal interreinforcement intervals (in sec) for each of the VI tapes used in the present study are listed below. The intervals occurred in the order listed for half of the sessions and in the reverse order during other sessions. VI 600-sec: 957, 120, 273, 785, 710, 752; VI 120-sec: 24, 113, 54, 56, 66, 80, 264, 195, 205, 83, 8, 146, 230, 40, 238; VI 40-sec: 38, 30, 10, 34, 12, 29, 112, 108, 25, 10, 121, 60, 22, 20, 25, 20, 9, 17, 55, 30, 33, 49, 20, 113, 8, 44, 9, 20, 7, 37, 10, 70, 63, 10, 9, 16, 38, 83, 8, 20, 25, 14, 150, 32, 78; VI 90-sec: 60, 85, 143, 45, 200, 95, 57, 16, 143, 90, 51, 149, 107, 22, 326, 30, 31, 56, 12, 65; VI 30-sec: 38, 32, 9, 22, 30, 5, 62, 7, 24, 24, 15, 16, 12, 65, 8, 48, 17, 34, 44, 6, 24, 91, 84, 72, 32, 20, 8, 9, 12, 22.

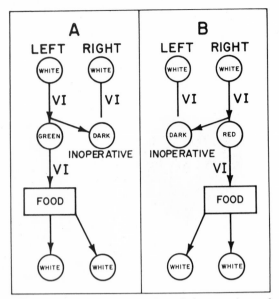

Fig. 2. Pictorial representation of the experimental procedure. Figure IIA indicates the sequence of events when responses on the left key were reinforced. Figure IIB represents the analogous sequence on the right key.

either VI programmer, it stopped operating, but the other VI programmer continued to operate. The next response on the appropriate key produced the terminal stimulus associated with that key and two additional events: (1) the VI programmer associated with the other key stopped operating; (2) illumination was removed from the other key, which became inoperative. Pecks in the presence of the terminal stimuli produced food according to different VI schedules. After food reinforcement, the initial links were reinstated. Pigeons 1 to 4 were first studied with a *chain* VI 30-sec VI 90-sec schedule on the left key and a *chain* VI 90-sec VI 30-sec schedule on the right key. After this phase, each of the six pigeons was studied with equal-valued VI schedules associated with the initial links. Three pairs of VI values were selected: *concurrent* VI 40-sec VI 40-sec, *concurrent* VI 120-sec VI 120-sec, and *concurrent* VI 600-sec VI 600-sec. These values were selected so that equation (2) would predict choice proportions greater than those predicted by equation (1) for one condition (VI 40-sec VI 40-sec), less than (1) for another condition (VI 600-sec VI 600-sec), and the same as (1) for the third condition (VI 120-sec VI 120-sec). Since there were six possible orders of exposure to these three conditions, each of the six pigeons was studied with a different order.

The schedules for the terminal links were again VI 30-sec and VI 90-sec; for each successive condition, however, these values were reversed. Thus, for the first and third conditions with equal initial links the VI 30-sec was associated with the left key; for the second condition, the VI 30-sec was associated with the right key as it had been in the first phase of the experiment, when the initial links were unequal.

Each experimental session terminated after 40 reinforcements of 4-sec access to grain. Each condition remained in effect until responding satisfied a visual stability criterion from day to day; this required about 28 daily sessions.

RESULTS

All data are averages taken from the last four sessions in each procedure. The absolute rate of responding for each pigeon on each key during the initial and terminal links is shown in Table I. These rates of responding are simply the total number of responses made on a key during the initial or terminal link, divided by the total duration of that link.

The proportion of choice responses (or the proportion of the absolute *rates* of responding that are presented in Table I, since durations of the two initial links are identical) to a key is the number of responses during the initial link of one key divided by the total number of responses during both initial links $\left[\text{or}\left(\dfrac{R_L}{R_L + R_R}\right)\text{ in equations (1) and (2)}\right]$. The choice proportions required by each formulation for each of the data points may be readily calculated from equations (1) and (2). For example, in the first phase of the experiment, equation (1) requires that the proportion of choice responses on the right key equal $\frac{1}{30}\text{ sec}/(\frac{1}{30}\text{ sec} + \frac{1}{90}\text{ sec}) = 0.75$, while equation (2) requires that this proportion equal $67.5\text{ sec}/(67.5\text{ sec} + 7.5\text{ sec}) = 0.90$. The predictions for each of the four conditions, the actual choice proportions obtained, and the deviations of the predicted values from the obtained values are presented in Table II.

DISCUSSION

The large deviations between the choice proportions obtained in this study and those required by formulation (1) demonstrate that

Table I

Absolute rates of responding (response/min) during the initial and terminal links for each key and for each pigeon in each of the four conditions. All VI values listed are in seconds. The sub headings "VI 30 key" and "VI 90 key" indicate the schedules of the *terminal* links. The notation (L) or (R) next to each entry indicates whether the data are from the left or right key, respectively.

	(i) *Chain VI 90 VI 30* vs. *Chain VI 30 VI 90*				(ii) *Chain VI 600 VI 30* vs. *Chain VI 600 VI 90*			
	Initial Link Rates		*Terminal Link Rates*		*Initial Link Rates*		*Terminal Link Rates*	
	VI 30 Key	*VI 90 Key*	*VI 30 Key*	*VI 90 Key*	*VI 30 Key*	*VI 90 Key*	*VI 30 Key*	*VI 90 Key*
Pigeon								
1	42.4 (R)	1.4 (L)	142.2 (R)	54.5 (L)	27.6 (R)	14.1 (L)	93.2 (R)	96.8 (L)
2	44.8 (R)	0.1 (L)	59.4 (R)	45.4 (L)	31.4 (L)	24.5 (R)	76.8 (L)	59.4 (R)
3	41.5 (R)	8.5 (L)	67.5 (R)	69.0 (L)	36.1 (L)	20.8 (R)	102.3 (L)	98.3 (R)
4	36.0 (R)	0.6 (L)	57.5 (R)	56.1 (L)	27.3 (R)	15.9 (L)	78.2 (R)	61.5 (L)
5	—	—	—	—	44.7 (L)	33.4 (R)	110.8 (L)	69.3 (R)
6	—	—	—	—	36.6 (L)	32.6 (R)	79.3 (L)	96.2 (R)

	(iii) *Chain VI 120 VI 30* vs. *Chain VI 120 VI 90*				(iv) *Chain VI 40 VI 30* vs. *Chain VI 40 VI 90*			
	Initial Link Rates		*Terminal Link Rates*		*Initial Link Rates*		*Terminal Link Rates*	
	VI 30 Key	*VI 90 Key*	*VI 30 Key*	*VI 90 Key*	*VI 30 Key*	*VI 90 Key*	*VI 30 Key*	*VI 90 Key*
1	37.1 (L)	12.9 (R)	95.9 (L)	85.8 (R)	45.3 (L)	3.7 (R)	95.1 (L)	124.7 (R)
2	46.9 (L)	13.6 (R)	46.3 (L)	59.1 (R)	54.3 (L)	0.1 (R)	50.8 (L)	85.9 (L)
3	53.2 (L)	8.0 (R)	96.9 (L)	83.4 (R)	74.1 (R)	0.1 (L)	89.6 (R)	87.6 (L)
4	35.1 (L)	14.5 (R)	64.4 (L)	59.5 (R)	57.2 (L)	6.8 (R)	42.1 (L)	64.8 (R)
5	67.2 (R)	2.2 (L)	70.6 (R)	88.3 (L)	76.3 (L)	3.0 (R)	68.4 (L)	87.3 (R)
6	62.4 (R)	13.6 (L)	77.0 (R)	81.5 (L)	57.3 (L)	4.9 (R)	86.3 (L)	53.0 (R)

this formulation is generally inadequate. It provides a fair approximation to the data only within an intermediate range of values. Since previous workers have found it convenient to work within this range of values, however, formulation (1) has, until now, provided a good description of choice.

A better description of choice is provided by formulation (2). In 15 of the 16 cases for which formulations (1) and (2) describe different choice proportions, (2) provides a closer fit to the obtained data. Perhaps more significant is the finding that for each of these 16 points, equation (2) accounts for the direction of the deviations from equation (1). For example, in each of the 10 cases for which formulation (2) requires a higher choice proportion than formulation (1), cols (i) and (iv) in Table IIB show that (1) underestimates these proportions; for each of the six cases in which (2) requires a lower choice proportion than (1), col (ii) in Table IIB shows that (1) overestimates these proportions. Table IIB indicates also that only for the condition described in col (iii) does formulation (1) provide even a rough approximation to the data; but this is the condition in which the choice proportions required by formulations (1) and (2) coincide precisely.

The absolute rates of responding shown in Table I reveal an additional finding of interest. The sum of the initial-link response rates on the two keys (*i.e.*, the overall rate of responding in the initial links) does not vary in a very orderly manner with the size of the VIs in the initial links. Considering the data from the conditions with equal initial links (cols ii-iv), only that for two of the six pigeons (Pigeons 3 and 4) shows a monotonic relation between absolute rate of responding and the length of the VIs. Thus, the dramatic changes in the distribution of choice responses on the two keys are not accompanied by commensurate changes in the overall rate of choice responding.

Although equation (2) provides a reasonable description of choice for every condition studied in the present experiment, some other formulation might provide an even better description, *e.g.*, with a significantly lower (absolute) mean deviation than the 0.06 associated with (2). Alternatively, it should be possible to improve the predictive accuracy of formulation (2). For example, at least one aspect of

Table II

IIA Proportion of choice responses to key providing higher rate of reinforcement in terminal link for each pigeon in each of four conditions. The average proportion for each condition and the proportions required by formulations (1) and (2) are listed below the line. All VI values listed are in seconds.

Pigeon	(i) *Chain VI 90 VI 30* vs. *Chain VI 30 VI 90*	(ii) *Chain VI 600 VI 30* vs. *Chain VI 600 VI 90*	(iii) *Chain VI 120 VI 30* vs. *Chain VI 120 VI 90*	(iv) *Chain VI 40 VI 30* vs. *Chain VI 40 VI 90*
1	0.97	0.66	0.74	0.93
2	1.00	0.56	0.77	1.00
3	0.83	0.63	0.87	1.00
4	0.98	0.63	0.70	0.89
5	—	0.57	0.97	0.96
6	—	0.53	0.82	0.92
Av. Proportion	0.94	0.60	0.81	0.95
Model I	0.75	0.75	0.75	0.75
Model II	0.90	0.55	0.75	1.00

IIB The deviations of the choice proportions above from the proportions required by formulation (1) and (2) for each pigeon for conditions (i)-(iv). For each of the 16 points in which (1) and (2) make different predictions, the smaller deviation is shown in italics. Col (v) on each side gives the mean of the *absolute* deviations for each pigeon. The means of the absolute deviations for each condition are listed below the line.

Pigeon	Formulation (1)					Formulation (2)				
	(i)	(ii)	(iii)	(iv)	(v)	(i)	(ii)	(iii)	(iv)	(v)
1	+0.22	−0.09	−0.01	+0.18	0.12	*+0.07*	+0.11	−0.01	*−0.07*	*0.06*
2	+0.25	−0.19	+0.02	+0.25	0.18	*+0.10*	*+0.01*	+0.02	*0*	*0.03*
3	+0.08	−0.12	+0.12	+0.25	0.14	*−0.07*	*+0.08*	+0.12	*0*	*0.07*
4	+0.23	−0.12	−0.05	+0.14	0.14	*+0.08*	*+0.08*	−0.05	*−0.11*	*0.08*
5	—	−0.18	+0.22	+0.21	0.20	—	*+0.02*	+0.22	*−0.04*	*0.09*
6	—	−0.22	+0.07	+0.17	0.15	—	*−0.02*	+0.07	*−0.08*	*0.06*
Mean of absolute deviations	0.20	0.15	0.08	0.20	0.16	*0.08*	*0.05*	0.08	*0.05*	0.06

formulation (2) may help account for the present deviations and it points to a potentially desirable refinement of this model. This is the method of computing T, which is calculated from the onset of the initial links. In fact, the longer the organism responds in the initial links in any given cycle the smaller is the expected time to achieve primary reinforcement. For example, when the schedules are *chain* VI 600-sec VI 30-sec on the left and *chain* VI 600-sec VI 90-sec on the right, T, as presently, calculated, is 6 min. As the elapsed time in the initial link increases, however, the real expected time to primary reinforcement progressively decreases from 6 min, and occasionally approaches 1 min. The latter extreme case occurs whenever the elapsed time since the onset of the initial links approaches the value of the longest interreinforcement interval on the VI 600-sec tapes. In other words, the VIs become effectively smaller the more time that has passed since the onset of the initial links. It is

conceivable that the organism's choice behavior reflects these changes in the expected time to primary reinforcement. If so, its choice proportions *within* an exposure to the initial links should show the same effects as occur when smaller VIs are used, namely, more responding in the initial link of the key with the higher rate of reinforcement in the terminal link. Alternatively, the organism's choice behavior may not reflect these more molecular dynamics of the reinforcement parameters. Although an additional experiment would be required to decide this question adequately, the analysis has a clear implication for the deviations obtained in the present experiment. In particular, it requires that the organism's choice proportions should be somewhat greater than those predicted by formulation (2). In other words, the deviations from (2), in Table IIB, should be positive. This is impossible, of course, for the six data points in col (iv) because for these points formulation (2) requires a proportion of 1.00. For 12 of the remaining 16 data points the deviations are indeed positive. This support for the analysis is sufficiently suggestive to warrant further experimentation.

The conditions for which formulations (1) and (2) make identical predictions may be specified more rigorously by setting them equal to one another. Hence, for $t_L < T$ and $t_R < T$:

$$\frac{T - t_L}{(T - t_L) + (T - t_R)} = \frac{\frac{1}{t_L}}{\frac{1}{t_L} + \frac{1}{t_R}};$$

$$(T - t_L)(t_R + t_L) = t_R(T - t_L) + t_R(T - t_R);$$

$$T = \frac{t_L^2 - t_R^2}{t_L - t_R};$$

$$O = (t_L - t_R)(t_L + t_R - T)$$

Thus, there are two solutions:

$$t_L = t_R$$
$$\text{and } T = t_L + t_R$$

When either of these conditions is met, formulations (1) and (2) make identical predictions. For example, whenever the terminal links are equal $(t_L = t_R)$ both formulations require choice proportions of 0.50. This implication appears somewhat implausible for the case of unequal initial links. With grossly unequal initial links and small but equal terminal links, for example, a higher rate of responding might be expected in the initial link that provides more frequent access to its terminal link. If this were so, refinement of formulation (2) would be required, at least for the case of unequal initial links. Two qualifications should be noted, however. In the first place, preference for the key with the shorter initial link might be due to the greater number of primary reinforcements it leads to; Fantino and Herrnstein (1968) showed this to be a significant variable affecting choice in concurrent-chain schedules. In the second place, the present experiment is admittedly not an adequate test of the generality of formulation (2) with unequal initial links. Indeed, only one data point in the present experiment employed unequal initial links. The present experiment does show that formulation (1) cannot describe choice when the initial links are unequal, whereas formulation (2) is compatible with the data thus far obtained.

The present results are germane to an important secondary question originally raised by Fantino and Herrnstein (1968). In their study, the number of primary reinforcements obtained during each cycle of the terminal link was varied, but the rate at which these reinforcements were scheduled in the terminal links was kept constant. The proportion of choice responses in the initial link varied directly (although nonproportionally) with the number of primary reinforcements given in the terminal links. Fantino and Herrnstein noted that, in principle, their results could be explained in terms of rate, rather than number, of reinforcements by calculating rate of reinforcement over total experimental time instead of just over time during the terminal links. Although the authors presented arguments against this interpretation of their results, it remained a logical possibility. Indeed, the possibility remained that in all experiments utilizing concurrent chains the main variable controlling choice behavior was the relative rate of reinforcement integrated over total experimental time and not over the terminal links only. This possibility is clearly refuted by the results from the first condition of the present experiment. In that condition the overall rate of reinforcement was 0.50 rfts/min for each key, since the schedules were *chain* VI 30-sec VI 90-sec and *chain* VI 90-sec VI 30-sec on the left and right keys respectively. Thus, if the variable controlling choice behavior were the rate of reinforcement integrated over total experimental time, the organism should distribute about half of its initial-link responses to each key. Instead, fairly large preferences were manifest for the right terminal link. Moreover, this preference for the right terminal link occurred despite two features of the experimental design that favored the left terminal link in this condition: (1) the greater number of conditioned and primary reinforcements obtained on the left; (2) the fact that, in a choice situation, VI 30-sec schedules maintain higher rates of responding in their presence than do VI 90-sec schedules. Thus, the data strongly reject the hypothesis that rate of reinforcement calculated over total experimental time is the important variable affecting choice.

The present experiment underscores the importance of testing conclusions originally formulated with a certain range of VI schedules for VI values outside this range. This point has been made before; for example, Hearst, Koresko, and Poppen (1964) showed that the shape of the generalization gradients obtained with VI 3-min or VI 4-min schedules was markedly different from the shape of gradients obtained by previous workers using only VI 1-min schedules.

In summary, previous experiments, particularly those of Autor (1960) and Herrnstein (1964a), indicated that the proportion of responses in the initial links matches the proportion of the rates of reinforcement in the terminal links. The present results show that this is not generally true. The results do support an alternative formulation that is consistent with extant data. This formulation states that choice behavior is determined by the degree of reduction in the expected time to primary reinforcement signified by entry into one terminal link, relative to the degree of reduction signified by entry into the other terminal link.

REFERENCES

Autor, S. M. *The strength of conditioned reinforcers as a function of frequency and probability of reinforcement.* Unpublished doctoral dissertation. Harvard University, 1960.

Fantino, E. Preference for mixed- *versus* fixed-ratio schedules. *Journal of the Experimental Analysis of Behavior*, 1967, **10**, 35-43.

Fantino, E. Effects of required rates of responding upon choice. *Journal of the Experimental Analysis of Behavior*, 1968, **11**, 15-22.

Fantino, E. and Herrnstein, R. J. Secondary reinforcement and number of primary reinforcements. *Journal of the Experimental Analysis of Behavior*, 1968, **11**, 9-14.

Ferster, C. B. and Skinner, B. F. *Schedules of reinforcement.* New York: Appleton-Century-Crofts, 1967.

Hearst, E., Koresko, M., and Poppen, R. Stimulus generalization and the response-reinforcement contingency. *Journal of the Experimental Analysis of Behavior*, 1964, **7**, 369-380.

Herrnstein, R. J. Secondary reinforcement and rate of primary reinforcement. *Journal of the Experimental Analysis of Behavior*, 1964, **7**, 27-36. (*a*)

Herrnstein, R. J. Aperiodicity as a factor in choice. *Journal of the Experimental Analysis of Behavior*, 1964, **7**, 179-182. (*b*)

Pliskoff, S. S. and Hawkins, T. D. A method for increasing the reinforcement magnitude of intracranial stimulation. *Journal of the Experimental Analysis of Behavior*, 1967, **10**, 281-289.

Rachlin, H. The effect of shock intensity on concurrent and single-key responding in concurrent-chain schedules. *Journal of the Experimental Analysis of Behavior*, 1967, **10**, 87-93.

Reynolds, G. S. Potency of conditioned reinforcers based on food and on food and punishment. *Science*, 1963, **139**, 838-839.

Received 31 July 1968.

SCHEDULES USING NOXIOUS STIMULI. IV: AN INTERLOCKING SHOCK-POSTPONEMENT SCHEDULE IN THE SQUIRREL MONKEY[1]

R. T. KELLEHER AND W. H. MORSE

HARVARD MEDICAL SCHOOL AND
NEW ENGLAND REGIONAL PRIMATE RESEARCH CENTER

Responding was studied under various schedules of electric shock postponement and presentation in the squirrel monkey. Under an interlocking shock-postponement schedule, successive responses decreased the time by which a response postponed the next scheduled shock until a shock immediately followed the nth response. Some parameters of this schedule, which can be formally related to fixed-interval schedules, engendered a pattern of positively accelerated responding between shocks. This pattern did not occur under comparable parameter values of an alternative fixed-ratio, avoidance schedule under which each response postponed shock by a fixed duration and every nth response produced shock. Subsequently, performances were studied under schedules of shock presentation. Responding was never maintained under fixed-ratio schedules of shock presentation, but was maintained with a pattern of positive acceleration under an alternative fixed-ratio, fixed-interval schedule and under a fixed-interval schedule.

Schedule-controlled responding often depends upon how durations terminated by responses (interresponse times) are related to scheduled events (Ferster and Skinner, 1957; Morse, 1966). Patterns of sequential responding tend to be minimal under schedules that minimize the selective grouping of responses before scheduled events. For example, under an avoidance schedule in which each response postpones the delivery of an electric shock for a specified time (response-shock interval), the defining characteristics of the schedule ensure that sequences of successive responses cannot immediately precede an electric shock. Although patterning of sequential interresponse times has been observed (Anger, 1963; Wertheim, 1965), responding under such avoidance schedules tends to be steady.

If all interresponse times under a continuous avoidance schedule are less than the response-shock interval, no shocks will occur, but responding can also be engendered or maintained under schedules in which a minimum number of shocks must occur. For example, responding has been maintained under conditions in which responses: (1) produce a shift from one shock frequency to a lower shock frequency (Herrnstein and Hineline, 1966; Sidman, 1962); (2) do not alter the shock frequency (Kelleher, Riddle, and Cook, 1963; Waller and Waller, 1963); or (3) increase the shock frequency (Byrd, 1969; Kelleher and Morse, 1968; McKearney, 1968, 1969; Morse, Mead, and Kelleher, 1967).

The present paper describes performances under interlocking and alternative shock-postponement schedules in which relations between interresponse times and shocks could vary over a wide range. Under the interlocking fixed-ratio, shock-postponement schedule, successive groups of responses decreased the time by which a response postponed the next scheduled shock (Fig. 1, solid line) (see also, Berryman and Nevin, 1962; Powers, 1968; Skinner, 1958). Under the alternative fixed-ratio, avoidance schedule, the response-shock interval was constant, and every nth response produced shock (Fig. 1, dashed line). Patterns of positively accelerated responding between shocks, resembling fixed-interval performances, developed under the interlocking sched-

[1]Dedicated to Professor B. F. Skinner in his sixty-fifth year with esteem and affection. This work was supported by PHS Research Grants MH 02094 and MH 07658 from the National Institute of Mental Health and by research career program awards 5-K3-GM-15,530 from the National Institutes of Health and 5-K3-MH-22,589 from the National Institute of Mental Health. We wish to thank Mrs. Regina N. Mead and Mr. Lionel King for assistance in conducting the experiments and Miss Eleanor Bates and Mrs. Carolyn Fishken for help in preparation of the manuscript. Reprints may be obtained from R. T. Kelleher, Department of Pharmacology, Harvard Medical School, 25 Shattuck Street, Boston, Massachusetts 02115.

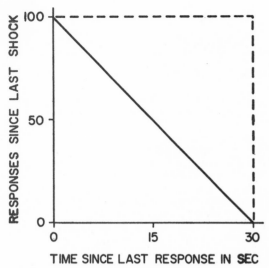

Fig. 1. Diagrammatic representation of interlocking shock postponement schedule (solid line) and alternative fixed-ratio, avoidance schedule (dashed line).

ule but not under the alternative schedule. Various schedules of response-produced shock were also studied.

METHOD

Subjects

Six mature male squirrel monkeys (*Saimiri sciureus*) with no previous training were used (S-67, S-68, S-69, S-70, S-72, and S-73). The monkeys were generally handled according to the procedures described by Kelleher, Gill, Riddle, and Cook (1963), except that the leash was sometimes removed during initial sessions. The monkeys had free access to food and water in their living cages.

Apparatus

A restraining chair similar to the one described by Hake and Azrin (1963) was used (see Kelleher and Morse, 1964). Each monkey was restrained in the seated position by a waist lock, its tail held motionless by a small stock. Electric current was delivered through the tail by two hinged brass plates that rested lightly on a shaved portion of the tail. A non-corrosive electrode paste (EKG Sol) ensured a low resistance electrical contact between the plates and the tail. The electric shock was 580 v ac, 60 Hz delivered to the plates through a series resistor for 200 msec. The response key (Lehigh Valley Electronics rat lever, LVE

1352) was mounted on the right-hand side of a metal wall facing the monkey. When the key was pressed with a force of 22 g (0.216 N) or more, a response was recorded. Each response produced the audible click of a relay. Just above the key was a stimulus panel that was transilluminated by a white light (6 w) during each session. General illumination during the session was provided by an overhead light (25-w GE type 101F bulb). The entire chair unit was enclosed in a ventilated refrigerator shell. Continuous white noise was used to mask extraneous sounds.

Schedules

Interlocking schedule. Figure 2 is a diagram of the interlocking schedule as it was actually arranged. The abscissa represents the time since the previous response; the ordinate represents cumulative responses since the previous shock. After a shock, each of the first nine responses postponed the next scheduled shock by 30 sec (or 10 sec); each of the tenth to the nineteenth responses postponed the shock for 27 sec (or 9 sec); shock postponement time continued to decrease every 10 responses until the delay was 3 sec (1 sec) after 90 responses, and 0 sec after 100 responses. The schedule can be specified in terms of the maximum number requirement (FR) and maximum shock postponement duration (R-S time). Threefold changes in the number require-

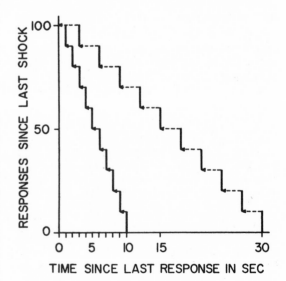

Fig. 2. Diagrammatic representation of interlocking shock postponement schedule at R-S times of 10 sec and 30 sec.

Table 1

Subject	Sessions	Schedule	Shock Intensity
S-69	1-58	interlocking FR 100, R-S time 10 sec	3 ma
	59-104	interlocking FR 300, R-S time 10 sec	3 ma
	105-120	FR 100 (FR 300, Session 105 only)	3 ma
	121-124	alternative FR 100, FI 5-min	3 ma
	125-149	interlocking FR 100, R-S time 10 sec	3 ma
	150-170	interlocking FR 100, R-S time 30 sec	3 ma
	171-233	interlocking FR 100, R-S time 30 sec (no S-S interval after Session 185)	10 ma
	234-245	FI 5-min	10 ma
S-70	1-112	interlocking FR 100, R-S time 10 sec	3 ma and 10 ma
	113-175	interlocking FR 100, R-S time 30 sec	10 ma and 3 ma
	176-246	interlocking FR 100, R-S time 10 sec (no S-S interval after Session 185)	3 ma
S-67	1-57	interlocking FR 100, R-S time 30 sec (modified after Session 44)	3 ma
	58-68	FR 100	3 ma
	69-75	FR 100 (shock interval 5 min)	3 ma
	76-118	alternative FR 100, FI 5-min	3 ma
	119-132	alternative FR 100, conjunctive FR 30 FI 5-min	3 ma
	133-157	alternative FR 100, FI 5-min (various shock intervals 10 sec to 6 min)	3 ma
	158-164	interlocking FR 300, R-S time 30 sec (no S-S interval)	3 ma
	165-234	FI 5-min	
S-68	1-45	interlocking FR 100, R-S time 30 sec	10 ma
	46-56	alternative FR 100, R-S interval 30 sec	10 ma
	57-85	alternative FR 300, R-S interval 30 sec	10 ma
	86-93	FR 300	10 ma
	94-97	alternative FR 100, FI 5-min (shock interval 10 min)	10 ma
	98-123	alternative FR 100, R-S interval 30 sec	10 ma
	124-143	interlocking FR 100, R-S time 30 sec	10 ma
	144-170	alternative FR 100, FI 5-min	10 ma
S-72	1-67	alternative FR 100, R-S interval 10 sec	3 ma and 10 ma
	68-71	FR 100	10 ma
	72-205	alternative FR 100, FI 5-min	10 ma and 3 ma
S-73	1-57	alternative FR 100, R-S interval 10 sec	3 ma and 10 ma
	58-73	alternative FR 100, FI 5-min (shock interval 5 to 10 min after Session 69)	10 ma and 3 ma
	74-119	alternative FR 100, R-S interval 10 sec	10 ma and 3 ma
	120-147	alternative FR 100, FI 5-min (shock interval 6 min after Session 124)	3 ma and 10 ma
	148-183	interlocking FR 100, R-S time 10 sec (no S-S interval)	10 ma
	184-191	FI 2-min	10 ma

ment (FR 100 and 300), the response-shock time (10 sec and 30 sec), and the shock intensity (3 ma and 10 ma) were studied. If no response occurred after a shock, the next shock was scheduled to occur after 10 sec (S-S interval), except as noted.

Alternative fixed-ratio, avoidance schedule. This schedule combined a fixed-ratio schedule of shock presentation with an avoidance schedule of shock postponement (Sidman, 1953), as diagrammed in Fig. 1. The response-shock interval and shock-shock interval were both 10 sec, the fixed-ratio was 100 responses, and shock intensities of 3 ma and 10 ma were studied. Shocks were delivered 10 sec after a previous response or immediately after 100 responses.

Schedules of shock presentation. Fixed-ratio, fixed-interval, and alternative fixed-ratio, fixed-interval schedules of shock pres-

entation were studied after performances had
been developed under the schedules described
above. Shocks were delivered immediately
after the terminal response of the schedule
except, as noted, when shock was delivered
at fixed time periods independently of responding (shock interval).

Procedure

Sessions lasted 1 hr and were conducted
daily, Monday through Friday. During the
session, the keylight and overhead light were
illuminated. During initial training under
the interlocking schedule and alternative
fixed-ratio, avoidance schedule, if no response
occurred after a shock, the next shock was
scheduled to occur under a 3-sec S-S interval.
The S-S interval was increased to 10 sec after
five to 10 sessions. Subsequently, the S-S interval was eliminated in some experiments under
the interlocking schedule. In some experiments under the alternative fixed-ratio, fixed-
interval schedule, shock intervals up to 10
min were used.

Four monkeys (S-67, S-68, S-69, and S-70)
were studied initially under the interlocking
shock postponement schedule; two monkeys

(S-72 and S-73) were studied initially under
the alternative fixed-ratio avoidance schedule.
Subsequently, threefold changes in the number requirement, the shock-postponement
duration, and the shock intensity were studied,
as well as performances under the fixed-ratio,
the alternative fixed-ratio, fixed-interval, and
the fixed-interval schedules. The sequence of
schedules and parameter values studied is
shown in Table 1. Unless otherwise specified,
there was an S-S interval of 10 sec under the
interlocking and the alternative fixed-ratio
avoidance schedules, and there was no S-S
interval or shock interval under the schedules
of shock presentation.

RESULTS

*Characteristics of performance under the
interlocking schedule.* Stable patterns of responding with identifiable features developed
under the interlocking schedule. A striking
characteristic of performance under the interlocking schedule was the gradual increase in
responding between shocks (Fig. 3). This pattern of increasing responding was clearest
when shocks were regularly spaced in time,

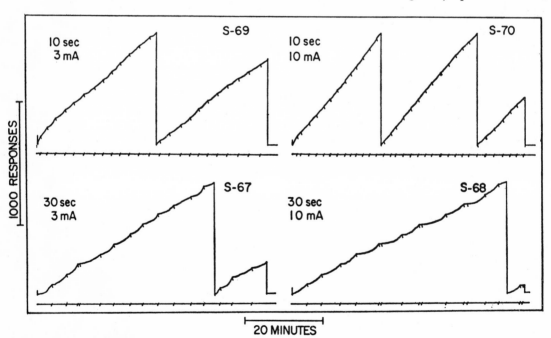

Fig. 3. Performances for four monkeys under the interlocking schedule after about 50 sessions (FR 100; R-S
time and shock intensity as indicated on the records). Ordinate: cumulative responses; abscissa: time. The recording pen reset to the baseline whenever 1100 responses accumulated and at the end of each session. Short
diagonal strokes on cumulative records and event records indicate presentations of electric shock. Note the
many instances of positively accelerated responding between shocks, especially at R-S 30 sec.

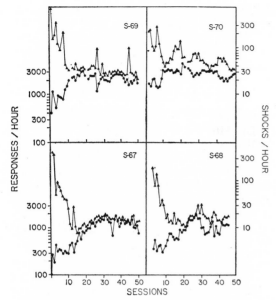

Fig. 4. Development of performance under the interlocking schedule. Ordinate (log scale): ●———● responses per hour, ▲———▲ shocks per hour; abscissa: sessions. Monkeys S-69 and S-70 (upper frames) were trained under interlocking FR 100, R-S time 10 sec. Monkeys S-67 and S-68 (lower frames) were trained under interlocking FR 100, R-S time 30 sec. The shock intensity was 3 ma for S-69 and S-67, 10 ma for S-68, and increased from 3 ma to 10 ma in Session 21 for S-70. The S-S interval was increased from 3 to 10 sec in Session 7 for S-67 and S-68 and in Session 11 for S-69 and S-70. Breaks in the curves indicate sessions for which data were lost. In all monkeys, response rates increased while shock frequency decreased for about 30 sessions; performances were relatively stable in subsequent sessions. Response rates and shock rates were higher with R-S 10 sec (upper frames) than with R-S 30 sec (lower frames).

but as the pattern developed, shocks tended to occur less regularly; thus, performance under the interlocking schedule fluctuated somewhat. Although there seemed to be optimal parameter values for the development of positively accelerated responding, this response occurred in each of the four monkeys initially studied under the interlocking schedule.

As performances developed under the interlocking schedule, rate of responding generally increased while shock frequency generally decreased (Fig. 4). Under the 10-sec R-S time, the average rate of responding was about 2500 responses per hour and shock frequency was about 35 shocks per hour; under the 30-sec R-S time, the average rate of responding was about 1200 responses per hour and shock frequency was 15 shocks per hour.

For Monkey S-70, responding developed with a shock intensity of 3 ma, but subsequently was not well maintained; when the shock intensity was increased to 10 ma, responding was more consistent throughout each session.

Variations in parameter values under the interlocking schedule. The effects of a threefold increase in the R-S time under the interlocking schedule are shown for S-70 in Fig. 5. Under the 10-sec R-S times, average response rates were about 2400 responses per hour (Fig. 5A) and 2600 responses per hour (Fig. 5C) and shock frequencies were about 36 per hour (Fig. 5A, C). When the R-S time was increased to 30 sec, average rate of responding decreased to about 1500 responses per hour and shock

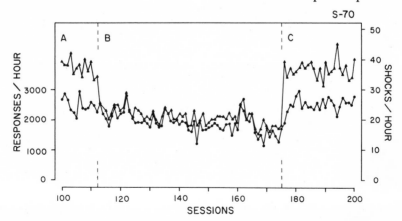

Fig. 5. Comparison of performances under the interlocking schedule at R-S 10 sec and R-S 30 sec (S-70). Ordinate: ●———● responses per hour, ▲———▲ shocks per hour; abscissa: sessions. A: terminal performance under R-S 10 sec; B: R-S 30 sec; C: R-S 10 sec. Shock intensity was decreased from 10 ma to 3 ma in Session 149. The S-S interval was eliminated in Session 186. Response rates and shock frequency were consistently lower when the R-S time was 30 sec than when it was 10 sec.

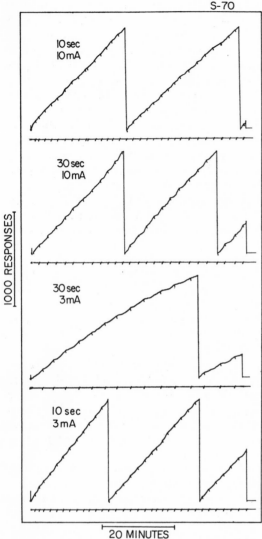

S-70

Fig. 6. Characteristics of performance under the interlocking schedule at R-S 10 sec and R-S 30 sec (S-70). Recording as in Fig. 3. The top record shows stable performance (Session 112) at R-S 10 sec. The transition from R-S 10 sec to R-S 30 sec is shown in the second record (Session 113); rates of responding remained relatively high, and positive acceleration between shocks became more pronounced. The third record shows stable performance under R-S 30 sec (Session 167). The bottom records shows stable performance with subsequent exposure to R-S 10 sec (Session 245).

frequency decreased to about 17 per hour (Fig. 5B); these values did not change further when the shock intensity was decreased from 10 ma to 3 ma. The pattern of responding changed rapidly after the R-S time was increased to 30 sec; the positively accelerated responding between shock presentations was more pro-

nounced (Fig. 6). When the R-S time was decreased to 10 sec again, the earlier performance was recovered (Fig. 5 and 6). Patterns of positively accelerated responding between shocks were more pronounced when the R-S time was 30 sec than when it was 10 sec in this monkey.

The effects of a threefold increase in the number requirement, R-S time, and shock intensity under the interlocking schedule were studied in Monkey S-69. When the number requirement was changed from 100 to 300 responses, rate of responding increased slightly, but shock frequency decreased from about 30 to 15 shocks per hour (Fig. 7A, B). Positively accelerated responding between shocks occurred at both number requirements (Fig. 8A-C). After intervening treatments, S-69 was studied again under the initial interlocking schedule (FR 100, R-S time 10 sec, 3 ma), and the earlier performance was slowly recovered (Fig. 7D-8D). Increasing the R-S time to 30 sec resulted in a decreased rate of responding to about 1400 responses per hour and shock frequency to about 15 per hour (Fig. 7E); however, patterns of positively accelerated responding were no more pronounced than under the 10-sec R-S time (Fig. 8E, F). The elimination of the S-S interval in Session 186 did not appreciably change the performance of S-69 (or S-70) even though shocks had been occasionally delivered under the S-S interval; for example, see Fig. 8B. Positively accelerated responding between shocks occurred at both fixed-ratio parameter values, both shock intensities, and both R-S times.

Comparisons of the interlocking schedule with an alternative fixed-ratio, avoidance schedule. Two monkeys (S-72 and S-73) were studied initially under an alternative fixed-ratio, avoidance schedule that had certain parameters in common with the interlocking schedule (FR 100, 10-sec R-S interval, 3 ma). As performances developed, average rates of responding were low; shock frequencies were high and variable, but became more stable after the shock intensity was increased from 3 to 10 ma (Fig. 9). Average rates of responding were about 1500 responses per hour and average shock frequencies were about 22 per hour. Neither of the monkeys trained under the alternative schedule developed positively accelerated responding between shock presentations.

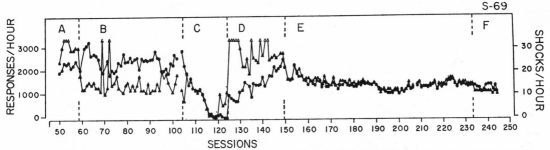

Fig. 7. Performance under interlocking schedules and various schedules of shock presentation (S-69). Ordinate: ● ─── ● responses per hour, △ ─── △ shocks per hour; abscissa: sessions. Open triangles indicate shock frequencies greater than 30 shocks per hour. A: terminal performance under interlocking FR 100, R-S time 10 sec; B: interlocking FR 300, R-S time 10 sec; C: FR 300 (Session 1 05 only), FR 100, and alternative FR 100, FI 5-min schedule after Session 121; D: interlocking FR 100, R-S time 10 sec; E: interlocking FR 100 R-S 30 sec; F: FI 5-min schedule of shock presentation. In Session 171, the shock intensity was increased from 3 to 10 ma; in Session 186, the S-S interval was eliminated. Responding decreased to near zero under the FR schedules and did not recover until the interlocking schedule was reintroduced.

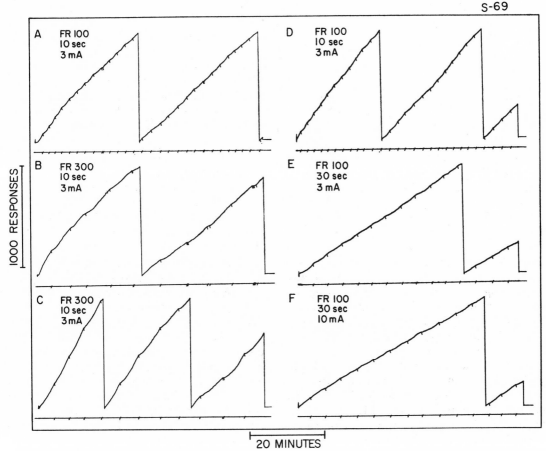

Fig. 8. Characteristics of performance under the interlocking schedule at various parameter values (S-69). Recording as in Fig. 3. A: stable performance under interlocking FR 100, R-S 10 sec (Session 58); B: transition to interlocking FR 300, R-S 10 sec (Session 59); C: terminal performance under interlocking FR 300, R-S 10 sec, showing some positively accelerated responding between shock presentations (Session 104); D: terminal performance under interlocking FR 100, R-S 10 sec (Session 149); E: under interlocking FR 100, R-S 30 sec (Session 170) rates of responding were lower than with R-S 10 sec; F: increasing the shock intensity from 3 to 10 ma had little effect (Session 232).

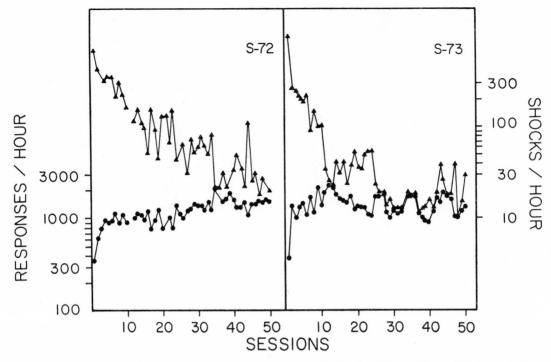

Fig. 9. Development of performance under the alternative fixed-ratio (FR 100), avoidance (R-S interval 10 sec, 3 ma) schedule. Ordinate (log scale): ●——● responses per hour, ▲——▲ shocks per hour; abscissa: sessions. Shock intensity was increased from 3 ma to 10 ma in Session 35 for S-72 and in Session 25 for S-73.

One monkey (S-73) studied initially under the alternative schedule (FR 100, R-S interval 10 sec) was studied at a later time under the interlocking schedule (FR 100, R-S time 10 sec). Figure 10 shows patterns of responding under the alternative schedule (on the left) and under the interlocking schedule (on the right). As performance developed under the interlocking schedule, positively accelerated responding between shock presentations became more pronounced. Rates of responding and shock frequencies were appreciably higher under the interlocking schedule than under the alternative schedule (Fig. 11).

Another monkey (S-68) studied initially under the interlocking schedule (FR 100, R-S time 30 sec) was next studied under the comparable alternative schedule (FR 100, R-S interval 30 sec). Average rates of responding decreased under the alternative schedule to about 400 responses per hour while shock frequencies decreased only slightly (Fig. 12A). When the response requirement under the alternative schedule was increased from 100 to 300, average rates of responding increased to about 800 responses per hour while shock

frequencies decreased to about three shocks per hour (Fig. 12B).

Within the first session after the change from the interlocking to the alternative schedule, the pattern of positively accelerated responding between shocks was less evident (Fig. 13, middle left) and in subsequent sessions disappeared (bottom left). The terminal performance (after intervening treatments) under the alternative fixed-ratio, avoidance schedule is shown at the upper right of Fig. 13; there was no positively accelerated responding between shocks. When S-68 was again studied under the interlocking schedule, the pattern of positively accelerated responding developed rapidly (Fig. 13, middle and bottom right), and rates of responding and shock frequency increased (Fig. 12E).

Performance under fixed-ratio, fixed-interval, and alternative fixed-ratio, fixed-interval schedules of shock presentation. Responding was never maintained indefinitely under the fixed-ratio schedules of shock presentation that were studied (FR 100 and FR 300). Monkeys were studied under fixed-ratio schedules after interlocking schedules (S-67 and S-69) or

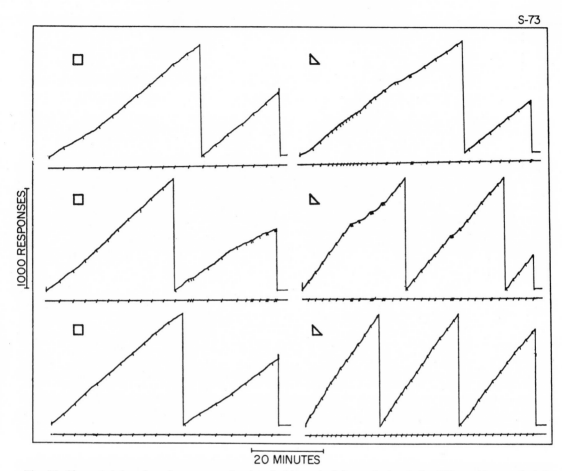

Fig. 10. Characteristics of performance under interlocking schedules and alternative FR, avoidance schedules (S-73). Recording as in Fig. 3. Under the alternative schedule (left records; denoted by squares) responding generally occurred at a steady rate (Sessions 56, 57, and 118). Under the interlocking schedule (right records; denoted by triangles) patterns of positively accelerated responding developed (Sessions 149, 164, and 183).

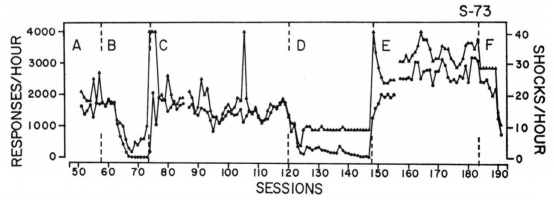

Fig. 11. Performance under alternative FR, avoidance schedules, interlocking schedules, and various schedules of shock presentation (S-73). Ordinate: ●——● responses per hour, ▲——▲ shocks per hour; abscissa: sessions. Open triangles indicate shock frequencies greater than 40 shocks per hour. A: alternative FR 100, avoidance R-S interval 10 sec; B: alternative FR 100, FI 5-min with shock interval of 5 to 10 min after Session 69; C: alternative FR 100, avoidance R-S interval 10 sec; D: alternative FR 100 FI 5-min with shock interval 6 min after Session 124; E: interlocking FR 100, R-S time 10 sec with no S-S interval; F: FI 2-min.

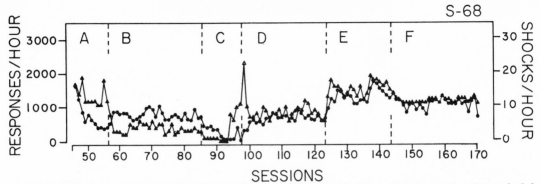

Fig. 12. Performance under alternative FR, avoidance schedules, interlocking schedules, and various schedules of shock presentation (S-68). Ordinate: ●——● responses per hour, ▲——▲ shocks per hour; abscissa: sessions. Open triangle indicates shock frequency greater than 20 shocks per hour. A: alternative FR 100, avoidance R-S interval 30 sec; B: alternative FR 300, avoidance R-S interval 30 sec; C: responding decreased to near zero under FR 300 (Sessions 86-93) and failed to recover under alternative FR 300 FI 5-min (Sessions 94-97); D: under alternative FR 100, avoidance R-S interval 30 sec, responding recovered; E: interlocking FR 100, R-S time 30 sec; F: alternative FR 100, FI 5-min schedule of shock presentation maintained responding.

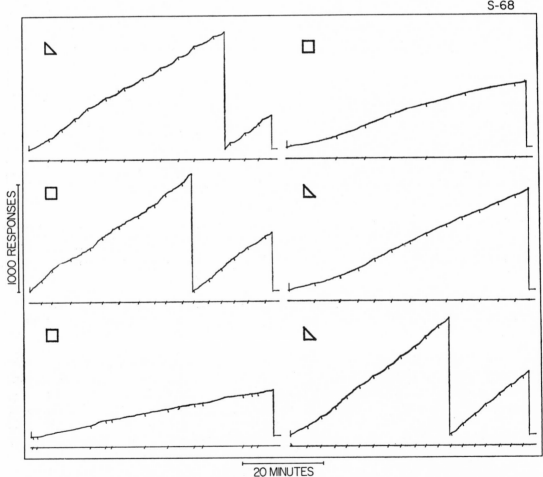

Fig. 13. Characteristics of performance under interlocking schedules and alternative FR, avoidance schedules (S-68). Recording as in Fig. 3. Responding was positively accelerated between shocks under interlocking FR 100, R-S time 30 sec (upper left record, Session 41), but not in the first session, under alternative FR 100, avoidance R-S interval 30 sec (middle left record, Session 46). Steady rates of responding were maintained under alternative FR 100, avoidance R-S interval 30 sec (lower left record, Session 56, and upper right record, Session 122). Responding increased under interlocking FR 100, R-S time 30 sec (middle right record, Session 124) and positively accelerated responding developed again (lower right record, Session 139).

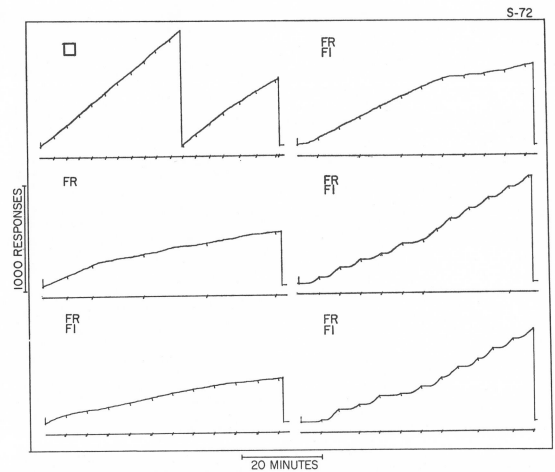

Fig. 14. Characteristics of performance under an alternative FR 100, avoidance schedule of shock postpone-ment (Session 67), an FR 100 schedule (Session 71), and an alternative FR 100, FI 5-min schedule (Sessions 72, 87, 119, and 123) of shock presentations (S-72). Ordinate: cumulative responses; abscissa: time. The recording pen reset to the baseline whenever 1100 responses accumulated and at the end of each session. Short diagonal strokes on cumulative records and event records indicate presentations of electric shock, except that shocks presented under the fixed-ratio component of the FR, FI schedule are not shown on the event record. Responding was not maintained under the FR 100 schedule of shock presentation, but was maintained with a characteristic pattern of positively accelerated responding under the alternative FR 100, FI 5-min schedule of shock presentation.

alternative fixed-ratio avoidance schedules (S-68 and S-72). In all instances, the rate of responding under the fixed-ratio schedules pro-gressively decreased to relatively low levels. The addition of a fixed-interval component (alternative fixed-ratio, fixed-interval sched-ules of shock presentation) failed to engender responding in two monkeys (S-68 and S-69), but increased the frequency of responding in Monkey S-72 (Fig. 14). When Monkey S-68 was again studied under the alternative fixed-ratio, fixed-interval schedule after 20 sessions under an interlocking schedule, responding was maintained (Fig. 12E, F), and patterns of posi-tively accelerated responding gradually de-

veloped. Terminal performances under the alternative FR 100, FI 5-min schedule of shock presentation are shown in Fig. 15 for Monkey S-72.

The rate of responding of Monkey S-67 under the fixed-ratio schedule of shock pres-entation gradually decreased to two responses per hour in Session 69 (Fig. 16B). The intro-duction of response-independent shocks, pre-sented every 5 min, gradually increased re-sponding (Fig. 16C and 17B). Responding further increased under the alternative FR 100, FI 5-min schedule of shock presentation, and the pattern of positively accelerated re-sponding became more pronounced. When

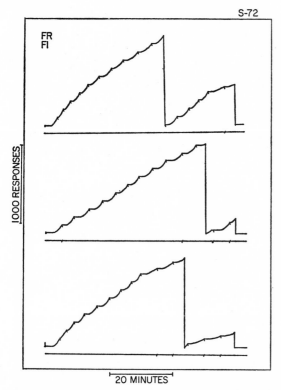

S-72

1000 RESPONSES

FR
FI

20 MINUTES

Fig. 15. Terminal performance under alternative FR 100, FI 5-min in Sessions 202, 203, and 204 (S-72). Recording as in Fig. 14.

the alternative schedule of shock presentation was modified so that shocks occurred under the 5-min fixed-interval component only after at least 30 responses had occurred (conjunctive FI 5-min, FR 30), rate of responding

decreased and the pattern was altered to a more abrupt acceleration of responding (Fig. 17D, E). Similar results have been obtained under a conjunctive FR, FI schedule of food presentation (Herrnstein and Morse, 1958). Responding abruptly decreased to near zero after a minor apparatus failure in Session 131 (Fig. 16D) and was not maintained at its previous level under alternative FR 100, FI 5-min (Fig. 16E). Under an interlocking FR 300, R-S time 30-sec schedule, rate of responding increased during seven sessions to about 1700 responses per hour (Fig. 16F, 17F).

Stable responding was maintained under a 5-min fixed-interval schedule of shock presentation in Monkey S-67 for more than 50 sessions. Eventually, the pattern of positively accelerated responding disappeared during the latter part of each session and the rate of responding decreased. It was observed that the monkey was pulling its leash, which greatly decreased responding in Sessions 222 and 223. When the leash was removed during subsequent sessions, characteristic patterns and rates of responding were recovered (Fig. 18). Several characteristics of performance under the fixed-interval schedule of shock presentation are shown in Fig. 19. The types of deviations from the pattern of positively accelerated responding between shocks are similar to the "run throughs", "knees", "bites", and "second-order effects" observed under fixed-interval schedules of food presentation by Ferster and Skinner (1957) and Skinner (1938).

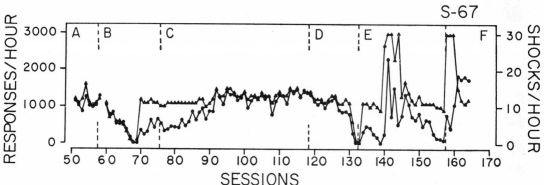

S-67

RESPONSES/HOUR

SHOCKS/HOUR

SESSIONS

Fig. 16. Performance under interlocking schedules and various schedules of shock presentation (S-67). Ordinate: ●——● responses per hour, ▲——▲ shocks per hour; abscissa: sessions. Open triangles indicate shock frequency greater than 30 shocks per hour. A: interlocking FR 100, R-S time 30 sec but modified so that R-S time was infinite until the tenth response; B: FR 100 with shock interval 5 min after Session 68; C: alternative FR 100, FI 5-min; D: alternative FR 100, conjunctive FR 30, FI 5 min; E: alternative FR 100, FI 5-min with various shock intervals; F: interlocking FR 300, R-S time 30 sec with no S-S interval. In Session 131, it was found that one of the two keylights had burned out.

S-67

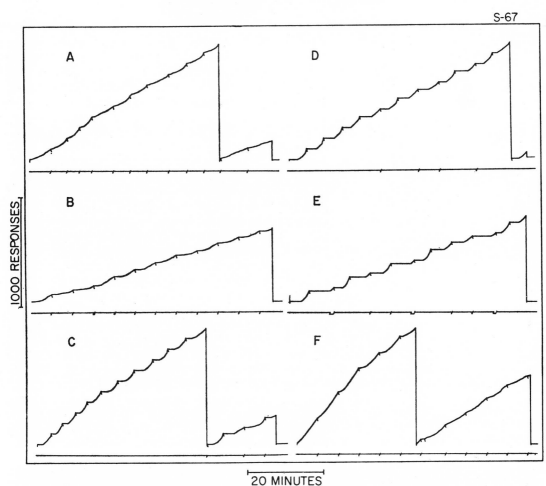

20 MINUTES

Fig. 17. Characteristics of performances under interlocking schedules of shock postponement and various sched-ules of shock presentation (S-67). Recording as in Fig. 14. A: FR 100 (Session 58); B: FR 100, shock interval 5 min (Session 75); C: alternative FR 100, FI 5-min (Session 118); D, E: alternative FR 100, conjunctive FR 30 FI 5-min (Sessions 124, 132); F: interlocking FR 300, R-S time 30 sec with no S-S interval (Session 164). A pattern of positively accelerated responding was maintained when shocks were presented every 5 min (B). Responding in-creased and the pattern was more pronounced under the alternative FR, FI schedule of shock presentation (C). The addition of the conjunctive component decreased responding and altered the pattern to a more abrupt ac-celeration of responding (D, E).

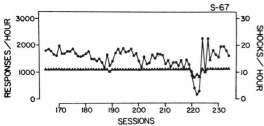

Fig. 18. Performance under FI 5-min schedule of shock presentation (Monkey S-67). Ordinate: ●——● re-sponses per hour, ▲——▲ shocks per hour; abscissa: sessions. In Session 221, it was found that one of the two keylights had burned out and that the monkey was persistently pulling at its leash. Beginning with Session 224, the monkey's leash was removed before each ses-sion, except for Session 225.

DISCUSSION

The pattern of positively accelerated re-sponding that develops under the interlock-ing schedule is significant for the analysis of schedule-controlled performances because the duration of the periodicity does not corre-spond to any simple time parameter of the schedule. The positively accelerated respond-ing that develops under fixed-interval sched-ules is often attributed (intuitively but wrongly) to a "temporal discrimination" of the interreinforcement interval, but there is no fixed interreinforcement interval under the interlocking schedule. Thus, the interlock-

S-67

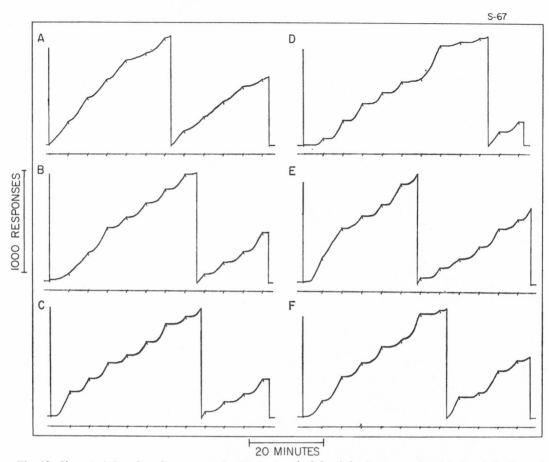

20 MINUTES

Fig. 19. Characteristics of performance under FI 5-min schedule of shock presentation (Monkey S-67). Recording as in Fig. 3. A: Session 165 (initial session); B: Session 177; C: Session 185; D: Session 186; E: Session 194; F: Session 195. Records were selected to illustrate common variations from the prototypic patterns of positively accelerated responding that occur under fixed-interval schedules (C); for example, instances of positively accelerated responding throughout two fixed-interval components (B, D), decelerations in responding (E), and "running through" (E, F).

ing schedule emphasizes that positively accelerated responding can have a dynamic basis.

The pattern of responding depends more upon interactions between features of the schedule and the individual's responding under the interlocking schedule than under many commonly used schedules (Ferster and Skinner, 1957; Skinner, 1966). A highly reproducible pattern of responding can produce a relatively constant duration between shock presentations under the interlocking schedule, just as there can be constant interreinforcement times under fixed-ratio schedules or the alternative fixed-ratio, avoidance schedule used in the present study. A constant interreinforcement duration in itself does not ensure a pattern of positively accelerated responding; rather, this pattern appears to develop under conditions favoring sequences of responding.

Under interval schedules, unlike ratio or continuous avoidance schedules, antecedent interresponse times change the likelihood that interresponse times will be reinforced. As the sum of antecedent interresponse times increases, the probability that the next response, with a fixed interresponse time, will be reinforced also increases (Morse and Herrnstein, 1955; Morse, 1966). The interlocking schedule is similar in that increasing numbers of responses, independently of interresponse-time duration, increase the likelihood that a shock will occur after a fixed time. In this respect, the formal properties of the interlocking schedule are like those of fixed-interval schedules. The left side of Fig. 20 shows certain relations that prevail under a 30-sec fixed-interval schedule. When the sum of previous interresponse times is 0, then a response after 30 sec will be reinforced; when their sum is 15 sec, a response after 15 sec will be reinforced; as the sum of antecedent interresponse times approaches 30 sec, responses with shorter and shorter interresponse times will be reinforced. The right side of Fig. 20 shows relations that prevail under interlocking FR 100, R-S time 30 sec. The first response postpones shock for 30 sec; the fiftieth response postpones shock for 15 sec; as the number of responses approaches 100, the duration of shock postponement becomes shorter and shorter. Thus, the interlocking schedule is a "number analogue" of the summation of interresponse time durations in fixed-interval schedules (see also Millenson, 1966). A major difference in the two representations is that the line in the fixed-interval diagram indicates the availability of reinforcement and the line in the interlocking diagram indicates the occurrence of shock. Although there are other important differences between fixed-interval and interlocking schedules, the similarities in the relations shown in Fig. 20 may elucidate the basis for the similar patterns of positively accelerated responding.

Under the interlocking and the alternative schedules of shock postponement, shock fre-quencies were decreased by responding. For example, under the interlocking FR 100, R-S time 30-sec schedule, the shock frequency could be reduced to about five shocks per hour by steady responding with 15-sec interresponse times, or to about two shocks per hour by optimum patterning of interresponse times. Average response rates and shock frequencies much exceeded these values under both interlocking and alternative schedules of shock postponement. Under the alternative fixed-ratio, fixed-interval schedule, the fixed-ratio schedule, and the fixed-interval schedule of shock presentation, and also under the interlocking schedule with no S-S interval, shocks were not presented unless responding occurred.

After a history of responding under other schedules, Monkeys S-67, S-68, and S-72 were maintained under the alternative fixed-ratio, fixed-interval schedule for many sessions. The fixed-interval component seemed to be essential for the maintenance of responding under this alternative schedule. Responding was never maintained under fixed-ratio schedules alone. Whenever a fixed-ratio schedule operated alone, the rate declined over consecutive sessions, but the addition of the fixed-interval component increased responding in S-72 (but not S-68 and S-69).

In Monkey S-67, after responding declined under the fixed-ratio schedule, the addition of a 5-min shock interval, and then a 5-min fixed-interval component, maintained a pattern of positively accelerated responding. Further, responding was not maintained in S-67 when the alternative fixed-ratio, fixed-interval schedule was changed to a conjunctive fixed-ratio, fixed-interval schedule. Finally, responding in S-67 was maintained for 70 sessions, and S-69 and S-73 for shorter periods, under a fixed-interval schedule of shock presentation alone. These diverse results indicate that fixed-interval schedules of shock presentation engendered responding, whereas fixed-ratio schedules of shock presentation did not maintain responding at the parameters used in this experiment.

Responding was not maintained in all subjects by the schedules of shock presentation. For example, although Monkeys S-72 and S-73 had comparable performances under the alternative fixed-ratio, avoidance schedule, the alternative fixed-ratio, fixed-interval schedule of

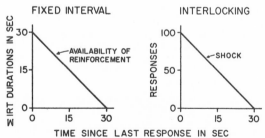

Fig. 20. Diagram illustrating a quantitative similarity in the effect of cumulative IRT durations under a fixed-interval schedule and cumulative responses under an interlocking schedule. Under FI 30-sec, a response after 30 sec will be reinforced without antecedent responses; a response after 15 sec will be reinforced if the sequence of antecedent responses had a total IRT duration of 15 sec; a response after 1 sec will be reinforced if the sequence of antecedent IRTs had a total duration of 29 sec. Under the interlocking FR 100, R-S time 30-sec schedule, the first response postpones shock for 30 sec; the fiftieth response postpones shock for 15 sec; the ninety-ninth response postpones shock for 1 sec; and the one hundredth response produces shock.

shock presentation maintained responding in Monkey S-72 but not in S-73. In the other instances in which responding was not maintained under the alternative fixed-ratio, fixed-interval schedule, the fixed-interval component was introduced after responding had already declined under the fixed-ratio schedule. At the present time not enough systematic data are available to evaluate quantitatively the antecedent conditions and present parameter values under which schedules of shock presentation will maintain responding.

Two different stable patterns of responding maintained under the same schedule parameters, one before and one after an intervening treatment, have been called metastable (Staddon, 1965). Performances under some of the conditions studied in the present experiments were reproducible after intervening treatments, whereas other performances were metastable. While performances under the interlocking and alternative fixed-ratio, avoidance schedules were reproducible, especially after changes in the R-S time parameter (see Fig. 5, 7), the effects of shock intensity under these schedules depended somewhat upon the subject's performance, and appeared to be more critical during the initial development of responding. For example, a shock intensity of 3 ma did not maintain a steady level of responding in S-70 or S-73 during initial training, but subsequently did maintain responding. Similarly, changing the shock intensity from 3 to 10 ma after 170 sessions had no appreciable effect on the performance of S-69. Previously we noted that the schedule conditions necessary to develop a characteristic performance were more critical than the conditions needed to maintain the performance (Morse and Kelleher, 1966). In general, performances under schedules of shock presentation appear to be more metastable than performances under schedules of shock postponement. Since the development of responding under schedules of shock presentation depends upon ongoing behavior, it is not surprising that responding might remain changed after a momentary disruption.

While it is generally accepted that schedules of food presentation engender patterns of responding with characteristics that depend upon the specific schedule contingencies, different schedules using electric shocks have been studied little until recently, perhaps be-cause performance under such procedures has been characterized in such general terms as "aversive control", "avoidance", or "escape" rather than in terms of the schedule itself. We have previously found that termination of a stimulus-shock complex under fixed-ratio and fixed-interval schedules engenders performances characteristic of these schedules (Morse and Kelleher, 1966). The present experiments extend and confirm several earlier studies (Byrd, 1969; Kelleher and Morse, 1968; McKearney, 1968, 1969; Morse, Mead, and Kelleher, 1967), showing that responding can be maintained under fixed-interval schedules of shock presentation alone. The performances that developed under the interlocking and the alternative fixed-ratio, avoidance schedules further indicate that different schedules using electric shock engender characteristic performances. The inherent properties of the interlocking schedule of shock postponement make it useful for analyzing positively accelerated responding.

REFERENCES

Anger, D. The role of temporal discriminations in the reinforcement of Sidman avoidance behavior. *Journal of the Experimental Analysis of Behavior,* 1963, **6,** 477-506.

Berryman, R. and Nevin, J. A. Interlocking schedules of reinforcement. *Journal of the Experimental Analysis of Behavior,* 1962, **5,** 213-223.

Byrd, L. D. Responding in the cat maintained under response-independent electric shock and response-produced electric shock. *Journal of the Experimental Analysis of Behavior,* 1969, **12,** 1-10.

Ferster, C. B. and Skinner, B. F. *Schedules of reinforcement.* New York: Appleton-Century-Crofts, 1957.

Hake, D. F. and Azrin, N. H. An apparatus for delivering pain shock to monkeys. *Journal of the Experimental Analysis of Behavior,* 1963, **6,** 297-298.

Herrnstein, R. J. and Hineline, P. N. Negative reinforcement as shock-frequency reduction. *Journal of the Experimental Analysis of Behavior,* 1966, **9,** 421-430.

Herrnstein, R. J. and Morse, W. H. A conjunctive schedule of reinforcement. *Journal of the Experimental Analysis of Behavior,* 1958, **1,** 15-24.

Kelleher, R. T., Gill, C. A., Riddle, W. C., and Cook, L. On the use of the squirrel monkey in behavioral and pharmacological experiments. *Journal of the Experimental Analysis of Behavior,* 1963, **6,** 249-252.

Kelleher, R. T. and Morse, W. H. Escape behavior and punished behavior. *Federation Proceedings,* 1964, **23,** 808-817.

Kelleher, R. T. and Morse, W. H. Schedules using noxious stimuli. III. Responding maintained with response-produced electric shocks. *Journal of the Experimental Analysis of Behavior*, 1968, **11**, 819-838.

Kelleher, R. T., Riddle, W. C., and Cook, L. Persistent behavior maintained by unavoidable shocks. *Journal of the Experimental Analysis of Behavior*, 1963, **6**, 507-517.

McKearney, J. W. Maintenance of responding under a fixed-interval schedule of electric shock presentation. *Science*, 1968, **160**, 1249-1251.

McKearney, J. W. Fixed-interval schedules of electric shock presentation: extinction and recovery of performance under different shock intensities and fixed-interval durations. *Journal of the Experimental Analysis of Behavior*, 1969, **12**, 301-313.

Millenson, J. R. Probability of response and probability of reinforcement in a response-defined analogue of an interval schedule. *Journal of the Experimental Analysis of Behavior*, 1966, **9**, 87-94.

Morse, W. H. Intermittent reinforcement. In W. K. Honig (Ed.), *Operant behavior: areas of research and application.* New York: Appleton-Century-Crofts, 1966. Pp. 52-108.

Morse, W. H. and Herrnstein, R. J. *An analysis of responding under three different forms of fixed interval reinforcement.* Paper presented at Eastern Psychological Association meetings, Philadelphia, 1955.

Morse, W. H. and Kelleher, R. T. Schedules using noxious stimuli. I. Multiple fixed-ratio and fixed-interval termination of schedule complexes. *Journal of the Experimental Analysis of Behavior*, 1966, **9**, 267-290.

Morse, W. H., Mead, R. N., and Kelleher, R. T. Modulation of elicited behavior by a fixed-interval sched-ule of electric shock presentation. *Science*, 1967, **157**, 215-217.

Powers, R. B. Clock-delivered reinforcers in conjunctive and interlocking schedules. *Journal of the Experimental Analysis of Behavior*, 1968, **11**, 579-586.

Sidman, M. Avoidance conditioning with brief shock and no exteroceptive warning signal. *Science*, 1953, **118**, 157-158.

Sidman, M. Reduction of shock frequency as reinforcement for avoidance behavior. *Journal of the Experimental Analysis of Behavior*, 1962, **5**, 247-257.

Skinner, B. F. *The behavior of organisms: an experimental analysis.* New York: Appleton-Century-Crofts, 1938.

Skinner, B. F. Diagramming schedules of reinforcement. *Journal of the Experimental Analysis of Behavior*, 1958, **1**, 67-68.

Skinner, B. F. Operant behavior. In W. K. Honig (Ed.), *Operant behavior: areas of research and application.* New York: Appleton-Century-Crofts, 1966. Pp. 12-32.

Staddon, J. E. R. Some properties of spaced responding in pigeons. *Journal of the Experimental Analysis of Behavior*, 1965, **8**, 19-27.

Waller, M. B. and Waller, P. F. The effects of unavoidable shocks on a multiple schedule having an avoidance component. *Journal of the Experimental Analysis of Behavior*, 1963, **6**, 29-37.

Wertheim, G. A. Some sequential aspects of IRTs emitted during Sidman-avoidance behavior in the white rat. *Journal of the Experimental Analysis of Behavior*, 1965, **8**, 9-15.

Received 22 July 1969.

FIXED-INTERVAL SCHEDULES OF ELECTRIC SHOCK PRESENTATION: EXTINCTION AND RECOVERY OF PERFORMANCE UNDER DIFFERENT SHOCK INTENSITIES AND FIXED-INTERVAL DURATIONS[1]

James W. McKearney

HARVARD MEDICAL SCHOOL

In squirrel monkeys responding under a schedule in which responding postponed the delivery of electric shock, the presentation of *response-dependent shock* under a fixed-interval (FI) schedule increased the rate of responding. When the schedule of shock-postponement was eliminated, so that the only shocks delivered were those produced by responses under the FI schedule, a pattern of positively accelerated responding developed and was maintained over an extended period. When responses did not produce shocks (extinction), responding decreased. When shocks were again presented under the FI schedule, the previous pattern of responding quickly redeveloped. In general, response rates were directly related to the intensity of the shock presented, and inversely related to the duration of the fixed-interval. These results raise fundamental questions about the traditional classification of stimuli as reinforcers or punishers. The basic similarities among FI schedules of food presentation, shock termination, and shock presentation strengthen the conclusion that the schedule under which an event is presented and the characteristics of the behavior at the time the event is presented, are of overriding importance in determining the effect of that event on behavior.

In animals that have responded under schedules in which responding postpones the delivery of electric shock, the periodic delivery of response-independent shocks can maintain responding, even when the shock-postponement schedule is no longer in effect (Sidman, Herrnstein, and Conrad, 1957; Sidman, 1958; Kelleher, Riddle, and Cook, 1963; Waller and Waller, 1963). Recently it has been shown that a pattern of responding initially elicited by recurrently presented shock can be altered to a pattern of maximal responding just before each shock, and maintained under a fixed-interval schedule of shock-presentation (Morse, Mead, and Kelleher, 1967). In another experiment (Kelleher and Morse, 1968) a 10-min fixed-interval schedule of shock-presentation was arranged concurrently with a variable-interval 2-min schedule of food presentation in squirrel monkeys. In addition, *each* response produced a shock during the

eleventh minute of each cycle (that is, for a 1-min period after delivery of shock under the FI schedule). After extended exposure to these concurrently arranged schedules, food presentations were eliminated, and a pattern of positively accelerated responding, characteristic of fixed-interval schedules, was maintained under the schedule of shock-presentation alone.

Previous experiments (McKearney, 1968) showed that, in monkeys previously trained to respond under a schedule of shock-postponement (Sidman, 1953), a pattern of positively accelerated responding can be engendered and maintained under a fixed-interval schedule of shock-presentation. The present paper amplifies and extends these findings, and reports the effects of eliminating scheduled shocks, and of varying shock intensity and parameter value of the fixed interval.

METHOD

Subjects and Apparatus

Three adult male squirrel monkeys (*Saimiri Sciureus*) were used. Two monkeys (S-65 and S-85) had been trained previously under various schedules of food presentation, but had no prior exposure to electric shock, and one (S-101) had been trained, several months previously, to terminate periodically presented

[1]Dedicated to B. F. Skinner in his sixty-fifth year. This work supported by grants MH 02094, MH 07658 and training grant 5—TI—MH 07084 from the U.S. Public Health Service. Some of these data were presented at the 1968 meeting of the Eastern Psychological Association (Washington, D.C.). I thank W. H. Morse, P. B. Dews, and R. T. Kelleher for helpful comments about the manuscript. Reprints may be obtained from the author, Dept. of Pharmacology, Harvard Medical School, 25 Shattuck St., Boston, Massachusetts 02115.

electric shock. The monkeys were housed individually, and were handled according to the general procedures reported by Kelleher *et al.* (1963).

Experiments were conducted with individual monkeys seated in a restraining chair similar to that described by Hake and Azrin (1963). The monkey's tail was held motionless by a small stock, and electric shocks were delivered through brass electrodes which rested on a shaved portion of the tail. The shock was 650 v ac, 60 Hz, of 250-msec duration, delivered to the electrodes through variable series resistance. The response key (Lehigh Valley Electronics rat lever, LVE 1352) was mounted on a wall facing the monkey. Each depression of the response key with a force of approximately 20 g or more produced the audible click of a relay within the chamber, and was recorded as a response. The restraining chair was enclosed in a sound-attenuating chamber (Industrial Acoustics Co., AC-3). A 25-w overhead light illuminated the chamber during experimental sessions. Continuous white noise was present to mask extraneous sounds.

Data were recorded on digital counters, elapsed time meters, and cumulative response recorders. From the total number of responses occurring in each tenth of the fixed interval over the entire session, the percentage of the interval taken for the first quarter of the responses to occur was determined by linear interpolation. This quarter-life measure provides an index of the temporal patterning of responding which is relatively independent of response rate (Herrnstein and Morse, 1957; Gollub, 1964).

General Procedure

The experiments were divided into several phases. First, all monkeys were trained to respond under a continuous avoidance schedule (Sidman, 1953). Then, concurrently with the avoidance schedule, the first response occurring after 10 min was immediately followed by shock (10-min fixed-interval shock-presentation). After this, the avoidance schedule was eliminated, and the monkeys responded under the fixed-interval schedule alone; during this phase, the effects of the addition and subsequent deletion of a timeout period following shock were studied. In the fourth phase, scheduled shocks were omitted; initially the timeout period was still available, but later

it also was eliminated. Phase 5 was concerned with the effects of varying shock intensities on performance under FI 10-min. In Phase 6, shocks were again eliminated, and in the last phase, performance under fixed intervals of 5, 3, and 1 min were studied. The various experimental phases are summarized in Table 1.

Table 1
Number of Sessions in Each Experimental Phase

Phases	S-65	S-85	S-101
1. avoidance	1-17	1-16	1-11
2. conc. avoid, FI 10-min	18-31	17-29	12-22
3. FI 10-min (with and without timeout)	32-101	30-101	23-82
4. extinction (with and without timeout)	102-152	102-136	83-121
5. FI 10-min (shock varied from 0.3-5.6 ma)	153-204	137-169*	122-184
6. extinction	205-211	204-221	185-189
7. FI 5-, 3-, and 1-min	212-290	222-284	190-265

*During sessions intervening between Phases 5 and 6 (Sessions 170-203), Monkey S-85 was subjected to several procedural variations which are described in the text.

Phases 1-3. All monkeys were first trained to press the key under a continuous avoidance schedule (Phase 1). Shocks (5.2 ma) were scheduled to occur every 10 sec, but each response postponed shock delivery for 30 sec. Sessions were usually 100 min long, and were conducted five days a week. After a number of sessions under the avoidance schedule, a 10-min fixed-interval (FI 10-min) schedule of shock-presentation was arranged concurrently with the avoidance schedule (Phase 2). Under the FI 10-min schedule, a shock was presented following the first response to occur after 10 min. In the third phase, the avoidance schedule was eliminated, and the FI 10-min was the only schedule in effect (Phase 3). At various times during Phase 3, a 30-sec timeout period followed each shock presentation; during the timeout period, the overhead light was off and responding had no scheduled consequences. A complete description of the procedures during Phases 1-3 was previously presented (McKearney, 1968).

Phase 4: elimination of scheduled shocks under FI 10-min. Beginning with Session 83

(S-101) or 102 (S-65 and S-85), shocks were eliminated. For the first four sessions, the 30-sec timeout was still available under the FI schedule, and was presented independently of responding if no response occurred within 2 min of the end of the 10-min FI. For the next 13 sessions, the 30-sec timeout was no longer presented independently of responding, but did follow the first response occurring after 10 min; for the remainder of the extinction sessions, the timeout period was eliminated.

Phase 5: reestablishment of responding under FI 10-min, with variations in shock intensity. After rates of responding had stabilized at low levels during Phase 4, shocks were again presented under the FI 10-min schedule. No timeout periods were presented. Shock intensity was either 0.3, 1.0, 3.0, or 5.6 ma, for varying numbers of sessions (see RESULTS). For all monkeys, the various shock intensities were given in ascending order.

During this phase, the shock intensity was increased to 10.0 ma for Monkey S-85. Responding was well maintained during the first session under this intensity, but during the second session the performance of this monkey was severely disrupted, and responding ceased over the next several sessions. Shock intensity was then reduced to 5.6 ma, and the schedule was modified in an attempt to restore responding. In the presence of a red stimulus light, shocks were scheduled to occur every 3 or 10 sec after the end of the 10-min FI. A response during this period produced a shock, and began a new fixed interval. After two sessions under this procedure, responding had recovered substantially, and the FI 10-min schedule, which was in effect before the disruption, was reinstated. Details of this modification are given in RESULTS.

Phases 6 and 7: extinction and development of performance under 5-, 3-, or 1-min fixed-interval schedules. After performance had stabilized under FI 10-min with 5.6-ma shock (Phase 5), shocks were again eliminated. During this phase (Phase 6), responding had no scheduled consequences. Following stabilization of rates of responding at low levels, shocks were again presented under varying parameter values of a fixed-interval schedule. Under the FI 10-min schedule in effect during previous phases, the overhead houselight was the only discriminative stimulus. In Phase 6, in addition to the overhead light, lumination from

6-w colored lights, mounted on the panel facing the monkey at approximately eye-level, served as discriminative stimuli. During FI 5-min, a green light was on, during FI 3-min an orange light, and during FI 1-min a white light. The number of sessions under each parameter value varied from monkey to monkey, and is given in RESULTS. Under FI 5-min and FI 3-min, the number of shocks delivered per session was kept constant; therefore, sessions varied in duration depending on the parameter value under study. For Monkeys S-85 and S-101, the number of shocks per session under FI 1-min was first 10 (as with other parameter values), and then 20 for the last five sessions. For Monkey S-65, the number of shocks per session was 20 for the entire time under FI 1-min.

RESULTS

Phases 1-3

Figure 1 summarizes rates of responding and quarter-life values for the three monkeys under the procedures of Phases 1-3. Under the continuous avoidance schedule, all monkeys developed a steady rate of responding characteristic of this schedule. When the FI 10-min schedule of shock presentation operated concurrently, there was no effect on the pattern of responding (quarter-life values were about 25%), but the rate of responding increased. After elimination of the avoidance schedule, the fixed-interval schedule of shock-presentation maintained a pattern of positively accelerated responding. When the 30-sec timeout was added, this pattern was accentuated (*i.e.*, quarter-life values increased), but subsequent removal and reinstatement of the timeout had no effect on the pattern that had developed. At the end of Phase 3, quarter-life values ranged from 66% to 70%. Figure 2 shows cumulative response records illustrating the terminal performance of the three monkeys under the 10-min FI schedule with timeout.

Phase 4

During the first four sessions after shock was eliminated (Fig. 3), the timeout was still available under the FI schedule, and was presented independently of responding if no response occurred within 2 min of the end of the

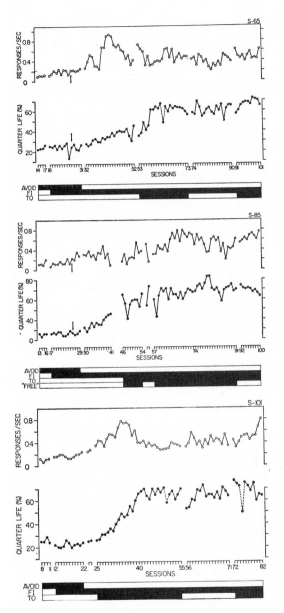

Fig. 1. Development of increased rates and a positively accelerated pattern of responding under a 10-min fixed-interval schedule of shock presentation. The solid black bars denote the procedures in effect during the various sessions. The mean number of shocks per session delivered under the avoidance schedule were 35.3, 12.0, and 8.4, respectively, for the last five sessions under simple avoidance, and the first and last five under the concurrent schedule. Note that when the avoidance schedule was eliminated, the rate of responding increased markedly but then decreased as positive curvature developed. Addition of the 30-sec timeout (TO) initially enhanced this curvature, but later deletion and reinstatement of timeout had no systematic effect. *Monkey S-65:* Before Session 27 (arrow), the shock delivered under the avoidance schedule was 5.2 ma, and the shock delivered under the FI 10-min schedule was 2.0 ma; in the sessions after the arrow, all shocks were 5.2 ma. For Session 56, the experimental chamber was moved to a new location, and the monkey was placed in the restraining chair in a slightly different way; for Session 63, the monkey's tail was improperly shaved. Both conditions resulted in slight disruptions of the behavior. *Monkey S-85:* Before Session 26 (arrow), the intensity of the shock under the avoidance schedule was 5.2 ma and that under the FI schedule was 2.0 ma; in Session 26 and thereafter, all shocks were 5.2 ma. During Sessions 42-45 (not shown) there was a disruption in performance and Monkey S-85 ceased responding for prolonged periods. Shock intensity was increased to 7.0 ma, and shocks were presented independently of responding if no response occurred within 1 min of the end of the FI 10-min; in addition, a 30-sec timeout period followed each shock. Under these conditions, the pattern of positively accelerated responding recovered (Sessions 46-54). In Session 55, shocks were no longer scheduled to occur independently of responding, and responding was well maintained. However, in Session 56, there were long pauses, and it was necessary to reinstate the response-independent shock procedure to maintain responding. Although response-independent shock was scheduled to occur in Sessions 57-91, few shocks were delivered under it (four in Session 57, two in 58, and one each in Sessions 61, 63, 74, 82, and 91). In Sessions 92-101, this contingency was eliminated, and responding was well maintained. *Monkey S-101:* The monkey escaped from restraint just before Session 50, and this resulted in a slight disruption of performance; the cause for the disruption during Session 75 is unknown. Note that Monkey S-101 was first studied for only two sessions (23-24) under FI 10-min without the 30-sec timeout.

interval. Under these conditions, rate of responding decreased abruptly for two monkeys (S-65 and S-101), but was relatively unchanged in the third (S-85); quarter-life values immediately decreased for all three monkeys, but positive curvature was still evident in the cumulative records (Fig. 4A). During the sessions when there was a possibility of response-independent presentation of the timeout, only in the case of Monkey S-101 was the

timeout ever presented in this way (three times in Session 85 and two in Session 86). Over the course of the sessions in which timeout was still available under the FI schedule, but not independently of responding, rates of responding and quarter-life values decreased further for all monkeys (Fig. 4B).

When the timeout was eliminated, rates of responding fell to near zero levels, and quarter-life values varied about 25% (Fig. 4C).

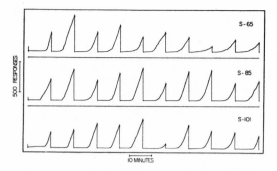

Fig. 2. Cumulative records of responding under 10-min fixed-interval schedule of electric shock presentation. Ordinate, cumulative number of responses; abscissa, time. The recording pen reset at shock presentation. A 30-sec timeout period followed each shock; the recorder was stopped during the timeout. Monkey S-65, Session 94; Monkey S-85, Session 97; Monkey S-101, Session 79.

Phase 5

The effects of reinstating scheduled shocks are summarized in the latter portions of Fig. 3. Cumulative records of terminal performances under each of the shock intensities are shown in panels D-G of Fig. 4.

At 0.3 ma, none of the monkeys responded appreciably (Fig. 4D). Quarter-life values, where rates of responding were sufficient to permit meaningful calculation, were approximately 25%; an exception to this was Monkey S-85 on the last day under the 0.3-ma shock (record D). In general, over the 1.0- to 5.6-ma shock range, rates of responding and quarter-life values increased and stabilized at values comparable to those obtained before extinction (Fig. 3).

Disruption and recovery of performance of Monkey S-85. After completion of the sessions under the 5.6-ma shock, shock intensity was increased to 10.0 ma for Monkey S-85. Performance was well maintained during the first session under the 10.0-ma shock (Fig. 5A). During the latter part of the second session, however, the performance of Monkey S-85 was disrupted (at *a* in Fig. 5B), and responding ceased. The next session was relatively normal (Fig. 5C), but in the following session (Fig. 5D), responding ceased after three fixed-interval cycles had been completed. During the next four sessions (not shown), various changes in procedure were made in an unsuccessful attempt to restore responding. In Sessions 174 and 175, shocks were presented independently

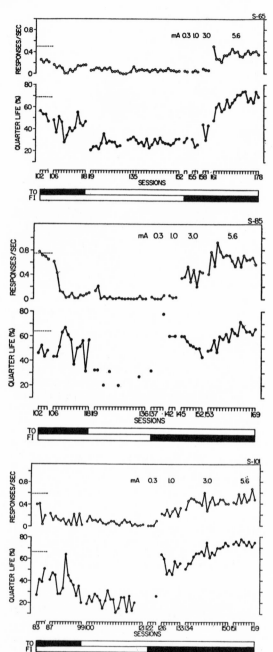

Fig. 3. Decreases in response rate and quarter-life after elimination of scheduled shocks (extinction), and redevelopment of responding under various shock intensities. The solid black bars denote the procedures in effect during the various sessions. The horizontal dashed lines at the left represent the mean rates of responding and mean quarter-life values for the last five sessions under FI 10-min. Quarter-life points were not plotted for certain sessions in which response rate was near zero.

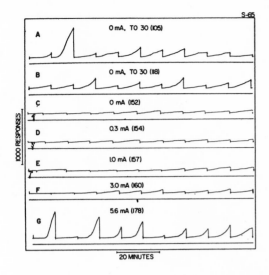

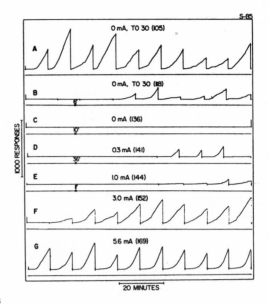

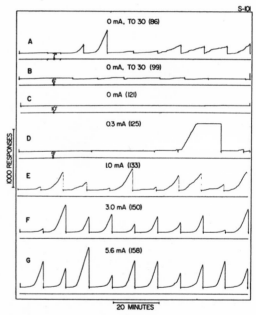

Fig. 4. Cumulative response records during various stages of extinction, and during redevelopment of responding under various shock intensities. *Monkey S-65:* A: Session 105, last session in which 30-sec timeout could be presented independently of responding; B: Session 118, last session in which 30-sec timeout was available under the FI 10-min; C: Session 152, last extinction session; D: Session 154, last session under FI 10-min, 0.3 ma; E: Session 157, last session under FI 10-min, 1.0 ma; F: Session 160, last session under FI 10-min, 3.0 ma; G: Session 178, eighteenth session under FI 10-min, 5.6 ma. Portions of records C, D, and E, during which there was no responding, have been eliminated; the numbers designate the number of minutes removed. *Monkey S-85:* A: Session 105, last session which 30-sec timeout could be presented independently of responding; B: Session 118, last session in which 30-sec timeout was available under FI 10-min; C: Session 136, last extinction session; D: Session 141, last session under FI 10-min, 0.3 ma; E: Session 144, last session under FI 10-min, 1.0 ma; F: Session 152, last session under FI 10-min, 3.0 ma; G: Session 169, seventeenth session under FI 10-min, 5.6 ma. As for Monkey S-65, portions of records B, C, D, and E, during which there was no responding, were eliminated. *Monkey S-101:* A: Session 86, last session in which 30-sec timeout could be presented independently of responding (indicated by marks on the event record); B: Session 99, last session in which 30-sec timeout was available under FI 10-min; C: Session 121, last extinction session; D: Session 125, last session under FI 10-min, 0.3 ma; E: Session 133, last session under FI 10-min, 1.0 ma; F: Session 150, last session under FI 10-

min, 3.0 ma; G: Session 158, eighth session under FI 10-min, 5.6 ma. As for the other monkeys, portions of records A, B, C, and D in which there was no responding have been removed.

of responding if no response occurred within 2-min of the end of the FI. In Session 176, a 30-sec timeout after each shock was also scheduled. None of these changes noticeably increased responding. In Session 178, the FI

schedule was modified as follows: in the presence of a red stimulus light, 5.6-ma shocks were scheduled to occur every 3 sec after the end of the 10-min FI. A response during this period terminated the condition, produced a

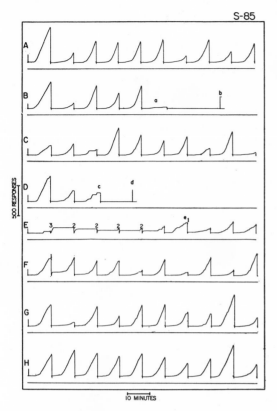

Fig. 5. Disruption and recovery of performance under FI 10-min schedule of shock presentation in Monkey S-85. A: Session 170, FI 10-min, 10.0 ma; B: Session 171, FI 10-min, 10.0 ma; disruption occurred at *a*, and session was terminated at *b*; C: Session 172, FI 10-min, 10.0 ma; D: Session 173, FI 10-min, 10.0 ma; shock reduced to 5.6 ma at *c*, session terminated at *d*; E: Session 178, modified FI schedule (see text); numbers refer to number of extra shocks delivered; shock-shock interval increased from 3 sec to 10 sec at *e*; F: Session 179, modified FI schedule; 10-sec shock-shock interval; one extra shock delivered at end of first interval only; G: Session 180, FI 10-min, 5.6 ma; H: Session 184, FI 10-min, 5.6 ma.

single 5.6-ma shock, and began a new fixed interval. Figure 5E shows the performance during the first session (178) under this modified schedule. For the first several cycles, responding was largely confined to the beginning and the end of each interval. In the sixth and seventh cycles of this session, and in subsequent cycles, responding in the early parts of the interval diminished, and a pattern of positively accelerated responding developed. After the sixth cycle, the shock-shock interval was increased to 10 sec. Note that during the last three cycles of Session 178, no shocks other than those following a response under the FI

schedule were delivered. The same modified schedule was in effect during the subsequent session (179). In this case (Fig. 5F), the only "extra" shock delivered was at the end of the first FI; during succeeding intervals, a pattern of positively accelerated responding was well maintained. In the next session (180), and in subsequent sessions, the 10-min FI schedule (5.6-ma shock), identical to that in effect before the disruption in performance, successfully maintained responding that, in both rate and pattern, was indistinguishable from that obtained before the disruption (Fig. 5G and 5H).

Phases 6 and 7

Beginning with Session 185 (S-101), 204 (S-85), or 205 (S-65), shocks were again omitted from the 10-min FI schedule; responding had no scheduled consequences. Rates of responding gradually declined to near-zero, and quarter-life values abruptly decreased to about 25% for all monkeys. The initial portion of Fig. 6 summarizes the effects on rate and quarter-life for Monkey S-85.

The effects of reinstating shock under a 5-min fixed-interval schedule were immediate; rates of responding increased sharply, and quarter-life values rose to approximately 60 to 65% (Fig. 6). Subsequently, in the presence of different colored stimulus lights, shocks were presented under FI 3-min and FI 1-min schedules. The number of sessions and the average rates of responding and quarter-life values under each of the fixed-interval parameters are summarized in Table 2.

For all monkeys, rates of responding increased as the duration of the fixed-interval was shortened; during this time, quarter-life values did not vary systematically, and were always close to 60%. Representative cumulative records of responding at each parameter are shown in Fig. 7. The relationship between fixed-interval duration and resultant rate of responding was an inverse linear one when the rate was plotted against the logarithm of the fixed-interval duration (Fig. 8).

DISCUSSION

In monkeys that have previously responded under schedules in which responding postpones the delivery of shock, the presentation of response-dependent electric shock under a fixed-interval schedule can enhance respond-

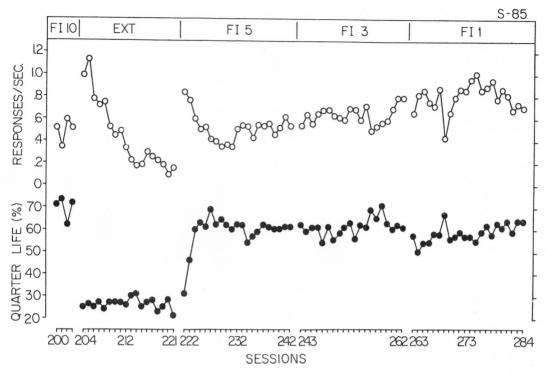

Fig. 6. Decreases in response rate and quarter-life after elimination of scheduled shocks (extinction), and re-development of responding under FI 1-min, 3-min, and 5-min (Monkey S-85).

ing, and lead to the development and maintenance of a pattern of positively accelerated responding. When shocks no longer followed responses (extinction), responding decreased (Phases 4 and 6). When shocks were again presented under the fixed-interval schedule, both rate and pattern of responding quickly recovered (Phases 5 and 7). In general, rates of responding were directly related to the intensity of the electric shock presented (Phase 5), and inversely related to the parameter value of the fixed interval (Phase 7).

Under a fixed-interval schedule of electric shock presentation, a shock is presented following the first response to occur after a fixed period of time has elapsed; responses during this fixed period have no scheduled consequences. Such a schedule is formally analogous to fixed-interval schedules under which food, water, or other stimuli are presented. The pattern of positively accelerated responding engendered under a fixed-interval schedule of shock presentation is similar in every respect to that engendered under fixed-interval schedules of food or water presentation (Skinner, 1938; Ferster and Skinner, 1957), or under

fixed-interval schedules of termination of stimuli associated with the delivery of electric shock (Morse and Kelleher, 1966).

When food is no longer presented under a schedule of food presentation, or when shocks are no longer delivered under schedules of stimulus-shock termination, responding decreases (Skinner, 1938; Morse and Kelleher, 1966); similarly, the present experiments have shown that responding decreases when shocks are eliminated under fixed-interval schedules of shock presentation. Rates of responding under schedules of food presentation have been reported to be directly related to the amount or concentration of the food presented (Stebbins, Mead, and Martin, 1959; Shettleworth and Nevin, 1965), and rates of responding under schedules in which responding terminates electric shock are directly related to the intensity of the shock (Dinsmoor and Winograd, 1958; Winograd, 1965). The rates of responding under the fixed-interval schedules of shock presentation studied here were also directly related to the shock intensity. Under fixed-interval schedules of food presentation, response rate is inversely related to the duration

Table 2

Rates of responding and quarter-life values under several parameters of fixed-interval schedules of electric shock presentation.

	Monkey S-65			Monkey S-85			Monkey S-101		
	No.[a]	Rate	Q[a]	No.	Rate	Q	No.	Rate	Q
FI 10-min	44[b]	0.399 (0.082)[c]	62.8 (5.5)	24	0.488 (0.079)	71.4 (6.9)	34	0.792 (0.040)	59.6 (6.1)
FI 5-min	52	0.664 (0.056)	60.8 (0.5)	21	0.533 (0.050)	60.6 (2.0)	32	1.069 (0.082)	64.8 (2.6)
FI 3-min	17	0.870 (0.095)	57.0 (3.9)	20	0.681 (0.035)	63.4 (7.1)	20	1.330 (0.071)	59.0 (4.1)
FI 1 (10 cycles)	—	—	—	17	0.896 (0.077)	60.2 (1.7)	17	1.687 (0.126)	58.8 (1.8)
FI 1 (20 cycles)	10	0.739 (0.140)	62.4 (2.8)	5	0.758 (0.067)	62.4 (2.1)	5	1.528 (0.157)	60.6 (2.1)

[a] no. = number sessions under particular schedule parameter.
[b] number of sessions under FI 10-min is the number under the 5.6-ma shock.
[c] response rate in responses per second (mean of last five sessions). Standard deviations in parentheses.
[d] Q = quarter-life in per cent (mean of last five sessions). Standard deviations in parentheses.

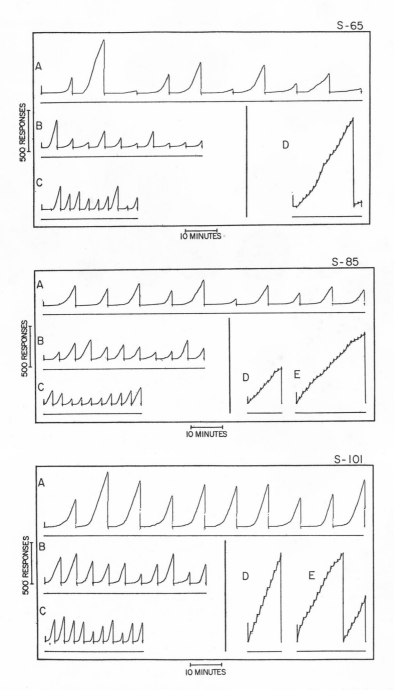

Fig. 7. Cumulative records of responding under several parameter values of FI schedules of shock presentation. The recording pen reset to the baseline after each shock, except under FI 1-min. *Monkey S-65:* A: Session 204, FI 10-min, 5.6 ma; B: Session 216, fifth session under FI 5-min, 5.6 ma; C: Session 268, fifth session under FI 3-min, 5.6 ma; D: Session 286, fifth session under FI 1-min, 5.6 ma (20 cycles per session). *Monkey S-85:* A: Session 201, FI 10-min, 5.6 ma; B: Session 226, fifth session under FI 5-min, 5.6 ma; C: Session 247, fifth session FI 3-min, 5.6 ma; D: Session 268, fifth session under FI 1-min, 5.6 ma (10 cycles per session); E: Session 286, fifth session under FI 1-min, 5.6 ma (20 cycles per session). *Monkey S-101:* A: Session 184, FI 10-min, 5.6 ma; B: Session 195, fifth day under FI 5-min, 5.6 ma; C: Session 227, fifth day under FI 3-min, 5.6 ma; D: Session 248, fifth day under FI 1-min, 5.6 ma (10 cycles per session); E: Session 264, fifth day under FI 1-min, 5.6 ma (20 cycles per session).

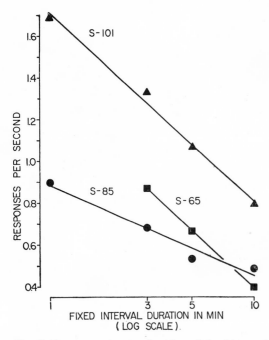

Fig. 8. Response rate as a function of fixed-interval duration. Ordinate, responses per second during the FI; abscissa, duration of FI (log scale). For FI 1-min, only the data from the sessions in which 10 shocks were delivered are plotted. Each point is the mean of the last five sessions under each parameter. Lines were fitted by the method of least-squares.

of the fixed interval (Skinner, 1938; Wilson, 1954; Ferster and Skinner, 1957); in the present experiments, over a 1- to 10-min range of FI durations, response rates were an inverse linear function of the logarithm of the fixed-interval duration. Thus, there appear to be no important differences among performances engendered under fixed-interval schedules of food presentation, shock termination, or shock presentation in the characteristic pattern of positively accelerated responding engendered, in the effects of elimination, reinstatement, and variations in intensity of the reinforcing stimulus, and in the effects of variations in parameter value of the fixed-interval schedule. This basic similarity strengthens and emphasizes previous conclusions (Kelleher and Morse, 1964; Morse and Kelleher, 1966; McKearney, 1968; Kelleher and Morse, 1968) that the schedule under which an event is presented, rather than the nature of that event, can be the most important determinant of the effects that event will have on behavior.

If the frequency of responding increases when the presentation of an event is made

dependent upon a response, that event is called a reinforcer (Skinner, 1938). Distinctions are often drawn between stimuli which maintain responses preceding their termination or postponement ("negative" reinforcers), and those maintaining responding preceding their presentation ("positive" reinforcers) (Keller and Schoenfeld, 1950; Reynolds, 1968). That such distinctions are frequently arbitrary and without empirical significance is demonstrated by the fact that, in the present experiments, electric shock first maintained responding that postponed it (Phases 1 and 2) and later maintained responding that led to its presentation (Phases 3-7). Thus, the electric shock met the defining criteria for both "types" of reinforcers.

To expect that any environmental event will have invariant effects is unreasonable; yet, for traditional behavior theories such invariance has usually been a tacit assumption. For a properly deprived animal, stimuli such as food or water are assumed to be inherently "positive", in the sense that the animal will work "for" them, and stimuli such as electric shock are thought to be invariably "negative" stimuli which animals will avoid or escape; exceptions are usually described as "paradoxical". However, there is evidence that a given stimulus can have different and even opposite effects in the same organism at the same time. For example, in the present experiments, electric shocks of the same intensity that functioned to maintain responses that postponed them later functioned to maintain responding preceding their presentation. Kelleher and Morse (1968) have recently shown that, in monkeys responding under a two-component FI 10-min, FR 1 schedule of electric-shock presentation, the presentation of electric shock maintained responding during the FI component, but suppressed responding during the FR 1 component. Clearly, the manner in which a stimulus is scheduled can be a more crucial determinant of its effects than any inherent qualities of that stimulus.

The development and maintenance of characteristic patterns of positively accelerated responding under fixed-interval schedules of shock presentation clearly depends also on the characteristics of the behavior existing at the time the schedule of shock presentation is imposed. It is equally clear, however, that no one particular reinforcement history or pattern of ongoing behavior is critical for the development of this behavior. For example, Morse *et al.* (1967) have shown that a pattern of responding (leash pulling in monkeys) initially elicited by delivery of electric shock can be altered to a pattern of maximal responding immediately before each shock, and then maintained under a fixed-interval schedule of shock presentation. In other experiments, monkeys responding under fixed-interval schedules of stimulus-shock termination or under interlocking shock-postponement schedules (in which successive responses postpone shocks for decreasing durations) have been maintained under fixed-interval schedules of electric shock presentation (Morse and Kelleher, 1969). In the latter experiments the subjects had previous experience in terminating or postponing electric shocks, but additional experiments (Kelleher and Morse, 1968) have shown that such experience is not necessary. After extended exposure to a concurrent variable-interval 2-min schedule of food presentation and two-component FI 10-min FR 1 schedule of shock presentation in squirrel monkeys, a pattern of positively accelerated responding developed and was maintained for extended periods under the fixed-interval schedule of shock presentation alone.

Complex interactions between ongoing behavior and the effects of new schedule conditions, and the general dependence of present and future behavior on past behavior are not peculiar to experiments involving the presentation of electric shock or similar events. For example, the effects of adventitiously presented reinforcers (Morse and Skinner, 1957; Herrnstein and Morse, 1957; Zeiler, 1968), of withholding the presentation of scheduled reinforcers (Ferster and Skinner, 1957), and of presenting stimuli correlated with periods of non-reinforcement (Ferster, 1958) are among the many interventions whose effects have been shown to depend upon the characteristics of behavior upon which they are imposed.

The direction and degree of the effects which environmental consequences have on a particular behavior depend importantly on the rate of occurrence, patterning in time, and physical topography of that behavior; these, and other aspects of behavior, are critically determined by the organism's history of reinforcement. The effects that a given stimulus will have when imposed upon a pre-existing sequence of behavior depend, as well, upon the schedule under which *it* is presented. The net effect, therefore, is the result of an interaction between the effects of the reinforcement schedules controlling the existing behavior, itself complexly determined, and the schedule under which the new event is presented.

REFERENCES

Dinsmoor, J. A. and Winograd, E. Shock intensity in variable-interval escape schedules. *Journal of the Experimental Analysis of Behavior*, 1958, 1, 145-148.

Ferster, C. B. The control of behavior in chimpanzees and pigeons by time-out from positive reinforcement. *Psychological Monographs*, 1958, 72 (whole No. 461).

Ferster, C. B. and Skinner, B. F. *Schedules of reinforcement.* New York: Appleton-Century-Crofts, 1957.

Gollub, L. R. The relations among measures of performance on fixed-interval schedules. *Journal of the Experimental Analysis of Behavior*, 1964, 7, 337-343.

Hake, D. F. and Azrin, N. H. An apparatus for delivering pain shock to monkeys. *Journal of the Experimental Analysis of Behavior*, 1963, 6, 297-298.

Herrnstein, R. J. and Morse, W. H. Effects of pentobarbital on intermittently reinforced behavior. *Science*, 1957, 125, 929-931. (a)

Herrnstein, R. J. and Morse, W. H. Some effects of response-independent positive reinforcement on maintained operant behavior. *Journal of Comparative and Physiological Psychology*, 1957, 50, 461-467. (b)

Kelleher, R. T., Riddle, W. C., and Cook, L. Persistent behavior maintained by unavoidable shocks. *Journal of the Experimental Analysis of Behavior*, 1963, 6, 507-517.

Kelleher, R. T. and Morse, W. H. Escape behavior and punished behavior. *Federation Proceedings*, 1964, 23, 808-817.

Kelleher, R. T. and Morse, W. H. Schedules using noxious stimuli. III. Responding maintained with response-produced electric shocks. *Journal of the Experimental Analysis of Behavior*, 1968, 11, 819-838.

Keller, F. S. and Schoenfeld, W. N. *Principles of psychology.* New York: Appleton-Century-Crofts, 1950.

McKearney, J. W. Maintenance of responding under a fixed-interval schedule of electric shock-presentation. *Science*, 1968, 160, 1249-1251.

Morse, W. H. and Skinner, B. F. A second type of superstition in the pigeon. *American Journal of Psychology*, 1957, 70, 308-311.

Morse, W. H. and Kelleher, R. T. Schedules using noxious stimuli. I. Multiple fixed-ratio and fixed-interval termination of schedule complexes. *Journal of the Experimental Analysis of Behavior*, 1966, 9, 267-290.

Morse, W. H., Mead, R. N., and Kelleher, R. T. Modulation of elicited behavior by a fixed-interval schedule of electric shock presentation. *Science*, 1967, 157, 215-217.

Morse, W. H. and Kelleher, R. T.   Schedules as fundamental determinants of behavior. In W. N. Schoenfeld (Ed.), *Theories of reinforcement schedules.* New York: Appleton-Century-Crofts, 1969 (in press).

Reynolds, G. S.   *A primer of operant conditioning.* Glenview, Ill.: Scott, Foresman and Co., 1968.

Shettleworth, S. and Nevin, J. A.   Relative rate of response and relative magnitude of reinforcement in multiple schedules. *Journal of the Experimental Analysis of Behavior*, 1965, **8**, 199-202.

Sidman, M.   By-products of aversive control. *Journal of the Experimental Analysis of Behavior*, 1958, **1**, 265-280.

Sidman, M., Herrnstein, R. J., and Conrad, D. G.   Maintenance of avoidance behavior by unavoidable shocks. *Journal of Comparative and Physiological Psychology*, 1957, **50**, 553-557.

Skinner, B. F.   *The behavior of organisms.* New York: Appleton-Century-Crofts, 1938.

Stebbins, W. C., Mead, P. B., and Martin, J. M.   The relation of amount of reinforcement to performance under a fixed-interval schedule. *Journal of the Experimental Analysis of Behavior*, 1959, **2**, 351-356.

Waller, M. B. and Waller, P. F.   The effects of unavoidable shocks on a multiple schedule having an avoidance component. *Journal of the Experimental Analysis of Behavior*, 1963, **6**, 29-37.

Wilson, M. P.   Periodic reinforcement interval and number of periodic reinforcements as parameters of response strength. *Journal of Comparative and Physiological Psychology*, 1954, **47**, 51-56.

Winograd, E.   Escape behavior under different fixed-ratios and shock intensities. *Journal of the Experimental Analysis of Behavior*, 1965, **8**, 117-124.

Zeiler, M. D.   Fixed and variable schedules of response-independent reinforcement. *Journal of the Experimental Analysis of Behavior*, 1968, **11**, 405-414.

Received 18 October 1968.

RESPONDING IN THE CAT MAINTAINED UNDER RESPONSE-INDEPENDENT ELECTRIC SHOCK AND RESPONSE-PRODUCED ELECTRIC SHOCK[1,2]

LARRY D. BYRD

UNIVERSITY OF NORTH CAROLINA[3]

Key-pressing responses in the cat were maintained under conditions in which brief electric shock was first postponed by responses (avoidance), then periodically presented independently of responses, and finally produced by responses on a fixed-interval schedule of 15 min (FI 15-min). A steady rate of responding occurred under shock avoidance and under response-independent shock; positively accelerated responding was engendered by the FI 15-min schedule. A second experiment studied responding under second-order schedules composed of three FI 5-min components. Responding was suppressed when a stimulus was presented briefly at completion of each FI 5-min component and a shock followed the brief stimulus at completion of the third component. Responding was maintained when each of the first two components was completed either with or without presentation of a brief stimulus and a shock alone was presented at completion of the third FI 5-min component.

The effects of electric shock upon operant responding have traditionally been investigated under conditions in which responding is maintained by terminating or postponing shock (Sidman, 1953), or suppressed by presenting shock (Azrin, 1956). Yet, under certain conditions, electric shock can enhance responding. Sidman, Herrnstein, and Conrad (1957) reported that under a schedule of continuous shock avoidance, rates of responding in the rhesus monkey increased in the presence of a stimulus (pre-shock stimulus) which terminated when a response-independent shock was presented. The enhancing effect was temporary, however; with continued training, higher response rates in the presence of the pre-shock stimulus gradually decreased and approached the rates in the absence of the stimulus. Frequency of responding declined when all shocks, except those delivered when the pre-shock stimulus terminated, were omitted, but the decline was slower in the

presence of the stimulus than in its absence. Later, Herrnstein and Sidman (1958) showed in the rhesus monkey that after training under a schedule of continuous shock avoidance, response rates were higher in the presence of a pre-shock stimulus than in its absence when responding was maintained under a schedule of food presentation.

More-recent investigations have shown that increased rates of responding in the presence of a pre-shock stimulus can persist in other species under different conditions. Waller and Waller (1963), studying responding in the dog under a multiple schedule of food presentation, shock avoidance, and extinction, found that rates of responding in the presence of a pre-shock stimulus consistently increased during the extinction periods and during the avoidance periods. Moderately high response rates in the presence of the pre-shock stimulus persisted even after avoidance responding was extinguished.

In a series of experiments, Kelleher, Riddle, and Cook (1963) found that responding in the squirrel monkey increased in the presence of a pre-shock stimulus presented during the food component of a multiple schedule of food presentation and shock avoidance. Responding during the pre-shock stimulus continued even when the schedules of food presentation and shock avoidance were changed to extinction, but responding ceased when a response-independent shock was not presented at termina-

[1]Dedicated to Professor B. F. Skinner in his sixty-fifth year.

[2]This work was supported in part by Grant MH 07534 from the U.S. Public Health Service to M. B. Waller, Principal Investigator. Preparation of the manuscript was supported by Grants MH 02094 and MH 07658 and by Training Grant 5-T1-MH 07084. The author wishes to thank Drs. P. B. Dews, R. T. Kelleher, and W. H. Morse for helpful comments.

[3]Reprints may be obtained from the author, New England Regional Primate Research Center, Harvard Medical School, Southborough, Mass. 01772.

tion of the stimulus. Later, responding was maintained when the pre-shock stimulus was continuously present and a response-independent shock was delivered to the subject every 10 min.

Rates of responding in the chimpanzee have also been shown to increase when a pre-shock stimulus was presented during the avoidance component of a complex multiple schedule of shock avoidance and food presentation (Belleville, Rohles, Grunzke, and Clark, 1963). Response rates increased immediately upon presentation of the pre-shock stimulus, and were consistently higher in the presence of the stimulus than in its absence.

Experiments in which response-independent shock was presented without a pre-shock stimulus also indicate that presentation of electric shock can enhance responding. Appel (1960a) reported that after training under a multiple schedule of shock avoidance and extinction, a rat seldom responded during the extinction component. When response-independent shock was presented at regular intervals during the extinction component, however, responding during extinction increased. Appel (1960b), studying responding in the rhesus monkey, reported similar results when response-independent shock was presented at variable times during the extinction component of a multiple schedule of shock avoidance and extinction.

Hearst (1962) trained rhesus monkeys to respond in the presence of a bright light under concurrent schedules of shock avoidance and food presentation, and then tested for generalization at decreased intensities of the light. In the absence of shock delivery and food presentation at the lower intensities, response rates decreased as the intensity of the light decreased. When response-independent shock was delivered at variable times during the lowest light intensity, response rates increased and approached the rates prevailing during the bright light.

All of these experiments studied the effects of presenting response-independent shock, either with or without a pre-shock stimulus, and all showed that response-independent shock can enhance responding in subjects having prior training under continuous shock avoidance. Furthermore, in the one experiment (Kelleher *et al.*, 1963) that studied the effect of response-produced shock, an enhanc-

ing effect was observed in one squirrel monkey during several sessions. That responding under fixed-interval schedules of shock presentation can be maintained in the squirrel monkey without prior training under shock avoidance has been shown by Kelleher and Morse (1968). However, there is no evidence that response-produced shock can maintain responding in subjects having histories of shock avoidance.[4]

The present paper describes two experiments which studied responding in the domestic cat when responses postponed shocks, when shocks were presented independently of responses, and when shocks were response-produced. These experiments demonstrated that responding in cats having prior training under continuous shock avoidance can be maintained when electric shock is response-produced under a 15-min fixed-interval schedule (FI 15-min) and when shock is presented independently of responses. These experiments also demonstrated that responding can be maintained under some second-order schedules of shock presentation, and that subjects' responding can be suppressed when a stimulus which is occasionally paired with shock is presented at completion of each of the components.

EXPERIMENT I: PERFORMANCE UNDER RESPONSE-INDEPENDENT SHOCK AND UNDER AN FI 15-MIN SCHEDULE OF SHOCK PRESENTATION

The first experiment attempted to determine if responding in the cat could be maintained by occasionally presenting a response-independent electric shock after training under a schedule of continuous shock avoidance, and whether responding would persist when shocks were response-produced under a fixed-interval schedule. Performance was studied when responding postponed shock presentation, when shocks were presented at regular intervals independently of responding, and when shock presentation was response-produced (FI).

---

[4]While the present paper was undergoing editorial review, a study similar to Exp. I appeared (McKearney, 1968) in which responding in squirrel monkeys was maintained under an FI 10-min schedule of shock presentation.

METHOD

Subjects

Two adult cats, *Felis domestica*, one a female (FC-I) and one a male (MC-II), served. FC-I weighed approximately 3.3 kilograms and MC-II weighed approximately 3.9 kilograms. Both had previously responded under a variable-interval schedule of food presentation and under a schedule of continuous shock avoidance. During the present investigation, food and water were continuously available in the home cages.

Apparatus

The experimental chamber was a cubicle measuring approximately 24 in. on each side. The four walls and the ceiling were wood. The floor consisted of 0.25-in. steel bars mounted 0.50 in. apart, center to center, to form a grid through which electric shock could be delivered. The shock source was a generator and scrambler (Grason-Stadler, Model E1064GS) modified to provide a 60 cps alternating current in excess of 4.0 ma. Modification consisted of replacing an 86,000 ohm series resistor with a multiple-position selector switch and appropriate resistors.

A small speaker through which an auditory stimulus could be presented was located at the bottom of one wall of the chamber. Also on this wall were a bar-type lever and a liquid feeder, both disconnected and unrelated to the present study. Mounted on the outer surface of an adjacent wall was a standard pigeon response key (R. Gerbrands Co.) which could be transilluminated by a white or a red 28-v dc lamp (G.E. #1028). Affixed to the surface of the response key was a cylindrical piece of transparent Plexiglas, 0.75 in. in diameter and approximately 0.75 in. in length. The response key was mounted so that the cylindrical Plexiglas extension passed through an opening 2.50 in. in diameter in the wall of the chamber, and the exposed end of the Plexiglas was flush with the inner surface of the wall. A force of at least 20 g operated the response key. Each response produced an audible click of a relay and caused the key to be illuminated with the white lamp for 0.05 sec. In the absence of responses the key was normally illuminated with the red lamp.

A 60-w, 115-v ac lamp mounted behind white, translucent glass in the center of the ceiling served as a houselight. The light went off and on once per second during each session. Usually there were six sessions per week, each lasting approximately 2 hr. Relay switching circuits and timers arranged the experimental conditions, and data were tabulated on counters and cumulative recorders as described by Ferster and Skinner (1957).

Procedure

Subjects were trained under a schedule of continuous shock avoidance (Sidman, 1953) in which a response postponed the presentation of shock for 60 sec (response-shock interval). If 60 sec elapsed without a response, a shock of 4.0-ma intensity and 0.75-sec duration was presented every 5 sec (shock-shock interval) until a response occurred.

After 15 sessions under continuous avoidance there were two sessions during which the schedule of shock avoidance remained in effect and, in addition, an electric shock was delivered every 15 min independently of shocks presented under the avoidance schedule, and independently of responding. Shocks presented during these two sessions were also 4.0 ma in intensity and 0.75 sec in duration. After these two sessions, the schedule of shock avoidance was omitted; thereafter, only a response-independent electric shock was presented every 15-min. The intensity of the shock was unsystematically varied and was either 4.0, 6.4, or 8.1 ma. Duration of shocks remained at 0.75 sec.

After 33 sessions under response-independent shock, the schedule was changed to a 15-min fixed-interval schedule of shock presentation (FI 15-min), *i.e.*, a shock was produced by the first response occurring after 15 min had elapsed since the previous shock. During 50 sessions under FI 15-min, shock intensity was, at various times, either 5.4, 6.4, or 8.1 ma for FC-I, and 4.0, 5.4, 6.4, or 8.1 ma for MC-II. Shock duration was 0.75 sec during the first 31 sessions, and 0.50 sec during the remaining 19 sessions.

Shock intensity was increased from 4.0 to 8.1 ma and shock duration was decreased from 0.75 to 0.50 sec to determine if a change in performance would accompany changes in these parameters, and to determine shock intensities appropriate to maintaining patterns of responding characteristic of the schedules studied.

RESULTS

Under the avoidance schedule, both subjects responded steadily and shocks occurred infrequently (Fig. 1 and 2). For each subject the mean number of shocks per session was approximately one; seldom did as many as three shocks occur during an individual session and occasionally none occurred. Mean rates of responding during the last three sessions were approximately 0.18 responses per second for FC-I and 0.11 responses per second for MC-II (Fig. 3).

When a response-independent shock was delivered every 15 min, rate of responding by FC-I was higher than under the avoidance schedule, but responding by MC-II was only slightly enhanced. Response rates during the last three sessions had increased to approximately 0.26 responses per second for FC-I and approximately 0.11 responses per second for MC-II (Fig. 3). Although a shock was pre-

sented at regular intervals there was only minimal evidence of a periodic change in response rate. For FC-I, and to a lesser extent for MC-II, the most noticeable change was an occasional slight decrease in response rate for a brief period immediately after a shock. Otherwise, the patterns of responding under response-independent shock, like those under continuous avoidance, showed relatively steady responding (Fig. 1 and 2).

The rates and patterns of responding changed after the FI 15-min schedule of shock presentation was introduced. FC-I developed a pattern of responding similar to the pattern typically engendered by an FI schedule of food presentation. Responses were infrequent during the initial part of the interval, and occurred with increasing frequency toward the end of the 15-min period (Fig. 1). MC-II showed less-marked contrast between responding during the initial and final segments of the interval; except for a brief pause after

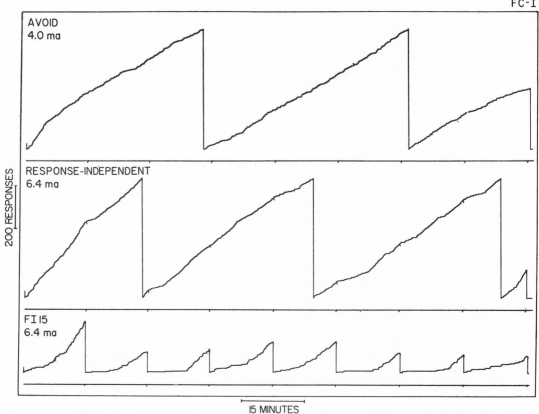

Fig. 1. Performance of FC-I under: (Avoid) continuous shock avoidance; (Response-Independent) presentation of a response-independent shock every 15 min; (FI 15) presentation of a response-produced shock every 15 min. A short diagonal mark of the response pen indicates presentation of a shock; the event pen marks successive 15-min periods. The response pen reset upon cumulation of 550 responses, or upon presentation of a shock.

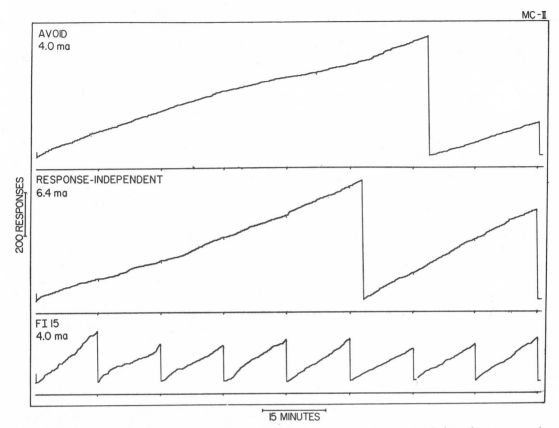

Fig. 2. Performance of MC-II under: (Avoid) continuous shock avoidance; (Response-Independent) presentation of a response-independent shock every 15 min; (FI 15) presentation of a response-produced shock every 15 min. A short diagonal mark of the response pen indicates presentation of a shock; the event pen marks successive 15-min periods. The response pen reset upon cumulation of 550 responses, or upon presentation of a shock.

shock presentation, responding tended to occur at a steadier rate (Fig. 2). After 50 sessions under FI 15-min, the mean response rates were 0.11 responses per sec for FC-I and 0.18 responses per sec for MC-II (Fig. 3).

Responding in both cats was relatively insensitive to changes in shock parameters under response-independent shock and under response-produced shock. Over the range studied, both cats responded at relatively steady rates under shock avoidance and under response-independent shock, and for FC-I, to a greater extent than for MC-II, responding was positively accelerated under FI 15-min.

EXPERIMENT II: PERFORMANCE UNDER SECOND-ORDER SCHEDULES OF SHOCK PRESENTATION

Experiment I demonstrated that in cats having histories of shock avoidance, responding can be maintained under an FI 15-min sched-

ule of shock presentation and under response-independent shock. After the determination that response-produced shock can maintain responding in cats, a second experiment was conducted to determine if responding would persist when shock was presented under second-order schedules (Kelleher, 1966a) and to examine the effect of presenting, at completion of individual components, a brief stimulus occasionally paired with shock. To the extent that the FI 15-min schedule of shock presentation engendered response patterns typical of an FI schedule of food presentation, it was of interest to determine whether a stimulus paired with shock, like a stimulus paired with food, would enhance responding. Kelleher (1966b) and others have shown second-order schedules to be especially sensitive procedures for assessing the effects of stimuli which are presented briefly during responding that is maintained under food presentation.

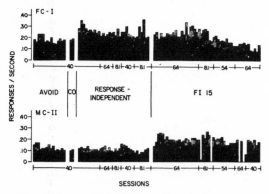

Fig. 3. Mean rates of responding during successive daily sessions under: (Avoid) continuous shock avoidance; (CO) continuous shock avoidance concurrent with presentation of a response-independent shock every 15 min; (Response-Independent) presentation of a response-independent shock every 15 min; (FI 15) presentation of a response-produced shock every 15 min. Changes in shock intensity (ma) are indicated below each abscissa. MC-II made no responses and produced no shocks during the twenty-eighth, forty-first, and forty-third sessions under FI 15-min, but immediately responded at beginning of the twenty-ninth, forty-second, and forty-fourth sessions.

METHOD

Subjects and Apparatus

The subjects and apparatus were the same as in Exp. I.

Procedure

The FI 15-min schedule studied in Exp. I was changed to a second-order schedule in which each fixed-interval component was completed by the first response occurring after 5 min (FI 5-min), and a 0.5-sec shock was presented upon completion of three FI 5-min components. Under the schedule studied first (Noise-Shock: Not Paired), a response-produced white noise of 0.75-sec duration was presented at completion of the first and second FI 5-min components, and a shock was produced by the response that completed the third component. A white noise was not presented at completion of the third FI 5-min component. Shock intensities for FC-I were 4.0 and 6.4 ma; for MC-II they were 1.3, 2.0, and 4.0 ma. Shock intensity was varied between 1.3 and 6.4 ma to determine if particular intensities in this range would further enhance positively accelerated responding, especially in MC-II.

After 38 sessions, the schedule was changed so that a response-produced white noise was presented when each of the three components

was completed; when the third component was completed, the white noise was immediately followed by shock (Noise-Shock: Paired). Intensity of the shock was 4.0 ma for FC-I and 1.3 ma for MC-II.

At the end of eight sessions, the schedule was changed so that responses at completion of the first and second FI 5-min components produced no stimulus change, and a response at completion of the third FI 5-min component produced a shock (Shock Only). A white noise was never presented during the 11 sessions under this procedure. Shock intensity remained at 4.0 ma for FC-I, and was either 1.3 or 2.0 for MC-II.

During the final phase of Exp. II, a white noise was presented at completion of each of the three FI 5-min components, and a shock immediately followed every third presentation of the white noise (Noise-Shock: Paired). Shock intensity was 4.0 ma for FC-I and 2.0 ma for MC-II. The experiment was terminated after two sessions under this schedule.

RESULTS

Responding by each subject was maintained at a mean rate of approximately 0.09 responses per second when a white noise was presented at completion of the first and second components only (Noise-Shock: Not Paired) (Fig. 4). FC-I showed a pronounced increase in the frequency of responding during each successive component of the three-component schedule. Rate of responding was lowest during the first or initial component and highest during the third or terminal component. (Fig. 5 and 7). MC-II did not show a uniform increase in frequency of responding during each successive component, but tended to respond at a relatively steady rate during each of the components (Fig. 6 and 7).

When a white noise was presented at completion of the terminal component, as well as at completion of the first and second components (Noise-Shock: Paired), responding decreased significantly (Fig. 4). FC-I responded at decreased rates during the first five sessions under this schedule, but made no responses during the sixth and subsequent sessions. Cumulative records of the performance of FC-I during the fifth session are shown in the second frame of Fig. 5. Responding by MC-II decreased to 0.05 responses per second, but did not cease during eight sessions under this

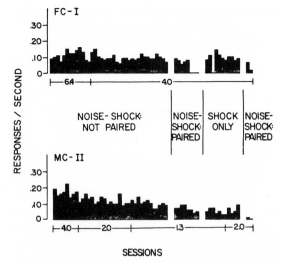

Fig. 4. Mean rates of responding during successive daily sessions under: (Noise-Shock: Not Paired) a white noise was presented at completion of the first and second FI 5-min components and a shock alone was presented at completion of every third component; (Noise-Shock: Paired) a white noise was presented at completion of each component and a shock immediately followed every third presentation of the white noise; (Shock Only) no stimulus change occurred at completion of the first and second components and a shock alone was presented at completion of every third component. Changes in shock intensity (ma) are indicated below each abscissa.

schedule. Records of the performance of MC-II during the seventh session are shown in the second frame of Fig. 6.

Omitting the white noise (Shock Only) did not immediately result in the recovery of responding by FC-I. During each of the first four sessions under this procedure, FC-I did not respond until a single 0.5-sec shock of 15.9 ma had been delivered; but once a response-independent shock had been presented, FC-I responded for the remainder of the session. During the third session, a shock was not delivered and FC-I made no responses. After a delay of approximately 6 min at the beginning of the fifth session, responding began without the presentation of a 15.9-ma shock, and responding persisted during the fifth and subsequent sessions. Responding was maintained at mean rates of 0.09 responses per second by FC-I and 0.06 responses per second by MC-II during the last three sessions under the Shock-Only procedure (Fig. 4). Although the trend was much more pronounced in FC-I, both subjects tended to increase the frequency of responding during successive components (Fig. 7). Cumulative records of terminal performances are presented in Fig. 5 and 6 for FC-I and MC-II respectively.

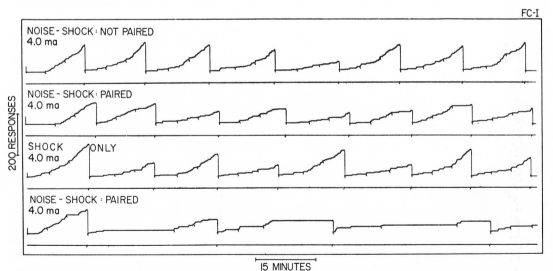

Fig. 5. Performance of FC-I under three second-order schedules of shock presentation. (Noise-Shock: Not Paired) a white noise was presented at completion of the first and second FI 5-min components and a shock alone was presented at completion of every third component. (Noise-Shock: Paired) a white noise was presented at completion of each component and a shock immediately followed every third presentation of the white noise. The second frame shows performance during the fifth session when the procedure was studied the first time. The bottom frame shows performance during the second session when the procedure was studied a second time. (Shock Only) no stimulus change occurred at completion of the first and second components and a shock alone was presented at completion of every third component. A short diagonal mark of the response pen indicates completion of an FI 5-min component. A mark of the event pen and resetting of the response pen indicate presentation of a shock.

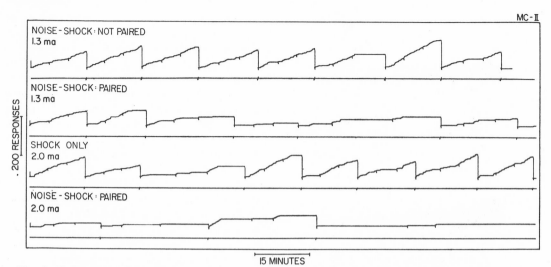

Fig. 6. Performance of MC-II under three second-order schedules of shock presentation. (Noise-Shock: Not Paired) a white noise was presented at completion of the first and second FI 5-min components and a shock alone was presented at completion of every third component. (Noise-Shock: Paired) a white noise was presented at completion of each component and a shock immediately followed every third presentation of the white noise. The second frame shows performance during the seventh session when the procedure was studied the first time. The bottom frame shows performance during the first session when the procedure was studied a second time. (Shock Only) no stimulus change occurred at completion of the first and second components and a shock alone was presented at completion of every third component. A short diagonal mark of the response pen indicates completion of an FI 5-min component. A mark of the event pen and resetting of the response pen indicate presentation of a shock.

The effect of changing to presentation of a white noise at completion of each component (Noise-Shock: Paired) was, as before, suppression of responding. Within two sessions the mean rate of responding had decreased to 0.02 responses per second for FC-I and to 0.004 responses per second for MC-II (Fig. 4). The effect upon responding can be seen in the records of MC-II during the first session after the change to this procedure (bottom frame of Fig. 6), and in the records of FC-I during the second session (bottom frame of Fig. 5). Both subjects showed a pronounced decrease in frequency of responding and a change in the pattern of responding.

Changes in shock intensity did not produce changes in patterns of responding under the present procedures, but the slightly decreased response rates for MC-II at 2.0 and 1.3 ma suggested that these intensities may be approaching the minimum necessary to maintain responding.

DISCUSSION

The present investigation demonstrated that responding in cats having prior training under shock avoidance can be maintained by response-produced electric shock. Responding in both subjects persisted under an FI 15-min schedule of shock presentation and under two second-order schedules of shock presentation. That response-produced shock could temporarily enhance responding in subjects with histories of shock avoidance was shown previously by Kelleher et al. (1963). One of three squirrel monkeys had positively accelerated responding during four sessions under an FI 2-min schedule of shock presentation.

The present investigation also demonstrated that responding in cats with histories of shock avoidance can be maintained under response-independent electric shock. These data are consistent with earlier experiments (Kelleher et al., 1963; Waller and Waller, 1963) which showed that after training under shock avoidance, responding was maintained in the presence of a stimulus terminating with a response-independent electric shock. These data are also consistent with previous experiments (Appel, 1960a, 1960b; Hearst, 1962) which showed that in subjects with histories of avoidance, response-independent shock engendered increased rates of responding during the extinction components of multiple schedules.

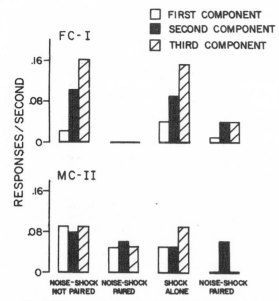

Fig. 7. Mean rates of responding during each of three components under: (Noise-Shock: Not Paired) a white noise was presented at completion of the first and second FI 5-min components and a shock alone was presented at completion of every third component; (Noise-Shock: Paired) a white noise was presented at completion of each component and a shock immediately followed every third presentation of the white noise; (Shock Only) no stimulus change occurred at completion of the first and second components and a shock alone was presented at completion of every third component. Mean response rates during the last session only are shown for the Noise-Shock: Paired procedure. Mean response rates during the last three sessions are shown for the Noise-Shock: Not Paired and for the Shock Only procedures.

Some earlier studies of electric shock reported that positively accelerated responding frequently developed in the presence of a stimulus which terminated with a response-independent shock (Sidman *et al.*, 1957; Herrnstein and Sidman, 1958; Kelleher *et al.*, 1963; Waller and Waller, 1963). In the present study, delivering a response-independent shock every 15 min engendered rather steady rates of responding similar to performance under continuous shock avoidance. Although response rate occasionally decreased immediately after a response-independent shock, positively accelerated responding did not develop in either cat until shocks were response-produced. Under the FI 15-min schedule and under two of the second-order schedules, responding by FC-I, and to a lesser extent by MC-II, was positively accelerated.

In Exp. II, responding was not maintained

under a three-component second-order schedule when a white noise was presented at completion of each component and the white noise was paired with shock at completion of the third component (Noise-Shock: Paired), but responding was maintained when the white noise was not paired with shock (Noise-Shock: Not Paired) and when the white noise was omitted (Shock Only). While this experiment may not offer an exhaustive analysis of the effects of pairing a stimulus with shock presented under second-order schedules, it does show clearly that responding can be maintained when shock is response-produced under a second-order schedule, and that responding can be suppressed when a stimulus paired with shock is presented at completion of each component. Before a reasonably complete explanation of these effects can be proposed, it must be determined whether the effect of shock and the effect of a stimulus paired with shock are alike or different. If the effects are similar, suppression of responding may be due to increasing shock frequency, in this case, three-fold. If the effects are dissimilar, the white noise paired with shock may suppress responding even though shock presentation enhances responding.

The similarity or dissimilarity of the effects of white noise and shock cannot be determined from the present study. However, because a stimulus paired with food presentation has been shown by Findley (1962), Kelleher (1966a, 1966b) and others to enhance responding, a stimulus paired with shock presentation might have been expected to enhance responding. Suppression of responding when white noise was paired with shock is not consistent with the enhancing effects of a stimulus paired with food presentation, and may suggest differences between response-produced food and response-produced shock in maintaining responding.

Perhaps the most sensitive indicator of the effectiveness of an event in modifying behavior is the pattern of responding engendered by the occurrence of that event. The present investigation showed that patterns of responding characteristic of fixed-interval schedules and of two second-order schedules can be maintained under response-produced electric shock. When shock was scheduled as the terminal stimulus event, responding by FC-I was positively accelerated under an FI 15-min schedule and under two second-order schedules comprising three components. MC-II displayed less sensitivity than FC-I to the schedules under which shock was presented, and tended to show less uniform changes in response rate. In terms of the stability of responding and the patterns of responding, response-produced shock maintained behavior in both cats.

REFERENCES

Appel, J. B. The aversive control of an operant discrimination. *Journal of the Experimental Analysis of Behavior*, 1960, **3**, 35-47. (a)

Appel, J. B. Some schedules involving aversive control. *Journal of the Experimental Analysis of Behavior*, 1960, **3**, 349-359. (b)

Azrin, N. H. Some effects of two intermittent schedules of immediate and non-immediate punishment. *Journal of Psychology*, 1956, **42**, 3-21.

Belleville, R. E., Rohles, F. H., Grunzke, M. E., and Clark, F. C. Development of a complex multiple schedule in the chimpanzee. *Journal of the Experimental Analysis of Behavior*, 1963, **6**, 549-556.

Ferster, C. B. and Skinner, B. F. *Schedules of reinforcement*. New York: Appleton-Century-Crofts, 1957.

Hearst, E. Concurrent generalization gradients for food-controlled and shock-controlled behavior. *Journal of the Experimental Analysis of Behavior*, 1962, **5**, 19-31.

Herrnstein, R. J. and Sidman, M. Avoidance conditioning as a factor in the effects of unavoidable shocks on food-reinforced behavior. *Journal of Comparative and Physiological Psychology*, 1958, **51**, 380-385.

Kelleher, R. T. Chaining and conditioned reinforcement. In W. K. Honig (Ed.), *Operant behavior: areas of research and application*. New York: Appleton-Century-Crofts, 1966. Pp. 160-212. (a)

Kelleher, R. T. Conditioned reinforcement in second-order schedules. *Journal of the Experimental Analysis of Behavior*, 1966, **9**, 475-485. (b)

Kelleher, R. T. and Morse, W. H. Schedules using noxious stimuli. III. Responding maintained with response-produced electric shocks. *Journal of the Experimental Analysis of Behavior*, 1968, **11**, 819-838.

Kelleher, R. T., Riddle, W. C., and Cook, L. Persistent behavior maintained by unavoidable shocks. *Journal of the Experimental Analysis of Behavior*, 1963, **6**, 507-517.

McKearney, J. W. Maintenance of responding under a fixed-interval schedule of electric shock-presentation. *Science*, 1968, **160**, 1249-1251.

Sidman, M. Avoidance conditioning with brief shock and no exteroceptive warning signal. *Science*, 1953, **118**, 157-158.

Sidman, M., Herrnstein, R. J., and Conrad, D. G. Maintenance of avoidance behavior by unavoidable shocks. *Journal of Comparative and Physiological Psychology*, 1957, **50**, 553-557.

Waller, M. B. and Waller, P. F. The effects of unavoidable shocks on a multiple schedule having an avoidance component. *Journal of the Experimental Analysis of Behavior*, 1963, **6**, 29-37.

Received 25 April 1968.

DISRUPTION OF A TEMPORAL DISCRIMINATION UNDER RESPONSE-INDEPENDENT SHOCK[1]

A. G. SNAPPER, D. A. RAMSAY, AND W. N. SCHOENFELD

FRANKLIN DELANO ROOSEVELT VA HOSPITAL AND QUEENS COLLEGE

The responding of rats was reinforced on one key after a 1-sec auditory stimulus and on a second key after a 5-sec stimulus. With errors punished by a short timeout, all subjects achieved a high level of accuracy. A chain of responses during the stimuli mediated the performance so that when the auditory signals were omitted accuracy decreased only slightly. Response-independent aversive stimulation superimposed upon this procedure both suppressed the total amount of behavior and reduced the accuracy of the discriminative performance, the intensity of the stimulus determining the error rate. The increase in errors under these conditions may have depended in part upon differential suppression of members of the response chain, but such suppression was not necessary, since error rate increased even in its absence. Furthermore, the locus of response disruption within the chain was not consistent from day to day either for any individual animal or across animals.

Some effects of aversive stimuli are specific to behavior that occurs in close temporal contiguity with the stimulus (such as escape behavior and response suppression by punishment). Other effects appear to be more temporally dispersed (such as long-lasting upset, and general reduction in food-intake or in discriminative stimulus control both within and between experimental sessions). Hearst (1965) reported that aversive stimuli have a generalized effect of breaking down a well-established discriminative performance. When either cued or non-cued response-independent shock was superimposed upon a multiple variable-interval extinction schedule of food reinforcement, responding during the extinction component was found to increase, although more reliably in the cued case. An apparently related finding is obtained when a conditioned emotional response (CER) procedure is added to an established differential-reinforcement-of-low-rates (DRL) performance (Blackman, 1967) in that the low rate of DRL responding increases during the stimulus correlated with shock. The Blackman (1967) study demonstrated discriminative breakdown primarily during the stimulus preceding shock, unlike Hearst's more generalized effect during stimuli not so correlated. In both cases, it is the rise in a low response frequency that is interpreted as breakdown of the discrimination. But the possibility exists that the aversive stimulation is merely exercising a greater energizing effect on low probability responding than on high response levels.

To resolve this question, the present experiment employed a discrimination in which a response on one key after a 1-sec auditory stimulus was reinforced and a response on a second key was reinforced after a 5-sec stimulus. Although responding developed during the stimuli at different rates on each key mediating the discrimination, the effects of response-independent shock upon the accuracy of the final response could be assessed independently of specific disruption of the mediating chains.

METHOD

Subjects

The free-feeding weights of six male albino rats (Charles River type CD), approximately 120 days old when the experiment began, were determined daily over two weeks, after which each rat was kept at 80% of its free-feeding weight through water deprivation.

[1]Dedicated to B. F. Skinner in his sixty-fifth year. This research was supported in part by NIMH Grant 13049 awarded to W. N. Schoenfeld, and by the Veterans Administration. Reprints may be obtained from A. G. Snapper, Psychology Research Laboratory, Veterans Administration Hospital, Montrose, New York 10548.

Apparatus

Two chambers (Scientific Prototype, Model 100), housed in sound-attenuating shells, were equipped with liquid reinforcement dispensers, 8-ohm Quam speakers, and two translucent response keys (Grason-Stadler, Model E8670A). The keys were 4.5 in. above the floor and 4 in. apart. Auditory stimuli consisted of white noise from a Grason-Stadler generator (Model 901B). Scheduling and recording were provided by a PDP-8 digital computer (Digital Equipment Corp.) with a specialized program written in terms of operant contingencies (Snapper, Knapp, and Kushner, 1967). Shocks consisted of 325 v ac, and were applied as a single sequential sweep across the 16 bars of the chamber grid, with current applied to each bar for about 20 msec (Snapper, 1966). Shock current levels, reported in the following section, were calculated on the assumption that the rats' resistances averaged 30 Kohms.

Procedure

All subjects were given daily 1-hr sessions with reinforcement consisting of 4-sec access to a 0.01-cc dipper cup filled with a mixture by volume of 50% water and 50% evaporated milk.

During the first two experimental sessions, each rat was trained to approach the dipper. In the third session, the left key was covered with black tape, and each subject was trained to press the right key after the white noise terminated. In this and all succeeding sessions, responses during the noise were never reinforced. The auditory stimulus was presented for 1 sec immediately after the end of reinforcement, and the first response after the noise ended produced the next reinforcement. After four successive sessions of this procedure, the right key was blocked and reinforcement was made contingent upon the first response to the left key after a 5-sec white-noise stimulus terminated. Again, responses during the stimulus, which began at the end of the reinforcement, were never reinforced. Altogether, seven sessions of training to the left key were given before the final stage of training began.

The terminal discriminative contingencies involved differential reinforcement for the appropriate response to the two keys, depending upon the duration of the immediately preceding auditory stimulus.

The details of this procedure are presented in the form of a state graph (Snapper *et al.*, in press) in Fig. 1. In this graph, conditions of stimuli and contingencies in effect throughout the experiment are shown by enumerated circles called states, only one of which is in effect at any time. Arrows leading from one state to the next show the response contingency or temporal requirement for the transition to new states with the accompanying requirement written above, or beside, the arrow. At the start of each session, State 1 ($1/S_1$ where S_1 represents the noise plus background stimuli) was entered. After 1 sec of the noise, during which responses had no effect, transition to State 2 occurred as shown by the arrow leading from State 1 to State 2. During State 2, S_2 represents the background stimuli of the chamber, minus the noise, and this state remained in effect until a response was made, either on the right or left key. If the right key was pressed, State 3 with its associated reinforcement was entered. After a 4-sec reinforcement, State 7 was entered and after 1.5 sec, either State 1 or State 4 began. If the left key was pressed, State 6 was entered, reinforcement was not presented, initiating the 15-sec delay before the next trial began. After both States 6 (error) and 7 (correct), initiation of State 1 or 4 as the next state was probabilistic with either transition being equally likely (indicated by 1.5-sec P, where P = Q = 0.5). If State 4 was entered, the noise was presented for 5 sec and, after the noise (State 5) a left-key response was reinforced; a right-key response was followed by the 15-sec timeout (State 6). Responses had effects only during States 2 and 5 (*i.e.*, after termination of the stimulus) and

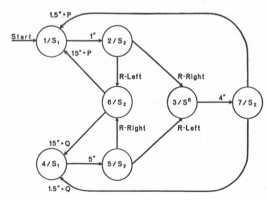

Fig. 1. State graph describing experimental contingencies in effect.

a non-correction procedure was used, in that after errors, the next duration could be either 1 or 5 sec.

In summary, then, a 1-sec and 5-sec noise were presented in random order with the former signalling reinforcement for right-key and the latter for left-key responses. Errors were followed by delayed onset of the next trial and only responses after noise led to reinforcement or timeout, responding during the stimulus having no scheduled effect. This baseline discrimination training was continued for three (F2, F7, and F9) of the six rats for a total of 61 sessions, and for the other three rats for 22 sessions. The last three sessions with each rat were taken to be a zero shock control value.

During the final phase of the experiment, five response-independent uncued shocks were delivered during each session. The interval between shocks ranged from 6 to 14 min with an average of 11 min in a random sequence, and shocks were presented independently of behavior so that they could fall during cues, reinforcements, or silent periods. Each subject was exposed to two consecutive sessions of this schedule at each of 15 shock values, starting at 0.5 ma and progressing in 0.5-ma steps up to the final value of 7.5 ma. Exceptions to this sequence, for reasons to be seen later, were: (a) the initial exposure to 0.5 ma for two sessions was followed first by one session with no shock, and then by two more sessions at 0.5 ma; (b) the two 3.5-ma sessions were separated by one non-shock day; (c) two sessions without shock were administered following the highest

shock level of 7.5 ma; and, (d) the final session of the experiment was a no-shock one in which the auditory stimuli were absent but the reinforcement contingencies remained in effect.

RESULTS

Baseline performance. By the final three sessions of discrimination training, each rat was responding correctly in at least 95% of the trials (*i.e.*, the first response after a 1-sec stimulus was on the right key, and that after the 5-sec stimulus on the left key).

Although responding during the stimulus had no effect upon the scheduled contingencies, each subject developed a stereotyped pattern or chain of responses on the two keys during the noise. Table 1 presents distributions of the frequencies of responses on the two keys during successive 0.5 sec of the 5-sec tone for the final baseline session. The rats responded on the right key for the first 1 or 2 sec after stimulus onset, and then switched to the left key toward the end of the 5-sec period. During the session, the number of 5-sec trials in which at least one response occurred during the stimulus averaged 90.6% for the six subjects. The final experimental session omitted the noise but left all of the response contingencies in force. During this test, all subjects (except for F10 which had a low response rate) made more errors than on the preceding non-shocked session, but fewer errors than would be expected by chance. (Table 2).

The high level of accuracy maintained despite the omission of the auditory stimuli sug-

Table 1

Distributions of responses on each key (R = right, L = left) during the 5-sec noise, in successive 0.5-sec intervals. Note that when the stimulus terminated, a left-key response was reinforced.

Stimulus Sub-Intervals (10ths)	Subjects											
	F2		F3		F6		F7		F9		F10	
	R	L	R	L	R	L	R	L	R	L	R	L
1	232	0	11	0	23	0	92	0	6	0	10	0
2	339	0	60	0	57	0	158	0	16	0	46	0
3	269	0	157	0	51	0	103	0	19	0	84	0
4	114	0	103	0	41	0	76	0	7	1	97	0
5	34	0	25	4	7	0	14	0	5	22	12	0
6	6	0	7	14	1	2	7	0	2	30	1	3
7	4	2	0	22	0	18	3	1	0	30	1	9
8	2	5	2	15	0	53	0	2	0	46	0	24
9	3	14	1	24	0	119	0	11	1	89	0	53
10	1	46	0	37	0	187	0	55	0	156	0	134
Total No. of Responses	999	67	366	116	180	379	453	69	56	374	251	223

gests that the discrimination was primarily based upon the right-left sequence of responses during the stimulus. In sessions during which the cue was present all subjects, however, did not respond during the cue on about 10% of the trials in which they responded accurately after the stimulus. The normal performance, then, probably depended upon both auditory and response-produced cues. This point is further substantiated by the low level of responding noted during the timeout periods following errors in control sessions.

Table 2

Per cent correct responses on each key during the last unshocked session (Noise) and during the final session, when the noise stimuli were removed (No Noise).

	Left Key		Right Key	
Subject	Noise	No Noise	Noise	No Noise
F2	96.1	90.0	97.4	86.4
F3	91.3	84.9	89.3	90.1
F6	93.3	74.8	95.3	72.8
F7	89.4	56.9	98.7	90.6
F9	94.4	89.9	92.7	91.1
F10	0	66.7	100.0	86.9

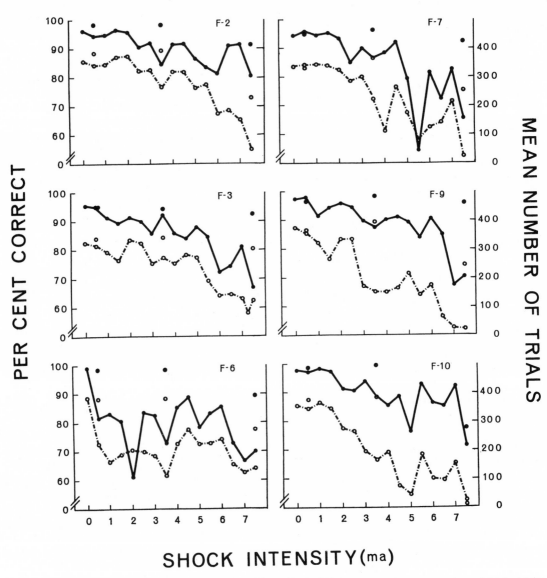

Fig. 2. Intensity of shock functions for the six subjects. Dashed lines represent mean number of trials (right-hand ordinate), while solid lines represent mean percentage of correct trials (left-hand ordinate). Unconnected filled and open circles represent interpolated non-shock sessions.

Effects of shock. Figure 2 presents for each subject the percentage of trials followed by correct responses and the average number of trials per session at each of the different levels of shock. The number of trials depended in part upon error rate (since each error was followed by a 15-sec timeout before the next trial began) and partly upon the latency of the first response after the stimulus. Figure 2 shows that, as shock intensity increased, the number of trials per session decreased for each subject, though at a different rate for the individual rats. Of special interest is the immediate increase in number of trials in the single shock-free session inserted at the 0.5- and 3.5-ma levels.

In general, the fall in percentage correct parallels that in the number of trials per session. Figure 2 indicates that the reduction in trial number was not completely determined by the increased error rate in any one session. For example, F7 showed considerable drop in the number of trials at 4 ma while error rate was relatively low. At other levels, including 5 and 7.5 ma, both measures were strongly affected by the response-independent shock. As said earlier, reduction in number of trials, when not correlated with an increased error rate, could have resulted from long response latencies after a few stimulus presentations, since the next trial would not occur until either a correct or incorrect response was made.

Recovery days (*i.e.*, shockless sessions inserted between shock sessions) produced a return toward both baseline discrimination accuracy levels and former total response rates, with the possible exception of the recovery session which followed the highest shock level of 7.5 ma. Visual observation of responding during response-independent shock sessions, along with the speedy recovery of baseline performance when shock was omitted, jointly indicated that errors did not occur in a session until the first response-independent shock was delivered. It appears, therefore, that the impact of shock upon discriminative performance was not conditioned, in the sense of being controlled by the specific paired stimuli, but rather was a general after-effect of the aversive stimulus.

Recordings of the chain of responses during the auditory stimulus permitted evaluation of whether increased errors arose from suppression of members of this chain (Blackman, 1967). Figure 3 plots the total number of responses on both keys during the auditory stimuli divided by the total number of stimuli per session. Increasing shock intensity slightly reduced responses during the stimulus for four of the animals, but produced no systematic trend for rats F3 and F9. Since the latter two subjects did make more errors as shock increased, suppression of the chain is not the only explanation of the increase in errors.

If the response-independent shock had exercised a consistent effect on the chain of responding during the stimulus (*i.e.*, had disrupted the chain in a consistent way such as fixation of responding on one key), then the percentage of errors made on one or the other key could be expected to demonstrate that consistency. These data, however, showed little consistency, either within or between subjects, as shock level increased. Although the average result for the group before shock was administered was close to 50%, some subjects made most of their errors after the shorter 1-sec stimulus and some after the longer 5-sec stimulus. As shock level increased, all subjects, except F2, sometimes made more errors on the right and sometimes on the left key. F2 tended throughout to make more errors, after the 5-sec noise (by pressing the right key), and it also showed the smallest increase in number of errors of all subjects. Distributions of the response frequencies on the two keys during the 5-sec stimulus (of the sort shown in Table 1) were also constructed for the shock sessions. These records also revealed little consistent change, thus substantiating the lack of systematic effect upon the chain of responding during the white-noise stimuli by the free-shock.

DISCUSSION

One feature of the baseline performance of the present experiment was the development of a measurable chain of responses that mediates the temporal discrimination. Although several recent experimenters (Catania, in press; Reynolds and Catania, 1962; Stubbs, 1968) have reported discriminations based on temporal aspects of a single stimulus with accuracy comparable to that of the present study, they have not noted mediating behavior. The present finding of an overt, stereotyped chain

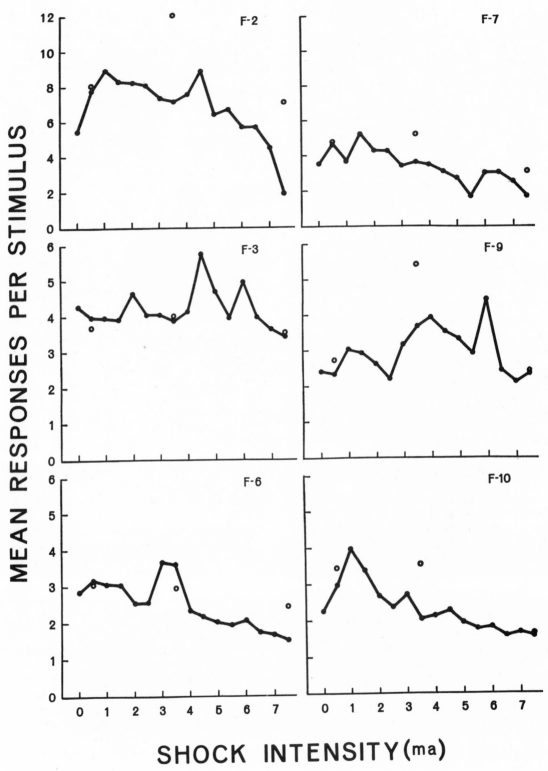

Fig. 3. Average number of responses per stimulus as a function of shock intensity. Open circles represent interpolated non-shock sessions.

during the auditory stimulus lends support to the suggestion that response chains do mediate some, if not all, temporal discriminations (Wilson and Keller, 1953; Rilling, 1967). The chain of responding that developed during the present experiment probably could have been eliminated by punishing responding during the stimulus, but this need not obviate the development of idiosyncratic "superstitious" responding not involving key presses. In terms of observing such chains it seems advantageous to permit them to develop toward the measured keys as in the present case.

The present results established that response-independent shock can increase error rate in a temporally ordered performance, and that the effect varies with the level of shock intensity. The procedure of gradually increasing shock intensities probably reduced the total amount of response suppression (Sandler, 1964), and may also have limited the total error rate. Furthermore, the increase in number of errors did not stem from differential suppression of the members of the chain of responses (Fig. 3): two of the six present rats showed no such suppression and the remaining four showed limited reduction in the number of responses per noise. We found little consistency among subjects in just where in the chain the errors occurred.

Unlike Hearst's (1965) study, where discriminative breakdown was related to the increase in rate of a previously low probability response, the present experiment indicated that a stimulus discrimination involving differential responding to two operanda may be disrupted by response-independent shock. One feature of the discriminative breakdown in both the present and Hearst's (1965) studies was the speed of recovery of performance when response-independent shocks were omitted. Apparently, the primary effect of an aversive stimulus does not become conditioned to the general experimental stimuli, but rather occurs only if the shock is delivered. This argues for the effect being a generalized unconditioned disruption of the discrimination rather than a conditioned suppression or facilitation of any particular part of the mediating response chain. Perhaps relevant to this point is the general procedural difference between the present study (as with Hearst's 1965 non-cued group) and those of Blackman (1967), Migler and Brady (1964), and Kruper (1968).

The latter experiments were primarily concerned with localized discriminative breakdown confined to the stimulus preceding shock. The specific sort of discriminative breakdown reported in those studies might depend upon the presentation of the pre-shock stimulus, for even in Hearst's (1965) cued group responding during the cue was abolished. However, Hearst's (1965) generalized effect (outside of the pre-shock stimulus) does appear to be more regular than ours, perhaps due to the simpler discrimination used as baseline.

An experiment that reported inconsistent effects of uncued but contingent shock is that of Edwards, Dubiner, and Crow (1967), in which a response-contingent punishment was delivered in the middle of a response chain requiring a fixed number of responses on one lever before a single response on a second lever was reinforced. The variability of runs of responses on the first lever increased under punishment but rapidly returned to unpunished levels when punishment was discontinued. The effect of punishment, in other words, was to cause breakdown of an inconsistent nature; *i.e.*, sometimes run lengths increased and sometimes decreased as against unpunished performance.

The present study and Hearst's (1965) found breakdown occurring under response-independent shock (but Migler and Brady, 1964, and Kruper, 1968, found little evidence of discriminative breakdown when cued response-independent shock was superimposed upon a complex discrimination). Hearst (1965) also observed similar, but smaller, effects under punishment, and Edwards *et al.* (1967) corroborated the latter finding. Thus, although there is still some uncertainty about the factors which produce breakdown of discrimination under aversive stimulation, the present study demonstrated that it is related to the variable of shock intensity under response-independent shock.

REFERENCES

Blackman, D. Conditioned suppression or facilitation as a function of the behavioral baseline. *Journal of the Experimental Analysis of Behavior*, 1968, **11**, 53-61.

Catania, A. C. Reinforcement schedules and psychophysical judgments: A study of some temporal properties of behavior. In W. N. Schoenfeld and J. Farmer (Eds.), *Theories of Reinforcement Schedules.* New York: Appleton-Century-Crofts, in press.

Edwards, D. D., Dubiner, D., and Crow, F. Response sequences in rats and pigeons. *Psychonomic Science,* 1967, **9**, 245-246.

Hearst, E. Stress-induced breakdown of an appetitive discrimination. *Journal of the Experimental Analysis of Behavior,* 1965, **8**, 135-146.

Kruper, D. Effects of a pre-aversive stimulus upon oddity performance in monkeys. *Journal of the Experimental Analysis of Behavior,* 1968, **11**, 71-75.

Migler, B. and Brady, J. V. Timing behavior and conditioned fear. *Journal of the Experimental Analysis of Behavior,* 1964, **7**, 247-256.

Reynolds, G. S. and Catania, A. C. Temporal discrimination in pigeons. *Science,* 1962, **135**, 314-315.

Rilling, M. Number of responses as a stimulus in fixed interval and fixed ratio schedules. *Journal of Comparative and Physiological Psychology,* 1967, **63**, 60-65.

Sandler, J. Some aspects of self-aversive stimulation in the hooded rat. *Journal of the Experimental Analysis of Behavior,* 1964, **7**, 409-414.

Snapper, A. G. A relay-transistor sequential grid scrambler. *Journal of the Experimental Analysis of Behavior,* 1966, **9**, 173-175.

Snapper, A. G., Knapp, J., and Kushner, H. On-line programming: I. Paper presented at the meeting of the American Psychological Association, Washington, D.C., September, 1967.

Snapper, A. G., Knapp, J., and Kushner, H. Mathematical descriptions of schedules of reinforcement. In W. N. Schoenfeld and J. Farmer (Eds.), *Theories of Reinforcement Schedules.* New York: Appleton-Century-Crofts, in press.

Stubbs, A. The discrimination of stimulus duration by pigeons. *Journal of the Experimental Analysis of Behavior,* 1968, **11**, 223-238.

Wilson, M. P. and Keller, F. S. On the selective reinforcement of spaced responses. *Journal of Comparative and Physiological Psychology,* 1953, **46**, 190-193

Received 28 June 1968.

POSITIVE CONDITIONED SUPPRESSION: CONDITIONED SUPPRESSION USING POSITIVE REINFORCERS AS THE UNCONDITIONED STIMULI[1]

N. H. AZRIN AND D. F. HAKE

ANNA STATE HOSPITAL

Research has revealed the phenomenon of conditioned suppression in which the rate of responding is reduced during a stimulus that is paired with noncontingent shock. The present study replicated this procedure, but used noncontingent positive reinforcers instead of the aversive shock. The lever-pressing responses of rats were reinforced with food or water. While the rats were responding, a stimulus was occasionally presented and paired with the delivery of a noncontingent positive reinforcer, which was either food, water, or brain stimulation for different rats. The result was a reduction in the rate of responding during the conditioned stimulus. This finding shows that conditioned suppression occurs during a signal for reinforcing as well as aversive stimuli.

Estes and Skinner (1941) discovered the phenomenon now known as conditioned suppression or conditioned anxiety. A baseline of lever-pressing responses was established by an intermittent schedule of food reinforcement; at infrequent intervals the rats were given an aversive shock that was immediately preceded by a neutral stimulus. The subsequent reduction in the rate of responding during the previously neutral stimulus supported their interpretation that anxiety was produced by the conditioned stimulus, as evidenced by the degree of disruption of ongoing operant responses. Later studies by many investigators, including Hunt and Brady (1955), Lyon (1964), Kamin, Brimer, and Black (1963), Stein, Sidman, and Brady (1958), Azrin (1956), Hendry and Van Toller (1965), Hake and Azrin (1965), also found a reduction in the rate of operant responding during a preshock stimulus. The shock has generally been designated as an unconditioned stimulus (UCS), the neutral stimulus as a conditioned stimulus (CS), and the pairing of the two events as an example of a classical conditioning procedure.

The anxiety interpretation of Estes and Skinner states that the reduction in the rate of responding during the conditioned stimulus is dependent upon that stimulus being paired with a "disturbing" or aversive event. Indeed, the reduction in response rate during the conditioned stimulus has been considered (Ferster and Skinner, p. 723, 1957) as a defining characteristic of an aversive stimulus. Another possible interpretation is that the reduction in response rate results from a general emotional state during presentation of a stimulus that is paired with any strong reinforcer, whether the reinforcer is positive or negative. These interpretations lead to different predictions about the possible effect of different types of unconditioned stimuli. Since the anxiety interpretation attributes the reduction in response rate to the degree of aversiveness of the unconditioned stimulus, this interpretation has led to the expectation that an unconditioned stimulus that was a positive reinforcer should produce an effect opposite to reduction, *i.e.*, an increase in response rate because of an "elation" or "joy" effect, as has been suggested by many including Millenson (1967), Rescorla and Solomon (1967), and Herrnstein and Morse (1957). The general emotional state interpretation, not being dependent on the qualitative aspect of the noncontingent stimulus, predicts that a positive reinforcer should produce suppression. Millenson (1967) has discussed both interpretations and the absence of definitive evidence in sup-

---

[1]Dedicated to B. F. Skinner in his sixty-fifth year. This investigation was supported by the Mental Health Fund of the Illinois Department of Mental Health. Rebecca Oxford performed the electrode implantation and histology as well as conducting that part of the study concerned with the "Food-ICS" rats. Jean Brown assisted in the electrode implantation and histology. Reprints may be obtained from either author, Anna State Hospital, Anna, Illinois 62906.

port of one over the other. The present study evaluated these interpretations by replicating the main features of the Estes and Skinner procedure but using food, water, or intracranial stimulation instead of aversive shock as the noncontingent stimulus. Intracranial stimulation was selected as one of the reinforcers because its mode of delivery is similar to pain-shock in that no consummatory response is required.

METHOD

The subjects were 18 experimentally naive male rats, 90 to 120 days old, of the Holtzman Sprague-Dawley strain.

Apparatus

Two chambers were used. One, about 11 by 9 by 9 in. high, was used for all but the two rats given intracranial stimulation. A response lever (Lehigh Valley Electronics Rat Lever #1352) was mounted 2 in. from the floor. A tray for delivery of food was located 0.25 in. to the right of the lever and a tray for water was 0.25 in. to the left. A downward force of 15 g on the lever defined a response, each of which received brief feedback in the form of a 100-msec interruption of the overhead lighting. The CS was a relay click that occurred six times per second.

A second larger chamber, 13 by 12 by 14 in. high, was used for the two rats given intracranial stimulation. It was similar to the first chamber except that it had no water delivery tray; the CS was a 10-Hz blinking red light located 5 in. above the response lever; a relay click provided the response feedback.

Procedure

The rats were divided into two groups. The eight in the water group received 0.1 cc of water as the contingent reinforcer for lever pressing and the 10 rats in the food group received one 45-mg food pellet as the contingent reinforcer. A buzzer sound accompanied the delivery of food; a distinctively different 500-Hz pure tone accompanied delivery of water. After about seven shaping and conditioning sessions for all rats, the lever-press response was being reinforced according to a 1-min variable-interval schedule of reinforcement during daily 2-hr sessions (1.5 hr for two rats in the food group). The CS was then presented for 10 sec at irregular intervals averaging 6 min between presentations (4 min for two of the rats) for a minimum of three and a maximum of six sessions. The rats were then subdivided further into five groups. Of the eight rats that were receiving water as the contingent reinforcer, two were given 0.5 cc of water also as the noncontingent stimulus (Water-Water Group), and six were given five pellets of food (Water-Food Group). Of the 10 rats that received food as the contingent reinforcer, three received five pellets of food as the noncontingent stimulus (Food-Food Group), five received 0.5 cc of water (Food-Water Group), and two received intracranial stimulation (Food-ICS Group). The noncontingent stimulus was delivered at the termination of the conditioned stimulus for 15 sessions (10 for the Food-ICS Group). The CS was 10 sec in duration plus the duration required for delivery of the noncontingent stimulus. The contingent reinforcer for lever pressing continued to be delivered according to the 1-min variable-interval schedule. Finally, the noncontingent stimulus was discontinued for 15 sessions (five sessions for the Food-ICS Group) during which the contingent reinforcer and the 10-sec CS continued to be presented.

For the rats that were not receiving water, whether as a contingent or noncontingent stimulus (Food-Food Group and Food-ICS Group), water was freely available in the experimental chamber during the session. Similarly, food pellets were freely available in the chamber for the rats not receiving food as a contingent or noncontingent stimulus (Water-Water Group). For the Water-Food group, food was freely available during the sessions in which food was not experimentally scheduled; food deprivation was initiated the day before the noncontingent food was scheduled. Similarly, water was freely available for the Food-Water Group during those sessions in which water was not experimentally scheduled; water deprivation was initiated the day before the noncontingent water was scheduled. These maintenance procedures were necessary because food-deprived rats responded very little for food unless water was also given during that session. Similarly, water-deprived rats responded very little for water unless food was available during the session. When food was used as a contingent or noncontingent stimulus the weight of the rat was reduced to 80% of free-feeding weight. When water was used, either as a contingent or noncontingent stimulus, the rat was restricted to 14 cc of water per day. The noncontingent food delivery was deliberately made greater than the contingent food (five pellets *vs* one pellet) to allow discrimination between them as different events. Similarly, the noncontingent water delivery was 0.5 cc, whereas the contingent water was 0.1 cc.

One week before their first session, the two rats in the Food-ICS Group had bipolar stainless steel electrodes implanted stereotaxically using a procedure similar to that described by Miller, Coons, Lewis, and Jensen (1961). The electrodes were 0.01-in. diameter covered with insulation except at the cross-sectioned tips. The waveform of the electrical stimulus was the same as that described by Valenstein and Meyers (1964): a 0.5-sec pulse train of 100-Hz biphasic rectangular pulses, each pulse having a duration of 0.2 msec with a 0.2-msec delay between positive and negative excursions. A pre-test was given to both rats, using a different response and different stimulus conditions, to determine the current intensity necessary to reinforce responding when the stimulation occurred at the same frequency of presentation as would be used in the experiment proper. A 0.5-sec pulse train of 0.095 ma for one rat and 0.065 ma for the other were found to reinforce a chain-pull response during a 10-sec white stimulus light, which was presented at irregular intervals averaging 4 min. Ten of these 0.5-sec pulse trains were delivered as the noncontingent stimulus during the experiment proper, each train following the previous one by 40 msec. The day after this experiment was completed, one rat was given a post-test in which it received the 10 pulse trains for the first chain-pull that occurred during a stimulus presented at irregular intervals averaging 4 min. The latency of chain-pulling averaged less than 2 sec for both rats in the pre-test and the one rat in the post-test. After the last session, the brain tissue was prepared and photographed according to the procedure described by Hutchinson and Renfrew (1967). Figure 1 shows that the electrodes were in the medial forebrain bundle just ventrolateral to the posterior hypothalamus for one rat and ventromedial to the medial lemniscus and dorsolateral to the ven-

tral tegmental nucleus for the other rat. Previous studies have reported positive reinforcing effects of electrical stimulation in or near these sites (Hawkins and Pliskoff, 1964; Valenstein and Meyers, 1964; and Valenstein, 1965).

RESULTS

Figure 2 shows responding during the CS relative to responding during the baseline us-

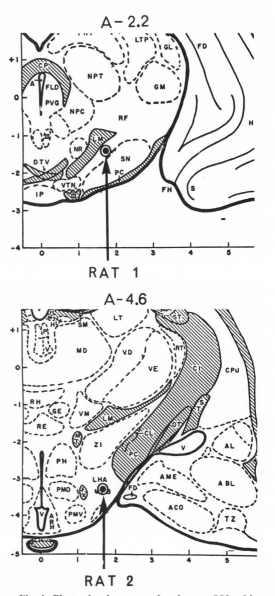

Fig. 1. Electrode placements for the two ICS subjects illustrated on frontal sections of the rat brain. The number above each section identifies the plate of the DeGroot (1963) rat stereotaxic atlas from which the sections were copied.

ing the ratio suggested by Annau and Kamin (1961) for measuring the degree of conditioned suppression. This ratio is equal to B/A+B where B is the number of responses during the 10-sec CS and A is the number during the 10-sec period preceding the CS. Hence, a ratio of 0.5 indicates no suppression; a ratio of 0.0 indicates complete suppression. For all five groups of rats, this suppression ratio was about 0.5 during the last three sessions before the noncontingent stimulus was presented. When the UCS was added, conditioned suppression occurred during the first or second session for all groups; the conditioned suppression continued during each day of UCS delivery for all groups except the Water-Water Group. When the UCS was discontinued, the suppression ratio increased on the first or second day when USC was absent, eventually returning to the non-suppressed level of about 0.5 seen initially.

Table 1 shows the mean response rate during the pre-CS and the CS periods. For indi-

vidual rats, the rate was as low as 10 and as high as 103 responses per minute at the start of the study. The mean response rate during the CS decreased by about one-half when the UCS was added and increased three-fold when it was discontinued. On the other hand, the baseline pre-CS response rate remained about the same when the UCS was added but did increase by about one-half when it was eliminated. The higher response rates at the end of the study during both the CS and pre-CS probably reflect the general increase usually found during continued reinforcement under a variable-interval schedule (Ferster and Skinner, 1957). Taken together these data show a large reduction in the rate of responding during the CS superimposed on an upward drift of the baseline response rate. The data of Table 1 show that the suppression seen in Fig. 2 was primarily attributable to the reduction of response rate during the CS rather than to an increase in the rate of baseline responding.

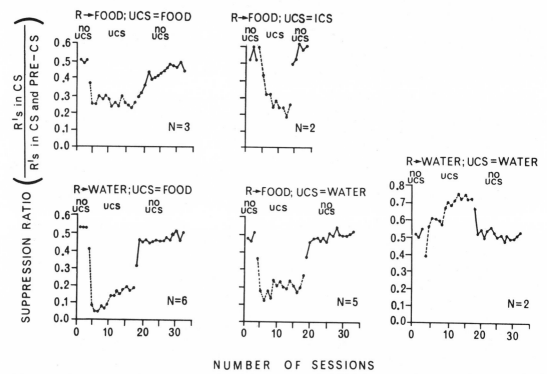

Fig. 2. Changes in the suppression ratio during a conditioned suppression procedure in which an unconditioned stimulus (UCS) was delivered automatically after 10 sec of conditioned stimulus (CS) presentation. Each graph is for a different group of rats. A suppression ratio of 0.0 shows complete suppression, 0.5 shows no suppression during the CS relative to the baseline. The designation above each graph describes the operant reinforcer delivered for the lever-pressing response (R), and also the nature of the UCS, one of which was intracranial stimulation (ICS). The initial "no UCS" period represents the last three sessions of that condition.

Table 1

Mean number of responses per minute for 18 rats during the Pre-CS and CS.

	Noncontingent UCS		
	Absent (Three Sessions)	Present (Five Sessions)	Absent (Five Sessions)
Pre-CS Period	56.4	54.0	76.8
CS Period	57.6	25.8	76.8

Analysis of the data for individual rats revealed that 15 of the 18 had suppression ratios of 0.02 to 0.40 calculated for the last five sessions of noncontingent stimulus presentation. Responding for six of these 15 rats was almost completely suppressed during the CS; the suppression ratios were less than 0.10. The two rats in the Water-Water Group (see Fig. 2) and one of the six in the Water-Food Group did not show response suppression; two showed slight response facilitation (0.60) and one showed substantial response facilitation (0.87). Each of these three rats had shown suppression during the first session in which the noncontingent stimulus was given; their suppression ratios were 0.35, 0.40, and 0.44 respectively for that session. A possible reason for the facilitation rather than suppression on subsequent days for these three rats is that adventitious reinforcement (Skinner, 1948) of some responses resulted from accidental correlations of the noncontingent stimulus with the lever press. To evaluate this interpretation, the two rats in the Water-Water Group that showed facilitation were given 23 additional sessions during which adventitious correlations were experimentally reduced by imposing a brief delay of 1.0 sec between the lever-press response and the noncontingent water delivery. The contingent water delivery continued to be given immediately after a lever press. For the rat that had shown the greatest facilitation, the mean suppression ratio for the last five days decreased from 0.87 to 0.41; for the other rat, which had shown only mild facilitation, the suppression ratio of 0.60 remained unchanged.

Gross observation of all rats during the CS revealed no pattern of competing responses. Some rats moved about rapidly, others moved only their head while still hovering above the response lever. Other rats seemed simply to "freeze" and others adopted no consistent pattern except to discontinue lever pressing.

DISCUSSION

The present findings revealed that the rate of responding was reduced during a stimulus that was paired with a positive reinforcer. Several features of the study indicated that the findings have generality over a range of conditions. The suppression was not dependent on the use of a specific operant reinforcer for the baseline responses, since both food and water were used for different rats; nor was it dependent on a specific conditioned stimulus, since both a clicker and a blinking light were used; nor was it dependent on the rate of the baseline responses, since the rates were as low as 10 and as high as 100 per min; nor was it dependent on a specific type of noncontingent reinforcer, since food, water, and ICS were used. The magnitude of the effect could be large, as seen by the near-zero suppression ratio for six of the rats. The effect was durable as seen by the continued reduction each day for as long as the procedure was maintained. The non-suppressive effect of the conditioned stimulus alone was evidenced by the usual rate of response when the unconditioned stimulus was absent. Especially important, almost all of the animals showed the effect. These findings indicate that the response reduction during a stimulus preceding a noncontingent positive reinforcer is substantial and general to a number of procedural variations.

The present results were similar in several ways to the findings of studies of conditioned suppression (see especially, Annau and Kamin, 1961) that have used aversive shock as the noncontingent reinforcer. The reduction in response rate occurred within one or two sessions, it was durable over continued sessions, the rate recovered rapidly when the noncontingent event was discontinued and the reduction was restricted largely to the CS period. Further evidence of comparability with the shock procedure must await subsequent studies that manipulate variables common to both procedures. At present, suppression during the aversive shock procedure seems best considered as one instance of the phenomenon, rather than as a model, since several types of positive reinforcers produced the suppression phenomenon, whereas only one type of negative reinforcer (shock) has produced it (Leitenberg, 1965). The phenomenon can be differentiated by designating it as negative conditioned suppression when a negative reinforcer such as shock is used, but as positive conditioned suppression when a positive reinforcer is used.

The findings failed to support the interpretation that competing behavior caused the suppression. First, gross observation failed to reveal any obvious competing type of activity, unless not responding is considered a competing reaction to responding. Secondly, the response lever was located so close to the food and water tray that the rats need not, and did not, leave the location of the lever to receive the noncontingent food and water deliveries. Thirdly, the intracranial stimulation required no consummatory response, nor did it elicit any strong unconditioned reactions. For the above reasons, the suppression cannot be accounted for by an appeal to incompatible conditioned reactions. It is still possible, and probable, that the interference is associated with autonomic changes during the CS such as has been found for cardiac changes (Stebbins and Smith, 1964; deToledo and Black, 1966) when shock has been used in the conditioned suppression procedure. Similarly, consistent patterns of salivation have been recorded during operant reinforcement by food (Shapiro, 1961, 1962; Kintsch and Witte, 1962). Although the autonomic changes have not been causally related to the operant changes (see review by Rescorla and Solomon, 1967), both changes may be the product of an underlying emotional state of heightened preparedness. This interpretation is similar to that made by Estes and Skinner (1941), except that the emotional state need not be negative.

The substantial facilitation, rather than suppression, that was found for one of the rats seemed to be the result of superstitious conditioning (Skinner, 1948) as evidenced by the suppression that resulted when adventitious correlations were prevented between the lever press and the noncontingent stimulus. Perhaps this preventive measure would have eliminated the slight facilitation shown by the other two rats had this feature been present at the start of the study. Additional evidence that faciliation was caused by a superstition was that facilitation occurred only after an initial suppression; all 18 subjects showed substantial suppression during at least the first or second day of pairing the conditioned stimulus with the noncontingent stimulus. Also, two of the three rats that showed facilitation

were receiving the same event as a noncontingent stimulus that was being given as a contingent reinforcer. This similarity would seem especially likely to produce a superstition.

The present results can be considered an example of respondent-operant interaction, a phenomenon which has received extensive theoretical attention by most dual-process learning theories (Skinner, 1938; Mowrer, 1960; Brown, 1961; Miller, 1951; and see review by Rescorla and Solomon, 1967). Several studies have found that Pavlovian pairing of a CS with food has resulted in an increase in the rate of food-reinforced responding when the CS was presented (Estes, 1948; Herrnstein and Morse, 1957; Morse and Skinner, 1958; Bower and Grusec, 1964). This increase, rather than decrease, seems to be accounted for by consideration of the similarity between the contingent and noncontingent reinforcer. The present study eliminated the possibility of similarity in the Food-Water, Water-Food, and Food-ICS procedure by making the contingent and noncontingent reinforcers qualitatively different from each other. Quantitative dissimilarity was attempted in the present Food-Food and Water-Water group by making the noncontingent event larger than the contingent event. In contrast, the noncontingent reinforcer and contingent reinforcer seen in previous studies were qualitatively and quantitatively identical and could thereby be expected to interact on the basis of discriminative rather than reinforcing properties. Adventitious reinforcement may also have been a factor in the Herrnstein and Morse (1957) study, as it was in the present study. In agreement with the present interpretation, Pliskoff (1961, 1963) found that food-reinforced responses were suppressed during a stimulus that preceded a period of high frequency reinforcement. As in the present study, the contingent and noncontingent events were at least quantitatively different.

REFERENCES

Annau, Z. and Kamin, L. J. The conditioned emotional response as a function of intensity of the US. *Journal of Comparative and Physiological Psychology*, 1961, **54**, 428-432.

Azrin, N. H. Some effects of two intermittent schedules of immediate and non-immediate punishment. *Journal of Psychology*, 1956, **42**, 3-21.

Bower, G. and Grusec, T. Effect of prior Pavlovian discrimination training upon learning an operant discrimination. *Journal of the Experimental Analysis of Behavior*, 1964, **7**, 401-404.

Brown, J. S. *The motivation of behavior.* New York: McGraw-Hill, 1961.

DeGroot, J. *The rat forebrain in stereotaxic coordinates.* Amsterdam: N. V. Noord-Hollandsche Uitgevers Maatschappij, 1963.

DeToledo, Leyla and Black, A. H. Heart rate: changes during conditioned suppression in rats. *Science*, 1966, **152**, 1404-1406.

Estes, W. K. Discriminative conditioning. II. Effects of a Pavlovian conditioned stimulus upon a subsequently established operant response. *Journal of Experimental Psychology*, 1948, **38**, 173-177.

Estes, W. K. and Skinner, B. F. Some quantitative properties of anxiety. *Journal of Experimental Psychology*, 1941, **29**, 390-400.

Ferster, C. B. and Skinner, B. F. *Schedules of reinforcement.* New York: Appleton-Century-Crofts, 1957.

Hake, D. F. and Azrin, N. H. Conditioned punishment. *Journal of the Experimental Analysis of Behavior*, 1965, **8**, 279-293.

Hawkins, D. T. and Pliskoff, S. S. Brain stimulation intensity, rate of self-stimulation, and reinforcement strength: an analysis through chaining. *Journal of the Experimental Analysis of Behavior*, 1964, **7**, 285-288.

Hendry, D. P. and Van-Toller, C. Alleviation of conditioned suppression. *Journal of Comparative and Physiological Psychology*, 1965, **59**, 458-460.

Herrnstein, R. J. and Morse, W. H. Some effects of response-independent positive reinforcement on maintained operant behavior. *Journal of Comparative and Physiological Psychology*, 1957, **50**, 461-467.

Hunt, H. F. and Brady, J. V. Some effects of punishment and intercurrent anxiety on a simple operant. *Journal of Comparative and Physiological Psychology*, 1955, **48**, 305-310.

Hutchinson, R. R. and Renfrew, J. W. A simple histological technique for localizing electrode tracks and lesions within the brain. *Journal of the Experimental Analysis of Behavior*, 1967, **10**, 277-280.

Kamin, L. J., Brimer, C. J., and Black, A. H. Conditioned suppression as a monitor of fear of the CS in the course of avoidance training. *Journal of Comparative and Physiological Psychology*, 1963, **56**, 497-501.

Kintsch, W. and Witte, R. S. Concurrent conditioning of bar press and salivation responses. *Journal of Comparative and Physiological Psychology*, 1962, **55**, 963-968.

Leitenberg, H. Is time-out from positive reinforcement an aversive event? A review of the experimental evidence. *Psychological Bulletin*, 1965, **64**, 428-441.

Lyon, D. Some notes on conditioned suppression and reinforcement schedules. *Journal of the Experimental Analysis of Behavior*, 1964, **7**, 289-291.

Millenson, J. R. *Principles of behavioral analysis.* New York: MacMillan, 1967.

Miller, N. E. Learnable drives and rewards. In S. S. Stevens (Ed.), *Handbook of experimental psychology.* New York: Wiley, 1951. Pp. 435-472.

Miller, N. E., Coons, E. E., Lewis, M., and Jensen, D. D. A simple technique for use with the rat. In D. E. Shear (Ed.), *Electrical stimulation of the brain.* Austin: University of Texas Press, 1961. Pp. 51-54.

Morse, W. H. and Skinner, B. F. Some factors involved in the stimulus control of operant behavior. *Journal of the Experimental Analysis of Behavior*, 1958, **1**, 103-107.

Mowrer, O. H. *Learning theory and behavior.* New York: Wiley, 1960.

Rescorla, R. A. and Solomon, R. L. Two-process learning theory: relationships between Pavlovian conditioning and instrumental learning. *Psychological Review*, 1967, **74**, 151-182.

Pliskoff, S. Rate-change effects during a pre-schedule-change stimulus. *Journal of the Experimental Analysis of Behavior*, 1961, **4**, 383-386.

Pliskoff, S. Rate-change effects with equal potential reinforcements during the "warning" stimulus. *Journal of the Experimental Analysis of Behavior*, 1963, **6**, 557-562.

Shapiro, M. M. Salivary conditioning in dogs during fixed-interval reinforcement contingent upon lever pressing. *Journal of the Experimental Analysis of Behavior*, 1961, **4**, 361-364.

Shapiro, M. M. Temporal relationship between salivation and lever pressing with differential reinforcement of low rates. *Journal of Comparative and Physiological Psychology*, 1962, **55**, 567-571.

Skinner, B. F. *The behavior of organisms: an experimental analysis.* New York: Appleton-Century-Crofts, 1938.

Skinner, B. F. "Superstition" in the pigeon. *Journal of Experimental Psychology*, 1948, **38**, 168-172.

Stebbins, W. C. and Smith, O. A. Cardiovascular concomitants of the conditioned emotional response in the monkey. *Science*, 1964, 881-883.

Stein, L., Sidman, M., and Brady, J. V. Some effects of two temporal variables on conditioned suppression. *Journal of the Experimental Analysis of Behavior*, 1958, **1**, 153-162.

Valenstein, E. S. Independence of approach and escape reactions to electrical stimulation of the brain. *Journal of Comparative and Physiological Psychology*, 1965, **60**, 20-30.

Valenstein, E. S. and Meyers, W. J. Rate independent test of reinforcing consequences of brain stimulation. *Journal of Comparative and Physiological Psychology*, 1964, **57**, 52-60.

Received 17 June 1968.

THE EFFECT OF INFORMATIVE FEEDBACK ON TEMPORAL TRACKING IN THE PIGEON[1]

J. E. R. STADDON

DUKE UNIVERSITY

Pigeons emitted interresponse times that were reinforced if they fell between an upper and a lower bound ($t <$ IRT $< t + t/10$). Brief stimuli followed each response; under some experimental conditions the color of these stimuli was correlated with whether the preceding interresponse time was longer or shorter than that specified by the schedule. Preliminary experiments indicated that these "feedback" stimuli acquired no discriminative properties even after prolonged training. A modified procedure, in which t varied cyclically throughout each experimental session, allowed the stimuli to acquire such properties: stimulus control was demonstrated under the training conditions, for two of the pigeons, and under transfer conditions for all three birds. A series of probe conditions, followed by a replication of the simple procedure using a multiple schedule, indicated that the controlling property of the stimuli was not the relation between stimuli, interresponse time, and value of t, but a variable determined by the interaction between the animals' responding and the cyclic procedure. This variable was probably the relative frequency of the less-frequent feedback stimulus.

CONTENTS

The behavior of pigeons can be brought under the control of a procedure that selectively reinforces responses terminating interresponse times (IRTs) lying between an upper and a lower limit (DRL LH schedules). Responding under these procedures typically falls considerably short of perfect effectiveness; the probability that a given response will be reinforced rarely exceeds 50%, and the "accuracy" of temporal discrimination, measured either as the variance of the distribution of IRTs or as the location of the modal IRT with respect to the reinforced interval, is not noticeably improved by requiring sharper discriminations of the animal. Thus, the results of Kelleher, Fry, and Cook (1959) indicate that a reduction in the limited hold (LH) on a DRL procedure tends to worsen temporal discrimination both by displacing the IRT mode

towards shorter values and by increasing the variance of the IRT distribution.

The relative inability of the usual differential reinforcement procedures to improve temporal discrimination of this sort leads one to ask whether performance under DRL schedules represents some kind of absolute limitation upon animals' ability to discriminate time intervals. Is there anything about the DRL schedule itself which might artificially restrict animals' opportunity to exhibit accurate temporal discriminations? At least two potential limiting properties can be distinguished. (1) An experiment by Reynolds (1966) indicated that the ability to discriminate, *i.e.*, show behavior correlated with, a given time interval must be distinguished from the ability to inhibit responding for the duration of that interval. The enforced-pause aspect of the spaced responding procedure may thus be an irreducible limiting factor. (2) An adventitious property of DRL LH procedures, however, as they are usually scheduled, is the infrequency of informative feedback available to the animal. Most of the informative feedback on DRL LH schedules is associated with the reinforcement; reinforcement implies that the previous IRT was correct and the animal should continue to emit IRTs of this duration. An unreinforced response, on the other hand, implies only that the previous IRT was incor-

[1]This paper is dedicated to B. F. Skinner in his sixty-fifth year.

rect; it carries no indication either of the correct IRT or the direction in which future IRTs should change. Thus, the rate of informative feedback depends largely upon the rate of correct responses, which, in turn, depends on the frequency of informative feedback, and so on. It is conceivable that this circular process may artificially limit pigeons' performance in spaced responding situations, either in terms of the accuracy of performance for a given DRL requirement, or by setting an upper limit on the DRL value that can gain discriminative control over the modal interresponse time (*cf.* Staddon, 1965), or both.

Empirical investigation of the effects of "informative" stimuli poses a number of subtle methodological problems. At the simplest level, however, a situation is required where response-contingent stimuli are presented that are (a) correlated with the difference between the just-emitted IRT and the IRT required, and (b) are not correlated with reinforcement. These two conditions were satisfied by a procedure that briefly presented a red or a green key following IRTs that were too short or too long, respectively, in terms of a given DRL LH schedule. The presentations were brief because a correlation with reinforcement would have qualified the stimuli as either discriminative, or conditioned reinforcers, or both, and thus might have confounded the outcome.

Asymptotic performances were obtained with this procedure in a series of experiments involving DRL LH schedules with DRL values over the range of 8.8 to 30 sec and limited holds from 10% to 30% of the DRL value. In a number of ABA sequences no reliable differences between asymptotic IRT distributions obtained with and without feedback stimuli were found.

This failure implies either that (a) pigeons cannot utilize the information provided by feedback stimuli, or (b) some kind of shaping procedure is necessary to demonstrate control of behavior by feedback stimuli, or (c) the DRL LH contingencies used were not sufficient to produce stimulus control, *i.e.*, the birds obtained sufficient reinforcement without attending to the stimuli; (b) and (c) are of course not mutually exclusive.

Further exploration of this technique focused on (c), the "difficulty" of the procedure. The manipulation finally chosen involved

shifting to a dynamic situation where, on *a priori* grounds, feedback might seem to be most useful. The situation involved a DRL *t* LH *0.t* schedule where the value of *t* changed systematically every 5 min, going through two cycles in a 2-hr experimental session. A series of transfer tests demonstrated clear control of responding by the feedback stimuli under these conditions, but indicated that the mechanism of control was not the obvious "speed up" or "slow down" effect intended. This conclusion was reinforced by a further experiment, using a more sensitive version of the original simple DRL LH procedure, that again failed to show any clear effect of the stimuli.

EXPERIMENT I: SEQUENTIAL STUDY OF FEEDBACK AND NO-FEEDBACK CONDITIONS[2]

METHOD

Subjects

Three adult, male, White Carneaux pigeons, maintained at 80% of their free-feeding weights, were used. These birds had been exposed to a variety of reinforcement schedules before the start of the experiment, including various exploratory procedures using feedback stimuli on DRL LH schedules.

Apparatus

The experimental chamber consisted of a standard 12- by 12- by 13-in. wire cage, one side of which was an aluminum panel on which a Gerbrands pigeon key and grain feeder were mounted. The translucent key was illuminated from behind by Christmas-tree lamps of various colors. These lamps also served as general illumination, both via the key and by reflection from the white-painted walls of the larger soundproofed enclosure containing cage and panel assembly. White noise masked most extraneous sounds. A force of at least 18 g was required to operate the key. Effective re-

[2]Experiment 1 is adapted from a thesis submitted to Harvard University in partial fulfillment of the requirements for the Ph.D. degree. The work was supported by grants from the National Science Foundation to Harvard University; preparation of this report was assisted by Grant MH 14194 from the National Institute of Mental Health. Reprints may be obtained from the author, Department of Psychology, Duke University, Durham, North Carolina 27706.

sponses produced an audible click from a relay behind the panel. During reinforcement (3-sec access to grain) the key lights were out and the magazine aperture was illuminated.

Scheduling was accomplished by a system of relays and timers. Responses were recorded on electric impulse counters and a cumulative recorder. IRT data were obtained by a graphic method first described by Blough (1963). The technique produces oscillograms in which each response is recorded as a dot; displacement of the dot along the ordinate is an exponential function of the preceding IRT and its displacement along the abscissa is proportional to the ordinal number of that response (*i.e.*, tenth, forty-fifth, *etc.*) within the session. The exponential time axis insures that responding that is random with respect to time will tend to produce a more or less uniform field of dots, whereas temporal discrimination, defined as a rising IRTs/Op function, will tend to produce clusters of responses around a given ordinate value. Thus, the data shown in Fig. 3 show a progressively changing temporal discrimination, since the ordinate value associated with clustering of responses shifts systematically through the experimental session.

Procedure

The schedule used throughout the experiment involved five DRL values, each one of the form: DRL *t* LH *0.t*-sec, *i.e.*, a 10% limited hold was used in all cases. These five values were presented in the following sequence (nominal values of *t* in sec[3]):

8; 10; 15; 20; 30; 30; 30; 20; 15; 10; 8.

Each component was in force for 5 min, independent of the number of reinforcements produced in the component; the scheduling timer did not stop during reinforcement. No differential stimuli, in the usual sense, were correlated with each value of the schedule and it must therefore be classified as a mixed DRL LH schedule of a cyclic rather than a random nature (cyclic DRL). Two cycles of this procedure constituted a session, which therefore lasted for 110 min. The session always started with the first 8-sec component. The 10% limited-hold aspect of the schedule was dic-

tated by the need to hold to a reasonable level the number of reinforcements the animal could produce within the 2-hr session. Earlier experiments indicated that even a 20% LH allowed some animals to produce as many as 90 reinforcements within a 2-hr period. Under these conditions, tracking behavior deteriorated sharply.

The major independent variable was the presence or absence of feedback (FB) stimuli. There were two stimuli, a red and a green key light. In the FB condition a response on the key had one of three outcomes: (1) after an IRT shorter than the minimum IRT specified by the cyclic-DRL component then in force, the white key light changed to green for 1.6 sec, followed by a return to the white key light; (2) after an IRT within the limits prescribed by the schedule in force, the key lights were extinguished and the reinforcer presented. Following reinforcement, the white key light reappeared at reduced intensity (caused by interposing a 300-ohm resistor in series with the light) for 1.6 sec, after which it returned to its normal intensity; (3) after an IRT longer than the maximum (10% longer than the minimum) specified by the schedule, the white key light changed to red for 1.6 sec, followed by a return to white. All key lights were turned off for 35 msec (the duration of the response pulse) after every response, to allow time for switching of the scheduling equipment. A typical sequence of events is illustrated in Fig. 1. In the "no-feedback" (NFB) situation, the number of possible outcomes that could result from a response was reduced from three to two: reinforcement, on the one hand, or the 1.6-sec appearance of the white light at reduced intensity, on the other. The same stimulus occurred after reinforcement in both procedures. Thus, the only difference between the FB and NFB situation was that in the latter, the white light at reduced intensity took the place of both green and red key lights.

In the extinction conditions with feedback, responses terminating IRTs that would normally have been reinforced were followed by the feedback stimulus that followed the preceding IRT.

Two major dependent variables will be discussed: (1) IRT distribution as a function of time and schedule component; (2) rate of responding as a function of time within each

---

[3]The nominal values of *t* do not reflect its actual value in all cases; actual values were:

nominal *t* (sec)	8	10	15	20	30
actual *t* (sec)	8.5	11.0	16.3	20.9	30.6.

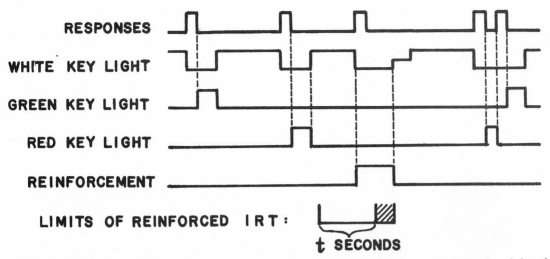

Fig. 1. The sequence of events following interresponse times greater than, less than, and within the reinforced IRT band. The effect of an IRT shorter than the 1.6-sec feedback stimulus duration is also shown. The time dimension is not to scale.

session; for this purpose the number of responses made during each of the eleven 5-min components during the second cycle of the session was recorded.

Table 1 shows the sequence of experimental conditions used. The first part of the experiment—Conditions 1 through 6—was designed to establish the existence of an effect of the feedback stimuli under both steady-state conditions and in extinction. The second part —Conditions 7 through 16—attempted to analyze further the mode of action of the stimuli by interpolating probe sessions separated by days under the basic feedback procedure.

RESULTS

The major result of the experiment was demonstration of control of the cyclic pattern of responding developed under this procedure ("tracking" of the cyclic DRL) by the feedback (FB) stimuli. This control is clearly evident under steady-state conditions for two of the birds and in extinction tests for all three. The relevant steady-state data appear in Fig. 2 which shows response rate within each 5-min component during the second cycle of the session for Conditions 1, 3, and 5 (NFB-1, FB-1, and NFB-2). Both 186 and 106 show the ex-

Table 1

Condition	Description		No. of Sessions (range)
1	no feedback	(NFB-1)	32
2	extinction without feedback	(EXT NFB-1)	1
3	feedback	(FB-1)	21-25
4	extinction with feedback	(EXT FB-1)	1
5	no feedback	(NFB-2)	29
6	extinction without feedback	(EXT NFB-2)	1
7	feedback	(FB-2)	27
8	extinction during second cycle	(½ EXT)	1
9	feedback	(FB-3)	3
10	reversed feedback for 2nd cycle	(½ REV)	1
11	feedback	(FB-4)	5
12	reversed feedback and extinction	(½ REV + EXT)	1
13	feedback	(FB-5)	6
14	green feedback stimulus only	(GREEN)	1
15	feedback	(FB-6)	3
16	red feedback stimulus only	(RED)	1

Experimental conditions and number of sessions. The basic procedure throughout the experiment was a DRL t LH $0.t$ schedule with t varying cyclically. Two cycles constituted a session.

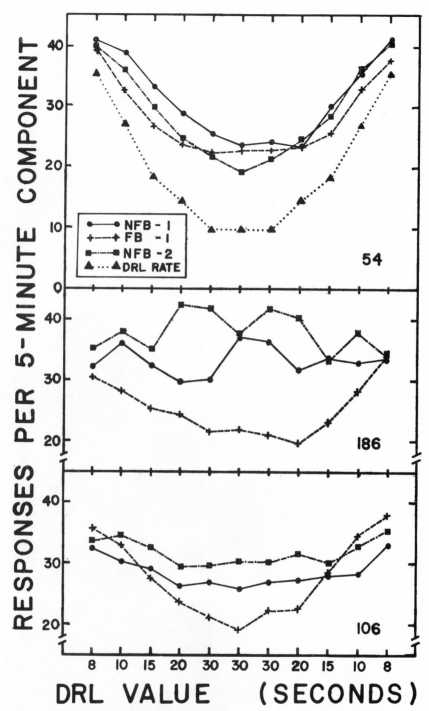

Fig. 2. Response rate in each component during the second cycle of the session for the first and second no-feedback (NFB-1 and 2) conditions and the first feedback condition (FB-1) for the three birds. Each point is the average of the last seven sessions under each condition. In this and all similar plots the rate in each component has been adjusted for the time taken by the reinforcement cycle. The curve labelled "DRL RATE" in the top panel indicates the number of responses that would be emitted in each component if every response terminated an IRT just long enough to qualify for reinforcement.

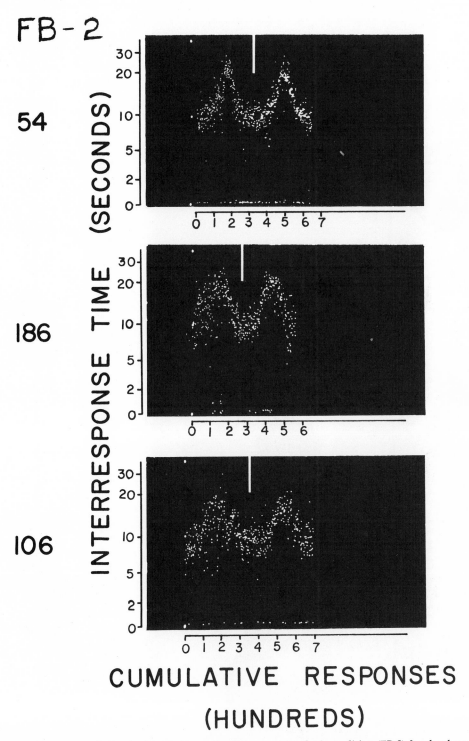

Fig. 3. Oscilloscope records for the last session under the second feedback condition (FB-2) for the three pigeons. Each point represents a response terminating an IRT given by the ordinate value. The ordinal number of the response is given by the value on the abscissa. Vertical white line at the top of each photograph indicates the end of the first cycle. See text for fuller discussion.

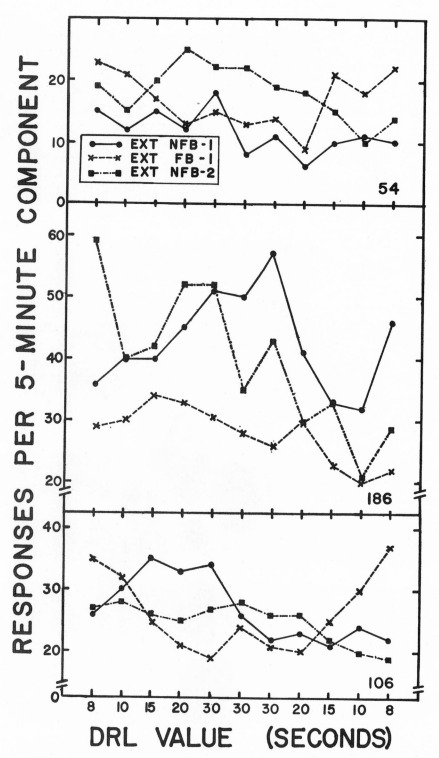

Fig. 4. Response rate in each component of the second cycle in extinction following feedback and no-feedback conditions; *i.e.,* in Conditions EXT NFB-1, EXT FB-1, and EXT NFB-2.

pected decline and increase in response rate as a function of time for the feedback condition, but to a lesser extent (106), or not at all (186), for either of the no-feedback conditions. Bird 54, however, tracked even without the aid of the feedback stimuli. The data in this figure indicate that the more proficient the bird was at this procedure, in terms of the regularity and amount of cyclic variation in the presence of cues both from reinforcement and the feedback stimuli, the less disruption was produced by removing the stimuli; *i.e.*, the same order of proficiency obtained both with and without feedback. Dot pictures taken for all these conditions indicate that the cyclic variations in response rate shown in Fig. 2 are due to systematic shifts in the modal IRT (*i.e.*, a change in temporal discrimination) rather than a nonselective change in the proportion of long *vs.* short IRTs such as that produced by extinction. A typical set of such dot pictures, taken from Condition 5 (the second feedback condition) is shown in Fig. 3.

The data shown in Fig. 2 might seem to suggest that Bird 54 was controlled solely by cues other than the feedback stimuli (*e.g.*, reinforcement, time since the beginning of the session, *etc.*). This conclusion is contradicted, however, by the results of the extinction sessions, which are depicted in Fig. 4 and 5. Figure 4 shows second-cycle response rate during extinction sessions with and without feedback following FB and NFB conditions, *i.e.*, EXT NFB-1, EXT FB-1, EXT NFB-2. All three pigeons show an effect of the feedback stimuli; in the case of Birds 54 and 106, the cyclic pattern of responding is disrupted by NFB and restored by FB, in the case of 186, responding occurs at a much lower rate in the feedback extinction condition, paralleling the results for this bird in the presence of reinforcement with and without feedback (Fig. 2).

The discriminative control exerted by the stimuli is even more apparent in the second-cycle conditions shown in Fig. 5. The relevant comparisons are between the ½ EXT condition, in which the feedback stimuli, but no reinforcement, occurred during the second cycle of the session, and the other two conditions in which the significance of the stimuli was reversed (*green* for "long", *red* for "short") but reinforcement was continued (½ REV), and the same condition without reinforcement (½ REV + EXT). Only in the ½ EXT con-

dition is the normal cyclic pattern of responding preserved and indeed the birds' tracking behavior during this condition was at least as accurate as during the condition when both reinforcement and feedback were available.

The feedback stimuli clearly exerted control over some aspect of the tracking behavior of all three pigeons in this experiment. Given the scheduled relationship between the red and green key lights and the birds' responding, the simplest mode of control by the stimuli would appear to be upon the direction of change of interresponse time: following an IRT shorter than the DRL requirement, the subsequent IRT should be longer; following a too-long IRT, the subsequent IRT should be shorter. The most direct method for testing a mechanism of this sort was provided by the second-cycle conditions when the significance of the green and red stimuli was reversed. If the birds' tracking were controlled by a negative feedback mechanism of the type described, with the stimuli providing the feedback signals, the second-cycle reversal conditions (½ REV and ½ REV + EXT) should convert a negative feedback mechanism into a positive feedback one, leading either to runaway acceleration (shorter and shorter IRTs) or deceleration (longer and longer IRTs). Figure 5 shows that neither result occurred for any animal. Indeed, for the ½ REV condition the rate for the first four or five components of the condition showed less change than usual, contradicting predictions based upon an IRT-by-IRT feedback control mechanism. The results of the ½ REV + EXT condition are more equivocal for Birds 54 and 106, but in neither case do they provide clear support for the simple feedback view. Unfortunately, the results of the other two probe conditions, GREEN and RED, are similarly uninformative, agreeing only in that they fail consistently to support the feedback hypothesis. Thus, while response rate in the GREEN condition (green feedback stimulus following all unreinforced responses) was lower than for the RED condition for Birds 186 and 106, in accordance with the scheduled "too short" significance of green, the opposite was true of Bird 54, which in other respects adapted best to this situation. In general, the tracking of all three birds was more disrupted by RED than by GREEN, the difference being greatest for 186 and least for

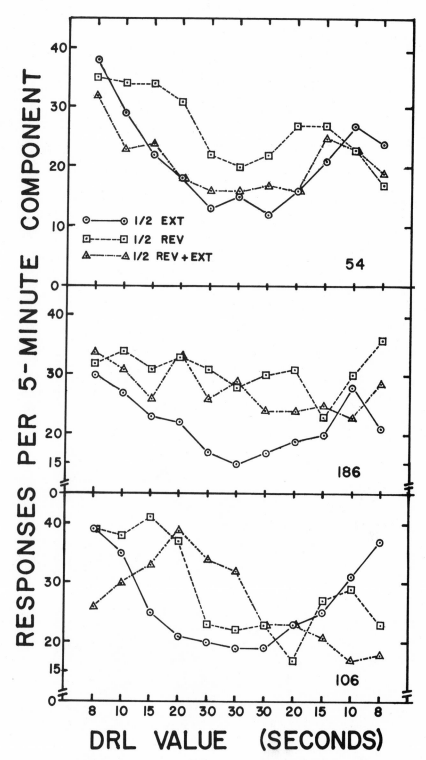

Fig. 5. Response rate in each component of the second cycle during the three second-cycle conditions: ½ EXT —extinction during the second cycle, feedback given; ½REV—reversed feedback during second cycle, reinforcement given; ½ REV + EXT—neither reinforcement nor feedback during second cycle.

54, again reflecting the order of proficiency of the birds at this task.

EXPERIMENT 2: FEEDBACK AND NO-FEEDBACK CONDITIONS WITHIN COMPONENTS OF A MULTIPLE SCHEDULE

After the cyclic DRL experiment, the possibility of discriminative control by feedback stimuli in the simple DRL LH situation was re-examined using a more sensitive procedure. In addition to four naive pigeons the two most proficient birds under the cyclic procedure (54 and 106) were used. This experiment thus constituted a test of whether or not their experience under the cyclic procedure allowed these birds to come under the control of feedback stimuli in the simple DRL LH situation. Two of the six pigeons showed small, idiosyncratic effects attributable to the feedback stimuli.

METHOD

Subjects

Six White Carneaux pigeons, four naive (223, 224, 225, 226) and two used in the previous experiment (54, 106) were maintained at 80% of their free-feeding weights.

Apparatus and Procedure

After one day of continuous reinforcement following key and magazine training for the four naive birds, all birds were exposed in the chamber of the previous experiment to 24 sessions of a DRL x LH y procedure with x and y varying from 5 sec and 1.5 sec, during early sessions, to 15 sec and 3 sec for the last 15 sessions. This was followed by 28 sessions when Birds 54, 106, 224, and 226 were exposed to DRL 15 LH 1.5-sec and Birds 223 and 225 to DRL 10 LH 1-sec.

Superimposed on this basic procedure was a two-component multiple schedule of feedback and no feedback. The components alternated at 5-min intervals and the first component of the session varied irregularly from day to day. Six cycles of this procedure constituted a session. During the feedback components, the same stimulus contingencies were in effect as in the feedback conditions in the first experiment, *i.e.*, a brief green or red stimulus following IRTs longer or shorter than the range specified by the DRL LH schedule. For

Birds 54 and 106, green signified "short" and red "long", as in the previous experiment. For the other four birds the significance of the colors was counterbalanced: green signifying "short" for Birds 223 and 224, and *vice versa* for Birds 225 and 226. The duration of the feedback stimuli was 1.5 sec for the DRL 15 LH 1.5 birds and 1 sec for the others. During the no-feedback component of the multiple schedule, the key light was dimmed after each response by interposing a 500-ohm resistor in series with the white key light. This stimulus also followed reinforcement during the feedback component.

On the day following Session 19 of the series of DRL 15 LH 1.5-sec sessions, Birds 54 and 226 were given an extinction session with the multiple feedback–no-feedback contingency remaining in force. As with the feedback extinction conditions in the previous experiment, after IRTs that would have been reinforced, the feedback stimulus appropriate to the preceding (one-back) IRT was presented.

Separate IRT distributions, with 16 IRT cells having a width of 1.5 sec for the DRL 15 LH 1.5-sec conditions and 1 sec for the DRL 10 LH 1-sec conditions, were obtained for the feedback and no feedback components.

RESULTS

Figure 6 shows data for the last 14 days of the final condition of the experiment. Each point is the mean of 14 daily points. Each daily point represents the difference (NFB − FB) between the number of IRTs in a given cell in the no-feedback and feedback components respectively. Thus, the curves of Fig. 6 represent the mean difference between the IRT distributions with and without feedback. The small IRT distributions along the right column of Fig. 6 are 14-day means with and without feedback; they show typical DRL LH performances for all the birds. The difference curves show few significant deviations from zero, however. With the exception of Bird 223, and possibly Bird 106, there were negligible differences between the feedback and no-feedback IRT distributions. Bird 223 did show a small but consistent difference between the feedback and no-feedback distributions, with the feedback distribution showing fewer short (< 6 sec) IRTs and more long (6 < IRT < 8 sec) IRTs. Overall, however, the effect of feedback under these conditions was much less ap-

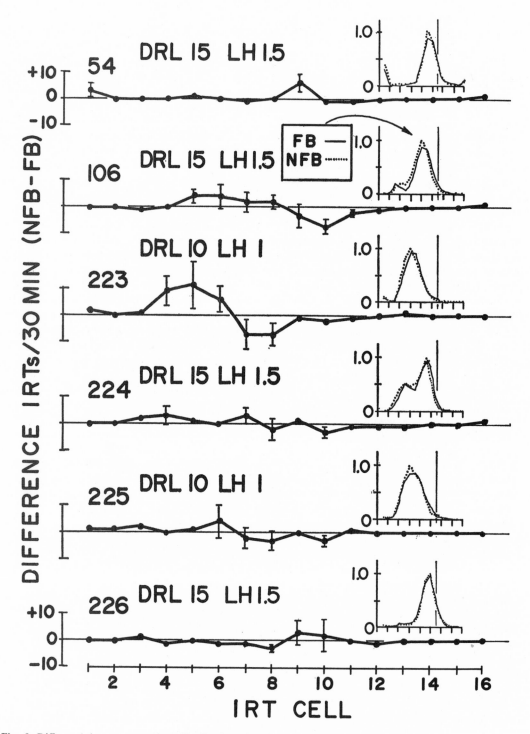

Fig. 6. Difference interresponse-time distributions for the six pigeons. The difference (NFB − FB) between the number of IRTs falling in each of 16 cells in the feedback and no-feedback components was computed for each of the last 14 days of the experiment. Each plotted point in the difference curve is the mean of these 14 differences. Vertical bars are 95% confidence intervals. IRTs falling in cell 11 were reinforced. The small, relative-frequency IRT distributions on the right are 14-day averages with and without feedback over the same period.

parent than under the cyclic procedure of the previous experiment, even for the two birds (54 and 106) that showed clear evidence of control by the feedback stimuli in that experiment.

Another comparison was afforded by the extinction sessions given to Birds 54 and 226. In the absence of cues provided by reinforcement, control by feedback might be expected to become more apparent. Such was not the case. Little breakdown in performance occurred during the extinction condition for either bird (*i.e.*, the form of IRT distribution closely resembled distributions obtained during training) and there were no significant differences between feedback and no-feedback components in this respect.

It remains possible that prolongation of the extinction condition, computation of more comprehensive average IRT distributions, or a number of other manipulations, both experimental and computational, would have shown an effect of the feedback stimuli. On the other hand, the results of this experiment strongly suggest that any effect is, at best, of small magnitude under these conditions.

GENERAL DISCUSSION

The present results indicate that feedback stimuli can assist pigeons to maintain a cyclic, temporal tracking performance and can sustain this behavior in the absence of reinforcement. The exact mode of action of the stimuli is unclear, however, although the results of the cyclic tracking procedure, together with the negligible effect of the stimuli in the stationary tracking experiment, suggest that they did not act in a simple negative feedback fashion, interresponse time by interresponse time.

One implication of these results is that the limitations on DRL performance alluded to earlier probably cannot be attributed to lack of informative feedback. A second implication concerns the relationship between "information" and the capacities of the organism. The information contained in a set of instructions is of little help to a hearer who does not speak the language; on the other hand the fact that instructions of some kind are being given may be of some help, although the detailed content is unavailable. In other words, a given situation may contain information on several levels and only those for which the organism

possesses the appropriate decoding system can come to control behavior. In the cyclic tracking situation with feedback, the stimuli contained two kinds of information: (a) Information corresponding to the scheduled contingencies concerning the relation between the just-emitted IRT and the tracking requirement. This information was associated with each stimulus occurrence. (b) Information contained in the pattern of feedback stimuli over time: because the pigeons adapted much better to the shorter (DRL 8 and 10) tracking requirements than to the longer (DRL 20 and 30) components, both the frequency of reinforcement and the relative frequency of the red ("too long") feedback stimulus increased during the shorter components. The effectiveness of the feedback stimuli in the cyclic situation, their relative ineffectiveness in the simple DRL LH situation, and the results of the various transfer and probe tests all suggest that the latter property of the stimuli was the effective one in this situation. The mechanism of action both of this relative frequency variable and of the other cues in the cyclic situation (beginning of session, reinforcement, and reinforcement frequency) remains obscure, however. A general implication of the results is that perhaps pigeons either cannot come under the control of a feedback "knowledge of results" relation of this sort, cannot rapidly and systematically shift the mode of their IRT distribution under discriminative control, or both.

REFERENCES

Blough, D. S. Interresponse time as a function of continuous variables: a new method and some data. *Journal of the Experimental Analysis of Behavior*, 1963, **6**, 237-246.

Kelleher, R. T., Fry, W. C., and Cook, L. Interresponse time distribution as a function of differential reinforcement of temporally spaced responses. *Journal of the Experimental Analysis of Behavior*, 1959, **2**, 91-106.

Reynolds, G. S. Discrimination and emission of temporal intervals by pigeons. *Journal of the Experimental Analysis of Behavior*, 1966, **9**, 65-68.

Staddon, J. E. R. The effect of "knowledge of results" on timing behavior in the pigeon. Unpublished doctoral dissertation, Harvard University, 1963.

Staddon, J. E. R. Some properties of spaced responding in pigeons. *Journal of the Experimental Analysis of Behavior*, 1965, **8**, 19-27.

Received 22 August 1966.

AUTOSHAPING OF KEY PECKING IN PIGEONS WITH NEGATIVE REINFORCEMENT[1]

Howard Rachlin

HARVARD UNIVERSITY

Pigeons exposed to gradually increasing intensities of pulsing electric shock pecked a key and thereby reduced the intensity of shock to zero for 2 min. Acquisition of key pecking was brought about through an autoshaping process in which periodic brief keylight presentations immediately preceded automatic reduction of the shock. On the occasions of such automatic reduction of shock preceding the first measured key peck, little or no orientation to the key was observed. Observations of pigeons with autoshaping of positive reinforcement also revealed little evidence of orientation toward the key.

Brown and Jenkins (1968) trained pigeons to peck a key by periodically illuminating the key for a few seconds, then presenting food reinforcement. If the pigeons pecked the illuminated key, the food was presented immediately after the peck. If the pigeons did not peck the key, food was presented anyway, after 8 sec (or, in one control procedure, after 3 sec) of illumination. With this procedure, all subjects, previously trained only with the food hopper, pecked the key within 160 trials. Brown and Jenkins called this process "autoshaping". Control procedures showed that in order to generate reliable pecking, food presentation was necessary and the key had to be illuminated just before the food was presented.

Sidman and Fletcher (1968) trained monkeys to press keys with a similar procedure. They paired a lighted key with food presentation and found that each of four monkeys pressed the key within 60 pairings of light and food. In both studies, the basic movements involved in the response to the key were similar to the movements involved in the response to the food. In the Brown-Jenkins experiment, the pigeons pecked both the food and the key. In the Sidman-Fletcher experiment, while the acts of pressing the key and picking up the food had different topographies, they both involved reaching and touching. Also, both key pecking of food-deprived pigeons and key pressing of food-deprived monkeys are common laboratory responses, easily shaped by more conventional techniques.

The present experiment extends autoshaping to a form of behavior that has been difficult to condition with negative reinforcers by normal laboratory techniques—key pecking by pigeons reinforced by escape from electric shock. Pigeons subjected to electric shock have been trained to peck a key by slowly increasing the shock from zero and reinforcing approaches to the key by periods of no shock (Rachlin and Hineline, 1967). However, as opposed to the ease of training pigeons to peck keys with positive reinforcement, the training of pigeons to peck a key with shock removal (negative reinforcement) often takes as much as 10 or 15 hr of patient shaping. Perhaps, as a result, there are almost no published studies of key pecking in pigeons established or maintained by negative reinforcement. Hoffman and Fleshler (1959) studied negative reinforcement in pigeons, but used a head-raising response, and reported that key pecking was impossible to obtain with the procedures used. Azrin (1959b) obtained key pecking with one pigeon, but only temporarily.

The primary purpose of the present experiment was to develop a practical laboratory method for training pigeons to peck a key with escape from shock as reinforcement. In addition, it extends the generality of the auto-

[1]Dedicated to B. F. Skinner in his sixty-fifth year. This research was supported by grants from the National Science Foundation and the National Institute of Health. The author is grateful to Philip N. Hineline for his criticism of the manuscript. Reprints may be obtained from the author, Department of Psychology, State University of New York, Stony Brook, Long Island, New York 11790.

shaping procedure. The present experiment differs from other autoshaping procedures in two respects: there is no specific consummatory response so the response being conditioned cannot resemble the consummatory response; the response being conditioned has a low operant level in the experimental situation. Because of these differences, some light may be thrown on the nature of the autoshaping process itself.

METHOD

Subjects

Twenty-six adult male White Carneaux pigeons were used; all were experimentally naive. Twenty-two were implanted with gold or stainless steel wire under the pubis bones (Azrin, 1959a) and given free access to food and water in their home cages. Four were not implanted and were kept at 80% of their free-feeding weight.

Apparatus

The experimental chamber was of standard dimensions (Ferster and Skinner, 1957), made of wire mesh, and coated with an insulating spray. The shock was 110 v ac transformed by a 0- to 110-v variable transformer, then stepped up by a 400-v transformer, and run through a 25 K ohm or larger resistor, through relay contacts which closed to produce a 35-msec pulse every second, and through a Gerbrands mercury swivel mounted on the ceiling of the chamber. The variable transformer was driven by a motor and a gear changer with a clutch arrangement. This apparatus provided for trains of shock with intensity linearly increasing with time, and for sudden reset of the intensity to zero. The experimental chamber was contained in a sound-resistant chest; white noise was supplied throughout the session. There was a houselight on the roof of the experimental chamber and a trans-illuminated key was mounted on the wall 10 in. above the floor. Mounted on the key was a hemispherical transparent plastic extension protruding 1.3 cm into the chamber. This extension allowed for greater latitude than an ordinary key for the kinds of movement that would be recorded as key pecks. For all but four subjects, a food hopper in the chamber was blocked off by a steel plate.

Procedure

The basic experimental paradigm is shown in Fig. 1. The naive, food-satiated pigeons were exposed to shock pulses at 1 per sec increasing from zero to a maximum, usually 6 ma. The time for the shock to reach maximum was 77 sec. The shock pulses remained at 6 ma for 7 sec more, and then shock was automatically terminated. A peck on the key, or any other action of the pigeons that would depress the key 1 mm during the 77-sec rise of the shock or during the subsequent 7 sec of constant intensity would also terminate shock. Hereafter, the sudden termination of shock, whether presented automatically after the 7 sec of constant intensity or presented as a result of a key peck, will be called negative reinforcement. During the periods of pulsing shock, the houselights were lit and at other times they were out. In addition, during the 7 sec of constant-intensity pulses just preceding negative reinforcement, the key was trans-illuminated with an orange light. At other times, the key was dark. The duration of the shock-off period following negative reinforcement was manipulated during the experiments. Pecks during this period had no scheduled consequences. At the end of the shock-off period, the houselights came on and the shock started increasing again from zero. The daily sessions lasted 90 min, except as noted.

Key presses were counted during the rise of the shock, during the period of constant intensity with the key lit, and during the shock-off period. Also, the number of 1-per-sec pulses between each two successive shock-off periods was recorded.

Hand shaping of key pecking for negative reinforcement had been facilitated by the addition of a hemispherical extension attached to the key, protruding 1.3 cm into the chamber (research in collaboration with P. N. Hineline). This extension was retained during most of the autoshaping experiments. With the extension, the pigeons could easily press the key by means other than pecking. During most of the following experiments the only way to tell whether a press was due to a peck or a wing-flap (the other frequent means of depressing the key) was occasional visual observation. Once key pressings became frequent, however, they became stereotyped, so a pigeon observed pecking at the key with its beak one

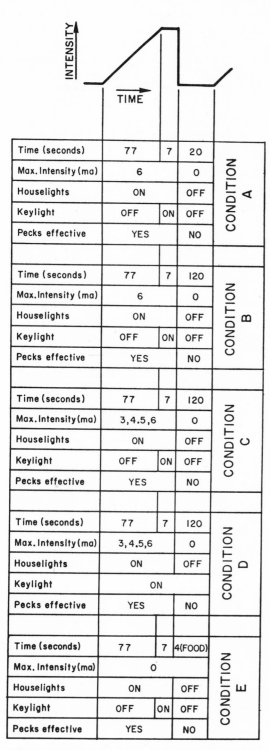

CONDITION A

Time (seconds)	77	7	20
Max. Intensity (ma)	6		0
Houselights	ON		OFF
Keylight	OFF	ON	OFF
Pecks effective	YES		NO

CONDITION B

Time (seconds)	77	7	120
Max. Intensity (ma)	6		0
Houselights	ON		OFF
Keylight	OFF	ON	OFF
Pecks effective	YES		NO

CONDITION C

Time (seconds)	77	7	120
Max. Intensity (ma)	3,4,5,6		0
Houselights	ON		OFF
Keylight	OFF	ON	OFF
Pecks effective	YES		NO

CONDITION D

Time (seconds)	77	7	120
Max. Intensity (ma)	3, 4,5,6		0
Houselights	ON		OFF
Keylight	ON		
Pecks effective	YES		NO

CONDITION E

Time (seconds)	77	7	4(FOOD)
Max. Intensity (ma)	0		
Houselights	ON		OFF
Keylight	OFF	ON	OFF
Pecks effective	YES		NO

Fig. 1. A diagram of the variation of shock intensity with time, and a table of experimental procedures. While the lines in the diagram are continuous, the shock is actually pulsing.

time was likely to peck at it the next time also. Photographs of the pigeons pressing the key confirmed this observation. In the earlier experiments, where photographs were not taken, only occasional visual observation was used to determine whether a given depression of the key was a peck or a wing-flap. Where the means of pressing the key is unknown, we will speak of key presses. Where pecks were observed, we will speak of key pecks. Where pigeons were observed to press the key with their wings, we will speak of wing-flaps.

EXPERIMENT I: 20-SEC SHOCK-OFF PERIOD

Four naive pigeons were exposed to the basic procedure with a shock-off period following negative reinforcement of 20 sec (condition A, Fig. 1). This condition continued for 20 sessions, during which two of the birds pressed the key, once each. One bird pressed the key during its fifth session, while the shock was at maximum intensity. The other pressed the key during its fourth session while shock was increasing.

EXPERIMENT II: 2-MIN SHOCK-OFF PERIOD

Several experiments with pigeons exposed to shock have led the present author and P. N. Hineline to speculate that adaptation to shock plays a large role in the escape and avoidance behavior of pigeons. If pigeons were adapting to shock during an increasing series of shocks, it is possible that the 20-sec shock-off period would not be sufficient time to lose the adaptation. The next series of shocks, presented to an adapted organism, would not be as aversive as the first; thus, escape behavior might not develop. It is also possible that 20 sec is not a sufficient magnitude of reinforcement. For this reason, six naive pigeons were given a procedure identical to that of Exp. I, except that each shock-off period following negative reinforcement lasted 120 sec. For four of the six pigeons, a camera and an electronic flash were fitted to the chamber to photograph the pigeon at the moment of each negative reinforcement. For these pigeons each session was about 90 min, covering 25 or more trials. Key presses shortened trials and hence increased the number of trials per session. For the other two pigeons each session was about 150 min. With this procedure, all six pigeons pressed the key during the first session. Of the six birds, one (S-100) came eventually to press the key consistently with its wings; one (S-27) usually pressed the key with its wings, and occasionally pecked the key, while the other four (S-7, S-26, S-28, and S-29) eventually pecked the key consistently. In this experiment, as well as in those to follow, there were very few presses during the shock-off period; at the most, two or three per session. Figure 2 shows, for one pigeon (S-7) that pecked the key, the development and subsequent fading

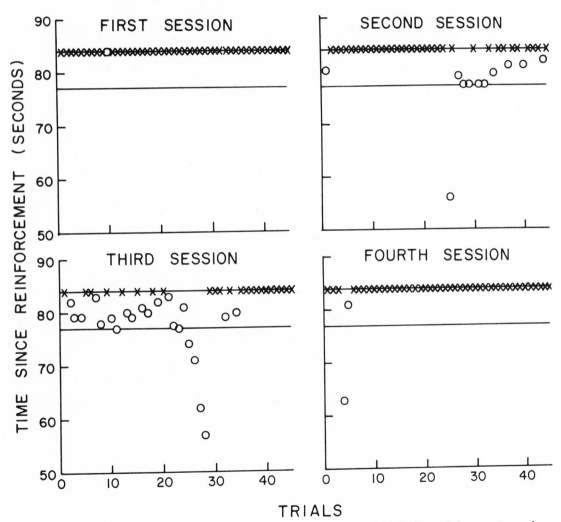

Fig. 2. The point at which reinforcement occurs measured since the end of the last reinforcement as a function of successive trials for subject No. 7. The lower horizontal line is at the time at which the shock reached maximum. The upper horizontal line is at the time at which automatic reinforcement occurred. Automatic reinforcements are indicated by a cross on the upper horizontal line. Presses of the key before this point are indicated by circles. If the circle is between the two horizontal lines, the press occurred on a lit key. If the circle is below the lower horizontal line, the press occurred on a dark key while the shock was rising. All presses, whether on lit or dark keys produced reinforcement.

out of key pecking. The first two or three presses were unobserved and could have been wing-flaps. The remaining presses were frequently observed and were all key pecks. Pecking started during the 7-sec period of constant intensity. However, by the third session several pecks were made during the period when the shock was rising. Within each session, pecking ceased to occur on the later trials. During the fourth session there were only two pecks. For this pigeon, in the fifth session, the automatic reinforcements were discontinued; the shock was held at 6 ma until a peck occurred. This caused pecking to start again, but it still decreased at the end of each session. At the ninth session, the maximum shock intensity was changed from 6 ma to 12 ma. The shock intensity rose at the same rate and took 154 sec to reach maximum, where it stayed until the key was pressed. This procedure decreased the latencies and, again, the shortest latencies for key pecking occurred at the beginning of the sessions.

The appearance of pecking and its subsequent disappearance and the increase in latencies as the session progressed were typical for those birds that pecked the key. The reappearance of pecking, after it had disappeared, when the shock was held at its maximum or when the maximum intensity was increased, was also typical. The bird that pressed the key consistently with wing-flaps started earlier than those that pecked, but pressing by this method was never as efficient, generally giving larger response latencies.

One may ask about this method of autoshaping: "How much shaping is involved?" "Does the key peck, when it appears, appear gradually?" According to Brown and Jenkins, ". . . the emergence of the key peck may be characterized as a process of autoshaping on which a direction is imposed by the species-specific tendency of the pigeon to peck the things it looks at. The bird notices the onset of the light and perhaps makes some minimal motor adjustment to it. The temporal conjunction of reinforcement with noticing leads to orienting and looking toward the key. The species-specific look-peck coupling eventually yields a peck to the trial stimulus."

If, as the above paragraph implies, adventitious reinforcement is responsible for the maintenance of orientation to the key and for the evolution of orientation into a peck, then on trials just before the first peck the pigeon's head will be close to the key at the moment of reinforcement. Assuming that "noticing" involves orientation toward the key, photographs of the pigeons at the moment of reinforcement ought to reveal whether "temporal conjunction" of noticing and reinforcement has taken place. Of the four birds photographed, three eventually pecked the key consistently. Figure 3 shows for these three pigeons, photographs of the first key peck (N), photographs of the pigeon at the moment of negative reinforcement on the trial before the first key peck (N-1), and on the trial before that (N-2). The pictures show no steady progression towards key pecking. In fact, rarely do the pigeons seem to be looking at the key, except when they actually peck it. The moment of reinforcement is not a random moment with respect to the 7 sec of keylight. That particular moment plays a critical role in Brown and Jenkins' argument. Even if noticing and reinforcement were in "temporal conjunction" at trial N-5, say, and noticing increased in frequency yet did not result in pecking as of trial N-1, then the conjunction of not noticing with reinforcement found here at trial N-1 should have *decreased* the probability of a peck at N (by the same mechanism by which the "temporal conjunction" of noticing and pecking is purported to increase the probability of a peck). In order to extend Brown and Jenkins' argument from positive to negative reinforcement, the pigeon ought to have been noticing or looking at the key on trial N-1 *at the moment of negative reinforcement.*

If we abandon the assumption that only adventitious reinforcement maintains orientation and causes pecking to evolve, the moment of negative reinforcement loses its relevancy to the question of orientation. It may well be that the pigeons in the present experiment were oriented toward the key at moments other than the particular one of the photographs. It is therefore still possible that orientation occurs, is maintained, and evolves into a peck by factors other than adventitious reinforcement.

EXPERIMENT III: POSITIVE REINFORCEMENT

Four naive pigeons were run, under condition E, Fig. 1, with no shock, but with posi-

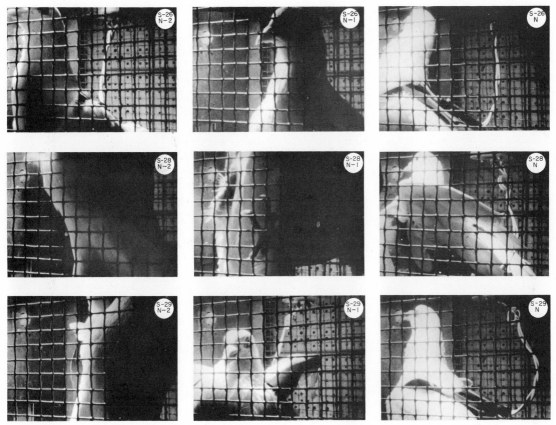

Fig. 3. Photographs of three pigeons at the moment of negative reinforcement. Photograph N shows the first peck on the key. Photograph N-1 shows the pigeons at the moment of automatic reinforcement on the trial before the first peck. Photograph N-2 shows the pigeons at the moment of automatic reinforcement, two trials before the first peck.

tive reinforcement instead. As in Exp. II, photographs were taken of the pigeons at the moment of each reinforcement, whether automatic or resulting from a peck. The purpose of this experiment was to see whether the failure to observe gradual shaping of the key peck as part of the autoshaping procedure was peculiar to negative reinforcement, and to compare negative and positive reinforcement with regard to the speed of conditioning under parallel conditions.

The first and most startling difference between positive and negative reinforcement is the relative speed of conditioning of the key peck with positive reinforcement. Despite the fact that these birds had no previous training with the food magazine, all four pecked the key within two sessions. Two of them pecked the key during the first session, after about 25 reinforcements, and the other two pecked the key after totals of 32 and 46 reinforcements.

Once pecking started, it was maintained consistently for all birds. The first peck by two birds occurred while the key was lit; the first peck of the other two birds was at a dark key. All pecks were effective. Within two or three trials after the first peck, all birds pecked almost immediately after each reinforcement. The schedule was now simply continuous reinforcement (CRF). Figure 4 shows photographs of the four pigeons at the first peck (N) and for the two reinforcements preceding the first peck (N-1 and N-2). As with negative reinforcement there is no discernible systematic progression toward the key peck except for one pigeon (S-30) that was oriented toward the key at N-2. The other pigeons do not seem to be looking at the key on the trials immediately preceding the peck. The topography of the peck itself seems to vary considerably between birds, but as far as can be judged from the pictures, pecks are not strikingly dissimilar from pecks for negative reinforcement.

EXPERIMENT IV: INCREASING MAXIMUM SHOCK INTENSITY

The procedure of this experiment (Fig. 1, Condition C) was identical to that of Exp. II (Condition B) except that the maximum intensity of shock was 3 ma for the first two sessions, 4.5 ma for the next two sessions, and 6 ma thereafter. Five naive pigeons were subjects. Three eventually pecked the key consistently and two hit the key with their wings. At 3 ma and 4.5 ma there were some stray presses but no consistent pressing from any of the birds. At 6 ma, four of the five birds pressed the key the first day. Two pecked and two flapped their wings. On the seventh session at 6 ma (the eleventh session of this procedure) after 250 trials with a total of 10 presses irregularly distributed among them, the fifth bird began to peck the key consistently. As opposed to the results of Exp. II, the

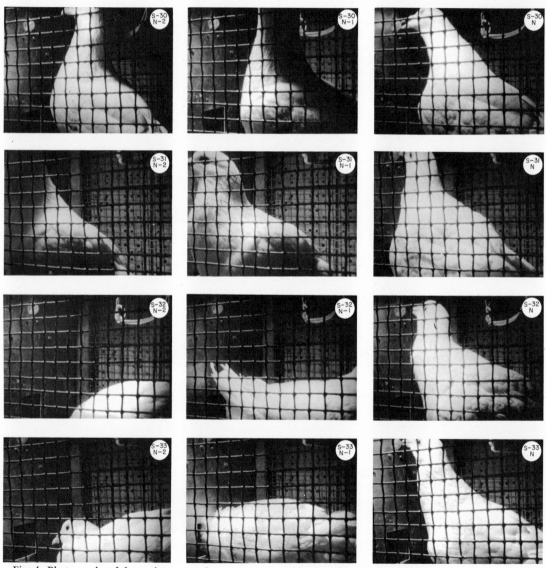

Fig. 4. Photographs of four pigeons at the moment of positive reinforcement. Photograph N shows the first peck on the key. Photograph N-1 shows the pigeons at the moment of automatic reinforcement of the trial before the first peck. Photograph N-2 shows the pigeons at the moment of automatic reinforcement, two trials before the first peck.

pecking and wing-flapping of the birds did not disappear. Therefore, there was no need to hold the shock at maximum to restore pecking and the autoshaping contingency with automatic negative reinforcement was maintained throughout.

Figure 5 portrays the performance of one bird that pecked and of one bird that hit the key with its wings. On the fourteenth day of this procedure, the extension was removed from the key. This did not affect the pecking, but greatly impaired performance when the presses were by means of wing-flaps.

EXPERIMENT V:
NO EXTENSION ON KEY

Experiment V was exactly the same as Exp. IV (Fig. 1, Condition C), except that three naive birds were run from the beginning with

no extension on the key. Without the extension, one bird pecked during the fifth session at 6-ma maximum (ninth session of the procedure) and the other two did not press the key. The pecking of the one bird faded out after a few sessions, but was restored by holding the shock at maximum and discontinuing the automatic negative reinforcements.

EXPERIMENT VI:
CONTINUOUS KEY LIGHT

Most of the birds that came to peck consistently did so at first during the 7-sec period when the keylight was on (Fig. 2 and 5 are typical). However, occasional presses before consistent pecking appeared occurred on the unlit key during the time the shock was rising. Experiment VI was conducted to see whether it was necessary to illuminate the key 7 sec be-

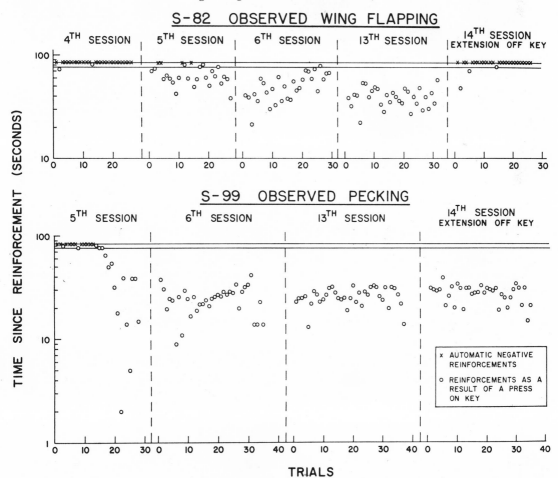

Fig. 5. The point at which reinforcement occurs measured since the end of the last reinforcement as a function of successive trials for two subjects for various sessions. See legend of Fig. 2 for interpretation.

fore negative reinforcement. In this experiment (Fig. 1, Condition D), four naive birds were run under conditions identical to Exp. IV (with the extension on the key) except that the key was continuously illuminated. With this procedure, two of the birds emitted wing-flaps and two did not press the key at all. One bird started to wing-flap when the maximum shock was at 4.5 ma (during the third session—after 55 trials) while the other did not wing-flap until the second session of 6-ma maximum shock. Once wing-flaps appeared they were sustained.

DISCUSSION

None of these experiments used enough subjects to be in any way statistically significant. They indicate what is possible, rather than what is probable. With regard to their primary purpose, however, the development of an efficient way to train pigeons to peck a key with negative reinforcement, they were at least partially successful. The method of Exp. II succeeded with four of six subjects, and the method of Exp. IV succeeded with three of five subjects in training key pecking and the other subjects pressed the key with their wings. Undoubtedly, parametric studies would reveal more efficient methods. Rachlin and Hineline (1967) found that pecking could be maintained both at faster and slower rates of increase of shock. Possibly some other rate of increase would yield faster shaping. Regarding the duration of the shock-off period after negative reinforcement, Exp. I showed that 20 sec is too short, but 120 sec may be longer than necessary. The rate of shock pulses at 1 per sec was also arbitrary. The extension on the key increased the probability of wing-flapping and pecking. However, with no extension on the key it was still possible to autoshape key pecking. A keylight that is sometimes dark seems to be necessary for generating key pecking, but wing-flapping will occur with a continuously present keylight, at least with the small number of birds in the present experiment.

Since autoshaping is a recently reported process, it is important to be specific about what sort of evidence might be required to establish that it has occurred. One possible criterion is that there be some shaping involved in the sense of a gradual approach to the key. In the present experiments, this criterion was not satisfied with negative or positive reinforcement. With positive reinforcement, Jenkins reports (personal communication) having seen repeated instances of orientation toward the key well before the first peck, and Brown (1968) had human observers report orienting responses corresponding to photocell beam interruptions in the vicinity of a key. Given the difficulty of determining exactly where a pigeon is looking from the photographs of Fig. 3 and 4, and the fact that one of the pigeons seems to be oriented toward the key, progressive approximations to the key peck in all cases of autoshaping cannot be ruled out. However, it must be noted that the present experiments, to the extent that they provide evidence at all, provide evidence against orientation to the key at the moment of negative reinforcement on trials before the first peck. If proof of such orientation is a criterion for calling a process "autoshaping", the present experiments, including Exp. III, are not autoshaping experiments.

Another possible criterion is that the occurrence of the first peck be a function of the pairing of the keylight and the reinforcement. The present experiments provide suggestive, but not conclusive, evidence that such pairing is necessary. The fact that Exp. I and VI (where keylight and shock were both present) produced no consistent pecking, is evidence that a keylight and shock are not sufficient for generating pecks. The wing-flapping of Exp. II and IV could be explained as a simple increase in probability by the shock as might occur if wing-flapping were a pain-induced aggressive response, such as those reported by Ulrich and Azrin (1962). However, the same cannot be said of pecking, since pecking did not appear in Exp. VI where the stimuli were equally painful and the keylight was present. Evidently, the briefly lit key is necessary for autoshaping of pecks with negative reinforcements. However, it is conceivable that the electric shock somehow sensitizes the pigeons so that they are more likely to peck at a briefly lit key. If this hypothesized sensitization were indeed effective, it could account for the present results without the necessity of the keylight and negative reinforcement being paired. A better test of the necessity for pairing keylight and reinforcement was made by Brown (1968) with positive reinforcement. He presented two keys, one with illumination paired with reinforcement and the other with illumination unrelated to reinforcement. The pigeon's first peck was invariably on the paired key, showing the relative power of pairing in autoshaping with positive reinforcement. Unfortunately a similar test with negative reinforcement has not yet been made.

A third possible criterion for calling a process "autoshaping" is that it provides an automatic method at least as efficient as hand shaping for generating the required behavior. This criterion was satisfied by the present experiments.

The ambient stimuli are important in determining not only whether key pressing occurs, but also the kind of key pressing obtained. Another experiment, not reported in the previous section, might be worth mentioning here in this connection. An attempt was made to take motion pictures of the movements of the pigeons in the box during the 7 sec that the keylight was on, just before negative reinforcement. In order to do this, five naive pigeons were exposed to the conditions of Exp. IV, except that when the keylight came on, a bright floodlight also came on to provide enough light for the motion pictures. With this procedure, none of the five subjects pecked the key, although four of them hit the key with their wings. The floodlights prevented the key from standing out in the total stimulus configuration in the box. Illuminating the key for a short period of time with a light contrasting significantly with its surroundings is required for key pecking to emerge with negative reinforcement. Obviously, key pecking will not occur unless something about the key draws the pigeons' attention to it. A randomly selected unmarked area of the wall equal to the area of the key would rarely be pecked by a bird being shocked, or by a hungry bird.

Despite the fact that there was no evidence of shaping in the sense of a gradual approach to the key, it is reasonable to assume that something about the key caused the pigeon to look at it before the peck. The same need not be true, however, with regard to wing-flapping. The fact that wing-flapping was obtained with the key continuously lit and with the photographic floodlights on indicates that, at first, the contact between the wing and the key could have been fortuitous. Later, however,

wing-flaps become stereotyped. Birds that developed early consistent wing-flapping did not peck the key.

Thus, behavior with a low operant level in the experimental situation is susceptible to autoshaping provided that a balance is struck between two somewhat contrary conditions:

a. The situation should be manipulated to increase the probability of the response in question, *e.g.*, by the extension on the key and by making the key distinct from its background;

b. But, in doing this, the class of behavior acting as an operant must not be broadened so extensively as to allow topographies with higher operant levels than the behavior-to-be-shaped to fall into that class.

For example, in the present experiment, wing-flapping, with a higher operant level than pecking in the experimental situation, could have the same effect on the environment as pecking (it could press the key). A still larger extension on the key would increase the probability of reinforcement from a peck, but it also would increase the probability of reinforcement from a wing-flap. Wing-flapping occurs more frequently than pecking with naive shocked pigeons, and when wing-flaps are successful they become stereotyped and interfere with the acquisition of the pecking response. So it is possible that a larger extension on the key would actually reduce the proportion of birds that would peck despite the fact that it increases the operant level of pecking. A balance must be reached, apparently, between increasing the operant level of the response to be shaped, and increasing the operant level of other, perhaps undesired, responses.

Finally, the difference between the rapid acquisition of key pecking with positive reinforcement (an average of 32 trials) and the slow acquisition of key pecking with negative reinforcement (about 90 trials in comparable cases) needs to be accounted for. A major factor, almost certainly, is the relatively high operant level of pecking in a situation where a hungry pigeon is fed *versus* the low level of pecking in a situation where a pigeon is shocked. However, another factor may be that even naive pigeons are experienced with food and with food deprivation. Also, they are experienced with making instrumental responses to obtain food (*e.g.*, hunting on the floor of their cages). It is possible that comparable experience with shock would reduce the number of trials necessary to autoshape key pecking with negative reinforcement.

REFERENCES

Azrin, N. J. A technique for delivering shock to pigeons. *Journal of the Experimental Analysis of Behavior*, 1959, **2**, 161-163. (a)

Azrin, N. J. Some notes on punishment and avoidance. *Journal of the Experimental Analysis of Behavior*, 1959, **2**, 260. (b)

Brown, P. L. Auto-shaping and observing responses (Ro) in the pigeon. *Proceedings, 76th Annual Convention, APA*, 1968, 139-140.

Brown, P. L. and Jenkins, H. M. Auto-shaping of the pigeon's key-peck. *Journal of the Experimental Analysis of Behavior*, 1968, **11**, 1-8.

Ferster, C. B. and Skinner, B. F. *Schedules of reinforcement*. New York: Appleton-Century-Crofts, 1957.

Hoffman, H. S. and Fleshler, M. Aversive control with the pigeon. *Journal of the Experimental Analysis of Behavior*, 1959, **2**, 213-218.

Rachlin, H. C. and Hineline, P. N. Training and maintenance of key-pecking in the pigeon by negative reinforcement. *Science*, 1967, **157**, 954-955.

Sidman, M. and Fletcher, F. G. A demonstration of auto-shaping with monkeys. *Journal of the Experimental Analysis of Behavior*, 1968, **11**, 307-310.

Ulrich, R. E. and Azrin, N. H. Reflexive fighting in response to aversive stimulation. *Journal of the Experimental Analysis of Behavior*, 1962, **5**, 511-520.

Received 27 December 1968.

AUTO-MAINTENANCE IN THE PIGEON: SUSTAINED PECKING DESPITE CONTINGENT NON-REINFORCEMENT[1]

David R. Williams[2] and Harriet Williams

UNIVERSITY OF PENNSYLVANIA

If a response key is regularly illuminated for several seconds before food is presented, pigeons will peck it after a moderate number of pairings; this "auto-shaping" procedure of Brown and Jenkins (1968) was explored further in the present series of four experiments. The first showed that pecking was maintained even when pecks turned off the key and prevented reinforcement (auto-maintenance); the second controlled for possible effects of generalization and stimulus change. Two other experiments explored procedures that manipulated the tendency to peck the negatively correlated key by introducing alternative response keys which had no scheduled consequences. The results indicate that pecking can be established and maintained by certain stimulus-reinforcer relationships, independent of explicit or adventitious contingencies between response and reinforcer.

Brown and Jenkins (1968) reported a method for automatically and rapidly establishing key pecking in pigeons. Although their "shaping" procedure was carried out without reference to the birds' behavior, it led uniformly to the development of key pecking. Brown and Jenkins suggested that adventitious reinforcement of key-orienting behavior, aided by a tendency for birds to peck at things they look at, might provide a full account of their findings. The consistent success of their procedure with a large number of subjects, however, suggests the operation of a more deterministic mechanism than one based primarily on adventitious reinforcement. The present experiments were carried out to explore the possibility that the auto-shaping procedure directly and actively engenders pecking.

The basic procedure of the present experiments was a variant of Brown and Jenkins' procedure in which pecks prevented reinforcement. As in their method, a response key was illuminated for several seconds before grain was presented. In the present experiment, key pecking turned off the key and blocked presentation of the reinforcer, so that pecking

actually prevented the reinforcing event. Because the effect of key pecking under this procedure was not irrelevant to reinforcement but rather reduced it, persistent responding would raise a strong presumption that key pecking can be directly maintained by variables which do not involve response-reinforcer relationships of either deliberate or accidental origin.

EXPERIMENT I

METHOD

Subjects

Thirteen naive Silver King pigeons, deprived to 80% of their free-feeding weight, served.

Apparatus

The pigeon chamber was 13 by 13 by 12 in.; one wall housed a standard three-key Lehigh Valley pigeon panel with keys which could be transilluminated by colored lights and vertical and horizontal striped patterns. The houselight and the keys used #1829 bulbs operated at 20 v dc. The keys were 8.5 in. above the floor of the compartment, and the grain hopper was centered 5 in. below the middle key.

Procedure

Upon initial placement in the experimental space, an experimentally naive bird was confronted by a raised grain hopper filled to the

[1]Dedicated to B. F. Skinner in his sixty-fifth year. This research was supported by a grant, NSF GB 5418, from the National Science Foundation. The authors are grateful to Thomas Allaway, Joseph Bernheim, and Elkan Gamzu for comments as helpful as they were astute. Reprints may be obtained from David R. Williams, Department of Psychology, University of Pennsylvania, Philadelphia, Pennsylvania 19104.

top with grain. The bird was allowed to eat for about 20 sec, after which the hopper was withdrawn. Over the course of several further presentations, which took place without reference to the bird's behavior, eating time was reduced to 4 sec. After these initial unsignalled presentations, birds were either placed directly on the negative procedure or first treated as described in Table 1, and then placed on the negative procedure.

Table 1

Number of sessions during which the procedures indicated were in force; procedures to the left were carried out first.

Bird	Hand-Shaping	Auto-Shaping	FR 1 Timeout
P-16	1	0	1
P-17	0	2	1
P-18	0	4	2

Auto-shaping: positive response contingency. Trials consisted of a 6-sec illumination of the center key, after which the key and the houselight were turned off, and the hopper was presented for 4 sec. Trials were separated by an intertrial interval averaging 30 sec, and ranging from 3 to 180 sec. Each peck on the lighted key turned off the key and the houselight, and presented the feeder directly. Intertrial pecks were recorded but had no scheduled consequences.

Auto-shaping: negative response contingency. The negative auto-shaping procedure exactly duplicated the positive auto-shaping procedure described above, except on trials where the lighted key was pecked. On those trials, the peck turned off the key, but the grain hopper was not presented. Neither the intertrial interval nor the onset of the next trial was altered by a peck; the key was simply darkened and the grain hopper was not presented. Intertrial pecks had no scheduled consequences.

Hand-shaping. After the general pretraining trials, the magazine was presented 50 additional times without warning on each of two successive days. The times between presentations were similar to the intertrial intervals in the auto-shaping procedure, but the response key was never illuminated. On the third experimental day, the key was illuminated on a trials basis, as in the auto-shaping procedure. The key remained on until the

reinforcer was presented according to the method of successive approximations described in Ferster and Skinner (1957). A total of 50 reinforcers was presented on this day.

FR 1 Timeout. Under this procedure, the key was illuminated for a 6-sec period, unless a peck occurred. If a peck occurred, the houselight and key light were turned off and the reinforcer was presented. If the key was not pecked, it was turned off and no reinforcer was presented. Intertrial intervals were the same as in the positive auto-shaping procedure.

RESULTS

Figure 1 shows results from four birds trained under auto-shaping with a negative response contingency. P-12 and P-19 received no prior training, whereas P-16 and P-17 had previously been trained on FR 1 Timeout. The ordinate of each panel represents the cumulative number of trials within each daily session on which a peck occurred, while the abscissa marks successive trials. A high slope indicated a high frequency of pecks on the negatively correlated key, and therefore a low frequency of reinforcement. Substantial responding clearly took place despite the negative correlation between pecking and reinforcement. Although P-12 did not begin pecking until 220 trials had been administered (and, therefore, 220 reinforcers presented), pecking was maintained at a remarkably high level for the next 18 days until another procedure (to be described in Exp. III) was instituted. Once pecking commenced, it persisted at a level such that only five to 20 reinforcers per day were presented out of a possible 50. P-19 began substantial pecking on the second day of training but did not maintain a high rate after Trial 150. Over the next 12 experimental sessions, pecking by this bird did not disappear but occurred only on a small percentage of the trials.

Because of prior training with a positive response contingency, P-16 and P-17 began the procedure with a high frequency of pecking. Over the first five sessions, the tendency of P-16 to peck decreased in a regular fashion. Some recovery took place after the fifth day, however, and substantial pecking continued throughout the next 15 days, waxing and waning over periods of several sessions. P-17 produced a similar overall pattern: during the

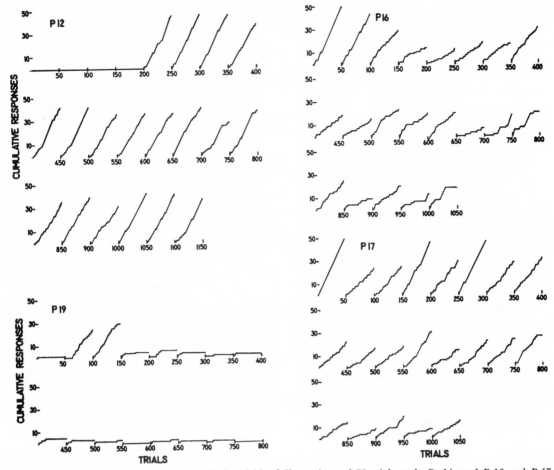

Fig. 1. Cumulative responses of four birds within daily sessions of 50 trials each. Pecking of P-16 and P-17 had previously been reinforced, while that of P-12 and P-19 had not. Throughout these sessions, each peck terminated the trial and prevented reinforcement.

first few days of the experiment the frequency of pecking declined markedly, but a series of recoveries and regressions characterized subsequent experimental days.

Results from the first 13 birds trained on auto-shaping with a negative response contingency are summarized in Fig. 2. It is evident that the procedure typically supported significant levels of responding whether or not key pecking had previously been reinforced (see Table 1 for particulars), and that the key pecking response could be established and maintained even though reinforcement was contingent on a failure to peck the key. Only one bird (P-19) regularly responded on less than 10% of the trials once pecking had begun.

The negative contingency was not wholly without effect. Two birds (P-019 and P-020) were changed from the negatively contingent

procedure to FR 1 Timeout with percentage reinforcement immediately after the sessions shown in Fig. 2. Under this new procedure, reinforcement was available on the same proportion of trials as had actually included reinforcement on the final three days with the negative contingency. Latency distributions from the last three days of contingent non-reinforcement, and from the last three sessions under percentage reinforcement, are compared in Fig. 3. Two changes are evident: under percentage reinforcements, pecking took place on a greater proportion of trials than before, and the pecks were generally of shorter latency. The longer latencies that characterized the distributions under the negative procedure were also a conspicuous feature of latency distributions from other birds trained with the negative procedure.

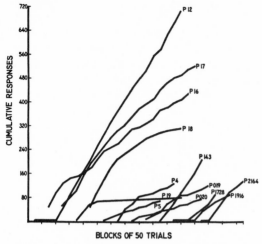

Fig. 2. Cumulative responses per session for the first 13 pigeons run with contingent non-reinforcement. Curves for the various birds are displaced along the abscissa.

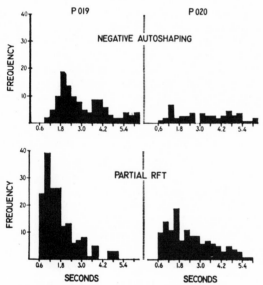

Fig. 3. Latency distributions for two birds (left and right columns) under contingent non-reinforcement and subsequent partial reinforcement. Latencies are indicated only for trials where pecks actually occurred.

EXPERIMENT II

The persistent pecking observed under the negative contingency might be attributed to generalization of feeder-oriented pecking or to reinforcement from stimulus change. A successive discrimination experiment carried out in a parametrically similar framework permitted assessment of these possibilities. On trials where the key was illuminated with the positive discriminative stimulus (S^D), a peck turned off the key and was reinforced; trials of this sort maintain feeding and feeder-oriented pecking in the situation. On trials where the other stimulus (S^Δ) was presented, no grain reinforcers could be produced but pecks did turn off the stimulus. Observation of pecking at S^Δ thus provided a means of assessing both the level of generalized pecking and the level of pecking maintained by the stimulus change itself. The main difference between discrimination training and auto-shaping with a negative contingency is that S^Δ is never paired with grain, but the negatively contingent key does receive such pairing on trials where pecks are not made. Differences between pecking S^Δ and pecking the negative key therefore indicate the effectiveness of the pairing procedure itself.

METHOD

Subjects

Six experimentally naive Silver King pigeons were deprived to 80% of their free-feeding weight.

Procedure

The apparatus and general procedures were identical to those described for Exp. I. Three birds (P-20, P-21, P-2) were trained initially by postitive auto-shaping, and three (P-7, P-8, P-9) by the hand-shaping procedure. After pecking commenced, all birds were trained on the FR 1 Timeout procedure for two days. Discrimination training was then introduced and consisted of 100 trials per day, of which half were positive and half were negative. The intertrial intervals were as in Exp. I. For birds P-7, P-8, and P-2 the discriminanda were red vs. green keys and for birds P-9, P-20, and P-21 they were horizontal vs. vertical stripes presented against a green background. On any trial the key was illuminated for 6 sec if no peck occurred. When a peck occurred, the key was turned off. On positive trials, 4-sec access to grain followed immediately, but no access to grain was provided on negative trials. The rate of trial presentation could not be influenced by pecking.

RESULTS AND DISCUSSION

Because all birds pecked on virtually every positive trial, those results are not presented. Figure 4 summarizes the data from S^Δ trials for all six birds, plotted on coordinates similar to those of Fig. 2 to facilitate comparison. Training was terminated for each bird after a session in which no pecks were made to S^Δ; those sessions are included in the figure.

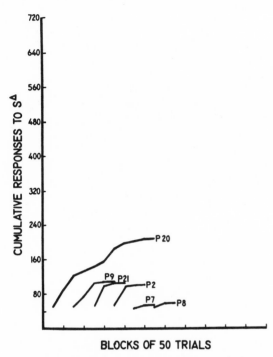

Fig. 4. Cumulative responses per session to S^Δ. Curves for the various birds are displaced along the abscissa; the scale is the same as that used in Fig. 2.

After responding on virtually all of the 50 S^Δ trials of the first session, birds with a hue discrimination ceased responding after one or two additional sessions; birds with the horizontal-vertical discrimination persisted somewhat longer, but did not show the sustained responding typical of the auto-maintenance performances shown in Fig. 2.

Since the persistent responding that characterizes auto-maintenance was not sustained by S^Δ, generalized pecking and reinforcement of pecking by stimulus change as such, seem inadequate to account for the auto-maintenance phenomenon. The main difference between S^Δ and a negatively correlated key is the pairing of the latter with grain on trials where pecks do not occur: this aspect of the procedure, then, appears to be responsible for the sustained pecking observed under the negative contingency.

The uniformly high tendency of all birds to peck S^D, even while S^Δ responses declined

and disappeared, demonstrates that some visual information from the key was received on every trial. If "noticing the key", followed by an automatic "look-peck coupling" were sufficient to sustain continued responding, pecking of S^Δ would have persisted, just as pecking to the response key did in Exp. I. It is clear that noticing a stimulus that is never followed by grain does not lead to pecking.

EXPERIMENT III

The previous experiments indicated that pairing a response key with grain sustains pecking at the key, even though the key peck prevents reinforcement. The phenomenon of auto-maintenance is both surprising and difficult to pursue because of the failure of the negative contingency to exert a strong suppressive effect. In this experiment, a procedure designed to abolish pecking on the negative key was explored. Two differently colored keys were simultaneously illuminated and darkened on every trial. The negative contingency was in force on one key, but the other key was functionally irrelevant: pecks there had no scheduled consequence or greater significance than, for example, pecks on the floor or houselight. The development of responding on the functionally irrelevant key in preference to the negative key would indicate behavioral sensitivity to some aspect of the negative contingency, and would thereby provide a means of identifying more clearly the circumstances that sustain pecking on the negative key.

METHOD

Subjects

Two experimentally naive birds, and four others shifted directly from Exp. I, were maintained at 80% of their pre-experimental weights.

Procedure

The negatively contingent procedure of Exp. I was carried out exactly as described there except that a second key was illuminated and darkened along with the negative key. The two keys were distinguished by color—red or green—and the color correlated with the negative contingency was counterbalanced across birds. The center and right key positions were used, and position of the two key colors reversed in an unpredictable manner during all sessions, so that key color and not position was correlated with the contingency.

RESULTS

Results of two birds trained from the beginning of the experiment with both negatively correlated and irrelevant keys are shown in Fig. 5. P-23 began pecking on the third day of training, and emitted substantial numbers of pecks on both the irrelevant and the negatively contingent key. The frequency of pecking the negative key declined during the next several sessions, and the significance of the key colors was reversed after a session in which the negatively contingent key was never pecked. On the day following reversal, no pecks were made on the irrelevant key (which had previously been negatively contingent) and the other key (previously irrelevant) was pecked on virtually every trial. During the next few days, however, this pattern reversed and by the end of the sessions shown, all pecking was again directed at the irrelevant key. Similar results were obtained for P-24; whenever the significance of the key color was reversed, pecking changed from the

negatively contingent to the irrelevant key during the course of several sessions.

This bird showed a marked preference for the key that was initially irrelevant, so the first shift was made after two sessions during which the irrelevant key sustained substantial pecking and no pecks were made on the negatively contingent key. It is evident that the contingency exerted stronger control than the marked bias for pecking a particular key color, and that the locus of pecking shifted from the negatively contingent to the irrelevant key after all reversals of conditions.

The irrelevant key was similarly effective in birds that had previously been trained only on the negative key. Figure 6 shows the development of control by the irrelevant key in two birds that served as subjects in Exp. I. In both cases the irrelevant key gradually gained

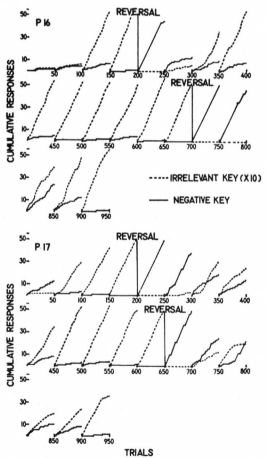

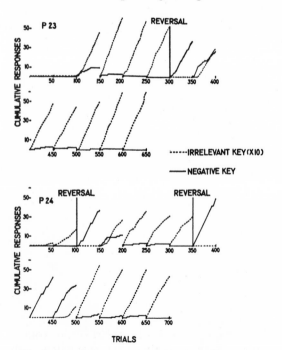

Fig. 5. Cumulative responses per trial to the negative and (on a reduced scale as indicated) the irrelevant key. The heavy vertical lines indicate when the significance of the key colors was reversed.

Fig. 6. Development of responding to the irrelevant key by two birds with a prior history of contingent non-reinforcement. The heavy vertical lines indicate where the significance of the key colors was reversed.

control during a series of sessions and, as with the naive birds, ultimately extinguished responding on the negatively contingent key. These results are typical of those of all four birds in which this procedure was carried out: in every case responding on the negatively contingent key ceased, and after reversal of stimuli, behavior shifted from the negatively contingent to the irrelevant key.

The continuing importance of the irrelevant key is suggested by the vigorous but gratuitous responding directed to it. It appears that the irrelevant key directs responding away from the negatively contingent key but does not produce an overall suppression. Direct evidence on this point was obtained by alternatively providing and omitting the irrelevant key in five-trial blocks. The negative contingency was effective only when the irrelevant key was present. When it was absent, the negative key was frequently pecked, though such responses prevented reinforcement. Apparently the irrelevant key provided a stronger stimulus for pecking than did the negative key. Even though it did not make the negative contingency effective by itself, the irrelevant key effectively demonstrated behavioral sensitivity to some aspect of the negative contingency.

EXPERIMENT IV

The only difference between the negative and irrelevant keys was the contingency scheduled on one and omitted on the other; as stimuli, both bore identical relationships to the grain reinforcer. The final experiment was carried out to determine whether intrinsic stimulus properties of the irrelevant key (as contrasted with those of other ostensibly suitable stimuli for pecking, such as the houselight) were responsible for its effectiveness, or whether the temporal relationship between the irrelevant key and the reinforcer was critical. In this experiment, a continuously illuminated but irrelevant key was substituted for the intermittent irrelevant key of Exp. III. As in the previous experiment, two keys were available on every trial, one scheduled with the negative contingency, the other with no contingency at all. The irrelevant key was also present between trials; it was darkened only during feeder presentations, and its location among the three key positions was changed at the start of each trial. If the mere availability of an irrelevant key is sufficient to support control by the negative contingency, a continuous key should substitute effectively for an intermittent one. However, if temporal relations between the irrelevant key and the reinforcer are important, the continuous key would not be an effective substitute. To assess the relative effectiveness of the continuous and intermittent irrelevant keys, additional birds received both continuous and intermittent irrelevant keys, while other birds were exposed only to the continuous key.

METHOD

Subjects

Four experimentally naive birds, and four others shifted directly from Exp. I, were maintained at 80% of their pre-experimental weight.

Procedure

The negatively contingent procedure of Exp. I was carried out exactly as described there with the addition of one or two other keys, distinguished by color from each other and from the negative key. For P-1916, P-2164, P-1909, and P-2096, a second key with no scheduled consequences was continuously illuminated except during feeder presentations. The position of this second key and the position of the negatively contingent key shifted at the start of each trial (defined by the presentation of the negatively contingent key). Both keys were distinctively colored and colors were counterbalanced for the four subjects. All three possible key locations were used, with two of the three being illuminated on any trial until a peck occurred or the reinforcer was presented. The negative key was darkened when pecked, but the continuous key did not go out. For P-1543, P-1728, P-1446, and P-1649, the procedure was exactly the same except that an intermittent irrelevant key was also present, and operated as in Exp. III. The intermittent irrelevant key had a third distinctive color, which was the same for all four birds, but the colors of the continuous and negative keys were counterbalanced. The location of all three key colors was shifted at the start of every trial, and following a peck or a reinforcement, the continuous key stayed in the same place until the onset of the next trial.

RESULTS

The two left panels (A and B) of Fig. 7 show responding over the course of the entire experiment for two birds trained first with the negative contingency alone; the right panels (C and D) show performance of two birds trained with a continuous key present from the start of the experiment. The two birds with only a continuous irrelevant key responded on the negative key for more than 30 sessions, and pecked far less on the continuous irrelevant key (Panels A and C). As in Exp. III, pecking on the negative key was controlled by the parallel presentation of an intermittent irrelevant key. Data from the other birds were entirely consistent with the results shown here: an irrelevant key presented along with the negative key enabled the contingency to gain control, but an irrelevant key that was continuously available did not.

The continuous key did not go entirely unpecked; P-1649, in fact, pecked more frequently on the continuous than on the intermittent key for the first four days after it was introduced. The timing of the pecks on the continuous key is of interest: not once during the experiment did a peck occur on the continuous key while the negatively correlated key was illuminated. Pecking was directed to the continuous key solely during the intertrial interval when it was the only key available.

Following the experiment proper, six birds were given additional training with the continuous key alone. The procedure was exactly as before except that the negative and intermittent irrelevant keys were never turned on. Because the location of the continuous key shifted when the trial began, it continued to signal the forthcoming presentation of grain; now, however, it was the only event to do so. Data from these sessions are shown to the right of the solid bars in Fig. 7. In all, four of the six birds trained under this procedure developed substantial pecking on the continuous key. Although pecking occurred throughout

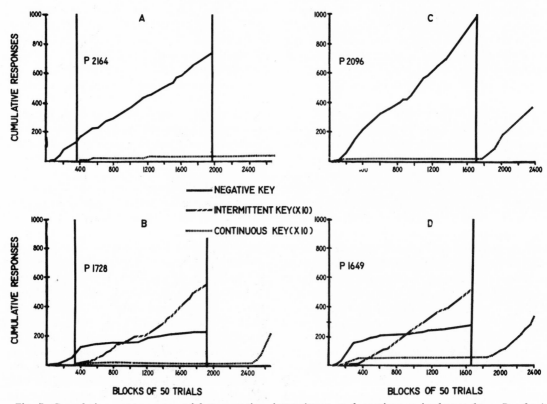

Fig. 7. Cumulative responses per trial to negative, intermittent, and continuous irrelevant keys. Panels A and B show cases where birds were trained first on the negative key only. Panels B and D show cases where three keys were present during the main part of the experiment. The heavy vertical lines within panels indicate changes in the variety of keys presented on each trial.

the session, it was concentrated in the 6 sec following a shift in the location of the key, when the presentation of grain was imminent.

The continuous key was not functionally similar to the intermittent key: it did not compete successfully with the negative key, nor was it pecked as often as the intermittent irrelevant key. The ineffectiveness of the continuous key is clearly consistent with the failure of other stimulus alternatives, such as the houselight, to substitute in function for the intermittent irrelevant key. If any of the effects reported in Exp. I and III were related to special characteristics of illuminated keys, the findings of those experiments would presumably have been disturbed by the presence of a continuously available key of similar appearance. The inability of the continuous key to compete with the negative key is particularly significant in light of the fact that responding finally developed, even in birds for which no key peck had ever been reinforced, when the continuous key was ineffective because it was a weaker stimulus for pecking, not because it was a wholly inadequate one. It could not have been weaker than the negative key because of extinction of pecking during the intertrial interval: due to the negative contingency, responses on the continuous key were inevitably more closely related to reinforcement than those on the negative key. On the other hand, the relative effectiveness of the negative key, compared to the continuous key, would seem also to be due to its association with the reinforcer: pairing of the negative key and the reinforcer established a relatively strong and directed tendency to peck on the negative key. Finally, the success of the intermittent irrelevant key in competing with the negative key would appear to depend in part on the fact that it bore the same stimulus-reinforcer relationship as the negative key, and to some consequence of the fact that reinforcement was never withheld in its presence.

GENERAL DISCUSSION

Successful auto-maintenance—persistent, directed key pecking despite contingent nonreward—does not seem to be a natural implication of either operant or respondent principles. Because actual pecking of the negative key produces nonreinforcement, it cannot be directly maintained by adventitious rela-

tionships. If it is supposed that unobserved behaviors preceding the actual striking of the key are adventitiously maintained, then either (a) one must assume that these adventitiously maintained precursors are inflexibly linked to pecking and account for why they are not extinguished or replaced by precursors for other responses, or (b) one must suppose that the precursors do not invariably lead to pecking but can precede other behaviors as well. If the latter assumption is made, then it is difficult to see why, by operant principles, the precursors do not become closely linked to some other behavior because of the consistent reinforcement such linkage would produce. Even if attention—heightened and directed by adventitious reinforcement and giving rise to behavior through a look-peck coupling—is assumed to be responsible for the initial pecks (Brown and Jenkins), it is difficult to see why the continual extinction of a specific response component would not lead to an operant shift in attention and inconsequential responding (when the negative key comes on, look at the continuous key and peck it). It is, for example, very difficult to see how the continuous key could ultimately control pecking but not compete with the negative key. It seems clear that stimulus-reinforcer relationships, and not only response-reinforcer interactions, play a special role in this phenomenon. Such a conclusion, of course, takes the phenomenon out of reach of a standard operant analysis, where the influence of stimuli depends on their discriminative function with regard to experimental contingencies.

Similarities to the respondent domain are easy to recognize: indeed, the auto-maintenance procedure is formally identical to the "omission training" procedure of Sheffield (1965) except that a key peck substitutes for a saliva drop. In the present case, the response at issue is topographically similar to the response made to food. However, even if one ignores the usual application of respondent analyses to autonomic rather than skeletal behavior, the directed quality of the induced pecking does not follow naturally from respondent principles (see also Brown and Jenkins, 1968). It is unclear, for example, why pecking would be directed at the key rather than the feeder, or indeed why it would be directed anywhere at all. Although respondent laws (which deal with laws of stimulus-reinforcer pairings) are no doubt pertinent to the present phenomenon, a detailed account of this phenomenon would seem to demand a serious augmentation of respondent principles to account for the directed quality of the response.

The most direct empirical precedent for the present phenomena is provided by the work of Breland and Breland (1961), who found, in several species, that response patterns that were related to a reinforcer could "drift" into a situation even though they delayed and interfered with actual production of the reinforcer. As in the present case, such behaviors were intrusive, counterproductive, and uncontrolled by their contingencies. In addition, it has been shown that pigeons trained to peck at other pigeons develop far more elaborate patterns of "aggressive" behavior than the actual contingency demands; the behavior is sometimes so vigorous that it continues into the period when reinforcement is available (Skinner, 1959; Reynolds, Catania, and Skinner, 1963; Azrin and Hutchinson, 1967). Similar effects have been reported in rats (Ulrich, Johnston, Richardson, and Wolff, 1963). When rats' running is reinforced, the speed at which they run is governed directly by the magnitude of the reinforcer, and fast running develops whether or not it produces more rapid reinforcement (Williams, 1966). These examples make it clear that contingencies of reinforcement alone do not determine when or how strongly some behaviors occur, even if the behaviors appear to be skeletal or "voluntary". As an instance of such direct control, the present phenomenon does not appear to be an isolated curiosity.

The place of this phenomenon in the general operant framework deserves explicit consideration. While it has always been recognized that many aspects of experiments, such as deprivation or physical details of the experimental space, influence the "operant level" of some responses, it now appears that many other variables, such as stimulus-reinforcer relationships, can also have an important influence on the unreinforced level of occurrence of some responses. That the stimulus-reinforcer pairing overrode opposing effects of differential reinforcement indicates that the effect was a powerful one, and demonstrates that a high level of responding does not imply the operation of explicit or even adventitious reinforcement. This point should be taken into careful account when effects of reinforcing contingencies *per se* are under investigation (see, for example, Herrnstein, 1966).

To relate the present work to the concept of "operant level" furnishes a context but does not provide an account. In further work, the concept of "arbitrariness", which is so frequently claimed for operants, will require close attention: is the action of reinforcement—direct or contingent—different when a response is "naturally" in the organism's repertory, or when it bears a special relationship to the reinforcer? More broadly, consideration should be given to ascertaining how frequently direct, as opposed to contingent, influences of reinforcers enter into the determination of "skeletal" or "voluntary" behavior in natural environments.

REFERENCES

Azrin, N. H. and Hutchinson, R. R. Conditioning of the aggressive behavior of pigeons by a fixed-interval schedule of reinforcement. *Journal of the Experimental Analysis of Behavior*, 1967, **10**, 395-402.

Breland, K. and Breland, M. The misbehavior of organisms. *American Psychologist*, 1961, **16**, 681-684.

Brown, P. L. and Jenkins, H. M. Auto-shaping of the pigeons's key-peck. *Journal of the Experimental Analysis of Behavior*, 1968, 11, 1-8.

Ferster, C. B. and Skinner, B. F. *Schedules of reinforcement.* New York: Appleton-Century-Crofts, 1957.

Herrnstein, R. J. Superstition: a corollary of the principles of operant conditioning. In W. K. Honig (Ed.), *Operant behavior: areas of research and application.* New York: Appleton-Century-Crofts, 1966. Pp. 33-51.

Reynolds, G. S., Catania, A. C., and Skinner, B. F. Conditioned and unconditioned aggression in pigeons. *Journal of the Experimental Analysis of Behavior*, 1963, **6**, 73-74.

Sheffield, F. D. Relation between classical conditioning and instrumental learning. In W. F. Prokasy (Ed.), *Classical conditioning.* New York: Appleton-Century-Crofts, 1965. Pp. 302-322.

Skinner, B. F. An experimental analysis of certain emotions. *Journal of the Experimental Analysis of Behavior*, 1959, **2**, 264. (Abstract).

Ulrich, R., Johnston, M., Richardson, J., and Wolff, P. The operant conditioning of fighting behavior in rats. *Psychology Records*, 1963, **13**, 465-470.

Williams, D. R. Relation between response amplitude and reinforcement. *Journal of Experimental Psychology*, 1966, **71**, 634-641.

Received 28 August 1968.

ATTENTION AND GENERALIZATION DURING A CONDITIONAL DISCRIMINATION[1]

G. S. Reynolds and A. J. Limpo

UNIVERSITY OF CALIFORNIA, SAN DIEGO

A conditional discrimination was established and analyzed, using four pigeons. The discrimination was among four compound stimuli projected on the response key—a white circle or triangle on a red or green background—during two conditions of illumination in the chamber, no illumination or flashing illumination. The two lighting conditions indicated whether the stimuli on the key containing triangles or those containing red would be the occasion for reinforcement. After the discrimination formed, generalization to intermediate and extreme values of the conditional stimulus and the attention of the birds to separate aspects of the stimulus on the key under each of the conditional stimuli were studied. All subjects generalized across values of the conditional stimulus, the lighting of the chamber. But subjects differed in the manner in which they treated the compound stimuli: two tended to attend to one or the other aspect of the stimulus on the key depending on the conditional stimulus, and two offered no evidence of such selective attention. Thus, the differential control of responding by the conditional stimuli cannot be attributed to a shift in attention between the figure and ground aspects of the compound stimuli.

Attention is a functional concept, defined in terms of the correlation between changes in the environment and in behavior. An organism attends to a feature of its environment if changes in the feature bring about changes in behavior; it does not attend to a feature of the environment if changes in the feature do not bring about changes in behavior. Attention is closely related to stimulus control and to generalization. An organism is said to attend to those stimuli or aspects of stimuli that control its behavior. A non-constant gradient of generalization implies attention to at least one of the environmental aspects that were changed in measuring the gradient, and a flat, constant gradient implies inattention to all of the changed aspects. For example, Jenkins and Harrison (1960) showed that the naive pigeon may be initially inattentive to its auditory environment (a flat gradient) but attentive (a non-flat gradient) after some experience, in that case differential reinforcement, with auditory stimuli.

Selective attention occurs when not all aspects of a stimulus are in control of behavior. It is clear that reinforcement in the presence of a stimulus with more than one independently manipulatable aspect does not guarantee that all aspects of the stimulus will individually come to control the organism's behavior (e.g., Reynolds, 1961). But attention to more than one aspect of a stimulus may occur, as when variation of two aspects of a stimulus produces a greater decrement in responding than does variation of only one aspect (e.g., Butter, 1963). What it is that directs and sustains the organism's attention has been little studied.

The present study attempted to control attention to either the figure or the ground of a series of stimuli by means of two additional, conditional stimuli. These two stimuli establish a conditional discrimination by setting the occasions on which either the figure or the ground of the series of stimuli is consistently associated with reinforcement or extinction. Further, this study attempted to analyze the function of the conditional stimulus by examining generalization to various values of it and to demonstrate directly that the control by the conditional stimuli cannot in this case be accounted for by a shift in the pigeons' attention between the figure and ground of

[1]Dedicated to B. F. Skinner in his sixty-fifth year. Reprints may be obtained from G. S. Reynolds, Department of Psychology, University of California, San Diego, P.O. Box 109, La Jolla, California 92037. This research was supported by NSF Grants GB-2541, GB-5064, and GB-6821 to the University of Chicago and to UCSD.

the series of stimuli depending on the value of the conditional stimulus.

METHOD

Subjects

Four adult male White Carneaux pigeons were maintained at 80% of their free-feeding weights. Each bird had several months of experience with the present procedure, except that auditory conditional stimuli were used and no tests of attention were made.

Apparatus

A standard chamber for conditioning the pigeon's operant behavior contained one key that could be operated by an effective force of 15 g. Reinforcement consisted of 3.5-sec access to mixed grain in a magazine located beneath the key. The key could be illuminated from behind with a white triangle, white circle, red background, or green background, either separately or in any combination. The houselight could be flashed at rates of 0.2, 0.5, 1.0, 2.0, 3.0 flashes per sec or not illuminated at all. Each flash was about 50 msec in duration. Standard scheduling and recording apparatus were located in a separate room.

Procedure

The procedure consisted of three parts: training on the conditional discrimination, measurement of generalization to intermediate and extreme values of the conditional stimulus, and the assessment of the direction of attention under the two values of the conditional stimulus used in training.

Formation of the discrimination. The birds were transferred directly from an auditory conditional discrimination to the following discrimination. They were exposed in each session to a total of eight stimuli consisting of four stimuli presented on the key, and for each stimulus on the key either no illumination of the houselight or flashes of the houselight at a rate of 2 per sec (the conditional stimulus). The stimuli on the key were the white triangle on a red or green background and the white circle on a red or green background. Each stimulus was presented for 2 min at a time, and there were eight presentations of each stimulus in a session, to a total session duration of 128 min. The stimuli were presented in three different orders from session

to session, to a total of 15 sessions, when an adequate discrimination had formed.

Reinforcement was on a VI 1-min schedule in the presence of stimuli containing the triangle when the houselight was flashing and in the presence of stimuli containing red if the chamber were dark. Thus, the stimuli-reinforcement correlations called for the pigeon to peck at the triangle on either a red or green background in the presence of flashing light and at the red background with either the triangle or circle as figure when the box was dark.

Measurement of generalization. In extinction, during each of two successive sessions the four stimuli on the key were each presented twice for 1 min each in the presence of each of the following conditions of lighting in the chamber: no light or flashing light at the original rate of 2 per sec; flashing light at the faster rate of 3 per sec; or flashing light at the rates of 0.2, 0.5, or 1.0 per sec. Each combination of light condition (six) and stimulus on the key (four) was presented twice on each day. The order of presentation was irregular with respect to both the light conditions and the key stimuli, except that no combination was repeated the second time until all had been presented once. A different irregular sequence was used in each session. The data consisted of the rates of responding in the presence of each of the 24 stimuli based on a total of 4 min of exposure to each stimulus.

Assessment of attention. After several sessions of reinforcement on the original procedure, interest turned to the specific aspect of the stimuli on the key that controlled the birds' behavior under the two conditional stimuli. The separate aspects of each stimulus, the triangle or circle on dark (unilluminated) backgrounds and the red and green backgrounds without figures, were presented singly with either no light in the chamber or with the light flashing at 2 per sec. Each stimulus was presented for 1 min twice during the session in a different irregular order each time, and the total number of responses in the presence of each was counted. No responses were reinforced.

RESULTS AND DISCUSSION

Formation of the discrimination. The conditional discrimination arranged for by the procedure developed more rapidly than one reported earlier (Reynolds, 1961), probably because of the experience of these subjects with the stimuli on the key, but the results are similar. After 15 sessions, all four pigeons responded predominantly in the presence of the triangle on a red or green background when the houselight was flashing (at 2 per sec) and predominantly in the presence of stimuli containing a red background with either a triangle or circle as figure when there was no light in the chamber. Thus, the birds responded to the triangle on the red background under both conditions, they responded little to the circle on a green background in either condition, and they responded to the circle on the red background and the triangle on the green background predominantly during the conditional stimulus that set the occasion for reinforcement in their presence.

Measurement of generalization. This portion of the experiment studied responding in extinction in the presence of each stimulus on the key during presentation of various values of the conditional stimulus covering a range from no illumination to three flashes of the houselight per second. Figure 1 shows, in a separate panel for each bird, the number of responses per minute emitted in the presence of each stimulus on the key as a function of a logarithmic scale of the rate of flashing of the houselight in the chamber. The triangles and circles denote responding in the presence of stimuli containing those figures, and filled and unfilled points denote responding in the presence of stimuli with red or green backgrounds, respectively. Dotted lines connect the data at two and at three flashes per second, a rate of flashing greater than that used in training.

Notice first that despite rates of responding around 40 per min by some pigeons in the presence of stimuli previously associated with extinction, the discrimination of all four pigeons is preserved in extinction. When there was no illumination in the chamber (N in the figure), the rate of responding was consistently highest in the presence of stimuli containing a red background (filled points), and when the light was flashing at 2 per sec, the rate of responding was consistently highest in the presence of stimuli containing a triangle (triangles).

While there are individual differences between pigeons, there is also evidence of generalization to intermediate values of the conditional stimulus. This is most evident for the two stimuli that had been differently associated with reinforcement under the two values of the conditional stimulus. As the rate of flashing increased toward 2 per sec, all four birds responded less in the presence of the circle on a red background (filled circles) and more in the presence of the triangle on a green background (unfilled triangles) than they did under conditions of no illumination, although the changes in these curves are by no means consistently monotonic. Each bird found a point of approximate response equality in the vicinity of 0.5 flashes per sec.

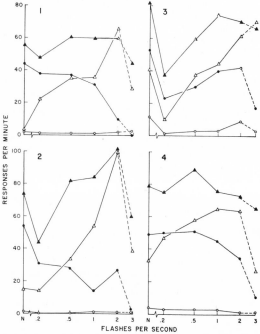

Fig. 1. Gradients of generalization for four pigeons. The number of responses per minute in extinction in the presence of each stimulus on the key as a function of a logarithmic scale of the rate of flashing of the houselight in the chamber. N indicates darkness. Triangles and circles in the graphs indicate that the stimulus on the key contained a triangle or a circle; filled points or unfilled points, that the stimulus on the key had a red or green background.

There is also an indication of generalization in the rates of responding obtained in the presence of a triangle on a red background, which had been consistently associated with reinforcement both in the presence of no illumination and two flashes of the houselight per second. All birds responded less frequently at 0.2 flashes per sec than at no illumination and all responded less frequently at 3.0 flashes per sec than at 2.0 flashes per sec. However, only one bird (2) responded less frequently at 1 than at 2 flashes per sec.

There are, on the contrary, no indications in these data of enhanced responding in the presence of the circle on green, the stimulus consistently associated with extinction, for either intermediate or extreme values of the conditional stimulus. Birds 1, 2, and 4 did not respond more in the presence of conditional stimuli not previously used in training, but since their overall tendency to peck at the circle on green was so low, it is impossible to say whether or not any of these values of the conditional stimulus control a lower rate of responding. Bird 3, however, exhibited a substantial rate of responding both with no illumination and with 2 flashes per sec. For this bird, the rates controlled by the intermediate values and the extreme value of the conditional stimulus are clearly lower. This effect is also seen in the decrease in the responding of all four birds in the presence of the circle on red when the conditional stimulus was changed from 2 to 3 flashes per sec.

There was no indication either during training or during the measurement of generalization of a correlation between responses and individual flashes of the light. Although flashing light clearly served as a stimulus in this experiment, there was no tendency to respond or not respond predominantly during or just after individual flashes. Increases and decreases in the number of individual flashes cannot therefore be appealed to in accounting for these data.

These data demonstrate that responding in the presence of the stimuli on the key was itself under the control of the conditional stimulus. The orderly shift from a pattern of responding in the presence of no illumination, marked by more responding to stimuli containing a red background, to a pattern of responding in the presence of 2 flashes per sec, marked by more responding to stimuli containing triangles, suggests that the pigeons' attention may have been shifted from the color of the background to the character of the figure by the change in the value of the conditional stimulus. This possibility is considered directly in the next part of the experiment.

First, however, two additional features of these results warrant brief discussion.

The joint control of responding by the stimulus on the key and the conditional stimulus is particularly revealed by the behavior in the presence of the triangle on the red background, the one stimulus consistently associated with reinforcement under each value of the conditional stimulus during training. The birds tended to respond less in the presence of values of the conditional stimulus which had not been explicitly associated with reinforcement during training. The presence of this generalization strengthens the conclusion that the conditional stimulus was effective in controlling responding jointly with the stimulus presented on the key.

These gradients do not reveal a release from inhibitory properties of extinction when the conditional stimulus is changed from values explicitly associated with extinction during training. When the rate of responding is sufficiently high for a decrease in responding to be detected, the presentation of intermediate or extreme values of the conditional stimulus invariably resulted in a decrease, rather than an increase, in the rate of responding. This occurred with intermediate values of the conditional stimulus for Pigeon 3 in the presence of a circle on a green background and for 3 flashes per sec for all birds in the presence of the circle on a red background. This effect can be interpreted as a decrease in the amount of induction to these stimuli when the conditional stimulus is changed. The present data therefore strengthen the notion that responding in extinction may be modulated up and down by changes in the amount of induction from responding reinforced in the presence of other stimuli (*cf.*, Reynolds, 1968).

Assessment of attention. This part of the experiment was undertaken in order to examine directly the direction of the pigeons' attention in the presence of each of the conditional stimuli used during training. Figure 2 shows, in a separate panel for each bird, the total number of responses emitted in the presence of each of the separate, singly presented aspects of the stimuli on the key (the triangle, the circle, red background or green background) in the presence of the original two conditional stimuli: no light in the chamber (unfilled bars) and two flashes of the houselight per second (filled bars).

If the conditional stimulus controls a simple shift in attention from the color of the background under conditions of no illumination to the character of the figure under conditions of 2 flashes per sec of the houselight, a number of results should be obtained. Figure 2 shows that these expectations are not fulfilled either consistently or on all occasions, nor are the differences in the tendencies to respond as great as found previously in cases of clearly selective attention (Reynolds, 1961). The expectations are stated and evaluated in the following paragraphs.

The triangle should certainly occasion more responses under the flashing condition (filled bars) than in the dark (unfilled bars) because the triangle was always the occasion for reinforcement under the flashing condition. Figure 2 shows that this occurred only with Birds 2 and 3, while the opposite occurred with Birds 1 and 4.

The red key should certainly occasion more responses in the dark (unfilled bars) than in the flashing condition (filled bars) because the red stimulus was always the occasion for reinforcement in the dark. Figure 2 shows that this occurred only with Bird 3, while the opposite occurred with Birds 1 and 4 and the number of responses in the two conditions were equal for Bird 2.

The circle might also be expected to occasion more responses in the dark (unfilled bars) than in the flashing condition (filled bars) because the circle was never the occasion for reinforcement under the flashing condition. Figure 2 shows, again, that this occurred with Birds 2, 3, and 4, while the opposite occurred for Bird 1, which did not respond at all in the dark.

Finally, the green stimulus might also be expected to occasion more responses under the flashing condition (filled bars) than in the dark (unfilled bars) because the green stimulus was never the occasion for reinforcement in the dark. Figure 2 shows that this occurred with Birds 1, 2, and 3, while the opposite occurred with Bird 4.

In these comparisons, the numbers of responses differ in the expected direction nine times, in the opposite direction six times, and there is one tie. When each bird is considered individually, however, Birds 2 and 3 (except for the tie of Bird 2) fulfill all four expectations, while Birds 1 and 4 do not.

A further analysis of these data casts additional doubt on an interpretation of the generalization gradients simply in terms of a shift in attention. Since the color red on the key was consistently associated with reinforcement in the dark condition (unfilled bars), the red key should occasion more responses than the green key. Figure 2 shows that while this was true for Birds 1, 2, and 4, Bird 3 pecked more on green. Moreover, Bird 4 pecked more frequently on the forms, which had not been consistently associated with reinforcement in the dark. In the flashing condition (filled bars), since the triangular form is consistently associated with reinforcement, the triangle should occasion more responses than the circle. Figure 2 shows that while this was true for Birds 2, 3, and 4, all four birds pecked more frequently on the colored keys not consistently associated with reinforcement.

These surprisingly high response rates on the colored stimuli, especially the green, argue against an interpretation on the basis of shifts in selective attention. Nevertheless, the responding on the green stimulus did not, in

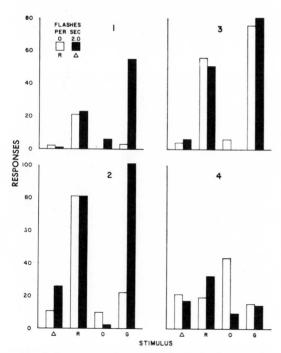

Fig. 2. Assessment of attention for four pigeons. The total number of responses in the presence of each of the separate aspects of the stimulus on the key is shown for two conditions of illumination of the chamber: no illumination (unfilled bars) and flashing light (filled bars).

six of the eight cases, obscure relationships predicted by selective attention: green occasions more responses than red in the dark, and the triangle occasions more than the circle in the flashing light.

Note also that Bird 4, the exception to complete color predominance, responded more to forms in the dark and to red in the flashing light, both of which were inappropriate to the overall reinforcement conditions. Nevertheless, this bird displayed some evidence of shifts in attention.

The data presented earlier on generalization demonstrated control over responding in the presence of the compound stimuli on the key by the conditional stimulus. The question to be raised now concerns the way in which that control is exercised.

It is clear from the present data that a single answer may not suffice for all four birds. This should not be surprising, because there have been demonstrations (*e.g.*, Reynolds, 1961) that attention may be capriciously directed. Although the conditional stimuli and their correlations with reinforcement would seem to have given the bird added reason for coming selectively under the control of particular aspects of the stimuli on the key, the analysis of Fig. 2 shows that radical shifts in attention did not occur when the conditional stimulus was changed. There is some evidence that Birds 2 and 3 tended to change the aspect of the stimuli on the key to which they attended in the presence of the conditional stimuli, but the magnitude of the shift, as measured by the differences in the number of responses, was not large. The attentional shifts observed in Birds 2 and 3 appear to be confined to either the figural stimuli or to the ground stimuli. However, both of these birds responded more frequently to the colors under conditions in which form was consistently associated with reinforcement. Birds 1 and 4 show no consistent evidence of a shift in attention.

This procedure established control of responding to compound stimuli by conditional stimuli as evidenced by the measurements of generalization to various values of the conditional stimulus. In addition, it may have been successful in controlling the attention of at least some of the subjects to some extent. It is not, however, an attention-controlling procedure of great power; the shifts in attention were not large and did not occur significantly in at least two subjects.

Perhaps a combination of extended training, different stimuli, and more sensitive procedures for testing attention would result in consistent and sizeable shifts in selective attention. However, the present data show that orderly generalization gradients and control by compound stimuli can be produced without consistent shifts in attention between the figure and ground aspects of compound stimuli.

The suprising lack of attentional shift in these pigeons contrasts with the apparent ease of human observers to shift attention between figure and ground in response to conditional stimuli.

REFERENCES

Butter, C. M. Stimulus generalization along one or two dimensions in pigeons. *Journal of Experimental Psychology*, 1963, **65**, 339-346.

Jenkins, H. M. and Harrison, R. H. Effect of discrimination training on auditory generalization. *Journal of Experimental Psychology*, 1960, **59**, 246-253.

Reynolds, G. S. Attention in the pigeon. *Journal of the Experimental Analysis of Behavior*, 1961, **4**, 203-208.

Reynolds, G. S. Induction, contrast, and resistance to extinction. *Journal of the Experimental Analysis of Behavior*, 1968, **11**, 453-457.

Received 13 December 1967.

CONTROL OF RESPONDING BY THE LOCATION OF AN AUDITORY STIMULUS: ROLE OF RISE TIME OF THE STIMULUS[1]

J. M. Harrison and M. D. Beecher

BOSTON UNIVERSITY

The control of responding by the location of tone bursts of 0.2- or 50-msec rise time was investigated in three albino rats. The apparatus consisted of an enclosure with two levers, two loudspeakers (in different locations), and a dipper feeder. The animal was exposed to tone bursts from either one or the other of the two speakers, and the speaker through which the tone bursts were delivered on any particular trial alternated in an irregular manner. Responses on one lever were reinforced with food in the presence of tone bursts from one speaker; responses on the second lever were reinforced with food in the presence of tone bursts from the second speaker. Responding came under the control of the location of 4-kHz tone bursts of 0.2-msec rise time within the first session. At this rise time, animals maintained a stable level of correct responding of greater than 95%. When the rise time was increased to 50 msec the percentage of correct responding fell to an average of 80 to 85%. It was concluded that location of an auditory stimulus is a powerful controller of responding in rats and that the degree of control is dependent upon rise time.

The location of a source of sound in the azimuth of an animal can be used to control responding of that animal (Neff, Fisher, Diamond, and Yela, 1965). Control of responding in the case of sounds of short duration depends upon similarities and differences between the sounds reaching the two ears (Neff, 1962). This implies that at one or more sites in the nervous system there are nerve cells innervated by the cochlea of both sides. Several anatomical considerations, summarized below, suggest that the first site at which this occurs is the superior olivary complex.

In mammals, the central end of the acoustic nerve terminates in the cochlear nucleus. Axons arising from nerve cells in the cochlear nucleus terminate (in part) in the three major nuclei of the superior olivary complex (Harrison and Irving, 1964; Harrison and Irving, 1966a; Harrison and Irving, 1966b; Warr, 1966). The lateral superior olivary nucleus (a nucleus of the complex) receives direct connections from the cochlear nucleus of the same side and receives indirect connections from the contralateral cochlear nucleus via the medial nucleus of the trapezoid body (a second nucleus of the complex) (Harrison and Irving, 1966a; Harrison and Warr, 1962; Warr, 1966). Thus, the lateral superior olivary nucleus is innervated by the cochlea of both sides, one necessary condition for this nucleus to be involved in control of responding by the location of a sound. Recent physiological work has further strengthened the suggestion that this nucleus may be involved in localization of sounds by showing that nerve cells of the nucleus are fired by sound to the ipsilateral ear and inhibited by sound to the contralateral ear (Boudreau and Tsuchitani, 1968).

Comparative anatomical studies of the mammalian superior olivary complex have shown that in echolocating mammals (Microchiroptera, Griffin, 1958; Cetacea, Turner and Norris, 1966) the lateral superior olivary nucleus is exceedingly large (Harrison and Irving, 1966c; Irving and Harrison, 1967). This finding supports the suggestion that the lateral superior olive may be involved in the control of responding by the location of a sound.

Other characteristics of the structure of the superior olivary complex suggest that control of responding by location of sounds may be a dominant attribute of audition. The lateral superior olive and the medial nucleus of the trapezoid body taken together comprise a substantial portion of the superior olivary complex. Thus, a substantial portion of the

[1]This work is dedicated to B. F. Skinner, with great admiration, in his sixty-fifth year. The research was supported in part by NSF grant GB 7617 and in part by Boston University Graduate School. We thank Paul Downey for help with the experiment. Reprints may be obtained from J. M. Harrison, Dept. of Psychology, Boston University, Boston, Massachusetts 02215.

complex is concerned with the bilateral innervation of the nerve cells of the lateral superior
olive. The involvement of so much of the
auditory system, at this level, to bilateral
innervation suggests that location may be a
dominant attribute of hearing.

On the basis of these considerations, preliminary behavioral experiments were carried
out to determine whether the location of a
sound was a potent discriminative stimulus.
The animal's head was not fixed in position
relative to the stimuli. The auditory system
has evolved in animals that are free to move
in their respective environments. This free
movement means that all possible relations
will exist between the positions of the animal's
head and the sounds, and it is under these
conditions that a localization mechanism (if
it is to be effective) must operate.

Stimuli of short duration were used in these
experiments because many auditory stimuli
present in the animal's natural environment
are of short duration (a snapping twig, for example). The control of responding by the
location of such stimuli depends upon the
differential stimulation of the two ears as described above. Sustained stimuli, such as a
continuous buzzer, for example, can be localized in cats with only a single functioning
ear (Neff and Diamond, 1958) and are thus not
suitable for experiments investigating binaural
hearing.

The preliminary experiments were carried
out in a box with a lever mounted on each
side of a liquid feeder. A relay was suspended
from the ceiling of the room near each lever
and was visually shielded from the animal.
Responses on one lever were reinforced when
the relay adjacent to that lever was activated to
give a train of clicks; responses on the other
lever were reinforced when its adjacent relay
was activated. Under these conditions rats
quickly reached a level of 90 to 100% correct
responses. However, when tone bursts produced from transistor radio earphones were
substituted for the relay clicks, only a 60 to
70% correct response level was reached. These
experiments indicated that the location of
sounds is a dominant aspect of audition, at
least for certain classes of auditory stimuli.

The relay clicks and earphone tone bursts
differ in a number of ways. One difference is
the kind of transients associated with the two
kinds of stimuli. The tone bursts had a rise

time in excess of 50 msec, while the relay produced sounds that had more rapid changes in
intensity. This experiment investigated the
effect of the rise time of an acoustic stimulus
upon the degree to which responding can be
brought under the control of the azimuth of
the stimulus.

METHOD

Subjects

Three male albino rats, approximately 300
days old, Sprague-Dawley strain, were fed
sufficient food, once per day, to reduce body
weight to approximately 75% of free-feeding
weight. During the experiment, body weight
was maintained at this level. Water was available at all times. It has been found that
animals with middle ear infection are not
suitable subjects.

Apparatus

The experimental chamber was a wire
mesh enclosure, 8 in. by 11 in. by 8 in. high.
Mounted in the front wall were two Gerbrands
rat levers, 4 in. apart and 3 in. above the
floor. A Gerbrands liquid food dispenser was
mounted between the two levers. A Gerbrands
pigeon key was mounted in the middle of the
back wall, 3 in. above the floor. The animal
enclosure was placed on a table in the middle
of a room 7 ft by 8 ft by 9 ft high. The walls,
ceiling, and door of the room were covered
with acoustic tile. Two loudspeakers (University Sphericon type T 202) were placed on
the table on either side of the animal enclosure
as shown in Fig. 1. The speakers were 18 in.

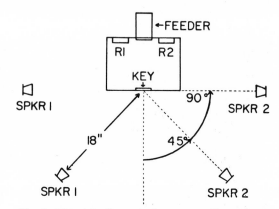

Fig. 1. Schematic diagram of apparatus (from above).
Speakers were situated in the 90° position for parts of
the experiment and in the 45° position for other parts.

from the midpoint of the key. Speaker position could be varied at any angle relative to the key. The positions marked 90° and 45° in Fig. 1 were used in this experiment. A houselight (10-w bulb), located on top of the wire mesh enclosure, was on continuously except during a blackout.

Standard operant conditioning equipment was used to schedule the experimental procedures. Cumulative records were taken of responding on the two levers.

The stimulus was a tone burst of 0.2 sec occurring at the rate of two bursts per second. The electrical signal that produced the tone bursts was generated by a General Radio oscillator (type 1210C), connected to a Grason-Stadler electronic switch (type 829C) and connected from there to a General Radio amplifier (type 1206B). The output of the amplifier was switched to one or the other of the two loudspeakers by the scheduling equipment. The electronic switch was appropriately operated by the equipment to produce the tone bursts described above.

Acoustic tone bursts in the animal enclosure produced by this equipment were examined with a 0.5-in. condenser microphone (Brüel and Kjaer, type 4133) connected to an oscilloscope via a wide band preamplifier (Tektronix type 122). It was found that acoustic tone bursts having a rise time of from 0.2 to 100 msec and a frequency range of 4 kHz to 40 kHz could be produced in the animal's enclosure. Two 3-msec, 10-kHz tone bursts, with different rise times, are shown in Fig. 2.

In the present experiment tone bursts of 4 kHz and 10 kHz and of various rise times were used. These were set at an intensity of 75 db (reference pressure 0.0002 microbar) using a General Radio sound level meter (type 1551C), with the microphone on an extension lead and placed in the position of the animal's head adjacent to the key.

Procedure

The basic procedure developed a discrimination in which the stimulus was produced by responding on the key. The essentials of the procedure are illustrated in Fig. 3, and details were as follows.

Responding on the key produced tone bursts from either the left or the right speaker on a fixed-interval schedule of 30 sec. The order of selection of either the left (L) or the right (R)

speaker was RLRRLLRLLR in all conditions except those noted below. Each presentation of the stimulus consisted of two tone bursts. The first lever response after onset of the stimulus, if the response occurred within 7.5 sec of the onset, was either reinforced (if correct) or followed by a blackout (if incorrect), and started the fixed-interval schedule timer. If a lever response did not occur within 7.5 sec of stimulus onset, the fixed-interval timer started at the end of this interval.

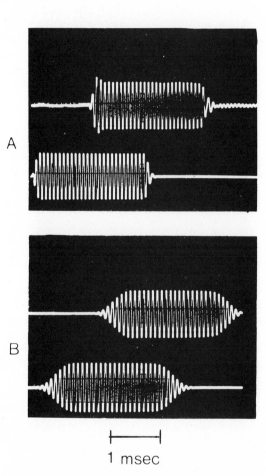

1 msec

Fig. 2. A. 3-msec, 10-kHz tone burst, rise time approximately 0.2 msec. Lower tracing in A shows electrical signal delivered to loudspeaker; upper tracing shows the resulting acoustic signal as recorded via microphone. The microphone faced the speaker at a distance of 16 in. The time difference between the onsets of the electrical and acoustic signals represents the time taken for the sound to travel from the speaker to the microphone. The reduced waveform observable at the end of the acoustic signal is an echo. B. 3-msec, 10-kHz tone burst, rise time approximately 0.5 msec. Lower tracing: electrical signal. Upper tracing: acoustic signal.

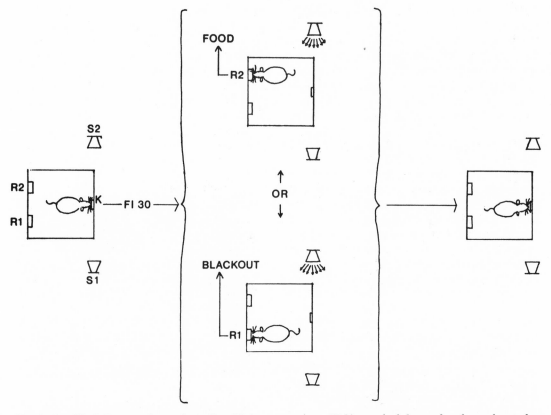

Fig. 3. Simplified diagram of procedure. Key (K) responses, on an FI 30-sec schedule, produced tone bursts from one or the other speaker. The case where tone bursts were produced from speaker S2 is shown. A response on lever R2 produced reinforcement, whereas a response on R1 produced a blackout. Dimensions are not to scale as in Fig. 1.

The first response on either lever that occurred within 7.5 sec of the onset of the tone bursts was reinforced as follows. A response on the lever to the left of the food cup (R1) was reinforced after tone bursts from the loudspeaker (S1) on the same side (correct response). A response on the lever to the right of the food cup (R2) was reinforced after tone bursts from the loudspeaker (S2) on that side. A response on R1 after tone bursts from S2 produced a 5-sec blackout (incorrect response). Similarly, a response on R2 after tone bursts from S1 produced a 5-sec blackout. Responses on either lever in the absence of either stimulus prevented, for 5 sec, the production of a stimulus by responding on the key. Reinforcement was 5-sec presentation of 0.1 cc of a 50% mixture of sweetened condensed milk and water.

After two incorrect responses in a row for tone bursts from the same speaker (unless a response, correct or incorrect, on the other

lever intervened), tone bursts from that speaker occurred on each succeeding presentation until a correct response occurred or until 10 consecutive errors had occurred. After either of these occurrences the speakers were again switched in the predetermined order. Sessions were 80 min long.

To test whether the behavior was under the control of the tone bursts, rather than electronic or mechanical artifacts, the oscillator gain control was turned down to −60 db and it was noted whether or not a response occurred when the equipment went through the procedure of presenting a stimulus. Responses never occurred during these tests.

RESULTS

The behavior of animal RB 13 is considered in detail; data from the other animals are presented in less detail as supporting evidence. The percentage of correct responses to S1 and

S2 was calculated for all S1s and all S2s for each session, and these numbers are presented in the figures for the three animals. The percentage of correct responses (for each stimulus) was calculated as follows:

$$\% \text{ correct (S1)} = \frac{\text{No. of R1 in presence of S1}}{\text{No. of R1 \& R2 in presence of S1}} \times 100$$

$$\% \text{ correct (S2)} = \frac{\text{No. of R2 in presence of S2}}{\text{No. of R1 \& R2 in presence of S2}} \times 100$$

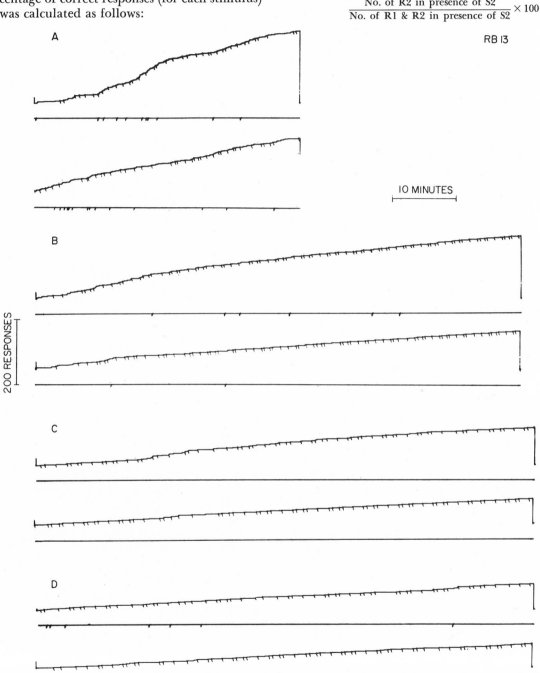

Fig. 4. Cumulative record of responses on right lever, R2 (upper record of pair) and on left lever, R1 (lower record of pair). Deflections of response pen indicate reinforcements (or correct responses), deflections of the event pen indicate blackouts (or errors). A. Session 1. 0.2-msec rise time, 90°, non-chain schedule. B. Session 2. Same conditions. C. Session 21. Same stimulus conditions, chain schedule (record of responses on key is not shown). D. Session 24. 50-msec rise time, 90°, chain schedule.

Development of the Behavior

Presses of RB 13 were shaped on both levers with food. The following day S1 and S2 (without limit to the number of tone bursts per stimulus presentation) were presented in the determined order once every 30 sec and the reinforcement and blackout contingencies were introduced. The loudspeakers were in the 90° position (see Fig. 1) and the tone burst had a frequency of 4 kHz with a rise time of 0.2 msec. By the end of this session the animal

was making only a small number of incorrect responses (Fig. 4, A). The animal continued on these conditions for the next six sessions during which a high level of correct responding was achieved on both levers (see Fig. 4, B, C and 5, Sessions 2 to 7). During Session 8 (see *a*, Fig. 5) key pressing was shaped and stimuli were produced by key responses on the fixed-interval schedule of 30 sec. The stimulus was limited to three bursts in Session 15 and to two bursts in all subsequent sessions. The animal continued to give an essentially errorless per-

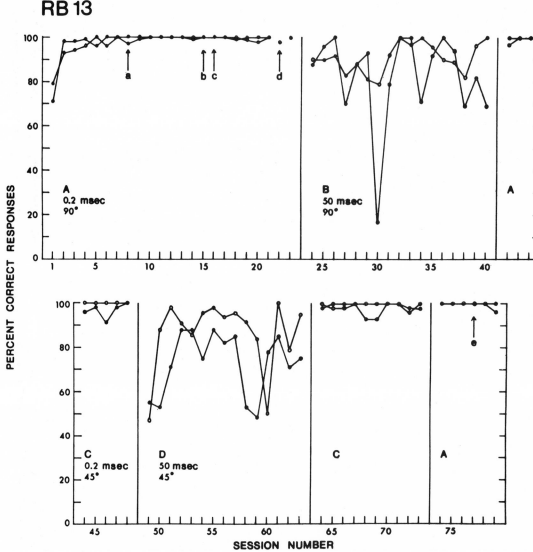

Fig. 5. RB 13. Percentage correct responses under different conditions (indicated by A,B,C, and D) of rise time (0.2 or 50 msec) and speaker angle (90° or 45°). Frequency 4 kHz in all conditions. Filled circles represent per cent correct in S2 (right speaker), open circles per cent correct in S1 (left speaker). Chain schedule begins at *a*. Stimulus limited to three tone bursts at *b*, and to two (final value) at *c*. In session indicated at *d*, only S2 was presented. At *e* speakers were interchanged (S2 still right, S1 still left) and remained so for succeeding sessions.

formance until the end of this part of the experiment. As a control procedure, in Session 22 (see *d*, Fig. 5) only the stimulus from the right speaker (S2) was presented. This was done by disconnecting the sequence stepper that controlled the selection of the speakers. Responding occurred on only the right lever.

From these data it is clear that the location of a 4-kHz tone burst with a rise time of 0.2 msec was an effective controlling stimulus. Stimulus control by location was rapidly obtained and the percentage of correct responses was high.

The development of the behavior in RB 14 is shown in the first segment (A) of Fig. 6. In

Session 22 (see *c* in Fig. 6) the animal was given a test in which all contingencies remained the same except that all tone bursts (whether scheduled as R or L) were channeled through one speaker (S2). Correct responding fell to an average of 53% (both stimuli combined).

The third animal, RB 4, had been run previously in variations of this experiment so the development of the behavior was not studied. Figure 7 (first segment, A) shows the last two days of responding on the initial conditions of this experiment (90° angle of the speakers and 0.2-msec rise time). The animal performed at the same high level of correct responding as did RB 13 and RB 14.

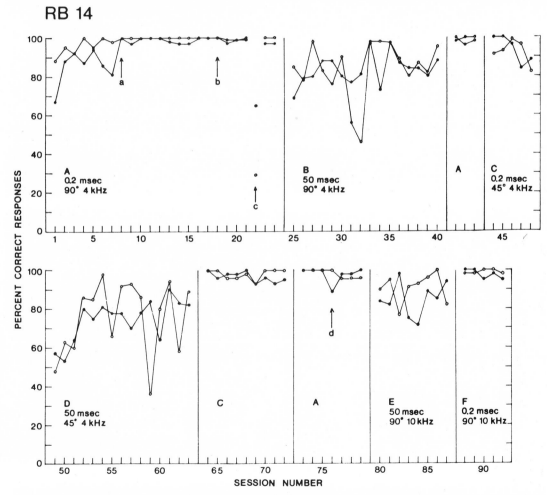

Fig. 6. RB 14. Percentage correct responses under different conditions (indicated by A, B, C, D, E, and F) of rise time (0.2 or 50 msec), speaker angle (90° or 45°) and frequency (4 or 10 kHz). Filled circles represent per cent correct in S2 (right speaker), open circles per cent correct in S1 (left speaker). Chain schedule begins at *a*. Stimulus limited to two tone bursts at *b* and for all following sessions. In session indicated at *c*, all stimuli were channeled through right speaker (normally S2). At *d* speakers were interchanged and remained so for succeeding sessions.

RB 4

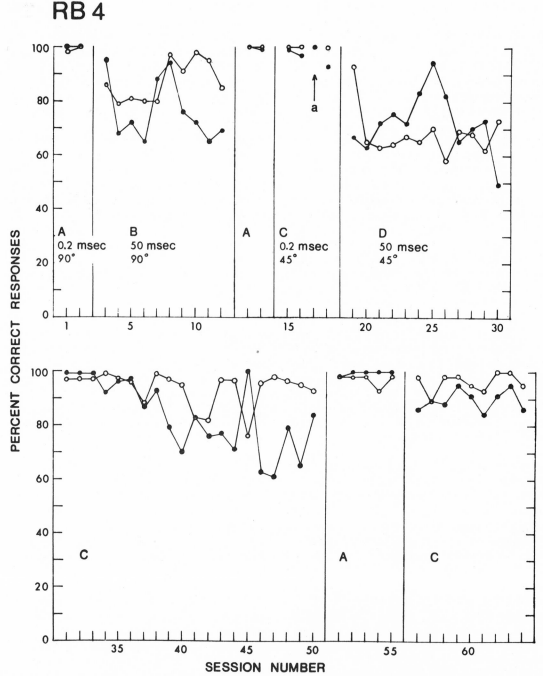

Fig. 7. RB 4. Percentage correct responses under different conditions (indicated by A,B,C, and D) of rise time (0.2 or 50 msec) and speaker angle (90° or 45°). Frequency was 4 kHz in all conditions. Filled circles represent per cent correct in S2 (right speaker), open circles per cent correct in S1 (left speaker). Animal had previous history on variations of this experiment before Session 1. In session indicated at *a*, only S2 was presented.

Effect of Slowing Rise Time to 50 msec

The rise time of the tone bursts for RB 13 was increased to 50 msec for Sessions 24 to 40 (segment B, Fig. 5). The percentage of correct responses immediately fell, showing considerable variability over these sessions. There was no indication of systematic increases in the percentage of correct responses over these sessions. The cumulative records of the first session under these conditions are shown in Fig. 4 (D). In Session 41 (second A segment, Fig. 5) the rise time of the tone bursts was returned to 0.2 msec and the percentage of correct responses returned to the 100% level by the second session.

In Session 44 (segment C, Fig. 5), the loud-speakers were changed to the 45° position (see Fig. 1). The rise time remained at 0.2 msec for the next five sessions. The animal showed a slight decrease in percentage of correct responses. In Session 49 (segment D, Fig. 5), and for the following 14 sessions, the rise time of the tone bursts was increased to 50 msec. The percentage of correct responses immediately decreased and showed considerable variability over the 15 sessions. The rise time was reduced to 0.2 msec in Session 64 (second C segment, Fig. 5) and the number of correct responses immediately increased to the previous level under this condition. The speakers were returned to the 90° position in Session 74 (final A segment, Fig. 5) and the rise time was maintained at 0.2 msec. The animal made virtually no errors. The speakers were interchanged in Session 77 (see e, Fig. 5) to determine if differences between the speakers were supporting the behavior. This had no effect upon the behavior.

It is clear from these data that the decrease in the percentage of correct responses produced by increasing the rise time of the tone bursts was not critically dependent upon whether the speakers were in the 45° or 90° positions. From inspection of Fig. 5 it appears, however, that the degree of control of responding under the 45° position for both fast and slow rise times was less than that for the 90° position.

Animal RB 14 (Fig. 6) was exposed to the same conditions as RB 13. Essentially the same results were obtained as those for RB 13.

In Session 80 (segment E, Fig. 6) for RB 14, the frequency of the tone bursts was raised from 4 kHz to 10 kHz. The speakers were in the 90° position and the rise time was 50 msec. From inspection of Fig. 6 it can be seen that the percentage of correct responses was about the same at 10 kHz as at 4 kHz (segment B). Finally, (segment F, Fig. 6) the rise time of the stimuli was reduced to 0.2 msec and the percentage of correct responses increased to the same level as that obtained at 4 kHz (segment

A). Thus, the effect of slowing the rise time of the stimuli was not critically dependent upon the use of a frequency of 4 kHz.

Animal RB 4 (Fig. 7) was exposed to the same changes of conditions as RB 13 and RB 14. In Session 3 (segment B, Fig. 7), the rise time was increased to 50 msec and percentage of correct responses immediately decreased in the same way as that found for the other animals. When the rise time was returned to 0.2 msec in Session 13 (second A segment, Fig. 7) the percentage of correct responses increased to its previous high value. The animal was then run with the speakers in the 45° position and the rise time at 0.2 msec. (first segment C, Fig. 7). The percentage of correct responses decreased slightly. In Session 19 (segment D, Fig. 7), the rise time was increased to 50 msec and the percentage of correct responses immediately decreased. In Session 31 (second C segment, Fig. 7), the rise time was reduced to 0.2 msec. The percentage of correct responses immediately increased. The animal was run for 20 sessions on this condition during which the number of correct responses gradually decreased. In Session 51 (final A segment, Fig. 7), the speakers were returned to the 90° position (0.2 msec rise time). The percentage of correct responses immediately rose to its previous high value. The speakers were returned to the 45° position (0.2-msec rise time) in Session 56 (final C segment, Fig. 7). The number of correct responses decreased but to a level higher than that under the 50-msec rise time condition.

Altering the rise time of the stimulus had the same effect with RB 4 as with the other animals. Under the 45° fast rise-time condition (second segment C, Fig. 7) however, control of responding was not as well maintained as with the other animals. However, the effect of altering the rise time upon responding was still evident in the 45° position.

In summary, these data show that increasing the rise time of tone bursts from 0.2 msec to 50 msec decreases the number of correct responses. This effect was obtained with different positions of the speakers (90° and 45°) and with different stimulus frequencies (4 kHz and 10 kHz).

DISCUSSION

The present results show that responding of unrestrained animals readily comes under the control of the azimuthal location of certain auditory stimuli. The degree of control was strong, the animals working at high levels of correct responding. This control was obtained in what might be considered a normal acoustic environment for a rat. The experimental room was not anechoic and it contained objects (feeder, levers, key, enclosure, *etc.*) that were not arranged in any particular way so as to produce a simple (free-field) signal at the ears. A different room, enclosure, and sound producer were used in the preliminary experiments discussed in the introduction; comparable results were obtained. Thus, the effect did not depend in any critical way upon some special feature of the present acoustic environment.

It is reasonable to conclude that the location of appropriate stimuli is a dominant attribute of audition, a conclusion in line with the anatomical analysis presented in the introduction.

The following points must be kept in mind when speculating about the reasons for the effects produced by changing the rise time of the signal.

In the rat, the pinnae stand above the head, so that the head does not lie between the ears as in man and other primates. Thus, intensity differences at the two ears are probably less dependent upon acoustic shadows cast by the head than in the primate. It seems probable, however, that the pinnae will cast shadows as well as having other acoustic effects relevant to location. In the absence of measurements of these effects it is impossible to estimate their role in the behavior observed in the present experiment. However, the magnitude of the effects, at the nominal frequency of the tone burst, is presumably unchanged by changing rise time.

Whatever time relations exist between the stimuli that reach the two ears in the complex acoustic environment of the experiment are unchanged by changing rise time. For stimuli of short rise time any difference in intensity of the stimuli at the two ears due to difference in time of arrival of the stimuli at the two ears will be larger than for stimuli of long rise time. Thus, it appears that differences in intensity due to the difference in rise time may be one variable involved in producing the behavioral effects observed in the present experiment. In the rat, the maximum difference in time of arrival of the stimuli is approximately 0.1 msec. In the cat, a difference in time of arrival of this magnitude (of clicks delivered one to each of left and right earphones) is sufficient to produce errorless localization (Masterton, Jane, and Diamond, 1967).

Masterton *et al.* (1967) have carried out two lesion experiments, the results of which are relevant to the present results. They found that lesions of the trapezoid body and superior olivary complex abolished the discrimination of pairs of clicks (delivered one to each ear by headphones) separated by an interval of 0.5 msec. In their cat M-329, the superior olivary complex and trapezoid body were destroyed on one side, and in cat M-330 the superior olivary complex and trapezoid body were extensively damaged on both sides. In both these animals discrimination of the click pairs was seriously disrupted. These results are consistent with the view that the superior olivary complex is involved in the discrimination of sound disparities at the two ears. Masterton *et al.* (1968) interpreted these data as indicating that the medial superior olivary nucleus is essential for the discrimination of location of auditory stimuli. The lesions of cats M-329 and M-330, however, interrupt a number of ipsilateral and contralateral pathways other than those to the medial superior olivary nucleus (Harrison and Beecher, 1967). In particular, they interrupt the axons to the lateral superior olivary nuclei or destroy the nuclei. It could well be that this damage, rather than that to the medial superior olivary nucleus, was responsible for the loss of the discrimination in their two cats.

REFERENCES

Boudreau, J. C. and Tsuchitani, C. Binaural interaction in the cat superior olive S segment. *Journal of Neurophysiology*, 1968, **31**, 442-454.

Griffin, D. R. *Listening in the dark*. New Haven: Yale University Press, 1958.

Harrison, J. M. and Beecher, M. D. Medial superior olive and sound localization. *Science*, 1967, **155**, 1697.

Harrison, J. M. and Irving, R. Nucleus of the trapezoid body; dual afferent innervation. *Science*, 1964, **143**, 473-474.

Harrison, J. M. and Irving, R. Ascending connections of the anterior ventral cochlear nucleus in the rat. *Journal of Comparative Neurology*, 1966, **126**, 51-64. (*a*)

Harrison, J. M. and Irving, R. Organization of the posterior ventral cochlear nucleus. *Journal of Comparative Neurology*, 1966, **126**, 391-403. (*b*)

Harrison, J. M. and Irving, R. Visual and nonvisual auditory systems in mammals. *Science*, 1966, **154**, 738-743. *(c)*

Harrison, J. M. and Warr, B. A study of the cochlear nuclei and ascending auditory pathways of the medulla. *Journal of Comparative Neurology*, 1962, **119**, 341-380.

Irving, R. and Harrison, J. M. The superior olivary complex and audition; a comparative study. *Journal of Comparative Neurology*, 1967, **130**, 77-86.

Masterton, B., Jane, J. A., and Diamond, I. T. Role of brainstem auditory structures in sound localization. I. Trapezoid body, superior olive and lateral lemniscus. *Journal of Neurophysiology*, 1967, **30**, 341-360.

Masterton, B., Jane, J. A., and Diamond, I. T. Role of brainstem auditory system in sound localization. II. Inferior collicus and brachicum. *Journal of Neurophysiology*, 1968, **31**, 96-108.

Neff, W. D. Neural structures concerned in the localization of sound in space. *Psychologische Beitrage*, 1962, **VI**, 492-500.

Neff, W. D. and Diamond, I. T. The neural basis of auditory discrimination. In H. G. Harlow and C. N. Woolsey (Eds.), *Biological and biochemical basis of behavior*. Madison: University of Wisconsin Press, 1958. Pp. 101-126.

Neff, W. D., Fisher, J. F., Diamond, I. T., and Yela, M. Role of auditory cortex in discriminations requiring location of sound in space. *Journal of Neurophysiology*, 1965, **28**, 500-512.

Turner, R. N. and Norris, K. S. Discriminative echolocation in a porpoise. *Journal of the Experimental Analysis of Behavior*, 1966, **9**, 535-546.

Warr, B. Fiber degeneration following lesions in the anterior ventral cochlear nucleus of the cat. *Experimental Neurology*, 1966, **14**, 453-474.

Received 10 June 1968.

INTERVAL REINFORCEMENT OF CHOICE BEHAVIOR IN DISCRETE TRIALS[1]

JOHN A. NEVIN

COLUMBIA UNIVERSITY

Pigeons were trained to peck at red or green keys presented simultaneously in discrete trials. In one experiment, reinforcements were arranged by concurrent variable-interval schedules. The proportion of responses to green approximately matched the proportion of reinforcements produced by pecking green. Detailed analysis of responding revealed a systematic decrease in the probability of switching from green to red within sequences of trials after reinforcement. This trend corresponded to sequential changes in the relative frequency of reinforcement, and not to sequential changes in probability of reinforcement. In a second experiment, reinforcements were scheduled probabilistically every seventh trial. Even though there were no contingencies on pecking during the first six post-reinforcement trials, choices of green on the first response after reinforcement matched the proportion of reinforcements for pecking green. These results extend the generality of overall matching under concurrent reinforcement.

The effects of reinforcement schedules have usually been studied by analyzing the average rate of emission of a single response, the pattern of responding in time after reinforcement, and the distribution of interresponse times. These measures are to some extent independent: the same average rate may result from quite different temporal patterns or interresponse-time distributions. However, these three aspects of behavior may be controlled by the same independent variables: frequency or relative frequency of reinforcement affects average response rates (e.g., Catania and Reynolds, 1968), the rate of responding at various times after reinforcement (Catania and Reynolds, 1968), and the probability of responding in time after a preceding response (Anger, 1956; Shimp, 1968; Staddon, 1968). The present paper attempts a similar analysis of the variables controlling choices between two simultaneously available responses.

Skinner (1950) first brought the analytic methods of free-operant research to bear on choice behavior by studying two continuously available responses maintained by independent schedules of reinforcement. More re-cently, asymptotic performances maintained by concurrent variable-interval (VI) schedules have been studied parametrically, and strikingly lawful data have been obtained. Within various procedural arrangements. Herrnstein (1961), Catania (1963), Reynolds (1963), and Pliskoff, Shull, and Gollub (1968) demonstrated that the overall relative frequency of one response matches the relative frequency of reinforcement produced by that response. There is relatively little information on detailed patterns of responding in these free-operant choice studies. Reynolds (1963) examined switches between keys as a function of obtained relative frequency of reinforcement, and found departures from a simple matching relation at this level of analysis. The boundary conditions for the overall matching relation have not been explored in detail, but it is known that independence of the two responses and schedules is important (Catania, 1966).

Traditionally, choice behavior has been studied in discrete-trial settings that provide well-defined response opportunities and permit direct estimation of response probabilities (Bush, Galanter, and Luce, 1963). This sort of design has been especially common in studies of discrimination learning in which responses to one stimulus are regularly reinforced and responses to another, simultaneously presented stimulus are never reinforced. Because the standard simultaneous discrimination procedure may be seen as a

[1]Dedicated to B. F. Skinner in his sixty-fifth year. This research was supported by NIMH Grant 08515 to Swarthmore College. I am indebted to Suzanne Roth, David Chadwick, Paul Beach, and Roberta Welte for their invaluable assistance in running animals and analyzing data. Reprints may be obtained from the author, Department of Psychology, Columbia University, New York, New York 10027.

limiting case of concurrent schedules with non-zero reinforcement frequencies for responding to both stimuli, similar methods may be valuable in the more general case.

Shimp (1966) studied discrete-trial choices with probabilistic reinforcement that mimicked certain contingencies of concurrent VI schedules and observed matching between the relative frequencies of choices and reinforcements. His analysis suggested that the subjects tended to respond to that alternative with the momentarily higher probability of reinforcement, which he termed momentary maximizing. He argued that matching resulted from this maximizing tendency. Herrnstein (in preparation) has also examined choices in discrete trials with concurrent VI reinforcement and observed overall matching. The present experiments provided further data on this situation. Specifically, choices were permitted in discrete trials. Reinforcements were scheduled concurrently at variable intervals (in effect, after variable numbers of trials), or after a fixed number of trials. Asymptotic performances were examined for dependencies on prior reinforcements and choice sequences in an attempt to understand the determinants of responding.

EXPERIMENT 1

METHOD

Subjects

Three experimentally naive male White Carneaux pigeons were maintained at 80% of their free-feeding weights.

Apparatus

The experiment was conducted in a Lehigh Valley three-key pigeon chamber with red and green keylights, houselight, grain magazine, and white noise source. The center key was always dark. The experiment was scheduled by standard relay equipment in a separate room. Data were recorded on counters and an event recorder.

Procedure

The subjects were trained to peck the side keys, and given equal numbers of regular reinforcements for pecking red or green on the right or left. They were then exposed to the following procedure. A trial began with illu-

mination of both keys, one red and one green. A peck on either key turned off both keylights for an intertrial interval of 6 sec. If no peck occurred within 2 sec, the keys were darkened for 6 sec. Pecks on dark keys extended the intertrial interval for 6 sec from the peck. The subjects rarely pecked dark keys more than four or five times per session. Responses on the green key were reinforced with 4-sec access to grain if a VI 1-min tape had scheduled reinforcement during the preceding intertrial interval, and responses on the red key were reinforced if an independent VI 3-min tape had made reinforcement available. The VI 1-min tape consisted of 11 arithmetically spaced intervals ranging from 10 to 110 sec, and the VI 3-min tape consisted of nine arithmetically spaced intervals ranging from 10 to 350 sec. The positions of the tapes were changed irregularly each day to prevent them from getting into phase with each other or with the beginning of a session. Once a reinforcement was scheduled for a particular color, it remained available until produced by a response to that color. Both tapes ran continuously during trials and intertrial intervals unless a reinforcement had become available, in which case the tape that set up reinforcement stopped until that reinforcement was produced.

For the first 23 sessions, red and green alternated irregularly on the right and left keys. Since reinforcements remained available until produced, it was possible for the birds to obtain all scheduled reinforcements by responding exclusively to one key, and all three subjects developed strong position preferences. To overcome this, the key colors changed sides every 3 min. If the keys were lighted at the expiration of a 3-min period, the change was postponed until the keys were dark. This procedure resulted in a substantial loss of reinforcements unless the birds pecked each key at least occasionally in each 3-min period. The latter arrangement was in effect for an additional 50 to 60 sessions. After this training, food reinforcement was omitted for 10 sessions, and then reinstated for 15 sessions. Throughout the study, sessions lasted 30 min and were scheduled daily unless a bird exceeded its 80% weight by 15 g.

RESULTS

Probability of responding given a trial, and probability of responding to green given that the subject responded, were computed for each session and averaged across subjects. The results for the final seven sessions of training, 10 sessions of extinction, and 15 sessions of reconditioning are presented in Fig. 1. The plot indicates that the birds virtually always responded given a trial, and that about 75% of their responses were to the green key, matching the scheduled relative frequency of reinforce-

ment. Probability of responding declined in an orderly curve during extinction, accompanied by a gradual reduction in choices of green until a level near 0.50 was reached. The original performance was rapidly reestablished when reinforcement was reinstated. The average was representative of all three birds, as indicated by the summary statistics shown in Table 1.

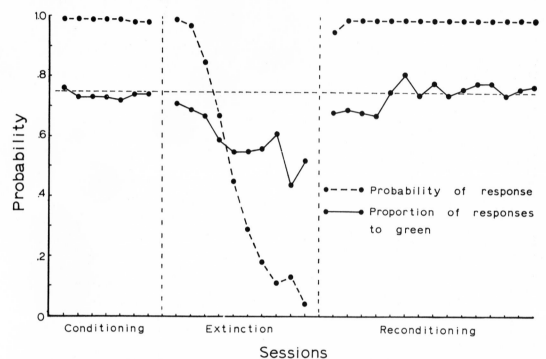

Fig. 1. Probability of responding given a trial, and probability of pecking green given that a response occurred, during the final seven of approximately 60 training sessions, 10 sessions of extinction, and 15 sessions of reconditioning. The data are averages for three pigeons. The light dashed line at 0.75 indicates the scheduled relative frequency of reinforcement.

Table 1

Summary Data for Selected Portions of Exp. I

	Bird No.	Responses			Reinforcements		
		G	R	$\dfrac{G}{G+R}$	G	R	$\dfrac{G}{G+R}$
Three sessions	58	542	133	0.80	84	24	0.78
preceding	59	468	192	0.71	81	27	0.75
extinction	60	490	222	0.69	83	28	0.75
Final three	58	66	45	0.59	–	–	–
sessions of	59	16	23	0.41	–	–	–
extinction	60	30	26	0.54	–	–	–
Final eight	58	1434	311	0.82	222	60	0.79
sessions of	59	1235	448	0.73	214	70	0.75
reconditioning	60	1297	464	0.74	212	69	0.75

Data for the final eight sessions of the experiment were analyzed in detail. As shown in Table 1, Birds 59 and 60 obtained exactly 75% of their total reinforcements for pecking green, and the proportion of responses to green matched this value almost perfectly. Bird 58 made 82% of its responses to green, and produced 79% of its reinforcements by pecking green, so that its relative frequency of responses to green departed only slightly from the obtained relative frequency of reinforcement.

All three birds exhibited position preferences. To show this, the relative frequency of responses to green was determined for five-trial blocks immediately before and after each change from green on the left to green on the right, and *vice versa*. The results are presented in Fig. 2. Although it is clear that key position affected the tendency to peck green, it is equally clear that the birds were not simply perseverating on the key most recently associated with the VI 1-min schedule. Instead, their probabilities of choosing green changed abruptly by about ±0.10 when the key colors changed sides.

Choices on trials immediately after reinforcement were broken down according to whether reinforcement had been produced by pecking red or green. Because of the 10-sec minimum interval on both tapes, at least two trials should elapse between reinforcements for successive pecks at a single color. In practice, intertrial pecks occasionally lengthened the intertrial interval so that two reinforcements could be produced by pecking the same color on two successive trials, but an analysis of the data showed that this was rare. The probabilities of reinforcement for pecking red or green on the first trial after reinforcement, subdivided according to reinforcement on the previous trial, were estimated by dividing the numbers of reinforcements produced by the numbers of responses recorded on these trials. As shown in Table 2, reinforcement was more probable for pecking red after reinforcement for pecking green than for pecking red, and *vice versa*. If the subjects conformed to this aspect of the schedule contingencies, the probability of pecking red after reinforcement on green should be high, and the probability of pecking red after reinforcement on red should be low. This was not the case. As shown in Table 2, only one subject exhibited an appreci-

able effect in that direction, and there was no difference in the pooled data.

Arithmetic variable-interval schedules make reinforcement increasingly probable as a function of time since reinforcement (Catania and

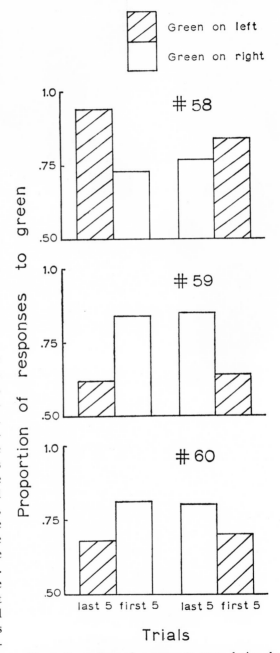

Fig. 2. Proportions of responses to green during the last five trials of a block with green on the left, the first five with green on the right, the last five with green on the right, and the first five with green on the left. Data were pooled for the final eight sessions of reconditioning.

Table 2

Obtained probabilities of reinforcement for pecking red or green on the first trial after reinforcement for pecking red or green, and the probability of pecking red rather than green on these trials. Data are given for individual subjects, and pooled across subjects for the final eight sessions of Exp. I.

	Probability of reinforcement				Probability of pecking red	
	Green after green	Green after red	Red after green	Red after red	After green reinforcement	After red reinforcement
#58	0.01	0.33	0.42	0.00	0.24	0.17
#59	0.03	0.20	0.18	0.08	0.34	0.41
#60	0.00	0.24	0.14	0.05	0.36	0.34
Pooled	0.01	0.26	0.33	0.05	0.31	0.32

Reynolds, 1968). Because of the differences in the mean and maximum interreinforcement intervals in the present schedules, the probability of reinforcement for pecking green increased more rapidly than that for pecking red. With the passage of successive trials after reinforcement, therefore, it became increasingly likely that the next reinforcement would be produced by pecking green rather than red. To check on the actual operation of the present VI schedules, the numbers of reinforcements produced by pecking red or green at each ordinal trial after reinforcement were determined for each subject. These numbers were pooled to calculate the proportion of reinforcements produced by pecking red at each trial number. This function is displayed in the upper panel of Fig. 3. The proportion of reinforcements produced by pecking red decreased from about 0.50 to about 0.15 over the course of nine trials. Too few long runs were available to permit reliable estimation beyond this point.

A similar analysis was performed to assess trends in the probability of pecking red rather than green at each ordinal trial number. Individual data are presented in the lower panel of Fig. 3. Beyond the initial decrease in the tendency to choose red after reinforcement, there is little evidence of a consistent trend in the data. These data were pooled without regard for the color of the key pecked to produce the previous reinforcement because the prior reinforcement evidently had no systematic effects on post-reinforcement choices (Table 2).

An alternative analysis leads to examination of prior responses rather than reinforcements. Because concurrent VI schedules run continuously until reinforcement is available, the probability of reinforcement for one response is an increasing function of time spent emitting the other response. In the present situation, for example, the probability of reinforcement for switching from green to red should be an increasing function of the number of consecutive trials on which the green key was pecked. The data were examined to determine whether this aspect of the schedules in fact had

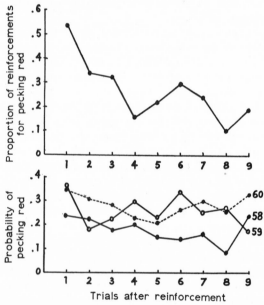

Fig. 3. Upper panel: the proportion of reinforcements obtained for pecking red as a function of the ordinal number of a trial after reinforcement. The function was determined from the number of reinforcements produced by pecking red or green at each ordinal trial, pooling across subjects, and dividing reinforcements for pecking red by total reinforcements for each trial. Lower panel: the probability of pecking red as a function of the ordinal number of a trial after reinforcement. Data for individual subjects are taken from the final eight sessions of Exp. 1.

an effect. The analysis was performed only for switches from green to red, because every subject recorded at least 25 runs of 10 or more consecutive pecks on green during the sessions under consideration, whereas they rarely pecked the red key on more than three or four successive trials. The numbers of responses producing reinforcement were determined separately for switching to red and for continuing on green as a function of the number of consecutive responses to green. The data were pooled across subjects and the probabilities of reinforcement calculated. The results are displayed in the upper panel of Fig. 4. The figure shows that the probability of reinforcement for switching to red increased with successive choices of green, as expected from the properties of VI schedules, while the probability of reinforcement for pecking green remained substantially constant. The latter statement apparently contradicts the statement that the probability of reinforcement for pecking red relative to that for pecking green decreased with successive trials (Fig. 3). The difference between these aspects of the schedule contingencies may be understood by appreciating that the analysis presented in Fig. 3 was based on trial sequences that began anew with each reinforcement, regardless of the key color pecked at any point in a sequence, whereas the analysis in Fig. 4 was based on trial sequences that began anew with each red-key response, without regard for whether it was reinforced or whether there were intervening reinforcements for pecking green.

The probability of switching from green to red, as a function of successive green pecks, is shown in the lower panel of Fig. 4 for individual subjects. In each case, the probability of switching from green to red decreased with successive choices of green. In this respect, then, none of the subjects conformed to the schedule contingencies.

As noted above, the data presented in Fig. 3 were pooled without regard for response sequences in an attempt to isolate the effects of prior reinforcement, and the data represented in Fig. 4 were pooled without regard for reinforcements in an attempt to evaluate the effects of prior choices. Both analyses are complicated by possible interactions between response sequences and reinforcements. A final analysis examined both determinants of responding. The probability of pecking red was

evaluated as a function of the number of consecutive responses to green after reinforcement, so that all responses after the first red-key peck in each post-reinforcement sequence of trials were excluded. This substantially reduced the sample size because there were few long runs of green-key pecks not interrupted by reinforcement. However, sufficient data were available to estimate trends over seven to nine trials for individual subjects. The resulting functions are presented in Fig. 5, which is simi-

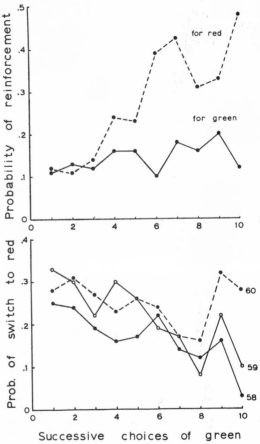

Fig. 4. Upper panel: the probability of reinforcement for pecking green, and for switching to red, as functions of the number of successive choices of green. The functions were obtained by pooling across subjects the numbers of reinforcements obtained for continuing on green or switching to red, and dividing by pooled numbers of responses to green or red at each number of previous successive choices. Lower panel: Probability of switching from green to red as a function of the number of successive responses to green. The functions were based on the final eight sessions of Exp. 1. Probability of switching was calculated on the basis of the number of opportunities for switching at each run length. All three birds had at least 25 opportunities to emit runs of 10 or more responses.

lar to Fig. 4 in showing systematic decreases in the probability of switching to red as a function of the number of green pecks.

This decreasing trend agrees with the inverse relation between the proportion (or relative frequency) of reinforcements for pecking red and the number of trials since the previous reinforcement (Fig. 3). It does not accord with changes in the probability of reinforcement as estimated from reinforcements per response. To show the separation between these aspects of the reinforcement contingencies within the present restricted set of data, the numbers of reinforcements obtained for pecking red or green after different numbers of consecutive green pecks after reinforcement were determined and pooled into three-trial blocks because of the small sample size. The probability of reinforcement for pecking red or green was determined by dividing the number of reinforcements by the number of responses emitted in each block. The relative probability of reinforcement was determined by dividing the probability of reinforcement for pecking red by the sum of the reinforcement probabilities in each block. Finally, the relative frequency of reinforcement for pecking red was determined by dividing reinforcements produced by red-key pecks by total reinforcements in each block. The results of these calculations are presented in Fig. 6. As in the larger sample considered in Fig. 3, the relative frequency of reinforcement for pecking red decreased with successive trials after reinforcement. As must be the case with arithmetic variable-interval

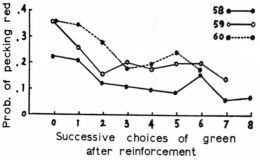

Fig. 5. Probability of pecking red as a function of successive choices of green after reinforcement. All responses after the first post-reinforcement response to red were excluded from the analysis. Probabilities were calculated on the basis of the number of opportunities for responding. No data points were plotted if there were fewer than 15 opportunities. Data for individual subjects were taken from the final eight sessions of Exp. 1.

schedules, the probabilities of reinforcement for pecking either red or green increased with successive trials after reinforcement, with the probabilitiy of reinforcement for pecking red remaining higher than that for green throughout the sequence of trials. These reinforcement probabilities covaried so that the relative probability of reinforcement remained constant over this range of trial sequences. This analysis suggests that choices were determined by the experienced relative frequency of reinforcement rather than by the probability of reinforcement.

EXPERIMENT 2

In Exp. 1, choices depended on maintained reinforcement, in that the probability of pecking green rather than red decreased to about 0.50 during extinction. That is, in the absence of any reinforcement contingencies, there was no systematic preference for green, despite its prolonged history of correlation with relatively

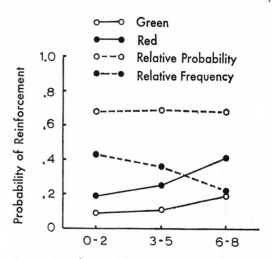

Successive Choices of Green After Reinforcement

Fig. 6. Probability of reinforcement for pecking green or red during blocks of three successive choices of green after reinforcement. The functions were obtained by dividing the pooled numbers of reinforcements for pecking green or red in each block of trials by the pooled numbers of responses to green or red, given that no previous response to red had occurred since reinforcement. Also shown on the same probability ordinate are the relative probability of reinforcement for pecking red (estimated by dividing the probability of reinforcement for pecking red by the sum of the reinforcement probabilities) and the relative frequency of reinforcement for pecking red (the number of reinforcements obtained by pecking red divided by total reinforcements obtained in each block of trials).

frequent reinforcement. As the foregoing analysis has shown, the contingencies of maintained reinforcement in that experiment were exceedingly complex and amenable to various analyses. The role of the contingencies may be separated from the maintenance of reinforcement by scheduling reinforcement at fixed intervals, without regard for responding during the interval. A procedure of this kind was employed in Exp. 2.

METHOD

Subjects and Apparatus

The subjects and apparatus were the same as in Exp. 1.

Procedure

The birds were exposed to the following reinforcement schedule for 37 sessions, beginning three weeks after completion of Exp. 1. Trials were scheduled as before, except that the left key was red and the right key green on every trial. On every seventh trial, reinforcement was made available for responses to either red or green by a probability randomizer set to assign 25% of all reinforcements to red, and 75% to green. Once a reinforcement was assigned to a color, it remained available until produced and no other assignments were made. This procedure guaranteed that obtained relative frequency of reinforcement approximately equaled the scheduled probability of reinforcement, and insured responding on both keys. No reinforcements were ever produced during the six trials immediately after reinforcement, and pecks during those trials in no way influenced the schedule.

Sessions lasted until 51 reinforcements were produced. No data were recorded until after the first reinforcement of each session. As before, sessions were run daily if the birds were within 15 g of their 80% weights.

RESULTS

The data for the last 10 sessions were analyzed to evaluate the probability of responding, and the probability of pecking the green key given a response, for each ordinal trial number after reinforcement. (Data for Bird 58 were lost for one session because of recording equipment failure.) These measures are given for all subjects in Fig. 7. In all cases, there was a systematic increase in the probability of re-

sponding as a function of trials after reinforcement. The probability of choosing green on the first trial after reinforcement, when responding was relatively infrequent, was substantially the same as on the seventh and subsequent trials when reinforcement was available and the birds nearly always responded. All subjects exhibited a slight elevation in choices of green at about the fourth or fifth trial after reinforcement, but otherwise there were no systematic effects.

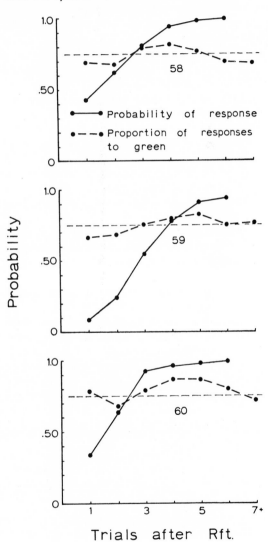

Fig. 7. Probability of responding given a trial, and probability of pecking green given a response, as a function of the ordinal trial number after reinforcement. Reinforcement was scheduled only on the seventh trial, and held until collected. The functions are based on pooled data for the final 10 of 37 training sessions. The light dashed line at 0.75 indicates the scheduled relative frequency of reinforcement.

Further analysis determined how the birds chose on their first response after reinforcement, regardless of the trial number on which it occurred, and whether this choice depended on the response previously reinforced. The results are summarized in Table 3, which indicates that the overall probability of pecking green on the first response after reinforcement approximately matched the proportion of reinforcements for pecking green. Except for Bird 60, the immediately preceding reinforcement had only a small effect. These initial responses had no scheduled consequences, except for the extremely rare instances in which the birds paused for six or more trials after reinforcement. Also, responses on early post-reinforcement trials in no way influenced the probabilities of reinforcement on subsequent trials. Therefore, matching evidently occurred in the absence of any explicit contingencies between responding and reinforcement.

DISCUSSION

These experiments replicate the common finding of approximate overall matching between the relative frequencies of responses and reinforcements during maintained concurrent reinforcement. In Exp. 1, overall matching occurred in a situation involving complex contingencies between sequences of choices and reinforcement, which in part controlled changes in response probabilities during sequences of trials. In Exp. 2, approximate matching occurred on initial post-reinforcement choices despite the absence of any scheduled contingencies between those responses

and reinforcement. Therefore, these findings extend the generality of the matching relation for concurrent reinforcement.

Examination of the detailed structure of responding in Exp. 1 revealed a complex picture of the control of choice behavior by reinforcement. It may be well to begin by considering some aspects of performance which evidently were not controlled by the schedule contingencies. Post-reinforcement choices were not affected by the color of the key pecked to produce reinforcement on the previous trial, even though the obtained probabilities of reinforcement depended on the previous reinforcement (Table 2). Also, the probability of switching from green to red did not accord with changes in reinforcement probability with consecutive pecks at green (Fig. 4).

These findings differ from those reported by Shimp (1966). In his Exp. III, reinforcement was scheduled probabilistically for choices in discrete trials. The contingencies in his study were similar to those of VI schedules in that reinforcement remained available until produced. He observed that both the initial post-reinforcement choices and the changes in choice probabilities during sequences of trials between reinforcements corresponded approximately to differences in reinforcement probabilities arranged by the schedule. For these reasons, Shimp argued that overall matching was a byproduct of a tendency to choose that alternative with the higher probability of reinforcement on each trial.

The apparent failure of control by similar aspects of the reinforcement schedules in Exp. 1 is not decisive against any particular view of the determinants of choice behavior. The pro-

Table 3

Choices of green and red on the first response after reinforcement, subdivided according to the immediately preceding reinforcement, during the final 10 sessions of Exp. 2.

Bird No.	Preceding reinforcement	First response		Proportion of responses to green	
		Green	Red	Subdivided	Pooled
58	Green	253	92	0.73	
	Red	71	27	0.72	0.73
59	Green	298	101	0.75	
	Red	63	28	0.69	0.74
60	Green	292	85	0.78	
	Red	68	43	0.61	0.74

cedure of Exp. 1 differed in many ways from Shimp's procedure, and further research on the parameters of choice experiments will be needed to elucidate those conditions which favor the development of control by various aspects of concurrent-schedule contingencies. The present results merely indicate that conformity to certain aspects of the reinforcement contingencies is not a necessary condition for matching.

On the positive side, Exp. 1 suggested that choices conformed better to changes in the relative frequency of reinforcement than to changes in the probability of reinforcement within sequences of trials between reinforcements. This finding accords with a number of studies that have identified frequency or relative frequency of reinforcement as prepotent over probability of reinforcement in the determination of responding. For example, Anger (1956) analyzed the distribution of interresponse times obtained after extended exposure to variable-interval reinforcement. He demonstrated that the conditional probability of responding at different post-response times covaried with the obtained relative frequencies of reinforcement and not with the probabilities of reinforcement at those times. In a study of performance on concurrent chained schedules, Herrnstein (1964) found that the relative frequency of reinforcement in a terminal link was a better predictor of choices in the initial link than the relative probability of reinforcement. Neuringer and Schneider (1968) studied performance in a single-response, discrete-trial procedure and found that post-reinforcement latencies were controlled by the frequency of reinforcement and not by the probability of reinforcement.

The findings of Exp. 2 are related to earlier work on discrete-trial simultaneous discriminations by Nevin (1967). In one of his experiments, reinforcement was available for pecking the brighter of two keys after a fixed number of trials in a fashion analogous to the schedule in Exp. 2. Under these conditions, the probability of responding increased with successive trials after reinforcement, but the probability of choosing the brighter key remained constant. Final performance in the present Exp. 2 was approximately the same in these respects. Thus, performances in conventional simultaneous discrimination experiments and concurrent-schedule experiments which provide reinforcement for both alternatives may be functionally similar.

This last possibility is brought into question by the present extinction data. Nevin (1967) found that the probability of pecking the brighter key did not change during experimental extinction, although the probability of responding decreased systematically. In Exp. 1, the probability of responding decreased in much the same way during the 10 sessions of extinction, and the probability of choosing green rather than red decreased at the same time to about 0.50. There is a fair amount of data from various situations indicating invariance during extinction in choices of a stimulus formerly correlated with reinforcement (*e.g.*, Cumming *et al.* 1967; Zeiler, 1968). It remains to be determined whether manipulation of the parameters of concurrent-reinforcement procedures will also lead to invariance in choice data during extinction.

REFERENCES

Anger, D. The dependence of interresponse times upon the relative reinforcement of different interresponse times. *Journal of Experimental Psychology*, 1956, **52**, 145-161.

Bush, R. R., Galanter, E., and Luce, R. D. Characterization and classification of choice experiments. In R. D. Luce, R. R. Bush, and E. Galanter (Eds.) *Handbook of Mathematical Psychology* Vol. 1. New York: Wiley, 1963. Pp. 77-102.

Catania, A. C. Concurrent performances: reinforcement interaction and response independence. *Journal of the Experimental Analysis of Behavior*, 1963, **6**, 253-263.

Catania, A. C. Concurrent operants. In W. K. Honig (Ed.) *Operant behavior: areas of research and application.* New York: Appleton-Century-Crofts, 1966. Pp. 213-270.

Catania, A. C. and Reynolds, G. S. A quantitative analysis of responding maintained by interval schedules of reinforcement. *Journal of the Experimental Analysis of Behavior*, 1968, **11**, 327-383.

Cumming, W. W., Berryman, R., Cohen, Leila R., and Lanson, R. N. Some observations on extinction of a complex discriminated operant. *Psychological Reports*, 1967, **20**, 1328-1330.

Herrnstein, R. J. Relative and absolute strength of response as a function of frequency of reinforcement. *Journal of the Experimental Analysis of Behavior*, 1961, **4**, 267-272.

Herrnstein, R. J. Secondary reinforcement and rate of primary reinforcement. *Journal of the Experimental Analysis of Behavior*, 1964, **7**, 27-36.

Neuringer, A. J. and Schneider, B. A. Separating the effects of interreinforcement time and number of interreinforcement responses. *Journal of the Experimental Analysis of Behavior*, 1968, **11**, 661-667.

Nevin, J. A. Effects of reinforcement scheduling on simultaneous discrimination performance. *Journal of the Experimental Analysis of Behavior*, 1967, **10**, 251-260.

Pliskoff, S. S., Shull, R. L., and Gollub, L. R. The relation between response rates and reinforcement rates in a multiple schedule. *Journal of the Experimental Analysis of Behavior*, 1968, **11**, 271-284.

Reynolds, G. S. On some determinants of choice in pigeons. *Journal of the Experimental Analysis of Behavior*, 1963, **6**, 53-59.

Shimp, C. P. Probabilistically reinforced choice behavior in pigeons. *Journal of the Experimental Analysis of Behavior*, 1966, **9**, 443-455.

Shimp, C. P. Magnitude and frequency of reinforcement and frequencies of interresponse times. *Journal of the Experimental Analysis of Behavior*, 1968, **11**, 525-535.

Skinner, B. F. Are theories of learning necessary? *Psychological Review*, 1950, **57**, 193-216.

Staddon, J. E. R. Spaced responding and choice: a preliminary analysis. *Journal of the Experimental Analysis of Behavior*, 1968, **11**, 669-682.

Zeiler, M. D. Stimulus control with fixed-ratio reinforcement. *Journal of the Experimental Analysis of Behavior*, 1968, **11**, 107-115.

Received 7 February 1969.

DISCRETE-TRIAL ALTERNATION IN THE RAT[1,2]

GEORGE A. HEISE, CONNIE KELLER, KHALIL KHAVARI,
AND NELL LAUGHLIN

INDIANA UNIVERSITY

The acquisition and maintenance by rats of single alternation, double alternation, and four other repeating patterns of reinforced and non-reinforced trials was studied in a discrete-trial lever-pressing situation. The rats learned all these patterns in a small number of experimental sessions. Single alternation was learned more rapidly than the more complex patterns. Rate of learning single and double alternation decreased moderately as inter-trial interval increased. Abrupt changes in the scheduling of trials, either by doubling the inter-trial interval or by shifting from fixed to variable trial spacing, temporarily disrupted the patterned performance. Two hypotheses concerned with the means by which the rats could have learned to conform to the pattern were examined: (1) "timing" of the interval between successive reinforcements; and (2) control of responding on a trial by the outcome of preceding trials, depending on the consistency with which these outcomes were associated with reinforced or non-reinforced trials in the pattern and on how many trials back these outcomes occurred. The second hypothesis accounted for the relative frequency of errors on trials at various locations in the sequences, and predicted most of the changes in error frequency observed in experiments in which "inter-trial stimuli" were added to the sequences.

The early investigations of alternation behavior in animals were undertaken primarily to assess the comparative "intelligence" of different species and to explore their capacity for "symbolic" behavior. The history and current status of the double-alternation research carried out with this objective has recently been summarized by Warren (1965), who concluded that available evidence fails to show that double-alternation performance differentiates lower from higher phylogenetic levels.

The results with rats seem to show that rats could learn spatial double alternation, but could learn temporal double alternation only with great difficulty, if they learned it at all (Munn, 1950). Probably the most convincing demonstration of double alternation in the rat (whether it should be called "spatial" or "temporal" is not clear) was provided by Schlosberg and Katz (1943) who trained rats to press a lever twice to the left and then twice to the right, for many successive sequences.

Recent research on single-alternation, double-alternation, and other patterns has been concerned more with identifying the factors controlling the sequential patterning of behavior (e.g., Capaldi, 1967) than with issues of animal intellectual capacity. In keeping with this trend, the present paper examines relationships between pattern complexity, inter-trial interval, and stimulus contingencies on the acquisition and maintenance by rats of single-alternation, double-alternation, and four other temporal sequences of discrete-trial lever pressing. A hypothesis concerned with the factors controlling the patterned behavior is presented, and is used to predict the relative frequency of errors on the trials in the various sequences.

METHOD

Subjects

Male albino rats (Sprague-Dawley derived) obtained from the Simonsen Laboratories,

[1]Dedicated to B. F. Skinner in his sixty-fifth year.

[2]This work was supported by MH 06997 and MH 14658 from the National Institutes of Mental Health to Indiana University. Preliminary experiments were made possible by a grant to the senior author from the Haverford College Faculty Research Fund, and by a donation of apparatus from Hoffmann La Roche, Inc. The assistance of Roy Webb and Fred Wightman is acknowledged. A preliminary version of this paper was presented at a Symposium on Discrimination Learning at the University of Sussex, England, on April 6, 1967. Reprints may be obtained from George A. Heise, Department of Psychology, Indiana University, Bloomington, Indiana 47401.

White Bear Lake, Minnesota, were 90 to 120 days old at the beginning of the experimentation. Most were water-deprived and their lever presses were reinforced with sugar-water; they had free access to water for 5 min after each experimental session. The remainder were food-deprived, and responding in experimental sessions was reinforced with food pellets; they received occasional supplemental feedings immediately after the experimental session as needed to maintain approximate normal free-feeding weight.

Apparatus

Four similar lever boxes, constructed from a commercial (Grason-Stadler E3125) prototype, were used. The essential features of each box were: manipulandum—a single Gerbrands lever; trial signal—a compound stimulus consisting of the concurrent presentation of a 6-w off-white panel light and a 1000-Hz tone at approximately 80 db; and a reinforcement device—either a dispenser for 45-mg Noyes pellets or a mechanism for presenting drops of 9% sucrose solution. Automatic controlling circuitry and a system of counters and event recorders were located in an adjoining room.

Procedure

A discrete-trial procedure was used, in which reinforced trials (S+) alternated in fixed sequence with non-reinforced trials (S−). The pattern of reinforced and non-reinforced trials recycled continuously throughout the experimental session of 480 trials; there were no "breaks" or other indications that the pattern was repeated. The sequence was "non-correction": the order of presentation of reinforced and non-reinforced trials was not affected by the animal's behavior.

Six patterns of reinforced and non-reinforced trials can be obtained with sequences of two, three, or four trials. Three of these patterns were selected for extensive experimental examination: single alternation (S+S− . . .), double alternation (S+S+S−S−. . . .), and "single-double" alternation (S+S−S− . . .). The other three patterns (S+S−S−S−. . . ., S+S+S−. . . ., and S+S+S+S−. . . .) were used to examine specific hypotheses about the factors controlling alternation performance, and received less extensive experimental treatment.

For all sequences, the same stimuli—the 1000-Hz tone and the lighted panel light—were always present during each trial. Neither stimulus was on during the inter-trial interval (ITI). In most of the experiments, a single response during a S+ trial (CRF) produced a drop of sugar-water reinforcement and terminated the trial. However, in one series of experiments (on the relation between ITI duration and alternation learning) 10 responses during the S+ trial (FR 10) were required for reinforcement; the reinforcer in these latter experiments was a food pellet.

The essential features of the trial sequence are presented in Fig. 1, which shows a segment of the single-alternation schedule. The schedule used with the other sequences was identical except for the order of presentation of reinforced and non-reinforced trials and for the response requirement (CRF or FR 10).

The maximum duration of a trial was 10 sec. S+ trials terminated with delivery of the reinforcement, or after 10 sec if the rat did not make the required response during the trial. The S− trials always lasted 10 sec whether or not the rat responded during the trial. The standard ITI was 10 sec except in an experimental series in which ITI duration was itself the independent variable. However, in order to minimize ITI responding, the onset of the next trial was postponed for the ITI duration (measured from the time of the response) whenever the rat pressed the lever during the ITI. (See example, Fig. 1)

The experimental procedure was designed specifically to separate the acquisition of lever

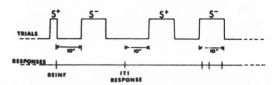

Fig. 1. Representation of trial sequence in 10-sec, CRF single alternation (*i.e.*, ITI was 10 sec, a single bar press during a trial was required for reinforcement, and responding on every other trial was reinforced). The "response" line shows simulated responding of a rat; the "trials" line shows effects of this behavior on the time of onset and duration of the alternation trials and on the duration of the intervals between trials (see text). The following features of the program are illustrated: termination of the trial and delivery of reinforcement when a response was made during a S+ trial; 10-sec duration of all S− trials whether or not the rat responded during the trial; and postponement of onset of the next trial for the ITI interval (10 sec in this example) if a bar press occurred during the ITI.

pressing (CRF or FR 10) and discrete trial performance from the acquisition of alternation *per se*. Accordingly, the procedure was divided into two distinct phases: (1) *preliminary training*, in which the rats were trained to press the lever on all trials, and (2) *alternation training*, in which the rats were trained to press the lever in accordance with the repeating pattern of reinforced and non-reinforced trials.

In *preliminary training*, responding on all trials was reinforced. Each rat remained in preliminary training until it pressed the lever (CRF or FR 10) on 90% or more of the 240 to 300 trials in each of three consecutive experimental sessions. The exact procedure during preliminary training varied somewhat among rats since they required different amounts of shaping to learn to press the lever, and different numbers of training sessions before attaining the 90% response criterion.

Alternation training usually began on the next session after the rat attained the preliminary training criterion. All alternation training sessions were 480 trials long. Each rat had the same trial stimuli, response requirement (FR 10 or CRF), ITI duration, *etc.*, as in its preliminary training. The only significant difference between preliminary and alternation training was that in the latter, responses in only some, rather than all, of the trials were reinforced, in accordance with one of the patterns of reinforced and non-reinforced trials. Thus, it could be assumed that differences between animals in learning the alternation patterns indicated differences in learning the pattern as such, uncontaminated by differences in adapting to the box, in initially learning to press the lever, or in learning to press the lever only during trials. These latter differences were presumably eliminated by bringing all the animals to a common criterion level of discrete trial responding during preliminary training.

Due to difficulties in scheduling experimental sessions, some of the rats that had reached criterion received additional preliminary training sessions before beginning the alternation phase. These extra sessions with responses reinforced in all trials probably did not affect subsequent alternation performance, since in a control experiment no differences in rate of single-alternation acquisition were found between a group which had the usual three criterion sessions at the end of preliminary training and a group that had 21 criterion sessions.

RESULTS

Performance on six alternation sequences. Figure 2 shows the acquisition curves obtained during alternation training for all the rats run on single alternation, single-double alternation, and double alternation under the usual experimental conditions: ITI was 10 sec; a single bar press during an S^+ trial produced reinforcement; and the reinforcer was a drop of sugar water. In Fig. 2, performance is plotted in terms of the ratio between the number of S^- trials on which the rat responded during a session and the number of S^+ trials on which it responded. This ratio is expressed in Fig. 2 as S^-/S^+ for single alternation, and $S_1^- + S_2^-/S_1^+ + S_2^+$ for double alternation. In single alternation and double alternation, the rat received an approximately equal number of S^- and S^+ trials (240 of each) during a session. Thus, the ratio was approximately 1.0 at the beginning of single-alternation or double-alternation training when the rat responded on nearly all its trials and gradually declined as the rat learned its pattern. In single-double alternation ($S^+S^-S^-$), on the other hand, the rat received twice as many S^- as S^+ trials during a session. Therefore, the number of S^+ trials per session on which the rat responded in single-double alternation was doubled in order to obtain a measure of single-double–alternation performance comparable to that used for single alternation and double alternation, and single-double–alternation performance is expressed in Fig. 2 as $S_1^- + S_2^-/2S^+$.

Clearly, each rat learned to respond in conformity to its particular alternation sequence and there was considerable similarity in performance between the different rats assigned to the same sequence. Figure 2 shows that acquisition of single alternation was more rapid than acquisition of double alternation (the slowest of the seven single alternation rats learned more rapidly than the fastest of the seven double-alternation rats) and the rate of acquisition of single-double alternation was intermediate. Acquisition of single-alternation patterned performance was superior not only when performance on the three patterns is compared with respect to the relative

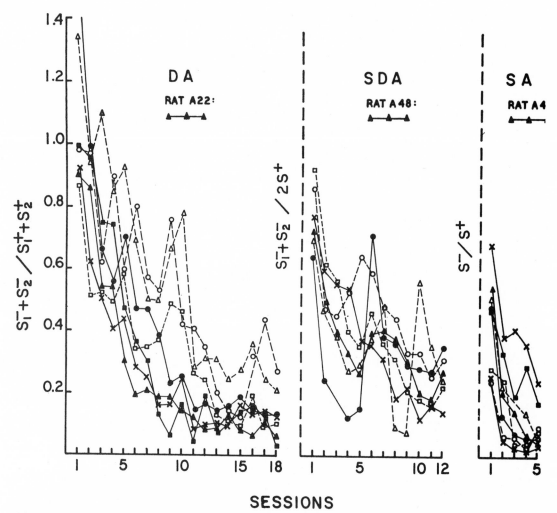

SESSIONS

Fig. 2. Alternation training curves for double alternation (DA) $(S_1^+ S_2^+ S_1^- S_2^-)$, single-double alternation (SDA) $(S^+ S_1^- S_2^-)$ and single alternation (SA) $(S^+ S^-)$ for all of the rats trained on each of these three sequences. Except for the differences in sequence, experimental conditions were the same for all rats shown here. The curves for rats A22 in DA, A48 in SDA, and A4 in SA are specifically designated because the within-session performances of these particular animals are presented in Fig. 3.

proportion of S^- and S^+ trials on which the rat responded, as in Fig. 2, but also when the different number of times that the single-alternation, single-double–alternation, or double-alternation pattern was repeated during the 480-trial session is taken into account. For example, the single-alternation pattern was repeated twice as many times during a session as the double-alternation pattern; yet even if the number of sessions marked on the abscissa of the single-alternation plot in Fig. 2 was doubled to compensate for this difference, the acquisition rate of the single-alternation rats would still be generally superior to that of the double-alternation rats.

Figure 3 shows the within- and between-session performance of individual rats on the various S^+ and S^- trials of single alternation, single-double alternation, and double alternation. As illustrated, the rats responded about as often on S^- as on S^+ trials at the beginning of their first alternation session. As alternation training proceeded, the rats continued to respond on most of their S^+ trials but gradually ceased to respond on S^- trials. In double alternation, and most markedly in single-double alternation, the rats responded less often (made fewer errors) on the first S^- in the sequence than on the second S^-. This differential responding on the S^- trials eventually

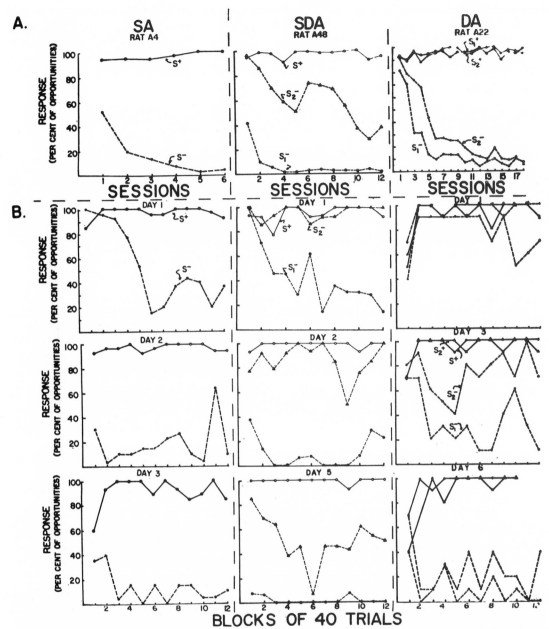

Fig. 3. Between session (Part A) and within session (Part B) performance of representative individual rats on the S+ (solid lines) and S- (dashed lines) components of SA (S+S-), SDA (S+S₁⁻S₂⁻), and DA (S₁+S₂+S₁⁻S₂⁻). The between-session performance of these same rats is shown as ratios in Fig. 2. The particular experimental sessions presented in Part B were selected in order to show the principal changes in S+ and S- responding that occurred during alternation training.

disappeared in double alternation, but persisted in single-double alternation.

Figure 4 shows the acquisition curves for representative rats trained on the remaining three patterns. Thus, the rats were able to learn all six repeating patterns obtained with groups of two, three, or four reinforced and

non-reinforced trials, although the rate of learning and number of trials to asymptotic performance varied considerably from pattern to pattern. Single alternation was learned more rapidly than any other pattern, while the S+S+S+S- pattern was learned most slowly.

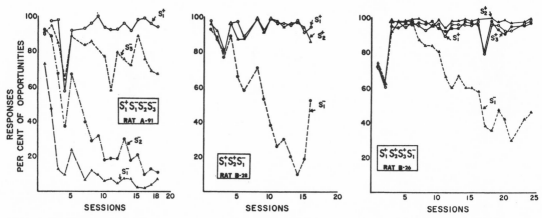

Fig. 4. Acquisition by representative rats of $S_1^+S_1^-S_2^-S_3^-$, $S_1^+S_2^+S_1^-$, and $S_1^+S_2^+S_3^+S_1^-$. Performance on S^+ trials is indicated by solid lines, performance on S^- trials by dashed lines.

It is evident from Fig. 3 and 4 that frequency of responding on a particular S^- component of the pattern depended on the pattern and on the location of the S^- trial within the pattern sequence. For example, if the pattern consisted of an S^+ trial followed by one or more S^- trials (*e.g.*, $S^+S^-S^-$, or $S^+S^-S^-S^-$) a response was least likely to occur on the S^- trial that immediately followed the S^+ trial, and then became increasingly probable on the succeeding S^- trials. The differing probabilities of response on the various components of four of the patterns are shown more directly in Fig. 5 (solid lines).

Figure 5 also shows (dotted lines) how the probabilities of response on the pattern components were altered by sounding an 80-db white noise (the Inter-trial Stimulus) during a designated inter-trial interval in the sequence. As illustrated, the inter-trial stimulus produced marked changes in the probabilities of response on certain pattern components. These effects of the inter-trial stimulus were for the most part predicted by the "discrimination hierarchy hypothesis", discussed in detail below.

Effects of inter-trial interval (ITI). The acquisition of single alternation at various ITIs between 5 and 160 sec was studied with six groups of rats; and double-alternation acquisition at ITIs between 10 and 80 sec was studied with four groups of rats. Each group had the same ITI in preliminary training as in alternation training. The reinforcer in these experiments on acquisition at different ITIs was a food pellet, and 10 responses during a trial

were required for reinforcement. The results are presented in Fig. 6.

In addition to demonstrating once again that single alternation is learned in far fewer trials than double alternation, Fig. 6 shows that the rate of learning single alternation or double alternation decreased as ITI increased. Nevertheless, the rats were able to learn the pattern when the ITI was as great as 160 sec in single alternation, or 80 sec in double alternation (although they did not learn the pattern as well in the same number of sessions as the groups that learned at shorter ITIs). Presumably, the rats could have learned single alternation or double alternation at even greater ITIs than those shown in Fig. 6. Longer intervals were not examined, however, because lengthy experimental sessions would have been required and because at the longer ITIs the rats sometimes failed to respond on a number of consecutive trials.

The role of temporal cues (*e.g.*, time since last trial or since last reinforcement) was examined in two ways: by abruptly increasing the ITI between regularly spaced trials; and by shifting from a fixed to a variable ITI without changing the average interval between trials. The effect of doubling ITI length on single-alternation performance is shown in Fig. 7. Five rats were first trained to stable single-alternation performance with an ITI of 5 sec, and then shifted successively to 10-sec, 20-sec, and finally to 40-sec ITI. Figure 7 shows that increasing the ITI from 10 to 20 sec, and from 20 to 40 sec temporarily disrupted performance, after which the performance grad-

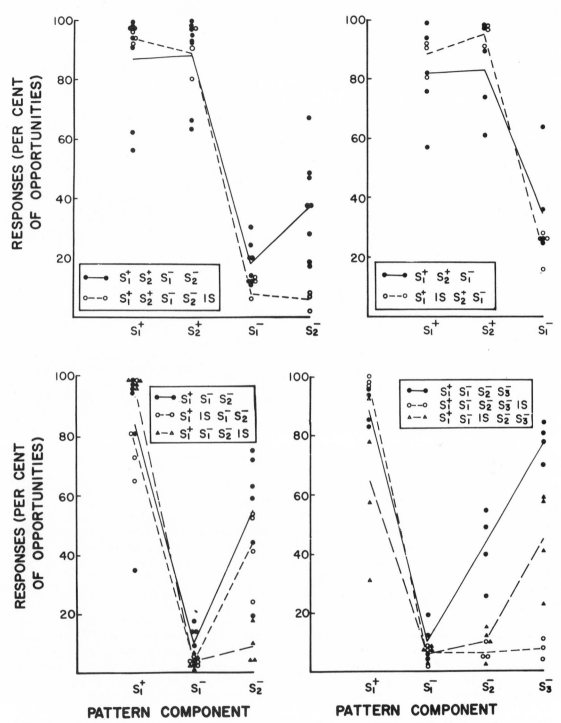

Fig. 5. Performance on the various stimulus components of four alternation patterns, and effects on responding produced by the presence of an "inter-trial stimulus" (IS) during acquisition. The data points for each animal were obtained during its seventh alternation session. The filled circles were obtained from the individual rats that learned an alternation pattern without an inter-trial stimulus; the solid lines show the mean performance for these animals. The triangles or open circles show performance of each of the rats that learned one of the IS-sequences. The dashed lines show the mean performance of the animals trained with the IS.

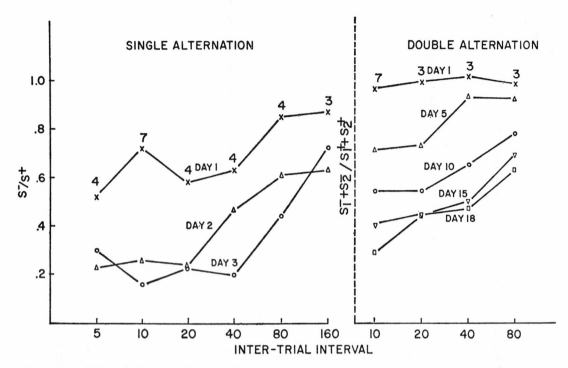

Fig. 6. Acquisition of alternation by SA and DA groups trained at the ITIs indicated on the abscissae. The numbers above the day 1 SA and DA curves indicate the number of rats in the group trained at each ITI. The mean performance of each of the SA groups is shown for days 1, 2, and 3 of alternation training, and the mean performance of each of the DA groups is shown for days 1, 5, 10, 15, and 18 (the final day) of alternation training.

ually returned approximately to pre-shift level.

A similar study of the effect on double-alternation performance of doubling ITI was carried out with three rats initially trained on double alternation with an ITI of 10 sec, and then shifted successively from 10-sec ITI to 20 sec, from 20 to 40 sec, and finally from 40 to 80 sec. Each shift to a higher ITI substantially disrupted performance followed by a gradual return to the approximate performance levels of the groups separately trained on each ITI (*cf.* Fig. 6).

Figure 8 shows the effects on single-alternation performance produced by shifting animals from 10-sec ITI regularly spaced trials to a variable ITI trial schedule in which the mean ITI remained 10 sec, while intervals between trials varied between 5 and 20 sec; and by shifting animals from 40-sec ITI regularly spaced trials to a 40-sec variable trial schedule in which the interval between trials varied between 20 and 80 sec. Figure 8 shows that for both single-alternation groups, the shift from fixed- to variable-trial spacing markedly dis-

rupted alternation performance, following which there was a gradual and incomplete return to preshift levels. A similar set of experiments, in which double-alternation rats were shifted from fixed to variable spacing of trials, yielded inconclusive results. Performance of some of the double-alternation rats was poorer after the shift but the performance of others was apparently unaffected.

DISCUSSION

Groups of rats learned to respond on discrete trials in accordance with six different repeating sequences of reinforcement and nonreinforcement. Since the stimuli presented during the trial before the response were always the same, the animals, in order to respond correctly, must have discriminated between persisting consequences of responding and not responding on preceding trials. Two hypotheses concerned with the types of discrimination that the animals might have made will be considered: (1) discrimination of temporal stimuli, *e.g.*, of time since last reinforce-

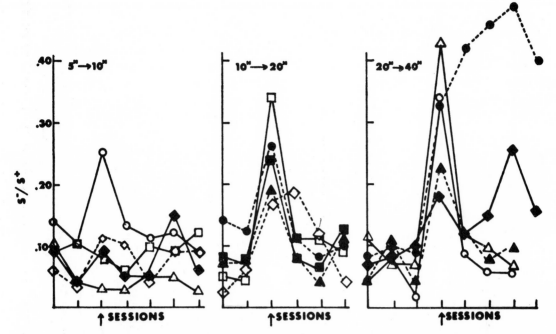

Fig. 7. Effect on SA performance of abruptly doubling the time between trials. The same rats were shifted at the beginning of the sessions indicated by the arrow from 5- to 10-sec ITI, then from 10- to 20-sec ITI, and finally to 40-sec ITI. Each curve shows the session-by-session performance of an individual rat. Experimental sessions required for recovery of stable baselines, intervening between those shown for the three panels, have been omitted.

ment; (2) discrimination of internally carried ("remembered") prior trial outcomes in accordance with a "discrimination hierarchy hypothesis".

(1) *Temporal discrimination.* According to this hypothesis, the rat discriminated the passage of time since its last reinforcement, and was thereby able to respond appropriately when the trials, and particularly the reinforcements, were equally spaced. Wall and Goodrich (1964) presented evidence to show that lever pressing on the discrete trials of three "recursive" sequences: S+S−, S+S−S−; and S+S−S−S− was controlled by temporal discriminations. They obtained the longest latency and lowest response probability on the trial immediately following the reinforced trial, with a progressive decline in response latency and increase in probability as proximity to the reinforced trial increased. On the basis of the similarity of their results to the free-operant fixed-interval (FI) "scallop", Wall and Goodrich argued that their discrete trial sequences were in essence ". . . . . FI schedules with limited opportunities for non-reinforced responding." Dews (1962) has shown that prob-

ability of responding during FI schedules depends primarily on the passage of time, and is independent of the presence or absence of opportunities to respond during the inter-reinforcement interval.

The present finding that single-alternation and double-alternation performance was usually disrupted by increases in ITI length (Fig. 7) or by shifts from fixed to variable ITIs (Fig. 8) could be regarded as evidence for the formation of temporal discriminations. However, the fact that temporal shifts disrupted alternation performance does not establish that the rats were making temporal discriminations before the shift. For example, double alternation performance was disrupted by temporal shifts; yet it seems unlikely that double alternation was controlled by temporal discriminations since the reinforced trials were not regularly spaced in time. Responding on the various sequences could have depended on other processes besides temporal discriminations that were also affected by changes in time, *e.g.*, memory of whether or not reinforcement occurred on the last or second-last trial.

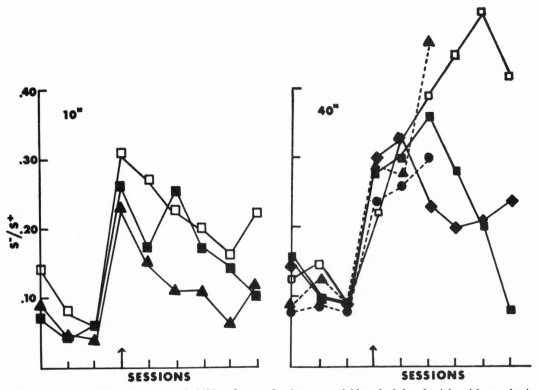

Fig. 8. Effects on SA performance of shifting from a fixed to a variable schedule of trials without altering the mean interval between trials. The shifts were made at the beginning of the sessions indicated by arrows. Each curve shows the performance over sessions of an individual rat. Left: 10-sec mean ITI. Right: 40-sec mean ITI.

In the present experiments, the rats were able to respond appropriately when temporal cues were absent or ambiguous. Rats learned three alternation patterns: S+S+S−, S+S+S−S−, and S+S+S+S−, in which the time between successive reinforcements varied within the sequence. They were able to perform adequately on single alternation and double alternation after they were shifted from fixed to variable scheduling of trials. Capaldi, Veatch, and Stefaniak (1966) have also reported that rats did not require temporal cues in order to learn single alternation in a straight runway. Their rats learned single alternation as rapidly when ITI varied as when it remained constant.

(2) *Discrimination hierarchy hypothesis.* Although it is possible that the rat uses temporal cues in responding on certain sequences, a more general hypothesis of sequential learning based on non-temporal cues is clearly required. Capaldi (1967) developed a hypothesis of "sequential stimulus after effects", which is based on the discrimination of non-temporal

cues. As the designation implies, Capaldi's hypothesis assumes that: (1) the outcomes of preceding trials persist to function as stimuli that control behavior on subsequent trials, and (2) the sequential ordering of reinforced and non-reinforced responding is of critical importance in predicting effects of preceding trial outcomes on subsequent behavior. With the aid of familiar associationistic principles, Capaldi and co-workers have been able to account for an impressive variety of discrete-trial straight runway phenomena, such as effect of reinforcement magnitude, variations in inter-trial interval, and, of particular interest here, single-alternation patterning. However, Capaldi's theory is closely tied to the conditions in the straight runway where, apparently, behavior patterning is much less readily obtained than in the present, lever box, situation. (For example, Bloom and Capaldi (1961) failed to obtain double-alternation performance with the straight runway).

A "discrimination hierarchy hypothesis" has been developed which accounts for the

Table 1

Representation of the six repeating sequences. The reinforced (S+) and non-reinforced (S−) trials appear in the order in which they occurred in the various sequences. The trials were numbered as indicated in accordance with their position in the sequence. The outcomes of the last (lag 0) and second last (lag 1) trials before each of the trials in the sequence are shown by "+" (for a reinforced trial) and "−" (for a non-reinforced trial). An inter-trial stimulus (IS) was inserted in some of the sequences at the inter-trial interval (ITI) indicated. These IS-sequences were designated as either Type A or Type B, depending on whether or not the added IS was expected to reduce errors on a trial in the sequence. An asterisk denotes those trials in the Type A IS-sequences for which a reduction in errors was expected (explanation in text).

			Position in Sequence				
	1 ITI	*2 ITI*	*3 ITI*	*1 ITI*	*2 ITI*	*3 ITI*	*4 ITI*
I (SA)¹				II (DA)²			
Sequence (NO IS)	S+	S−		S+	S+	S−	S−
Outcome: Lag 0	−	+		−	+	+	−
Lag 1	+	−		−	−	+	+
Type A IS-Sequence				S+	S+	S−	S−* IS
Outcome: Lag 0				IS	+	+	−
III (SDA)³			IV				
Sequence (NO IS)	S+	S−	S−	S+	S−	S−	S−
Outcome: Lag 0	−	+	−	−	+	−	−
Lag 1	−	−	+	−	−	+	−
Type A IS-Sequence	S+	S−	S−* IS	S+	S−	S−*	S−* IS
Outcome: Lag 0	IS	+	−	IS	+	−	−
Type B IS-Sequence	S+ IS	S−	S−	S+	S− IS	S−*	S−
Outcome: Lag 0	−	IS	−	−	+	IS	−
V			VI				
Sequence (NO IS)	S+	S+	S−	S+	S+	S+	S−
Outcome: Lag 0	−	+	+	−	+	+	+
Lag 1	+	−	+	+	−	+	+
Type A IS-Sequence	S+ IS	S+	S−*				
Outcome: Lag 0	−	IS	+				

¹SA—single alternation
²DA—double alternation
³SDA—single-double alternation

relative frequency of errors on trials at various locations in the sequences studied in the present experiments, and also predicts most of the changes in error frequency produced by altering the stimuli present in the sequence. As in Capaldi's theory, the present analysis treats the patterned behavior as a series of discriminations of preceding trial outcomes. The hypothesis also assumes that the rat can discriminate not only whether the immediately preceding trial (the "lag-0" trial) was one in which responses were reinforced or nonreinforced, but also, if necessary, whether the second trial back (the "lag-1" trial) or even the third trial back (the "lag-2" trial) was one in which responses were reinforced or non-reinforced. The outcomes of the lag-0 and lag-1 trials that precede each of the trials in the six

sequences studied are shown in Table 1. The trials in the sequences are designated as S+ or S− depending on whether or not responding on them was reinforced; the outcomes of the trials of various lags that precede each of the trials in the sequence are designated as "+" or "−" depending on whether or not responding on these preceding trials was reinforced.

The hypothesis asserts that responding on a particular S+ or S− trial in a sequence is controlled by the outcome of its "+" or "−" lag-0 trial if this "+" or "−" lag-0 outcome is *consistently* associated with S+ or S− whenever it is the lag-0 outcome on a trial in the sequence. If, on the other hand, the lag-0 trial outcome on a trial is *ambiguous, i.e.,* if the lag-0 trial outcome, either "+" or "−", is associated as a lag-0 outcome with both S+ and S− trials in the sequence, then it is assumed that responding on trial will be controlled by the next higher lag trial outcome that *is* consistently associated with S+ or S−.

To illustrate: in single alternation (*cf.* Table 1), an S+ trial always precedes an S− trial and *vice versa*. Thus, in single alternation a "+" lag-0 trial outcome is consistently associated with S− trials, a "−" lag-0 outcome is consistently associated with S+ trials, and it is assumed that responding on the S+ and S− trials is controlled by the "−" and "+" lag-0 trial outcomes respectively. In double alternation, on the other hand, Table 1 shows that the lag-0 trial outcomes are all ambiguous: both "+" and "−" lag-0 trial outcomes are associated with both S+ and S− trials. However, the lag-1 trial outcomes for both the S+ and S− trials in double alternation *are* consistent: "+" as a lag-1 outcome in double alternation is always associated with S− and "−" as a lag-1 outcome is always associated with S+. In double alternation, therefore, the lag-1 trial outcome, whether the second trial back was S+ or S−, is assumed to control the behavior.

The hypothesis has specific implications concerning the relative frequency of errors on S− trials within the various sequences studied. (The rats seldom made errors on S+ trials, reflecting presumably a general tendency toward errors of commission rather than omission.) According to the hypothesis, the rats should respond more frequently (*i.e.*, make more errors) on those S− trials in the sequence for which the lag-0 outcomes are ambiguous. This result will be expected because responding on these S− trials will be controlled by higher lag trial outcomes that *are* consistent; and the higher the lag of the trial outcomes that control the behavior, the greater the possibility that responding can be evoked by lower lag trial outcomes associated with S+ elsewhere in the sequence.

In addition, the hypothesis also leads to definite predictions concerning the effects of experimentally manipulating stimuli in the sequence on the relative frequency of errors in the sequence. These predictions were tested in a series of experiments in which groups of rats learned alternation sequences in which a white-noise stimulus (the inter-trial stimulus) was sounded throughout an ITI in the sequence. The inter-trial stimulus

was introduced into the sequence at the beginning of alternation training, since it did not reliably affect responding if it was inserted after the rats had learned patterned responding without the inter-trial stimulus.

In the "Type A" sequences in Table 1, the inter-trial stimulus was placed in the ITI preceding a S+ trial. According to the hypothesis, the inter-trial stimulus at this location was expected to decrease the frequency of errors on certain specified S− trials in the sequence; these S− trials are designated by an asterisk in Table 1. Note that the decreased errors were predicted for S− trials that did not directly follow the inter-trial stimulus; on the contrary, most of the S− trials for which decreases in errors were expected immediately preceded the inter-trial stimulus.

For the two "Type B" (control) sequences in Table 1, the inter-trial stimulus was placed in an ITI in the sequence where the ambiguity of the lag-0 trial outcomes was left unchanged by introduction of the inter-trial stimulus. Hence the inter-trial stimulus was expected *not* to change the distribution of errors on trials in these sequences.

The extent to which the discrimination hierarchy hypothesis provided an accurate description of the relative frequency of errors on S− trials within the different sequences, and the extent to which differences in errors on S− trials between groups trained with and without the inter-trial stimulus conformed to theoretical expectation can be evaluated by examining the various sequences in turn.

S+S−S− (*Table 1, Sequence III*). The "+" lag-0 trial outcome associated with S− on Trial 2 (as designated in Table 1) of this sequence is consistent and should control responding on this trial; but the "−" lag-0 trial outcome associated with S− on Trial 3 of this sequence is ambiguous because a "−" lag-0 trial outcome is also associated with S+ on Trial 1. Responding on Trial 3 will therefore be controlled primarily by its consistent lag-1 trial outcome. Consequently, more errors would occur on Trial 3 than on Trial 2 because the lag-0 trial outcome on Trial 3 is associated with reinforcement on 50% of its appearances in the sequence and would be expected to evoke some responding.

In the S+S−S− IS Type A sequence, in contrast, the inter-trial stimulus is the lag-0 trial outcome for Trial 1. The "−" lag-0 trial outcome for Trial 3 is now consistently associated only with an S⁻ trial and should control the behavior on this trial. Hence, there should be fewer errors on Trial 3 of the Type A IS-sequence than on Trial 3 of this same sequence with no inter-trial stimulus. Figure 5 shows that this prediction was confirmed.

The S⁺ IS S⁻S⁻ Type B sequence was studied to test whether the inter-trial stimulus reduced errors not by eliminating ambiguity, as asserted by the discrimination hierarchy hypothesis, but rather by "marking" the rat's place in the sequence. The inter-trial stimulus was placed in the sequence where the lag-0 trial outcome for the following trial was consistent when there was no inter-trial stimulus in the sequence. If the inter-trial stimulus served primarily to orient the animal in the sequence, it should have reduced errors no matter where it was in the sequence. According to the hypothesis, on the other hand, placing an inter-trial stimulus after S⁺ in this sequence should not have affected performance because it did not change the ambiguity of lag-0 stimuli: as indicated in Table 1, one consistent lag-0 stimulus (the inter-trial stimulus) merely took the place of another consistent lag-0 trial outcome. Figure 5 shows, in support of this latter interpretation, that the inter-trial stimulus placed after the reinforcement did not alter the pattern of responding.

S⁺S⁺S⁻S⁻ (Double Alternation: Table 1, Sequence II). During both acquisition (Fig. 3) and maintenance (Fig. 5) of double alternation, the rats made many more errors (*i.e.*, responded more frequently) on Trial 4 than on Trial 3. As previously explained, double-alternation responding is controlled by lag-1 trial outcomes. Table 1 shows that the lag-0 and lag-1 trial outcomes are the same (both "+") on Trial 3, whereas on Trial 4 the controlling lag-1 outcome is "+" while the lag-0 trial outcome is "−". This "−" lag-0 trial outcome on Trial 4 has been associated with S⁺ on 50% of its appearances as a lag-0 outcome in the double-alternation sequence. Hence, more responding would be expected on Trial 4 than on Trial 3, due to the incompatible lag-0 trial outcome present on Trial 4.

Introduction of the inter-trial stimulus between Trial 4 and Trial 1 of the double-alternation sequence eliminates the ambiguity of the lag-0 outcome on Trial 4, since, in the IS-sequence, a "−" trial outcome is associated

as a lag-0 trial outcome only with Trial 4. Hence, responding on Trial 4 of the inter-trial stimulus sequence should be controlled by this lag-0 outcome, whereas in the double-alternation sequence with no inter-trial stimulus, responding on Trial 4 is controlled by a lag-1 trial outcome. Figure 5 shows that, as predicted, the rats made fewer errors on Trial 4 of the IS-sequence than on Trial 4 of the double-alternation sequence with no inter-trial stimulus.

S⁺S⁻S⁻S⁻ (Table 1, Sequence IV). Table 1 shows that the lag-0 outcomes on Trial 3 and 4 of this sequence are ambiguous, and, in addition, the lag-1 trial outcome is also ambiguous on Trial 4. The lowest lag trial outcome that is consistent on Trial 4 is the lag-2 trial outcome. Therefore, errors should occur on Trial 3 due to the incompatible lag-0 trial outcome for that trial, and a still greater number of errors should occur on Trial 4 due to interference by both the lag-0 and lag-1 outcomes. Figure 5 shows that, as expected, errors rarely occurred on the trial immediately following reinforcement, and then increased progressively with succeeding S⁻ trials.

Table 1 shows that inserting an inter-trial stimulus between Trial 4 and Trial 1 of this sequence eliminates the ambiguity of the lag-0 trial outcome for *both* Trial 3 and Trial 4. Consequently, there should be fewer errors on each of these trials in the Type-A IS-sequence than in the sequence with no inter-trial stimulus. The results presented in Fig. 5 confirm this prediction.

However, the results obtained with the Type-B IS-sequence (S⁺S⁻ IS S⁻S⁻) were only partially predicted. As expected, Fig. 5 shows that errors on Trial 3, immediately following the inter-trial stimulus, were decreased by the inter-trial stimulus; but it was not predicted that errors would also decrease on Trial 4 of this sequence. The "−" lag-0 trial outcome for Trial 4 remains ambiguous in the Type-B IS-sequence: it is associated with S⁺ as a lag-0 trial outcome for Trial 1 as well as with S⁻ for Trial 4. However, it might be noted *post hoc* that the inter-trial stimulus could have converted the controlling trial outcome for Trial 4 from a lag-2 to a lag-1 outcome (the inter-trial stimulus), thus accounting for the modest reduction of errors on Trial 4.

S⁺S⁺S⁻ (Table 1, Sequence V). The hypothesis predicted unequivocally that an inter-trial stimulus placed between Trial 1 and Trial 2 should decrease errors on Trial 3. With no inter-trial stimulus, the "+" lag-0 trial outcome associated with S⁻ on Trial 3 is also associated with S⁺ on Trial 2. Hence, replacing the "+" lag-0 stimulus on Trial 2 with the inter-trial stimulus should have made the lag-0 trial outcome for Trial 3 consistent, responding on Trial 3 would then have been controlled by the lag-0 trial outcome, and errors should have decreased. But, according to Fig. 5, the results failed to support the prediction. The rats that learned the sequence with the inter-trial stimulus present made as many errors on Trial 3 as those that learned the sequence without the inter-trial stimulus.

Evaluation of the discrimination hierarchy hypothesis. The hypothesis has been shown to be useful for describing, predicting, and controlling the patterns of responding in the various sequences. Nevertheless, unequivocal failure of prediction was specifically noted for one IS-sequence, and partial failure of prediction was reported for another IS-sequence.

More general inadequacies of the theoretical analysis should also be noted. The generally high level of performance on S⁺ trials was not satisfactorily explained. Nor was it stated precisely what aspect of the "outcome" of the S⁺ trials controlled behavior on subsequent trials, whether it was the responding, the reinforcement, or perhaps the mere occurrence of the S⁺ trial irrespective of the behavior and its consequences. The conceptual status of the S⁻ trials, also, was vague: what were the stimulus properties of S⁻ trials on which the rat failed to respond, in contrast to the stimulus properties of S⁻ trials on which the rat did respond? In presenting the hypothesis it was simply assumed, without explicit theoretical justification, that the stimulus properties of these two types of S⁻ trials were identical.

The discrimination hierarchy hypothesis is a trial-by-trial rather than a "pattern as a whole" approach to sequential patterned responding. Nevertheless, in order to predict the pattern of responding, it was necessary to consider the control of responding on individual trials in the context of all the trials in the sequence. The contingencies that controlled the rat's behavior on a given trial depended on relations between the outcomes of the preceding one, two, or even three trials.

Hence, a different type of hypothesis might also have been examined, one that emphasizes learning of the "general pattern". For example, Restle (1967) described experiments in which human subjects learned repeating patterns by "grouping" the trials. It should be possible to devise analogous experiments to discover if rats, like Restle's humans, also "recode" sequences and learn to respond in accordance with rather general "rules".

REFERENCES

Bloom, J. M. and Capaldi, E. J. The behavior of rats in relation to complex patterns of partial reinforcement. *Journal of Comparative and Physiological Psychology*, 1961, **54**, 261-265.

Capaldi, E. J. A sequential hypothesis of instrumental learning. In K. W. Spence and J. T. Spence (Eds.), *The psychology of learning and motivation: advances in research and theory*. Vol. 1. New York: Academic Press, 1967. Pp. 67-156.

Capaldi, E. J., Veatch, R. L., and Stefaniak, D. E. Stimulus control of patterning behavior. *Journal of Comparative and Physiological Psychology*, 1966, **61**, 161-164.

Dews, P. B. The effect of multiple S^Δ periods on responding on a fixed-interval schedule. *Journal of the Experimental Analysis of Behavior*, 1962, **5**, 369-374.

Munn, N. L. *Handbook of psychological research on the rat.* Boston: Houghton Mifflin, 1950.

Restle, F. Grammatical analysis of the prediction of binary events. *Journal of Verbal Learning and Verbal Behavior*, 1967, **6**, 17-25.

Schlosberg, H. and Katz, A. Double alternation lever pressing in the white rat. *American Journal of Psychology*, 1943, **56**, 274-282.

Warren, J. M. Primate learning in comparative perspective. In A. M. Schrier, H. F. Harlow, and F. Stollnitz (Eds.), *Behavior of nonhuman primates*. Vol. 1. New York: Academic Press, 1965. Pp. 249-281.

Wall, A. M. and Goodrich, K. P. Differential responding on reinforcement and non-reinforcement trials occurring in fixed repeating patterns. *Psychonomic Science*, 1964, **1**, 193-194.

Received 8 November 1968.

THE RELEASE OF CATECHOLAMINES BY SHOCKS AND STIMULI PAIRED WITH SHOCKS[1]

S. H. Ferreira[2], L. R. Gollub[3], and J. R. Vane[4]

INSTITUTE OF BASIC MEDICAL SCIENCES,
ROYAL COLLEGE OF SURGEONS OF ENGLAND

One monkey and five baboons were surgically prepared so that heart rate and blood pressure could be monitored continuously, and an extra-corporeal blood path was established to detect the secretion of epinephrine (adrenaline) and norepinephrine (noradrenaline). A respondent conditioning procedure was used in which a tone was paired with electric shocks. Epinephrine, but not norepinephrine was released by shocks, and a corresponding release was demonstrated by the tone alone. Heart rate and blood pressure changes were also elicited by shocks and by the tone.

Many physiological reactions can be conditioned to arbitrary stimuli through the procedure of respondent conditioning (Kimble, 1961; Bykov, 1957), and of these, cardiovascular responses have been extensively studied. For example, after an exteroceptive stimulus such as a light or sound has momentarily preceded an electric shock on several occasions, heart rate (Gantt, 1966) and blood pressure (Newton and Perez-Cruet, 1967) increase when that stimulus is presented alone. Paralysis of the subject with tubocurarine does not prevent this conditioning or its extinction (Black, 1965).

Some of these cardiovascular changes may be induced by the sympathetic nervous system, which is presumed to be activated during aversive conditioning. For example, as early as 1911 Cannon and de la Paz found that blood from a cat exposed to a barking dog contained a substance ("adrenal secretion") that relaxed an intestinal muscle strip. Mason, Mangan,

Brady, Conrad, and Rioch (1961) measured release of catecholamines and other hormones during several different aversive conditioning procedures, using a fluorometric technique. They found an increase in the plasma concentrations of 17-hydroxycorticosteroids and of norepinephrine during an electric shock avoidance schedule, during a conditioned "anxiety" procedure, and release of epinephrine as well during an "ambiguous" stimulus that preceded either food reinforcement or aversive conditioning schedules in an irregular manner (*cf.* Brady, 1967).

We have used the continuous bioassay procedure developed by Vane (1964) to assess the release of catecholamines in primates during classical aversive conditioning procedures. Simultaneous recordings of heart rate and arterial blood pressure were also made.

METHOD

Subjects

One cynamologus monkey (*Macaca iris*) and five male baboons, weighing 5 to 10 kg, had continuous access to food and water.

Surgical Preparation

The experiments were relatively complex and several problems were encountered in the first three, with the monkey and two baboons, the major one being formation of blood clots in the implanted arterial catheter. In the most successful experiments the catheter was pushed quite far down the artery, about 7 cm, so that

[1]Dedicated to B. F. Skinner in his sixty-fifth year. The authors gratefully acknowledge the technical assistance of Miss Heather Carswell, and the loan of apparatus by Dr. A. N. Nicholson. Preparation of the manuscript was supported by USPHS grant MH-01604 from the National Institute of Mental Health.

[2]Smith & Nephew Research Fellow. Present address, Faculty of Medicine of Ribeirao Preto, Ribeirao, Preto, Sao Paulo, Brasil.

[3]Special Research Fellow, USPHS, No. 1-F3, MH-33, 004-01. Present address, and, request reprints from, Department of Psychology, University of Maryland, College Park, Md. 20742.

[4]The order of the authors' names was determined alphabetically.

there was turbulence around the tip, and the lumen of the catheter was partially filled by a nylon rod until the animal was used. The operative procedure was as follows. The baboon was anaesthetized with Phencyclidine (Sernylan, 2 mg/kg intramuscularly), supplemented, as needed, by pentobarbital sodium (Nembutal, 5 mg/kg intramuscularly). A skin incision was made in the neck over the region of the left external jugular vein, and that vein and the left carotid artery were exposed by blunt dissection. Two catheters, 25 cm in length, were made from Portex polyethylene tubing (internal diameter 2 mm, external diameter 3 mm) and a nylon rod of a diameter which just moved easily into the catheter was inserted down its whole length. A short, tight-fitting length of silicone-rubber tubing was tied as a cap to the end of the nylon rod, and formed a seal on the catheter by ligation. The space between the catheter and the rod was filled with strong heparin saline solution (5000 i.u./ml).

The carotid artery and jugular vein were cannulated and the catheters were inserted 7 cm down each vessel towards the heart. The distal end of each vessel was ligated. Next, a mid-line incision was made in the scalp, at the top of the head, in the same plane as the ears, and a trocar was passed under the skin from this incision to the neck wound. The two catheters were threaded through the trocar, which was then removed. Lengths of tubing of about 10 cm emerged from the scalp. The positions of the catheters were fixed only by the stitches in the scalp, which were also tied around them. The muscle layers and skin incision in the neck were closed by cat gut and nylon sutures as was the skin incision on the scalp. The whole operation was carried out under sterile conditions and, as a precaution, the animal was afterwards given benzyl penicillin (1 million units intramuscularly).

Apparatus

While the animal was still anaesthetized, it was placed in a restraining chair (Nicholson, 1965) where it had free access to food and water. The chair was inside a large wooden box (60 by 60 by 120 cm in height) which had a fan for air circulation, a loudspeaker for presenting the masking white noise and auditory stimuli, two white lights, and a hole to receive the lens of a television camera. Electrome-chanical equipment for presenting the various stimuli was in an adjoining room.

In some animals, conditioning was begun on the day after the operation and mean blood pressure and heart rate were measured during the session. Blood pressure from the carotid arterial catheter was recorded with a Statham P23Db strain gauge attached either to a Beckman Offner Dynograph or to a Texas Rectiriter recorder. Heart rate was either recorded on a second channel of the Dynograph with a heart rate input coupler, using the pulse pressure from the strain gauge as a trigger, or counted manually.

Hormone Assay Procedure

On the last day of each experiment, catecholamines in the blood stream were measured, using the blood-bathed organ technique. Blood from the carotid arterial catheter was pumped at a constant rate by a roller pump so that it superfused a strip of muscle from the rat stomach (Vane, 1957) and a longitudinal section of chicken rectum (Mann and West, 1950). (In several experiments, a section of rat colon was also used, to detect angiotensin (Regoli and Vane, 1964) but no evidence of changes in blood concentration of angiotensin was obtained.)

Heparin (Pularin, Evans, 1000 i.u./kg intravenously) was injected into the animal before the external circulation of blood was started. After superfusing the tissues, the blood was returned through the cannula in the jugular vein. With these organs superfused in series, it was possible to distinguish between the release of epinephrine and norepinephrine (Armitage and Vane, 1964). The rat stomach strip relaxes both to epinephrine (adrenaline) and to norepinephrine (noradrenaline), whereas the chick rectum relaxes only to epinephrine. If there is a relaxation of both, it is necessary to match the relaxation on the chick rectum with a control injection of epinephrine. If this matching injection also gives a matching effect on the rat stomach strip, there could not have been any norepinephrine release. However, if the relaxation of the rat stomach strip is greater than is shown by the control, there must also be some norepinephrine present. Our experience with this method shows that it is unlikely to detect less than 10% of norepinephrine in a mixture but would certainly detect more than 15%. The amounts of catecholamines released were determined by comparing the responses of the blood-bathed organs with the effects of intravenous injections of epinephrine and norepinephrine. Generally, the technique could estimate the release of less than 200 ng epinephrine/kg body weight. The movements of the assay organs actuated auxotonic levers (Paton, 1957) attached to "Ether" strain gauges, and were displayed on two or three channels of the Dynograph. Blood pressure, heart rate, and the presentations of conditioned and unconditioned stimuli were also displayed on the Dynograph.

When blood was being withdrawn to superfuse the assay tissues, nylon tubing (1-mm external diameter) was inserted down the arterial catheter via a Y-junction piece, and was connected to the Statham pressure transducer.

Electric shocks were delivered via silver coin electrodes strapped to the animal's shaved tail by elastic bandage. Redux electrode paste helped maintain a good electrical contact. Voltage (50 Hz) was adjusted with a variable transformer, and current was monitored.

General Procedure

Several different methods of pairing tones with electric shock were used. With the exception of the first subject (a Cynamologus monkey), all preparations were short term. The subject was received on Monday or Tuesday of the week of the experiment and was placed in the restraining chair; the operation described above was performed the next day. Preliminary conditioning, with recording of blood pressure and heart rate only was, in some cases, performed on the following day and, in all cases, the cannulae were tested; for some subjects, a second day of recovery and conditioning was allowed. The measurement of catecholamine release and cardiovascular change was conducted the next day. The specific stimuli, and pairing procedures used, varied among the subjects, and are therefore described in detail for each baboon for which data are presented.

RESULTS

In the three fully successful experiments, the animal was healthy and appeared fairly normal throughout; cannulae were sufficiently patent to allow the withdrawal of blood

rapidly enough for the assay tissues, and blood pressure records were obtained. The results from the other experiments were similar in all respects, but were intermittently marred by technical difficulties, such as occlusion of the catheter by a clot.

The first successful experiment, with a 10-kg baboon, showed elicitation of heart rate and blood pressure changes and of release of epinephrine to a tone paired with shock as well as to shock alone. On the day after the operation, a discriminative training procedure was used. Two tones (1500 Hz and 2700 Hz, each of 11-sec duration) were presented, but only one of them (1500 Hz) preceded the electric shock (1-sec duration, 6 ma).

On the first trial, the 1500-Hz tone was presented alone, and there was no change either in blood pressure or heart rate. Nine conditioning trials were then given, during each of which the systolic and diastolic blood pressures increased by about 10 mm Hg and then returned to base line over the next minute. Concurrent with the increase in blood pressure was a sharp fall in heart rate of between five and 10 beats per minute from a basal level of about 200 per minute. By the sixth trial the heart rate and blood pressure changes occurred during the tone and simply continued after the shock had been presented. On the ninth trial the 1500-Hz tone was presented alone and changes in blood pressure and heart rate were essentially the same as on the preceding trials. Because no evidence of differential responding was seen after about a dozen interspersed presentations of the 2700-Hz tone, the procedure was changed to use only the 1500-Hz tone.

On the next day the blood-bathed organ method was used to determine catecholamine outputs during further trials. Blood was superfused at 10 ml/min over a rat stomach strip, a rat colon, and a chick rectum and was then returned intravenously. During the period in which the assay organs were stabilizing, tones and shocks were presented to the baboon. Changes in heart rate and blood pressure were small compared with those obtained on the previous day and there was no observed behavioral response to the shock. We believed that the mechanical pressure on the tail by the straps holding the shock electrodes had been tight enough to cause a mechanical anaesthesia. Therefore, with this subject only, shocks were delivered via light clip electrodes, one attached to each ear. The cardiovascular responses were then similar to those obtained on the previous day, and there was also a release of catecholamines when shocks were given. The cardiovascular response consisted of a rise in both systolic and diastolic pressure of about 20 mm of mercury and a fall of heart rate of 10 to 15 beats per minute. The first paired presentation of tone and shock released some catecholamines into the circulation. By calibration with known amounts of catecholamines, the material released was shown to be 5 μg of epinephrine. The second pairing elicited a similar release of epinephrine. On the third trial, only the tone was presented. The cardiovascular changes were very similar to those obtained before, but the release of epinephrine was reduced to 3 μg. Two more paired presentations each induced the release of about 5 μg epinephrine and a smaller release was again obtained with the tone alone. A further pairing trial 35 min later released 5 to 7 μg of epinephrine. The injection of 7-μg epinephrine intravenously induced blood pressure and heart rate changes almost identical to those seen on a conditioning trial. As in all these experiments, successive trials were conducted only when all technical aspects of the experiments were judged to be appropriate. This criterion included return to baseline and stable movements of the assay tissues, and of heart rate and blood pressure. The intertrial intervals were therefore irregular, and were at least 8 min, and as much as 30 min.

Figure 1 was taken from a later stage in the experiment. In the left part of the figure, the effects of intravenous injections of epinephrine (7 and 3.5 μg), and norepinephrine (8 μg) are shown. The rat stomach strip (top tracing, RSS) relaxed after all three injections, whereas the chick rectum (second tracing, CR) relaxed only after epinephrine. Due to the time taken for the blood to reach the assay tissues, the effects of catecholamines upon them occurred about 35 to 45 sec after the drugs were given, whereas the cardiovascular effects of these drugs were more sudden, beginning within 10 sec. Later in the experiment, by running the paper at 10 times the normal speed, it was possible to see that the rise of blood pressure started within 2 sec of the conditioned stimulus and the fall of heart rate within 4 sec. Note that the third event shown was the presentation of the tone alone (CS). This produced a

relaxation of the assay tissues similar to that produced by 3.5 μg of epinephrine, but a change in heart rate and blood pressure which were somewhat larger.

The right-hand section of Fig. 1 shows the effects of presenting the tone and shock stimuli both alone and in sequence. Each presentation of the tone alone released about 3.7 μg of epinephrine; paired presentation of tone and shock released 5.5 μg, and shock alone released 6.6 μg. The difference between the effect of shock alone and shock preceded by tone was greater as estimated from the response of the chick rectum than from the rat stomach strip.

In these experiments, the release of epinephrine was estimated by injecting calibrating doses of epinephrine in one shot intravenously. The shape of the curves of relaxation of the assay tissues following these injections and following release from the adrenal glands shows that the medullary release must also have reached the venous circulation in a similar sudden burst.

At the end of the experiment, the tone was presented alone on a number of trials. On each successive presentation there was a smaller epinephrine release, and smaller changes in heart rate and blood pressure, until, after 11 trials, all responses to the tone were extinguished.

A second baboon was prepared surgically, exposed to conditioning procedures with measurement of heart rate and blood pressure on the next day, and to the full experimental procedure on the third. On the second day, the mean blood pressure was 90 mm of mercury and the mean resting heart rate was about 118 per min. A 1500-Hz tone, 7-sec long, was paired with a 7-10 ma shock, 1-sec long, to the tail. After the fifth trial, the tone alone produced increases in heart rate of 24 beats per minute and increases in systolic and diastolic blood pressure of about 20 mm of mercury.

On the next day, the circulating catecholamines and cardiovascular function were assessed. Further conditioning trials were conducted and presentations of tone alone and shock alone were also given. The results with this subject were similar to those described above. There was release of epinephrine only, of about 1 to 2 μg, an increase in blood pressure of about 12 mm of mercury, and an increase in heart rate of about 20 beats per minute. Calibrating intravenous injections of

RELEASE OF ADRENALINE BY CONDITIONED AND UNCONDITIONED STIMULI
♂ BABOON 10 Kg

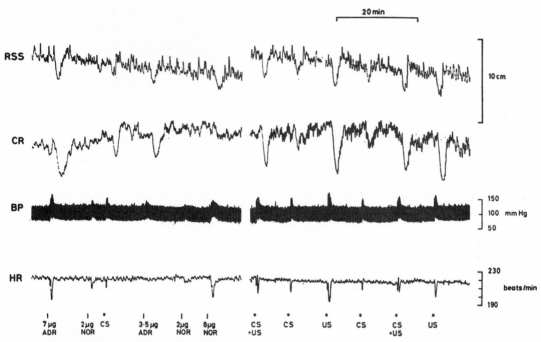

Fig. 1. Two sections of polygraph recordings from a male baboon (10 Kg). Records are, from top, movement of rat stomach strip muscle (RSS), movement of section of chick rectum (CR), arterial blood pressure (BP), and heart rate (HR). Scales on top and to right of records indicate absolute values. Time of occurrence and types of event are indicated at bottom of record: introduction of epinephrine (adrenaline-ADR) and norepinephrine (noradrenaline-NOR) into venous blood catheter, presentation of tone (CS) and electric shock (US).

epinephrine (1 to 5 μg) decreased the heart rate when the blood pressure was increasing, implying that the increased heart rate during the conditioning trials was not due to circulating epinephrine but must have been due to stimulation of sympathetic nerves to the heart or to vagal inhibition.

The assay organs in this experiment reliably detected intravenous injection of less than 2-μg epinephrine. However, during some of the conditioning trials, even though the changes in heart rate and blood pressure were fairly regular, there was not always a detectable output of epinephrine to the tone or shock. There appeared to be no other difference between this animal and the others which would account for the difference in hormonal output.

Because the two complete experiments reported above, and the preceding ones which were technically less satisfactory, were consistent in showing cardiovascular changes and

output of epinephrine during the delay conditioning procedure, a different procedure was used in the next experiment. The baboon was received on a Monday, cannulated on Tuesday, and recordings of heart rate and blood pressure were made on Wednesday and Thursday. On these two days, appetitive delay conditioning, in which food (apples) was paired with a tone (1500 Hz), was performed. The animal readily accepted the food, and oriented its head toward the place where the food was delivered when the tone was turned on. But there were no detectable changes in heart rate or blood pressure as a function of any of the experimental manipulations, which included presentation of food alone, presentation of auditory stimulus alone, paired presentations, and a final series of trials with tone and no food (extinction).

On the third post-operative day, the animal would not accept pieces of apple, probably because it had been given too much food, including apples, on the night before. Two conditioning procedures with shock were, therefore, used. First, a delay conditioning procedure, similar to that used with the other two baboons, was instituted. The auditory stimulus was a 4000-Hz tone and electric shock was applied to the tail. Changes in blood pressure, heart rate, and epinephrine release were again demonstrated for presentations of paired tone and shock, shock alone, and tone alone. The pattern of heart rate changes was, however, different from that described for the other animals. In this case, there was an initial momentary decrease in heart rate followed by an increase.

Later in the experiment a different conditioning procedure was instituted in which a 2-min auditory stimulus (4000 Hz) was pre-sented and was sometimes accompanied by eight irregularly spaced electric shocks to the tail. On some trials, no auditory stimulus was presented, but eight irregularly spaced electric shocks were presented over a 2-min interval. Figure 2 shows a comparison of the effects produced by eight shocks which are and are not accompanied by a specific exteroceptive stimulus. During the first period shown, shock was presented alone; about 2 μg of epineph-rine was released and blood pressure and heart rate increased. A similar effect was produced by the second unaccompanied series of shocks. The third series of shocks was accompanied by a tone which had been associated with the chain of eight shocks on previous trials. There was a smaller increase in heart rate during this series of shocks and also a smaller output

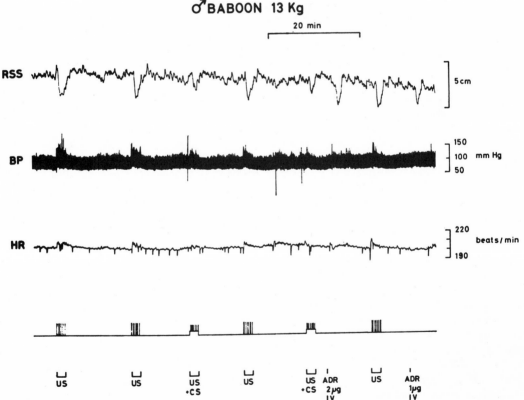

Fig. 2. Polygraph recording from experiment with male baboon (13 Kg). From top, records are movement of section of rat stomach strip (RSS), arterial blood pressure (BP), and heart rate (HR). Scales are shown at the top and to the right of the recordings. Events are indicated on the bottom tracing and by symbols below: administration of epinephrine into the venous blood return (ADR) presentation of electric shocks alone (US) and presentation of electric shocks accompanied by a continuous tone (US + CS). Single large excursions on the BP record are artifacts due to movements by the animal which constricted the arterial catheter.

of epinephrine into the circulation. Next, the shocks were given alone and the increase of heart rate and output of epinephrine were once again larger.

Shocks with tone again produced a smaller change in epinephrine secretion and in heart rate. Intravenous injections of 1 and 2 μg of epinephrine showed that the previous releases had been within this range. This section of tracing shows that when the series of shocks was paired with a tone to which the animal had been conditioned, there was less output of epinephrine into the circulation than when the shocks were given without warning.

DISCUSSION

These experiments showed that increases in systolic and diastolic blood pressure and in heart rate were elicited by an auditory stimulus paired with electric shock, and by shock alone. Because no explicit test was made to rule out sensitization or pseudo-conditioning, it cannot be concluded unambiguously that the response to the tone was specifically conditioned rather than being due to pseudo-conditioning. The procedure followed was a delayed conditioning paradigm, which has previously been shown to produce cardio-vascular changes. Such changes have been widely reported in dogs (*e.g.*, Gantt, 1966), and increases in heart rate and blood flow under similar procedures have been reported in monkeys (Smith and Stebbins, 1965). As in the experiments of Smith and Stebbins (1965) and Stebbins and Smith (1964), visual observation of the animals did not reveal any substantial increases in gross body movement during the conditioned stimulus. In fact, there was often a lessening of activity during the tones. Although undetected increases in muscle tension might have developed during the conditioned stimulus, successful cardiovascular conditioning has been obtained or maintained in dogs when muscle activity has been abolished by crushing anterior spinal nerve roots (Royer and Gantt, 1966) or by the use of neuromuscular blocking agents (*cf.* Black, 1965). The cardiovascular responses elicited by the tone were, therefore, unlikely to have been artifacts of, or dependent on, an operant skeletal response, but, most likely, were conditioned respondents (*cf.* Rescorla and Solomon, 1968).

Elevated blood levels of catecholamines and 17-hydroxycorticosteroids have been previously reported in monkeys undergoing conditioning by Mason *et al.* (1961).[5] In that experiment, monkeys were exposed to several different aversive conditioning procedures, *i.e.*, a shock avoidance schedule, a conditioned emotional response procedure (an auditory stimulus that preceded shock was occasionally presented while the monkey was working for food reinforcement), and a multiple schedule in which a waiting period preceded, on an irregular and unpredictable basis, exposure to an avoidance schedule, to food reinforcement, to shock punishment, or to the conditioned emotional response procedure. Plasma levels of epinephrine and norepinephrine were determined by the Weil-Malherbe and Bone method using chemical separation and fluorometric identification, and of corticosteroids (17-OH-CS), by the Nelson-Samuels method, on blood samples withdrawn immediately before an experimental session, and after 10 and 30 min. They reported: "While norepinephrine and 17-OH-CS elevations occurred in virtually all the conditioned emotional disturbances investigated in this study, the instances in which marked epinephrine elevations occurred—that is levels above 2.5 μg/1., were relatively rare". The only situation that produced consistent increases in epinephrine level was the "ambiguous" waiting period. The authors suggest that norepinephrine is released under "stereotyped, predictable situations, in which the conditions associated with the administration of the noxious stimulus to the animal are unambiguous and familiar" (P. 352), whereas, epinephrine is released in conditions which "all possess an appreciable degree of uncertainty, novelty, or unpredictability" (P. 350).

That finding differs considerably from the present results, but so do the methods. At no time during the present experiments was a release of norepinephrine detected, and even with a mixed output of epinephrine and norepinephrine the latter would have been detectable in proportions of 10 to 20%. The blood-bathed organ method primarily detects phasic releases of hormones, and relatively stable levels, or a very slow release, are less

[5]See also the recent supplement to *Psychosomatic Medicine*, Vol. 30, No. 5, Part II, which summarizes a variety of research by Mason and his colleagues on endocrine changes accompanying various conditioning procedures.

easily seen. In the experiment by Mason *et al.* (1961), norepinephrine increased to as much as 13.6 $\mu g/l.$, a level which, had it occurred in the present study, would have been detected easily.

Almost every detail of the present experimental procedure was different from those of Mason *et al.* (1961), *e.g.*, different species, methods of conditioning, amounts of exposure to conditioning procedures, and time intervals. It would therefore be fruitless to speculate as to which one distinguishing variable is at the root of the difference. One can conclude, however, that an emphasis on the degree of unpredictability or ambiguity of the conditioning procedure is not generally applicable to the present results. It might be relevant to note Mason, Tolson, Brady, Tolliver, and Gilmore (1968) on urinary levels of catecholamines in monkeys under an avoidance schedule. In that study, levels of epinephrine in trained monkeys approximately tripled, whereas those of norepinephrine increased by only 30% during the first 24 hr of an avoidance session. Even though the original data (Mason *et al.*, 1961) on differences in catecholamine output were collected in the same laboratory and in a similar conditioning situation, these authors also acknowledge the presumed importance of the many small differences in procedure that could have produced these markedly different results.

The present study represents perhaps a third pattern of adrenal hormone release, to a third set of behavioral conditioning procedures. We can conclude that shocks and tones paired with shocks in this experiment elicited epinephrine alone, or a mixture of epinephrine and not more than 10 or 15% of norepinephrine. The lower limit of sensitivity to a hormone mixture is at the mean relative level of norepinephrine output detected in the urine of monkeys under avoidance training by Mason *et al.* (1968). The possible congruence of these results should not be overlooked. Altogether, the involvement of the adrenal medulla in response to aversive conditioning procedures seems well established, although the specific variables controlling different types of hormone release are not at all known.

One additional result of the present experiment that deserves some comment was the tendency for lower cardiovascular and hormonal response when a conditioned stimulus preceded the shock than when the shock occurred alone. Similar findings have been reported for the GSR conditioning in man (Kimble, 1961). Rats or dogs also spend more time in a compartment in which shocks are preceded by a stimulus, than in one in which equally frequent shocks are presented alone (Lockard, 1963; Perkins, Levis, and Seymann, 1963; Wagner, 1966). Katcher and Turner (1968) reported, however, that neither heart rate nor blood pressure in curarized dogs differed to signalled and unsignalled shocks. The generality of this finding requires further research.

It also remains to be determined what the interaction is between the cardiovascular and hormonal responses described in this paper and other activities of the organism. Recent work by Miller and his colleagues (Miller, 1969) seriously calls into question any distinction among recordable activities on the basis of type of effector tissue or innervation. The present procedure describes a method for measuring on-line activity of the adrenal medulla, for application of either respondent or operant conditioning procedures. Whether the activity of the adrenal medulla or related autonomic processes during operant avoidance or escape conditioning of some other behavior plays any important role is still largely a matter of speculation (*cf.* Herrnstein, 1969).

REFERENCES

Armitage, A. K. and Vane, J. R. A sensitive method for the assay of catecholamines. *British Journal of Pharmacology and Chemotherapy*, 1964, **22**, 204-210.

Black, A. H. Cardiac conditioning in curarized dogs: the relationship between heart rate and skeletal behavior. In W. F. Prokasy (Ed.), *Classical conditioning*. New York: Appleton-Century-Crofts, 1965. Pp. 20-47.

Brady, J. V. Emotion and the sensitivity of psychoendocrine systems. In D. C. Glass (Ed.), *Neurophysiology and emotion*. New York: Rockefeller Univ., 1967. Pp. 70-95.

Bykov, K. M. *The cerebral cortex and internal organs.* W. H. Gantt (Trans.). New York: Chemical Publishing Co., 1957.

Cannon, W. B. and de la Paz, D. Emotional stimulation of adrenal secretion. *American Journal of Physiology*, 1911, **27**, 64-70.

Gantt, W. H. The meaning of the cardiac conditional reflex. *Conditional Reflex*, 1966, **1**, 139-142.

Herrnstein, R. J. Method and theory in the study of avoidance. *Psychological Review*, 1969, **76**, 49-69.

Katcher, A. H. and Turner, L. H. Interactions between heart rate and blood pressure responses to signalled and unsignalled shock. *Psychophysiology*, 1968, **4**, 506.

Kimble, G. A. *Hilgard and Marquis' conditioning and learning.* New York: Appleton-Century-Crofts, 1961.

Lockard, J. S. Choice of a warning signal or no warning signal in an unavoidable shock situation. *Journal of Comparative and Physiological Psychology*, 1963, **56**, 526-530.

Mann, M. and West, G. B. The nature of hepatic and splenic sympathin. *British Journal of Pharmacology and Chemotherapy*, 1950, **5**, 173-177.

Mason, J. W., Mangan, J. G., Brady, J. V., Conrad, D., and Rioch, D. McK. Concurrent plasma epinephrine, norepinephrine, and 17-hydroxycorticosteroid levels during conditioned emotional disturbances in monkeys. *Psychosomatic Medicine*, 1961, **23**, 344-353.

Mason, J. W., Tolson, W. W., Brady, J. V., Tolliver, G. A., and Gilmore, L. I. Urinary epinephrine and norepinephrine responses to 72-hr avoidance sessions in the monkey. *Psychosomatic Medicine*, 1968, **30**, 654-665.

Miller, N. E. Learning of visceral and glandular responses. *Science*, 1969, **163**, 434-445.

Newton, J. E. and Perez-Cruet, J. Successive-beat analysis of cardiovascular orienting and conditional responses. *Conditional Reflex*, 1967, **2**, 37-55.

Nicholson, A. N. A restraining chair for long term experimental studies in conscious monkeys. *Medical Electronics and Biological Engineering*, 1965, **3**, 77-80.

Paton, W. D. M. A pendulum auxotonic lever. *Journal of Physiology (London)*, 1957, **137**, 35-36.

Perkins, C. C., Lewis, D. J., and Seymann, R. Preference for signal-shock vs shock-signal. *Psychological Reports*, 1963, **13**, 735-738.

Regoli, D. and Vane, J. R. A sensitive method for the assay of angiotensin. *British Journal of Pharmacology and Chemotherapy*, 1964, **23**, 351-359.

Rescorla, R. A. and Solomon, R. L. Two-process learning theory: relationships between Pavlovian conditioning and instrumental learning. *Psychological Review*, 1967, **74**, 151-182.

Royer, F. L. and Gantt, W. H. Effect of movement on the cardiac conditional reflex. *Conditional Reflex*, 1966, **1**, 190-194.

Smith, O. A. Jr. and Stebbins, W. C. Conditioned blood flow and heart rate in monkeys. *Journal of Comparative and Physiological Psychology*, 1965, **59**, 432-436.

Stebbins, W. C. and Smith, O. A., Jr. Cardiovascular concomitants of the conditioned emotional response in the monkey. *Science*, 1964, **144**, 881-883.

Vane, J. R. A sensitive method for the assay of 5-hydroxytryptamine. *British Journal of Pharmacology and Chemotherapy*, 1957, **12**, 344-349.

Vane, J. R. The use of isolated organs for detecting active substances in the circulating blood. *British Journal of Pharmacology and Chemotherapy*, 1964, **23**, 360-373.

Wagner, A. R. *Instrumental-motivational processes in the classical conditioning of skeletal behavior.* Paper read at the XVIII International Congress of Psychology, Moscow, August, 1966. Cited by Rescorla, R. A. and Solomon, R. L., 1967.

Received 9 August 1968.

B. F. SKINNER'S VERBAL BEHAVIOR: *A RETROSPECTIVE APPRECIATION*[1]

KENNETH MACCORQUODALE

THE UNIVERSITY OF MINNESOTA

In his *Annual Review* chapter on the learning literature for 1957, Kendler observed, in obvious bemusement, that "Skinner is an enigma. . . . Never in the history of psychology has one person authored two such contrasting books. *Verbal Behavior* is practically void of facts and filled with speculation. *Schedules of Reinforcement*, on the other hand, is filled with facts and void of speculations" (Kendler, 1959, p. 59). *Contemporary Psychology* acknowledged the importance of *Verbal Behavior* by giving it two prestigious reviewers, Charles Osgood and Charles Morris, representing psychology and semantics, respectively. Both expressed doubt that Skinner's atheoretical system is adequate for verbal behavior, although the point of the book was to show that it is. Such dubiety is perfectly familiar to Skinnerians, and one with which many otherwise orthodox Skinnerians probably secretly sympathize in the case of verbal behavior, suddenly becoming closet mentalists, so to speak.

In spite of their own reservations, both Osgood and Morris were aware of the book's importance. Osgood said: "*Verbal Behavior* is certainly one of the two or three most significant contributions to this field in our time . . . full of insights into human behavior" (Osgood, 1958, p. 212). Morris wrote: "Skinner's book is both elegant and admirable" (Morris, 1958, p. 213). Both predicted a promising future for the book. As Osgood put it: ". . . if the bird proves a little too big for its nest, that merely demonstrates the viability of fledglings" (Osgood, 1958, p. 214). Morris put it more sedately: "It is an impressive book, and its influence will be deservedly great" (Morris, 1958, p. 214).

So it has indeed been, although in a somewhat oblique way. Its influence was partly mediated, of all things, by Chomsky, of all people, who wrote a third, relentlessly negative, review (Chomsky, 1959) that is as well-known among psychologists as the book itself, and even more widely read, to judge by the subsequent uncritical acceptance of its misconceptions concerning *Verbal Behavior*'s content.

In this retrospective review, which will be frankly but, I hope, critically favorable, I will attempt to clarify why *Verbal Behavior* is vulnerable to some misunderstanding, and then to reconstruct the salient points of the book's argument, since I feel that it is its own best justification. Along the way I will comment on those aspects which have, in my experience, raised the most sensible questions. *Verbal Behavior* deserves a careful reading, both for the insights it contains concerning speech, which are considerable, and for the light it casts upon the analysis of behavior as a scientific system, wherever applied.

Verbal Behavior is in part vulnerable to misunderstanding because its intentions and its claims to validity are not firmly specified at the outset. It is neither a grand new theory, nor a new microtheory; it has no new experimental evidence, no cumulative records, no analyses of variance. Many readers, accustomed to having their psychology as well-laced with nearly raw data as possible, simply did not know how to categorize it, although Schoenfeld (1969) has reminded us that *Verbal Behavior* is most like Kantor's *Psychology of Grammar*, against which it might be evaluated. But, alas, Kantor's is not a familiar book.

Skinner characterized *Verbal Behavior* as an "extension to verbal behavior", and "an exercise in interpretation rather than a quantitative extrapolation of rigorous experimental results" (Skinner, 1957, p. 11). In an earlier

[1]Dedicated to B. F. Skinner in his sixty-fifth year. Reprints may be obtained from the author, Dept. of Psychology, 112 Elliott Hall, University of Minnesota, Minneapolis, Minnesota 55455.

version he had called it, rather more informatively, a *plausible reconstruction* of how an accomplished speaker's verbal behavior could have been conditioned and maintained by the same kinds of controlling variables and reinforcing contingencies that have been shown to condition and maintain nonverbal behavior, without recourse to new principles, new variables or, above all, to hypothetical entities, either as causal mediators or as attributes of speech as a dependent variable.

I think that *Verbal Behavior* is best conceived as a *hypothesis* that speech is within the domain of behaviors which can be accounted for by existing functional laws, based upon the assumption that it is orderly, lawful, and determined, and that it has no unique emergent properties that require either a separate causal system, an augmented general system, or recourse to mental way-stations.

The word *hypothesis* may be unwelcome and incautious in this context, but it seems to me to fit precisely, and to put *Verbal Behavior* on familiar ground, where it can be evaluated against relevant criteria. Like all hypotheses, this one asserts more than the author has yet demonstrated experimentally, and it sounds dogmatic. We expect and tolerate this in hypotheses. I do not know when a hypothesis is premature. Usually they are published after they have been experimentally tested, which *Verbal Behavior* has not been. Neither has it stimulated many relevant experiments on its own terms. What little research has followed is highly focussed upon the effects of reinforcing verbal responses having preselected grammatical properties, such as plural nouns. In spite of the fact that there is no formal response property likely to sustain response induction in such classes, the reinforcement operation has proven surprisingly (and perhaps disconcertingly) powerful.

For his part, Skinner seems not hopeful for an eventual experimental test of the hypothesis, principally because of the vicissitudes of identifying and controlling all of the variables presumably at work, and because of the practical impossibility of knowing any speaker's relevant ontological history. The available longitudinal observations of adult-child interactions in naturalistic settings provide very, very restricted samplings of the speech of a very small number of rather elderly children, and represent monumental labor. Parenthetically, they also contain much information to reassure Skinner, although they are not experimental either.

These practical constraints upon the experimental testability of *Verbal Behavior* do not transmute it, or the analysis upon which it rests, into a theory, pure speculation, or metaphysics. *Verbal Behavior* is, actually, full of relevant empirical observational, naturalistic data. Although they are not experimental and were not generated for the purpose of testing the hypothesis, they do constitute a test of it, in that they are consistent with it and do not contradict it. In this respect, however, they are precisely as powerful as an experimental test would be.

Supposing that *Verbal Behavior* is a hypothesis, what may we demand of it? Not that it must have been proved, of course, nor be consistent with our common preconceptions concerning the relation between mind and speech. These are not the aims of a hypothesis. We can expect that existing terms and processes in the underlying explanatory apparatus will be plausibly applied to speech conceived in purely behavioral terms, without modification in any defining characteristics and without invoking new, *ad hoc* variables.

Verbal Behavior is vulnerable also because its preconceptions concerning speech are at such variance with tradition. Speech is the last stronghold of mentalism. Now Skinner is telling us that it is not needed even there. One's initial conviction that a purely functional account is viable for all behavior depends heavily upon acquaintance with Skinner's methodological papers, which many readers simply lack. They are referred to *Science and Human Behavior* (Skinner, 1953) for rehabilitation, a surprising but exactly appropriate choice, although Skinner says of *Verbal Behavior* that "the present account is self-contained" (Skinner, 1957, p. 11).

The morale of even the most devoted functional analyst may need some bolstering as the analysis relentlessly proceeds to encompass speech. He may wince at hearing himself called a mere "locus—a place in which a number of variables come together in a unique confluence to yield an equally unique achievement" (Skinner, 1957, p. 313), and something to be "got rid of" (Skinner, 1957, p. 312), so far as his autonomous control over his own speech is concerned. One wonders about him. If he is not willing to entertain the *possibility*, at least, that the analysis is sufficient for his own speech, and may diminish the importance of his *self*, why did he start out on this path in the first place? The destination is clearly not a surprise, however much the assertion that we have already arrived at it may be. Why does he deny more than locus status to the rat or pigeon? What does he suppose happens to the effects of his own past reinforcements and to the evoking power of his environment when he suspends natural science and takes over control of his speech?

A third aspect of *Verbal Behavior*'s vulnerability is that the explanatory processes described are usually not identified by their technical names. This stratagem was no doubt meant to make things easier and more palatable for the nonscientific reader, but it disconcerts the scientific one, who wonders if a technical term which seems apt in a given context has been avoided for some reason which eludes him. Chomsky curiously complained that Skinner borrows the technical vocabulary to create a spurious atmosphere of objectivity; I have concluded quite the opposite, and would have preferred more.

Speech as Behavior

There is something paradoxical in the mere existence of a separate treatment of speech, since the purpose of the effort is to show that neither the form of the behavior nor the necessary explanatory system is in any way separate or unique. Verbal behavior is, in effect, a subclass, not a new class, of behavior. By Skinner's definition, any behavior is verbal if it is "reinforced through the mediation of other persons" (Skinner, 1957, p. 2). The traditional topographical verbal repertoires—speaking, writing, and gesturing—are reinforced by persons whose mediating behavior has been *"conditioned precisely in order to reinforce the behavior of the speaker"* (Skinner, 1957, p. 225. Italics in original). At first blush, this seems an unnecessarily oblique way of defining the domain, but it is appropriately functional and consistent with the hypothesis. Moreover, it reveals itself, on close inspection, to be a sanitized way of isolating those repertoires that are traditionally said to be symbolic. What is symbolic about verbal behavior is, first, that it is without direct, mechanical reinforcement contingencies, but second, that

it is responded to discriminatively by other, appropriately conditioned, people in ways which are reinforcing to the speaker. This fact gives verbal behavior essentially all of its unique characteristics.

The verbal repertoires which reinforcement mediators have been conditioned to discriminate are such that "in studying speech we have to account for a series of complex muscular activities which produce noises. In studying writing or gesturing, we deal with other sorts of muscular responses" (Skinner, 1957, p. 13), and nothing more. Gone are intention, ideas, information, reference, meaning, and all other conceptual dimensions attributed to verbal behavior. As usual the muscles are not named; since speech is operant, what counts is effect, not form. Direct quotation and transcription suffice for adequate recording of speech. These may seem crude as scientific data, but in fact they stimulate the recipient of the report in much the same way that they stimulated the observer of the original behavior.

The Response Unit

In the analysis of verbal behavior it becomes necessary to respect the difference between the operant and a response, a distinction which tends to become blurred in discussions of nonverbal laboratory behavior. The bar press and the key peck appear to be identifiable on purely formal grounds. A response is what repeats and can be counted. However, the recycling aspect of bar pressing and key pecking is an intentional artifact of the experimental situation which does not occur in verbal behavior, whose formal properties tell us nothing about where the boundaries of its component responses are located. The verbal response can best be identified as whatever is strengthened in a verbal operant or, put another way, whatever is strengthened as a consistent effect of a controlling variable. Linguistically a response may be a phoneme, word, or phrase. Quite obviously, then, at present writing the verbal response is definable only abstractly, but the method for deriving an example from actual speech is available. It is empirical and nonarbitrary.

Common sense and our preconceptions tell us that once a verbal response has been conditioned it is available for "use" in a rather wide variety of circumstances. The conception of the verbal operant encourages no such prediction. According to *Verbal Behavior*, if the response *milk* has been conditioned to milk as a stimulus, it will not *therefore* be strengthened as a request by an appropriate state of deprivation, unless of course the two situations have some elements in common to sustain a form of generalization from one to the other. Skinner is very clear about this. However *a priori* probable it may seem that the speaker who "knows the word for milk" will automatically be able to ask for it by name, he may very well not. Correct or not, Skinner's prediction is interesting because it is deduced from the analysis; he is not merely composing a technical paraphrase of common sense.

Considering how familiar the concept of the operant is, it reemerges as a surprisingly apt and powerful entity when applied to verbal behavior. It would tell us, if we knew what operants a speaker "has", precisely what we need to know in order to predict, control, and understand why he speaks. A lexicon of the responses in his repertoire would tell what he might say, but not the conditions under which he would say them. A record of response *orders*, no matter how precisely recorded and internally analyzed, and no matter how conceptualized and categorized in terms of surface and underlying grammars, can reveal nothing concerning the structure of controlling variables. These are illuminated by knowledge of the circumstances in which they have occurred. In fact, questions concerning both the meanings and the grammars of such puzzling response specimens as *They are eating apples* are answered by identifying their controlling variables.

We probably have come to use the terms *operant* and *response* interchangeably because it is reassuring to do so. A response, as a unique, dated occurrence, is unquestionably objective, and easily satisfies our insistence upon natural science dimensionality for all of our terms. The operant, on the other hand, is a relation, and therefore dubious. But all of an operant's component parts, the antecedent and response terms, are objective and measurable, and so is the fact that one follows the other with a specifiable frequency. Nothing is imaginary.

The objectivity of some of the responses mentioned in *Verbal Behavior* may be suspect. For example, much speech is said to be covert or subvocal, and is ordinarily unobservable.

However, covert behavior is presumed to have muscular locus, with reduced but real and instrumentally measurable amplitude. It is at least potentially observable, although the operant research tradition has left these repertoires almost completely uninvestigated.

Covert speech is said to occur in a situation that would otherwise strengthen the corresponding overt form. Its covertness is separately accounted for as due to some additional threat of punishment for speaking aloud. It tends also to be the form of speech addressed to the self, since the effort-reinforcement ratio can thus be reduced without loss in probability or amount of reinforcement. In *Verbal Behavior* it plays two important roles. It is a common form of the dependent variable, and on occasion it is said to be a causal variable. In the latter role, it is likely to be incorrectly viewed as an explanatory fiction. Properly speaking, it is an hypothesized and presumably demonstrable event, not an hypothetical, theoretical one.

In speech, as in any other behavior, the "basic datum to be predicted and controlled" is the probability that a given response will occur at a given time (Skinner, 1957, p. 28). The range of probabilities considered in *Verbal Behavior* extends *below* the threshold of actual occurrence (overt or covert; this is not the issue) to include responses which are merely *potential* or *incipient*. This range of probabilities is somewhat troublesome, but it does appear to describe what happens. For example, any stimulus object seems to strengthen an *array* of verbal responses. But, while several response probabilities may increase simultaneously, several responses cannot occur at once. Those which lose out must be considered as having been merely incipient or potential. Such probabilities raise several methodological issues which Skinner does not elaborate in *Verbal Behavior*. Some of these must be recalled in later portions of this review (see especially *Autoclitic Behavior*).

Reinforcement

Reinforcement is central to the thesis of *Verbal Behavior*. Skinner obviously supposes that speech is conditioned and maintained only by speech-contingent reinforcement. This is not to say that genetic contributions to speech are absent or negligible. A human organism learns to talk because he is genetically equipped to do so. If he were not, he would not learn. He inherits his vocal musculature and a strong predisposition to make vocal noise. He learns because he is genetically susceptible to reinforcement and its collateral induction and generalization effects. None of this, however, is speech, which is the product of these genetic capabilities and experience.

There is considerable emphasis in *Verbal Behavior* upon *conditioned generalized reinforcement*. Whatever objectivity speech achieves is due to the availability of such reinforcers, as we shall note later in more detail. Knowledge of generalized reinforcers is more observational than experimental, but, while one might wish for more, there is nothing *prima facie* improbable or *ad hoc* about the role they are said to play in speech.

Another emphasis, on the other hand, is new and initially puzzling. The mediator of much reinforcement for verbal behavior is said to be the speaker himself. He can self-reinforce, as when he delivers to himself a conditioned generalized reinforcer, such as a covert *good* or *that's right* contingent upon some other verbal response in his own speech. A special case is *automatic* self-reinforcement. The dice player calls his point and is said to be automatically self-reinforced for doing so by "hearing good news at the earliest opportunity". "Boasting is a way to 'hear good things said about oneself'" (Skinner, 1957, p. 165). Similarly, the inexperienced reader reinforces himself by making tentative responses until he hears one to which he can respond as a listener.

The idea takes some getting used to, and Skinner for the most part leaves the reader to work it out by himself. A single speaker also becomes accomplished as a listener and reinforcement mediator. If he hears himself say something that is reinforcing in his verbal community, he will not be exempt as a listener from its reinforcing consequences. But since both speaker and hearer are the same, this reinforcement is no longer mediated and non-automatic, hence it is automatic and self-reinforcement. A similar and more conventional version of this process occurs in nonverbal behavior when "the musician playing for himself ... plays music which, as listener, he finds reinforcing. In other words, he 'plays what he likes' just as the self-reinforcing speaker 'says what he likes'" (Skinner, 1957, p. 165).

It would be a mistake to paraphrase automatic self-reinforcement by saying that such behavior "reinforces itself". It generates stimulus *consequences* that would be reinforcing if they originated from another source, and does not reinforce itself any more than any other behavior does.

The Controlling Variables

If a pigeon is conditioned to peck with food reinforcement when the key is illuminated, pecking is conjointly controlled by food deprivation and illumination, and to alter either is to alter the probability of the response. Considered as verbal behavior, what does the peck "tell" the observer about the pigeon's current motivational and environmental circumstances? Nothing unequivocal. It says, in effect, *The light is on* and *I am hungry*. The laboratory pigeon never gives an objective and disinterested report of its environment. If sufficiently deprived, it may lie and say that the light is on when it is not. It may fail to report that the light is on unless it is *also* deprived.

Verbal behavior is different. Some verbal responses are under essentially exclusive environmental control. Neither their form nor the probability of their emission is affected by the speaker's motivational condition. Other verbal responses are, similarly, controlled by motivational conditions and are essentially independent of environmental influence. This polarization of motivational and environmental variables and the speech they control is an emergent dynamic property of verbal behavior, but it does not depend upon a new term or process in the operant conditioning paradigm, as the reinforcement histories for stimulus and deprivation controlled responses show, according to Skinner's reconstruction.

Motivational Variables: the Mand

Skinner defines a mand as "a verbal operant in which the response is reinforced by a characteristic consequence and is therefore under the functional control of relevant conditions of deprivation or aversive stimulation" (Skinner, 1957, p. 35-36). *Milk, please, taxi*, and *stop that* are typical mands; each produces its own characteristic consequence when received by an appropriately conditioned reinforcement mediator. A particular deprivation or aversive stimulus automatically acquires control over its mand because the reinforcer it specifies is ineffective under other conditions. In these respects the mand is very like most nonverbal behavior. But more importantly, unlike most nonverbal behavior, the *form* of the mand does not covary with stimuli in the speaker's environment.

All of the examples of deprivations and aversive stimuli cited in *Verbal Behavior* are wholly objective. The motivational conditions responsible for mands that specify conditioned reinforcers, *Take me for a ride*; *Let me fix it*, presumably involve some other reinforcer that originally was paired with the conditioned reinforcer specified in the mand. No riding drive or fixing drive is implied; drive, the suspect term which seems to come and go between books, does not appear in *Verbal Behavior*.

However, one new (to me) dynamic process of motivational control is invoked to explain *magical mands*, "which cannot be accounted for by showing that they have ever had the effect specified or any similar effect upon similar occasions" (Skinner, 1957, p. 48). One supposes, for example, that *Would God I were a tender apple blossom* has never been reinforced by the effect it specifies. "The speaker," Skinner says, "appears to create new mands on the analogy of old ones" (Skinner, 1957, p. 48), which does describe the process but does not really explain it. It is as if reinforcement of a sufficient variety of mands creates a kind of superoperant containing all of the remaining motivational states, pre-coupled with whatever responses specify the reinforcers appropriate to them. Unfortunately, *Verbal Behavior* does not coordinate this analogic process with any familiar principle of behavioral control. Magical mands are merely said to be *extended*, a word Skinner uses in this book to characterize behavior whose strength is due to either response induction or stimulus generalization, both ways of "creating by analogy" to be sure. To the best of my knowledge, however, we do not yet have any experimental evidence to justify including deprivation among the variables that sustain generalization. Even if we did, the heterogeneity of the deprivation states among which generalization would have to extend seems excessive. The existence of magical mands seems so ubiquitous that the informality of Skinner's explanation suggests a real weakness in the formulation.

Mands comprise a rather small fraction of all speech, which is interesting because it follows that the large remainder is essentially free of control by motivation, the variable which even Skinnerian psychologists tend to think lies somewhere behind everything.

Stimulus Variables: S^Ds

The larger part of speech is controlled by discriminative stimuli (S^Ds). It includes the generic *tact* case, such as naming, assertion, and announcement, and also the speech involved in reading, echoing, intraverbal responding, and certain audience effects. Such speech is often entirely objective and disinterested, independent of, and sometimes antithetical to, the speaker's motivations. The scientist is a highly discriminating tacter, reporting what he observes whether it refutes his theory or not. The reader simply talks away, saying anything, any time, good news or bad, whether he believes or even understands a word he speaks. There is, so to say, nothing of the *speaker* in such verbal behavior. This is remarkable and it must be explained.

In conditioning these operants, the reinforcing community solves an obvious problem in behavioral engineering: it must maintain a three-term contingency between the speaker's environment, the form of his verbal response, and the presentation of reinforcement. So much is no problem of course, except that it must be done so as to prevent the spontaneous emergence of an additional contingency between any particular motivational state of the speaker and the probability and form of reinforcement. The verbal community accomplishes this through the use of *conditioned generalized reinforcers*. For verbal behavior, the common conditioned generalized reinforcers are themselves verbal. The reinforcement mediator says something: *um-hm, right, thank you, correct, yes, very interesting*—a short list whose items are interchangeably applicable to any stimulus-response contingency *provided* they stand in some sort of conventional correspondence. If their use is restricted to these circumstances, purely environmental control results, while careless use of them produces inexact stimulus-response correspondences such as exaggeration, ambiguity, and outright lying.

The largest and most important class of stimulus-controlled speech occurs in the *tact*, whose controlling relations are "nothing less than the whole of the physical environment—the world of things and events which a speaker is said to 'talk about' " (Skinner, 1957, p. 81). Formally, the tact is defined as "a verbal operant in which a response of given form is evoked (or at least strengthened) by a particular object or event or property of an object or event" (Skinner, 1957, p. 82).

A tact conditioned to one stimulus will, of course, generalize to other stimuli. Again avoiding the technical term, Skinner says that such generalized behavior is *extended*, and again he runs the risk of appearing to name the effect but not explain it, although the informed reader should see at once that generalization is involved. Skinner shows, in a very illuminating discussion, how such literary examples of extension as metaphor, simile, and metonymy, with all of their traditional mentalistic, high-art, creative-act connotations, are nothing but rather simple instances of generalized stimulus control. Metonymic extension is particularly important because it accounts for many instances in which a tact appears to be strengthened by a missing stimulus, such as when a speaker says *no orange* when confronted by the empty fruit bowl. A missing stimulus cannot control any response. To suppose it could generates endless absurdities: there is no elephant either, but no one is likely to mention the fact. *Orange* in this context is often a simple tact, metonymically controlled by the fruit bowl in whose presence it has been reinforced on occasions when it held an orange. The *no* is autoclitic, not metonymic, and will be discussed below.

Abstraction involves tacting in response to some single isolated property of a stimulus such as its shape, color, or configuration. The process is often conceived as involving a prior nonverbal act of decomposing the environment into its parts—called universals—which are then tacted. Skinner's reconstruction implies, however, that functionally it is not the speaker who acts to abstract a property out of its context, but rather the property which abstracts or strengthens one response out of the speaker's repertoire.

Skinner says that "abstraction is a peculiarly verbal process because a non-verbal environment cannot provide the necessary restricted contingency" (Skinner, 1957, p. 109), *i.e.*, the discrimination learning necessary for abstraction *must* be mediated by another organism. Feral organisms thus do not abstract, because colors, lengths, and shapes as such do not have innate functional identities, and the feral environment does not maintain any correlation between them and reinforcement for some conventional response. The full pursuit of this empirical view of perception contains much food for thought and can be the subject of endless debate. It is probably true for *conditioned* responses controlled by abstract properties of stimuli, which do appear to require mediated reinforcement. However, some abstract stimuli appear to have innate functional identities for some feral organisms, since they evoke (or is it elicit?) species-specific behavior from them.

Tacting Private Stimuli

It is somewhat curious that Skinner, the most thoroughgoing behaviorist, is the only one who has been willing to discuss private stimuli, which he has done with characteristic consistency since 1945. Since speakers do learn to tact such stimuli, from, as Skinner puts it, "*heartburn* to *Weltschmerz*" (Skinner, 1957, p. 132), the variables controlling those tacts must be located in the interests of the completeness of the verbal account. The analysis in *Verbal Behavior* is essentially unchanged from his 1945 version, and need not be reconstructed here. In *Verbal Behavior*, however, he gives especially detailed consideration to tacts that describe the speaker's own behavior. These include responses like *beautiful*, *familiar*, and *similar*, which *refer* to external stimuli, but the possibility that external stimuli directly control them is contraindicated by the fact that these responses are evoked by stimuli among whose members no generalization gradients or common objective properties can be presumed. Skinner suggests that the recurrent element in situations called *beautiful*, *familiar*, or *similar* is to be found in the speaker's responses, not the situations themselves.

This, of course, is the mediation paradigm. It has been in operant psychology a long time. It presupposes that a speaker *can* discriminate his own behavior as a covert, essentially private, event.

Other Kinds of Stimulus Control

In addition to the tact, Skinner recognizes four specialized classes of stimulus control.

Echoic speech "generates a sound pattern similar to the stimulus" (Skinner, 1957, p. 55), and is conditioned, not innate. In a *textual* operant, "a vocal response is under the control of a nonauditory verbal stimulus" (Skinner, 1957, p. 66), such as printed, written, or pictorial matter. *Intraverbal* operants are composed of stimulus-response relationships which do not show the fine-grained, point-to-point control of echoics and textuals. The *audience* gains control as an S^D whose effects upon speech are always supplementary, according to a process to be discussed below.

The important question to ask about this array of stimuli is whether they are consistent with the traditional physical definition of the S^D. So far as I can determine they all are. However, either of two rather easily made mistakes might lead to the erroneous criticism that one has, in fact, found a hypothetical stimulus in *Verbal Behavior*. The first is to restrict *stimulus* to simple points or dimensions. When a speaker tacts a painting as *Dutch*, he is responding to complex and subtle relations among many simple stimulus dimensions, not to any element of Dutchness. The relations he is tacting are as physical as the elements that comprise them, however, and no hypothetical stimulus dimension is involved. The other mistake is to identify the *referent* of a tact as its S^D. Tacting is not reference. Reference is a relation between the environment and some of the words in a language; its existence is independent of any speaker. Although the notion of reference has its uses elsewhere, Skinner shows that in a functional analysis it is merely mischievous. The principal difficulty is that a word that *refers*, while it is indeed controlled by its referent in some tact relationships, also occurs at other times, controlled by other stimuli to which it does not refer. So, one may say *Eisenhower* because he has just read the name or heard it; his response refers to the man but is controlled by the text or the echoic stimulus. Attempting to preserve the reference-tact identity in these circumstances conduces to the hasty conclusion that the Eisenhower that controls the response is now a hypothetical, mental one. In a functional analysis, of course, it is the controlling stimulus, not the referent, which is of interest. The speaker who says *I am going to Europe this summer* refers to an event but does not tact it because it does not exist yet. The envoy who reports home what the ambassador said is not speaking echoically, although he is referring to the ambassador's speech. In such instances, other S^Ds, real and concurrent, must be presumed to control.

Combining the Variables: Recomposing the Environment

These five kinds of stimulus control, plus motivation, constitute all of the variables Skinner provides to account for the emission of speech, and the functions that relate them to speech are all simple enough to be observed in lower organisms. Everything considered, the basic explanatory apparatus seems very meager, while verbal behavior is very complex.

But the power of a simple functional law must not be underestimated. A process observed in a simple organism such as a pigeon or rat may recur in the behavior of a human child or adult with vastly different parameter values. Grammatical behavior may be very rapidly conditioned in children and at a very early age. Neither the complexity nor the rapidity nor the age of the child proves that the underlying conditioning processes are different from those involved in conditioning the key peck. The fact that rats and pigeons never learn to talk does not prove that their conditioning processes are insufficient. No one has ever tried to teach one to behave verbally using the processes specified in *Verbal Behavior* (although Wenrich appears to have trained a rat to tact, Premack is undertaking to condition abstract tacting in a chimpanzee, and the Gardners are teaching theirs to mand).

More importantly, the power of a single variable is seen to multiply when we take into account its multiplicity of effects. Two forms of what Skinner calls *multiple causation* are identified in *Verbal Behavior*. First, a single variable controls many responses, giving a speaker a great deal to say even in a static environment. No train of ideas is needed to keep him talking. Although multiple concurrent effects of a single deprivation condition are familiar, multiple S^D effects are not. In the laboratory experiment, an initially neutral stimulus is ordinarily selected to become the controlling variable for a single response, thus conducing to an informal "one-stimulus one-response" rule which is, however, artifactitious and not a necessary consequence of the discrimination process.

If one stimulus controls many responses the problem of accounting for the sheer bulk of speech is solved, but the solution generates another problem because, if several responses are concurrently strong, additional variables are needed to control the order of their emission and whatever response selection, and rejection, occurs. Ordering is a problem of great magnitude and interest. It is discussed below.

As for response selection, two traditional but repugnant solutions suggest themselves. One is to give in at last and let the speaker "choose his words" from among those currently made available to him by the variables. Skinner rejects this because such choice behavior must, in turn, be accounted for. The other is less solution than stratagem: predict that the response which has the most favorable reinforcement history will occur first, and then account for mispredictions, when the occasional low-strength response intrudes, as due to oscillation (that is, chance).

Skinner's alternative is to account for response selection in terms of variables already at hand. Some responses no doubt select themselves on the basis of their superior reinforcement history. The unexpected response, the neologism, slip, or intrusion is accounted for by another form of multiple causation in which a given response is concurrently strengthened by more than one variable, or "said once for two reasons". Their separate strengths are said to combine, additively and algebraically in fact. Skinner calls this process *supplementary strengthening*. The most subtle and interesting examples occur within *thematic groups*. A thematic group might be defined as the array of responses strengthened by a single S^D in the tact or intraverbal relationship. If a normally weak response in such a hierarchy receives sufficient additional strength from a supplementary variable, it will occur instead of other, normally stronger, responses. One of Skinner's examples (Skinner, 1957, p. 237) quotes a legend underneath a picture of the kitchen at 10 Downing Street: *A bad meal cooked here can derange British history*. The oddity of *derange* in this sentence compels attention. An existing tendency to say *derange* as part of a thematic group including *disrupt, disturb, deflect*, and so forth, may have received the necessary supplementary strength from the rather prominent *range* in the picture.

Anticipating the criticism that the explanation is far-fetched, Skinner says "it is often difficult to prove the multiple sources, but examples are so common that anyone who has bothered to notice them can scarcely question the reality of the process" (Skinner, 1957, p. 237). This is true, and the doubter is urged to bother. Everyday speech is full of them.

A similar process occurs when the supplementary variable is echoic or textual, and is then called *formal strengthening*. A thematically weak response may on occasion be collaterally strengthened by an echoic or textual stimulus that controls a response of similar form. Rhyme, alliteration, assonance, and meter result. During a performance of *Richard III*, John Barrymore is reputed to have been able to speak appositely, immediately, *and* in unrhymed iambic pentameter when a spectator laughed at the line *A horse, a horse, my kingdom for a horse*. Without hesitating Barrymore thundered on *Make haste, and saddle yonder braying ass*. The theme was apparently determined by the laugh, but its form was influenced by the poetic context in which it occurred.

Other effects of multiple causation include blends and distortions, as when the hungry lady, apparently as *ravenous* as she was *famished*, confided to her dinner companion that she was *ravished*. *Ad hoc* causes for these pathological effects need not be assumed. The fact that we tend to hear and remember better the "Freudian" slips that suggest pathological motivation and dulled speaker vigilance is probably due to a selective process related to hearer behavior, and does not reflect a general characteristic of all misspeaking, much of which probably passes unnoticed.

Autoclitic Behavior

Mands and tacts, along with audience, echoic, textual, and intraverbal responses, constitute the raw material of speech. Additional verbal phenomena of great interest and complexity remain to be accounted for. These are generally called *grammar*, and include *ordering* as well as certain response forms such as *and, but, is, some, except, no*, and so forth. These behaviors are said to be *autoclitic*, a neologism intended to suggest that they are controlled by other behavior. Thus, grammar is conceived to be causally dependent upon, and temporally secondary to, first having something to say, in the form of mands, tacts, echoics, and so forth. Grammar is accounted for within the existing analysis and does not invoke a separate causal variable. It is a phenomenon on the dependent variable side, not a cause in itself. So once again the speaker is excluded as a causal instigator.

A few examples will show how the autoclitic process works. *Descriptive autoclitics* simply comment upon the responses they accompany and which control them. *I see it is going to rain* contains the autoclitic *I see*, which identifies the controlling variable for *it is going to rain*, while *He said it is going to rain* identifies a different one. Since *it is going to rain* may be said for any of a number of reasons, the hearer needs to know which one is involved in a current instance. Other autoclitics specify the strength of the behavior they accompany, such as *I am certain that* ... as opposed to *One might almost say that*.... Autoclitic identification of the effect of his verbal behavior upon the speaker himself occurs in *Happily his fall broke no bones*. Adverb or not, *happily* modifies the speaker, not *broke*. The *no* in *no orange*, discussed earlier, is autoclitically controlled by the metonymic response *orange*. In the vernacular, *orange* is about the fruit basket, but *no* is about the response *orange*, however odd it may be to trace their strengths to separate variables.

Ordering is the second large class of autoclitic phenomena, although not all ordering is autoclitic. For example, *The boy's hat* could be acquired as a single functional unit, and speech which is controlled echoically, textually, or intraverbally requires no autoclitic behavior.

Much actual autoclitic ordering depends upon "partially conditioned autoclitic 'frames'" (Skinner, 1957, p. 336). Having separately acquired *The boy's gun*, *the boy's shoe*, and *the boy's hat*, the boy's first appearance with a bicycle can be tacted as *the boy's bicycle*, with the boy and his bicycle controlling their respective tacts, and the relation between them controlling the order of their emission. Similar frames include the orders of tacting actor-action and adjective-noun relations.

Thus Skinner proceeds. The autoclitic hypothesis is the most subtle, complex, and innovative aspect of *Verbal Behavior*. Anyone who wants a real intellectual workout is invited to take it on. Its plausibility depends upon one's being able to accept the notion that a speaker can respond discriminatively to (1) what he is *about* to say ["responses cannot be grouped or ordered until they have occurred *or are at least about to occur*" (Skinner, 1957, p. 332; italics added)]; (2) why he is about to say it; and (3) how strong the operant is. The discriminations concern complex relations between speech and its causes, and they are very rapid. In this respect it is important not to relapse into conceiving of discrimination as a separate prebehavioral *act*. Ordering *is* discriminative behavior, not the result of it, so that the complex discriminations in autoclitic behavior need not be allotted prebehavioral time. Skinner apparently considers the discriminability of one's own behavioral predispositions sufficiently well-established not to warrant explicit discussion in his treatment of autoclitic behavior.

Even so, the discrimination of *incipient* speech does raise serious questions, especially concerning its physical form and locus. I can suggest two possible resolutions. First, the incipient speech that controls autoclitic behavior might be conceived to occur covertly first, and then to be autoclitically edited as one would rewrite a sketchy manuscript. However, ongoing speech rarely seems to be marked by the pauses such a process would require. The second and I believe correct and satisfactory resolution of the problem is to understand that any autoclitic which refers to incipient speech is in fact controlled by the variable which makes that speech incipient. Thus, a speaker can autoclitically say *I was about to remark* ... under the influence of the situation in which he ordinarily says whatever follows, but before he has in any sense done so. The situation that strengthens the tacts *the boy* and *runs* also contains the relation that determines the order of their emission as *the boy runs*. If I am correct in this, autoclitic behavior is not, strictly speaking, controlled by other behavior, but by other operants. There is a difference.

Thinking

Verbal Behavior converges upon an analysis of thinking, with which the book ends. Although this chapter will fascinate those who have watched the evolution of Skinner's preoccupation with this subject, thinking turns out not to be peculiarly verbal at all. Its final disposition is most clearly defined in these terms, "thought is simply behavior—verbal or nonverbal, covert or overt" (Skinner, 1957, p. 494). More specifically, it is behavior "which automatically affects the behaver and is reinforcing because it does so" (Skinner, 1957, p. 438). As behavior, then, thinking has no unique response properties and no unique sources of control. The speaker therefore loses out again as the autonomous instigator. Thought, his last chance for privacy and self-determination, for creativity and personal style, finds its way into the determinism of the operant paradigm.

Last Words

Thus, the argument in *Verbal Behavior* proceeds, inexorably and relentlessly, to the final overthrow of the speaker as an autonomous agent. Chomsky, recoiling from this conclusion, apparently saw—quite correctly—that the argument in *Verbal Behavior* follows quite impeccably from its premises. He therefore attacked the premises and essentially ignored what followed from them in *Verbal Behavior*. Unfortunately for his purposes, Chomsky did not grasp the differences between Skinnerian and Watsonian-Hullian behaviorism, and his criticisms, although stylistically effective, were mostly irrelevant to *Verbal Behavior*.

He was simply wrong. This is a *great* book. The reader who is well acquainted with the technical experimental analysis of behavior will find real pleasure in watching its elegant argument unfold. It provides a rare opportunity, in psychology, to discover the potential that has existed all along, unsuspected, in the underlying formulation. In the language of the book itself, *Verbal Behavior* serves as a supplementary variable, prompting verbal responses which were at some strength before he read the book. One might, almost, have been able to write it himself. Yet he would

not have. What is most astonishing and exciting about the book is that the speech it prompts is at such wide variance with the residues of one's prescientific, traditional beliefs about this subject matter and, more importantly, about his *self*. The psychologically sophisticated reader may, with Chomsky, recoil from the conclusions in *Verbal Behavior*, but I do not believe he can rationally reject them.

His comfort will have to come from the fact that Skinner cannot prove, any more than any other scientist can, that all of the variance has been accounted for. The remainder may be where the speaker directly controls. Unaccounted-for variability is not the very best basis for theory construction but it is always a safe one, temporarily. History tells us, however, that this variability will be traced to non-theoretical sources, most probably those which are already acknowledged.

Like it or not, the camel's nose *is* in the tent. Mark my words.

REFERENCES

Chomsky, N. *Verbal Behavior*, by B. F. Skinner. *Language*, 1959, **35**, 26-58.

Kendler, H. H. Learning. In Paul R. Farnsworth and Quinn McNemar (Eds.), *Annual Review of Psychology*. Palo Alto, California: Annual Reviews, Inc., 1959. Pp. 43-88.

Morris, C. *Verbal Behavior*, by B. F. Skinner. *Contemporary Psychology*, 1958, **3**, 212-214.

Osgood, C. E. *Verbal Behavior*, by B. F. Skinner. *Contemporary Psychology*, 1958, **3**, 209-212.

Schoenfeld, W. N. J. R. Kantor's *Objective Psychology of Grammar* and *Psychology and Logic*: a retrospective appreciation. *Journal of the Experimental Analysis of Behavior*, 1969, **12**, 329-347.

Skinner, B. F. Are theories of learning necessary? *Psychological Review*, 1950, **57**, 193-216. Also in B. F. Skinner, *Cumulative record*. New York: Appleton-Century-Crofts, 1959.

Skinner, B. F. *Science and human behavior*. New York: Macmillan Company, 1953.

Skinner, B. F. *Verbal behavior*. New York: Appleton-Century-Crofts, 1957.

"AVOIDANCE" IN BEHAVIOR THEORY[1,2]

W. N. SCHOENFELD

QUEENS COLLEGE, THE CITY UNIVERSITY OF NEW YORK
AND CORNELL UNIVERSITY MEDICAL COLLEGE

I. Some years ago, I tried to formulate an account of the acquisition and maintenance of operant avoidance behavior. In that paper, I could draw upon all that was known at the time about avoidance, since the number of available studies was small. The literature has grown enormously since then, and it would no longer be practicable today to review it all in any meaningful way in a single paper. Actually, I do not think that is what is most needed in this area. In any case, I became dissatisfied with my own theoretical treatment of avoidance, and now it seems to me that the outline of a more adequate formulation has become clearer in the light of the remarkable experimental advances made since my first writing. The relevant information is in the current literature, and I am here only recognizing its implications for a new theoretical approach to the avoidance problem. This new approach is essentially a restatement leading not to the "solution" of the problem, but to its dissolution; framed in proper terms, the phenomenon of avoidance simply disappears as a separate category of behavior, or at least becomes a derivable spin-off from a more general treatment of behavior. It seems to me that because "aversive" responding is not different in either principle or process from the acquisition and maintenance of other types of responding, it is involved in the broader question of "reinforcement" in general.

II. Behavioral science has drawn many words from the layman's vocabulary, even though such words are seldom good ways to describe the response material of conditioning theory. They reflect social attitudes and beliefs about behavior; they are defined by social criteria; they group acts by their social outcomes; and, they are almost always mistaken in what they accept as their behavioral referents. More often than not, they only obstruct a proper analysis of behavior by clouding issues, generating profitless debates, and sidetracking research. These words range from seemingly simple responses to broad action patterns: memory, lying and stealing, thinking, aggression-submission, cooperation, courtship, motivation, stress. Even as seemingly specific a word as "swim" can mislead: if it is asked how a rat can know how to swim the first time it is put in water, the reply might be that it is not swimming at all, just doing what it knows, walking, but that "swimming" is how the rat walks in a medium like water, and that a continuous series of modifications could be traced in its walking through media and on surfaces of different densities and firmnesses. Some words like "pain" have been extended quite far in anthropomorphic application to animals. In fact, of course, "pain" is a socially taught verbal response reporting the occurrence of certain stimuli and preceding responses; animals do not have "pain" even when responding under those circumstances that we generalize with what we would ourselves report socially as causing "pain" to us. In other cultures, and in varying situations in our own culture, we might report those same stimuli and responses quite differently, whereupon animals would have those other feelings imputed to them.

Other words from the lay lexicon refer to a restricted response range that is conventionally set off for special naming within a broader continuum of behavior effects. Aversive behavior words like "avoidance" and "escape" are of this sort. As a lay word, "avoid-

---

[1]Dedicated to B. F. Skinner in his sixty-fifth year.

[2]This work was supported in part by Public Health Service Research Grant MH 12964 from the National Institute of Mental Health. Reprints may be obtained from the author, Dept. of Psychology, Queens College of the City University of New York, Flushing, N.Y. 11367.

ance" has a kind of commonsense meaning of doing something to prevent a hurtful experience. In a general way, "avoidance" like this does occur, but it is careless to permit the lay sense to define the scientific problem. To import the term into a science of behavior as defining a problem for study is to import along with it the same problems the layman eventually encounters in understanding and using it. An example may be found in the *t*-system wherein a recycling time interval, T, has some part, t^D, in which a response may have an experimentally specified environmental consequence. If T is very short, and if t^D is made coextensive with a stimulus like strong electric shock and is given an appropriate value, then the shock itself will appear continuous to a subject, and an "avoidance" response, if allowed to produce a timeout, is identical to an "escape" response. Avoidance and escape are thus products of the parameter of T length, and each term will be used by the lay community for that part of the T range where it seems acceptable to tradition and valid on anthropomorphic-empathic grounds.

Of course, scientific study historically begins with words from the lay vocabulary, even though they must be refined and perhaps rejected as knowledge accumulates, and as discoveries are made that permit sharper definitions of phenomena, of their determining conditions, and so on. This has happened with the word "avoidance". We can often obtain responding, or produce response changes, of various sorts by applying known experimental operations to the stimuli and responses composing the behavior stream. If we wish, we can also by our procedures and apparatuses permit certain environmental outcomes to occur as consequences of an ordained response, and if the resulting behavioral changes match a lay term in our vocabulary, such as "avoidance", we apply it. But then, as research into the matter develops, new or "strange" observations crop up that puzzle us, such as the effects of "free" stimulations, or the parametric kinships among conditioning procedures once thought of as unrelated. At present, a set of behavioral phenomena are familiar to us, as they are to laymen, under the guise of "avoidance". It is within this rubric that we at one time formulated the "problem of avoidance", and were led to ask the question of what the reinforcement for avoidance responding might be. But the question in this form was an en-

trapment. We are beginning to see that set of phenomena as part of a larger but continuous range along which appear related behavioral phenomena that impress us as strange just yet. Once these are linked to the familiar, once they are seen as parts of the same parametric continua of experimental operations and variables, the strangeness disappears. And with the strangeness, the problem also disappears. We have been carrying the avoidance problem down this road for many years, traveling what seemed a long distance toward this goal, but the conceptual distance, as science has often found, is quite short.

III. The problem of operant avoidance behavior has seemed to be identifying the reinforcement for it. The "avoidance paradox" arose from the definition of avoidance as behavior leading to non-occurrence of certain stimuli, with the consequent need to rationalize stimulus non-occurrence as reinforcing. This difficulty originally suggested to me that the very existence of avoidance as a behavior phenomenon might be doubted, but—amusingly enough in view of my present belief—I dismissed those misgivings and concentrated on a possible solution. It was organized along a few main lines. The emphasis was placed on the cued avoidance case, although the place of non-cued avoidance was plain. Avoidance was reached as the last in a progression of paradigms starting with experimental anxiety (more currently called CER or "conditioned suppression"), followed by escape, and then avoidance. The paradigms were based upon a sequence of two stimuli $S_1 \rightarrow S_2$ (where S_1 is the traditional "neutral" stimulus or cue, S^N, and S_2 the "aversive" stimulus or negative reinforcer, S^{-R}), and upon the experimentally defined role of the response (R) to these two stimuli. The progressive paradigms were treated as operationally discontinuous, but the behavioral products were taken as continuous, and this continuity provided the basis for identifying the reinforcement for avoidance. (My present approach to avoidance not only removes the operational discontinuity but reaffirms the behavioral continuity and extends it to include all behavior, not just anxiety and escape.) The reinforcing function was assigned to proprioceptive-kinesthetic stimuli, and the avoidance response was the behavior that survived after all other responses were suppressed by the "punishing" stimulus.

At least two weaknesses in that explanation were caused by approaching avoidance through the question of what its reinforcement is, and they did not escape the notice of later theorists. They were tolerated at the time because no alternative seemed available while the question was in that form. One was that the actual role of proprio-kinesthetic stimuli is not ascertainable; although the class of stimulus called proprioceptive is known to exist, such stimuli are not yet accessible for measurement or experimental manipulation. The second was that the idea of suppressing all behavior except the avoidance response left open the problem of specifying "all behavior" without invoking infinity. Even if the behavior stream were broken into a finite number of blocks of responses within which all responses were affected in some measure by reinforcement or extinction of any one response member, it still is not prudent to rely on elimination of all blocks save the one containing the avoidance response, partly because no experimental information is available on the sizes and boundaries of the "other response" classes, and partly because the speed with which avoidance is often learned has implications for the speed with which weakening of all the other blocks would have to be accomplished.

But now there are more persuasive reasons for relinquishing that early explanatory approach. In the intervening years, we have learned so much more about avoidance behavior and its properties that it is no longer necessary to try to reach avoidance responding from supposedly simpler paradigms like anxiety and escape. Indeed, it might be more useful to work from avoidance to the other forms of "aversive" behavior, since some things we have learned about acquisition and reinforcement from the avoidance case can be transferred to the other cases. For example, avoidance responding without reduction in frequency of aversive stimulus falls into the purlieu of experimental anxiety, and broadens the latter category both theoretically and in experimental prediction of behavioral possibilities extending beyond the simple response suppression view of the CER paradigm.

The intervening years have also provided the opportunity to learn more about reinforcement schedules in general, including those involving "positive" reinforcers (S^{+R}), and thereby to observe and conceptualize more broadly—as in the t-τ systems—the kinships and overlaps among schedules once thought to be different in kind. We have before us today attempts from several researchers to systematize schedules along new theoretical lines, and to deal with the stimulus and response contents of the behavior stream in new ways.

All these factors are working toward a reassessment of the avoidance problem. New experimental information exerts pressure on older formulations, and, conjoined with the latters' weaknesses, creates the need for new theoretical efforts.

IV. There are a number of considerations, both specific and general, that inform a recasting of the avoidance problem. The following seem just now to be the more important ones.

(1) Preliminary considerations alone show the difficulty of even defining avoidance behavior, and suggest that avoidance need not be regarded as a separate behavioral problem. The individual response itself is not an issue, since any response may be selected from the behavior stream to do the "avoiding" and be measured. The strategy that was adopted historically was to define avoidance in terms of outcome; that is, in terms of what the response accomplishes. For the free operant non-cued avoidance case ("Sidman avoidance"), this outcome is usually defined as a reduction in S_2 frequency; in a trial-by-trial procedure, where each trial is an opportunity for S_2 to occur, the outcome is an increase in inter-S_2 time. There are two experimental findings, however, that undermine any such reliance on outcome as a defining criterion of avoidance. Indeed, these findings are crucial for any theory of avoidance, and we will call upon them several times. The first, already well validated by experiment, is that behavior acquired under "avoidance" procedures can be maintained indefinitely by "free" S_2s delivered non-contingent upon any stated response and without reduction in frequency. In fact, there are schedules under which responding is maintained even though shock frequency is increased. The second, as yet reported only by isolated investigators but probably soon to be firmly established, is that a pre-selected response, which would be the recognized "avoidance" response if acquired in an experiment where reduction of shock frequency were its "contingent" outcome, can also be acquired *ab initio* under certain conditions by the sim-

ple procedure of intruding "free" S_2s into the behavior stream. Moreover, any avoidance schedule can involve, as a parameter, proportions of "free" to "contingent" S_2s varying from zero to unity. Facing these facts, it cannot be correct to define "avoidance" in terms of reduction in number of S_2s.

This conclusion is supported by several other thoughts. To look to reduction in S_2 frequency as the cause of avoidance responding is once again to appeal to the non-occurrence of a stimulus as reinforcing. The absurdity of this appeal is evident because at any moment an infinite number of stimuli are not occurring, and we would therefore have to assume that all behavior is avoidant. There is also the unacceptable implication that avoidance behavior is unique because no parallel case can be drawn from schedules involving "positive reinforcement"; it is not the *reduction* in frequency of food delivery on partial schedules which achieves a relatively greater durability of a response as compared to the 100% or regular reinforcement schedule. Furthermore, avoidance regarded as an outcome would have "food-procurement" as a parallel in positive reinforcement (rather than, say, bar pressing) as the "response" being manipulated. Even if one wished to deal with outcomes in this way, there is the problem of how outcome itself is to be defined. For example, if the "timeout from S_2" in the free operant case involves the cancellation of many scheduled S_2s, shall an "avoidance" be tallied for each forestalled S_2, or is each timeout or train of timeouts to be taken as a single "avoidance"? Or, if the outcome schedule depends upon a number of responses ("ratio" avoidance responding) rather than a single response, how shall "avoidances" be tallied? Still other questions flow from the measurement of the avoidance response. A traditional one for the free operant non-cued case is that of response rate, while a traditional one for trial procedures is that of latency. We have long realized, of course, that the proper gauge of conditioning is not response rate alone, but rather the degree of control over the response exercised by the experimental variable. Thus, DRL procedures that lower response rate demonstrate control as well as procedures which raise rate, and both DRL escape and DRL avoidance responding may be achieved experimentally. Avoidance is not response-specific; it needs to be analyzed in terms of the actual stimulus-response events of which it is the product; that is, in terms of what the organism is *doing* rather than of the outcomes of his behavior.

(2) Avoidance schedules are conventionally classed as "aversive", leading us to ask first what aversive schedules are and then how they might resemble positive reinforcement schedules.

An aversive schedule involves S^{-R} and therefore generates "anxiety" and "escape" behavior as well as "avoidance". The difficulties of defining either anxiety or escape are like those encountered in defining avoidance, and need not be rehearsed. Similarly, to define an aversive schedule we must first define the terms "aversive stimulus" and "reinforcer". The effort to define S^{-R} in terms of the behavior it can support does not advance our understanding; even if possible circularities are overcome, the behaviors themselves are suspect. The fact is that we are involved here with parametric aspects of certain experimental procedures, and with parameters of response measurement. This is a decisive point, and we shall return to it later.

A reinforcement schedule is an elaboration of the single and primitive operation of intruding a stimulus into the behavior stream. It is desirable to define a stimulus in physical terms; that is, as a physical event. The effects of any intruded stimulus on responding (whether "reinforcing" or "emotionalizing", *etc.*) depend on what behavior changes we are willing to accept as classes of effect, and what we are willing to include as part of any effect, as well as on a number of other variables such as the state of the organism, or the response composition of the behavior stream at the moment of S intrusion. Among these latter variables is one fundamental to any discussion of aversive schedules; namely, stimulus intensity.

For any stimulus, the intensity continuum ranges from zero to indefinitely large magnitudes. This continuum may be divided into sub-ranges, although these may have fluctuating and overlapping boundaries. Progressing from zero, they are: imperceptible intensities, intensities that make up the usual psychophysical range, "positively reinforcing" intensities, "aversive" intensities, and finally, fatal intensities. This is true of simple stimuli like tones, lights, or touches as well as complex stimuli or "objects" like food pellets. Thus, an "intense" (heavy) pellet would be aversive if dropped onto a rat instead of to one side; on the other hand, an electric shock would *not* be aversive if delivered to one side instead of to the animal. (But if the side-delivered shock were eventually encountered, and each encounter were cued, the cues would secondarily function as or "be" the shock, just as the sight, smell, *etc.*, of the pellet "is" the pellet as "object".)

In short, no stimulus is aversive in itself without regard to the parameter of its intensity and the circumstances of its delivery. Joining this observation to the difficulty of defining aversive responding, we must conclude that "aversive schedules" are only arbitrarily, even conventionally and nominally, classified under that title. This conclusion holds equally for an aversive schedule which the animal seeks to escape in favor of some other "preferred" schedule. In the latter sense, of course, any circumstance affecting the animal may be labelled "aversive" since *some* other circumstance will always be preferred.

The thoroughly parametric nature of aversive conditioning operations (in common with all conditioning operations) cannot be exhaustively considered here, but a few of the many examples may be cited: (a) In free operant non-cued "Sidman avoidance", the S^{-R} terminating an S—S interval might be different (in type, or intensity, *etc.*) from that terminating an R—S interval, and the probability of occurrence of each of those stimuli (the mean lengths of the S—S and R—S intervals) may be systematically varied either together or independently. (b) The "Sidman avoidance" paradigm is the same as that of the delayed punishment procedure which employs a reset of delay for intervening responses. While the delayed punishment procedure involves an initial response, "Sidman avoidance" does also, since with zero operant level no animal would ever learn that avoidance response (although the first shocks might re-make the operant level repertory to bring out at least one of the specified responses.) (c) Distinctions between cued and non-cued avoidance procedures are based on the temporal spacing of the stimuli in the $S_1 \rightarrow S_2$ sequence. (d) In cued escape paradigms, if the interval before the next $S_1 \rightarrow S_2$ trial is short, and if the probability of S_2 occurrence is set between unity and zero, then the "escape" response appears like an "avoidance" response. One may multiply such cases of parametric variation leading from one supposed type of aversive behavior to another.

Positive reinforcement is also of a thoroughly parametric nature and is on the same continua as aversive conditioning. At least some of the many similarities between the two types of schedule can be indicated, although an exhaustive list cannot be given, probably because at bottom the two schedules are not really different types at all. In both schedules an intruding stimulus is used, either as reinforcer or as cue, its presence alternating with its absence. In both schedules, all stimulus operations involve stimulus "presentation" and stimulus "removal", with both always simultaneously present as stimulus "change". In both schedules, the definition of the measured response class is arbitrary, and the exclusion from that class of closely related responses probably makes even the 100% reinforcement schedule effectively an intermittent schedule. In both schedules, because the behavioral stream has no "holes" in it or places empty of responses, behavioral change of any sort always means that some responses have gone up in strength, while others have gone down. This is, of course, the basis of the familiar theories of extinction known as "counter-conditioning" or "interference". Both schedules share characteristic problems of response acquisition and maintenance: in acquisition under positive reinforcement schedules, animals would be lost through failure to condition as they often are under aversive schedules if prior discriminative training were not given and prior behavior chains were not built up; the maintenance of aversive responding by "free" aversive stimulations is paralleled by maintenance of responding through "free positive" (often called "superstitious") reinforcements. In both schedules, either the same stimulus or an intensity variant of it may serve as the intruding stimulus or "reinforcing" stimulus event, and the same delivery schedule may be employed; a "positive reinforcer" may be an electric shock of appropriately weak intensity, and may be delivered on a "Sidman avoidance" schedule. (Schedules like these have actually been studied experimentally, although under the headings of "delayed reinforcement" and "reinforcement of not-R".)

Considerations of this sort inevitably weaken the assertion of a separate identity for aversive schedules, including avoidance, since the differences between any two schedules can be arranged parametrically with respect to the details of independent variables and behavior measurements.

V. In treating the problem of avoidance conditioning, the first question to ask is not the traditional one of what the reinforcement for such responding is, but how avoidance responding is acquired—that is, what the determining conditions or variables are—and how it is maintained. We have tried to show that some familiar assumptions about conditioning an avoidance response are false. Given that a response has been arbitrarily chosen by the experimenter as the "avoiding" response, that response can be controlled by operations other than the frequency of aversive stimulation, or indeed of any stimulus contingent upon the response. (By "contingent" I mean a relationship whereby the temporal distribution of stimulus deliveries is determined by the temporal distribution of responses.) Avoidance conditioning commonly involves some arrangement by the experimenter of how, and under what schedule, certain stimuli are to be applied to an organism, and then simply projecting the organism into that arrangement. This rather insouciant casting of one's behavioral bread upon scientific waters may occur in some measure in all schedules but is prominent in avoidance procedures including cued or non-cued avoidance training, free operant or trial-by-trial procedures, "Sidman avoidance", or *t-τ* system aversive schedules. This way of proceeding does not look at the experimental variables as they actually impact the animal, and it does not insure that the appropriate variables are brought to bear at any given instant in the training. It is not like the "shaping" whereby a pre-specified avoidance response is reached. As a reuslt, of course, many animals fail to condition and are lost to the study. The failures are perhaps less instructive than the successes; why do some animals condition or shape up, and not others? Clearly, if we knew the conditions that produced the successful learning we could salvage every subject. Under these circumstances, we should not be surprised that a thoughtful researcher, by simply exposing an animal to a sequence of non-contingent aversive stimulations, has successfully produced acquisition of what under parametric variations of the procedure we would call the "avoidance" response, and that he has therefore concluded that a response does not need a history of avoidance training for "free" aversive stimulations to be effective.

With regard to supporting an avoidance response, the familiarity of "free" S_2s as a maintaining schedule makes us readier to accept the possibility that with proper values of the relevant parameters the "free" procedure could maintain responding indefinitely. But it would be gratuitous for theory to endorse a distinction between the mechanisms of response acquisition and response maintenance, especially since we are beginning also to see that no such distinction need be made on the experimental level.

In addition to the parametric and classificatory aspects, our understanding of avoidance acquisition and maintenance must stand upon the temporal relations and the associated probability relations between the experimentally manipulated stimuli and those responses chosen from the behavior stream for observation. This conclusion is neither as onerous nor as vague as it may appear at first; in fact, it has always guided our research on behavior under "positive reinforcement". Now it opens the way for operationally and theoretically linking aversive conditioning to the general theory and practice of reinforcement schedules. Efforts along this line have already been made by the *t-τ* systems of schedule classification within which some currently popular aversive and positive schedules prove to be special cases. In addition to this linkage, a full treatment of aversive conditioning will surely involve new considerations about the behavior stream; there are already signs that this theme is re-emerging as a concern of behavior theory.

VI. The burden of this paper can now be summarized by two statements: (1) Any avoidance response, whether specified in advance or not, may be conditioned or controlled by an appropriate selection of values of the three parameters, among others, of operant level of the response, stimulus frequency, and stimulus intensity. (2) Since the same variables apply to "positive" and "negative" reinforcement schedules, separate or unique treatment is not required for either within a general theory of behavior.

Received 7 March 1969.

HISTORICAL NOTE

THE DAVIS PLATFORM[1]

Bird watchers (the out-of-doors variety) operate happily on a schedule of intermittent reinforcement. Of the various rewards available to them, probably the one with the greatest effect is that of happening upon the unexpected. Such was the case for the writer, who in reading a new work on the finch family, found a report of what may well have been the first rough Skinner box, complete with key and food magazine. While there is clearly no historical tie between this early device made by a naturalist interested in problem-solving in wild birds and B. F. Skinner's careful instrumentation, still one is reminded of the observation that novel ideas often turn up in very different places at almost the same time.

The account appears in the final volume of Bent's monumental *Life Histories of North American Birds.* A series of bulletins of the United States National Museum, the first was published in 1919 and only in 1968 did the last volume (that on finches) appear. All in all, the series consists of over 10,000 pages of description of such things as the habits, nesting, incubation, young, plumage, food, behavior, voice, enemies, field marks, migration, and distribution of hundreds of species.

It is in the chapter on the pine siskin (written by R. S. Palmer) that one finds the unexpected reference to an early experiment on operant conditioning. The material is taken from a piece by E. R. Davis first published in 1926 in *Bird Lore.* Davis reports that in the fall of 1925 a flock of 100 siskins took up residence at the feeders about his home in Leominster, Massachusetts. Though normally a resident of the more remote wilderness areas, these birds ". . . grew to be exceedingly sociable and to lose every vestige of fear. Whenever I would appear at the window, or step outside the door, down they would come and, settling upon my head, shoulders, and arms, would peer anxiously about for the food that they had learned to know I held . . . [p. 382]." One is reminded of Skinner's situation on the top of a flour mill in Minneapolis in the early 1940s: "All day long, around the mill, wheeled great flocks of pigeons. They were easily snared . . . and proved to be an irresistible supply of experimental subjects [1958, p. 94]."

Wrestling with the ancient question about whether animals can "reason", Davis writes that the siskins learned to fly into his open bedroom windows and to wake him in the early morning by pulling his hair. He then put seed in a glass-covered box by his bedside.

Unable to get at the seed, they would pull his hair, fly to the seed, and then fly back to pull his hair again until he awakened and removed the glass cover. Davis then goes on to describe his early version of the Skinner box:

"Another experiment that I made to test their power of reasoning was a device consisting of a platform, with a rear wall on which was placed an ordinary push button. An arrangement on the other side of the wall would, when the button was pressed, allow a small quantity of seed to pass down a little chute and be delivered at their feet. It was ludicrous and interesting in the extreme to see the birds attempt to solve this new problem. Immediately I put it out, one after another came and inspected it; they were mystified at finding nothing to eat on the strange-looking affair. They would critically examine it in every corner, then fly away only to return for a yet closer inspection. They couldn't quite understand why I had put out something that contained no food—everything, heretofore, had had food connected with it in some manner.

"For quite awhile the thing remained a puzzle to them. Finally, one of them happened to notice that push-button, which was a different colored wood from the rest of the contraption. He sidled up to it, looked it over for a moment, then up and gave it a 'biff.' This released the catch on the other side and down at his feet came a little handful of seeds. This frightened him, of course, and he flew away, only to return a minute later, eat the seeds that had fallen down the chute, and then tried the "press-the-button" arrangement again. It was not long before several of the flock had learned the secret, but it was quite awhile before they became used to the seeds falling down at their feet, so that they were not afraid, and would proceed to eat them without first flying away a few inches [p. 385]."

The account ends with a note that the last of the flock left for its breeding range by the middle of June. Whether any returned the next winter to demonstrate retention of the button pressing is not recorded. Most probably they did not, for many members of the family *fringillidae* are noted for the unpredictable pattern of their annual wanderings.

C. W. HUNTLEY
Union College

---

[1]Dedicated to B. F. Skinner in his sixty-fifth year. Reprints may be obtained from C. W. Huntley, Dept. of Psychology, Union College, Schenectady, N.Y. 12308.

REFERENCES

Bent, A. C. and Collaborators. *Life histories of North American cardinals, grosbeaks, buntings, towhees, finches, sparrows, and allies.* Washington: Smithsonian Institution Press, United States National Museum Bulletin No. 237, 1968.

Davis, E. R. Friendly siskins. *Bird Lore*, 1926, **28,** 381-388.

Skinner, B. F. Reinforcement today. *American Psychologist*, 1958, **13,** 94-99.

ON CERTAIN SIMILARITIES BETWEEN THE PHILOSOPHICAL INVESTIGATIONS OF LUDWIG WITTGENSTEIN AND THE OPERATIONISM OF B. F. SKINNER[1]

WILLARD F. DAY

UNIVERSITY OF NEVADA

It is my purpose to point out certain similarities between the *Philosophical Investigations* of Ludwig Wittgenstein and the work of B. F. Skinner. In doing this, I hope to stimulate a somewhat deeper appreciation of Skinner's views than is generally found among psychologists at the present time. I hope also to influence the critical appraisal of Skinner's work, so that it might come to bear more cogently upon the position as it has actually developed. I feel that much of the current criticism (*e.g.*, Chomsky, 1959) misses its mark largely because it seems to take for granted that Skinner adopts philosophical perspectives which are in fact inimical to his views. It is my opinion that Skinner's position is more compatible with the later views of Wittgenstein than with other philosophical approaches more widely accepted among psychologists.

Ludwig Wittgenstein is acknowledged by some (*e.g.*, Warnock, 1958, p. 62) to have exerted an influence more powerful than that of any other individual upon the contemporary practice of philosophy.[2] The nature of this influence is suggested by the following comments of G. H. von Wright.

> It has been said that Wittgenstein inspired two important schools of thought, both of which he repudiated. The one is so-called logical positivism or logical empiricism, which played a prominent role during the decade immediately preceding the Second World War. The other is the so-called analytic or linguistic movement . . . [which] dominates the British philosophy of today and has spread over the entire Anglo-Saxon world and to the countries in which Anglo-Saxon influence is strong.

It is true that the philosophy of Wittgenstein has been of great importance to both of these trends in contemporary thought: to the first, his early work *Tractatus Logico-Philosophicus* and discussions with some members of the Vienna Circle; to the second, besides the *Tractatus*, his lectures at Cambridge and also glimpses of the works which he did not publish in his lifetime. It is also partly true that Wittgenstein repudiated the results of his own influence. He did not participate in the world wide discussion to which his work and thought had given rise. He was of the opinion—justified, I believe—that his ideas were usually misunderstood and distorted even by those who professed to be his disciples. He doubted that he would be better understood in the future. He once said that he felt as though he were writing for people who would think in a quite different way, breathe a different air of life, from that of present-day men. For people of a different culture, as it were. (von Wright, 1955, p. 527).

Wittgenstein died in April, 1951. His book *Philosophical Investigations*, which contains his later views principally of concern to us here, was published posthumously in 1953.

In what follows I shall list, and comment briefly upon, 10 specific similarities between the later work of Wittgenstein and the systematic position of B. F. Skinner. However, the preceding remarks of von Wright suggest at once certain preliminary similarities in the professional fortunes of Wittgenstein and Skinner. Both Wittgenstein and Skinner published an early book, each of which was striking in originality of thought and seriousness of purpose, and each of which was destined to exert a dynamic influence in its own field. The reference here, of course, is to Wittgenstein's *Tractatus* and Skinner's *The Behavior of Organisms*. Then also, both of these works bear an interesting relation to logical positivism, although to be sure they are related to that point of view in considerably different ways. The *Tractatus* played a conspicuous role in the very formulation of logical positivism, and although the position it as-

---

[1]Dedicated to B. F. Skinner in his sixty-fifth year. Reprints may be obtained from Willard F. Day, Dept. of Psychology, University of Nevada, Reno, Nevada 89507.

[2]For a short and current assessment of the development and significance of Wittgenstein's thought see Pears, 1969.

sumes is more properly associated with the logical atomism of Bertrand Russell than to logical positivism, the work was accepted with only slight reservation by the Vienna Circle as a powerful and exciting exposition of their point of view (see Ayer, 1959, p. 4 ff.). *The Behavior of Organisms*, on the other hand, is related to logical positivism in that it was written by Skinner at a time when he was keenly interested in operational and behaviorist methodology, an interest which he shared at that time with many other experimental psychologists, and which was considerably nourished by notions of logical positivism that were more widely discussed among experimental psychologists than understood. Finally, both Wittgenstein and Skinner came in their later work to develop points of view which are markedly incompatible with what is generally taken to be the logical positivist position. For Wittgenstein, this development involved an explicit repudiation of earlier views. The *Philosophical Investigations* contains a powerful attack upon his own *Tractatus* (see Malcolm, 1954, p. 559). For Skinner, the development has involved principally an unfolding of various implications of his system, some of which would lead Skinner now to present his ideas in a considerably different fashion than in *The Behavior of Organisms*. There is little need for Skinner explicitly to repudiate the troublesome sections of *The Behavior of Organisms*, such, for example, as the discussion of static and dynamic laws. His verbal behavior is simply different now from what it was in 1938, the difference being undoubtedly accountable for in terms of his more extensive experience in the laboratory, his having worked through some of the implications of the analysis of verbal behavior, and his having become aware that writing books is hardly the most efficient technique for manipulating the scientific behavior of psychologists.

Antipathy to Logical Positivism

The preceding point that Skinner's system has developed into an approach fundamentally different from theories consonant with logical positivism is not widely recognized among psychologists, or among philosophers either, for that matter. In fact, it is the frequent practice of simply dismissing Skinner's perspective as a rather bizarre form of logical positivism, when the philosophical implications of his work are brought up for discussion, that leads me to call attention in this paper to a number of striking similarities between his views and those of Wittgenstein. More specifically, I fear that the widespread influence of logical positivism still present in the outlook of many experimental psychologists leads even those who profess to be Skinner's disciples to misread his work, and hence to fail to understand it thoroughly.

It is true, one should perhaps not work too strenuously the udder of logical positivism in seeking similarities between Skinner and Wittgenstein. Although many of our current professional ills can undoubtedly be attributed to various habits of thinking about the nature of science and of psychology that have been picked up by psychologists over the past 50 years, such cultural influences are legitimately labeled logical-positivistic only for lack of a better word. It has been easy for psychologists to magnify out of all reasonable proportion the importance of logical positivism as a philosophical doctrine, either by accepting uncritically the writings of a number of logical positivists with whom they happen to be familiar, or by looking to the position as a kind of representation of Satan himself. Be that as it may, I offer as a first similarity between the later work of Wittgenstein and Skinner their inharmonious relation to logical positivism. The point merits elaboration.

With respect to Wittgenstein, it need simply be noted that philosophers of the linguistic movement are in general particularly careful to contrast their position sharply with that of logical positivism. Although both Ayer (1959, p. 5 ff.) and Gellner (1959, p. 86) have, for rather different reasons, stressed certain similarities in the two positions, the followers of Wittgenstein have been outspoken in their criticism of logical positivism. For particulars, one should consult Urmson's book *Philosophical Analysis*, which is devoted largely to a detailed criticism of both logical positivism and logical atomism from the perspective of linguistic analysis.

As for Skinner, his most explicit attacks upon logical positivism are to be seen indirectly through his almost bitter repudiation of what operationism was to become for psychology. To be sure, Skinner was strongly stimulated by the publication of Bridgman's

Logic of Modern Physics, and he has stated: "At that time—1930—I could regard an operational analysis of subjective terms as a *mere exercise in scientific method* . . . It never occurred to me that the analysis could take any but a single course or have any relation to my own prejudices" (1945, pp. 291-292). Skinner was apparently surprised to find that a professional interest in operationism was to lead quickly to the arena of intense philosophical debate, a debate with which he was totally unsympathetic. At the center of that arena, of course, stood logical positivism. In 1930 Herbert Feigl, the eminent logical positivist and member of the Vienna Circle, had come to Harvard, and according to Boring "it was he [Feigl] who introduced the Harvard psychologists to the ideas of their own colleague, Bridgman, to the work of the Vienna Circle, to logical positivism and to operational procedures in general" (1950, p. 656). S. S. Stevens at Harvard assumed leadership of the new approach, and he published ultimately in 1939 his paper on *Psychology and the Science of Science*, which Boring has called "the handbook of the new 'psycho-logic' ". Skinner's repudiation of this "new approach" is bitingly expressed in the following remarks.

> What happened instead was the operationism of Boring and Stevens. This has been described as an attempt to climb onto the behavioristic bandwagon unobserved. I cannot agree. It is an attempt to acknowledge some of the more powerful claims of behaviorism (which could no longer be denied) but at the same time to preserve the old explanatory fictions. It is agreed that the data of psychology must be behavioral rather than mental if psychology is to be a member of the United Sciences [note Skinner's mockery of the positivistic interest in Unified Science; see Ayer, 1959, p. 6], but the position taken is merely that of "methodological" behaviorism. According to this doctrine the world is divided into public and private events; and psychology, in order to meet the requirements of a science, must confine itself to the former. This was never good behaviorism, but it was an easy position to expound and defend and was often resorted to by the behaviorists themselves. It is least objectionable to the subjectivist because it permits him to retain "experience" for purposes of "non-physicalistic" self-knowledge. The position is not genuinely operational because it shows an unwillingness to abandon fictions (1945, pp. 283-284).

It seems clear that Skinner erred in feeling that his own interpretation of the *Logic of Modern Physics* would be shared by others. By 1945 he was to state, in commenting upon

the achievement of operationism, "Bridgman's original contention that the 'concept is synonymous with the corresponding set of operations' cannot be taken literally, and no similarly explicit but satisfactory statement of the relation [involved in definition] is available" (1945, p. 270). In fact, the paper from which the preceding quotation has been taken, *The Operational Analysis of Psychological Terms*, can be viewed throughout as a forceful indictment of logical positivism. Consider the following reference to Carnap: "The early [behaviorist] papers on the problem of consciousness by Watson, Weiss, Tolman, Hunter, Lashley, and many others, were not only highly sophisticated examples of operational inquiry, they showed a willingness to deal with a wider range of phenomena than do current streamlined treatments, particularly those offered by logicians (*e.g.*, Carnap) interested in a unified scientific vocabulary" (1945, p. 271). Or this reference to Feigl: "To be consistent the psychologist must deal with his own verbal practices by developing an empirical science of verbal behavior. He cannot, unfortunately, join the logician in defining a definition, for example, as a 'rule for the use of a term' (Feigl)" (1945, p. 277). In still other remarks Skinner's dissatisfaction with the vague ineffectuality of the philosophical reasoning of the period is made clear. Consider the following.

> The operationist, like most contemporary writers in the field of linguistic and semantic analysis, is on the fence between logical 'correspondence' theories of reference and empirical formulations of language in use. He has not improved upon the mixture of logical and popular terms usually encountered in casual or even supposedly technical discussions of scientific method or the theory of knowledge (*e.g.*, Bertrand Russell's recent *An inquiry into meaning and truth*). *Definition* is a key term but it is not rigorously defined. . . . Instead, a few roundabout expressions recur with rather tiresome regularity whenever this relation is mentioned. We are told that a concept is to be defined '*in terms of*' certain operations, that propositions are to be '*based upon*' operations, that a term denotes something only when there are '*concrete criteria for its applicability*,' that operationism consists in '*referring any concept for its definition to* . . . concrete operations . . . ,' and so on (1945, p. 270).

It is thus clear that Skinner came to view the relation between his own work and the common expression of logical positivism as anything but harmonious. However, the specific ways remain to be identified in which the views of Skinner and Wittgenstein are jointly incompatible with that position. As a second point in common, then, I call attention to the fact that in their outlook both Wittgenstein and Skinner are essentially non-reductionist.

Anti-reductionism

There is little need to comment at length upon the non-reductionist character of Wittgenstein's later work. The *Philosophical Investigations* contains a painfully careful exposition of the defects of his own earlier atomism (see Strawson, 1954, p. 74 ff.). The strength of the opposition of the linguistic movement to reductionist analysis can be sensed from the fact that one of the significant chapters in Urmson's book is entitled *The Impossibility of Reductionism* (1956, p. 146).

Few seem to realize, however, the non-reductionist character of Skinner's position. Even so, the point has been clearly stated by Verplanck (1954, p. 269 ff., p. 302, p. 307 ff.) and by Wolman (1960, p. 127 ff.). Verplanck emphasizes Skinner's antipathy to "any explanation of an observed fact which appeals to events taking place somewhere else, at some other level of observation, described in different terms, and measured, if at all, in different dimensions" (Skinner, 1950, p. 193). For Skinner, facts are little more than what we observe to be the case, and they are generally to be explained by relating them to other facts, not by reconstructing them out of more primary sense-data, as in phenomenalism. Moreover, Verplanck has called attention to Skinner's affinities to non-reductionist Gestalt Psychology, as follows:

> Skinner's approach, then, bears no more than a terminological resemblance to Hull's or Pavlov's, but it is at least first cousin to Kantor's system, which explicitly rather than implicitly accepts a metaphysical position, naive realism, and rejects even the logical possibility of a reductionism. His approach has affinities to Tolman's. Tolman postulates that the so-called laws of perception, derived from phenomenological studies, apply to the rat; Skinner does what amounts to the same thing implicitly, by starting with what comes to him, to all other experimenters, and until proven otherwise, to the experimental animal. Hull, on the contrary, seems to wish . . . to derive 'perceptual' laws on the basis of his reductively stated postulates. Skinner wants to start with a point-at-able world, with point-at-able operations, and to carry on from there. (Verplanck, 1954, p. 308).

That Skinner's concepts have often been misunderstood and misinterpreted probably stems from his choice of a set of terms. . . . To the "Tolmanite", conditioned responses are *mere*, or *mechanical*. To the "Hullian", *expectancy* and *cognition* carry the suggestion of the capricious intervention of entities extraneous to behavior. Skinner has attempted to avoid such considerations, and to eliminate the preconceptions (about what organisms ought or ought not to do) that may flow from the use of terms with extensive connotations. He wishes to find out how animals behave and seeks a vocabulary that will let him talk about how they behave. Because of the existence in Sherrington and Pavlov of sets of data of the kind he believes are needed, he has adopted many of their terms and applied some of their laws in defining his area. As a consequence he has been misinterpreted. In his choice of terminology, Skinner has assured that his works and those of his followers will be read easily by the followers of Hull and Guthrie and only with emotion, if not with difficulty, by those who have selected the organismic-field-Gestalt-force family of words to work with. Skinner's conditioned responses seem to many readers just as *mere* as those of Pavlov or Hull, with the extraordinary result that he has been classed with Hull rather than with Tolman, with Guthrie rather than with Lewin, in his general position (Verplanck, 1954, p. 307).

Indeed, it is tempting to conclude that Skinner is more appropriately classed phenomenologist rather than behaviorist, from the argument implied by the following quotations. Verplanck states: "It is apparent that Skinner's positivism is closer to that of Mach and Pearson than to that of the more recent logical positivists and scientific empiricists" (1954, p. 269). Skinner himself supports this claim by specifically acknowledging his indebtedness to Mach several places in print (e.g., 1931, p. 427; 1945, p. 291; 1961a, p. 319). But Boring states: "Mach fits into the phenomenological tradition and can properly be regarded as a grandparent of Gestalt psychology" (1961, p. 200).

Actually, however, Skinner's position with respect to issues of reductionism is as different from conventional ones as Wittgenstein's, and it is properly understood only within the context of his system as a whole. As with Wittgenstein, the treatment turns about the analysis of verbal behavior, or of the functions of words, and particularly about issues involved when we talk about our own private experience. For Skinner, the treatment of reductionism is made indirectly through a consideration of abstraction and of what he calls "tacting" (see 1957, p. 109 ff.). He comments specifically upon the traditional issue of reductionism as follows:

> The fact that the process of abstraction appears to generate a world composed of general properties, rather than of particular events, has led, however, to inconsistent interpretations. On the one hand the particular event has been regarded as immediate experience, while the process of abstraction has been said to *construct* a physical world which is never directly experienced. On the other hand the single occasion has been viewed as a momentary unanalyzed contact with experience (1953a, p. 277).

Yet Skinner's concern with the problems that make reductionism philosophically significant is more directly expressed by him as a concern with dualism, to which topic I now turn. I offer as a third similarity between Skinner and Wittgenstein the fact that neither position is dualistic. In fact, both views are vigorously *anti*-dualistic, and for much the same reason.

Anti-dualism

Skinner generally states his objection to dualism in such words as these:

> It is usually held that one does not see the physical world at all, but only a nonphysical copy of it called "experience". When the physical organism is in contact with reality, the experienced copy is called a "sensation", "sense datum", or "percept"; when there is no contact, it is called an "image", "thought", or "idea". Sensations, images, and their congeries are characteristically regarded as psychic or mental events, occurring in a special world of "consciousness" where, although they occupy no space, they can nevertheless often be seen. We cannot now say with any certainty why this troublesome distinction was first made, but it may have been an attempt to solve certain problems which are worth reviewing.
>
> There are often many ways in which a single event may stimulate an organism. Rain is something we see outside our window or hear on the roof or feel against our face. Which form of stimulation *is* rain? It must have been difficult to suppose that any one discriminative response could identify a physical event. Hence it may have been tempting to say that it identified a transient but unitary sensation or perception of the event. Eventually the least equivocal form—stimulation through contact with the skin—became most closely identified with reality. A form vaguely seen in a darkened room was not "really there" until one could touch it. But this was not a wholly satisfactory solution. Stimulation arising from contact may not agree perfectly with that arising visually or audibly, and we may not be willing to identify one form with reality to the exclusion of the others. There still are psychologists, however, who

argue for the priority of one form of stimulation and, hence, insist upon a distinction between experience and reality. They are surprised to find that "things are not what they seem" and that a room which looks square from a given angle may be found upon tactual or visual exploration to be askew. This difficulty offers no particular problem here. It is obvious that a single event may stimulate an organism in many ways, depending upon the construction of the organism and its capacity to be stimulated by different forms of energy. We are much less inclined today to ask which form of energy *is* the thing itself or correctly represents it.

> Another problem which the distinction between physical and non-physical worlds may have been an attempt to solve arises from the fact that more than one kind of response may be made to stimulation arising from a physical event. Rain is something you may run to escape from, catch in your hands to drink, prepare crops to receive, or call "rain". Which response is made to "rain in itself"? The solution was to construct a passive comprehension of rain, which was supposed to have nothing to do with practical responses. So far as we are concerned here, the problem is disposed of by recognizing that many verbal and nonverbal responses may come under the control of a given form of stimulation (1953a, pp. 276-277).

Yet Skinner's position is not only specifically anti-dualistic. It is essentially in sympathy with the following discussion of the reasons which underlie Wittgenstein's opposition to dualism. The remarks are taken from David Pole's critical work, *The Later Philosophy of Wittgenstein*.[3]

> The philosophical position Wittgenstein is seeking to break down might be roughly identified as Dualism; though at the risk of leaving the impression that he proposes to replace it by something that would be called Monism. But Monism, mentalistic or materialistic, is for Wittgenstein only another, deeper error. . . . We ordinarily speak of people as perceiving physical things, tables and chairs and the like; the dualist speaks of the mind as perceiving inward entities, ideas, images or acts of will. . . . [It] seems . . . that two separate mistakes must be involved. . . . First, we suppose ourselves

---

[3] I shall rely heavily in what follows on Pole's (1958) analysis of the character of Wittgenstein's later thought. Direct quotation from the *Philosophical Investigations* is often awkward, especially when taken out of context and addressed to an audience not trained in philosophy. Wittgenstein's style in the *Philosophical Investigations* is evocative rather than expository, so that one faces a certain problem in learning how to read the work, as the quotation found below, under *Anti-mentalism*, may well illustrate. Relevant passages in the *Philosophical Investigations* are cited by Pole.

to be dealing with two ontological realms, when we are in fact dealing with two parts of language; secondly we misinterpret the one, the language-game of inward experience, and force on it the grammar of the language-game of the public world of things. The language in which we speak of private experience is in fact part of a larger, public language, and is learnt in social contexts . . . .

The dualist conceives us as learning these concepts not in any social context, but privately, from our own experience. It follows from the picture he draws that one might live and move wholly in one's own private world; philosophers have often thought of this as our starting point, from which we progress to the discovery of outer things. And indeed it has puzzled them how in the circumstances we are able to make that discovery at any stage: and still more, how we penetrate the private world of any other person. This doctrine supposes the possibility of a private language—a language that will permit references to nothing but the speaker's own experiences. . . . Such a language will be necessarily private. . . . Wittgenstein denies that such a language is possible.

Such is the dualist picture, but it is unworkable; and struggling to free ourselves, we are only the more entangled. Dualism leads on to Behaviorism. For we have been told to think of a man's inner experience, his mental images, his feelings and the like, as forming a class of objects which lie hidden from the rest of us in some closed place; they are objects which only he can perceive. . . . If so they play no part in our lives; if his outward behaviour meets all our ordinary needs, and is all, so to speak, that we shall ever treat with, then the inward object drops out of consideration as irrelevant. . . . The behaviourist, therefore, rejects them as a fiction; and indeed a fiction would serve as well as an entity of which we can know nothing.

Yet Wittgenstein himself has been thought a behaviourist. For, one asks, if Dualism is rejected . . . what other alternative remains? But Wittgenstein does not mean to offer any alternative, any other or newer theory or picture (Pole, 1958, pp. 63-67).

Thus, Wittgenstein sees as the inherent error in dualism a faith in purely private language, which he maintains is impossible. Skinner is strongly in agreement. I shall return to this point shortly. But first, a fourth point of similarity between Wittgenstein and Skinner is suggested by the comments on behaviorism at the conclusion of the preceding quotation. Neither Wittgenstein nor Skinner rejects private events as necessarily meaningless or fictitious entities, in contrast to the usual behaviorist hypothesis. The question may well be raised as to how great the differences have to be between Skinner and what is generally taken to be behaviorism before he can no longer be considered a behaviorist?

The Significance of Private Events

Skinner contrasts sharply his position on private events with conventional behaviorism in the following remarks, which constitute in full the only reference to operationism indexed in *Science and Human Behavior.*

Operational definitions of sensation and image. Another proposed solution to the problem of privacy argues that there are public and private events and that the latter have no place in science because science requires agreement by the members of a community. Far from avoiding the traditional distinction between mind and matter, or between experience and reality, this view actually encourages it. It assumes that there is, in fact, a subjective world, which it places beyond the reach of science. On this assumption the only business of a science of sensation is to examine the public events which may be studied in lieu of the private.

The present analysis has a very different consequence. It continues to deal with the private event, even if only as an inference. It does not substitute the verbal report from which the inference is made for the event itself. The verbal report is a response to the private event and may be used as a source of information about it. A critical analysis of the validity of this practice is of first importance. But we may avoid the dubious conclusion that, so far as science is concerned, the verbal report or some other discriminative response *is* the sensation (1953a, pp. 281-282).

Skinner's avowed interest in private events is by no means merely lip-service. In fact, at the present time perhaps the most exciting of all Skinnerian empirical research centers around frankly perceptual problems, as in the focal concern with what children are actually looking at as they learn to draw an empirical inference or to match color to sample. Anyone familiar with the Hively study (1962) on matching to sample will recognize the relevance to Skinnerian research of the following remarks by Pole on Wittgenstein:

Now ostensive definition may seem to be a process whose significance is unambiguous and self-evident; a sound is simply correlated with an object. Children are taught it this way. 'That', one says, pointing, 'is an orang-outang.' And Adam, we may suppose, simply uttered the sound when the first of the species was brought before him.

What we have here is a particular nexus of sounds, gestures and objects; it is false, however, that all this is of itself unambiguously significant. One might point to the door and say 'Go!' Here the same performance has a totally different function. This is not an ostensive definition—and yet it might serve as one after a fashion; for one way of teaching the meaning of 'go' in the imperative might be this. If a mother points to the milk and says 'white' clearly the child may take 'white' to mean 'milk', and *vice versa*. There are different kinds of game to be learnt here which are by no means uniformly simple and self-evident. The child's error may be corrected, perhaps, by his mother's pointing in turn to the paper and the tablecloth, repeating the word—a fairly complex procedure whose significance has to be grasped. Again one might set objects in pairs as an ostensive definition of 'two'; one might even in certain cases find it the best way to give an ostensive definition to point to something strikingly different and say, 'That is *not* a such and such.'

From all this there are various things that may be learnt. The variety of ways in which words acquire their meanings is reflected in the variety of their uses; the ways in which the forms of language may be meaningful are no less numerous (Pole, 1958, p. 14).

The Impossibility of a Purely Private Language

Let us return now to what I offer as a fifth similarity between Wittgenstein and Skinner, namely, the care with which both argue the impossibility of a purely private language. For Skinner this argument is the central theme of his paper *The Operational Analysis of Psychological Terms*. In this paper he states:

> We have not solved the . . . problem of how the community achieves the necessary contingency of reinforcement. How is the response 'toothache' appropriately reinforced if the reinforcing agent has no contact with the tooth? There is, of course, no question of whether responses to private stimuli are possible. They occur commonly enough and must be accounted for. But why do they occur, what is their relation to controlling stimuli, and what, if any, are their distinguishing characteristics?
>
> There are at least four ways in which a verbal community which has no access to a private stimulus may generate verbal behavior in response to it (1945, p. 273).

Skinner then proceeds to elaborate upon what he conceives to be the ways in which the public community commonly teaches people to talk about their own private experience. As he concludes he is led to make the following comments:

> There is apparently no way of basing a response entirely upon the private part of a complex of stimuli. *A differential reinforcement cannot be made contingent upon the property of privacy.* This fact is of extraordinary importance in evaluating psychological terms.
>
> The response 'red' is imparted and maintained (either casually or professionally) by reinforcements which are contingent upon a certain property of stimuli. Both speaker and community (or psychologist) have access to the stimulus, and the contingency can be made quite precise. . . .
>
> We can account for the response 'red' (at least as well as for the 'experience' of red) by appeal to past conditions of reinforcement. But what about expanded expression like '*I see* red' or '*I am conscious of* red'? Here 'red' may be a response to either a public or a private stimulus without prejudice to the rest of the expression, but 'see' and 'conscious' seem to refer to events which are by nature or by definition private. This violates the principle that a reinforcement cannot be narrowed down to a specifically private event by any known method of differential reinforcement. . . . To say 'I see red' is to react, not to red (this is a trivial meaning of 'see'), but to one's reaction to red. 'See' is a term acquired with respect to one's own behavior in the case of overt responses available to the community. But according to the present analysis it may be evoked at other times by *any private accompaniment* of overt seeing. Here is a point at which a non-behavioral private seeing may be slipped in [by others] (1945, pp. 275-276).

The Wittgenstein argument is outlined by Pole as follows:

> But if some one uses the word 'pain' and so doing, speaks to and communicates with other people, it must be the ordinary word, with its public meaning, not the word we gave meaning to by a private reference, that he uses. If we still cling to the dualist picture and, allowing a public meaning to the word 'pain', yet claim that there is something, even if its nature is inexpressible, that remains behind, we shall still find that the words we are using, so long as we use any at all—here the word 'something'—belong to public speech.
>
> In all this the privacy of sensations is not in doubt; for that is a part of the language-game. 'Sensations are private' is for Wittgenstein a grammatical proposition that we might use in teaching the word. Only one who feels pain can report it, and if he sincerely says that he is in pain he cannot be wrong. Somewhat similarly, someone who has learnt the five-times table can repeat it; but we have seen that in order to repeat it correctly, it is not necessary that he should be at the same time glancing or gazing mentally at a private image. He does not look inward and proceed accordingly. These two cases, that of reporting one's feelings and that of repeating what one has learnt, are very different in other ways; but in both what must be rejected is the notion that a correct report or performance can only follow on an act of inward inspection. . . .
>
> Here we have the crux of Wittgenstein's argument. To speak a language, on his view, is to take part in a certain form of social activity which, moreover, is governed by rules. Hence conduct may be condemned as wrong or irregular; the procedures of an individual may diverge from accepted procedures. We have a standard to which to refer

it. In the case of a private language no such appeal can be possible; there can be no such things as divergent or irregular practice, and hence the notion of such a language is nonsensical (Pole, 1958, pp. 73-75).

It might be helpful to add that when Wittgensteinians speak of the necessity for public "criteria of identification," for public "means of determining right and wrong", or for "condemning conduct as wrong or irregular", they are pointing up what Skinnerians consider to be the function of differential reinforcement in establishing verbal discriminations.

The Behavioral Nature of Language

However, it is not only in connection with the verbal reporting of private experience that Wittgenstein and Skinner are similar in their approach to language. As a sixth similarity, it is to be noted that in both perspectives language is viewed as something natural, with an emphasis on the *effects* of verbal behavior and on the situation in which verbal behavior occurs. Wittgenstein's emphasis upon effects is analogous to Skinner's emphasis upon reinforcement. For Skinnerians, "effects" or "consequences" are much better words for "reinforcement" than is "reward", the popularly used substitute. There is clearly no need to illustrate this point from Skinner. Yet the following quotations from Pole on Wittgenstein are relevant.

> Language, we may say, is the instrument of human purposes and needs; thus, very broadly, Wittgenstein thought of it. . . . It is easy to think of human language as if it were some kind of gift of the gods, like Promethean fire; to give it a status that sets it apart from all the rest of our doings and concerns. Wittgenstein saw it differently. Language is part of the social behavior of the species; it belongs as much to our natural history as walking, eating or drinking. It is created, or evolves, like an institution. Parliaments and the party-system, social and religious ceremonies, cricket matches and competitive examinations are forms or functions of social life; and it is on these analogies that language is to be thought of. And they, in turn, may be compared to the hiving of bees and the nesting and migration of birds. Language presupposes, therefore, a non-linguistic context. It operates against a background of human needs in the setting of a natural environment. These together determine its character. And we must see it and understand it in this way, as involved in a pattern that goes further, if we are to understand it at all (Pole, 1958, pp. 2-3).

> The uses of words are infinitely various: there are orders, questions and reports, prayers and recitations. We lose sight of their variousness and seek to assimilate them. Every word must have a meaning, we say; and then we suppose that this meaning is in all cases some sort of object related to the word, as St. Paul's is related to the name 'St. Paul's'. But in effect we have said no more, Wittgenstein urges, than if we should say that every tool in the tool-box has its use; the use in each case is different. . . .

> Wittgenstein often bids us consider the situations in which our words were first learnt; we shall see then what setting they belong to, what part they play in our lives. One may ask what difference the first introduction of a given word made to the pattern of activities it was brought into. . . . Here we touch on a last important point: for Wittgenstein there is no compulsion about the use of words. We suppose that their existing use obliges us to apply them in such ways in other contexts; we think that the meaning itself demands it. But we may use them as we like; and further they have no more meaning than we have found work for them to do. In face of a philosophical 'must', of some statement that we seem compelled to adopt, we shall ask to be shown its application—what connexions it makes and allows, what language-game it belongs to. 'What can I do with this?' is Wittgenstein's question. . . . In all this Wittgenstein's general aim is to break up the rigidity of our terms of thought. But he disclaims any thesis of his own, he offers no doctrine. He merely describes the various workings of language and lays them before us (Pole, 1958, pp. 27-28).

Opposition to Reference Theories of Language

As a seventh point of similarity, let me call attention to the opposition of both Wittgenstein and Skinner to correspondence or reference theories of language. In developing their views on language, both Wittgenstein and Skinner take as their point of departure objections to the common belief that the chief function of words is to stand for, to name, or to *refer* to objects. Pole on Wittgenstein has the following to say:

> The view Wittgenstein is attacking is that which sees the working of language generally in terms of the function of naming. A name stands over against an object; in some such way, it is supposed, all significant language must be related to some independently existing entity. It is a picture which widely dominates philosophical thinking. It leads us to see the relation of language to reality as essentially uniform, as a relation of correspondence or confrontation. . . . [This] view Wittgenstein . . . repudiates (Pole, 1958, p. 10).

Wherever non-natural qualities, subsistent entities and the like, are invoked to vindicate the meaningfulness of forms of discourse, the same model is at work: we have a notion, Wittgenstein said, that the meaning of a word is a sort of object

—that to every word there corresponds a meaning, related to it much as St. Paul's is related to the name 'St. Paul's'. . . . It will suffice to recall Wittgenstein's recommendation to seek, not for objects corresponding to words and sentences, but for their function in human life as parts of language. . . . There are other views or assumptions concerning language that those of Wittgenstein's replace or dispense with. [But the] outcome . . . is condensed in a single saying of Wittgenstein's: 'For a large class of statements—though not all—in which we employ the word "meaning" it can be defined thus: the meaning of a word is its use in the language.'

The equation of meaning and use, in the light of our previous discussion, will, I hope, not need much further explanation. If we are asked the meaning of any word . . . we must answer it by exhibiting its function; we must show the kind of work that it does (Pole, 1958, pp. 15-19).

As for Skinner, much of the introduction to his book *Verbal Behavior* is devoted to a discussion of this point. Consider the following:

The existence of meanings [as substantive psychological entities] becomes even more doubtful when we advance from single words to those collocations which "say something". What is said by a sentence is something more than what the words in it mean. Sentences do not merely refer to trees and skies and rain, they say something about them. This something is sometimes called a "proposition" —a somewhat more respectable precursor of speech but very similar to the "idea" which would have been said to be expressed by the same sentence under the older doctrine. To define a proposition as "something which may be said in any language" does not tell us where propositions are, or of what stuff they are made. Nor is the problem solved by defining a proposition as all the sentences which have the same meaning as some one sentence, since we cannot identify a sentence as a member of this class without knowing its meaning—at which point we find ourselves facing the original problem.

It has been tempting to try to establish the separate existence of words and meanings because a fairly elegant solution of certain problems then becomes available. Theories of meaning usually deal with corresponding arrays of words and things. How do the linguistic entities on one side correspond with the things or events which are their meanings on the other side, and what is the nature of the relation between them called "reference"? Dictionaries seem, at first blush, to support the notion of such arrays. But dictionaries do not give meanings; at best they give words having the same meanings. The semantic scheme, as usually conceived, has interesting properties. Mathematicians, logicians, and information theorists have explored possible modes of correspondence at length. For example, to what extent can the dimensions of the thing communicated be represented in the dimensions of the communicating medium? But it remains to be shown that such constructions bear any close resemblances to the products of genuine linguistic activities.

In any case the practice neglects many important properties of the original behavior, and raises other problems. We cannot successfully supplement a framework of semantic reference by appealing to the "intention of the speaker" until a satisfactory psychological account of intention can be given. If "connotative meaning" is to supplement a deficient denotation, study of the associative process is required. When some meanings are classed as "emotive", another difficult and relatively undeveloped psychological field is invaded. These are all efforts to preserve the logical representation by setting up additional categories for exceptional words. They are a sort of patchwork which succeeds mainly in showing how threadbare the basic notion is. When we attempt to supply the additional material needed in this representation of verbal behavior, we find that our task has been set in awkward if not impossible terms. The observable data have been preempted, and the student of behavior is left with vaguely identified "thought processes".

The impulse to explicate a meaning is easily understood. We ask, "What do you mean?" because the answer is frequently helpful. Clarifications of meaning in this sense have an important place in every sort of intellectual endeavor. For the purposes of effective discourse the method of paraphrase usually suffices; we may not need extra-verbal referents. But the explication of verbal behavior should not be allowed to generate a sense of scientific achievement. One has not *accounted for* a remark by paraphrasing "what it means".

We could no doubt define ideas, meanings, and so on, so that they would be scientifically acceptable and even useful in describing verbal behavior [as in conventional operationism]. But such an effort to retain traditional terms would be costly. It is the general formulation which is wrong. We seek "causes" of behavior which have an acceptable scientific status and which, with luck, will be susceptible to measurement and manipulation. To say that these are "all that is meant by" ideas or meanings is to misrepresent the traditional *practice* [i.e., for Wittgenstein, *use*]. We must find the functional relations which govern the verbal behavior to be explained; to call such relations "expression" or "communication" is to run the danger of introducing extraneous and misleading properties and events. The only solution is to reject the traditional formulation of verbal behavior in terms of meaning (Skinner, 1957, pp. 8-10).

The chapter on "The Tact" in *Verbal Behavior* contains a section specifically devoted to "The Problem of Reference," and it begins as follows:

Semantic theory is often confined to the relation between response and stimulus which prevails in the verbal operant called the tact. Words, parts of words, or groups of words on the one hand and things, parts of things, or groups of things on the other stand in a relation to each other called "reference", "denotation", or "designation". The relation may be as empty as a logical convention or it may provide for the "intention" of the speaker. But how a word "stands for" a thing or "means" what the speaker intends to say or "communicates" some condition of a thing to a listener has never been satisfactorily established. The notion of the verbal operant brings such relations within the scope of the methods of natural science. How a stimulus or some property of a stimulus acquires control over a given form of response is now fairly well understood. The form of a response is shaped by the contingencies prevailing in a verbal community. A given form is brought under stimulus control through the differential reinforcement of our three-term contingency [i.e., a discriminative stimulus in the presence of which a response is followed by reinforcement]. The result is simply the probability that the speaker will emit a response of a given form in the presence of a stimulus having specified properties under certain broad conditions of deprivation or aversive stimulation. *So far as the speaker is concerned*, this *is* the relation of reference or meaning. There would be little point in using this formula to redefine concepts such as sign, signal, or symbol or a relation such as reference, or entities communicated in a speech episode such as ideas, meanings, or information (Skinner, 1957, pp. 114-115).

I suggest that it is the difficulty that most psychologists face in overcoming their tendency to view language as a process of referring to things that stands most in the way of their proper understanding of Skinner's analysis of verbal behavior.

The Nature of Meaning

However, two sentences in the preceding quotation suggest an eighth, and for Wittgensteinians a most important, similarity between Wittgenstein and Skinner. Wittgenstein and Skinner are very much alike in their analysis of the nature of meaning itself. For both, there are no such *things* as meanings, where meanings are taken to be mental entities somehow focally involved in communication. For both, a search for meaning can lead only to the study of word usage, to the analysis of verbal behavior as it is actually seen to take place. For both, the meaning *is* the usage. There is little need to illustrate the point from Wittgenstein, other than perhaps to refer the reader again to the quotations from Pole offered above in illustration of Wittgenstein's views on reference. Indeed, it is largely because of the lengths to which Wittgenstein has teased out the implications of his famous dictum "the meaning is the use" that his views are accorded their current philosophical importance.

However, with respect to Skinner, consider first the relevant sentences from the preceding quotation. "The result is simply the probability that the speaker will emit a response of a given form in the presence of a stimulus having specified properties under certain broad conditions of deprivation or aversive stimulation. *So far as the speaker is concerned*, this *is* the relation of reference or meaning." The first of these sentences describes what is seen as the usage of words when verbal behavior is analyzed in terms of the Skinnerian language-game. Thus the second sentence states directly 'that meaning is usage.'

Consider the following quotation taken from *The Operational Analysis of Psychological Terms:*

The doctrine that words are used to express or convey meanings merely substitutes 'meaning' for 'idea' (in the hope that meanings can then somehow be got outside the skin) and is incompatible with modern psychological conceptions of the organism. Attempts to derive a symbolic function from the principle of conditioning (or association) have been characterized by a very superficial analysis. It is simply not true that an organism reacts to a sign 'as it would to the object which the sign supplants' (Stevens [1939], p. 250). Only in a very limited area (mainly in the case of autonomic responses) is it possible to regard the sign as a simple substitute stimulus in the Pavlovian sense. Modern logic, as a formalization of 'real' languages, retains and extends this dualistic theory of meaning and can scarcely be appealed to by the psychologist who recognizes his own responsibility in giving an account of verbal behavior. . . .

A considerable advantage is gained from dealing with terms, concepts, constructs, and so on, quite frankly in the form in which they are observed—namely, as verbal responses. There is then no danger of including in the concept that aspect or part of nature which it singles out. . . . Meanings, contents, and references are to be found among the determiners, not among the properties, of response. The question 'What is length?' would appear to be satisfactorily answered by listing the circumstances under which the response 'length' is emitted (or, better, by giving some general description of such circumstances). . . .

What we want to know in the case of many traditional psychological terms is, first, the specific stimulating conditions under which they are emitted (this corresponds to 'finding the referents') and, second (and this is a much more important systematic question), why each response is controlled by its corresponding condition. The latter is not necessarily a genetic question. The individual acquires language from society, but the reinforcing action of the verbal community continues to play an important role in maintaining the specific relations between responses and stimuli which are essential to the proper functioning of verbal behavior. How language is acquired is, therefore, only part of a much broader problem (Skinner, 1945, pp. 270-272).

When Skinner says, "The question 'What is length?' would appear to be satisfactorily answered by listing the circumstances under which the response 'length' is emitted (or, better, by giving some general description of such circumstances)", or "What we want to know in the case of many traditional psychological terms is . . . the specific stimulating conditions under which they are emitted (this corresponds to 'finding the referents')", he is not holding a brief for ostensive definition. He is demanding an analysis of word usage to establish the meaning of a term.

Skinner's interest in the relation between meaning and use is much more for him than a mere statement of theoretical perspective. The relation as he sees it is brought into daily use in the laboratory as a working tool of considerable practical importance. In connection with his practical interest in programmed instruction, Skinner is very much concerned at present with the meaning of such terms as "thinking", "inductive reasoning", and "reading". He must know, for example, what is generally meant by "a knowledge of French" in order to know how to teach French effectively. In this, of course, there is no single entity that can be identified as the referent of "a knowledge of French", nor does a constructed referent emerge out of a complex variety of instances. The method Skinner uses to clarify one aspect of the meaning of "a knowledge of French" is to describe whatever observable situations act as discriminative stimuli to control usage of the phrase in identification. That is, he attempts to describe whatever stimulation we might respond to with such verbalizations as "That is an illustrative instance of a knowledge of French", or "That is the sort of thing we normally take to be evidence of a knowledge of French." To do this is to employ the technique referred to in the above quotation as one which "corresponds to 'finding the referents'".[4] Consider the following.

----

[4]Needless to say, emission of the phrase "a knowledge of French" is not restricted to verbalizations which function as identifications, and descriptions of the discriminative control of verbal identifications are only a small part of the analysis of verbal behavior in general.

We can define terms like "information", "knowledge", and "verbal ability" by reference to the behavior from which we infer their presence. *We may then teach the behavior directly.* Instead of "transmitting information to the student" we may simply set up the behavior which is taken as a sign that he possesses information. Instead of teaching a "knowledge of French" we may teach the behavior from which we infer such knowledge (1961b, p. 383).

Traditionally, for example, something called a "knowledge of French" is said to permit the student who possesses it to do many things. One who possesses it can (1) repeat a French phrase with a good accent, (2) read a French text in all the senses of reading listed [earlier in the paper], (3) take dictation in French, (4) find a word spoken in French on a printed list, (5) obey instructions spoken in French, (6) comment in French upon objects or events, (7) give orders in French, and so on. If he also "knows English", he can give the English equivalents of French words or phrases or the French equivalents of English words or phrases.

The concept of "a knowledge of French" offers very little help to the would-be teacher. As in the case of reading, we must turn to the behavioral repertoires themselves, for these are all that have ever been taught when education has been effective. The definition of a subject matter in such terms may be extraordinarily difficult. Students who are "competent in first-year college physics", for example, obviously differ from those who are not—but in what way? Even a tentative answer to that question should clarify the problem of teaching physics. It may well do more. In the not-too-distant future much more general issues in epistemology may be approached from the same direction. It is possible that we shall fully understand the nature of knowledge only after having solved the practical problems of imparting it (1961b, p. 391-392).

Anti-mentalism

Many people may well feel that Skinner's search for the meaning of "knowledge" is destined inevitably to be a superficial one, even when it is restricted to an interest in the "knowledge of French" as in the above illustration. It may seem to many that Skinner's method is limited to a concern with trivial indices of knowledge, or with what may be judged as mere behavioral representations of a deeper knowledge within. It is true that Skinner might make his survey of the signs of knowledge arbitrarily broad or increasingly subtle, as more and more careful analysis is made of conditions that govern the usage of the word in identification. Nevertheless, even though the very most subtle signs of knowledge were to be described, would they constitute in sum or in part a picture of knowledge *in itself?* Is there no difference between *evidence* of knowledge, no matter how subtle that evidence may be, and knowledge itself as it *really is?*

It is Wittgensteinian to reply that questions such as those derive "from our interpreting the language of experience in terms of the language of public objects; for the private realm we [seek] is an attempt to see mental life in the image of the world of common things" (Pole, 1958, p. 65). A Skinnerian might reply, "But after all, knowledge consists only of whatever it is that makes us think we know anything." Even so, Wittgenstein himself responds to questions of this kind, as in the following remarks taken from the *Philosophical Investigations.* The quotation will also serve to illustrate a ninth similarity between Wittgenstein and Skinner, namely, their essentially compatible approach to issues of mentalism.

303. "I can only *believe* that someone else is in pain, but I *know* it if I am."—Yes: one can make the decision to say "I believe he is in pain" instead of "He is in pain". But that is all.—What looks like an explanation here, or like a statement about a mental process, is in truth an exchange of one expression for another which, while we are doing philosophy, seems the more appropriate one.

Just try—in a real case—to doubt someone else's fear or pain.

304. "But you will surely admit that there is a difference between pain-behavior accompanied by pain and pain-behavior without any pain?"—Admit it? What greater difference could there be?—"And yet you again and again reach the conclusion that the sensation itself is a *nothing*."—Not at all. It is not a *something*, but not a *nothing* either! The conclusion was only that a nothing would serve just as well as a something about which nothing could be said. We have only rejected the grammar which tries to force itself on us here.

The paradox disappears only if we make a radical break with the idea that language always functions in one way, always serves the same purpose: to convey thoughts—which may be about houses, pains, good and evil, or anything else you please.

305. "But you surely cannot deny that, for example, in remembering, an inner process takes place." What gives the impression that we want to deny anything? When one says "Still, an inner process does take place here"—one wants to go on: "After all, you *see* it." And it is this inner process that one means by the word "remembering".—The impression that we wanted to deny something arises from our setting our faces against the picture of the 'inner process'. What we deny is that the picture of the inner process gives us the correct idea of the use of the word "to remember". We say that this picture with its ramifications stands in the way of our seeing the use of the word as it is.

306. Why should I deny that there is a mental process? But "There has just taken place in me the mental process of remembering. . . ." means nothing more than: "I have just remembered . . . .". To deny the mental process would mean to deny the remembering; to deny that anyone ever remembers anything.

307. "Are you not really a behaviourist in disguise? Aren't you at bottom really saying that everything except human behaviour is a fiction?"—If I do speak of a fiction, then it is of a *grammatical* fiction.

308. How does the philosophical problem about mental processes and states and about behaviorism arise?—The first step is the one that altogether escapes notice. We talk of processes and states and leave their nature undecided. Sometime perhaps we shall know more about them—we think. But that is just what commits us to a particular way of looking at the matter. For we have a definite concept of what it means to learn to know a process better. (The decisive movement in the conjuring trick has been made, and it was the very one that we thought quite innocent.)—And now the analogy which was to make us understand our thought falls to pieces. So we have to deny the yet uncomprehended process in the yet unexplored medium. And now it looks as if we had denied mental processes. And naturally we don't want to deny them.

309. What is your aim in philosophy?—To shew the fly the way out of the fly-bottle (Wittgenstein, 1953, pp. 102^e-103^e).

Wittgenstein is pointing out that the difficulties faced by psychologists or philosophers in their concern with mental processes arise from habitual ways of talking about, of conceptualizing, of thinking about mental events as objects of study. He notes that the language in terms of which we conceptualize much profitable inquiry, as for example in physical science or in practical technology, often breaks down when it is brought to bear upon an interest in mental experience. He calls attention also to our learned aspirations and expectations, which lead us to think it is even possible for us to have knowledge of mental processes and to hope that we shall sometime know more about them in pursuing conventional modes of inquiry. Thus we bear in our very behavior what is easily viewed as an intellectual commitment.

In this, Wittgenstein resists ontology.[5] That is, he resists making claims about the nature of reality, or about the ultimate constituents of which reality is composed. What then is

---

[5]Whether or not Wittgenstein succeeds in avoiding ontological commitment has been argued (Pole, 1958, p. 18 n.1, p. 100 ff.; Gellner, 1959, p. 103 ff.).

Wittgenstein doing? He is trying to help—flies out of fly-bottles, philosophers out of puzzles (Pole, 1958, p. 98). But what is the status of this reply? In saying that Wittgenstein is trying to help, are we making an ontological claim? Is "trying to help" what Wittgenstein is *really* doing, as opposed, say, to enjoying the display of his own brilliance? Of course, to say that someone is trying to help can be viewed not as a statement about the inherent nature of his motivation but rather simply as a *description*. "Trying to help" may be taken as only one of presumably a variety of descriptions that are applicable.

At the core of much interest in psychological explanation is the hope that an account can be given of the way in which certain ultimate constituents of our psychological nature are interrelated. With sufficient sophistication this would be theory, and it is ontological in character. Such an account Wittgenstein resists. When pressed for an account of the nature of what he is doing, Wittgenstein gives, in the end, only the broadest possible description: he is behaving. "There comes a point, Wittgenstein writes, where he is inclined to say, 'This is simply what I do.' " (Pole, 1958, p. 51).

> 217. "How am I able to obey a rule?"—if this is not a question about causes, then it is about the justification for my following the rule in the way I do.
> If I have exhausted the justifications I have reached bedrock, and my spade is turned. Then I am inclined to say: "This is simply what I do." (Wittgenstein, 1953, p. 85ᵉ).

What has all this to do with mentalism? Skinner frequently attacks an outlook in psychology which he calls "mentalism", and at times he contrasts his position with that of conventional behaviorism on the basis of this issue (see, *e.g.*, Skinner, 1964, p. 106). It is less important here to give evidence of Skinner's antipathy to mentalism than it is to clarify what he means when he speaks of it. For Skinner there are two sides to the coin of mentalism. The first of these is the dualistic separation of the physical and the mental into two ontological realms, an issue which we have already discussed. The second side of the coin, and the one which bears the similarity to Wittgenstein now under consideration, has to do with the practice of reifying terms generally thought to refer to psychological or behavioral processes. For Skinner, it is mentalistic to look at such words as "attending", "inferring", "observing", "trying", "deciding", "remembering", *etc.*, as identifying psychological acts, states, or processes which correctly map the underlying structure of our psychological nature. It is here that he resists ontology. For Skinner these terms are viewed as part of the language with which we ordinarily make sense out of behavior, and if we are to account for the behavior to which they are relevant we must first analyze the control of these terms as aspects of verbal behavior. Wittgenstein captures very nicely the spirit of Skinnerian anti-mentalism on paragraphs 305-306, quoted above from the *Philosophical Investigations*. It will suffice to give only one illustration of Skinner's efforts to avoid the ontological implications of mentalism. Consider the following discussion of "tendencies" and "readinesses" to behave.

> A science must achieve more than a description of behavior as an accomplished fact. It must predict future courses of action; it must be able to say that an organism will engage in behavior of a given sort at a given time. But this raises a special problem. We want to believe that a prediction is in some sense a description of a condition at the moment—before the predicted event has taken place. Thus, we speak of tendencies or readinesses to behave as if they corresponded to something in the organism at the moment. We have given this something many names—from the preparatory set of experimental psychology to the Freudian wish. Habits and instincts, dispositions and predispositions, attitudes, opinions—even personality itself—are all ways of representing, in the present organism, something of its future behavior.
> This problem cannot be avoided in any scientific account, but it can be expressed much more rigorously. We are dealing here with a question of probability—specifically, the probability that an organism will emit behavior of a given sort at a given time. But probability is always a difficult concept, no matter in what field of science it arises. What is a probability? Where is it? How may we observe it? We have tried to answer these difficult questions by giving probability the status of a thing—by *embodying* it, so to speak, within the organism. We look for neurological or psychic states or events with which habits, wishes, attitudes, and so on, may be identified. In doing so we force extraneous properties on behavior which are not supported by the data and which may be quite misleading (Skinner, 1953b, p. 69).

Interest in Description

A tenth similarity, and one that is the last to be mentioned here, is that both Skinner and Wittgenstein have viewed their work as essentially descriptive in nature. Skinner is widely held among psychologists to regard his system as purely descriptive, as opposed to hypothetical or theoretical, in approach (*e.g.*, Hilgard, 1956, p. 101). Concerning the basically descriptive character of his system, Skinner has had the following to say in *The Behavior of Organisms:*

> So far as scientific method is concerned, the system set up in the preceding chapter may be characterized as follows. It is positivistic [in the Machian sense]. It confines itself to description rather than explanation. Its concepts are defined in terms of immediate observations and are not given local or physiological properties. A reflex is not an arc, a drive is not the state of a center, extinction is not the exhaustion of a physiological substance or state. Terms of this sort are used merely to bring together groups of observations, to state uniformities, and to express properties of behavior which transcend single instances. They are not hypotheses, in the sense of things to be proved or disproved, but convenient representations of things already known. As to hypotheses, the system does not require them—at least in the usual sense (Skinner, 1938, p. 44).

However, a number of psychologists have found it difficult to conclude that Skinner's system is as purely descriptive as one might hope. Consider, for example, the following comments by Chaplin and Krawiec:

> Skinner's willingness to grapple with the age-old problems of human behavior demonstrates the lure of theory. Despite his "antitheory" bias, Skinner, in company with every psychologist who has tried to organize and systematize the data of behavior, finds it necessary to bridge the all-too-frequent gaps in our knowledge of human behavior by appealing to theory. We do not mean to imply that Skinner has fallen into what he himself considers the traditional "errors" of seeking explanations in the nervous system, on the one hand, or appealing to intervening variables, on the other. Rather, Skinner's theorizing takes two forms: First, he accepts the ready-made skeleton of conditioning theory as the structural framework of his system, and, second, by a process of logical reasoning, he is willing to extend or extrapolate the principles of operant conditioning to everyday problems of human behavior. This, we submit, is theory (Chaplin and Krawiec, 1960, p. 250).

Hilgard appears to feel that even were Skinner to succeed in formulating a purely descriptive system, the system itself would then not genuinely mediate practical application. It is as if he believed that predictions can legitimately be made only through the deductive implications of theory. Is it the case that Skinner's system is hopelessly dependent in its utility upon some such factor as the experimenter's ingenuity, his insight, or what Chaplin and Krawiec identify above as "logical reasoning"? In the influential 1956 edition of his *Theories of Learning*, Hilgard concludes his analysis of Skinner's position in the following way.

> The practical use of the system is based on the complementary principles of control through presenting and withholding food reward for a hungry animal. The supplementary principles of stimulus discrimination and response differentiation suffice to inaugurate the method of successive approximations. Beyond that, all that is needed is the experimenter's ingenuity. It is not necessary to worry about anything precise in the way either of experimental data or of correlated principles. From the point of view of a theoretical achievement this is really a pretty modest extension of Thorndike's law of effect. Whether or not a child can be taught to write a limerick by the same methods can only be known when the limerick gets written. The theory does not propose to predict[6] (Hilgard, 1956, p. 119).

Professional usage of "logical reasoning", "extrapolation", and "analogy" in commenting upon Skinner's practices of prediction and explanation has possibly been stimulated by Verplanck (but see also Skinner, 1953a, p. 39).

> Does the system mediate the application of knowledge to new situations? Does it predict?
>
> Some systems or theories of behavior lay great stress on their ability to predict the outcome of planned experiments—often taken to be *experimenta crucis*. It is not surprising, however, that a theory of restricted empirical basis, "informally stated", and "inductively" developed does not generate rigorous predictions about the behavior to be observed in novel situations. In fact, such statements as these must be qualified. Several aspects of Skinner's view of the problem of prediction and extrapolation must be treated individually. Although one of our more conservative theorists when he is making statements *about* prediction, Skinner is more willing than most to extrapolate his concepts from the situations in which they have been developed to some of the more intricate cases of human behavior. This willingness is clearly indicated in the title of the treatise, *The Behavior of Organisms*, which deals with the white rat in the Skinner-box.
>
> Two situations may be distinguished in which a systematist may wish to make predictions. The first

---

[6]Hilgard would possibly attempt to substantiate this cryptic remark by reference to Skinner's challenging remarks on prediction in *The Behavior of Organisms* (1938, p. 10 f.).

is that in which a logical or operational analysis shows that the "same" variables that have already been isolated and studied in the laboratory are operative elsewhere in the "same" relationships that have been investigated. The data are in, and the theorist simply asserts the genotypicality of the situation, applies his theory, and "predicts" the course of events. In the other situation, familiar variables may be encountered, but in novel configurations, the theorist is required to generate statements that go beyond those he has already made. Or, again, new variables may be encountered, and again, prediction may be called for. While Skinner will predict, or rather extrapolate freely where a logical analysis reveals familiar variables acting in familiar ways, he will not predict at all under other circumstances. As a consequence it is possible to find no predictions at all of the behavior of rats, or of pigeons, when novel combinations of stimuli are presented to them in the Skinner-box, and many predictions among Skinner's writings with respect to human behavior in a social environment. The great difficulty is that these predictions are usually unverifiable, because of the complexity of the situation and the consequent impossibility of meaningful experimental test. Prediction, then, is represented by extrapolation, by analogy; its use for the generation of propositions that may be put to experimental test is avoided (Verplanck, 1954, pp. 310-311).

It is clear, then, that various psychologists have been unable to view Skinner's system as one that successfully avoids theory and is purely descriptive in nature. Moreover, the imputation has been made that in certain ways practical application of the system is not free from dependence upon extra-systematic, unspecified, and vague mental operations. Very much the same kind of criticism has been directed at Wittgenstein's attempt to avoid metaphysical involvement by what purports to be simple description. An explicit charge of mysticism has been made by Bertrand Russell (1959, p. 14; see also Ayer, 1959, p. 5). A similar view by Gellner (1959) is elaborated into an accusation of general intellectual inadequacy. Even Pole, whose remarks have been quoted here at length in exposition of Wittgenstein's views, is led to the following critical conclusion.

> Wittgenstein disclaimed any intention of propounding a philosophy of language [*i.e.*, theory of the nature of language]. To me it seems that he has done so whether he intended it or not. To tell us that languages resemble games; that the use of language is as much part of our natural history as eating or walking; that it is a particular form of public activity, interwoven with others and subject to rules; that language consists of an infinity of different parts, like so many tools, each working in its own way, in its own context—all this, I suggest, is to do as much in the way of a general characterization as one could ask of any philosopher who had made that his avowed object. If so much is granted, a metaphysician will naturally wish to know why language should be the only subject matter that lends itself to such treatment. Surely there may be other fields of inquiry where no less illumination may be got from a non-empirical, reflective investigation. But that is a line of argument I shall not pursue. My concern here is rather to ask whether the present picture of language, upon which, for Wittgenstein, everything turns, is not itself inadequate and vulnerable to criticism.

Wittgenstein characterizes his own work as descriptive. He explains nothing, he says, he merely lays before us the different parts or segments of language, and points out the actual use of different terms. He thus establishes for himself something like a Socratic immunity from criticism; he professes to know nothing—or nothing beyond what other people can see for themselves. But the claim, or rather the disclaimer, may be subject to suspicion in the one case no less than the other. What Wittgenstein seems in fact to require of us, when he sets out these things, is to understand the working of a mechanism; for he tells us time and again to think of a word as a tool—there is no saying of his that occurs more often. Wittgenstein's crucial concept is of a language-game, a complex or system of linguistic activities; and every such game must be understood individually, for each works to its own end and in its own particular setting. Our endeavour in each case must be to see or grasp a unique pattern, a system of relations; and language contains at least as many such games as—to take not too remote an analogy—there are concepts to be unfolded in the Hegelian Dialectic.

Now it seems that it would be possible to describe the action of a machine, to specify all its movements correctly, without understanding its working principle. And again one might describe all the procedures followed by the various players in a game without in any way appreciating the pattern. Yet that is what above all Wittgenstein requires us to appreciate. For consider the great purpose of all this—this descriptive setting-forth of language-games. It is to bring us to see that some particular move which we took for a move in the game has no proper place in it. Such a move is to be shown as failing to connect with the rest of the pattern. Wittgenstein compares it to a wheel spinning idly, disengaged from the machine it should belong to. Here we have a luminous metaphor—and yet no more than a metaphor. For there can be no way of testing whether this or that linguistic wheel has failed to engage, except to grasp the pattern in each case; to arrive at some sort of insight into that unique set of relations which it professes but fails to form a part of. . . . [It must be] agreed that Wittgenstein in fact requires something more than a mere description, or the acceptance of a description, [in order for his views to find application] (Pole, 1958, pp. 79-82).

In what follows I shall comment briefly upon the preceding criticisms of Wittgenstein and Skinner. To consider Skinner first, it seems clear that a particularly troublesome aspect of his published work centers about the way in which his system mediates prediction. However the problem of prediction is but one part of the even more sensitive problem of how his system mediates explanation in general. The above quotation from Chaplin and Krawiec misses its mark by speaking as if any specialized use of language in interpretation and explanation must be taken to be theoretical. Ontological properties are attributed not only to theory, presumably as distinguished from description, but also to such entities as logical reasoning and extrapolation, possibly taken either as mental processes or as *a priori* forms of knowing. Verplanck's intelligent remarks on prediction and explanation can easily be read from two different points of view: on the one hand that of Chaplin and Krawiec, and on the other hand that of Skinner. In a Skinnerian reading, Verplanck's statements about prediction are taken as having been emitted by him chiefly under the control of his own observation of practices of scientific prediction; in other words, these statements are read as descriptions. "Logical analysis", "extrapolation", and "analogy" are read in the Skinnerian fashion as loosely distinguished classes of responding, verbal or otherwise.

The issue here is whether explanations and predictions are properties of scientific systems in themselves or whether they are aspects of human functioning. Are predictions about what is to be observed properties of formally organized words and symbols or are they varieties of human behavior? For neither Skinner nor Wittgenstein is the problem in this regard to determine which one of these alternatives is *really* the case. We have only to decide which of the two language-games we wish to play. For Skinner, the preference is to view explanations and predictions as aspects of human behavior. Their nature can be understood only after examining the variety of factors controlling usage of the words "explanation" and "prediction". To raise questions concerning how a particular explanation happens to have been given is to inquire about the behavior of the person offering the explanation. To raise questions concerning how predictions happen to be made is to inquire about the behavior of making a prediction. To raise questions concerning how predictions *should* be made is to invite behavioral control in the form of advice. To raise questions concerning the *adequacy* of an explanation is to inquire about the effects of the explanation upon the behavior of persons who entertain the explanation. Of course, to adopt such a perspective as Skinner's does not diminish general interest in such questions as whether or not professional psychologists happen to agree with, to be stimulated by, or to like Skinner's explanations, or whether or not a study of his work enables them to predict and control more effectively those human activities in which they are interested.

The critical comments by Hilgard quoted above, while relatively unappreciative of the breadth and originality of Skinner's thought, are nonetheless not unperceptive. They reflect at heart a concern with Skinner's obvious affront to the time-honored canons of respectable procedure in psychological science. Thus, Hilgard stands as the champion of those who find distasteful the apparent untestability of many Skinnerian explanations. Yet for Skinner, his explanations are after all no more than instances of his own verbal behavior. If what he has to say, either by way of what is likely to be called explanation or not, poses a problem to psychologists, then he sees only one avenue of interesting and effective comment as open: an analysis must be made of the variables that may be considered to have controlled his emission of the troublesome verbal behavior in question. This is, of course, to take a uniquely Skinnerian course of action; but it is also to bring intellectual activity to bear upon the problem as it exists as an aspect of the observable world. How would one approach the task of attempting to determine the variables which control, for example, that aspect of Skinner's verbal behavior that appears to be explanatory? It is immediately seen that no one actually knows very much about how to give an empirically oriented accounting of what people happen to say, whether the particular verbal behavior is generally accorded intellectual significance or not. Nor do we know very much by way of fact about what scientists do when they succeed in effecting a new measure of control over natural events, or when they come to feel they have attained a more adequate understanding of observed phenomena, or when they conclude that an explanation that has been offered is a satisfactory one.

It is distinctively Skinnerian to urge the empirical study of whatever intellectual activities happen to characterize successful scientific behavior. It is true that many scientists, and notably psychologists, *think* they know what science is (to speak in terms of the name-relation), or *think* they know what is involved in legitimate scientific explanation and in the application of scientific method. However, their *thoughts* in this respect have still to be accounted for just as much as Skinner's even if the value in trusting such conventional views were not to be questioned. It is hardly necessary to elaborate upon how sharply conventional attitudes towards scientific explanation have been questioned, even recently and by the most competent of scientists (see Polanyi, 1958). To fail to view the problem of explanation in this fashion, as *inescapably* an empirical and behavioral problem, is perhaps to miss the force of what well may be Skinner's major contribution to psychological thought.

However still, asks the philosopher, how is it that some of Skinner's statements work upon us as explanations whereas others do not? This is the kind of question that plagues Pole when he reads Wittgenstein. When Wittgenstein says "This is simply what I do," he stops talking. Wittgenstein can say no more; yet the listener to whom he speaks remains transfixed by the meaning and significance of his remark. How is it that he can stop talking? Will he not take the next step and inquire *how* the miracle of language has taken place? Pole itches to know, as do many others, the how and what of language. Very much as a psychologist he asks, in effect, "What are the properties intrinsic to human functioning that enable effective communication to take place?" Effective communication seems to *depend upon* certain conditions.

Wittgenstein would certainly contend that to raise questions of this kind is to play a particular type of language-game. To use language of this sort involves us in speaking of a world broken apart into effects and their antecedent conditions. Of course, this particular game is one that interests Skinner, unlike Wittgenstein. In contrast to a view popularly

attributed to Hume, Skinner holds that certain events are *seen* to have their effect upon other events. One can *see* effects and dependencies in nature. For Skinner, natural controlling contingencies are observed to take place. Yet the perception in this is not totally trusted: the disposition is there to regard whatever is seen as dependent upon a previous history of reinforcement. What is seen in observation is simply a part of the behavior-game a man plays, a behavior-game that is often critically and dangerously linguistic. Thus, he considers his own perceptions of natural contingency to be under the control of the same natural processes he hopes through observation to be able to understand. He hopes, moreover, that the observation of natural contingency will have, in turn, its own effect upon the success with which he is able to understand and control other events. For Skinner, an individual whose behavior is controlled more by the *observation* of natural contingency than by any other kind of factor is, in an interesting way, properly called a scientist. To my view, such a statement of simple hopes, and fears, and faiths, even when coupled with strong conviction, is not ontology. Such a statement is a verbal description of behavior. With this comment I shall rest my case.

REFERENCES

Ayer, A. J. Editor's introduction. In A. J. Ayer (Ed.), *Logical positivism*. Glencoe, Ill.: Free Press, 1959.

Boring, E. G. *A history of experimental psychology.* 2nd. ed.; New York: Appleton-Century-Crofts, 1950.

Boring, E. G. *Psychologist at large.* New York: Basic Books, 1961.

Chaplin, J. P. and Krawiec, T. S. *Systems and theories of psychology.* New York: Holt, Rinehart & Winston, 1960.

Chomsky, N. Review of *Verbal behavior. Language,* 1959, **35,** 26-58.

Gellner, E. *Words and things.* London: Victor Gollancz, 1959.

Hilgard, E. R. *Theories of learning.* 2nd ed.; New York: Appleton-Century-Crofts, 1956.

Hively, W. Programming stimuli in matching to sample. *Journal of the Experimental Analysis of Behavior,* 1962, **5,** 279-298.

Malcolm, N. Wittgenstein's *Philosophical investigations. Philosophical Review,* 1954, **63,** 530-559.

Pears, D. F. The development of Wittgenstein's philosophy. *The New York Review of Books,* 1969, **12**(1), 21-30.

Polanyi, M. *Personal knowledge.* Chicago: University of Chicago Press, 1958.

Pole, D. *The later philosophy of Wittgenstein.* London: Athlone Press, 1958.

Russell, B. Introduction to E. Gellner, *Words and things.* London: Victor Gollancz, 1959.

Skinner, B. F. The concept of the reflex in the description of behavior. *Journal of General Psychology*, 1931, **5**, 427-458.

Skinner, B. F. *The behavior of organisms.* New York: Appleton-Century-Crofts, 1938.

Skinner, B. F. The operational analysis of psychological terms. *Psychological Review*, 1945, **52**, 270-277, 291-294.

Skinner, B. F. Are theories of learning necessary? *Psychological Review*, 1950, **57**, 193-216.

Skinner, B. F. *Science and human behavior.* New York: Macmillan, 1953. (*a*)

Skinner, B. F. Some contributions of an experimental analysis of behavior to psychology as a whole. *American Psychologist*, 1953, **8**, 69-79. (*b*)

Skinner, B. F. *Verbal behavior.* New York: Appleton-Century-Crofts, 1957.

Skinner, B. F. *Cumulative record.* Enl. ed.; New York: Appleton-Century-Crofts, 1961. (*a*)

Skinner, B. F. Why we need teaching machines. *Harvard Educational Review*, 1961, **31**, 377-398. (*b*)

Skinner, B. F. Behaviorism at fifty. In T. W. Wann (Ed.), *Behaviorism and phenomenology.* Chicago: University Chicago Press, 1964. Pp. 79-108.

Stevens, S. S. Psychology and the science of science. *Psychological Bulletin*, 1939, **36**, 221-263.

Strawson, P. F. Philosophical investigations. *Mind*, 1954, **63**, 70-99.

Urmson, J. O. *Philosophical analysis.* Oxford: Clarendon Press, 1956.

Verplanck, W. S. *Burrhus F. Skinner.* In W. K. Estes, S. Koch, K. MacCorquodale, P. E. Meehl, C. G. Mueller, Jr., W. N. Schoenfeld, and W. S. Verplanck, *Modern learning theory.* New York: Appleton-Century-Crofts, 1954. Pp. 267-316.

Warnock, G. J. *English philosophy since 1900.* London: Oxford Univ. Press, 1958.

Wittgenstein, L. *Philosophical investigations.* New York: Macmillan, 1953.

Wolman, B. B. *Contemporary theories and systems in psychology.* New York: Harper, 1960.

Wright, G. H. von Ludwig Wittgenstein—A biographical sketch. *Philosophical Review*, 1955, **64**, 527-545.

ON THE LAW OF EFFECT[1]

R. J. HERRNSTEIN

HARVARD UNIVERSITY

Experiments on single, multiple, and concurrent schedules of reinforcement find various correlations between the rate of responding and the rate or magnitude of reinforcement. For concurrent schedules (*i.e.*, simultaneous choice procedures), there is matching between the relative frequencies of responding and reinforcement; for multiple schedules (*i.e.*, successive discrimination procedures), there are contrast effects between responding in each component and reinforcement in the others; and for single schedules, there are a host of increasing monotonic relations between the rate of responding and the rate of reinforcement. All these results, plus several others, can be accounted for by a coherent system of equations, the most general of which states that the absolute rate of any response is proportional to its associated relative reinforcement.

A review of the evidence for the law of effect would quickly reveal that the simple notion of "stamping-in" (Thorndike, 1911, *e.g.*, p. 283) does not suffice. Animals do not just repeat the first successful act; they are likely to improve upon it until they find something like the optimal performance. In Thorndike's puzzle box, in the maze, or in Skinner's operant conditioning chamber, animals tend toward faster, easier, and more congenial movements, unless the performances are virtually optimal to begin with. Although some theorists find enough stereotypy to suggest a quasi-mechanical process of stamping-in (*e.g.*, Guthrie and Horton, 1946), others have remained unconvinced (*e.g.*, Tolman, 1948). Something more than the static form of the law of effect is needed for a really persuasive theory. The temptation to fall back on common sense and conclude that animals are adaptive, *i.e.*, doing what profits them most, had best be resisted, for adaptation is at best a question, not an answer. And it is not hard to find evidence that violates both the Thorndikian principle of stamping-in and common-sense motions of adaptation, as the following two examples show.

Ferster and Skinner (1957) reported that an animal, when shifted from an interval to a ratio schedule, typically showed a change in its rate of responding. As regards stamping-in, the rate should remain unchanged for ratio schedules reinforce all rates of responding with equal probability (Morse, 1966). Although the deviation from the theory is large and reproducible, its direction is somewhat unpredictable. For example, in an experiment with pigeons (Ferster and Skinner, 1957, pp. 399-407), one subject's rate of responding increased while the other's virtually ceased, when the schedule changed from a variable interval to a variable ratio matched for numbers of responses per reinforcement. While both of these findings—both the increase and the decrease in the rate of responding in the shift from interval to ratio schedule—violate the Thorndikian law of effect, only the increase is plausibly seen as adaptive. By responding faster on the ratio schedule, one animal increased its reinforcements per unit time, but, by the same token, the other one reduced its rate of reinforcement by responding more slowly. If the acceleration is adaptive, then the

[1] The preparation of this paper and the original work described herein were supported by grants to Harvard University from the National Science Foundation, the National Institute of Mental Health (NIMH-15494), and the National Institutes of Health (NIH-GM-15258). This paper is dedicated to B. F. Skinner in his sixty-fifth year, in partial payment for an intellectual debt incurred over the past decade and a half. There are also more recent debts to be acknowledged, which I do gratefully. J. A. Nevin and H. S. Terrace have generously made available unpublished data, some of which have been included. W. M. Baum and J. R. Schneider have criticized and undoubtedly improved the paper, in substance and in style. Reprints may be obtained from the author, Psychological Laboratories, William James Hall, Harvard University, Cambridge, Massachusetts 02138.

deceleration is not, and both findings are well substantiated.

A related finding, also violating both the Thorndikian law of effect and adaptiveness, has been obtained with the conjunctive schedule, schematically shown in Fig. 1. This graph plots on the coordinates of a cumulative record the region over which responses are unreinforced. For the conjunctive schedule, it is the entire plane minus the shaded area within the right angle. In other words, the conjunctive schedule reinforces the first response after the occurrence of a certain number of responses (n on the figure) *and* the passage of a certain period of time (t). The schedule is specified by its component members: fixed interval and fixed ratio in the present instance. The conjunctive schedule in Fig. 1 would be called a "conjunctive fixed-interval t, fixed-ratio n + 1." In the simple fixed-interval schedule, rapid responding is implicitly penalized, for faster responding increases the work per reinforcement. In contrast, ratio schedules exact no such penalty for responding quickly, for the amount of work per reinforcement is held constant. In fact, ratio schedules may favor rapid responding by arranging a direct proportionality between the rate of responding and the rate of reinforcement. The conjunctive schedule concatenates these features of ratio

and interval schedules, since the rate of reinforcement is directly proportional to the rate of responding only for rates of responding no larger than n/t, beyond which the rate of responding covaries with the responses per reinforcement.

The relevant finding was obtained in an experiment (Herrnstein and Morse, 1958) that held the interval component constant at 15 min, but varied the ratio component from zero (which is a simple fixed-interval schedule) to 240. Figure 2 shows the relation between rate of responding and the number requirement imposed by the ratio component. Although the pigeons were responding more than an average 300 times per reinforcement on the fixed-interval schedule, a number requirement as small as 10 (for one of the pigeons) or 40 (for either), caused a detectable slowing down of responding. The range of rates of responding within individual fixed intervals is large enough so that number requirements even this small are likely to make contact with the behavior. Larger requirements caused progressively larger decrements in responding. This falling rate of responding reduced the rate of reinforcement, as Fig. 3 shows. Here for the two pigeons are the average interreinforcement times as the number requirement was increased. For the fixed-interval schedule, the interreinforcement time was as small as the procedure permits, which is to say, 15 min. Even the smaller requirements produced some reduction in the rate of reinforcement. For one pigeon, the rate of re-

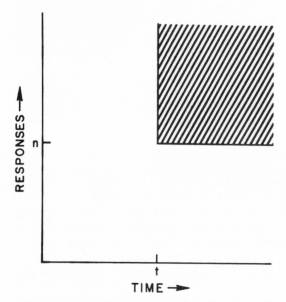

Fig. 1. The shaded area shows the region of reinforced responding on a conjunctive schedule of reinforcement. The ordinate is cumulated responding; the abscissa is elapsed time.

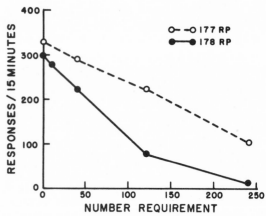

Fig. 2. For two subjects, the rate of responding as a function of the size of the number requirement in a conjunctive schedule with a time requirement of 15 min throughout.

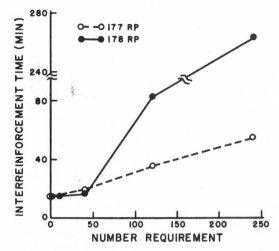

Fig. 3. For two subjects, the interreinforcement time as a function of the size of the number requirement in a conjunctive schedule with a time requirement of 15 min throughout.

inforcement fell very sharply as the number requirement was increased; for the other, the decline was more gradual, but in either case, the requirement took its toll throughout.

The conjunctive schedule lends itself poorly to a Thorndikian analysis, for what could be getting stamped-in when responding and response requirement vary inversely? Moreover, the conjunctive schedule makes poor sense as regards the animal's best interests, for the animal may be emitting substantially more (in Fig. 2, it was 30-fold more) behavior on the fixed interval than the number requirement demands, and yet the behavior is nevertheless depressed.

These problem cases are troublesome only within the confines of theory. In the broader sphere of common sense, reinforcement is affecting what might be termed the "strength" of behavior, as reflected in its rate. For example, consider the change from interval to ratio schedules. If the first effect is a higher rate of reinforcement, the rate of responding might increase. But this would further increase the rate of reinforcement, further "strengthening" responding, causing it to rise again, which again pushes the rate of reinforcement upwards, and so on. If, on the other hand, the first effect is a lower rate of reinforcement, then the rate of responding should fall. The rate of reinforcement would then also fall, further weakening the responding, and so on again. This dynamic process occurs

with ratio, and not interval, schedules because only the ratio schedule arranges a proportionality between the rate of reinforcement and the rate of responding. The proportionality is the basis for an instability in ratio schedules that should produce either maximal responding or none at all, an implication that is confirmed by the tendency of ratio responding to be "two-valued" (Ferster and Skinner, 1957, chap. 4).

The conjunctive schedule similarly exemplifies the notion of strength. However slightly the number requirement increases the interreinforcement interval, it should reduce the strength, and therefore the output, of responding. If the strength of responding is sufficiently reduced so that the rate of responding is less than n/t (see Fig. 1), then the conjunctive schedule becomes identical to a ratio schedule, and responding may reasonably be expected to vanish altogether, as it does with too-large ratios. One of the pigeons in Fig. 2 had, in fact, virtually stopped responding at the largest ratio studied, even though the number requirement was still less than the responses per reinforcement freely emitted on the simple fixed-interval schedule.

Those two examples, and others like them, show that neither stamping-in, nor adaptation, nor the two of them together, can account for what is here being called the strength of behavior. This paper specifies more formally than heretofore the shape of this intuitively obvious concept, while staying within the general outlines of the law of effect.

REINFORCEMENT AS STRENGTHENING

Reinforcement as strengthening is not being offered as a new idea, for "to reinforce" means to strengthen, and only by metaphor, to strengthen behavior. The earliest psychological usage concerned Pavlovian conditioning, where "reinforcement" of a reflex in a physiological sense was already familiar in classical work on facilitation and inhibition. The use of "reinforcement" in the vocabulary of instrumental learning was promoted in the mid-1930s, particularly by Skinner and primarily as a substitute for the traditional term "reward", whose very age tainted it with the suspicion of mentalism. Mentalism notwithstanding, "reward" was more neutral than "reinforce", for while reward simply names a class of events that have some effect on the organism, "reinforcement" implies what the effect is, namely a strengthening. The extra connotation was tolerable only so long as it was not contrary to fact, which it was not. The leading advocates of the law of effect—Thorndike, Skinner, and others—had from the beginning spoken in terms of a "strengthening" of behavior.

What, though, does it mean to strengthen behavior? Thorndike's answer was the notion of stamping-in, which may, in fact, be adequate for the acquisition of new behavior. But for behavior already learned, stamping-in seems inappropriate. The response form as such is then no longer changing, and yet, as the examples in the previous section show, reinforcement is still affecting what might be considered the strength of the behavior. The answers of others, like Skinner and Hull, addressed themselves sensibly if not successfully to the underlying problem, which is one of measurement. To say that behavior is strengthened is to imply some dimension of behavior along which it changes when its strength changes.

The measurement problem is empirical, not conceptual, which is not to deny the virtue of clear and original thinking. It is, rather, to point out that the only persuasive argument for any measure of response strength is to show orderly relations between the parameters of reinforcement—its frequency, quantity, quality, and so on—and the designated parameter of behavior. The traditional measures of response—probability, rate, amplitude (i.e., work or effort), latency, resistance to extinction—have all failed to gain unequivocal support simply because orderly data with *quantitative* and *general* significance have not been forthcoming. Although there is no doubt that behavior is affected by its consequences, the law of effect is still expressed qualitatively, rather than as a relation between measurable variables, which it clearly must be at some level of analysis.

The notion of response probability comes closest to being a generally accepted measure of strength, cutting, as it does, across theories as diverse as those of Tolman (1938) and Hull (1943), Brunswik (1955) and Skinner (1953). But the agreement is more apparent than real, for the abstractness of "probability" masks the diversity of methods used for its extraction. For example, in some experiments, particularly those concerned with acquisition, the changing probabilities of response are estimated by the proportion of subjects doing something at successive points in training. In other experiments, single subjects are the basis for estimation of the probability by integrating over successive trials. In still others, the probability is estimated by the proportion of trials, or proportion of subjects, showing the choice of one response alternative out of a known set of alternatives. Not even the use of relative frequencies—the measure in modern probability theory—is common to all theorists, for according to Skinner, the rate of responding is the proper estimate of the organism's probability of responding. This is not an estimator in the formal sense—a mathematical probability is a dimensionless quantity between 0 and 1.0, and response rate is neither dimensionless nor bounded in principle—but rather an index of the animal's disposition to respond over some interval of time. Given the present state of knowledge, this abundance of measures is more likely to confuse than to enrich.

To reduce the confusion, and hopefully to advance the state of knowledge, the present approach focuses initially on a single relative-frequency measure as its index of strength. No "probability" will be inferred simply because to do so might suggest an equivalence with other empirical measures for which there is no evidence. The measure is exemplified by an experiment in which pigeons had two keys to peck (Herrnstein, 1961). The keys were available continuously during experimental sessions and pecking was reinforced with two variable-interval schedules, mutually independent and running simultaneously. The relative frequency is obtained by dividing the number of pecks on one key by the sum to both. In the context of operant conditioning this is a concurrent schedule, but it is clearly a version of the familiar "choice" experiment. It is, however, different in two significant respects. First, it uses continuous exposure to the alternatives instead of discrete trials. Second, reinforcements come on interval, instead of ratio, schedules. In the typical choice experiment, as well as in gambling casinos, the over-all probability of winning is constant for a given play (or response alternative), so that the number of wins is proportional to the number of plays. With interval schedules, there is no such proportionality, as noted earlier. Instead, the probability of winning on any given play is inversely related to the rate of play (response), and the number of wins is virtually independent of the number of plays, given a high enough rate of play.

The pigeons, then, had a pair of keys to peck, and the experiment rewarded their efforts with brief access to food at irregular intervals. The schedules set a maximum rate of reinforcement throughout the experiment at 40 per hour, but the number allocated to one key or the other was systematically varied, to see how the distribution of responses was affected. The question was whether, to use the vocabulary of this paper, response strength as relative frequency was some plausible function of reinforcement frequency. The answer was both plausible and attractively simple, as shown in Fig. 4. The ordinate is the proportion of responses on the left key; the abscissa is the proportion of reinforcements delivered thereon. The points fall near the diagonal, which is the locus of perfect matching between the distribution of responses and of reinforcements. A simple equation summarizes the finding (P is number of pecks, R is number

of reinforcements, and the subscripts denote the two alternatives).

$$\frac{P_L}{P_L + P_R} = \frac{R_L}{R_L + R_R} \qquad (1)$$

Unless the number of pecks far exceeds the number of reinforcements, the matching function (equation 1) is trivially true. For example, if the variable-interval schedules were assigning reinforcements to the two keys more quickly than the pigeons pecked, then every peck would be reinforced. The data point would necessarily fall on the diagonal, but the result would have little empirical content. If reinforcements were being assigned at the rate of one for every other response, or one for every third response, the possible range of variation for the points would still be narrowly constrained around the diagonal, and the findings would still be essentially vacuous. In fact, the possible range of variation is exactly fixed by the actual numbers of reinforcements and responses. Since there are at least as many responses on each key as there are reinforcements, the smallest relative frequency of response for a given relative frequency of reinforcement $R_L/(R_L + R_R)$ is

$$\frac{R_L}{P_L + P_R} \qquad (2)$$

This fraction approaches $R_L/(R_L + R_R)$ as the total number of responses approaches the total number of reinforcements. The largest relative frequency of response for a given relative frequency of reinforcement is also dependent upon the fact that there can be no fewer responses than reinforcements. Thus, the ratio of responses for a given $R_L/(R_L + R_R)$ can go no higher than 1.0 minus the minimum value for the other key—$R_R/P_L + P_R$)—which may be written as

$$\frac{P_L + P_R - R_R}{P_L + P_R} \qquad (3)$$

This fraction, too, will approach $R_L/(R_L + R_R)$ as the total number of responses approaches the total number of reinforcements, which is to say when the responses on the separate keys each equal the reinforcements thereon. The result, then, is that as the number of responses approaches the number of reinforcements, the possible range of variation for the ratio of responses converges on to the matching relation in Fig. 4. In the case of the experiment sum-

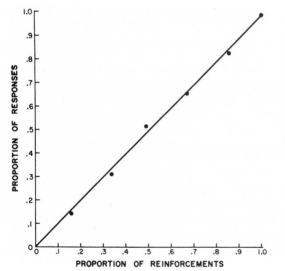

Fig. 4. The relative frequency of responding to one alternative in a two-choice procedure as a function of the relative frequency of reinforcement thereon. Variable-interval schedules governed reinforcements for both alternatives. The diagonal line shows matching between the relative frequencies. From Herrnstein (1961).

marized here, however, the ratio of responses to reinforcements was approximately 100. At 0.5 on the abscissa, therefore, the possible range of variation of responding was from 0.005 to 0.995. At other values of the abscissa, the possible range was comparably broad. The close agreement between the matching relation and the distribution of responding says something, therefore, about the animal, not just about the procedure itself. What this is, and how it operates in a variety of situations, will occupy the remainder of the paper.

RESPONSE STRENGTH AND CHOICE

The experiment summarized in Fig. 4 had an additional procedural wrinkle. Each time the pigeon shifted from one key to the other, there was a brief period of time during which any reinforcement called for by the variable-interval schedule was delayed. This "change-over delay" (COD) lasted for 1.5 sec, and was imposed in order to prevent the pigeons from switching after virtually every response. It was found, without the COD, that the distribution of responses tended to stay around 50-50, without regard to the distribution of reinforcements. If the matching relation were an accident of the duration of the COD, it would hardly be a principle of either response strength or choice. The most direct test of the COD is contained in an experiment in which it was varied systematically to see whether the matching relation was a peculiarity of only a certain range of durations.

The experiment, by Shull and Pliskoff (1967), varied a number of conditions besides the duration of the COD. Instead of pigeons, their experiment used albino rats. The reinforcer, instead of brief access to food for a hungry animal, was the opportunity for the rat to get electric current passed through its brain in the region of the posterior hypothalamus. A reinforcement consisted of the lighting of a small light in the presence of which the rat could press the lever 20 times, each time obtaining 125 milliseconds of a 100-Hz train of sine waves of 150 to 300 microamps across the electrodes implanted in its head. The variable-interval schedule resumed at the end of the last burst of current. The schedule itself was a variation of the simple concurrent procedure, one that had been originally described

by Findley (1958). Instead of a pair of response alternatives associated with a pair of variable-interval schedules, the Findley procedure had the two variable intervals associated with a pair of stimuli, but responses on only one of the two levers could produce reinforcement. At any one time, only one of the two stimuli was present, and while it was present, reinforcements from only its associated variable interval were forthcoming. The second lever in the chamber switched from one stimulus to the other, along with its associated variable-interval schedule. Actually, the two variable-interval programmers ran concurrently and continuously, just as they do in a conventional concurrent procedure. Shull and Pliskoff varied the COD, which is here the minimum possible interval between a response to the switching lever and the first reinforced response. Their finding was that matching occurred as long as the COD was greater than a certain minimal duration, as was found in the earlier study, but that beyond that value, matching was maintained whatever the duration of the COD in the range examined (0 to 20 sec). As the COD is made larger, however, it begins to affect measurably the obtained rates of reinforcement by interacting with the schedules themselves, as might be expected. Matching is always with respect to obtained, rather than pre-specified, reinforcement rates.

The experiment by Shull and Pliskoff extended the generality of the matching relation more than merely by showing that the COD is not the controlling variable. It extended the finding to rats, to Findley's procedure, and to intracranial stimulation as the reinforcer. Other studies have extended it further. Reynolds (1963a) showed matching with three response alternatives instead of two. Holz (1968) found matching even when each of the responses was punished with electric shock, in addition to being reinforced by the usual variable-interval schedules. Holz varied the intensity of the punishment until it was so severe that the pigeons stopped responding altogether. However, as long as they were responding, and as long as the punishment for the two responses was equally intense, the distribution of responses matched the distribution of reinforcements. Catania (1963a) and Neuringer (1967b) found matching with respect to total amount of food when the two reinforcers differed not in their rate of occurrence, but in the grams of food per reinforcement. In another study, Catania (1963*b*), using the Findley procedure, found matching both for the proportion of responses and for proportion of time spent with each of the two stimuli. Baum and Rachlin (1969) showed matching (correcting for a position bias) when the "responses" consisted of standing on one side of a chamber or the other. The proportion of time spent in each location was found to be distributed as the associated proportion of reinforcements. Along these lines, Brownstein and Pliskoff (1968) found that the Findley procedure can be further modified so that when the animal selects one stimulus condition or the other, reinforcement comes along independently of any response. The pigeons here are simply choosing between one rate of reinforcement or the other. Their finding, too, is described by the matching relation, suitably adapted. The proportion of time spent in each stimulus condition is equal to the proportion of reinforcement received therefrom. Nevin (1969) noted that matching is found in human psychophysical studies when the proportion of "yes" responses is plotted against either the proportion of trials containing a signal or the relative size of payoff (*i.e.*, the frequency or magnitude of reinforcement). Shimp (1966), and the present author in unpublished work, have found matching in discrete-trial procedures of various sorts.

The list of confirmatory studies could be extended, but without profit at this point. It has been consistently found that responding is distributed in proportion to the distribution of reinforcement, as long as the responding and the reinforcements across the alternatives are not unequal qualitatively. Thus, the matching relation would not be expected if the reinforcer for one response were a preferred food and that for the other were a nonpreferred food, unless the scale values for the reinforcers expressed the difference quantitatively. Nor would it be expected if the two responses differed in some important way, *e.g.*, that one involved considerably more work than the other. In fact, the matching relation may be used to construct equivalences between qualitatively different responses or reinforcers, although no such undertaking has come to the author's attention. It should, however, be possible to scale reinforcers against each other or responses against each other by

assuming that the subject must be conforming to the matching relation whenever it is in a choice situation of the general type employed in these experiments, and by adjusting the measures of response or reinforcement accordingly.

The main opposition to the matching relation is found in the literature on so-called "probability learning". If an experiment arranges a certain probability (excluding 1.0, 0.5, and 0) of reinforcement for each of a pair of response alternatives, and if the subject distributes its responses in proportion to these pre-assigned probabilities, then the matching relation, as defined here, is violated. Imagine that the two probabilities are 0.4 and 0.1. In a sequence of 100 responses, probability learning requires 80 responses to the better alternative and 20 responses to the poorer one. The number of reinforcements would be $80 \times 0.4 = 32$ for the one, and $20 \times 0.1 = 2$ for the other. With respect to the matching formula, this is a violation, for

$$\frac{80}{80 + 20} \neq \frac{32}{32 + 2} \tag{4}$$

The literature does not, however, claim strict conformity to probability learning. Instead, responding is often confined exclusively to one or the other of the two alternatives, typically toward the alternative with the higher probability of reinforcement. But even when the two reinforcement probabilities are equal, responding tends to become exclusive for one of the choices. These deviations from probability learning are said to be instances of "optimizing" or "maximizing", since exclusive preference is the optimal strategy in the sense that the subject will, on the average, maximize its winning if it stays with the better bet. Even when the two probabilities are equal, nothing is lost by exclusive preference, and perhaps something is gained, for the subject is thereby spared the effort of switching from one alternative to the other.

Maximization in the probability type experiment actually conforms to the present matching function. Equation (1) is satisfied when all or none of the responses and all or none of the reinforcements occur for one of the alternatives and is therefore consistent with all of the experiments that deviate from probability learning and find maximization instead. Not all the experiments, however, find exclusive preference, and it is not yet clear whether apparently minor procedural factors are inadvertently affecting outcomes, as some have suggested (Bush and Mosteller, 1955), or whether there is, in addition, a phyletic factor. Bitterman (1965) argued that the higher organisms tend to maximize, while the lower ones, like fish and pigeons, tend to "probability learn". However, the experiments by Bitterman and his associates often use procedural features, such as forced trials to the alternatives, that complicate the calculation of the obtained frequencies of reinforcement, if not the psychological processes at work. In any event, pigeons do not invariably show probability learning; Herrnstein (1958) showed maximizing in pigeons given a choice between differing probabilities of reinforcement.

It is, in other words, not clear how much of the literature of probability learning actually violates equation 1, since it is not clear how much of this literature can be taken as firm evidence for probability learning. Nevertheless, suppose for the sake of argument that there is some valid evidence for probability learning, which is to say, that the responses are in the same ratio as the *probabilities* of reinforcement. How does this differ from the findings with rate of reinforcement, according to which the responses are in the same ratio as the *numbers* of reinforcement? The two findings turn out to be closely related mathematically, as the following set of equations shows, starting with the equation for probability learning:

$$\frac{P_L}{P_R} = \frac{\dfrac{R_L}{P_L}}{\dfrac{R_R}{P_R}} \tag{5a}$$

$$P_L{}^2 R_R = P_R{}^2 R_L \tag{5b}$$

$$P_L \sqrt{R_R} = P_R \sqrt{R_L} \tag{5c}$$

$$P_L \sqrt{R_R} + P_L \sqrt{R_L} = P_R \sqrt{R_L} + P_L \sqrt{R_L} \tag{5d}$$

$$\frac{P_L}{P_L + P_R} = \frac{\sqrt{R_L}}{\sqrt{R_L} + \sqrt{R_R}} \tag{6}$$

Natapoff (in press) has shown that the matching of response frequencies to reinforcement frequencies (equation 1) is just one, and in some sense the simplest, of a family of functions that may relate these two variables under the assumptions of symmetry of choice, which is to assume that the factors that affect choice operate invariantly across the alternatives.

Another, and closely related, function, according to Natapoff, would be equation 6 above, according to which the match is between response frequencies and the square root of reinforcement frequencies. This latter finding is, as the mathematical argument demonstrates, merely another version of probability learning. Although we do not know with certainty if, and when, probability learning actually occurs in simple choice procedures, it may eventually be useful to be able to relate the two kinds of matching to each other mathematically.

The only other significant departure from matching known to the present author is an experiment with pigeons (Herrnstein, 1958) in which reinforcement was dependent upon a required number of responses on the two keys. The sum of the two requirements was kept constant at 40, but the two components varied: 2, 38; 5, 35; 10, 30; and 20, 20. No further restrictions were imposed on the order or manner in which the requirements were reached. The pigeon could work in any sequence of alternation between the two keys, and could emit any number in excess of the requirement on one of the keys, but, having met one requirement, it was rewarded as soon as it met the other. Figure 5 shows the proportion of responses on the left key as a function of the proportion of the total requirement on that key. It also shows the proportion of reinforcements on that key. The procedure clearly produced a kind of matching, but not to the distribution of reinforcements, since the proportion of reinforcements was so much more variable than the proportion of responses. Instead, the pigeons responded so as to minimize the number of responses (and also probably the time) per reinforcement.

There are undoubtedly many other procedures that would give comparable departures from matching. For example, if reinforcement were made conditional upon a pair of *rates* of responding on the two keys (instead of upon a pair of numbers of responses thereon), there probably would be some accommodation in responding and matching in the present sense would probably be violated. Such procedures need not be particularly complicated, the two examples so far notwithstanding. For example, consider a procedure that simply reinforced alternation of left and right responses, with reinforcement occurring only for right re-

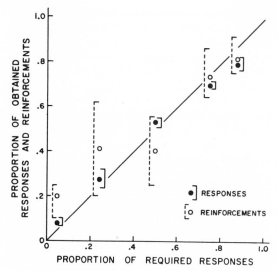

Fig. 5. The filled circles and solid brackets show the average and range of the relative frequency of responding to one alternative in a two-choice procedure. Reinforcement was for the occurrence of at least a minimum number of responses to each of the two alternatives. The abscissa shows what fraction of the total response requirement was allocated to the alternatives being plotted. The open circles and broken brackets are for the relative frequency of reinforcement against the same abscissa. The diagonal line shows matching between the abscissa and the ordinate. From Herrnstein (1958).

sponses. The distribution of responses would here approach 50-50, but the distribution of reinforcements would be 0-100. This last example is instructive, for it suggests why matching neither occurs nor should be expected in such cases. Reinforcement for alternation is likely to give not two separate responses, but rather a single, albeit biphasic, response—respond-left–respond-right—that is reinforced every time it occurs. In the more complex case summarized in Fig. 5, there is a similar issue of response definition, as there is in any procedure in which reinforcement is conditional upon combinations of responses across the alternatives.

A procedure that reinforces multiphasic responses across the alternatives is thus not properly described by tallies of the individual response frequencies. Instead of so many left responses and so many right responses, there should be so many left-rights or the like. The point is worth noting for it is probably why matching depends on the COD in some (but not all) procedures. If the response alternatives are situated near each other, the subject's

left-right or right-left sequences may be adventitiously reinforced. If so, the usual tally of left and right responses cuts across the response classes actually being maintained by the reinforcement and matching in the ordinary sense is no longer an appropriate expectation. By interposing a delay between a response to one alternative and reinforcement for the other, the COD discourages these adventitious response clusters.

In virtually all of the published experiments showing matching, the alternative responses were reinforced by schedules that differed only in the reinforcement parameter, whether frequency or amount. This may not, however, be necessary. For example, it remains to be shown whether matching would be found if the concurrent procedure used a variable-interval schedule pitted against a variable ratio. The procedure is peculiar not only because of its asymmetry, but also because it is intermediate as regards the degree to which the subject's behavior governs the distribution of reinforcement, and is therefore of some general interest. With two variable-interval schedules, the distribution of reinforcements is not likely to be affected by the distribution of responses, given the usual rates of responding. On the other hand, with two variable-ratio schedules, the distribution is virtually entirely under the subject's control. In the combination procedure, the animal is in control of reinforcement frequency for one alternative, but not for the other, again assuming that response rate is high enough. Finally, the experiment is peculiar because matching, while well established for interval schedules and their analogues, cannot occur for ratio schedules except trivially. For example, suppose ratios of 50 and 200 are scheduled for two alternatives. Equation 1, the matching function, can be satisfied only if the animal ceases responding to one of the alternatives, thereby obtaining all of its reinforcements thereon. The ratio schedules assure that the distribution of responses will follow the relation:

$$\frac{P_L}{P_L + P_R} = \frac{50R_L}{50R_L + 200R_R} \qquad (7)$$

The coefficients on the reinforcement frequencies express the fact that a ratio schedule fixes a proportionality between numbers of responses and numbers of reinforcements. In the present example, equation 7 agrees with equation 1 only when either R_L or R_R goes to zero. In general, agreement can be obtained only at these limiting values, plus the 50% value when the two ratios are equal to each other. In contrast, the present experiment, combining interval and ratio schedules, permits matching at all values, as follows:

$$\frac{P_L}{P_L + P_R} = \frac{rR_L}{rR_L + xR_R} \qquad (8)$$

Here, r is the required proportionality for the alternative with the ratio schedule. For the other alternative, reinforced on a variable-interval schedule, there is no required proportionality. By responding faster or slower, the subject can here emit more or fewer responses per reinforcement (x). In order to obtain agreement between equation 8 and equation 1, the subject must adjust its rate of responding on the variable-interval schedule such that r = x.

An experiment combining the two schedules was performed with four pigeons. As in the earlier study, there was a change-over delay (2 sec) between the two alternatives. Responding to one alternative was reinforced on variable-interval schedules that were changed from time to time (in the range of 15 sec to 2 min). Responding to the other was reinforced on variable-ratio schedules, also varied from time to time (in the range of 20 to 160). Since the distribution of reinforcements is here affected by the distribution of responses at all rates of responding, the values of the two schedules do not fix a particular distribution of reinforcement. The relative frequency of reinforcement, the nominal independent variable, was largely up to each subject. For most of the pairs of values, the findings trivially confirmed matching, by giving responding exclusively to one alternate or the other. This has also been the outcome when both alternatives were variable-ratio schedules (Herrnstein, 1958). However, for some pairs of values, the responding was distributed between the two responses with something between exclusive preference and total abstinence. Figure 6 shows the proportion of responses to one of the two alternatives (the variable-interval key) as a function of the proportion of reinforcements actually obtained from that key. The data for four pigeons have been averaged here, but the individual points were not systematically different. The finding is that even when the two alternatives reinforce according to different schedules, the distribution of responding still obeys the matching rule, or something close to it. The bunching of the points on the lower part of the function appears to be a reliable outcome of the procedure. It says that preferences for the variable-interval alternative (*i.e.*, above 0.5 on the ordinate) are exclusive, while for the variable-ratio alternative (*i.e.*, below 0.5 on the ordinate) they may be exclusive or non-exclusive.

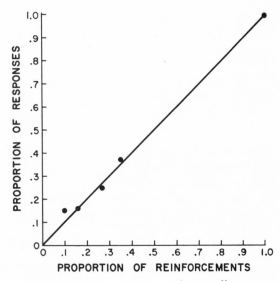

Fig. 6. The relative frequency of responding to one alternative in a two-choice procedure as a function of the relative frequency of reinforcement thereon. For one alternative, reinforcement was on a variable-interval schedule, while, for the other, it was on a variable-ratio schedule. The ordinate plots the variable-interval alternative. The diagonal shows matching between ordinate and abscissa.

The matching in Fig. 6 is surprising not only because of the peculiar procedure, but also in light of the well-known effects of the two kinds of schedules on responding in isolation. Variable-ratio responding is typically a good deal faster than variable-interval responding, at equal frequencies of reinforcement (Herrnstein, 1964). In the present experiment, the momentary rates of responding were about twice as high for the ratio schedules as for the interval schedules. Nevertheless, each of the subjects maintained approximately the required invariance of responses per reinforcement across the ratio and interval schedules (see equation 8) even while the parameter values of both schedules were being changed.

CHOICE AS BEHAVIOR AND VICE VERSA

Intuitively, response strength should covary in some reasonably orderly way with the parameters of reinforcement. The foregoing section presents the case for replacing intuition with the relative frequency of response. The argument is simply that since relative responding is so directly controlled by relative reinforcement, the former is the proper measure of the effects of the latter. The investigation of strength need not, however, stop here. Several theorists (Shimp, 1966; Neuringer, 1967a) have argued that matching is not fundamental, but is to be explained as the outcome of a more molecular interaction between behavior and its consequences, somehow based on "maximizing" in the probability-learning sense. The developments along this line will not be further examined here, for a persuasive case one way or the other is yet to be made. Suffice it to note that there is no logical assurance that this sort of reductionism will ever explain anything. The issue is empirical, and it is possible that behavior is more (or more simply) orderly at the level of the matching relation than at the level of interresponse times or sequences of choices, which is where the molecular theories operate. In contrast, logic demands that if the *relative* frequency of response is governed by the frequency of reinforcement, it must also govern somehow the *absolute* rate of responding. Since relative frequencies in the free-operant procedure are merely ratios of rates of responding, the one could hardly be affected without the other being affected as well.

The link between sheer output of behavior and what is usually called "choice" is peculiarly apparent with the free-operant method. In conventional choice experiments using discrete trials, the total number of responses is a trivial by-product of the procedure, depending simply on the number of trials per unit time. When the experimenter stipulates what the sheer output of behavior is going to be, he is unlikely to find it interesting. In the operant paradigm, however, where the output is as free to vary as anything else, if not more so, it becomes an interesting, and inescapable, dependent variable. Yet the matching relation holds for both continuous-responding and discrete-trial procedures. In the former, the

question of sheer output cannot honestly be disregarded; in the latter, the question is precluded by the procedure. Since it seems unlikely that the two situations can be fundamentally different when they both produce matching, "choice" in the discrete-trial procedure should be explained the same way as the output of behavior for the free-operant procedure. It is hard to see choice as anything more than a way of interrelating one's observations of behavior, and not a psychological process or a special kind of behavior in its own right. For continuous-responding procedures, the correspondence between choice and behavior is clear, for the measure of choice is just the ratio of the simple outputs for the alternative responses.

What, then, can be said about these simple rates of responding? In the first concurrent procedure considered above (see Fig. 4), the two responses were freely occurring operants, reinforced on variable-interval schedules, and the matching relation was the ratio of their rates of occurrence. Figure 7 shows the absolute rates of responding of which the matching relation was the ratio. For absolute rates of responding there are twice as many degrees of freedom as for relative rates, since the two keys give values separately in the former in-

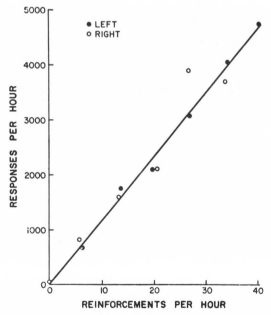

Fig. 7. The rate of responding for each of two alternatives in a two-choice procedure as a function of the rate of reinforcement for each. Variable-interval schedules were used for both. From Herrnstein (1961).

stance, but complementarily in the latter. Even though the functions in Fig. 7 are, therefore, not as firmly demonstrated as in Fig. 4, the trend of the data is clear. (One point from the original experiment for one subject has been omitted since there are reasons to believe that it was aberrant.) The absolute rate of responding on each key is directly proportional to the absolute rate of reinforcement. This elegantly simple relation may be expressed in the equation:

$$P = kR \qquad (9)$$

Note that this relation is consistent with the basic matching relation, as it would have to be unless something were amiss. If each response alternative were obeying this rule, then any combination of responses with the same proportionality to reinforcement (*i.e.*, the same k) should show matching, as simple algebra proves:

$$\frac{P_L}{P_L + P_R} = \frac{kR_L}{kR_L + kR_R} = \frac{R_L}{R_L + R_R} \qquad (10)$$

Equation 9 makes a plausible and impressively simple fundamental law of response strength. Its main trouble is that it has been tried before and failed, for, in another form, it merely restates Skinner's first published guess about response strength (1938, p. 130f), when he asserted the constancy of what he called the extinction ratio. From his early work, he surmised that the number of responses per reinforcement with interval schedules might be a constant, which is equation 9 solved for k. Thus, if the animal's response is reinforced once every 5 min it should respond twice as fast as when the response is reinforced every 10 min, and so on. Skinner's own data failed to support this simple principle, and later (1940) he revised the general principle of the "reflex reserve", so that the constancy of the extinction ratio was no longer of any theoretical importance in his system. The mass of data collected since shows no such relation as equation 9 in single-response procedures, as Catania and Reynolds (1968) demonstrated most exhaustively.

In the experiment summarized in Fig. 7, the over-all frequency of reinforcement was held constant at 40 per hour while the proportion allocated to one alternative or the other was varied. As long as the total number of reinforcements ($R_L + R_R$) is constant, there is

no way to distinguish in a single experiment between the prediction of equation 9 and the following:

$$P_L = \frac{kR_L}{R_L + R_R} \qquad (11)$$

When the sum $R_L + R_R$ is itself a constant, equation 11 is equivalent to equation 9, the only difference being the value of k, which is an arbitrary constant in either case. As regards Fig. 7, then, equation 11 is as good as equation 9. The two equations make divergent predictions only when $R_L + R_R$ is not a constant, which is actually more typical in concurrent procedures. The difference is that equation 11 predicts a "contrast" effect, which is to say a reciprocal relation between the reinforcements for one alternative and the responses to the other, whereas equation 9 predicts independence of responding to one alternative and reinforcements for the other. The data unequivocally support equation 11, for contrast effects are reliably found in concurrent procedures (Catania, 1966).

Although equation 11 conforms at least qualitatively to the literature on concurrent procedures, it, like equation 9, seems to run into trouble with single-response situations, for when there is only one response alternative being reinforced the equation degenerates into the following constancy:

$$P = k \qquad (12)$$

Responding in single-response situations is notoriously insensitive to variations in the parameters of reinforcement, but it is not totally insensitive. Equation 12, however, is the result of a gratuitous assumption, albeit one that is easily overlooked. It assumes that because the experimenter has provided just one response alternative, there is, in fact, just one. A more defensible assumption is that at every moment of possible action, a set of alternatives confronts the animal, so that each action may be said to be the outcome of a choice. Even in a simple environment like a single-response operant-conditioning chamber, the occurrence of the response is interwoven with other, albeit unknown, responses, the relative frequencies of which must conform to the same general laws that are at work whenever there are multiple alternatives. In fact, it seems safe to assume that all environments continually demand choices in this sense, even though in many cases the problem of identifying and measuring the alternatives may be insoluble. That problem is, however, the experimenter's, not the subject's. No matter how impoverished the environment, the subject will always have distractions available, other things to engage its activity and attention, even if these are no more than its own body, with its itches, irritations, and other calls for service.

The notion that started this section, that choice is not a psychological mechanism so much as a certain measure extracted from observations of behavior, has a complement. For while choice is nothing but behavior set into the context of other behavior, there is no way to avoid some such a context for any response. An absolute rate of responding is occurring in such a context, whether or not the experimenter happens to know what the other alternatives and their reinforcers are. With this in mind, equation 11 may be rewritten for a nominal single-response situation, but recognizing the possibility of other sources of reinforcement, as follows,

$$P = \frac{kR}{R + R_o} \qquad (13)$$

in which R_o is the unknown, aggregate reinforcement for other alternatives.[2] In practical terms, R_o is a second free parameter to be extracted from the data, but it is one that has a definite empirical interpretation. The question is whether equation 13 fits the data.

Figure 8 is a test of equation 13 with data obtained by Catania and Reynolds (1968). The six pigeons in the experiment were submitted to variable-interval schedules with rates of reinforcement ranging from about 10 to about 300 per hour. The effects on performance were varied, as the points in Fig. 8 show. However, with few exceptions, the points fall on or near the smooth curves, which are plots of equation 13. The parameter values for the individual subjects are shown in each panel, k first and R_o second, with k in responses per

[2]This same equation for absolute rate of responding in single-response situations can be found in Norman (1966), except that Norman offers the equation as an approximation, rather than as an exact relationship between the variables. Norman's analysis does not appear to be applicable to multiple-response situations and his interpretation of the parameters is entirely different from the present one. The two accounts are, therefore, readily distinguishable, notwithstanding the convergence at this point.

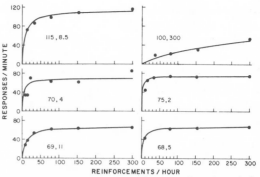

Fig. 8. The rate of responding as a function of the rate of reinforcement for each of six subjects on variable-interval schedules. The first number in each panel is k in responses per minute and the second is R_o in reinforcements per hour for the various smooth curves. From Catania and Reynolds (1968).

minute and R_o in reinforcements per hour. The fit of points to function for each animal shows that the mathematcial form of equation 13 is suitable for the single-response situation, notwithstanding its origin within the context of choice experiments. The variety of parameter values further shows that inter-subject variability is also amenable to description in these formal terms. There appears to be no other comparably simple mathematical expression for the relation between absolute input and output for simple, repetitive responding, let alone one that also predicts the distribution of choices over multiple alternatives.

Figure 9 is another test for equation 13, showing the results of an unusual procedure for varying reinforcement frequency. The parameter values are again for k in responses per minute and R_o in reinforcements per hour, in that order. Chung (1966) reinforced his pigeons' responses after a given duration had elapsed since the first response after the last reinforcement—in the terminology of reinforcement schedules, a tandem fixed ratio 1, fixed interval of various durations. From time to time, the duration was changed, giving a new determination of rate of responding. The actual rate of reinforcement was substantially controlled by the subjects, for the sooner after reinforcement the animals responded, the sooner the required time interval would begin. Chung's experiment is worth noting here not only because the procedure is unusual, but because it achieved reinforcement rates of about 2000 per hour, seven times Catania and Reynolds' (1968) maximum. Nevertheless,

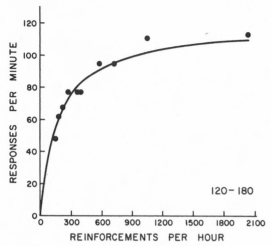

Fig. 9. The rate of responding as a function of the rate of reinforcement for subjects on a tandem fixed-ratio, fixed-interval schedule. The first number is k in responses per minute and the second is R_o in reinforcements per hour for the smooth curve. From Chung (1966).

Chung's results are well described by equation 13, although the parameter value for R_o (180) is substantially higher here than for five of Catania's and Reynolds' six subjects.

Equation 13 is readily expanded into a general principle of response output, whether the response is presumably in isolation or not. The matching relation can be derived by taking into account the reinforcement from both alternatives:

$$\frac{P_L}{P_L + P_R} = \frac{\dfrac{kR_L}{R_L + R_R + R_o}}{\dfrac{kR_L}{R_L + R_R + R_o} + \dfrac{kR_R}{R_L + R_R + R_o}}$$

$$= \frac{R_L}{R_L + R_R} \qquad (14)$$

This assumes that k and R_o are the same for the responses under observation, a reasonable supposition as long as the responses are equivalent in form and effort. If choice were, however, asymmetric—for example, if one response was to depress a lever while the other was to pull a chain—the equivalence of neither k nor perhaps R_o could be assumed. Matching would not be predicted, but the present formulation would apply in principle nevertheless.

In recent experiments on choice, the symmetry assumption has been supportable, which is to say, the matching relation has been found. The next question is whether the absolute rates of responding also conform to the

present formalization. Equation 14 contains the expressions for the absolute rates of responding, restated here for convenience (for the left key):

$$P_L = \frac{kR_L}{R_L + R_R + R_o} \qquad (15)$$

For the first study of matching (Herrnstein, 1961), the agreement between fact and theory is clear, since that is where the discussion began (see Fig. 7). When the total reinforcement is held constant, as was the case in that experiment, the absolute rate of responding should be directly proportional to the absolute rate of reinforcement. When the over-all rates of reinforcement are not constant, there should be "contrast" effects, with the rate of responding on each alternative varying directly with the associated rate of reinforcement, but inversely with the rates of reinforcement elsewhere.

Catania's work (1963b) provides a quantitative evaluation of equation 15. Catania used pigeons on the Findley procedure. The two alternatives were the usual variable-interval schedules, each one signalled by a particular color on the response key. The variable intervals ran concurrently, but, in accordance with the Findley procedure, there was only one color (and, therefore, but one variable interval) making direct contact with the subject at any one time. A peck on the second key changed the color and brought the second variable interval into contact with the subject. The difference between this sort of concurrent schedule and the more familiar type is in the "switching" response: for the Findley procedure it is the pecking of a key, for the other, it is actually moving back and forth between the keys. Figure 10 shows that the difference does not affect the matching relation. Both the proportion of responses and the proportion of time equal the proportion of reinforcement for each alternative.

Equation 15, however, calls for absolute rates of responding, not proportions, and these are plotted in Fig. 11. There were two series of reinforcement rates in the experiment. In one, the sum of the reinforcement rates for the two alternatives was always 40 per hour, just as in Fig. 7 (Herrnstein, 1961). In the other, the sum varied, but was held at 20 per hour for one of the two schedules. Equation 15 predicts a direct proportionality

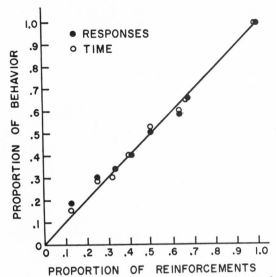

Fig. 10. The relative number of responses emitted (filled circles) and the relative amount of time spent (open circles) on one alternative in a two-choice procedure as a function of the relative frequency of reinforcement thereon. The diagonal shows matching between ordinate and abscissa. From Catania (1963b).

for the first condition and a curvilinear relation for the second. The left portion of Fig. 11 shows responding as a function of reinforce-

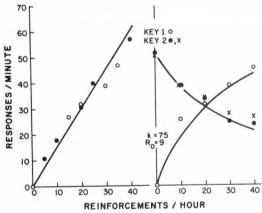

Fig. 11. The rate of responding as a function of the rate of reinforcement for each alternative in a two-choice procedure. For the left panel, the overall frequency of reinforcement was held constant at 40 reinforcements per hour, while varying complementarily for the two alternatives. Each point is here plotted above the reinforcement rate at which it was obtained. For the right panel, the frequency of reinforcement for Key 2 was held constant at 20 reinforcements per hour, while varying between 0 and 40 for Key 1. The points here are plotted above the reinforcement rate on Key 1 at the time it was obtained. The values of k and R_0 were used for the smooth curves in both panels. From Catania (1963b).

ment when the total reinforcement rate was held constant at 40 per hour. For each alternative, the points approximate a straight line passing through the origin, as theory predicts. The selected line has the parameters k = 75 (responses per minute) and $R_0 = 9$ (reinforcements per hour). Note that these values are easily within the range obtained in Fig. 8 for a single-response situation involving variable-interval schedules. The right-hand panel shows responding as a function of reinforcement rate on Key 1[3] for the second series, when the reinforcement for one key (Key 2) was held constant at 20 per hour while Key 1 reinforcements ranged from 0 to 40 per hour. The contrast effect is the decreasing rate on Key 2 as reinforcement for Key 1 increases. The smooth curves again plot equation 15, with the parameters again at k = 75 and $R_0 = 9$. The crosses on the right panel show the results of a second procedure with the same three pigeons. Responding to Key 2 was still reinforced 20 times per hour, while that to Key 1 was again varied from 0 to 40 per hour. The change was that the pigeons switched to Key 1 only when a light signalled that reinforcement was due there, so that the number of responses to Key 1 was virtually equal to the number of reinforcements. Otherwise, the procedure was unchanged. As the decreasing rate of Key 2 responding shows, and as equation 15 implies, contrast depends upon the reinforcement for the other alternative, not on the responding there. The crosses may actually deviate slightly from the filled circles, for reasons that will be considered in the next section, but aside from this, Catania's data provide substantial confirmation for Equation 15 and the system from which it emerges.

Catania accounted for his results with a power function between absolute responding and the relative number of reinforcements, as follows:

$$P_1 = \frac{kR_1}{(R_1 + R_2)^{5/6}} \qquad (16)$$

Like equation 15, this one, too, predicts matching when k and the denominators can be cancelled out, which is to say, when choice

---

[3]With the Findley procedure, the designations, "Key 1" and "Key 2", do not identify two separate response keys. Rather, they represent the two possible states of the key to which responses were reinforced.

is between otherwise equivalent alternatives. Given the variability in the data, it would be hard to choose between equation 16 and the present formulation as contained in equation 15. The most easily testable difference between Catania's hypothesis and the present one is in regard to responding in single-response situations, for which equation 16 implies a power function with an exponent of $1/6$, while equation 15 implies equation 13. The data, the best of which we owe to Catania and Reynolds (1968), distinctly favor the latter alternative, since no power function handles the data from individual pigeons in single-response procedures while equation 13 makes a plausible fit, as shown in Fig. 8 and 9.

Equation 13 is for single-response procedures; equation 15, for two-response procedures. The general case, for a situation containing n alternative sources of reinforcement, is:

$$P_1 = \frac{kR_1}{\sum\limits_{1=0}^{n} R_1} \qquad (17)$$

This mathematical form is not used throughout because it hides R_o, the parameter in the denominator. It does, however, reveal the most general implications of the theory. Matching will take place over any set of alternative responses for which k and ΣR are fixed, the typical choice procedures, for example. Inversely, when matching is not obtained, the alternatives either have different asymptotic rates (k) or are operating within different contexts of reinforcement (ΣR), or both. It is not hard to conceive of situations that exhibit either or both of these asymmetries, even though they are somewhat unfamiliar in experiments on choice. The next section summarizes research in a field that shows the latter asymmetry, the absence of a fixed context of reinforcement.

The idea of a "context" of reinforcement is fundamental to the present analysis, for that is what the denominator is best called. Equation 17 says that the absolute rate of responding is a function of its reinforcement, but only in the context of the total reinforcements occurring in the given situation. When the total is not much more than the reinforcement for the response being studied, then responding will be relatively insensitive, for the ratio $R_1/\Sigma R_i$ will tend toward 1.0. This explains, at least partly, why for over three decades, interesting functional relations between reinforcement and responding have been so scarce. Experimeters have naturally tried to make the behavior they were observing important to the subject, and they have probably succeeded. If the response was to be reinforced with food or water, then the state of deprivation, the size of the reinforcer, and the experimental isolation of the subject have probably guaranteed that ΣR will be only negligibly larger than R_1. To do otherwise, which is to make ΣR substantially larger than R_1, is to risk unexplained variability, for then P_1 will be at the mercy of fluctuations in the other (usually unknown) reinforcers in the situation. Investigators have made a tacit decision in favor of stability, but at the cost of sensitivity to the independent variable.

Equation 17 explains the unique advantage of concurrent procedures. Because ΣR and k are eliminated when comparable responses are being measured as relative frequencies, the stability-sensitivity dilemma is avoided. The peculiar discrepancy between single and multiple response situations has been noted, with the one stubbornly insensitive and the other gratifyingly orderly and interesting (Catania, 1963a; Chung and Herrnstein, 1967). For magnitude, frequency, and delay of reinforcement, it has been shown that matching in multiple-response procedures and virtual insensitivity in single-response procedures are the rule. The discrepancy is a corollary of equation 17, which implies that responses at comparable levels of strength, as in symmetric choice experiments, will not only be sensitive to shifts in reinforcement between them, but equally affected by uncontrolled changes in extraneous reinforcers and therefore relatively orderly with respect to each other.

INTERACTION AT A DISTANCE

Equation 17 says that the frequency of responding is proportional to its relative reinforcement. The interval over which these responses and reinforcements are counted has so far been taken for granted. In simple choice, the interval is the experimental session itself, which is usually homogeneous with respect to rates of reinforcement and responding. The literature of operant conditioning contains, however, many experiments in which neither behavior nor its consequences are evenly distributed over sessions, and many of these experiments show interactions between successive (as well as simultaneous) conditions of reinforcement. An early and clear instance was Reynolds' (1961a) experiment, in which the rate of responding by pigeons on a variable-interval schedule increased when the schedule alternated with a period of non-reinforcement. The procedure started with 3-min alternation between red and green light on the response key, but responding was reinforced on the variable-interval schedule throughout. As expected, the rate of responding was approximately steady. When reinforcement was discontinued during, let us say, the red periods, responding during the green periods rose by about 50%, even though the rate of reinforcement was unchanged therein. In another part of the experiment, a variable-ratio schedule was used instead of a variable-interval schedule, with comparable results.

This "contrast" effect, as Reynolds termed it, has been widely confirmed, under many circumstances. For present purposes, the question is whether or not such changes in rate of responding belong with the present account of response strength. To anticipate the answer, the conclusion will be affirmative: the contrast effect is largely, if not entirely, derivable from an adaptation of equation 17.

If Reynolds had used a concurrent procedure, instead of a multiple schedule, a contrast effect would have been in order. With a variable interval of 3 min (VI 3-min) for responding on each key, the rate of responding is governed by the equation (measuring in reinforcements per hour),

$$P = \frac{k20}{40 + R_o} \qquad (18)$$

With extinction on the other key, the rate on this key should rise, since it would now be governed by,

$$P = \frac{k20}{20 + R_o} \qquad (19)$$

If R_o, the unscheduled, extraneous reinforcement, is assumed to be vanishingly small, the contrast effect is a doubling, i.e., 100%. The larger is R_o, the smaller is the contrast effect. In Reynolds' experiment, the contrast effect was only about 50%, which implies $R_o = 20$ reinforcements per hour, assuming, for the moment, that equations 18 and 19 are appropriate. Although R_o may have been this large in his experiments, the more typical range for pigeons in the standard chamber is 1 to 10, with only infrequent instances falling outside. This, and other considerations, suggest that the multiple schedule, in which the alternatives succeed each other, differs in some way from simultaneous choice as regards the analysis of response strength.

For simultaneous choice, each source of reinforcement is assumed to exert a full effect on every response alternative. However plausible this assumption is for concurrent procedures, it is less so for multiple schedules, in which the various sources of reinforcement are not simultaneously operative. As the components of a multiple schedule become more separate, the interaction across components is likely to diminish; in the limiting case, diminish to no interaction at all. Thus, if the components alternate slowly and are denoted by distinctive stimuli, the interaction might be smaller than if the alternation is rapid and the stimuli marginal.

There are many ways to translate this continuum of interactions into a formal expression, but one of the simplest is to assume that the reinforcement in one component affects the responding in the other by some constant fraction of its full effect. For the two-component multiple schedule, then, the rate of responding in one component would be given by:[4]

$$P_1 = \frac{kR_1}{R_1 + mR_2 + R_o} \qquad (20)$$

This is identical to the equation for one of the alternatives in a two-choice procedure

---

[4]Note that the time base for calculating the rate of responding in multiple schedules is the duration of the component during which the responding may occur. For concurrent schedules, the time base is the entire experimental session (excluding feeding cycles, timeouts, etc.). In general, the time base for calculating a rate of responding should be the time during which responding may occur, which differs as indicated in multiple and concurrent procedures. Also, note that the quantity R_o in equation 20 represents a composite of the extraneous reinforcement during one component (component #1 in the example in the text) plus the extraneous reinforcement in the other component, with the latter suitably decremented by the multiplicative factor m. In a fuller account, R_o should be written out as $R_{o1} + {}_mR_{o2}$. Such detail is clearly premature at this point.

(equation 15), except for the additional parameter, m, which should vary between 0 and 1.0, depending upon the degree of interaction across components. Equation 15 may, in fact, be considered a special case of equation 20, where $m = 1$.

The remainder of this section is a consideration of multiple schedules along the lines implied by equation 20. It should be noted at the outset that this equation is just one way to extend the present formulation to situations in which interactions are sub-maximal. As the following discussion shows, the data are not quite adequate either to confirm equation 20 or to demand an alternative. For present purposes, however, it suffices to demonstrate that many of the effects of multiple and concurrent procedures follow from a single conception of response strength.

Equation 20 assumes not only a simple mechanism to govern the degree of interaction, but it tacitly describes the most symmetrical sort of multiple schedule, as shown by the absence of subscripts on the parameters, k, m, and R_o. This is tantamount to assuming that the response alternatives have equal asymptotic rates (k), that the interaction one way is the same as the interaction the other (m), and that the unscheduled reinforcement is the same during the two components (R_o). This is for a multiple schedule, in other words, with the same response-form in both components (k), with the same rule for the alternation from one component to the other as for the alternation back (m), and with the extra-experimental factors held constant (R_o). It is possible to violate any of these conditions, but that should only complicate the analysis, not change it. Reynolds' experiment appears to satisfy these restrictions, and his results would follow from equation 20 if m was between 0.55 and 0.75, assuming R_o between 1 and 10 reinforcements per hour.

Equation 20 says that the contrast effect depends upon the reinforcement in the other component. Reynolds addressed himself to this issue at an early stage (1961b). He showed contrast when a "timeout" period was substituted for extinction. During a timeout, pigeons do not peck the key, and, in Reynolds' experiment, they received no reinforcement. Timeout and extinction should have the same effects on responding in the other component if they both reduce reinforcement in the inter-

acting component to zero, and if equation 20 is correct. Reynolds then went on to show that as long as reinforcement in the interacting component is sustained, with or without responding, contrast is prevented. In one procedure, reinforcement was for 50 sec of non-responding, a technique that suppresses responding, but does not eliminate reinforcement. Contrast was not observed. As Reynolds concluded, and as equation 20 implies, "The frequency of reinforcement in the presence of a given stimulus, *relative to the frequency during all of the stimuli that successively control an organism's behavior*, in part determines the rate of responding that the given stimulus controls." (p. 70, his italics)

The importance of reinforcement rate is clearly shown in Bloomfield's study of two multiple schedules (1967a). One multiple schedule consisted of 2-min alternations of VI 1-min with a DRL, the latter a procedure in which the response is reinforced only after specified periods (varied from 5 to 15 sec) of non-responding. In the other schedule, VI 1-min alternated with a fixed-ratio schedule (varied from 10 to 500). The two halves of the experiment shared a standard variable-interval schedule alternating with a schedule that yielded various different rates of reinforcement. Moreover, for both fixed-ratio and DRL schedules, the rate of reinforcement is a continuous joint function of the emitted rate of responding and the experimental parameter. However, the difference is that the functions are opposite, for on a fixed-ratio schedule, the rate of reinforcement is proportional to the rate of responding, while on the DRL, the rate of reinforcement is inversely related to the rate of responding given the levels of responding obtained by Bloomfield. Nevertheless, both of Bloomfield's multiple schedules support the implication of equation 20, that reinforcement rate determines contrast. The rate of responding during the variable-interval component was an inverse function of the rate of reinforcement in the other component, without regard to whether the other schedule was a fixed ratio or a DRL. Neither the direction nor the magnitude of the contrast effect was apparently affected by the rate of responding or the schedule *per se* in the interacting component.

The question now is whether the dependence of contrast on reinforcement is in quantitative, as well as qualitative, agreement with equation 20. Reynolds (1961c), using multiple VI FR schedules, concluded not only that the relative rate of responding was a function of the relative rate of reinforcement, but that the function was linear, with a positive intercept and slope less than 1.0. This was to be distinguished from concurrent procedures, where the matching relation holds (slope $= 1.0$; intercept $= 0$).

Reynolds' linear relation is at variance with equation 20. The predicted relation between the relative frequency of responding and the relative frequency of reinforcement is considerably more complex than linear, as follows:[5]

$$\frac{P_1}{P_1 + P_2} = \frac{\dfrac{kR_1}{R_1 + mR_2 + R_o}}{\dfrac{kR_1}{R_2 + mR_2 + R_o} + \dfrac{kR_2}{R_2 + mR_1 + R_o}}$$

$$= \frac{1}{1 + \dfrac{R_2(R_1 + mR_2 + R_o)}{R_1(R_2 + mR_1 + R_o)}} \quad (21)$$

As a function of the relative frequency of reinforcement, $R_1/(R_1 + R_2)$, this expression plots as a family of reverse-S-shaped functions, the curvature of which is dependent upon the relative magnitudes of $R_{1,2}$, R_o, and m. Complex as this is, it would be even worse without the assumptions of symmetry that qualify equation 20. The more general formulation will not, however, be explicated here, since there appear to be virtually no data to test it. Figure 12 shows a representative sampling from the family expressed in equation 21. The ordinate is the relative rate of responding in one component of a multiple schedule and the abscissa is the relative rate of reinforcement therein. When the interaction between components is absent, which is to say, when there is no contrast effect, then the parameter $m = 0$. When interaction is maximal, as in concurrent procedures, $m = 1.0$. The shape of the function depends jointly on the degree of interaction (m) *and* on R_o, which is the reinforcement from sources other than the multiple schedule itself. If both this quantity and the interaction term, m, go to zero, then the relative rate of responding during a component will be insensitive to changes in the rela-

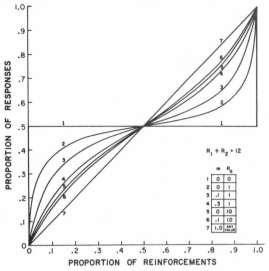

Fig. 12. Hypothetical curves relating the relative frequency of responding and the relative frequency of reinforcement in a two-component multiple schedule. The rate of reinforcement summed across the two components is assumed to be held constant at 12 reinforcements per unit time, while the other parameters vary as indicated on the figure. See text for discussion of equation 21.

tive rate of reinforcement. For any given value of m, the function is made steeper by larger values of R_o. As long as m is less than 1.0, the function approaches the matching line (7) asymptotically as R_o increases. On the other hand, with $m = 1.0$, the matching line is obtained, notwithstanding the value of R_o. The effect of R_o at $m < 1.0$ depends upon the relative magnitudes of R_o and the over-all scheduled rates of reinforcement, which is 12 reinforcements per unit time for Fig. 12. When R_o is relatively small, it exerts a smaller effect than when it is relatively large.

Points on the functions in Fig. 12 may easily be taken for linear, particularly if they fall in the middle of the range, as Reynolds' (1961c) did. The most complete set of data to test equation 21 is Reynolds' experiment (1963b) on multiple VI VI. Three pigeons were each run through three sequences of values. In the first, one of the schedules was held constant at VI 3-min while the other varied; in the second, both varied; in the last, one was again held constant, but at VI 1.58-min. Figure 13 shows for each pigeon how well equation 21 handles the data for all three series. The smooth curves plot equation 21, with different parameters for the three pi-

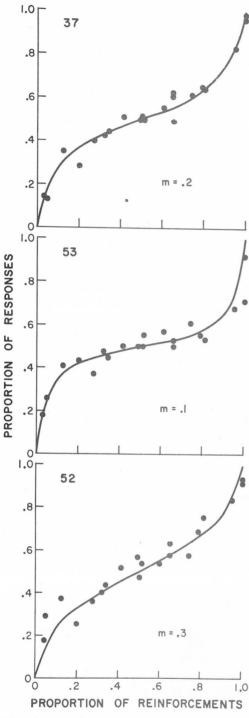

geons. For 37, m = 0.2; for 52, m = 0.3; and for 53, m = 0.1. R_o was arbitrarily set at 0 for all pigeons for convenience in calculation and presentation. If non-zero values of R_o had been used, then no single predicted curve could have been drawn for each pigeon, since the over-all frequency of reinforcement was not held constant, and the effect of R_o depends upon the over-all frequency of reinforcement. In any case, the typical value of R_o can exert only negligible effects on the relative rate of responding, at these rates of reinforcement. The fit of the points to the data justifies both the omission of R_o and the general formulation underlying equation 21.

Although the fit in Fig. 13 supports the present account, reverse-S curves are not necessarily evidence for contrast. Figure 12 shows that curves of this general shape may be obtained even when m = 0, which is to say, when the reinforcement in each component affects the responding in that component only. To show contrast effects directly, absolute, not relative, rates of responding are in order. Although Reynolds' absolute rate data contain evidence for contrast, they were too variable, both within and between subjects, to permit a useful test of the present formulation. The most comprehensive data for this purpose appear to be in an unpublished experiment by J. A. Nevin.

Nevin used pigeons on a three-component multiple schedule, of which two were conventional VI 1-min and VI 3-min, signalled by the color of the illumination on the response key. Each lasted for 1 min, after which the chamber was darkened for 30 sec. The independent variable was the rate of reinforcement during the timeout, which was set at five nominal values, from zero to one every 10 sec. The absolute rate of responding during a component should follow from equation 20, modified to take into account the presence of three, instead of two, components. For the component with VI 1-min (60 reinforcements per hour), the equation is, to a first approximation,

$$P_1 = \frac{k\,60}{60 + m\left(\dfrac{20 + x}{2}\right) + R_o}; \qquad (22)$$

for the VI 3-min (20 reinforcements per hour) component, it is

$$P_2 = \frac{k\,20}{20 + m\left(\dfrac{60 + x}{2}\right) + R_o}. \qquad (23)$$

The quantity, x, is the independent variable, which is to say, the reinforcement rate during timeout. The interaction term, m( ), is the average rate of reinforcement during the two components that might cause contrast. This formulation disregards at least two factors that are likely to have some effect. First of all, it tacitly assumes equivalent interactions between responding in a given component and reinforcement in either of the two other components. A more realistic assumption would be that the component closer in time exerts a greater effect, as, in fact, some work has indicated (Boneau and Axelrod, 1962; Pliskoff, 1963). Secondly, it tacitly assumes that the durations of the components (1 min as opposed to 30 sec for the timeout) are immaterial as regards contrast, whereas a component's effect probably increases with its duration. Placing values on these two complicating factors would be totally arbitrary at present, as well as somewhat unnecessary, since they may at least be presumed to operate in opposite directions, the nearer component being the briefer.

Figure 14 shows the absolute rate of responding during the two variable-interval components, averaged over the four subjects. The two curves are plots of equations 22 and 23. Narrow bands, rather than lines, are drawn for the predicted values because of variation in the obtained rates of reinforcement on the

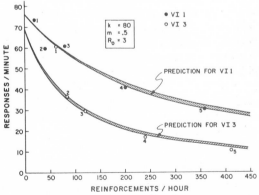

Fig. 14. The rate of responding in one component as a function of the rate of reinforcement summed across the other two components in a three-component multiple schedule. The filled circles and the upper curve are for the component held constant at a variable interval of 3 min. Both curves drawn with lower curve are for the component held constant at a variable-interval of 3 min. Both curves drawn with the parameters as indicated in the box. From Nevin (unpublished).

nominal VI 1-min and VI 3-min. The abscissa is the rate of reinforcement summed across two of the three components, omitting the component from which responding is plotted (*i.e.*, two times the term in parenthesis in equations 22 and 23). The numbers alongside the points identify the two values from each of the five multiple schedules studied. Generally, the point on the lower curve is shifted 40 reinforcements per hour to the right of the upper point, which is the difference between the VI 1-min and the VI 3-min. These decreasing functions are pure contrast, since the rates of reinforcement were close to constant in each of the variable-interval components (except for the last point on the lower curve). Equations 22 and 23, with parameters set at $R_0 = 3$ reinforcements per hour, m = 0.50, and k = 80 responses per minute, appear to be satisfactory except for the first point for VI 3-min.

Contrast is generally (*e.g.*, Reynolds, 1963*b*) more pronounced with lower constant rates of reinforcement. Thus, the upper function in Fig. 14 is shallower than the lower. In fact, as the reinforcement rate during the timeout increases, the proportion between the rates of responding in the two components should, according to equations 22 and 23, approach asymptotically the ratio between the rates of reinforcement, in this instance 3:1. The ratios of responding are, moving to the right along the abscissa, 1.19:1, 1.6:1; 2.24:1, 2.54:1; 2.69:1. The greater susceptibility to contrast of less frequently reinforced behavior has been noted by Bernheim and Williams (1967), as well as in various experiments on pigeons in multiple schedules. Their finding, based as it was on rats in running wheels, serves particularly to extend the applicability of the present analysis.

Although it is premature to argue for the exact function by which the interaction between components is diminished, the simple multiplicative factor of equation 20 does well with most of the published literature. Parameters have been calculated for three other multiple schedules in which reinforcement varied over a range large enough to allow some assessment. The fit of the data to theory was no worse than in Fig. 14, with no deviation greater than six responses per minute, and 15 (out of 18 independent data points) less than three responses per minute. Table 1 shows the parameter values for the three experiments, all of which used pigeons as subjects. Lander and Irwin's (1968) was a conventional two-component multiple schedule. Nevin's (1968) had as its independent variable the duration of reinforced non-responding in one of its two components. The shorter the duration, the higher the rate of reinforcement. The parameters predict the rate of responding in the other component, which was a conventional variable interval. Rachlin and Baum's (1969) experiment used two keys, of which one always provided reinforcement on VI 3-min. The reinforcer was 4-sec access to food. The light on the other key was extinguished except when a second VI 3-min programmer completed an interval, at which time it was lit until the next response collected the reinforcement.[6] The amount of these reinforcements was varied 16-fold during the course of the experiment. Responding on the other key varied inversely with magnitude of reinforcement, as if amount and frequency of reinforcement could be traded off against each other in equation 20.

Equation 20 appears to run into trouble mainly in regard to transitory effects. For example, Terrace (1966a, —b) found a transient contrast effect going from a simple variable-interval schedule to the same variable interval alternating with extinction. Equation 20 does not predict any change in rate here, since the interaction term is zero before and after the change. Terrace's procedure differs from Reynolds', which goes from a multiple schedule

consisting of a pair of matched variable intervals to one consisting of the variable interval alternating with extinction and for which equation 20 predicts contrast. Terrace's contrast effect vanishes with mere exposure to the conditions or with repeated alternations between the variable interval in isolation and the multiple schedule consisting of the variable interval and extinction. On the other hand, Bloomfield (1967b), using Reynolds' paradigm and addressing himself specifically to the persistence of contrast, found the effect undiminished even with several alternations back and forth between *mult* VI VI and *mult* VI EXT. Equation 20, then, is apparently consistent with the long-term effects, but not with the temporary contrast in the Terrace paradigm.

Terrace (1966b) concluded that the temporary contrast effect is emotional, based on the aversiveness of extinction. He noted the one-to-one correspondence between contrast and peak shift in discrimination learning, and also that the peak shift is often taken as evidence for an inhibitory or aversive effect of non-reinforcement. Any procedure that produces a peak shift also produces contrast; any procedure that prevents or diminishes the peak shift, prevents or diminishes contrast, according to Terrace. Aversiveness as negative reinforcement solves the problem, for adding a negative quantity to the denominator of $kR_A/(R_A + R_o)$ increases the value of the expression, given that it remains positive. And there is other evidence that extinction is temporarily aversive as, for example, summarized by Terrace in his defense of the view. There is also evidence for representing aversiveness as a negative quantity. Brethower and Reynolds (1962) used a *mult* VI VI with equal reinforcement schedules in the two components, and added punishment with electric shock to one

---

[6]Catania's findings (1963b) with just this procedure are plotted as x's on Fig. 11. It was noted before (see p. 257) that the x's are slightly above the predicted line, which is where they should be if m < 1.0; in fact, m < 1.0 (m = 0.45 in the Rachlin-Baum study) because the alternating conditions of reinforcement and stimulation make this more properly a multiple schedule than a concurrent, notwithstanding the use of two response keys.

Table 1

	k (Responses per Minute)	m	R_o (Reinforcements per Hour)	Procedure
Lander and Irwin (1968)	77	0.2	4	VI 3-min VI x-min
Nevin (1968)	85	0.35	2	VI 3-min DRO x
Rachlin and Baum (1969)	70	0.45	10	VI 3-min CRF (varying amount of reinf)

of the components. They found a contrast effect in which magnitude was an increasing function of the shock intensity.

A corrollary of the foregoing is that equation 20 predicts a difference between the rate on a simple variable-interval schedule and the rate on a multiple schedule in which each component uses this same variable interval, as follows:

$$\frac{kR_A}{R_A + R_o} \gtreqless \frac{kR_A}{R_A + mR_A + R_o} \qquad (24)$$

Only if $m = 0$ will the two expressions be equal; otherwise the variable interval in isolation will produce the higher rate. This surprising prediction appears, in fact, to be correct. In Bloomfield's experiment (1967*b*), responding on a variable interval alone was faster than responding on a multiple comprising two components of the same variable interval, although the experiment was not specifically designed for this comparison. A direct test of the inequality above (24) is in an unpublished study by Terrace. Four pigeons were trained initially with a simple VI 1-min in the presence of a given stimulus. Then, when responding was judged to be stable, this stimulus alternated every 1.5 min with a different stimulus, but reinforcement was continued on VI 1-min. For each pigeon, and for at least several weeks of daily sessions, the rate of responding dropped during the stimulus common to the first and second procedures. The average decrement was about 30%, which for these reinforcement rates implies $0.31 < m < 0.36$ (setting $R_o = 0$-10). At this point, however, the discussion begins to go beyond the boundaries set by well established data.

ENVOI

Temporary changes in responding clearly require further study, as the foregoing section shows. There are other, even more short-term, changes in responding (*e.g.*, Williams, 1965; Nevin and Shettleworth, 1966; Bernheim and Williams, 1967) in multiple schedules that must for now also remain on the boundary of the present formulation. Another boundary, touched on earlier, is the definition of response classes (see p. 251). The key pecking of pigeons, for example, is relatively unambiguous, but even its properties, as some experiments show (Herrnstein, 1958), can get entangled with the measurement of response strength. Nevertheless, within these boundaries, the present formulation is a quantitative law of effect that cuts across traditional distinctions between choice and sheer output of behavior, as well as between simultaneous and successive conditions of work. The territory circumscribed is sizeable, expandable, and susceptible to precise measurement.

REFERENCES

Baum, W. H. and Rachlin, H. C. Choice as time allocation. *Journal of the Experimental Analysis of Behavior*, 1969, **12**, 861-874.

Bernheim, J. W. and Williams, D. R. Time-dependent contrast effects in a multiple schedule of food reinforcement. *Journal of the Experimental Analysis of Behavior*, 1967, **10**, 243-249.

Bitterman, M. E. Phyletic differences in learning. *American Psychologist*, 1965, **20**, 396-410.

Bloomfield, T. M. Behavioral contrast and relative reinforcement in two multiple schedules. *Journal of the Experimental Analysis of Behavior*, 1967, **10**, 151-158. (*a*)

Bloomfield, T. M. Some temporal properties of behavioral contrast. *Journal of the Experimental Analysis of Behavior*, 1967, **10**, 159-164. (*b*)

Boneau, C. A. and Axelrod, S. Work decrement and reminiscence in pigeon operant responding. *Journal of Experimental Psychology*, 1962, **64**, 352-354.

Brethower, D. M. and Reynolds, G. S. A facilitative effect of punishment on unpunished behavior. *Journal of the Experimental Analysis of Behavior*, 1962, **5**, 191-199.

Brownstein, A. J. and Pliskoff, S. S. Some effects of relative reinforcement rate and changeover delay in response-independent concurrent schedules of reinforcement. *Journal of the Experimental Analysis of Behavior*, 1968, **11**, 683-688.

Brunswik, E. Representative design and probabilistic theory in a functional psychology. *Psychological Review*, 1955, **62**, 193-217.

Bush, R. R. and Mosteller, F. *Stochastic models for learning.* New York: Wiley, 1955.

Catania, A. C. Concurrent performances: a baseline for the study of reinforcement magnitude. *Journal of the Experimental Analysis of Behavior*, 1963, **6**, 299-300. (*a*)

Catania, A. C. Concurrent performances: reinforcement interaction and response independence. *Journal of the Experimental Analysis of Behavior*, 1963, **6**, 253-263. (*b*)

Catania, A. C. Concurrent operants. In W. K. Honig (Ed.), *Operant behavior: areas of research and application.* New York: Appleton-Century-Crofts, 1966. Pp. 213-270.

Catania, A. C. and Reynolds, G. S. A quantitative analysis of the responding maintained by interval schedules of reinforcement. *Journal of the Experimental Analysis of Behavior*, 1968, **11**, 327-383.

Chung, S.-H. *Some quantitative laws of operant be-*

havior. Unpublished doctoral dissertation, Harvard University, 1966.

Chung, S.-H. and Herrnstein, R. J. Choice and delay of reinforcement. *Journal of the Experimental Analysis of Behavior,* 1967, **10**, 67-74.

Ferster, C. B. and Skinner, B. F. *Schedules of reinforcement.* New York: Appleton-Century-Crofts, 1957.

Findley, J. D. Preference and switching under concurrent scheduling. *Journal of the Experimental Analysis of Behavior,* 1958, **1**, 123-144.

Guthrie, E. R. and Horton, G. P. *Cats in a puzzle box.* New York: Rinehart, 1946.

Herrnstein, R. J. Some factors influencing behavior in a two-response situation. *Transactions of the New York Academy of Sciences,* 1958, **21**, 35-45.

Herrnstein, R. J. Relative and absolute strength of response as a function of frequency of reinforcement. *Journal of the Experimental Analysis of Behavior,* 1961, **4**, 267-272.

Herrnstein, R. J. Secondary reinforcement and rate of primary reinforcement. *Journal of the Experimental Analysis of Behavior,* 1964, **7**, 27-36.

Herrnstein, R. J. and Morse, W. H. A conjunctive schedule of reinforcement. *Journal of the Experimental Analysis of Behavior,* 1958, **1**, 15-24.

Holz, W. C. Punishment and rate of positive reinforcement. *Journal of the Experimental Analysis of Behavior,* 1968, **11**, 285-292.

Hull, C. L. *Principles of behavior.* New York: Appleton-Century, 1943.

Lander, D. G. and Irwin, R. J. Multiple schedules: effects of the distribution of reinforcements between components on the distribution of responses between components. *Journal of the Experimental Analysis of Behavior,* 1968, **11**, 517-524.

Morse, W. H. Intermittent reinforcement. In W. K. Honig (Ed.), *Operant behavior: areas of research and application.* New York: Appleton-Century-Crofts, 1966. Pp. 52-108.

Natapoff, A. How symmetry restricts symmetric choice. *Journal of Mathematical Psychology,* in press.

Neuringer, A. J. *Choice and rate of responding in the pigeon.* Unpublished doctoral dissertation, Harvard University, 1967. (*a*)

Neuringer, A. J. Effects of reinforcement magnitude on choice and rate of responding. *Journal of the Experimental Analysis of Behavior,* 1967, **10**, 417-424. (*b*)

Nevin, J. A. Differential reinforcement and stimulus control of not responding. *Journal of the Experimental Analysis of Behavior,* 1968, **11**, 715-726.

Nevin, J. A. Signal detection theory and operant behavior. Review of D. M. Green and J. A. Swets' *Signal detection theory and psychophysics. Journal of the Experimental Analysis of Behavior,* 1969, **12**, 475-480.

Nevin, J. A. and Shettleworth, S. J. An analysis of contrast effects in multiple schedules. *Journal of the Experimental Analysis of Behavior,* 1966, **9**, 305-315.

Norman, M. F. An approach to free-responding on schedules that prescribe reinforcement probability as a function of interresponse time. *Journal of Mathematical Psychology,* 1966, **3**, 235-268.

Pliskoff, S. S. Rate-change effects with equal potential reinforcements during the "warning" stimulus. *Journal of the Experimental Analysis of Behavior,* 1963, **6**, 557-562.

Rachlin, H. and Baum, W. M. Response rate as a function of amount of reinforcement for a signalled concurrent response. *Journal of the Experimental Analysis of Behavior,* 1969, **12**, 11-16.

Reynolds, G. S. An analysis of interactions in a multiple schedule. *Journal of the Experimental Analysis of Behavior,* 1961, **4**, 107-117. (*a*)

Reynolds, G. S. Behavioral contrast. *Journal of the Experimental Analysis of Behavior,* 1961, **4**, 57-71. (*b*)

Reynolds, G. S. Relativity of response rate and reinforcement frequency in a multiple schedule. *Journal of the Experimental Analysis of Behavior,* 1961, **4**, 179-184. (*c*)

Reynolds, G. S. On some determinants of choice in pigeons. *Journal of the Experimental Analysis of Behavior,* 1963, **6**, 53-59. (*a*)

Reynolds, G. S. Some limitations on behavioral contrast and induction during successive discrimination. *Journal of the Experimental Analysis of Behavior,* 1963, **6**, 131-139. (*b*)

Shimp, C. P. Probablistically reinforced choice behavior in pigeons. *Journal of the Experimental Analysis of Behavior,* 1966, **9**, 443-455.

Shull, R. L. and Pliskoff, S. S. Changeover delay and concurrent performances: some effects on relative performance measures. *Journal of the Experimental Analysis of Behavior,* 1967, **10**, 517-527.

Skinner, B. F. *The behavior of organisms.* New York: Appleton-Century, 1938.

Skinner, B. F. The nature of the operant reserve. *Psychological Bulletin,* 1940, **37**, 423 (abstract).

Skinner, B. F. *Science and human behavior.* New York: Macmillan, 1953.

Terrace, H. S. Behavioral contrast and the peak shift: effects of extended discrimination training. *Journal of the Experimental Analysis of Behavior,* 1966, **9**, 613-617. (*a*)

Terrace, H. S. Stimulus control. In W. K. Honig (Ed.), *Operant behavior: areas of research and application.* New York: Appleton-Century-Crofts, 1966. Pp. 271-344. (*b*)

Thorndike, E. L. *Animal intelligence.* New York: Macmillan, 1911.

Tolman, E. C. The determiners of behavior at a choice point. *Psychological Review,* 1938, **45**, 1-41.

Tolman, E. C. Cognitive maps in rats and men. *Psychological Review,* 1948, **55**, 189-208.

Williams, D. R. Negative induction in instrumental behavior reinforced by central stimulation. *Psychonomic Science,* 1965, **2**, 341-342.

Received 3 December 1969.

WHAT PSYCHOLOGY HAS TO OFFER EDUCATION—NOW[1,2]

SIDNEY W. BIJOU

UNIVERSITY OF ILLINOIS

Some day, the question, "What does psychology have to offer education—now?" will be answered by psychologists with some measure of agreement. But at present the answer to this question depends almost entirely on the particular orientation of the individual to whom the question is put, for psychologists differ enormously in their conception of the subject matter and objectives of their discipline. Some say its subject matter is the domain of the mind, others, that it is the observable interaction of an individual's behavior with environmental events. When the question of the objectives of psychology arises, some claim them to be the understanding and explanation of psychological phenomena, others, the prediction and control of behavior. Psychologists also differ markedly in their choice of research methodology, with one segment stressing statistical designs that compare achievement of groups, and others emphasizing changes in the behavior of an individual organism. In addition, psychologists vary greatly in their approach to theory construction, with some favoring the hypothetico-deductive method, and others, the empirico-inductive procedure.

In spite of these great individual variations, there would probably be three basic approaches to the question of what psychology has to offer education: that which would be taken by the *great majority,* that of the *large minority,* and that of the *small minority.* The great majority would probably say that psychology presently offers education something like this: "We can offer an impressive collection of facts about the abilities of the child and his growth and development; we can offer an extensive literature on the analysis of stimuli, on the psychology of simple and complex learning, and on perception; we can offer a considerable body of knowledge on measurement, test construction, and statistical procedures for the experimental study of groups; and we can offer some promising theories of intelligence, socialization, personality, development, and psychopathology."

The concepts and principles of this large majority have accrued not only from psychology, but from sociology, anthropology, and physiology as well. They have evolved from many theories, mostly from psychoanalytic, cognitive, and learning theory. They have been established on findings from many research methods, experimental, correlational, clinical, and field observational or ecological. Consequently, many of the concepts and principles are not rooted in objectively defined raw data, nor are they systematically related to each other. Those with this orientation are eclectic with respect to a research methodology. In general, group experimental designs serve to test theories and hypotheses while correlational methods serve to assess traits and abilities. Since these psychologists, for the most part, view teaching as an intuitive art, their predominant view is that psychology can offer educators the kind of information and ideas that will help them evaluate their philosophy of education, and can acquaint teachers with recent research findings and their possible implications for instruction.

If, on the other hand, another group of psychologists, whom we shall call the large minority, were asked what psychology can offer education, the reply might be: "We can offer some tentative ideas about the nature of the child; we can present firm convictions about

[1]Invited address, Division of School Psychologists, American Psychological Association, 76th Annual Convention, September 1, 1968, San Francisco, California. The analysis presented was generated in large measure from research supported by the U. S. Office of Education, Division of Research, Bureau of Education for the Handicapped, OEG-0-9-2322030-0762(032). Reprints may be obtained from S. W. Bijou, Child Behavior Laboratory, 403 East Healey, Champaign, Illinois 61820.

[2]Dedicated to Professor B. F. Skinner in his sixty-fifth year.

the stages of cognitive and intellectual development; and we can offer theoretical formulations about perception, learning, the will to learn, and the general mechanisms of coping and defending. We can also offer a philosophy of science which postulates that behavior is determined both by observable and by hypothetical internal variables."

Subgroups in this large minority attempt to relate their concepts and principles in a systematic manner. However, the concepts and principles developed by one group do not synchronize with those developed by the others, mainly because these systematists do not anchor all of their terms to objectively verifiable data. Research, as with the first group, is designed mainly to test a theory or an hypothesis and consists for the most part of comparing the achievements of groups. Practical application often involves terms and processes that are not related to the principles applied. That is to say, attempts to apply research findings to classroom practices are all too often bolstered by hypothetical variables or precepts. Because hypothetical variables and processes are central to the theories in this group, educators who subscribe to this approach are prone to attribute school failures to such presumed internal conditions as lack of drive, perceptual disability, or clinically inferred brain damage.

Still another group of psychologists, which at present is only a small minority, responding to the question of what psychology can contribute to education now would say: "We can offer a set of concepts and principles derived exclusively from experimental research; we can offer a methodology for applying these concepts and principles directly to teaching practices; we can offer a research design which deals with changes in the individual child (rather than inferring them from group averages); and we can offer a philosophy of science which insists on observable accounts of the relationships between individual behavior and its determining conditions."

Faced with this complex state of affairs—a house of psychology divided on what it has to offer education—I should like to elaborate on the offer of the last-mentioned group of psychologists, the behavioral analysis group. I shall discuss what I believe to be the promise of this approach, its influence on the role of the school psychologist, and what educators

can do if they choose to pursue the leads offered by this group.

THE OFFER OF THE SMALL MINORITY

The offer of the behavioral analysis will be presented in terms of its philosophy of science, concepts and principles, core research method, and procedure for the application of concepts and principles to teaching.

The Philosophy of Science

The philosophy of science (assumptions) of any approach merits close scrutiny because it influences the kinds of problems selected for study, the basic method of gathering data, the forms in which the data are presented, and the interpretation of the findings. For the purpose of this paper, I shall limit my discussion to only five of the basic assumptions of a behavioral analysis. More comprehensive accounts may be found in Kantor (1959) and Skinner (1947, 1953, and 1963).

1. The subject matter of psychology is the interaction between the behavior of an integral organism and environmental events. These interactions are analyzed in *observable, measurable,* and *reproducible* terms and therefore are amenable to scientific investigation.

2. The interactions between the behavior of an individual and environmental events are lawful. Given an individual with his unique biological endowment, changes in his psychological behavior are a function of his interactional history and the current situation in which he is behaving.

3. As in all of the sciences, the subject matter of psychology exists in *continuities.* Continuities are assumed to exist in the stages of development, in the rates of development (normal, retarded, and accelerated), in the relationships between normal and pathological development, in the problems and procedures of basic and applied research, and in the analysis of psychological phenomena from raw data to theoretical formulation.

4. Complex interactions evolve from simple interactions and begin with the infant's initial relationships with people and objects. This does not mean that com-

plex behaviors are assumed to be sums of simple behaviors. How a specific form of complex behavior, such as mathematical problem solving, is established is a problem for experimental study. The final analysis of any class of complex behavior would probably involve many concepts and principles such as minute stimulus control, subtle variations in setting conditions, and intricate schedules of reinforcement.

5. A psychological theory and its technology are open and flexible systems. That is, a new concept, a new principle, or a new technique may at any time be added to the existing list, provided that it can display the proper credentials: it must be tied unequivocally to observable events; it must be functional; and it must not overlap with the concepts, principles, or techniques already catalogued.

The Concepts and Principles

The concepts of behavioral analysis refer only to observable behavioral events and environmental conditions, and to the relationships between them. Furthermore, these concepts, derived entirely from experimental investigations, are functional in character; that is to say, behavioral events are defined by their effects on the environment, such as producing or removing a stimulus, and environmental events are defined by their effects on the behavior, such as providing an occasion for a class of operant behavior.

The behavioral concepts of this approach are, for the most part, divided on the basis of whether they are sensitive to antecedent or consequent stimulus events; the former are referred to as respondent behavior, and the latter as operant behavior. There is, among adherents to this approach, an acknowledged penchant for measuring respondent behavior in terms of its latency or magnitude and operant behavior in terms of its rate or frequency of occurrence (Skinner, 1966a).

The environmental concepts also fall into two categories: stimuli with functional properties, and setting factors. A conditioned stimulus in a respondent interaction and a discriminative stimulus in an operant interaction are examples of stimulus functions. Satiation and deprivation of reinforcing stimuli,

disruption of sleep cycles, and drug intervention are examples of setting factors.

The principles of the behavioral approach are statements describing demonstrated relationships among behavioral and environmental variables. These statements, which have been accumulating steadily over the past sixty years, are the *facts* of the science of psychology as generated by an experimental analysis of behavior. They have been organized variously, but with slight differences among them (*e.g.,* Ferster and Perrott, 1968; Millenson, 1967; Reynolds, 1968; and Skinner, 1953). Reynolds (1968), for example, groups the principles as follows: acquisition and extinction of operant behavior, stimulus control of operant behavior, conditioned reinforcers, schedules of reinforcement, respondent behavior and respondent conditioning, aversive control, and emotion and motivation.

Research

Experimental analysis of the interactions between changes in individual behavior and environmental events is the core strategy in research (Sidman, 1960). Here, research is not planned to test a theory or an hypothesis but to demonstrate functional relationships (Skinner, 1966b), or to evaluate a practical application of the concepts and principles (Baer, Wolf, and Risley, 1968).

The strategy of teaching-oriented applied research does not consist of designing a study to determine whether Method A is better than Method B for the teaching of subject-matter X. It is, instead, a search for ways to engineer an educational environment so that each child can learn specified tasks, and then, after that goal is attained, to compare achievement in that engineered situation with achievement in some other school situation.

Application to Education

The concepts and principles of behavioral analysis are applied directly to the classroom teaching situation: to the observable behavior of the pupil in relation to the teacher's techniques of instruction, the instructional materials, the contingencies of reinforcement, and the setting conditions. The analysis of teaching and the methodology of application are clearly set forth by Skinner in *The Technology of Teaching* (1968).

Teaching, according to Skinner, is a situation in which the teacher arranges the contingencies of reinforcement to expedite learning by the child. The teacher is the arranger, and since she generally works in the classroom by herself, we may think of her as the "Lone Arranger". The teacher arranges the contingencies to develop appropriate study behavior, for example, attending to the materials to be learned, and hopefully she arranges the contingencies so that this behavior becomes part of a child's way of dealing with future study tasks. She also arranges contingencies by scheduling the formal academic subjects (the visible programs), and manners and moral behavior (the invisible programs) in such a way that each child makes progress at approximately his own pace and with minimum frustration or aversive consequences. She finds it necessary, at some times, also to arrange contingencies to reduce or eliminate behaviors that compete with acquiring the desired academic and social behaviors.

Two comments about arranging the educational environment are appropriate at this point; one pertains to scheduling the contingencies of reinforcement; the other, to scheduling the stimulus material. The fact that academic and social behaviors are operants, and hence sensitive to consequent stimulation, has led many teachers and researchers to use, indiscriminately, contrived contingencies such as tokens, candies, points, stars, *etc*. Such artificial reinforcers are not always necessary, and in many instances in which they have been used, they have not been functional. In other words, a child's rate of learning has not increased through the use of candies, or by whatever else he receives in exchange for a collection of tokens or a sum of points. Contrived reinforcers are appropriate only when the usual reinforcers applied in the classroom (confirmation, indications of progress, privileges, preferred work, approval, and the like) are not meaningful to a child. If, at times, contrived reinforcers are considered necessary in order to initiate learning, they can be scheduled so that they are gradually replaced by the reinforcers indigenous to the situation and the activity being learned. These are called by Ferster (1967) "natural", "intrinsic", or "automatic" reinforcers. As Skinner (1968) pointed out, the critical task in most teaching is not the incorporation of more and more new reinforcers but the effective utilization of those currently available to the teacher.

Let us turn to the scheduling of stimulus materials. The fact that a school task can be learned with a minimum of frustration and on the basis of positive reinforcement via a program of differential reinforcement of successive approximations to the ultimate form of a response (skill), or the desired response in the proper situation (knowledge), has led to an over-emphasis on the role of teaching machines, and to a misconception about the school subjects that can be properly programmed. Teaching machines, from the most primitive to the most elaborate, are of value in teaching only insofar as they assist the teacher in arranging the contingencies that expedite learning, *i.e.*, aid the teacher in presenting the material properly, in providing for explicit responses, and in arranging for optimum timing of effective contingencies of reinforcement. The programming of any academic subject for a child is straightforward: (1) state in objective terms the desired terminal or goal behavior, (2) assess the child's behavioral repertory relevant to the task, (3) arrange in sequence the stimulus material or behavioral criteria for reinforcement, (4) start the child on that unit in the sequence to which he can respond correctly about 90% of the time, (5) manage the contingencies of reinforcement with the aid of teaching machines and other devices to strengthen successive approximations to the terminal behavior and to build conditioned reinforcers that are intrinsic to the task, and (6) keep records of the child's responses as a basis for modifying the materials and teaching procedures.

The research to date suggests that behavioral principles can be applied to the teaching situation with gratifying results. Further advances in basic and technological knowledge should, of course, lead to even more effective application.

IMPLICATIONS FOR THE SCHOOL PSYCHOLOGIST

Now let us look briefly at the offer from the mini-minority of psychologists as it relates to the school psychologist. Let us suppose that we have a school in which the teachers are happily applying behavioral principles to all aspects of education. In such a situation, the school psychologist would perform at least four functions.

First, he would work in close cooperation with kindergarten and first-grade teachers to help newly admitted children make a smooth transition from their homes to the classroom, with the objective of preventing school retardation and behavior problems. Specifically, the school psychologist would help these teachers to assess the repertories of their children and would help them to arrange suitable individual pupil programs. He would also help these teachers and their assistants to modify the programs when the child encounters difficulties and to assess their reinforcement contingency practices.

Second, he would work with counselors, teachers, school social workers, and parents on mitigating or eliminating problem behavior, setting up remedial programs that would be based on the same set of concepts and principles that are applied to teaching. In other words, the school psychologist would be engaging in behavior modification or *action counseling* as described and practiced by Krumboltz and his colleagues (1966).

Third, the school psychologist would assist teachers in dealing with problems of classroom management and subject-matter programming. His efforts with respect to classroom management would be comparable to the work of Thomas, Becker, and Armstrong (1968). On request from the teacher, he would observe the behavior of a problem child or group of children in the classroom, and on the basis of data collected he would analyze the contingencies that are operating in the situation, work out a course of action with the teacher, and evaluate it in terms of data from observational procedures. Data indicating that the new procedure was ineffective would lead to reassessment and alteration of the plan until a satisfactory solution is found. In helping the teacher to program instructional material, the school psychologist's task would consist of analyzing each child's daily academic records and modifying teaching procedures, contingency arrangements, and sequences of materials. With respect to assisting the teacher to develop and maintain other essential school behavior, such as paying attention, his procedures would be similar to those described by Hall, Lund, and Jackson (1968).

Fourth, and finally, the school psychologist would conduct in-service training for the teacher's assistants. In many instances these people would be clerks, like the instructional material clerks in the University of Pittsburgh type of programming; or they might be aides who would conduct individual and small group tutorials. The school psychologist would also be responsible for keeping the teachers and others informed of advances in technology of teaching and the specific ways of incorporating them into the school system.

It is obvious that the school psychologist described here would not be simulating the role of a child psychiatrist, would not be performing as a part-time clinical psychologist, would not be a full-time psychometrician; rather, he would be a person informed and skilled in the application of behavioral principles to all aspects of teaching both normal and handicapped children.

REQUIREMENTS FOR THOSE IN EDUCATION WHO WISH TO ACCEPT THE OFFER

Now I should like to suggest what educators might do if they wish to accept the offer of psychologists with a behavioral analysis orientation.

First, they should learn with precision the more specific aspects of this approach. A thorough grounding is necessary because behavioral analysis does not offer a touchstone. It is necessary because the approach has an apparent simplicity that can be deceptive, and many alluring features that can be misleading. Lastly, it is necessary because effective application requires a minute analysis of the teaching situation, and ingenuity in rearranging contingencies in order to eliminate difficulties and to expedite the establishment and maintenance of the desired behavior. It is therefore essential that the practitioner learn from *first sources:* (1) the nature of the concepts and principles and referential supporting data, (2) the methodology of practical application and the basic literature on the behavioral technology of teaching, (3) the individual research methodology, and (4) the assumptions of behavioral analysis and their implications for educational practices.

Second, the practitioners should obtain experience in applying these principles. Those who would use this approach should arrange to observe demonstrations in actual educational settings and should seek out opportunities to practice the techniques under supervision. Such first-hand experience provides occasions in which one must face and deal with the problems of contingency management and subject-matter programming; it also provides opportunities to be reinforced by the visible changes that result from one's efforts. If there are no preschool or elementary school demonstration classes within easy reach, educators who teach in colleges and universities might apply these principles to their classes (Ferster, 1968; and Keller, 1968). They might do this even if there are opportunities to observe the application of behavioral principles to the education of young children. Not only will it give them a new source of satisfaction but their students would probably appreciate a learner-centered approach to instruction.

SUMMARY AND CONCLUSIONS

A small but rapidly growing group of psychologists can now offer educators (1) a set of concepts and principles derived entirely from the experimental analysis of behavior, (2) a methodology for the practical application of these concepts and principles, (3) a research method that deals with changes in individual behavior, and (4) a philosophy of science that says: "Look carefully to the relationships between observable environmental and behavioral events and their changes."

Application of behavioral principles to education would revise the role of the teacher; she would become a facile manager of the contingencies of reinforcement and an effective instructional programmer. Application would also change the style of educational research from comparing the achievement of groups of children to analyzing the specific conditions and processes in the teaching of a particular subject as they relate to the behavior of an individual pupil, and application of these principles would change the role of the school psychologist. He would be an expert in the behavioral technology of teaching. As such, he would collaborate with kindergarten and first-grade teachers to prevent school problems by arranging remedial procedures for individual children. He would also serve as a consultant to all teachers on problems of classroom management and program-

ming, and through in-service classes would train teacher's aides to assist the teacher in reaching her goals.

To act on this offer from the small minority of psychologists, educators are advised to learn the details of this approach from primary sources. In addition, they should seek first-hand experiences in applying the techniques so they can understand the problems involved and the approaches to their solutions.

What sorts of changes would be expected to result from an acceptance to this offer? It is difficult to foresee all the details of the changes but certain broad indications are clear. First, the teacher would probably derive new satisfaction from teaching because she would be in a situation that allows her to see concretely the progress of each child in her class, and she would know what to do when a child is not making reasonable progress. She could not help but gain new confidence in herself as a teacher because she would know *what* she is doing and *why* she is doing it. She would in addition be more secure in the knowledge that her teaching practices are based on demonstrated principles, and that with the help of the school psychologist she can refine and extend her methods in accordance with new research findings. Finally, she would have opportunities to try new ways of teaching standard subjects, and to explore ways of teaching subjects not now programmed.

Second, putting this offer into operation would probably provide a common basis for the discussion of problems among those working with the teacher—the principal, the psychologist, the counselor, and the school social worker. It would make no difference whether the problem were the persistent deviant behavior of a child, curriculum difficulties, an unruly classroom, an uncooperative parent, or the behavior of groups of children in the cafeteria or on the playground. A common approach to all aspects of education, especially one based on experimental concepts and principles, would certainly advance teaching as a profession.

Third, systematic application of behavior principles would be expected to reduce dramatically the number of children who reach the fourth grade without learning to read at a socially functional level. Present estimates of this group range from 20% to 40% of the school population. In terms of numbers, this is a staggering figure. With its emphasis on the prevention of academic and behavioral retardation, it is not unrealistic to think that the behavioral analysis approach could reduce that percentage to almost zero. And for the same reason, it would be expected to reverse the trend of spiralling increases in budgets for remedial services.

Fourth, the ultimate result, of course, would be a better educated community—the first requisite in equipping an industrial society to manage the advances of science and technology to achieve *humanitarian goals* (MacLeish, 1968).

REFERENCES

Baer, D. M., Wolf, M. M., and Risley, T. R. Some current dimensions of applied behavior analysis. *Journal of Applied Behavior Analysis,* 1968, **1,** 91-97.

Ferster, C. B. Arbitrary and natural reinforcement. *Psychological Records,* 1967, **17,** 341-347.

Ferster, C. B. Individualized instruction in a large introductory psychology college course. *The Psychological Record,* 1968, **18,** 521-532.

Ferster, C. B. and Perrott, Mary C. *Behavior principles.* New York: Appleton-Century-Crofts, 1968.

Hall, R. V., Lund, Diane, and Jackson, Deloris. Effects of teacher attention on study behavior. *Journal of Applied Behavior Analysis,* 1968, **1,** 1-12.

Kantor, J. R. *Interbehavioral psychology.* (2nd rev. ed.) Bloomington, Ind.: Principia Press, 1959.

Keller, F. S. "Good-bye, teacher . . ." *Journal of Applied Behavior Analysis,* 1968 **1,** 79-90.

Krumboltz, J. (Ed.) *Revolution in counseling.* New York: Houghton Mifflin, 1966.

MacLeish, A. The great American frustration. *Saturday Review,* 1968, **51,** No. 28, 13-16.

Millenson, J. R. *Principles of behavioral analysis.* New York: Macmillan, 1967.

Reynolds, G. S. *A primer of operant conditioning.* Glenview, Ill.: Scott, Foresman, 1968.

Sidman, M. *Tactics of scientific research.* New York: Basic Books, 1960.

Skinner, B. F. Behaviorism at fifty. *Science,* 1963, **140,** 951-958.

Skinner, B. F. Current trends in experimental psychology. In W. Dennis (Ed.), *Current trends in psychology.* Pittsburgh: University of Pittsburgh Press, 1947. Pp. 16-49.

Skinner, B. F. Operant behavior. In W. K. Honig (Ed.), *Operant behavior: Areas of research and application.* New York: Appleton-Century-Crofts, 1966. Pp. 12-32. (*a*)

Skinner, B. F. *Science and human behavior.* New York: Macmillan, 1953.

Skinner, B. F. *The technology of teaching.* New York: Appleton-Century-Crofts, 1968.

Skinner, B. F. What is an experimental analysis of behavior? *Journal of Experimental Analysis of Behavior,* 1966, **9,** 213-218. (*b*)

Thomas, D. R., Becker, W. C., and Armstrong, M. Production and elimination of disruptive classroom behavior by systematically varying teacher's behavior. *Journal of Applied Behavior Analysis,* 1968, **1,** 35-45.

Received 23 October 1968.
(Revised 24 November 1969.)

INDEX

All numbers refer to the first page of the article in which the entry appears.